A TREASURY OF PHILOSOPHY

A Treasury of Philosophy

Edited by

DAGOBERT D.
RUNES

Volume I

INCORPORATED
NEW YORK

CONTENTS

v

xv

A Few Words to the Reader

Man is a meditative creature, and wherever we come across his traces we find indications of his perennially philosophical mind.

What philosophy be has been defined a great many times. None of the definitions, however, seems to be entirely satisfactory, and even now, standing at the end of this book —like all prefaces, this is being written, not at the beginning, but at the completion of a work—I can say only that "philosophy is the search for the indefinable."

Of the almost four hundred searchers represented in this collection, none has really set out to solve an issue or a problem once and for all, as do mathematicians, physicists, chemists, or engineers. Rather, all these men whom I have brought together under the roof of this volume have, at certain times in their lives, sat down to meditate upon the wondrous themata that came to their minds in uncharted realms: the essence of being, the nature of man, the principles of ethics, the "where from" of existence, the "where to" of human purpose, the "where in" of beauty, the undercurrents of emotional life, the structure of reason, the limitations of knowledge, and the quest for God.

There are about ten thousand men and a score of women who have some claim to be classed as philosophers. If there was any notable difficulty in my task, I would point only to the process of selecting the few hundred from the many thousands. Many, even of the well-known, were not thinkers but rather teachers, others were not pundits but rather preachers—and some were just clever.

I have taken care to include in this anthology a considerable number of Hebrew, Chinese, and other Oriental minds who have generally been ignored by our Western-focussed historians. I have also listed American philosophers who still seem to be step-children in the house of European lexicographers. In going through European reference books, I sometimes felt that their authors had not heard of the discovery of America!

In my efforts to keep this book within the prescribed limits of space, and perhaps also through the unavoidable coloring of choice by personal taste, I may have done injustice by omitting one philosopher or another, and I shall, in this sense, welcome suggestions from serious readers.

I should like to thank, for their advice and valuable assistance, the Doctors Vergilius Ferm, John White, and Kurt F. Leidecker, without whose cooperation my task could not have been accomplished.

And now, may I wish the readers of this Treasury the same benign pleasure in perusing the following pages that I experienced in assembling them.

D. D. R.

A TREASURY OF PHILOSOPHY

ABAILARD, PETER

ABAILARD, PETER (1079-1142). Abailard's life is a portrait of the triumphs and vicissitudes of philosophy, faith, and love. He was born in a little town in Brittany, and having been ordained as priest, returned there to tutor Héloïse, the niece of Canon Fulbert. His secret love affair with her, and Astrolabius, the son she bore him, caused him considerable misfortune, for when the canon discovered the secret relationship he had the priest physically mutilated. Abailard persuaded Héloïse to take the veil: he himself retired to a quiet place near Troyes.

His disciples, however, sought him out, and once again the handsome, eloquent schoolman attracted students from all over Europe. He established an oratory called the Paraclete. His subtle argumentation persuaded his listeners to found their beliefs on reason. He tabulated the contradictions of the Bible and the Church Fathers for easy reference; he made freedom of the will the basis of all ethics; he opposed the teachings of the famous schoolmen, and expounded those concepts which hold that the Aristotelian precepts, called universals in scholastic philosophy (such as genus and species), have only intellectual significance.

The story of his "calamities" (he wrote a book by that title) was never-ending. His interpretation of the Trinity was twice condemned as heretical. Finally, weary of the fight, he burned his book on the Trinity and lived out his life, a subdued follower of the faith. Upon his death Héloïse, twenty-one years younger than he, claimed his body and buried him. The ashes of both lovers now rest at the Père-Lachaise in Paris.

ON SIN

WHEN the Scripture says: 'Go not after your own desires' (Eccles. xviii, 30), and: 'Turn from your own will' (ibid.), it instructs us not to fulfil our desires. Yet it does not say that we are to be wholly without them. It is vicious to give in to our desires; but not to have any desires at all is impossible for our weak nature.

The sin, then, consists not in desiring a woman, but in consent to the desire, and not the wish for whoredom, but the consent to the wish is damnation.

Let us see how our conclusions about sexual intemperance apply to theft. A man crosses another's garden. At the sight of the delectable fruit his desire is aroused. He does not, however, give way to desire so as to take anything by theft or rapine, although his mind was moved to strong inclination by the thought of the delight of eating. Where there is desire, there, without doubt, will exists. The man desires the eating of that fruit wherein he doubts not that there will be delight. The weakness of nature in this man is compelled to desire the fruit which, without the master's permission, he has no right to take. He conquers the desire, but does not extinguish it. Since, however, he is not enticed into consent, he does not descend to sin.

What, then, of your objection? It should be clear from such instances, that the wish or desire itself of doing what is not seemly is never to be called sin, but rather, as we said, the consent is sin. We consent to what is not seemly when we do not draw ourselves back from such a deed, and are prepared, should opportunity offer, to perform it completely. Whoever is discovered in this intention, though his guilt has yet to be completed in deed, is already guilty before God in so far as he strives with all his might to sin, and accomplishes within himself, as the blessed Augustine reminds us, as much as if he were actually taken in the act.

God considers not the action, but the spirit of the action. It is the intention, not the deed wherein the merit or praise of the doer consists. Often, indeed, the same action is done from different motives: for justice sake by one man, for an evil reason by another. Two men, for instance, hang a guilty person. The one does it out of zeal for justice; the other in resentment for an earlier enmity. The action of

2

hanging is the same. Both men do what is good and what justice demands. Yet the diversity of their intentions causes the same deed to be done from different motives, in the one case good, in the other bad. [1]

ABRAVANEL, ISAAC

ABRAVANEL, ISAAC (1437-1508). A Spanish Sephardic Jew who was in the court of Alfonso V, King of Portugal, but had to flee, at great loss of personal fortune, when a new ruler ascended the throne. From Lisbon he went to the House of Castile, and when the Jews were banished from Spain, he went to Naples, once again in the service of a king, until he was banished by the French rulers. He then fled to Venice where he remained until his death. He was buried in Padua.

Abravanel is generally considered the last great Aristotelian. Sometimes a philosophic eclectic, he was principally concerned with the teachings of the Bible and the modifications of doctrine expounded by the Jews. He was a believer in the Torah and considered the history of the Jews a revelation of God. His studies of the Bible are frequently used as reference by Christian scholars.

THE INTERRUPTED WORK

THUS spake Isaac, the son of my Lord, of the prince and great man in Israel, Judah Abravanel, of the root of Jesse the Bethlehemite, of the seed of David, a leader and commander to my people, of a people scattered abroad and dispersed, one of those exiled from Jerusalem to Spain:

Behold, in expounding the books, that is to say, Joshua, Judges, Samuel, and Kings, I encountered in reverse order what Hiel the Bethelite encountered when he built up Jericho, he who laid the foundation thereof with the loss of his firstborn, and with the loss of his youngest son he set up the gates of it. But I opened my mouth to God in former days that were better than these, settling on my leas in the kingdom of Portugal, the land of my birth, to expound those four books, since I saw that those who had expounded them had done so inadequately. But with the burden of the king and

3

princes it came up upon my neck, and I could not complete it until the hand of the Lord touched me, and the king of Portugal held me for his enemy, not for any injustice in my hands. He stood with his right hand as an adversary to destroy me utterly; he took all that was mine, durable and lawful possessions, and I saved myself, I alone, fleeing to the kingdom of Castile from the oppressing sword. And when I arrived there, a stranger in the land, a wayfaring man that turneth aside to tarry for a night, I sought to repay that which God had lent me by expounding the three first books, Joshua, Judges, and Samuel.

All this happened at the beginning of the two hundred and forty-fourth year, in the sixth millennium of the creation. And when I was about to begin expounding the Books of the Kings, I was called to come in unto the king, to the king of Spain, the greatest of all the kings on earth, who ruled over the kingdoms of Castile, Aragon, Catalunia, and Sicilia, and the other islands of the sea. I came to the court of the king and the queen, was with them many days, and the Lord gave me favor in their eyes, in the eyes of the princes that sat first in the kingdom, and I wrought in their service for eight years.

And both riches and honor, which if a man do, he lives by them, I gained in their towns and in their castles. Therefore the Torah was slacked and the work hindered. Because I served the kings of peoples who are not of the children of Israel, I left mine heritage, the kingdom of Judah and of Israel, and the expounding of their books.

In the year two hundred and fifty-two, [1492] the king of Spain conquered the entire kingdom of Granada and the great city of Granada, great among nations and princess among the provinces, and in his might and pride he turned from his former ways. He imputed his might unto his God. "And Esau said in his heart": For wherewith could I reconcile myself unto my master, who has girded me with strength to battle, wherewith shall I come before the Lord, who has put this city into my hands, if not that I bring under his wings the people that walks in darkness, the scattered sheep of Israel, and either lead back to his law and his faith the backsliding daughter, or banish them from my countenance and cast them into another land, so that they may no longer dwell in my land nor tarry in my sight.

And because of this the king's commandment and his decree went forth, and a herald loudly proclaimed: "To you it is commanded, to all the families of the house of Israel, that if you 'go through the water,' if you fall down and worship the gods of those peoples, you shall eat the good of the land, as we are doing this very day, and you shall dwell and trade therein. But if you refuse and rebel, if you do not mention the name of my God, and if you do not worship my God, rise up, and get you forth from among my people, out of the lands of Spain, Sicily, Mallorca, and Sardinia, which are under my rule, and three months after, there shall not a hoof be left behind of all who call themselves by the name of Jacob, or by the name of Israel, in any of the provinces of my kingdom."

Now since I was in the court of the king's house, I wore myself out with crying and my throat dried. Oftentimes I spoke to the king, I entreated him with my mouth, and said: "Help, O king, wherefore dealest thou thus with thy servants? Ask me never so much dowry and gift, gold and silver and all that a man of the house of Israel has, will he give for his land."

I called for my lovers that see the king's face, to plead for my people. The nobles took counsel together, with all their might to implore the king to reverse the letters of his anger and fury, and to destroy the scheme he had devised against the Jews. But like the dead adder he stopped his ear and answered nothing at all to anyone. And the queen stood at his right hand to accuse. With her much fair speech she caused him to yield, and bring to pass his act, to begin and also make an end. We labored but our fears were not mitigated. I was not at ease, neither was I quiet, neither had I rest; but trouble came.

5

And they went without strength, three hundred thousand on foot, the people among whom I am, young and old, little children and women, in one day, from all the provinces of the king. "Whither the spirit was to go, they went."

I too chose out their way, the way of a ship in the midst of the sea. I, among the captives, came with all my house— "the children are my children, and the flocks are my flocks" —came here to Naples, to that exalted city, whose kings are merciful kings, and I spoke with my own heart: I will pay that which I have vowed, I will expound the Books of the Kings, which I have not done until now; and I shall do this also because "it it time to work for the Lord," to commemorate the destruction of our holy and glorious house, and the exile that has come upon our people, as they are written in this book, and as I will expound with the help of God.

Now, after this: Hiel the Bethelite, in the building of Jericho, had laid "the foundation thereof with his first-born, and with his youngest son set up the gates thereof," but I, a man that hath seen affliction, began my explanation of these four books, and founded it upon the least of the banishments and exiles that came upon me, that is, the particular exile from the kingdom of Portugal, and with the greatest of the exiles, the bitter and hasty exile, the great and dreadful destruction, devoured and swallowed, driven from abiding in Spain—with this I "set up the gates" of this commentary and completed it. [2]

ABRAVANEL, JUDAH

ABRAVANEL, JUDAH (c. 1460-1530). Abravanel was one of the outstanding figures of the period of transition between the Middle Ages and the Renaissance. He lived not only at the conjunction of two eras, but also in contact with three cultures—Jewish, Spanish, and Italian. He and his father, Don Isaac Abravanel fled in 1483 from their native Portugal to Spain, and thence to Italy in 1492. Judah practised medicine, but he was mainly interested in philosophy, mathematics, and astronomy. For a time he lectured at the

Universities in Naples and Rome. The intellectuals of both cities requested his friendship; his was a close association with Pico della Mirandola. During his sojourn in Italy, Judah assumed the name of Leone, the translation of Judah, the Lion.

His most famous work, *Dialoghi di Amore* (Dialogues about Love), was published in Italian, and soon after translated into Hebrew, Latin, French, Spanish, and English. A portion of the book was incorporated in a rabbinical commentary on the Song of Songs. The Dialogues are landmarks in the history of aesthetics and of great consequence to the history of metaphysics and ethics. The book promulgates love as a cosmic principle inseparable from being; its spirit, the mirror of reality. The Dialogues stressed the spiritual character of physical beauty and helped develop the field of aesthetic idealism. He maintained that true happiness is the "union of the human intellect with the Divine intelligence," and that it is directly connected to aesthetic enjoyment. There is a pantheistic strain in Abravanel's philosophy, but he always emphasized his orthodox Judaism, and tried to reconcile his pantheistic feelings with the Biblical concept of God.

KNOWLEDGE, LOVE AND DESIRE

KNOWLEDGE must precede all love; for we could not love anything we had not first known to be good. Nor can we love anything before we conceive of it as an actuality. Our mind is a mirror and model, or to be more specific, an image of real things. Therefore we can love nothing, until we can perceive its existence as reality.

It cannot be denied that knowledge precedes desire. Knowledge is not only concerned with what *is*, but also that which *is not*. For our mind judges things as it perceives them to be; it judges things which are not, in the same fashion. Thus I would say that love presupposes a knowledge of things which are, and a desire of those things which are not or which we lack.

Knowledge without love is of those things which are not beautiful, and therefore not desirable; or of bad and ugly things that are hated; or of things which are neither desired nor hated. All other knowledge of good and beautiful things either has love or desire as its end.

7

Every degree of being in the universe is subordinate to another, and graded from the lowest to the highest. In man himself, the lesser faculties are subordinate to the greater; to wit: those of the vegetable soul to those of the sensitive; those of the sensitive to those of the intellectual. The intellectual is the finest and highest faculty, not only in Man, but in all of the lower world. Even in the intellectual, activities are graded from the lowest to the highest in order of intelligible objects. The highest and final intelligible object is the highest being, and the ultimate end to which all things are ordered. The acme and objective of intellectual activity is that celestial, angelic intellect, to which all others are subordinate. In the same way . . . the various loves in the created universe are subordinate, from the lowest to the highest, up to that final and supreme love, that of the universe for its creator.

[2A]

ACOSTA, URIEL

ACOSTA, URIEL (1590-1647). Born in Portugal, the descendant of a Marrano family, religiously observant of Catholicism, the young Acosta prepared himself for the priesthood. But, tortured by doubts about the Christian religion, he decided to flee to Holland. Here he embraced Judaism, not because he was convinced of the truth of his new faith, but he was resolved to deny his former beliefs. He defied Jewish orthodoxy, the very basis of Judaism, because he was incapable of integrating himself into the Jewish community or of understanding its precarious situation and vital needs. His attacks upon the fundamental doctrines of Christianity, which he wrote as a member of the Jewish congregation of Amsterdam angered the congregation because they felt the Christian authorities who had given the Jews refuge would be offended. Banished, he recanted, revolted anew, was banished anew, and ostracized for seven years. No longer able to endure solitude, he was willing to withstand the most severe penance in order to be allowed to re-enter the Jewish community. But the rigors of the ceremony destroyed his will to survive. Soon thereafter, he committed suicide, unrepenting and irreconcilable. To some extent, he was the victim of his temper, but more so of an era in which it was impossible for an independent thinker to live unharmed outside a religious community.

Many novelists and dramatists, Jew and non-Jew, have idealized his life and thoughts, for the poetic transfiguration of his fate is the tragedy of an uprooted man in revolt against tradition and any community based on tradition—the tragedy of a humiliated man, unable to live in isolation, whose only alternative was death. He entitled his autobiography *Exemplar Humanae Vitae* (Example of a Human Life), but his life was certainly anything but typical.

THE HUMAN SOUL

SINCE we have to deal with the mortality or immortality of the human soul, it is appropriate to ask what that soul is. Many ignorant fools speak of it as though it were a virgin personified; others describe it as something emergent from purgatory. We say that the human soul is man's vital spirit, by means of which he lives. This spirit is in the blood, and with it man acts and moves in the world. Man lives as long as the vital spirit works in his body. He dies when the spirit is either naturally or accidentally extinguished. The only difference between the animal soul and the human soul is that the human soul is endowed with reason, while the animal soul lacks reason.

We know that we have something called the soul, and we must ask what it is that creates this soul in the human body. Man creates, by a natural process, the soul of another man, just as an animal creates the soul of another animal similar to itself. That can be the only indubitable answer . . . . Those who assert that the soul is different from the body; that it was created by a God who deposed it, are not worth being heeded. . . . Man would not die if his vital spirit, his soul, could not die.   [3]

ADAMS, JOHN

ADAMS, JOHN (1735-1826). The second president of the United States regarded himself as "one of those Protestants who do not believe in anything." He repudiated Platonism, the doctrines of the Christian churches, deism, materialism, and scoffed at the belief in the perfectibility of human nature and the progressive development of the human intellect. An austere, cynical, selfless, and stubborn man, he opposed democracy because he distrusted the people, yet he devoted himself to the welfare of the entire nation. He maintained that an aristocratic class could provide for the interests of the poor more adequately than the masses of plain people whose very interests might be at stake.

Adams was a political philosopher despite his contemptuous attitude toward philosophy. His concepts of government were based upon the arguments of Aristotle and Montesquieu. He admired the ideas of these men, even though they were philosophers, and in the same way, he revered Bolingbroke, Hume and Voltaire as "comets" of thought. He staunchly defended the governmental system of checks and balances against the demands for centralized power or an extension of democracy.

Adams played a leading part in the opposition to the Stamp Act of 1765 and in the organization of the War of Independence; but he remained a Tory in his persistent sympathy for the British form of government. Thus the constitution for the State of Massachusetts, written by him, was very conservative. As President, Adams resisted Alexander Hamilton's requests for a declaration of war against France and the negation of the lower-class demands. Adams' domestic policy of taking the middle course was a failure; his Presidential experiences reinforced his feelings of detached cynicism. After he left the Capitol, he declared that "a fine load of manure was a fair exchange for the honors and virtues of the world."

ON SELF-DELUSION

NOTHING in the science of human nature is more curious or deserving of critical attention than the principle, referred to by moralists, as self-deceit. This principle is the spurious offspring of self-love. It is, perhaps, the greatest source and the worst part of the vices and calamities of mankind. The most distorted minds are ingenious in contriving excuses for their crimes. They will explain that compulsion, necessity, the strength or suddenness of temptation, or the violence of passion caused them to commit the crime. These excuses also serve to assuage their consciences and to make them, by degrees, even more insensible.

Indeed it must be confessed . . . that those eyes, which

have been given us to see, are willingly suffered, to be obscured, and those consciences, which by the commission of the Almighty God have a rightful authority over us, are often deposed by prejudices, appetites, and passions; disagreeable qualities that ought to have an inferior position in our intellectual and moral systems. . . .

Let not writers and statesmen deceive themselves. The springs of conduct and opinion are not always clear and pure, nor are those of our political antagonists so polluted and corrupt, as they would have the world believe.

[4]

ADLER, ALFRED

ADLER, ALFRED (1870-1937). Adler is important for his formulation of the theory of "individual psychology," the most widely accepted technique (next to psychoanalysis, founded by Sigmund Freud) in the treatment of neuroses. This concept is largely based upon the general theory of psychology and human character. Because "individual psychology" is based on medical practice as well as philosophy, it is easily distinguishable from the various social psychologies.

Adler, a disciple and collaborator of Freud, is said to have influenced his teacher in some ways. Like Freud, Adler attributed primary importance to infantile experiences. But, whereas Freud considered sexuality or its repression as the formative force of character and the cause of certain types of neuroses, Adler stated that the formative force is the desire of the individual to secure authority in the social milieu. Neurosis, according to Adler, is the effect of inferior feelings that result from the individual's failure to gain superiority or dominance. Inferior feelings may be caused either by physical or mental shortcomings. Consequently, the individual tends to compensate or even over-compensate. He assumes superior attitudes which cause abnormal behavior patterns.

Freud endeavored to discover the sexual components of the healthy or neurotic personality, while Adler deviated from this over-emphasis of sexuality. He maintained that no component could be evaluated accurately without regard for the unity of character which manifests itself in the individual's "style of life." The weak individual, unable to overcome his shortcomings or to discipline himself, adopts a "style of life" which enables him to enjoy illusions of superiority. He expects social prestige because of his imagined superiority instead of actual efficiency. Consequently he becomes a stranger to reality, pursuing "fictive goals." The function of the psychologist, according to Adler, is to induce the patient (whose fundamental "style of life" cannot be changed after early childhood) to avoid conflicts with society by recognizing its dangers, to act in accordance with reality and abstain from a reversion to delusions. Because of the emphasis on early childhood, Adler and his disciples were interested in educational reform.

His principal works are *The Neurotic Constitution* (1912) and *Individual Psychology* (1924).

THE STYLE OF LIFE

IF we look at a pine tree growing in the valley we will notice that it grows differently from one on top of a mountain. It is the same kind of a tree, but there are two distinct styles of life. Its style on top of the mountain is different from its style when growing in the valley. The style of life of a tree is the individuality of a tree expressing itself and moulding itself in an environment. We recognize a style when we see it against a background of an environment different from what we expect, for then we realize that every tree has a life pattern and is not merely mechanical reaction to the environment.

It is much the same with human beings. We see the style of life under certain conditions of environment, and it is our task to analyze its exact relation to the existing circumstances, since our mind changes with alteration of the environment. As long as a person is in a favorable situation we cannot see his style of life clearly. In new situations, however, where he is confronted with difficulties, the style of life appears clearly and distinctly. . . . The style of life is a unity because it has grown out of the difficulties of early life and out of the striving for a goal.   [5]

ADLER, FELIX

ADLER, FELIX (1851-1933). Brought to the United States at the age of six by his father, a rabbi, Felix Adler was also educated for the rabbinical office. He received his doctorate from Heidelberg University and returned to preach at the Temple Emanu-El in New York City. It was here that he failed to refer to God in his sermons. Although he was not disloyal to Judaism, as a rationalist he could not accept the rituals in any literal sense.

He left the rabbinate and his friends established a professorship of Hebrew and Oriental literature for him at Cornell University.

It was his belief that the principle of the good life can be achieved independently of religious ritual and dogma that led him to found the American Ethical Union and the Society for Ethical Culture in New York. (From there it spread to many groups throughout America and the Continent.) He maintained that the idea of a personal God is unnecessary; that the social and ethical behavior of man, if it makes for harmonious relationships among men, constitutes the Godhead; that man's personality because of its unique and inviolable nature is the central force of the religion. He advocated more than mere religious tolerance: men should reverently respect the religious differences among themselves.

In his books *Creed and Deed* (1878) and *Moral Instruction of Children* (1892) he was able to fuse his heterogeneous influences: Judaism, Christianity, Kant, Emerson, and the cogent socialistic ideas of his lifetime. He is noted for his social efforts in such areas as kindergarten and manual training schools, and the abolition of child labor.

IMMORTALITY

TRUE disinterestedness is the distinguishing mark of every high endeavor. The pursuit of the artist is unselfish, the beauty he creates is his reward. The toil of the scientist in the pursuit of abstract truth is unselfish, the truth he sees is his reward. Why should we hesitate to acknowledge in the domain of ethics what we concede in the realm of art and science? To say that unselfishness itself is only the more refined expression of a selfish instinct, is to use the term selfish with a double meaning, is a mere empty play on words. We have the innate need of harmony in the moral relations; this is our glory, and the stamp of the Divine upon our nature. We cannot demonstrate the existence of disinterested motives any more than we can demonstrate that there is joy in the sunlight and freedom in the mountain breeze. The fact that we *demand unselfishness* in action alone assures us that the standard of enlightened self-interest is false.

And indeed, if we consult the opinions of men where they are least likely to be warped by sophistry, we shall find that disinterestedness is the universal criterion by which moral worth is measured. If we suspect the motive we condemn the act. If a person gives largely for some object of public usefulness, or charity, we do not permit the munificence of the gift to deceive our judgment. Perhaps he is merely desirous of vaunting his wealth, perhaps it is social standing he aims at, perhaps he is covetous of fame. If these suspicions prove well founded, the very men who accept his bounty will, in their secret hearts, despise him, and by a certain revulsion of feeling we shall resent his action all the more, because, not only is he destitute of honorable purpose, but he has filched the fair front of virtue, and defiled the laurel even in the wearing of it.

We do not even accord the name of goodness to that easy, amiable sympathy which leads us to alleviate the sufferings of others, unless it be guided by wise regard for their permanent welfare. The tattered clothes, the haggard looks, the piteous pleading voice of the pauper on the public highway may awaken our pity, but the system of indiscriminate alms-giving is justly condemned as a weakness rather than a virtue.

On the other hand, obedience to duty, when it involves pain and self-abnegation, seems to rise in the general estimation. Clearly because in this instance even the suspicion of interested motives is removed, since hardship, injury in estate and happiness, and even the possible loss of life, are among the foreseen consequences of the act. It is for this reason that the Book of Martyrs has become the golden book of mankind, and that the story of their lives never fails to fill us with mingled sorrow and admiration and pride. They are monuments on the field of history, and milestones on the path of human progress. We regard them and gain new courage and confidence in our better selves. The blazing pyre on the

Campo Fiore, whereon Giordano Bruno breathes his last, becomes a beacon-light for the truth-seeker; the dying Socrates
still pours benignant peace over many a sufferer's couch; the
Man of Sorrows, on Calvary, comforts the hearts of the Christian millions. In the presence of these high examples the inadequacy of the selfish standard becomes clearly apparent.
We recognize what a sublime quality that is in man which
enables him, not only to triumph over torment and suffering,
but to devote his very self to destruction for the sake of honor
and truth. Freely must Virtue be wooed, not for the dowry
she may bring; by loyal devotion to her for her own sake
only, can she be won!

If thus it appears that not only is there nothing in the
nature of Virtue to warrant a claim to reward, but that it is
her very nature to disclaim any reward, it will become plain
that the problem, as stated in the beginning, rests upon an
entirely false foundation. That the unrighteous and unprin-
cipled should enjoy temporal happiness, does not offend the
law of justice. That you, my good sir, honest in all your deal-
ings, truthful in all your acts, should be unhappy, is greatly
to be deplored. Why evil and happiness should have been
allowed at all to enter a world created by an all good and
all powerful Being may fairly be asked. Why those who possess the treasure of a clear conscience should not also possess
the lesser goods of earth is a question with which morality is in nowise concerned.

Virtue can have no recompense, save as it is its own
recompense, and vice can receive no real punishment, save
as it is its own avenger. The hope of immortality, in so far
as it is based upon the supposed necessity of righting in a
future state what is here wrong, is therefore untenable, for
it is based upon the assumption of a wrong which exists in
the imagination merely. *And he who claims a reward because
of his virtue, has thereby forfeited his right to maintain the
claim, since that is not virtue which looks for reward.*

[6]

AHAD HAAM. See Ginzberg, Asher.

ALBERTUS MAGNUS

ALBERTUS MAGNUS (1193-1280). Considered the first representative of humanism during the Middle Ages, Albertus Magnus was born in Germany, a descendant of the Counts of Bollstadt in Bavaria. He was educated in Padua and Bologna. Endowed with an encyclopedic mind, he was rightly called "Doctor Universalis."

His reputation as a professor of theology at the University of Paris was known throughout Europe, and he was highly esteemed as a scholar of Arab and Jewish philosophy (studies which had been encouraged under the influence of Emperor Frederick II). In fact, no other Christian scholar of the Middle Ages quoted as many Jewish philosophers as did Albertus. He learned much from Solomon ibn Gabirol's *Fons Vitae* (Source of Life), although he recognized that this book was not in accordance with the accepted precepts of philosophy.

In physics and cosmology, he was a disciple of Maimonides. As a trained scientist he stressed the importance of observation and experiment. Interested in the study of metals and inorganic elements, Albertus is perhaps best remembered as a scientist for his observation of the comet in 1240 and for his contributions to experimental science.

In 1223, Albertus entered the Dominican Order, despite the protestations of his former teachers. He believed in the defense of knowledge for its intrinsic value, and that philosophy was an integral part of that knowledge, rather than an accessory study. He maintained that his essential ideas were best expressed in his theological works. He was more the compiler than the systematic thinker, the commentator rather than the creator of constructive and consistent philosophies. Although he always presented a speculative philosophy with great clarity, he never succeeded in integrating contemporary philosophies into Christian thought.

He taught at Cologne from 1248 to 1254 and after served as Bishop of Ratisbon for two years. His most famous pupil was Thomas Aquinas, and they were devoted friends until Aquinas' death in 1274. One of Albertus' last works was written in defense of his former pupil.

ANALOGY BETWEEN GOD AND MAN

THERE is no excellence among the creatures which is not to be found in a much higher style, and as an archetype, in the Creator; among created beings it exists only in footmarks and images. This is true also of the Trinity. No artistic spirit can accomplish his work without first forming to himself an outline of it. In the spirit, therefore, first of all, the idea of its work is conceived, which is, as it were the offspring of the spirit in every feature resembling the spirit, representing it in its acting. Thus, therefore, the spirit reveals himself in the idea of the spirit. Now, from the acting spirit this idea passes into reality, and for this purpose the spirit must find a medium in outward action. This medium must be simple, and of the same substance with him who first acted, if indeed the latter is so simple that being, nature, and activity are one in him. From this results the idea in reference to God, of the formative spirit, of the planned image, and of the spirit by which the image is realized. The creation in time is a revelation of the eternal acting of God, the eternal generation of his Son. The revelation of God in time for the sanctification of nature, is an image of the eternal procession of the spirit from the Father and the Son. Our love is only a reflection of the divine love; the archetype of all love is the Holy Spirit, who, like all love, proceeds from God. The one love spread abroad through all holy souls proceeds from the Holy Spirit. Love in God neither diminishes nor increases, but we diminish or increase it in ourselves according as we receive this love into our souls, or withdraw from it.

[7]

ALBO, JOSEPH

ALBO, JOSEPH (c. 1380-1445). Very little is known about the life of Albo, but the few facts that are available present interesting aspects of medieval Jewish life midst Gentile surroundings. Albo was the representative of the Jewish community of Daroca, where the impact and resultant clash of Jewish, Christian, and Islamic thought gave rise to a number of intellectual disputes. He participated in the great religious controversy at Tortosa (1413-14), where he vigorously defended the Jewish viewpoint of the Talmud.

He attained popularity among medieval Jews because of his book

Sefer-Ha-Ikkarim (Book of Principles), a defense of Judaism against philosophical criticism and Christianity. Although no new ideas are introduced, the book is important to the general philosophy of religion because it established the criterion whereby the primary fundamental doctrines of Judaism may be distinguished from those of secondary importance. Albo stated that three principles are basic to every revelational religion: a belief in God, the concept of divine revelation, and divine retributive justice.

LAUGHTER

"LAUGHTER" (Heb. *sehok*) is a homonymous term. It applies to joy, as in the expression, "Then Abraham fell upon his face and laughed." Here "laughed" means "was glad," as is also the interpretation of Onkelos.

Laughter may also denote scorn, as in the expression, "I am as one that is a laughing-stock to his neighbour." And sometimes laughter and scorn are combined, and the words are used synonymously, as in the expression, "He that sitteth in heaven laugheth, the Lord hath them in derision," for laughter is often due to the feeling of contempt for that which deserves it, as when a person observes a defect in the words or deeds of another, while being conscious of superiority in himself, as not likely to err in word or deed as his neighbor has done. Thus laughter arises from the feeling of contempt when he observes his neighbor doing or saying something that is unbecoming to human nature or the person's dignity.

In the same way, laughter and derision are ascribed to God in the expression, "He that sitteth in heaven laugheth, the Lord hath them in derision." The reason is because He hears them saying, "Let us break their bands asunder," words a human being should not use; as our Rabbis say: The reason that the Psalm of Absalom stands next to that dealing with Gog and Magog, is that if any one should say, Is it possible that a servant should rebel against his master? you say to him, Is it possible that a son should rebel against his father? And yet the latter actually happened, so the former will happen. It is clear from this that it is an unusual thing for a man to say, and that he who says it deserves derision and contempt. In such cases, then, laughter is attributed to God or man.

Sometimes a person laughs when he deceives another in a matter about which the latter should have taken caution and did not. Accordingly the cause of laughter in all cases is a feeling of superiority in the person laughing, when he sees another commit a folly or exhibit ignorance or foolishness. When the scientists say that laughter is a human property, i.e. the cause of laughter is not known, they mean to say that we do not know why laughter is accompanied by certain bodily motions or why laughter is caused by touching the armpits or feeling other sensitive places in the body. But derision as a cause of laughter is well known, as we have shown in explaining the verse, "He that sitteth in heaven laugheth."

[8]

ALCOTT, AMOS BRONSON

ALCOTT, AMOS BRONSON (1799-1888). Alcott is frequently referred to as a dreamer because of his unsystematic, deeply veiled philosophy. Yet, like his friend, Emerson, he is truly representative of the New England transcendentalist movement. He was best received at small gatherings, where people listened patiently to his rambling ideas, eager to catch the secret meaning of his orthodoxy. His critics like to dwell upon his personal oddities with the result that his virtues and thoughts are little known. However, many of his lectures throughout the East and Middle West were published in *The Dial*. He is also the author of *Orphic Sayings, Tablets*, and *Concord Days*. Principally a distributor of ideas, a reiterator of previously formulated concepts, he was a teacher by conversation rather than indoctrination. He established several schools based upon these ideas, and was a member of the short-lived Utopian experiment at Fruitlands. Through his solid friendships with Ralph Waldo Emerson and William T. Harris, he was able to realize his dream of a school of philosophy at Concord, Massachusetts.

It is frequently said, despite his contributions to American letters and philosophy, that his life was a failure—largely because his household larder was empty most of the time. This in no way detracted from his family's allegiance to him. His daughter, Louisa May Alcott, portrayed him as the grandfather in *Little Women*. In spite of his critics, this peripatetic lover of wisdom remains one of New England's most lovable sons.

TABLE TALK

LIKE its suburban neighbor beside the Charles, our village, scated along the banks of its Indian stream, spreads a rural cradle for the fresher literature; and aside from these advantages it well deserves its name for its quiet scenery and plain population. Moreover, few spots in New England have won a like literary repute. The rural muse has traversed these fields, meadows, woodlands, the brook-sides, the river; caught the harmony of its changing skies, and portrayed their spirit in books that are fit to live while Letters delight, and Nature charms her lovers. Had Homer, had Virgil, fairer prospects than our landscape affords? Had Shakespeare or Goethe a more luxuriant simplicity than ours? Only the wit to say or sing these the poet needs; and of this our neighborhood has not less than many sounding cities. Plain as our landscape is, it has special attractions for the scholar who courts quiet surroundings, scenery not too exciting, yet stimulating to genial and uninterrupted studies. If the hills command no very broad horizon, the prospect is sufficiently sylvan to give an agreeable variety without confusing the mind, while the river in good part compensates for the sameness, as it winds sluggishly along the confines of the village, flowing by the monument into the distance through the meadows. Thoreau, writing of it jocosely says: "It is remarkable for the gentleness of its current, which is hardly perceptible, and some have ascribed to its influence the proverbial moderation of the inhabitants of Concord, as celebrated in the Revolution and on other occasions. It has been suggested that the town should adopt for its coat-of-arms a *field verdant* with the Concord River circling nine times round it."

*   *   *

Not in stirring times like ours, when the world's affairs come posted with the succesive sun rising or setting, can we ignore magazines, libraries, and ephemera of the press. Newspapers intrude into every house, almost supersede the primers and text-books of the schools, proffering alike to hand and eye intelligence formerly won only by laborious studies and much expense of time and money. Cheap literature is now in vogue; the age, if not profound, has chances for attaining some superficial knowledge, at least, of the world's doings and designings; the experiments of the few being hereby popularized for the benefit of the many everywhere, the humblest even partaking largely of the common benefit.

*   *   *

Life and literature need the inspiration which idealism quickens and promotes. The history of thought shows that a people given to sensationalism and the lower forms of materialism have run to ruin. Only that which inspires life and nobility of thought can maintain and preserve itself from speedy and ignoble decay. And we have too palpable evidences of corruption, public and private, to leave us in doubt as to the tendency of not a little of the cultivation and teachings in our times. . . The idealists have given deeper insight into life and nature than other schools of thought. If inclined to visionariness, and seemingly sometimes on the verge of lunacy even, they have revealed depths of being, a devotion to the spirit of universality, that render their works most edifying. They, more than any other, hold the balance between mind and matter, and illuminate literature, while they furthered the science, art, and religion of all times. An age deficient in idealism has ever been one of immorality and superficial attainment, since without the sense of ideas, nobility of character becomes of rare attainment, if possible.

*   *   *

If the speaker cannot illuminate the parlor, shall he adorn the pulpit? Who takes most of private life into the desk comes nearest heaven and the children who have not lapsed out of it. Is it not time in the world's history to have

21

less familiarity with sin and the woes of the pit? Commend me to him who holds me fast by every sense, persuades me—against every bias of temperament, habit, training, culture—to espouse the just and lovely, and he shall be in my eyes thereafter the Priest of the Spirit and the Sent of Heaven. It is undeniable that, with all our teaching and preaching—admirable as these often are— the current divinity falls behind our attainments in most things else; the commanding practical sense and adventurous thoughts of our time being unawakened to the concerns wherein faith and duty have their seats, and from whose fountains life and thought are spiritualized and made lovely to men. Though allegory is superseded in good part by the novel, the field for this form of writing is as rich and inviting as when Bunyan wrote. A sacred allegory, treating of the current characteristics of the religious world, would be a powerful instrumentality for awakening and stimulating the piety of our times.

*   *   *

Every dogma embodies some shade of truth to give it seeming currency. Take the theological trinity as an instance which has vexed the literal Church from its foundation, and still perplexes its learned doctors. An intelligible psychology would interpret the mystery even to the unlearned and unprofessional. Analyse the attributes of your personality—that which you name yourself—and you will find herein the threefold attributes of instinct, intelligence, will, incarnate in your own person:—the root plainly of the trinitarian dogma.—Not till we have fathomed the full significance of what we mean when we pronounce "*I myself,*" is the idea of person clearly discriminated, philosophy and religion established upon immutable foundations.

*   *   *

Ever present and operant is *That* which never becomes a party in one's guilt, conceives never an evil thought, consents never to an unrighteous deed, never sins; but holds itself impeccable, immutable, personally holy — the Conscience — counsellor, comforter, judge, and executor of the spirit's decrees. None can flee from the spirit's presence, nor hide himself. The reserved powers are the mighty ones. Side by side sleep the Whispering Sisters and the Eumenides. Nor is Conscience appeased till the sentence is pronounced. There is an oracle in the beast, an unsleeping police; and ever the court sits, dealing doom or deliverance. Our sole inheritance is our deeds. While remorse stirs the sinner, there remains hope of his redemption. "Only he to whom all is one, who draweth all things to one, and seeth all things in one, may enjoy true peace and rest of spirit." None can escape the *Presence*. The *Ought* is everywhere and imperative. Alike guilt in the soul and anguish in the flesh affirm His ubiquity. Matter—in particle and planet, mind and macrocosm—is quick with spirit.

*   *   *

Born daily out of a world of wonders into a world of wonders, that faith is most ennobling which, answering to one's highest aspirations, touches all things meanwhile with the hues of an invisible world. And how vastly is life's aspect, the sphere of one's present activity, widened and ennobled the moment there step spiritual agents upon the stage, and he holds conscious communication with unseen powers! "He to whom the law which he is to follow," says Jacobi, "doth not stand forth as a God, has only a dead letter which cannot possibly quicken him." The religious life transcends the scientific understanding, its light shining through the clouds to those alone whose eyes are anointed to look behind the veils by lives of purity and devotion.

*   *   *

Personal Identity is the sole Identity. "That which knows and that which is known," says Aristotle, "are really the same thing." The knowing that *I am* affirms also the personality

23

immanent in all persons; and hence of the Supreme Person, since distinct from personality neither mind nor God were thinkable. And it were impossible to have like conceptions in our minds, if we did not partake of one and the same intellect.

> Were God not *God*, I were not *I*;
> Myself in Him myself descry.

An impersonal God were an absurdity. Personality is essential to the idea of spirit, and man, as man, were unthinkable without the presupposition of personality. It is the *I* that gives subsistence to nature and reality to mind. Where the *I* is not, nothing is. Religion and science alike presuppose its presence as their postulate and ground. It is the essence of which substance is the manifestation. Qualities are inherent in substance, and substance is one and spiritual. Personal Identity is spiritual, not numerical, souls being one, bodies not one. Any number of bodies can never attain to unity, since it is the one in each that defines and denotes it. The personality is inclusive of the one in each and in all.

*   *   *

Our sleep is a significant symbol of the soul's antecedence. Shall I question that I now am, because I am unconscious of being myself while I slept; or because I am conscious of being then unconscious? I am sure of being one and the same person I then was, and thread my identity through my successive yesterdays into the memory out of which my consciousness was born; nor can I lose myself in the search of myself. At best, our mortality is but a suspended animation, the soul meanwhile awaiting its summons to awaken from its slumbers. Every act of sleep is a metamorphosis of bodies and a metempsychosis of souls. We lapse out of the senses into the pre-existent life of memory through the gate of dreams, memory and fancy opening their folding-doors into our past and future periods of existence:—the

24

soul freed for the moment from its dormitory in space and time. The more of sleep the more of retrospect; the more of wakefulness, the more of prospect. Memory marks the nadir of our consciousness, imagination its zenith. Before the heavens thou art, and shall survive their decay. Were man personally finite, he could not conceive of infinity; were he mortal he could not conceive of immortality. Whatever had a beginning comes of necessity to its end, since it has not the principle of perpetuity inherent in itself. And there is that in man which cannot think annihilation, but thinks continuance. All life is eternal; there is no other. Despair snuffs the sun from the firmament.

> For souls that of His own good life partake
> He loves as His own self; dear as His eye
> They are to Him. He'll never them forsake.
> When they shall die, then God Himself shall die.
> They live, they live in blest eternity.   [9]

ALCUIN, FLACCUS ALBINUS

ALCUIN, FLACCUS ALBINUS (c. 735-804). Well-known as a teacher, poet, and monastic, Alcuin achieved his greatest fame as the educator of Charlemagne. The emperor probably met him on his journeys through Italy. Alcuin had returned to Parma from England because of a declining interest in education there, and when Charlemagne invited him to take charge of his court school, the Schola Palatina, he gladly accepted. There, and later at Tours, where he had been given the monastery of St. Martin, Alcuin lived the life of a teacher, always abreast of the literary developments of the period. According to him, he "dispensed the honey of the Holy Scripture, intoxicated his students with the wine of ancient learning, fed them the apples of grammatical refinement, and adorned them with the knowledge of astronomy."

The erudition of Charlemagne is directly traceable to the influence of his versatile teacher. Alcuin was a lover of poetry, and wrote quite acceptable hexameters. But posterity remembers him best as a great letter writer; more than three hundred of his letters have been preserved. Each was written to a distinguished friend, addressed either by some name which characterized the recipient,

25

or a Latin paraphrase of the real name. They are still interesting for their philosophical content as well as for their references to historic events.

DIALOGUE ON THE VIRTUES

Charlemagne—I wonder that we Christians should so often depart from virtue, though we have eternal glory promised as its recompense by Jesus Christ, who is Truth itself whilst the heathen philosophers steadily pursued it merely on account of its intrinsic worth, and for the sake of fame.

Alcuin—We must rather deplore than wonder, that most of us will not be induced to embrace virtue, either by the fear of punishment or the hope of promised reward.

Charlemagne—I see it, and must, alas! acknowledge that there are many such. I beg you, however, to inform me as briefly as possible, how we, as Christians, are to understand and regard these chief virtues.

Alcuin—Does not that appear to you to be wisdom, whereby God, after the manner of human understanding, is known and feared, and his future judgment believed?

Charlemagne—I understand you; and grant that nothing is more excellent than this wisdom. I also remember that it is written in Job, *Behold, the wisdom of man is the fear of God!* And what is the fear of God but the worship of God.

Alcuin—It is so: and further, what is righteousness but the love of God, and the observance of his commandments?

Charlemagne—I perceive this also, and that nothing is more perfect than this righteousness, or rather that there is no other than this.

Alcuin—Do you not consider that to be valor whereby a man overcomes the "Evil One," and is enabled to bear with firmness the trials of the world?

Charlemagne—Nothing appears to me more glorious than such a victory.

Alcuin—And is not that temperance which checks desire, restrains avarice, and tranquillizes and governs all the passions of the soul?

[10]

ALDEN, JOSEPH

ALDEN, JOSEPH (1807-1885). Principally known as a pedagogue, Alden began his career at the age of fourteen when he became a teacher in a district school. His skill and ability were soon recognized. He became a professor at Williams College in 1835 and remained there until 1852. He was appointed president of Jefferson College in 1857, and was principal of the State Normal School at Albany, New York from 1867 to 1882.

He excelled in directing and developing logical thought in young people and was equally successful as an administrator and author. He published more than seventy books, most of which dealt with philosophy, religion, and government in such a manner that they were popularly acceptable for classroom use. Aware that his talents were chiefly of a didactic nature, Alden refrained from pretentious expression and adopted his aims to his methods. Of his many books, *Christian Ethics or the Science of Duty* (1866), *The Science of Government* (1867), and *Thoughts on the Religious Life* (1879) were the most widely read.

CONCEPTIONS OF THE INFINITE

THERE has been a great deal written about the absolute and the infinite which conveys no meaning to such as have not the faculty of understanding the unintelligible. For example, Mansel says: "That which is conceived of as absolute and infinite must be conceived of as combining within itself the sum not only of all actual but of all possible modes of being."—There is no such thing as a general infinite. There are infinite things or attributes, just as there are true propositions. But the infinite and the true are not independent entities. We cognize infinite objects, and can thus form an abstract idea of infinity. The idea is not definable. As we say, "Truth is that in which all true proportions agree," so we may say, that the infinite is that in which all infinite objects agree.

27

That is infinite which has no limit. That which we cognize as limitless is to us infinite. We must distinguish between the infinite and the indefinite. God's wisdom is infinite; it transcends all our powers of expression. So of his mercy and his benevolence. Infinite existence is everlasting existence. When we speak of God as the Infinite Existence, we mean that all his attributes are infinite. The human mind can form no adequate apprehension of infinite things; and yet it is not, properly speaking, a negative apprehension which we have of it. The fact that we cannot know everything about a subject or object does not prove that we cannot know anything about it. The fact that we cannot by searching find out God to perfection, does not prove that we cannot know many things respecting him. God is infinite: that is, His existence and attributes are without limit—transcend all our power of apprehension. We know nothing than can be added to them.

[11]

ALEXANDER, SAMUEL

ALEXANDER, SAMUEL (1859-1938). A teacher at Oxford, Glasgow and Victoria Universities, Alexander's fame rests principally on his book *Space, Time and Deity*, which evolved out of his Gifford Lectures at Glasgow given in 1915. This book has been referred to as the most significant British metaphysical contribution since that of Hobbes. Classed as both idealist and realist, he tended more toward realism as he grew older. In 1889, his prize essay *Moral Order and Progress* (which he disowned some twenty years later) fanned the Anglo-Aristotelian-Hegelian movement in British ethics toward the direction of a sophisticated evolutionary theory.

PHILOSOPHY AND THEOLOGY

PHILOSOPHY approaches theology, in the character of the philosophy of religion, in the same spirit as it approaches the other sciences, the spirit of criticism and comprehension. Necessarily, in Bacon's fine phrase, philosophy takes all knowledge for its province; not in the sense of arrogating an impossible erudition, but in the sense that it asks whether the ideas used in any science are compatible with those used in other sciences or in the ordinary unscientific possessions of the mind. No topic raised in the sciences, so far as it does not fall strictly within that art which is the special province of the science—and is therefore subject to the rules of the scientific artist (what philosopher in his senses would question the demonstration of the binomial theorem? He leaves such doubts to the skilled craftsman, the mathematician)—is exempt from his enquiry. His dearest privilege indeed is to organize knowledge, to find a comprehensive view of the whole. But comprehension means scrutiny. Of theology it asks, granted that the object of religion is such and such, what place is there in the rest of the universe for such a being? Is the being so described consistent with other well-attested facts? Hence, as in regard to the ordinary things of sense, it asks whether these are indeed real, apart from our awareness of them, or exist only in so far as there is a knower of them; so it asks of theology, may not the object of religion be a fancy projected into reality by the wishes of man?

Philosophy is critical of theology in another fashion, which is more to my immediate purpose. Theology is exposed to a peculiar danger. The more it penetrates by reflection into the notions of religion the more it tends to employ conceptions on the borderland of philosophy. Some theologies do more or less without philosophy; it is always said that the Jews are not a philosophical people on the whole, and are content with moral notions. But Christian theology has been, in its more abstract parts, very philosophical, and has attracted to itself some of the greatest speculative intellects. Now the danger arises thus: the demands of the religious consciousness—I mean, of course, the clarified religious consciousness— are insistent and must be met, and they lead to ideas which are mysterious indeed, but whose mystery passes more or less unnoticed by the ordinary mind; which are indeed pictorial embodiments of these insistent claims. Thus the intimate harmonising of God and man, their communion in the relation of child to father, is embodied in the idea of a God-made man, which is found in other religions, but in none with such grace and winningness as in Christianity. But the purely religious data of the Incarnation, the Atonement, the Resurrection, data which are the starting points of Christian theology, lead on to the subtlest metaphysical conceptions, such as that of the Trinity, which are introduced to satisfy rationally the data contained in the religious consciousness, which is not of itself rational at all in its inception. It is in the employment of philosophical conceptions that theology has to tread most warily and to beware of taking them over except after scrutiny. Much of the theology which I have read of to-day (and it is very little) seems to me not to avoid this danger; one instance is the indiscriminate appeal made to the idea of value or the valuable, as something which must be accepted as admitting no further analysis, although psychologists and writers on morals have offered such analyses more than once.

[12]

AL-FARABI

AL-FARABI (c. 870-950). Born of a Turkish family, educated by a Christian physician at Baghdad, Al-Farabi has been ranked with Aristotle as one of the greatest of all teachers.

A versatile man, his chief occupation was that of philosopher, either by way of comment or original contribution. He is best known for his analyses of the Greek philosophers. Whatever he wrote was syncretistic in nature, for he sought for the compatible concepts of God, soul, time, and space among the diverse philosophies. Thus he found Plato and Aristotle in perfect accord, and historians of philosophy have ever since despaired over his treatise *On the Agreement of the Philosophy of Plato and Aristotle.*

He wrote many works on various aspects of the soul: its intellect, the unity of the soul, its substance, and many of its problems. All his thinking was characterized by an idealism bordering on mysticism.

Al-Farabi was principally influenced by Plotinus whose belief that the materially comprehensive world emanated from God still exerts influence over Moslem scholastic thought, and by Aristotle

30

who assumed there was a Prime Mover of the universe and therefore the world had no beginning in time, that time is relative to motion and could not have preceded God, who himself was the first mover.

Al-Farabi was not only a great philosopher but also a noted musicologist. Dervishes in the East can still be heard singing the chants he composed. He was also a Utopian whose *Model City* envisioned his desires for the heavenly city on this earth.

ON CONCEPTS

I. KNOWLEDGE is divided into (a) generally accepted concepts (concepts of the sun, moon, intellect, and the soul), and (b) those concepts that require verification (such as making certain that the heaven consists of spheres, one in the other; or that the world has been created in time).

It is necessary for every concept to have a prior concept. The concluding concept may be established without connecting it to a concept preceding it. This is true of being: the necessary and the possible. These concepts do not require one to previously perceive that something comprises them. These three are rather distinct, correct concepts, innate to understanding. If someone desires to verbally clarify these concepts, then this is only a stimulus to understanding; but they cannot be clarified beyond the clarity of the concepts themselves.

II. It is impossible for us to understand the verifications of concepts without previously having understood other things. For instance, if we wish to know that the world has been created in time, then we must have the prior certainty that the world is composite. However, all that is composite has also been originated in time; consequently we know also that the world has been originated in time. Without doubt, this verification ultimately ends in another which then does not require another to precede it for confirmation.

These, then, are the basic principles that are clearly present in the intellect: of two sides of an opposite, one must always be true, the other false; the whole is greater than any part of it. Logic is the science by which we get acquainted with these methods so that they assist us in our concepts of things and guide us to their verification. The two methods mentioned here aid us in distinguishing between complete and deficient concepts, between the certain and those only approximately certain; as well as the preponderant opinion and the doubtful one. By doing this we become aware of all the aspects of the complete concept as well as the certain verification of those that do not contain any doubt.

III. Thus we maintain: All that there is is divided into two categories. In the first category it is unnecessary to cogitate the nature of the things, since they are of a possible existence. If we reflect on the nature of the second category of things, we find that their being is a necessary one and we say accordingly, it is of necessary existence. It is not absurd to postulate that some things of possible existence are not present; for in order for a thing to exist, it must have a cause; however, if it becomes a necessary being, then it attains necessary existence through something other than that which it itself is. From this it follows that it is necessary for it to belong to that which naturally always has a possible existence and became a necessary being only by virtue of something else. This possibility either never ceases or it takes place at a particular time. The possibility cannot move forever as cause and effect, as it were, in a circle; instead it must end in something necessary to itself. The latter would be that which would be present at first.

IV. However, if we postulate that which is necessary as not present, then we state an absurdity. For its being has no cause, and furthermore, it cannot have its being by virtue of something else. It is the first cause of the being of things, and its being must of necessity be the prime being. We are compelled to imagine the same in every way free of want. Its being is thus complete. Moreover, its being must of necessity be the most perfect one, free from causes, i.e., matter, form, creation, and the final goal.   [13]

ALGHAZZALI, ABU HAMID MOHAMMED IBN GHAZZALI

ALGHAZZALI, ABU HAMID MOHAMMED IBN GHAZZALI
(1059-1111). Alghazzali was a Persian philosopher born in the
northeastern part of the empire. The greatest teachers of Islam have
bestowed upon him innumerable encomiums, among them, "the guide
to the True Faith," "the embodiment of religious thought," "the living reaffirmation of Islam." To this day his writings are considered
classic throughout the Moslem world.

Alghazzali, never a bigoted orthodox, both advocated and practiced tolerance. He often advised his co-religionists to take the pious
Jew as their model in religious reverence. In fact, Jewish philosophers of the Middle Ages soon became aware that Alghazzali's
principles and teachings were closely akin to those of Judaism, a
fact that has often been confirmed by modern Christian scholars.

Alghazzali was deeply influenced by Sufism despite his faithful
study of the Koran. His doctrine of emanation was derived from neo-
Platonic writings. He classified those who denied this doctrine as
children, for both confuse marionettes or wooden idols with reality.
His criticisms of causality pre-dated David Hume's parallel theories
by several centuries, and he exerted great influence over William
of Ockham and other Christian philosophers. He compared the pursuit of knowledge to the process involved in digging a well: both involved probing; the desired object in both cases was necessary to
life.

THE NATURE OF MAN

THOUGH man shares with the other animals external and internal senses, he is at the same time also endowed with two
qualities peculiar to himself, knowledge and will. By knowledge is meant the power of generalization, the conception of
abstract ideas, and the possession of intellectual truths. By
will is meant that strong desire to acquire an object which
after due consideration of its consequences has been pronounced by reason to be good. It is quite different from
animal desire, nay, it is often the very opposite of it.

In the beginning children also lack these two qualities.
They have passion, anger, and all the external and internal

33

senses, but will finds its expression only later. Knowledge differs according to the capacity for it, according to the latent powers in a man. Hence there is a variety of stages amongst Prophets, the Ulamas, the Sufis and the Philosophers. Further progress is possible even beyond these stages, for divine knowledge knows no bounds. The highest stage is reached by one to whom all truths and realities are revealed intuitively, who by virtue of his exalted position enjoys direct communion and close relation with the Most Holy. The real nature of this position is known only to him who enjoys it. We verify it by faith. A child has no knowledge of the attainments of an adult; an adult is not aware of the acquisitions of a learned man. Similarly a learned man is not cognizant of the holy communion of the saints and the prophets, and of the favors bestowed on them. Although the divine blessings descend freely, those are fit recipients of them, whose hearts are pure and wholly devoted to Him. "Verily," says the Hadis, "the desire of the virtuous is to hold communion with me, and I long to look at them." "He who approaches me a span, I approach him an arm." The divine favors are not withheld, but hearts bedimmed by impurity fail to receive them. "Had it not been that the devils hover round the hearts of men, they would have seen the glories of the Kingdom of the Heaven."

The superiority of man consists thus in his being cognizant of divine attributes and actions. Therein lies his perfection; thus he may be worthy of admission to God's presence.

The body serves as a vehicle for the soul, and the soul is the abode for knowledge which is its fundamental character as well as its ultimate object. The horse and the ass are both beasts of burden, but a superiority of the former is found in its being gracefully adapted for use in battle. If the horse fails in this it is degraded to the rank of mere burden bearing animals. Similarly with man. In certain qualities man resembles a horse and an ass, but his distinguishing trait is his participation in the nature of the angels, for he holds a middle position between the beast and the angel. Considering the mode of his nourishment and growth he is found to belong to the vegetable world. Considering his power of movement and impulses he is a denizen of the animal kingdom. The distinguishing quality of knowledge lifts him up to the celestial world. If he fails to develop this quality and to translate it into action he is no better than a grunting pig, a snarling dog, a prowling wolf, or a crafty fox.

If he wishes for true happiness, let him look upon reason as a monarch sitting on the throne of his heart, imagination as its ambassador, memory as treasurer, speech as interpreter, the limbs as clerks, and the senses as spies in the realms of color, sound, smell, etc. If all these properly discharge the duties allotted to them, if every faculty does that for which it was created—and such service is the real meaning of thanksgiving to God—the ultimate object of his sojourn in this transitory world is realized.

Man's nature is made up of four elements, which produce in him four attributes, namely, the beastly; the brutal, the satanic, and the divine. In man there is something of the pig, the dog, the devil, and the saint. The pig is the appetite which is repulsive not for its form but for its lust and its gluttony. The dog is passion which barks and bites, causing injury to others. The devil is the attribute which instigates these former two, embellishing them and bedimming the sight of reason which is the divine attribute. Divine reason, if properly attended to, would repel the evil by exposing its character. It would properly control appetite and the passions. But when a man fails to obey the dictates of reason, these three other attributes prevail over him and cause his ruin. Such types of men are many. What a pity it is that these who would find fault with those who worship stones do not see that on their part they worship the pig and the dog in themselves: Let them be ashamed of their deplorable condition and leave no stone unturned for the suppression of these evil attributes. The pig of appetite begets shamelessness, lust, slander, and such like: the dog of passion begets pride, vanity, ridicule, wrath and tyranny. These two, controlled by the satanic power produce deceit, treachery, perfidy, meanness etc. but if divinity in man is uppermost the qualities of knowledge, wisdom, faith, and truth, etc. will be acquired.

Know then that mind is like a mirror which reflects images. But just as the mirror, the image, and the mode of reflection are three different things so mind, objects, and the way of knowing are also distinct. There are five reasons which may prevent the object from being reflected in the mirror. 1. There may be something wrong with the mirror. 2. Something other than the mirror may prevent the reflection. 3. The object may not be in front of it. 4. Something may come between the object and the mirror. 5. The position of the object may not be known, so that the mirror may be properly placed. Similarly, for five reasons, the mind fails to receive knowledge. 1. The mind may be imperfect, like the child's. 2. Sin and guilt may bedim the mind and throw a veil over it. 3. The mind may be diverted from the real object. For example, a man may be obedient and good, but instead of rising higher to the acquisition of truth and contemplation of God is contented with bodily devotions and aquirement of means of living. Such a mind, though pure, will not reflect the divine image for his objects of thought are other than this. If this is the condition of such mind, think what will be the state of those minds which are absorbed in the gratification of their inordinate passions. 4. An external screen, may as it were, come before the objects. Sometimes a man who has subjugated his passions still through blind imitation or prejudice fails to know the truth. Such types are found amongst the votaries of the Kalam. Even many virtuous men also fall a prey to it and blindly stick to their dogmas. 5. There may be ignorance of the means for the acquisition of truth. Thus for illustration, a man wants to see his back in a mirror: if he places the mirror before his eyes he fails to see his back; if he keeps it facing his back it will still be out of sight. Let him then take another mirror and place one before his eyes and the other facing his back in such a position that the image of

36

the latter is reflected in the former. Thus he will be able to see his back. Similarly the knowledge of the unknown from the known.

The divine dispensation is liberal in the distribution of its bounties, but for reasons mentioned above, minds fail to profit by them. For human minds partake of the nature of the divine and the capacity to apprehend truth is innate. The Koran says: "Surely we offered the trust to the heavens and the earth and the mountains, but they declined to bear it up and were afraid of it and man took it up. Surely he is not just (to himself) and is ignorant." In this passage the innate capacity of man is hinted at and refers to the secret power of knowing God, latent in human minds by virtue of which they have preference over other objects and the universe. The Prophet says: "Every child is born in the right state (Fit-rat) but his parents make him a Jew, a Christian, or a Magian." And again: "Had it not been that evil spirits hover round the hearts of the sons of Adam they would have seen the kingdom of heaven." Ibn Umar reports that the Prophet was once asked as to where God is found either on earth or in heaven. "He is in the hearts of his faithful servants," replied the Prophet.

It will not be out of place to throw some light here on the following terms which are often vaguely applied while dealing with the question of human nature.

1. Qalb (heart) has two meanings. (a) A conical shaped piece of flesh on the left side of the chest, circulating blood, the source of animal spirits. It is found in all animals. The heart thus belongs to the external world and can be seen with the material eyes. (b) A mysterious divine substance which is related to the material heart like the relation between the dweller and the house or the artisan and his implements. It alone is sentient and responsible.

2. Ruh (spirit) means (a) a vapory substance which issues from the material heart, and quickens every part of the body. It is like a lamp which is placed in a house and sheds its light on all sides. (b) The soul which is expressed

in the Koran as "divine commandment" and is used in the same sense as the second meaning of Qalb, mentioned above.

3. Nafs (self) which means (a) the substratum for appetite and passion. The Sufis call it the embodiment of vices. (b) The ego which receives different names in accordance with the qualities acquired from changes in its conditions. When in subjugating passions it acquires mastery over them and feels undisturbed, it is called *the peaceful self* (Nafsi mutmainna). The Koran says: "Nafs that art at rest. Return to thy Lord well pleased with Him, well pleasing." When it upbraids man for his actions it is called *conscience* (Nafsi lauwama). When it freely indulges in the gratification of his passions, it is called *the inordinate self* (Nafsi ammara).

[14]

AL-KINDI

AL-KINDI (died 873 A.D.). The son of a South Arabian governor, Al-Kindi was given the best possible education at Basra and Baghdad. His life was spent in the service of the court as tutor, astrologer, translator and editor of many Greek philosophical works. We possess few of his writings in the original Arabic, probably because, at one time, his extensive library was temporarily confiscated. His optical and astronomical calculations were valued for centuries. He was the first to apply mathematics not only to the physical world but also to Materia Medica where he calculated the effect of medicines from the proportions and qualities represented in the various mixtures.

From Latin translations of his works and literary activities, we learn that his eclecticism was equally characteristic of many Arab philosophers throughout the Middle Ages. He respected Plato, Aristotle and Pythagoras, but remained blind to their essential doctrinal differences. He, thus, shared the tendencies of most Neo-Platonists and Neo-Pythagoreans. In philosophy, he regarded God as the intelligent cause of the universe, the Greek *nous*, that has communicated itself from above through successive emanations of the soul to the sphere in which we live. Through this process, man became free and immortal, though his body remained subject to the influence of the stars.

ON THE SUBJECT OF INTELLECT

I HAVE taken note that you ask that a brief discussion of the intellect [and the object of comprehension], according to the theory of Plato and Aristotle, be communicated to you. Their theory is that intellect falls into four types. The first is the intellect which is always active; the second is the intellect potentially in the mind; the third is the intellect when it becomes an efficient agent by virtue of [its] power in the mind; the fourth is the intellect which we call demonstrative, and it is this intellect which Aristotle approximates to sensation, because of the propinquity of sensation to truth and because it is in complete communion with it.

For Aristotle has said that there are two kinds of form. One of them has matter and it is that which underlies sensation; but the other is that which is devoid of matter and is that which forms the substratum of intellect. Indeed, the former has to do with things, while the latter is above that.

Now, the form that resides in matter, is actually perceived; for if it were not actually perceived it would not lie within the range of sensation. Now, if the mind apprehends it, then it is as such in the mind. But it does not apprehend it unless it was first potentially in the mind. Therefore, when the mind apprehends it, it becomes actual in the mind. However, it is not in the mind as something is in a vase, nor does it chase through the body; for the mind is not the body, nor is it limited. Therefore, it is in the mind, and the mind is one, identical with itself, and not anything other than itself; nor is it again different by virtue of a twisting of terms.

Similarly, the faculty of feeling does not exist except in the soul. But it is not part of the soul as a member is part of the body; rather, it is the soul itself, and as such is feeling. Likewise, the form of the sense datum is not in the mind as something distinct or different. Therefore, as Aristotle has declared, the sense datum in the mind is the perceiving agent in conformity to what is in the mind. But, the sense datum as a material thing is outside the perceiving mind. Now, therefore, that which is in matter is the sense datum, not the perceiving agent.

Similarly, Aristotle has explained intelligence as the mind when it apprehends the object of comprehension, or THE form which has neither matter nor sensuous representation and is one with mind, and is then in actuality in the mind; for it was not previously in actuality, but [only] potentially in the mind. This form, therefore, which hasn't any matter or sensuous representation as yet, is the intellect which the mind has attained through primal intelligence, the concept of all, ever active. However, this does not become contributive, unless the mind has attained the power to receive it, since the mind is [only] potentially an agent of intelligence, whereas primal intelligence is always active. For nothing assimilates anything through its own receptivity except that which belonged to it potentially and not in actuality. Nothing, to be sure, that a thing possesses potentially works as an efficient cause by itself; for if it were self-existent, it would always be in activity; since its essence would always be its own and spontaneous. Therefore, nothing that exists potentially becomes an efficient cause unless by virtue of something that is an efficient cause. Hence, the mind is potentially an agent of intelligence, yet it becomes an efficient cause at the instigation of primal intelligence, looking to which it becomes an agent of intelligence in actuality. And, when an intelligible form is conjoined with it, it is not one thing, and the intelligible form another, because it is not divisible, allowing it to be changed. But when a union is brought about with the intelligible form, then it and the intellect are one, if you will allow the agent of intelligence and that which is comprehended. Thus, the intellect and the object of comprehension are one when they exist in the mind. In truth, the intellect as such, which is always active and draws forth the mind so it may become an agent of intelligence in fact, after it was potentially in-

40

telligent, and the object of comprehension as such are not one and the same thing. Therefore, the object of comprehension in the mind and the first type of intellect derived from primal intelligence are not the same; however, the intellect derived from the mind and the object of comprehension are one and the same.

But the intellect, which in simplicity is more like the soul, is much higher in comparison with the thing comprehended than sensation, as compared with the sense datum. The first type of intellect, therefore, is the cause of all that is comprehended. But the second type of intellect is potentially in the mind.

Intellect is, thus, either of the first type in that it is for all that is comprehended, or it is of the second type and then it is potentially in the mind; at all events, the mind is not an actual agent of intelligence. The third type of intellect, however, is the one that is working efficiently in the mind which has already acquired it. And, it is kept there in such a manner that, when it wills, it may use it and cause it to be in one other than itself. In the same way, writing is ready and easy for a scribe because he has already become proficient in it and it has become second nature to him. Consequently, he communicates and practices it whenever he is so inclined. The fourth type of intellect is that which goes forth from the mind which, when you desire to communicate it, will work an effect in someone other than yourself.

The second type of intellect derives, therefore, from the the third and fourth, for the reason that the third is an acquisition of the mind and causes it to appear whenever it wishes, either at the first instance of its acquisition in us, or in the second instance of its appearance outside us. Then the mind uses it. Therefore, the third is the one that is an acquisition of the mind, which is prior to it, and, if it so wills, becomes spontaneous in it. But the fourth is that which appears to work as an efficient cause from the mind.

These are, therefore, the parts into which the foremost

philosophers have divided the intellect. May this explanation suffice for what you had in mind.

[15]

ALLEN, ETHAN

ALLEN, ETHAN (1738-1789). Ten years prior to the publication of Thomas Paine's *Age of Reason,* Ethan Allen's book, *Reason The Only Oracle of Man,* (1784), enunciated the principles of deism operative in American life. Condemned by the clergy and New England universities, it was admiringly referred to by freethinkers as "Ethan's Bible." When a fire at the publishing house destroyed the stock of copies, the orthodox welcomed the incident as "an act of God."

Though Allen was a contemplative man, he led an active life, engaging in farming, mining, manufacturing, and real-estate transactions. He was a soldier during the French and Indian War, and, during the War for Independence, he commanded the Green Mountain Boys of Vermont and captured from the British Fort Ticonderoga, the main approach to Canada. He was a pioneer in the development of American economic life and built a blast furnace in the Litchfield Hills of Connecticut, his native state. Vermont was his adopted state, and he vociferously defended its boundary and land claims against those of New York and New Hampshire.

Allen was reared in Arminianism. This religious belief, though tolerant of Calvinist orthodoxy, emphasized human duties more than theological speculation. Allen rebelled against any accepted dogma, publicly protesting that he was not a Christian but a deist. He opposed authority of all kinds and declared that tradition was fallible, reason the highest gift of God, and faith less reliable and unimportant. He viewed human beings as "the most selfish, oddest, and most cunning medley of beings of that size in the universe." And though his opinions of contemporary human conditions were equally pessimistic, he was confident that the ultimate victory of virtue would make for human progress. He was convinced that the existence of Man was necessary for the maintenance of the world created by God and, therefore, there "can be no ultimate failure." He held that the future was beyond human comprehension and that goodness and happiness would prevail in the last stage of human development, for so had God ordained.

THE period of life is very uncertain, and at the longest is but short: a few years bring us from infancy to manhood, a few more to a dissolution; pain, sickness and death are the necessary consequences of animal life. Through life we struggle with physical evils, which eventually are certain to destroy our earthly composition; and well would it be for us did evils end here; but alas! moral evil has been more or less predominant in our agency, and though natural evil is unavoidable, yet moral evil may be prevented or remedied by the exercise of virtue.

Morality is of more importance to us than any or all other attainments; as is a habit of mind, which, from a retrospective consciousness of our agency in this life, we should carry with us into our succeeding state of existence, as an acquired appendage of our rational nature, and as the necessary means of our mental happiness. Virtue and vice are the only things in this world, which, with our souls, are capable of surviving death; the former is the rational and only procuring cause of all intellectual happiness, and the latter of conscious guilt and misery; and therefore, our indispensable duty and ultimate interest is, to love, cultivate and improve the one, as the means of our greatest good, and to hate and abstain from the other, as productive of our greatest evil. And in order thereto, we should so far divest ourselves of the incumbrances of this world, (which are too apt to engross our attention) as to acquire a consistent system of the knowledge of religious duty, and make it our constant endeavour in life to act conformably to it.

The knowledge of the being, perfections, creation and providence of GOD, and of the immortality of our souls, is the foundation of religion. And as the Pagan, Jewish, Christian and Mahometan countries have been overwhelmed with a multiplicity of revelations diverse from each other, and which, by their respective promulgators, are said to have been immediately inspired into their souls, by the spirit of God, or immediately communicated to them by the intervening agency of angels (as in the instance of the invisible Gabriel to Mahomet) and as those revelations have been received and credited, by far the greater part of the inhabitants of the several countries of the world (on whom they have been obtruded) as supernaturally revealed by God or Angels, and which, in doctrine and discipline, are in most respects repugnant to each other, it fully evinces their imposture, and authorizes us, without a lengthy course of arguing, to determine with certainty, that not more than one if any one of them, had their original from God; as they clash with each other; which is ground of high probability against the authenticity of each of them.

A revelation, that may be supposed to be really of the institution of God, must also be supposed to be perfectly consistent or uniform, and to be able to stand the test of truth; therefore such pretended revelations, as are tendered to us as the contrivance of heaven, which do not bear that test, we may be morally certain, were either originally a deception, or has since, by adulteration become spurious. Furthermore, should we admit, that among the numerous revelations on which the respective priests have given the stamp of divinity, some one of them was in reality of divine authority, yet we could not otherwise, as rational beings, distinguish it from others, but by reason.

Reason therefore must be the standard by which we determine the respective claims of revelation; for otherwise we may as well subscribe to the divinity of the one as of the other, or to the whole of them, or to none at all. So likewise on this thesis, if reason rejects the whole of those revelations, we ought to return to the religion of nature and reason.

Undoubtedly it is our duty, and for our best good, that we occupy and improve the faculties, with which our Creator has endowed us, but so far as prejudice, or prepossession of opinion prevails over our minds, in the same proportion, reason is excluded from our theory or practice. Therefore if

44

we would acquire useful knowledge, we must first divest ourselves of those impediments; and sincerely endeavour to search out the truth; and draw our conclusions from reason and just argument, which will never conform to our inclination, interest or fancy; but we must conform to that if we would judge rightly. As certain as we determine contrary to reason, we make a wrong conclusion; therefore, our wisdom is, to conform to the nature and reason of things, as well in religious matters, as in other sciences. Preposterously absurd would it be, to negative the exercise of reason in religious concerns, and yet, be actuated by it in all other and less occurrences of life. All our knowledge of things is derived from God, in and by the order of nature, out of which we cannot perceive, reflect or understand any thing whatsoever; our external senses are natural and so are our souls; by the instrumentality of the former we perceive the objects of sense, and with the latter we reflect on them. And those objects are also natural; so that ourselves, and all things about us, and our knowledge collected therefrom, is natural, and not supernatural.

We may and often do, connect or arrange our ideas together, in a wrong or improper manner, for the want of skill or judgment, or through mistake or the want of application, or through the influence of prejudice; but in all such cases, the error does not originate from the ideas themselves, but from the composer; for a system, or an arrangement of ideas justly composed always contain the truth; but an unjust composition never fails to contain error and falsehood. Therefore an unjust connection of ideas is not derived from nature, but from the imperfect composition of man. Misconnection of ideas is the same as misjudging, and has no positive existence, being merely a creature of the imagination; but nature and truth are real and uniform; and the rational mind by reasoning, discerns the uniformity, and is thereby enabled to make a just composition of ideas, which will stand the test of truth. But the fantastical illuminations of the credulous and superstitious part of mankind, proceed from weakness, and as far

45

as they take place in the world, subvert the religion of REASON
and TRUTH. [16]

AL-MUKAMMAS, DAVID IBN MERWAN

AL-MUKAMMAS, DAVID IBN MERWAN (died c. 937). Born in
Babylonia, author of the earliest known Jewish philosophical work of
the Middle Ages—a commentary to the Sefer Yetzirah (the Book
of Formation)—chiefly responsible for the development of the Cabala, Al-Mukammas' manuscripts lay forgotten for centuries. The
aforementioned was discovered in 1898 in the Tsarist Library;
fragments of another work on the unity of God were found in the
basement of a Cairo synagogue. Al-Mukammas established three ascending categories of science: practical philosophy, theoretical philosophy, and knowledge of the Torah.

THE THREE GRADES OF SCIENCE

THE science of ethics and the mind clarifies the opinions of
men and guides them in the path of understanding.

The study of applied mathematics is an aid to the thorough understanding of the practical arts; the study of rational mathematics is a guide to the understanding of the
speculative arts. For the science of mathematics is one of the
gates which lead to a knowledge of the substance of the soul.
This knowledge is the beginning of science, the constituent
element of wisdom, and the root of the practical and theoretical arts.

Philosophy is the knowledge of all things according to
the measure of their form, the secret of their nature, and the
impartation of truth. . . . The "impartation of truth" includes that science, superior to all other sciences, namely
the science of the Torah. These three are essential gradations of philosophy.

No one who acknowledges the existence of God, prophet,
or law, can deny the authority of the Torah. To deny it is
an important omission. Some deniers add or invent mysterious things for the purpose of self-aggrandizement. For it

46

was God's own goodness that prompted Him to benefit man by giving him laws for his guidance; not the innate merits of man that gave him prior claim to God's protection, since God neither benefits from man's obedience, nor receives injury from his disobedience.

[17]

ANAXAGORAS

ANAXAGORAS (c. 500-428 B.C.). Renowned as the last of the great Ionian philosophers, Anaxagoras was born at Klazomene on the Lydian coast of Asia Minor. A friend of Pericles and a teacher of Thucydides, Euripides, and other noted Greeks, he was the first philosopher to choose Athens as his home. He was held in great reverence until, at the instigation of a bigot, he was accused of blasphemy in speculating that the sun was a red, hot mass of stone and the moon an earthy substance. Although he was condemned to death, his influential friends helped him escape.

FRAGMENTS

ALL things were together infinite both in number and in smallness,—for the small, too, was infinite. And when all things were together, none of them could be distinguished because of their smallness. For air and æther prevailed over all things, being both of them infinite; for amongst all things these are the greatest both in quantity and size.

For air and æther are separated off from the mass that surrounds the world, and the surrounding mass is infinite in quantity.

And since these things are so, we must suppose that there are contained many things and of all sorts in all (the worlds) that are brought together, germs of all things, with all sorts of shapes, and colours and savours, and that men have been formed in them, and the other animals that have life, and that these men have inhabited cities and cultivated fields, as with us; and that they have a sun and moon and the rest, as with us; and that their earth brings forth for them many things of all kinds, of which they gather together the

47

best and use them for their dwellings. Thus much have I said with regard to separating off, but elsewhere too.

. . . As these thus revolve and are separated off by the force and speed. And the speed makes the force. And their speed is like nothing in speed of the things that are now among men, but in every way many times as quick.

.　　.　　.　　.　　.　　　.　　.　　.　　.

But before they were separated off, when all things were together, not even was any colour distinguishable; for the mixture of all things prevented it,—of the moist and of the dry, and the warm and the cold, and the light and dark [and much earth being in it], and of a multitude of innumerable germs in no way like each other. For none of the other things either is like any other.

In everything there is a portion of everything except Nous, and there are some things in which there is Nous (mind) also.

All other things partake in a portion of everything, while Nous is infinite and self-ruled, and is mixed with nothing, but is alone, itself by itself. For if it were not by itself, but were mixed with anything else, it would partake in all things if it were mixed with any; for in everything there is a portion of everything, as has been said by me in what goes before, and the things mixed with it would hinder it, so that it would have power over nothing in the same way that it has now being alone by itself. For it is the thinnest of all things and the purest, and it has all knowledge about everything and the greatest strength; and Nous has power over all things, both greater and smaller, that have life. And Nous had power over the whole revolution, so that it began to revolve in the beginning. And it began to revolve first from a small beginning; but the revolution now extends over a large space, and will extend over a larger still. And all the things that are mingled together and separated off and distinguished are all known by Nous. And Nous set in order all things that were to be and that were, and all things that are now and that are, and this revolution in which now revolve the stars and the sun and the moon, and the air and the æther that are separated off. And this revolution caused the separating off, and the rare is separated from the dense, the warm from the cold, the light from the dark; and the dry from the moist. And there are many portions in many things. But no thing is altogether separated off nor distinguished from anything else except Nous. And all Nous is alike, both the greater and the smaller; while nothing else is like anything else, but each single thing is and was most manifestly those things of which it has most in it.

.   .   .   .

And when Nous began to move things, separating off took place from all that was moved, and so far as Nous set in motion all was separated. And as things were set in motion and separated, the revolution caused them to be separated much more.

The dense and the moist and the cold and the dark came together where the earth is now, while the rare and the warm and the dry (and the bright) went out towards the further part of the æther.

From these as they are separated off earth is solidified: for from mists water is separated off, and from water earth. From the earth stones are solidified by the cold, and these rush outwards more than water.

But Nous has power over all things that are, and it is now where all the other things are, in the mass that surrounds the world, and in the things that have separated off and that are being separated off.

Nor are the things that are in one world divided nor cut off from one another with a hatchet, neither the warm from the cold nor the cold from the warm.

And when those things are being thus distinguished, we must know that all of them are neither more nor less; for it is not possible for them to be more than all, and all are always equal.

Nor is there a least of what is small, but there is always a smaller; for it is impossible that what is should cease to be by being divided. But there is always something greater than what is great, and it is equal to the small in amount, and, compared with itself, each thing is both great and small.

And since the portions of the great and of the small are equal in amount, for this reason, too, all things will be in everything; nor is it possible for them to be apart, but all things have a portion of everything. Since it is impossible for there to be a least thing, they cannot be separated, nor come to be by themselves; but they must be now, just as they were in the beginning, all together. And in all things many things are contained, and an equal number both in the greater and in the smaller of the things that are separated off.

The Hellenes are wrong in using the expressions coming into being and passing away; for nothing comes into being or passes away, but mingling and separation takes place of things that are. So they would be right to call coming into being mixture, and passing away separation.

The earth is flat in shape, and remains suspended because of its size and because there is no vacuum. For this reason the air is very strong, and supports the earth which is borne up by it.

Of the moisture on the surface of the earth, the sea arose from the waters in the earth, . . . and from the rivers which flow into it.

Rivers take their being both from the rains and from the waters in the earth; for the earth is hollow, and has waters in its cavities. And the Nile rises in summer owing to the water that comes down from the snows in Ethiopia.

The sun and the moon and all the stars are fiery stones ignited by the rotation of the æther. Under the stars are the sun and moon, and also certain bodies which revolve with them, but are invisible to us.

We do not feel the heat of the stars because of the greatness of their distance from the earth; and, further, they are not so warm as the sun, because they occupy a colder region. The moon is below the sun, and nearer to us.

The sun surpasses the Peloponnesos in size. The moon has not a light of her own, but gets it from the sun. The course of the stars goes under the earth.

The moon is eclipsed by the earth screening the sun's light from it. The sun is eclipsed at the new moon, when the moon screens it from us. Both the sun and the moon turn in their courses owing to the repulsion of the air. The moon turns frequently, because it cannot prevail over the cold.

Anaxagoras was the first to determine what concerns the eclipses and the illumination of the sun and moon. And he said the moon was of earth, and had plains and ravines in it. The Milky Way was the reflection of the light of the stars that were not illuminated by the sun. Shooting stars were sparks, as it were, which leapt out owing to the motion of the heavenly vault.

Winds arose when the air was rarefied by the sun, and when things were burned and made their way to the vault of heaven and were carried off. Thunder and lightning were produced by heat striking upon clouds.

Earthquakes were caused by the air above striking on that beneath the earth; for the movement of the latter caused the earth which floats on it to rock.

But Anaxagoras says that perception is produced by opposites; for like things cannot be affected by like. He attempts to give a detailed enumeration of the particular senses. We see by means of the image in the pupil; but no image is cast upon what is of the same colour, but only on what is different. With most living creatures things are of a different colour to the pupil by day, though with some this is so by night, and these are accordingly keen-sighted at that time. Speaking generally, however, night is more of the same colour with the eyes than day. And an image is cast on the pupil by day, because light is a concomitant cause of the image, and because the prevailing colour casts an image more readily upon its opposite.

It is in the same way that touch and taste discern their objects. That which is just as warm or just as cold as we are neither warms us nor cools us by its contact; and, in the same way, we do not apprehend the sweet and the sour by means of themselves. We know cold by warm, fresh by salt, and sweet by sour, in virtue of our deficiency in each; for all these are in us to begin with. And we smell and hear in the same manner; the former by means of the accompanying respiration, the latter by the sound penetrating to the brain, for the bone which surrounds this is hollow, and it is upon it that the sound falls.

And all sensation implies pain, a view which would seem to be the consequence of the first assumption, for all unlike things produce pain by their contact. And this pain is made perceptible by the long continuance or by the excess of a sensation. Brilliant colours and excessive noises produce pain, and we cannot dwell long on the same things. The larger animals are the more sensitive, and, generally, sensation is proportionate to the size of the organs of sense. Those animals which have large, pure and bright eyes see large objects and from a great distance, and contrariwise.

And it is the same with hearing. Large animals can hear great and distant sounds, while less sounds pass unperceived; small animals perceive small sounds and those near at hand. It is the same too with smell. Rarefied air has more smell; for, when air is heated and rarefied, it smells. A large animal when it breathes draws in the condensed air along with the rarefied, while a small one draws in the rarefied by itself; so the large one perceives more. For smell is better perceived when it is near than when it is far by reason of its being more condensed, while when dispersed it is weak. But, roughly speaking, large animals do not perceive a rarefied smell, nor small animals a condensed one.

[18]

52

ANAXIMANDER

ANAXIMANDER (610-c. 547 B.C.). Known as Anaximander of Miletus, he was the earliest Greek philosophical essayist. A pupil of Thales, he was also the first Greek cartographer, and has been credited with the invention of a number of astronomical instruments.

His treatise *On Nature* dealt with the development of matter. In the search of the basic principles from which all things in existence were derived, Anaximander ignored those elements experienced by perception. He upheld the concept of *apeiron,* wherein the universe developed from the infinite by means of rotation.

Neither Anaximander nor his contemporaries analyzed the concept of the infinite. However, he did advance theories concerning infinite space, the infinite possibilities of combinations of qualities, and the infinite power of production.

FRAGMENTS

ANAXIMANDER of Miletus, son of Praxiades, a fellow-citizen and associate of Thales, said that the material cause and first element of things was the Infinite, he being the first to introduce this name for the material cause. He says it is neither water nor any other of what are now called the elements, but a substance different from them which is infinite, from which arise all the heavens and the worlds within them.

And into that from which things take their rise they pass away once more, "as is ordained; for they make reparation and satisfaction to one another for their injustice according to the appointed time."

And besides this, there was an external motion, in the course of which was brought about the origin of the worlds.

He did not ascribe the origin of things to any alteration in matter, but said that the oppositions in the substratum, which was a boundless Body, were separated out.

He says that something capable of begetting hot and cold was separated off from the eternal at the origin of this world. From this arose a sphere of flame which grew round the air encircling the earth, as the bark grows round a tree.

When this was broken up and enclosed in certain rings, the sun, moon, and stars came into existence.

Rain was produced by the moisture drawn up from the earth by the sun.

The sea is what is left of the original moisture. The fire has dried up most of it and turned the rest salt by scorching it.

The earth swings free, held in its place by nothing. It stays where it is because of its equal distance from anything.

Living creatures arose from the moist element as it was evaporated by the sun. Man was like another animal, namely, a fish, in the beginning.

Further, he says that in the beginning man was born from animals of a different species. His reason is, that, while other animals quickly find food for themselves, man alone requires a prolonged period of sucking. Hence, had he been originally such as he is now, he could never have survived.

The first living creatures were produced in the moist element, and were covered with prickly integuments. As time went on they came out upon the drier part, and, the integument soon breaking off, they changed their manner of life.

[19]

ANAXIMENES

ANAXIMENES (c. 585-525 B.C.). Along with Thales and Anaximander, Anaximenes was one of the triumvirate of important Milesian philosophers. His importance is due to his formulation of the method whereby change is represented as the result of the processes of condensation and rarefication. This theory anticipated the development of physical laws and mechanics and physics.

He also attempted to define the fundamental substance that constitutes the universe. Anaximenes endeavored to synthesize the doctrines of his two Milesian predecessors by stating that the qualities of air were sufficient to explain whatever exists perceptually and intellectually. He maintained that air was as infinite as Anaximander's *apeiron* and as real as the water which Thales considered the fundamental cosmic matter.

ANAXIMENES of Miletus, son of Eurystratos, who had been an associate of Anaximander, said, like him, that the underlying substance was one and infinite. He did not, however, say it was indeterminate, like Anaximander, but determinate; for he said it was Air.

From it, he said, the things that are, and have been, and shall be, the gods and things divine, took their rise, while other things come from its offspring.

"Just as," he said, "our soul, being air, holds us together, so do breath and air encompass the whole world."

And the form of the air is as follows. Where it is most even, it is invisible to our sight; but cold and heat, moisture and motion, make it visible. It is always in motion; for, if it were not, it would not change so much as it does.

It differs in different substances in virtue of its rarefaction and condensation.

When it is dilated so as to be rarer, it becomes fire; while winds, on the other hand, are condensed Air. Cloud is formed from Air by "felting;" and this, still further condensed, becomes water. Water, condensed still more, turns to earth; and when condensed as much as it can be, to stones.

He says that, as the air was "felted," the earth first came into being. It is very broad, and is accordingly supported by the air.

In the same way, the sun and the moon and the other heavenly bodies, which are of a fiery nature, are supported by the air because of their breadth. The heavenly bodies were produced from the earth by moisture rising from it. When this is rarefied, fire comes into being, and the stars are composed of the fire thus raised aloft. There were also bodies of earthy substance in the region of the stars, revolving along with them. And he says that the heavenly bodies do not move under the earth, as others suppose, but round it, as a cap turns round our head. The sun is hidden from sight, not because it goes under the earth, but because it is concealed by the higher parts of the earth, and because its distance from us becomes greater. The stars give no heat because of the greatness of their distance.

Winds are produced when condensed air rushes into rarefied; but when it is concentrated and thickened still more, clouds are generated; and, lastly, it turns to water.

[20]

ANSELM OF CANTERBURY, SAINT

ANSELM OF CANTERBURY, SAINT (1033-1109). A prominent figure in the struggle for power (in this period) between the secularists and ecclesiastics, Anselm was of even greater importance as a Christian philosopher. Although he was not a Scholastic, this school of church philosophy embodied many of his concepts.

Anselm, first as abbot and later as archbishop, defended the authority of the Pope to William Rufus and Henry I, kings of England. This resulted in his exile. But regardless of whether he was living in poverty or splendor, he always maintained an ascetic existence. His monastic life of contemplation and meditation was frequently interrupted by political activity.

His philosophy, largely a justification of Church practices and dogma, was publicized because he felt its position needed strengthening. He was convinced that the comprehension of divine truth was the result of faith, not reason. He stated that believing is a necessary condition of knowledge, and that in order to believe, one need not probe. In his most famous book, *Cur Deus Homo* (Why God Made Man), he tried to answer questions concerning the doctrine of man's redemption. He stated that man is created for an immortal life but is frustrated by sin, and that the Messiah has the power of redemption because His virginal birth excludes Him from the inheritance of sin. His theory of atonement and satisfaction has determined Christian thought and piety throughout the centuries. Anselm is held responsible for the ontological argument for the existence of God. This thesis, elaborated in his *Monologium*, was accepted by theologians and such eminent philosophers as Descartes and Leibniz.

NO GREATER BEING

AND so, Lord, do thou, who dost give understanding to faith, give me, so far as thou knowest it to be profitable, to under-

56

stand that thou art as we believe; and that thou art that which we believe. And, indeed, we believe that thou art a being than which nothing greater can be conceived. Or is there no such nature, since the fool hath said in his heart, there is no God? (Psalms xiv. 1). But, at any rate, this very fool, when he hears of this being of which I speak—a being than which nothing greater can be conceived—understands what he hears, and what he understands is in his understanding; although he does not understand it to exist.

For, it is one thing for an object to be in the understanding, and another to understand that the object exists. When a painter first conceives of what he will afterwards perform, he has it in his understanding, but he does not yet understand it to be, because he has not yet performed it. But after he has made the painting, he both has it in his understanding, and he understands that it exists, because he has made it.

Hence, even the fool is convinced that something exists in the understanding, at least, than which nothing greater can be conceived. For, when he hears of this, he understands it. And whatever is understood, exists in the understanding. And assuredly that, than which nothing greater can be conceived, cannot exist in the understanding alone. For, suppose it exists in the understanding alone: then it can be conceived to exist in reality; which is greater.

Therefore, if that, than which nothing greater can be conceived, exists in the understanding alone, the very being, than which nothing greater can be conceived, is one, than which a greater can be conceived. But obviously this is impossible. Hence, there is no doubt that there exists a being, than which nothing greater can be conceived, and it exists both in the understanding and in reality.

[21]

ANTISTHENES

ANTISTHENES (c. 445-365 B.C.). Son of a lower-class Athenian father and either a Thracian or Phrygian-slave mother, Antisthenes was the founder of the Cynic school of Greek philosophy. The name of his school was derived from the building in which he taught, the *Cynosarges* (dog's tomb), for Cynic philosophy bears no relation to the modern meaning of cynicism in which human values or moral scruples are held in contempt. He was originally a disciple of Gorgias, the sophist, who came to Athens in 427 B.C. Later he became one of the most faithful pupils of Socrates, tramping five miles each day to the city in order to listen to his master's words. He was present when Socrates drank the cup of hemlock.

Antisthenes was opposed to Plato's doctrine of ideas and to Aristippus' philosophy of pleasure. He interpreted the teachings of Socrates as the doctrine of virtue which can be taught with disregard of feelings, independence of judgment, contempt for conventional opinions, and discrimination between social status, birth and wealth. Later Cynics, exaggerating Antisthenes' statements, were strongly opposed to Stoics and Epicureans.

APOPHTHEGMS

O Plato, I can see a horse but I do not see horseness.
I would rather be mad than feel pleasure.
Virtue is a matter of action.
Virtue is sufficient in itself to secure happiness.
The wise man is self-sufficient.
The wise man does not follow established laws but only the law of virtue.
It is better to side a handful of good men in their struggle against an army of bad men than to side an army of bad men in their battle against a handful of good men.

[22]

AQUINAS, THOMAS

AQUINAS, THOMAS (1225-1274). Recognized as the leading philosopher of the Roman Catholic Church, Aquinas' authority was officially established by Pope Leo XIII in the encyclical *Aeterni Patris* (1879).

All non-Catholic philosophers and historians regard the doctrines promulgated by Aquinas as the quintessence of the Scholastic spirit of the Middle Ages. He surpassed all Christian predecessors in his ability to deal with the crucial problems of reason and faith by mediating variant tendencies within the Church and systematizing its theology so that it was consistent and precise.

Aquinas subordinated philosophy to theology; natural law to the revelations of Christ; human society to the dogma of the Church. He endeavored to demonstrate that these subordinations benefit philosophy, natural law, and human society, and that the dignity of each of these is reinforced in its subordination to theology. Aquinas tried to show that reality has value because it is created by God. For this reason he opposed Averroism because it rejected the theological control of philosophy; and Platonism because it depreciated the real world. He accepted Aristotelian philosophy because it was compatible with the doctrines of Christianity and met the desires and needs of human society. Many of his pronouncements were directly influenced by Jewish thinkers. His proof for the existence of God was adapted from Maimonides, and one of his proofs for the unity of God was taken from Bahya ibn Pakuda.

He was the son of the Count of Aquino, and a relative of the emperor, Frederick II. He was glorified as the "Doctor Angelicus," and, after his death, canonized as a saint.

WHETHER THE INTELLIGIBLE SPECIES ARE DERIVED BY THE SOUL FROM CERTAIN SEPARATE FORMS?

Objection 1. It seems that the intelligible species are derived by the soul from some separate forms. For whatever is such by participation is caused by what is such essentially; for instance, that which is on fire is reduced to fire as the cause thereof. But the intellectual soul forasmuch as it is actually understanding, participates in the thing understood: for, in a way, the intellect in act is the thing understood in act. Therefore what in itself and in its essence is understood in act, is the cause that the intellectual soul actually understands. Now that which in its essence is actually understood is a form existing without matter. Therefore the intelligible species, by which the soul understands, are caused by some separate forms.

Objection 2. Further, the intelligible is to the intellect, as the sensible is to the sense. But the sensible species which are in the senses, and by which we feel, are caused by the sensible object which exists actually outside the soul. Therefore the intelligible species by which our intellect understands, are caused by some things actually intelligible, existing outside the soul. But these can be nothing else than forms separate from matter. Therefore the intelligible forms of our intellect are derived from some separate substances.

Objection 3. Further, whatever is in potentiality is reduced to act by something actual. If, therefore, our intellect, previously in potentiality, actually understands, this must needs be caused by some intellect which is always in act. But this is a separate intellect. Therefore the intelligible species, by which we actually understand, are caused by some separate substances.

On the contrary, If this were true we should not need the senses in order to understand. And this is proved to be false especially from the fact that if a man be wanting in a sense, he cannot have any knowledge of the sensibles corresponding to that sense.

I answer that, Some have held that the intelligible species of our intellect are derived from certain separate forms or substances. And this in two ways. For Plato, as we have said, held that the forms of sensible things subsist by themselves without matter; for instance, the form of a man which he called *per se* man, and the form or idea of a horse which he called *per se* horse, and so forth. He said therefore that these forms are participated both by our soul and by corporeal matter; by our soul, to the effect of knowledge thereof, and by corporeal matter to the effect of existence: so that, just as corporeal matter by participating the idea of a stone, becomes an individual stone, so our intellect, by participating the idea of a stone, is made to understand a stone. Now participation of an idea takes place by some image of the idea in the participator, just as a model is participated by a copy. So just as he held that the sensible forms, which are in corporeal matter, are derived from the ideas as certain images thereof: so he held that the intelligible species of our intellect are images of the ideas, derived therefrom. And for this reason, as we have said above, he referred sciences and definitions to those ideas.

But since it is contrary to the nature of sensible things that their forms should subsist without matter, as Aristotle proves in many ways, Avicenna setting this opinion aside, held that the intelligible species of all sensible things, instead of subsisting in themselves without matter, pre-exist immaterially in the separate intellects: from the first of which, said he, such species are derived by a second, and so on to the last separate intellect which he called the *active intelligence*, from which, according to him, intelligible species flow into our souls, and sensible species into corporeal matter. And so Avicenna agrees with Plato in this, that the intelligible species of our intellect are derived from certain separate forms; but these Plato held to subsist of themselves, while Avicenna placed them in the *active intelligence*. They differ, too, in this respect, that Avicenna held that the intelligible species do not remain in our intellect after it has ceased actually to understand, and that it needs to turn (to the active intellect) in order to receive them anew. Consequently he does not hold that the soul has innate knowledge, as Plato, who held that the participated ideas remain immovably in the soul.

But in this opinion no sufficient reason can be assigned for the soul being united to the body. For it cannot be said that the intellectual soul is united to the body for the sake of the body: for neither is form for the sake of matter, nor is the mover for the sake of the moved, but rather the reverse. Especially does the body seem necessary to the intellectual soul, for the latter's proper operation which is to understand: since as to its being the soul does not depend on the body. But if the soul by its very nature had an inborn aptitude for receiving intelligible species through the influence of only certain separate principles, and were not to receive them from the senses, it would not need the body in order to understand: wherefore to no purpose would it be united to the body.

61

But if it be said that our soul needs the senses in order to understand, through being in some way excited by them to the consideration of those things the intelligible species of which it receives from the separate principles: even this seems an insufficient explanation. For this excitation does not seem necessary to the soul, except in as far as it is overcome by sluggishness, as the Platonists expressed it, and by forgetfulness, through its union with the body. Consequently the reason of the union of the soul with the body still remains to be sought.

And if it be said with Avicenna, that the senses are necessary to the soul, because by them it is roused to turn to the *active intelligence* from which it receives the species: neither is this sufficient explanation. Because if it is natural for the soul to understand through species derived from the *active intelligence,* it follows that at times the soul of an individual wanting in one of the senses can turn to the active intelligence either from the inclination of its very nature, or through being aroused by another sense, to the effect of receiving the intelligible species of which the corresponding sensible species are wanting. And thus a man born blind could have knowledge of colors; which is clearly untrue. We must therefore conclude that the intelligible species, by which our soul understands, are not derived from separate forms.

Reply Objection 1.   The intelligible species which fall to the share of our intellect are reduced, as to their first cause, to a first principle which is by its essence intelligible—namely, God. But they proceed from that principle by means of the forms of sensible and material things, from which we gather knowledge, as Dionysius says.

Reply Objection 2.   Material things, as to the being which they have outside the soul, may be actually sensible, but not actually intelligible. Wherefore there is no comparison between sense and intellect.

Reply Objection 3.   Our passive intellect is reduced from potentiality to act by some being in act, that is, by the active intellect, which is a power of the soul as we have said; and not by a separate intelligence, as a proximate cause, although perchance as remote cause.

[23]

ARCESILAUS

ARCESILAUS (c. 315-240 B.C.). From 270 to 240 B.C., Arcesilaus directed the Platonic Academy at Athens and helped it to regain its former splendor. During his administration, the doctrine of the Academy turned to a scepticism similar to that of Pyrrho and Timon, although it had developed independently of them and was somewhat milder in form.

Arcesilaus studied mathematics with Autolycus, a predecessor of Euclid at Sardes, Asia Minor. He was also an experienced musician, and a brilliant speaker and teacher. He regarded himself as the true disciple of Plato, haranguing against Speusippus and Xenocrates whom he accused of distorting Plato's doctrines. According to Arcesilaus, the correct understanding of Plato results in doubt, suspension of judgment, and a complete spiritual freedom equivalent to the supreme good. With a vehemence equal to that of other Platonists, Arcesilaus attacked the Stoics, who, in turn, severely criticized him. Epicurus was the only contemporary philosopher he acknowledged. Only a few sayings of Arcesilaus are extant.

ASSENT AND SUSPENSION

SUSPENDED judgment of particular objects is good, but assent of particulars is bad.

Whereas these statements are not made dogmatically, but in accordance with the appearance of things, they are made as statements of real facts. Therefore suspension is really good and assent bad.

Suspension is accompanied by quietude.

What the Stoics call apprehension, assent, and apprehensive presentation occurs neither in a wise man nor in a fool.

He who suspends judgment about everything, will regulate his inclinations, aversions, and his general actions with application of the rule of Reason, and by proceeding in accordance with this criteria he will act rightly. For happiness is attained through wisdom; wisdom consists in right actions, and right actions, when performed, possess reasonable justification. [24]

ARDIGO, ROBERTO

ARDIGO, ROBERTO (1828-1920). A former Catholic priest and influential leader of Italian positivism, Ardigo abandoned theology in 1869 and resigned from the Church in 1871. He was appointed a professor of theology at the University of Padua in 1881, and from that time until 1900, when an idealistic reaction had taken place, exerted considerable influence in philosophic circles. His positivism, inspired by Auguste Comte, differed from that of his master. Ardigo considered thought more important than matter and insisted on psychological disquisitions. He stated that thought is dominant in every action, the result of every action, and that it vanishes only in a state of general corruption; according to him, thought is a natural formation, unrelated to an alleged absolute; facts are the contents of consciousness, in which the subjective and objective elements are developed from an originally indistinct state. His principal works are *Psychology As A Positive Science* (1870) and *The Moral of the Positivists* (1879).

TRUTH AND REASON

TRUTH is essentially the conscious datum because consciousness incontestably attests to reality. Conscious datum is the only reality. Simple or complex sensations and the rhythm of concurring groups of sensations are facts. Truth is essentially the result of sensation because in consciousness the only datum that can be met is that of sensation.

Reason is the rhythm of experiences of the species or the individual remembered by the organism. When it functions it makes itself partly known in consciousness, but a part remains concealed. The individual does not make this rhythm, and therefore often succumbs to the delusion that the rhythm is dictated by an eternal truth which always illuminated his mind and the mind of every man in the same way. [25]

ARISTIPPUS

ARISTIPPUS (c. 435-366 B.C.). All the writings of Aristippus are lost, but if the ancient sources about him are not entirely misleading, he seems, of all the disciples of Socrates, to have been the least congenial with his teacher. The only Socratic point in Aristippus' doctrine was the praise of inner freedom and true independence. Unlike Socrates, he denied social responsibility, was indifferent to reason, and conceived of wisdom as that which is concerned with the enjoyment of pleasure and the avoidance of pain. He is said to have been the first disciple of Socrates to request fees for his lessons. When this action aroused Socrates' indignation, he offered his master part of his gain as a royalty.

Aristippus was born in Cyrene, North Africa. Early in life, he settled in Athens to study first with Protagoras and then with Socrates. The little that is known about him through anecdotes reveal him to have been wily, greedy, and ever eager to ridicule Plato. He also seems to have been optimistic, of a serene disposition, and kindly disposed to his fellow-men, except those whom he regarded as his competitors.

PLEASURE AND PAIN

THERE are only two states of the soul, namely pleasure and pain. Pleasure is a soft and easy motion. Pain is a rough and violent one. There is no other pleasure than that of the body. No pleasure is more pleasant than another one. But a pleasure may be composed of a multitude of elementary pleasures. Pleasure is agreeable, and pain is repellent to all living creatures.

[26]

ARISTOTLE

ARISTOTLE (384-322 B.C.). Still accepted by thousands as the world's leading philosopher, Aristotle possessed one of the few really encyclopedic minds ever produced by the West. His was an unique combination of philosophic insight and keen powers of observation. He was a great thinker, systematic historian, and natural scientist. Although his contributions to the subject matter of physics are important and still used, his subsequent reflections on the causes and principles of physical matter established the field of metaphysics, literally those things beyond or after physics.

The substance of his philosophy, influenced by the highly developed state of Greek art, is that there are two dichotomies: matter and form. Everything is either matter or form. For example, in a brass statue, brass is matter with a variety of potentialities and possibilities; the statue is form, the actuality. It is the form or shape of one of the possibilities of brass. Development is the process by which matter becomes form, and every form the matter for the next highest form. God, the prime mover, is pure form or thought. In man, reason represents the highest form. Entelechy is the formative principle in which purpose and cause unite for a final end.

To Aristotle, man's happiness consisted in virtue—the mean between two extremes. "Even if happiness is not sent by the Gods, but is the result of virtue and of learning of discipline of some kind, it is apparently one of the most divine things in the world; for it would appear that that which is the prize and end of virtue is the supreme good, and in its nature divine and blessed."

He conceived the perfect state to be a democracy in which the masses are restricted and where education is aimed at the development of bodily vigor and the virtues.

Aristotle was born at Stagira, and went to Athens to become a pupil (and later a critic) of Plato. He spent some years in the company of the tyrant, Hermias, whose niece he married. Shortly afterwards, he accepted the task of educating the son of Philip of Macedonia, who became known to posterity as Alexander the Great. After the death of Plato, he returned to Athens to found a school. He taught art, politics, physics, systems of natural science, logic, and philosophy at the Lyceum. In his last years, he was condemned as godless and banished from Athens. He died shortly thereafter.

THE PROCESS OF CHANGE

EVERYTHING which comes into being is brought about by something, that is, by a source from which its generation comes. And it is composed of something. Now this latter is best described not as the absence of the thing but as the matter from which it comes. And it becomes a particular thing, as a sphere or a circle or some other thing. Now one does not "make" the material—as the bronze—of which a thing is composed; so one does not make the sphere, except in a secondary sense, in so far as the bronze circle is a circle and one makes it. For the act of making a particular thing is a process of making it out of some material in general. I mean that to make the bronze round is not to make the "round" or the "sphere," but quite a different thing—that of putting this form into what did not have it previously. If one made the "form," one would make it out of something else, for this would underlie it, as when one makes a sphere out of bronze. This is done by making of a particular kind of substance, namely bronze, a special sort of thing, namely a sphere. And if one makes this "sphere" also in the same way, it is evident that he will make it in the same manner, and the process of origination will go on to infinity. It is evident therefore that the form, or whatever one ought to call the shape of the perceived object is not "made." It does not "become," nor does it have an origin. Nor is there any for the essential conception of a thing. For this is what is implanted in another entity, either by training or by nature or by force. But one does cause the "bronze sphere" to *be*. For one makes it out of bronze and the form of "sphere." One puts the form into this matter, and it is then a bronze sphere. But if there is an origin for "the idea of sphere in general" it will be something generated from something else. That which is generated will have to be analyzed again in turn, and each reduced to something further, then that to something else; I mean in one aspect into matter, in another into form. A sphere is a figure whose surface is everywhere equally distant from a center. One aspect of it is the material into which the form is to be put; the other the form which is to be put into it. The whole is what results, namely, the bronze sphere.

It is evident from what we have said that the part which is spoken of as the form or the essence does not originate; but the combination which derives its name from this does; and in everything which originates there is matter, and it is now this thing, now that. Is there then a "sphere" beside the particular spheres? Or is there a "house" beside the houses of brick? Or would there never be any particular things if this were so? The genus gives the general character, but is not a definite particular thing. But one makes and produces such and such a thing out of "this" particular substance. And when it has been produced it is "this thing of such and such a kind." This concrete existing thing is "Kallias" or "Socrates," just as the other was "this bronze sphere," but it is man and animal in general just as the other was a bronze sphere in general. It is evident then that the formal principle, as some are accustomed to speak of forms, if they are something aside from the particulars and beside the acts of generation and the essences, is of no use. For not by virtue of them would there be particular instances of them. In some cases indeed it is evident that that which causes is the same sort of thing as that which is caused, yet not identically the same, nor one numerically, but in form—as in the case of the products of nature. Man begets man, (and so it is), except where something arises of different nature, as when a horse begets a mule. Yet these cases also are really similar to the others; but what is common to a horse and an ass has not been given a name as a "proximate genus"; perhaps it would be "mule."

So it is evident that it is not at all necessary to supply forms as patterns, (for they would have to be found in these cases especially, since these are certainly substances). The begetter is adequate to the production of the effect and to the embodiment of the form in the matter. And the compound— such and such a form in this flesh and these bones—is Kallias or Socrates. They differ because of their matter, for it is different, but they are the same in form. For the form is indivisible.

Of things which come into existence some are generated by nature, some by art, some by chance. And all things which are generated are generated by something and from something and as some particular thing. Some particular thing, I mean with respect to each category, such as substance, quantity, quality or place. Origination by nature occurs in the case of those things whose origin is through the processes of nature. The substance of which they are formed we call matter; the source from which they arise is some thing in nature; the kind of thing which they become is "man" or "plant" or some other thing of the kind which we are especially accustomed to call "substances." All things which have an origin, whether by nature or by art, have a material. Each of them might exist or not exist; and the seat of this double possibility is the material part of them. In general that out of which and in accordance with which they arise is some natural thing. For that which comes into being has some natural character as that of a plant or an animal. And that under the influence of which it arises is a natural object which with reference to its form may be said to be homogeneous. And this form is found in another individual; as one man begets another man. In this way arise the things which come about by nature; but other originations are called artificial creations.

Artificial creations result from acquired skill, or external power, or deliberate planning. Some of these also come about spontaneously and by chance, in nearly the same manner as some things are generated by nature. For there some kind of things arise in some instances from seed, in other instances without seed. Into these things we shall have to look later; but those things arise by art, the forms of which are in some one's mind. And by form I mean the essential conception of the thing and its fundamental essence. And indeed in a certain sense opposites have the same form. The opposed essence is that of the absence of the given thing, as health is the absence of disease. For by the absence of the former disease becomes manifest. But health is the determining principle, in the soul and in knowledge. The healthy condition of one who has been ill comes about as follows: since such and such a condition is health it is necessary, if there is to be health, that some other condition exist, as uniform temperature, and if there is to be uniform temperature then warmth. And in this manner one continues one's analysis until one arrives at a certain thing which one can do as the

69

first step. The activity which comes from this is an artificial productivity, in this case the production of health. So in this sense it is true that health comes from health, and a house from a house, that which has material content from that which does not. The essence of the physician's art and of the builder's art is the form of health and the form of the house. And the essence without matter I call the essential conception.

One aspect of the process of production and of action is called the intellectual contemplation, the other the practical effecting of them. The one which has to do with the principle and the form is intellectual contemplation. That which refers to the aim of the intellectual contemplation is the practical application. And each of the intermediate steps has the like phases. For instance, if one will be healthy it is necessary to have an even temperature. What does the maintenance of an even temperature involve? This: it will result if one is kept warm. And what will do this? The following; but this exists only as a possibility. Yet it is in one's power. So then the action and the source from which the development of the healthy state springs, if it is from an artificial source, is the "form" in one's mind; but if from chance, still it results from something which at sometime or other is the source of activity used by him who acts with conscious skill. In the case of medical treatment perhaps the source is in causing warmth, and one produces this by rubbing. So the warmth in the body is either a part of health or there follows it something of a kind which is a part of health, or is so after some intermediate stages. And this last step is what causes the essential part and what is thus a part is to health as the stones are to a house; and likewise with other things.

As we have said, nothing can arise unless something pre-exists. Therefore that some part necessarily exists is evident. For the material part is a part. And it enters into a thing and pervades its changes. And so it is also with the things mentioned in our statement. We tell what bronze circles are by distinguishing two phases; saying of the material that it is

70

bronze; and of the form that it is such and such a shape. And this is the genus under which it is placed first. The brazen circle includes matter in its notion. Some things receive names from the matter out of which they come when they arise, being said, of course, to be not " that substance" but "of that substance," as the image of a man is said to be not "stone" but "of stone." But a healthy man is not designated from that out of which he has come. The reason for this is that he has come from a condition opposite to his present one, as well as out of a substance which we call his material being. Thus it is both a man and a sick man who becomes well. But the statement is made rather with reference to the negative state; one becomes healthy from being ill rather than from being a man. Consequently the well person is not said to be ill, but a man and a healthy man. But in those things to which there is no evident opposite, or none with a name, as of any kind of form in bronze, or the bricks or boards of a building, generation is said to be out of these, as in the other case it was out of the condition of illness. Wherefore, as in that case that from which this comes is not used in the name, so here the image of the man is not called "wood" but is styled "wooden," or "brazen" not "bronze," or "stony" not "stone"; and a house is said to be "of brick" not "bricks." Nor does the image come from wood, nor the house from bricks, if one looks at the matter exactly; and one could not say this without qualification, for it is necessary that generation come through the changing of a source—through its not remaining permanent. For these reasons then we use such modes of expression.

[27]

AURELIUS AUGUSTINUS
(Saint Augustine)

AURELIUS AUGUSTINUS (SAINT AUGUSTINE) (354-430). Born in Tagaste, near Carthage, North Africa, Augustine was the son of a pagan father and a pious Christian mother, Monica (who was later canonized). By the time he was thirty-three, he had embraced Christianity, although much earlier he had been an adherent of Manicheanism and scepticism. Shortly after his conversion, he was ordained, and from 395 until his death he served as bishop of Hippo, North Africa. He died when the Vandals besieged his episcopal town.

Living in the period of the disintegration of the Roman Empire, Augustine, through his writings, contributed much to strengthening the position of the Christian church. He defended its established doctrines against heretical attacks, and gave it a philosophy of ethics, metaphysics, and a lasting philosophy of history. His writings show him to have been trained in rhetoric, a sincere confessor, a man of both passion and serenity, and humble, though in an authoritative position.

His works deal with the problems of divine omnipotence, predestination, God, the Trinity, and creation. They consistently affirm that the Catholic Church is the only reliable guide of human reason; that founded by Christ, it practices His teachings. In addition to hundreds of sermons and pamphlets, most of which are devoted to the refutation of heresy, he made world-wide lasting contributions to the history of philosophy and literature. His major works are: *Expositio Fideis Christianae* (397); *De Trinitate* (c. 416); a commentary on *Genesis* the first parts of which were published in 414; *De Civitate Dei*; and *Confessiones*. He spent the years from 410 to 427 in writing *The City of God* (De Civitate Dei). In this work, he enunciated the famous doctrine of the four epochs of human history, a doctrine that was impressed upon the consciousness of Western civilization until the time of Hegel and Comte. However, it is not the originality of his ideas but the profundity of psychological analysis that makes Augustine a great figure in the history of philosophy. His autobiographical *Confessions* has been regarded for many centuries as a manual of self-analysis. His influence, though immeasurable, is especially notable in the teachings of Luther, Pascal, Descartes, and Leibniz.

WHAT WE ARE TO BELIEVE

WHEN, then, the question is asked what we are to believe in regard to religion, it is not necessary to probe into the nature of things, as was done by those whom the Greeks call *physici;* nor need we be in alarm lest the Christian should be ignorant of the force and number of the elements,—the motion, and order, and eclipses of the heavenly bodies; the form of the heavens; the species and the natures of animals, plants, stones, fountains, rivers, mountains; about chronology and distances; the signs of coming storms; and a thousand other things which those philosophers either have found out, or think they have found out. For even these men themselves, endowed though they are with so much genius, burning with zeal, abounding in leisure, tracking some things by the aid of human conjecture, searching into others with the aids of history and experience, have not found out all things; and even their boasted discoveries are oftener mere guesses than certain knowledge. It is enough for the Christian to believe that the only cause of all created things, whether heavenly or earthy, whether visible or invisible, is the goodness of the Creator, the one true God; and that nothing exists but Himself that does not derive its existence from Him; and that He is the Trinity—to wit, the Father, and the Son begotten of the Father, and the Holy Spirit proceeding from the same Father, but one and the same Spirit of Father and Son.

[28]

AURELIUS, MARCUS ANTONINUS

AURELIUS, MARCUS ANTONINUS (121-180). While thousands cheered hysterically when the victorious gladiator plunged his sword into his vanquished opponent, a boy in the imperial box buried himself even deeper in a book on moral philosophy. The boy, an adopted son of Antoninus Pius, became Roman emperor in 161 A.D. Ascetic in his ways, his stoical outlook had been carefully nursed by excellent teachers, and he tried to apply it during his reign, turbulent though the times proved to be.

Like his foster father, he believed that no price was too great which might buy peace and good will. Never before in the Western world had a philosopher sat on the throne, none, surely, that had tried so consistently to extol the virtues of the intellect, none that dismissed pleasure and fought with righteous zeal the ignorance which is at the base of the fear, desire and sorrow that constitute the evil in this world. Even the Christians, whom he never understood and who suffered in consequence, acknowledged the saintliness of his character and could not help but admire his half agnostic,

73

half faith-inspired belief in God or gods as the font of wisdom and power.

While the political situation worsened throughout the empire which was no longer protected by Roman armies but by foreign armed bands, while his adoptive brother, Lucius Verus, wasted himself and the empire's opportunities in debauchery in the East, while Rome was gripped in the Oriental plague and the Italian peninsula threatened by the Marcomanni, throughout all this Antoninus remained true to himself. He honored his faithless, scheming wife, Faustina, by consecrating a temple to her at Halala where she died and one at Rome, and by establishing a foundation for poor girls. Her damning letters he nobly burned unread.

His best-known work, the *Meditations*, this emperor-saint wrote on the battlefield. His life and writings show Stoicism at its best although he was judged wanting in ability to cope wih empire problems where force was deemed necessary for their successful solution.

VANITAS

MEN seek retreats for themselves, houses in the country, sea-shores, and mountains; and thou too art wont to desire such things very much. But this is altogether a mark of the most common sort of men, for it is in thy power whenever thou shalt choose to retire into thyself. For nowhere either with more quiet or more freedom from trouble does a man retire than into his own soul, particularly when he has within him such thoughts that by looking into them he is immediately in perfect tranquillity; and I affirm that tranquillity is nothing else than the good ordering of the mind. Constantly then give to thyself this retreat, and renew thyself; and let thy principles be brief and fundamental, which, as soon as thou shalt recur to them, will be sufficient to cleanse the soul completely, and to send thee back from all discontent with the things to which thou returnest. For with what art thou discontented? With the badness of men? Recall to thy mind this conclusion, that rational animals exist for one another, and that to endure is a part of justice, and that men do wrong involuntarily; and consider how many already, after mutual enmity, suspicion, hatred, and fighting have been stretched dead, reduced to ashes; and be quiet at last.—But

74

perhaps thou art dissatisfied with that which is assigned to thee out of the universe.—Recall to thy recollection this alternative; either there is providence or atoms [fortuitous concurrence of things]; or remember the arguments by which it has been proved that the world is a kind of political community [and be quiet at last].—But perhaps corporeal things will still fasten upon thee.—Consider then further that the mind mingles not with the breath, whether moving gently or violently, when it has once drawn itself apart and discovered its own power, and think also of all that thou hast heard and assented to about pain and pleasure [and be quiet at last].—But perhaps the desire of the thing called fame will torment thee.—See how soon everything is forgotten, and look at the chaos of infinite time on each side of [the present], and the emptiness of applause, and the changeableness and want of judgment in those who pretend to give praise, and the narrowness of the space within which it is circumscribed [and be quiet at last]. For the whole earth is a point, and how small a nook in it is this thy dwelling, and how few are there in it, and what kind of people are they who will praise thee.

This then remains: Remember to retire into this little territory of thy own, and above all do not distract or strain thyself, but be free, and look at things as a man, as a human being, as a citizen, as a mortal. But among the things readiest to thy hand to which thou shalt turn, let there be these, which are two. One is that things do not touch the soul, for they are external and remain immovable; but our perturbations come only from the opinion which is within. The other is that all these things, which thou seest, change immediately and will no longer be; and constantly bear in mind how many of these changes thou hast already witnessed. The universe is transformation: life is opinion.

Take away thy opinion, and then there is taken away the complaint, 'I have been harmed.' Take away the complaint, 'I have been harmed,' and the harm is taken away.

* * *

Do not act as if thou wert going to live ten thousand years. Death hangs over thee. While thou livest, while it is in thy power, be good.

How much trouble he avoids who does not look to see what his neighbor says or does or thinks, but only to what he does himself, that it may be just and pure; or as Agathon says, look not round at the depraved morals of others, but run straight along the line without deviating from it.

He who has a vehement desire for posthumous fame does not consider that every one of those who remember him will himself also die very soon; then again also they who have succeeded them, until the whole remembrance shall have been extinguished as it is transmitted through men who foolishly admire and perish. But suppose that those who will remember are even immortal and that the remembrance will be immortal, what then is this to thee? And I say not what is it to the dead, but what is it to the living. What is praise, except indeed so far as it has a certain utility? For thou now rejectest unseasonably the gift of nature, clinging to something else.

Everything harmonizes with me, which is harmonious to thee, O Universe. Nothing for me is too early nor too late, which is in due time for thee. Everything is fruit to me which thy seasons bring, O Nature: from thee are all things, in thee are all things, to thee all things return.

Occupy thyself with few things, says the philosopher, if thou wouldst be tranquil.—But consider if it would not be better to say, Do what is necessary, and whatever the reason of the animal which is naturally social requires, and as it requires. For this brings not only the tranquillity which comes from doing well, but also that which comes from doing few things. For the greatest part of what we say and do being unnecessary, if a man takes this away, he will have more leisure and less uneasiness. Accordingly on every occasion a man should ask himself, Is this one of the unnecessary things? Now a man should take away not only unnecessary acts, but also unnecessary thoughts, for thus superfluous acts will not follow after.

Try how the life of a good man suits thee, the life of him who is satisfied with his portion out of the whole, and satisfied with his own just acts and benevolent disposition.

Hast thou seen those things? Look also at these. Do not disturb thyself. Make thyself all simplicity. Does any one do wrong? It is to himself that he does the wrong. Has anything happened to thee? Well; out of the universe from the beginning everything which happens has been apportioned and spun out to thee. In a word, thy life is short. Thou must turn to profit the present by the aid of reason and justice. Be sober in thy relaxation.

Either it is a well arranged universe or a chaos huddled together, but still a universe. But can a certain order subsist in thee, and disorder in the All? And this too when all things are so separated and diffused and sympathetic.

*   *   *

The words which were formerly familiar are now antiquated: so also the names who were famed of old, are now in a manner antiquated, Camillus, Caeso, Volesus, Leonnatus, and a little after also Scipio and Cato, then Augustus, then also Hadrianus and Antoninus. For all things soon pass away and become a mere tale, and complete oblivion soon buries them. And I say this of those who have shone in a wondrous way. For the rest, as soon as they have breathed out their breath they are gone, and no man speaks of them. And, to conclude the matter, what is even an eternal remembrance? A mere nothing. What then is that about which we ought to employ our serious pains? This one thing, thoughts just, and acts social, and words which never lie, and a disposition which gladly accepts all that happens, as necessary, as usual, as flowing from a principle and source of the same kind.

[28 A.]

AUROBINDO, SRI

AUROBINDO, SRI (1872-1950). The son of a prominent Bengalese physician, Sri Aurobindo was educated in England, where he was sent at the age of seven. Returning to India at the age of twenty-one, he served the State of Baroda for the next three years in various administrative and teaching capacities; in 1906 he resigned from the Baroda State Service. He anticipated Gandhi in organizing the national action of passive resistance during his next few years of political activity in Bengal. Imprisoned by the government for one year on a false political charge, he left Bengal upon his release in 1910, went to live in French Pondicherry, and from then on devoted his interests exclusively to philosophical writing and teaching.

Two books synthesize his teachings: "The Life Divine", his philosophy, and "The Synthesis of Yoga", his system of Yoga. He also completed three volumes of poetry, and from 1914 to 1921, he was the editor of ARYA, a philosophical journal. In 1926, he retired to the *Ashrama*, where he lived in isolation except for a few public appearances during the course of each year.

THE INDIAN CONCEPTION OF LIFE

THE VALUE of the Indian conception for life must depend on the relations and gradations by which this perfection is connected with our normal living. Put over against the latter without any connection, without any gradations leading up to it, it would either be a high unattainable ideal or the detached remote passion of a few exceptional spirits, or discourage the springs of our natural life by the too great contrast between this spiritual being and natural being. Something of the kind has happened in later times and given some room for the current Western impression about the exaggerated asceticism and other-worldliness of Indian religion and philosophy. But we must not be misled by the extreme over-emphasis of certain tendencies. To get to the real meaning of the Indian idea of life we must go back to its best times and look not at this or that school of philosophy or at some side of it, but at the totality of the ancient philosophical thinking, religion, literature, art, society. The Indian conception in its soundness made no such mistake; it did not imagine that this great thing can or even ought to be done by some violent, intolerant, immediate leap. Even the most extreme philosophies do not go so far. Whether the workings of the Spirit in the universe are a reality or only a half reality, self-descriptive *Lila* or illusory *Maya*, whether it be an action of the Infinite Energy, *Sakti*, or a figment of some secondary paradoxical consciousness in the Eternal, *Maya*, life as an intermediate reality is nowhere denied by any school of Indian thinking. Indian thought recognized that the normal life of man has to be passed through conscientiously, developed with knowledge, its forms perused, interpreted, fathomed, its values worked out, possessed and lived, its enjoyments taken on their own level, before we can go on to self-existence or a supra-existence. The spiritual perfection which opens before man is the crown of a long, patient, millennial outflowering of the spirit in life and nature. This belief in a gradual spiritual progress and evolution is the secret of the almost universal Indian acceptance of the truth of reincarnation. By millions of lives in inferior forms the secret soul in the universe, conscious even in the inconscient, *cetano acetanesu*, has arrived at humanity: by hundreds, thousands, perhaps millions of lives man grows into his divine self-existence. Every life is a step which he can take backward or forward; by his action, his will in life, by the thought and knowledge that governs it, he determines what he is yet to be, *yatha karma yatha srutam*.

This conception of a spiritual evolution with a final spiritual perfection or transcendence of which human life is the means and an often repeated opportunity, is the pivot of the Indian conception of existence. It gives to our life a figure of ascent, in spirals or circles, which has to be filled in with knowledge and action and experience. There is room within it for all human aims, activities and aspirations; there is place in the ascent for all types of human character and nature. The spirit in the world assumes hundreds of forms, follows many tendencies, gives many shapes to his play or *lila*, and all are part of the mass of necessary experience; each has its justification, its law, its reason of being, its utility. The claim of sense satisfaction is not ignored, nor the soul's need of labour and heroic action, nor the hundred forms of the pursuit of knowledge, nor the play of the emotions or the demand of the aesthetic faculties. Indian culture did not deface nor impoverish the richness of the grand game of human life or depress or mutilate the activities of our nature. On the contrary it gave them, subject to a certain principle of harmony and government, their full, often their extreme value; it bade man fathom on his way all experience, fill in life opulently with colour and beauty and enjoyment and give to his character and action a large rein and heroic proportions. This side of the Indian idea is stamped in strong relief over the epic and the classical literature, and to have read the *Ramayana*, the *Mahabharata*, the dramas, the literary epics, the romances, the lyric and the great abundance of gnomic poetry, to say nothing of the massive remains of other cultural work and social and political system and speculation without perceiving this breadth, wealth and greatness, one must have read without eyes to see or without a mind to understand. But while the generous office of culture is to enrich, enlarge and encourage human life, it must also find in it a clue, give it a guiding law and subject it to some spiritual, moral and rational government. The greatness of the ancient Indian civilization consists in the power with which it did this work and the high and profound wisdom and skill with which, while basing society, ordering the individual life, encouraging and guiding human nature and propensity, it turned them all towards the realization of its master idea and never allowed the mind it was training to lose sight of the use of life as a passage of the Infinite and a discipline for spiritual perfection.

Two main truths are always kept in sight by the Indian mind whether in the government of life or in the discipline of spirituality. First, our being in its growth has stages

80

through which it must pass. Then again, life is complex, the nature of man is complex, and in each life man has to figure a certain sum of its complexity. The initial movement of life is that form of it which develops the powers of the ego in man; *kama, artha,* self interest and desire are the original human motives. Indian culture gave a large recognition to this primary turn of our nature. These powers have to be accepted; the ego-life must be lived and the forces it evolves in the human being brought to fullness. But to get its full results and inspire it eventually to go beyond itself, it must be kept from making any too unbridled claim or heading furiously towards its satisfaction. There must be no internal or external anarchy. A life governed in any absolute or excessive degree by self-will, by passion, sense-attraction, self-interest, desire cannot be the whole natural rule of a human or a humane existence. The tempting imagination that it can, with which the Western mind has played in leanings or outbursts of what has been called Paganism, not at all justly, for the Greek or Pagan intelligence had a noble thought for self-rule, law and harmony,—is alien to the Indian mentality. It perceived very well the possibility of a materialistic life and its attraction worked on certain minds and gave birth to the Carvaka philosophy; but this could not take hold or stay. Even it allowed to it when lived on a grand scale a certain perverse greatness, but a colossal egoism was regarded as the nature of the Asura and Raksasa, the Titanic, gigantic or demoniac type of spirit, not the proper life for man. Another power claims man, overtopping desire and self-interest and self-will, the power of the Dharma.

The Dharma, religious law of action, is not as in the Western idea, only a religious creed and cult inspiring an ethical and social rule, but the complete rule of our life, the harmony of the whole tendency of man to find a right and just law of his living. Every thing has its dharma, its law of life imposed on it by its nature, but the dharma for a man is a conscious imposition of a rule of ideal living on all his members. This Dharma develops, evolves, has stages, gradations of spiritual and ethical ascension. All men cannot follow in all things one common and invariable rule of action. Nature, the position, the work, aim and bent, the call of life, the call of the spirit within, the degree and turn of development, the *adhikara* or capacity differ too much in different men; life is too complex to admit of such an ideal simplicity. Man lives in society and by society, and every society has its own general dharma, its law of right stability and right functioning, and into this law the individual life must be fitted; but the individual's part in society, his own nature, the needs of his capacity and temperament all vary, and the social law on its side must make room for this variety. The man of knowledge, the man of power, the productive and acquisitive man, the priest, scholar, poet, artist, ruler, fighter, trader, tiller of the soil, craftsman, labourer, servant cannot all have the same training, be shaped in the same pattern, follow the same way of living or be all put under the same tables of the law. Each has his type of nature and there must be a rule for the perfection of that type, or each his function and there must be a canon and ideal of the function. The main necessity is that, that there must be in all things some wise and understanding canon and ideal; a lawless impulse of desire and interest and propensity cannot be allowed; even in the frankest following of desire and interest and propensity there must be a rule, a guidance, an ethic and science arising from and answering to some truth of the thing sought, a restraint, an order, a standard of perfection. The rule and training and result differ with the type of the man and the type of the function. The idea of the Indian social system was a harmony of this complexity of *artha, kama* and *dharma*.

[28B]

ANONYMOUS

AUTHOR OF THE IMITATION OF CHRIST, AN UNKNOWN CARTHUSIAN MONK. Carlyle said about this work, "None, ex-

cept the Bible, is so universally read and loved by Christians of all
tongues and sects," a statement confirmed by all lovers of devotional
literature. Whoever wrote the book described the trials and temptations, the joys of mystical intercourse with Christ, and the readiness
to suffer with him. The debates about the author of this work began
around 1430 and have continued up to the present day. For a long
time, it was attributed to Thomas á Kempis (1380-1471), who
signed a copy of his writing in 1441. But none of his other numerous books is comparable to the *Imitatio*, and the oldest extant manu-
script was written in 1383 when Thomas á Kempis was three years
old. However, he may be considered as the editor who improved the
Latin phraseology. The assumption that the *Imitatio* is based upon
the diaries of Gerard Root is also untenable. In all probability, the
author was a Carthusian monk who, after many wordly experiences,
composed this work, which has been described by Matthew Arnold
as "the most exquisite document of Christian spirit after the New
Testament."

THE THOUGHTS OF DEATH

1. VERY quickly will it be over with thee here; see then how
matters stand with thee. A man is here to-day, and to-morrow
he is no longer seen.

And when he is taken away from the sight, he is also
quickly out of mind.

Oh! the dullness and hardness of the human heart, which
thinks only of what is present and does not look rather forward to things to come.

Thou oughtest in every action and thought so to order
thyself, as if thou wert immediately to die.

If thou hadst a good conscience, thou wouldst not much
fear death.

It were better for thee to avoid sin, than to escape
death.

If thou are not prepared to-day, how wilt thou be to-
morrow?

To-morrow is an uncertain day; and how dost thou
know that thou shalt be alive to-morrow?

2. What good is it to live long, when we advance so
little?

Ah! long life does not always make us better, but often rather adds to our guilt.

Would that we had behaved ourselves well in this world, even for one day!

Many reckon up the years of their conversion; but oftentimes the fruit of amendment is but small.

If it be frightful to die, perhaps it will be more dangerous to live longer.

Blessed is he that has always the hour of his death before his eyes, and every day prepares himself to die.

If thou hast at any time seen a man die, think that thou also must traverse the same path.

3. In the morning, think that thou mayest not live till night; and when evening comes, presume not to promise thyself the next morning.

Be therefore always prepared, and live in such a manner, that death may never find thee unprepared.

Many die suddenly, and when they little think of it: For in such an hour as ye think not the Son of Man will come.

When that last hour shall come, thou wilt begin to have quite other thoughts of thy whole past life, and be exceeding sorry that thou hast been so negligent and remiss.

4. How happy and prudent is he who strives now to be such in this life, as he desires to be found at his death.

A perfect contempt of the world, a fervent desire to advance in virtue, a love of discipline, labor in penitence, readiness in obedience, self-denial, and patience in affliction for the love of Christ, will give us great assurance of dying happily.

Thou mayest do many good things whilst thou art well; but when thou art sick, I know not what thou wilt be able to do.

Few are improved by sickness; so they also that rove about much, seldom become holy.

5. Trust not in thy friends and kinsfolk, nor put off the welfare of thy soul to hereafter; for men will forget thee sooner than thou thinkest.

It is better now to provide in time, and send some good before thee, than to depend upon the help of others.

If thou art not now careful for thyself, who will be careful for thee hereafter?

The present time is very precious. Now is the acceptable time; now is the day of salvation.

But oh, the sorrow that thou dost not spend this time more profitably, wherein thou mayest earn life for ever! The time will come, when thou wilt wish for one day or hour to amend; and I know not whether thou wilt obtain it.

6. O dearly beloved, from how great a danger mayest thou deliver thyself, from how great a fear mayest thou rescue thyself, if thou wilt but now be always fearful, and looking for death!

Strive now so to live, that in the hour of thy death thou mayest be able to rejoice rather than fear.

Learn now to die to the world, that thou mayest then begin to live with Christ.

Learn now to despise all things, that thou mayest then freely go to Christ.

Chasten thy body now by penitence, that thou mayest then have a sure confidence.

7. Ah, fool! why dost thou think to live long, when thou art not sure of one day?

How many thinking to live long have been deceived, and snatched unexpectedly away?

How often hast thou heard related, that such a one was slain by the sword; another drowned; another, from a height, broke his neck; one died eating, another playing?

Some have perished by fire; some by the sword; some by pestilence; and some by robbers.

And so death is the end of all; and man's life suddenly passeth away like a shadow.

8. Who will remember thee when thou art dead? and who will pray for thee?

Do now, beloved, do now all thou canst, because thou knowest not when thou shalt die, nor does thou know what shall befall thee after death.

Whilst thou hast time, gather up for thyself everlasting riches; think of nothing but thy salvation; care for nothing but the things of God.

Make now to thyself friends, by honoring the saints of God, and imitating their actions; that when thou failest, they may receive thee into everlasting habitations.

9. Keep thyself as a pilgrim and a stranger upon earth, whom none of the affairs of this world concern.

Keep thy heart free, and raised upwards to God; for here thou hast no continuing city.

Send thither thy daily prayers with sighs and with tears; that after death thy spirit may be worthy happily to pass to our Lord. Amen.   [29]

AVENARIUS, RICHARD

AVENARIUS, RICHARD (1843-1896). Empirio-criticism was a radical positivist doctrine formulated by Avenarius. He maintained that scientific philosophy must be confined to the descriptive, generalized definitions of experience; that pure experience must be kept free of metaphysics or materialism. This doctrine assumes that there is a constancy in the mutual relationship between the ego and its environment; that only parts of our environment constitute pure experience; that those occasions where experience is said to transcend the environment must be regarded and repudiated as an extraneous element or invention of the mind. Substance and causality are such inventions. Avenarius accepted a parallelism between brain changes and states of consciousness, but emphasized that neither thoughts nor sensations are to be explained as functions of the brain. He stated that since men are equal, the experience of each ego has equal validity, provided that individual variations are recognized; that the experience of each ego can be used to construct a natural concept of the world. His opposition to the materialist assertions of Karl Vogt resulted in a violent attack upon empirio-criticism by Lenin. Avenarius, whose principal works are *Critique of Pure Experience* (1888-90) and *The Human Concept of the World* (1891) influenced Ernst Mach and, to some extent, William James.

THE TWO AXIOMS OF EMPIRIO-CRITICISM

IT is perhaps not unsuitable to advance two assumptions which I should like to call empirio-critical axioms: The first is the axiom of the contents of knowledge, the second the axiom of the forms of knowledge.

One could formulate these two axioms in the following manner.

(1) Each human individual originally supposes an environment with multiple elements; other human individuals with multiple assertions as well as a certain dependence of that which is asserted in the environment. All the contents of knowledge of the philosophical concept of the world (whether it be critical or uncritical) are alterations of this original supposition.

That means whatever the conclusions of a Plato, Spinoza or Kant might be . . . these philosophers came to their results by positive or negative additions to the particular supposition which they too made at the beginning of their development.

(2) The scientific cognition has essentially no other forms or means than the nonscientific cognition. All the special forms or means of knowledge are transformations of prescientific ones. That means that whatever methods mathematics or mechanics may have developed they must be reducible to simple and general human functions.

One who accepts the first proposition will most likely admit that it is also advisable in our research, to proceed from this original assumption and not from later transformations. . . .

To proceed from "consciousness" or "reasoning" in order to develop one's own opinion on cognition or even to judge other people's opinion on it would mean, in order not to use a more drastic comparison, to start with the end.

If one admits, however, that one has to proceed from the original supposition as we have mentioned . . . one should also admit that it would be inadvisable to proceed from the environment and the asserting individual, in his relationship to the environment. When the influences of irritation on the nervous center are noticed, one cannot immediately proceed from the changes of this organ to "consciousness," "reasoning," and the "images" of the individual. The changes, and their various ramifications, which the irritation has produced in the organ must be followed up. After that, one may go on to the phenomena dependent upon these changes.

Whoever admits the second proposition will be inclined to admit that it is advisable not to reflect immediately or exclusively on complicated and special forms and means of a highly developed scientific knowledge. One must keep in mind the ordinary life, the natural, unprejudiced cognition which draws upon its own resources; scientific cognition is developed from this. Thus is shown the relationship of the scientific form of knowledge to its prescientific form.

[30]

AVENPACE (Ibn Badjdja)

AVENPACE (IBN BADJDJA) (End of 11th Century—1138). Avenpace was a high dignitary in Islamic Spain, for twenty years when he was poisoned by his enemies who decried him as an atheist and scorner of the Koran. He was a reputed musician and well acquainted with the natural sciences, mathematics and astronomy. Avenpace wrote commentaries on several works of Aristotle, whom he interpreted in accordance with Neo-Platonism, and treatises among which *The Hermit's Guide* was most famous. It was used by Averroës and the Jewish author Moses of Narbonne, as well as by Albertus Magnus and Aquinas. He distinguished between "animal" and "human" activities, regarded the human intellect as the emanation of the Agens Intellect, the supreme Being, and described their mystical union.

ON HUMAN PERFECTION

THE word "regime," in its most popular sense, signifies a concurrence of actions which are directed toward a certain end. The word regime cannot, therefore, be applied to a single action, since it is used for a complex of actions, as military regime or political regime. Thus, we say that God governs and rules over the world. For this regime, according to vulgar opinion, is similar to that of the governments of states, though, from the philosophical point of view, these words are a simple homonym. This regulated concurrence of actions which demands reflection, cannot be formed but by a solitary man. The regime of the solitary man must be the image of the perfect government of a state, where judges and physicians are absent because they are useless. . . . In a perfect state, every individual will have the highest degree of perfection of which man is capable. There, everyone thinks in accordance with the highest justice, and does not neglect, when he is acting, any law and custom. There will be no fault, no joke, no ruse.

In an imperfect state the solitary man shall become the element of the future perfect state.

He who acts under the influence of reflection and justice only, without regard to the animal soul, must be called divine rather than human. Such a man must excel in moral virtues so that when the rational soul decides in favor of a thing, the animal soul, far from objecting, decides in favor of the same thing. It is the nature of the animal soul to obey the rational soul. This is, however, not the case with men who are not in the natural state but who allow themselves to give way to rage. He who allows himself to give way to passions acts in accordance not with human but with animal nature. He is even worse than the animal which obeys its own nature.

[31]

89

AVERROËS (Ibn Roshd)

AVERROËS (IBN ROSHD) (1126-1198). Due to a mistake made in translating the works of Mohammed ibn Ahmed ibn Mohammed ibn Roshd from the Arabic into Latin, this great Islamic philosopher for about two centuries deeply influenced Christian thinkers, by whom he was known under the name Averroës. In reality, Averroës taught that there is one eternal truth which, according to the various levels of education, can be formulated and comprehended in two ways, namely, the way of revelation, by the Koran, or the way of natural knowledge, with the aid of Aristotle and other philosophers. He maintained on occasion that there is a double truth, and that a proposition may be theologically true and philosophically untrue, and vice versa. Christian Averroism flourished in the thirteenth century, especially at the University of Paris where Siger of Brabant was the leader of that school. In 1277, Averroism was condemned by the Church. Averroës also influenced Jewish philosophers of the Middle Ages.

Apart from his ascendancy over Christian and Jewish philosophy, Averroës has become important as the last great philosopher of Islamic Spain, and as the last and greatest of all Arabian Aristotelians. He studied medicine and jurisprudence, and was a judge in Sevilla and Cordova. Although he was fully acquainted with natural sciences, his approach to philosophy was determined to a great extent by his legal training. As a jurist, Averroës insisted on the literal meaning of religious and secular documents, and was eager to refute misinterpretations, particularly those which were advanced by theologians. In this way, Averroës studied, explained and annotated Aristotle whom he glorified as a "man chosen by God." Violently attacked by the Mohammedan clergy, Averroës' doctrines were condemned and his books burned.

His theories of the evolution of pre-existent forms and of the intellect anticipated modern concepts.

ON METAPHISICS

It has already been demonstrated in natural science that everything that is moved presupposes a moving principle; that, furthermore, the moved is moved only in so far as it exists potentially and that the mover carries out a movement in so far as he is *in actu;* and that the mover, if one time he carries out a movement but the next time does not produce such, must, in a certain manner, be passively moved, since active motion exists only potentially in him if he does not actually move. If we thus assume in this case that the first mover of the world one time carries out a movement, but not the next time, then we have to conclude inevitably that a further mover, prior to this one, must exist in the world. This one is, therefore, not the prime mover. Now, if we thus assume in the case of the second one that he moves one time and does not move the next time, we necessarily get the same result with respect to it as we got in the first case. Therefore, it is an irrefutable consequence that either this succession yields an infinite chain or that we admit that in the "here" [i.e., the world] there exists a mover who is in no manner moved nor may yet be moved, neither as concerns his essence, nor yet *per accidens*. Since matters lie thus, this mover is consequently of necessity eternal; the object that is put in motion by him is likewise eternally in motion; for if something existed that, at a given time, were potentially in a position to be moved by the eternal mover, then a mover who would precede the eternal mover, would inevitably have to exist "beyond." For this reason, the mover whose existence has been demonstrated in the 16th Book of Zoology, would not possess the qualification sufficient for carrying out a special movement without the aid of the mover of the whole world.

If it is thus clear that an eternal motion exists in the "here," and if it is impossible that there is an eternal motion, leaving out of account the circular and spatial one—this has been discussed in natural science—then it is evident that this demonstration yields the necessity of an eternal, spatial motion existing in the "here." However, this is in no manner ascertainable by sensual perception, if you except the motion of the heavenly body. The motion of this body must, therefore, be the eternal motion of which we are in search. The mover of this body is at the same time the eternal mover whose existence has become intelligible through former discussions. The existence of an eternal, continuous motion with respect to time has likewise been proved; for, time, as has been demonstrated, is one of the accidents of motion. Time cannot be slowly composed, not even by him who is raised above time. The reason for this lies in what follows: Let us admit that time arises by degrees; then it would exist after it was nonexistent previously, indeed already prior to its existence. The earlier and the later are, however, two designations for parts of time. Therefore, time would have to exist before there was any. Furthermore, if time were something that originates, then it would happen that time which might be a present time did not precede a particular thing. However, it is quite impossible to imagine that no past preceded a particular thing which is in actuality and exists in a "present" moment, let alone that we could imagine such a state of affairs were we to reflect on the real nature of time. An error in these ideas can occur only when we think of time in terms of a line; for, in so far as the line possesses spatial motion—this exists in actuality—it is by necessity finite, not to mention the fact that one cannot even imagine infinity in connection with it. Now, if you should imagine time in this sense as a straight line, it is impossible for it to be infinite. This type of error belongs to those that fall under the topic of spatial motion and substitution. Farabi has composed long dissertations concerning this problem with respect to things that exist and change.

This being so, and it being evident that time forms an eternal continuum, it follows inevitably upon an eternal motion which is continuous and uniform; for a motion which in the proper sense of the word is uniform, is the continuous motion. If, now, there exists in the "here" an eternal motion, it follows that there must also be present an eternal mover who is ever the same; for, if there were many moving principles existing, the motion would not be one and the same, nor would it be continuous. Now, that this first mover cannot be of a material nature, has become intelligible by virtue of the fact that his motion, which takes place in time, proceeds without end. However, every mover that exists in some matter must have quantity adhering to him, that is, must possess a body. Every potentiality, however, which has its seat in something quantitative, is divisible, corresponding to the divisibility of quantity. It follows likewise in the determination of finiteness and infinity, as has been demonstrated in natural science, be it that one presupposes this potentiality as blended with the body or only as "engraved" upon it. Of such nature are heat in fire and cold in water. This potentiality is in some sort of necessary internal dependence on the *hyle*, that is to say, a dependence absolutely necessary for its existence. Thus with respect to the psychic principle. Since, now, in essence, form is material, no material force can exist which, as moving principle, is infinite. All this was demonstrated in natural science. . . .

[32]

AVICENNA

AVICENNA (979-1037). Nearly a thousand years have passed and the name of Avicenna is still revered in the East. One of the wisest of physicians, he is referred to in the West as the Galen of the Moslem world. The name Avicenna is the Latinized form of the Hebrew, Aven Sina; or the Arabic, Abu Ali al-Husain ibn Abdullah ibn Sina. While still a youth in his teens, Avicenna was called upon to cure the Sultan of Bokhara. The potentate, in gratitude, opened his library to the young man. This good fortune enabled Avicenna, (who had memorized the Koran by the age of ten) to write the *Canon,* the basis of his medical fame, before he had attained his legal majority.

In addition to his medical accomplishments, he studied logic, metaphysics, mathematics, and physics. He studied Aristotelian and neo-Platonic philosophy with Al-Farabi. As a result of this, Avicenna wrote voluminously on Aristotle. He said that cause and effect are simultaneous and therefore God and the world are co-eternal; that God created intelligence or the soul, and these emanate from the heavens and reach the earth in huge chains; that intelligence is sustained by God, and though that is innately eternal, its multiple extensions are not dependent on Him, for He is not concerned with matter.

Avicenna was probably a pantheist. His work, *Philosophia Orientalis*, in which his position was apparently clarified, is lost. His mysticism is said to have been derived from Mazdaism. For a time he occupied the office of Vizier at Hamadan.

MENTAL ESSENCE

As to the mental essence, we find it in infants devoid of every mental form. Then, later on in life, we find in it self-evident axiomatic mentally-grasped notions, without effort of learning and without reflections. So that the arising of them within it will not fail of being either through sense and experience, or else through divine outpouring reaching to it. But it is not licit to hold that the arising of such primary mental form will be through experience, seeing that experience does not afford and supply a necessary and inevitable judgment, since experience does not go so far as to believe or disbelieve definitely the existence of something different to the judgment drawn from what it has perceived. Indeed experience, although it shows us that every animal we perceive moves on chewing the lower jaw, yet it does not supply us with a convincing judgment that such is the case with every animal; for were this true, it would not be licit for the crocodile to exist which moves his upper jaw on chewing. Therefore not every judgment we have arrived at, as to things, through our sensuous perception, is applicable to and holds good of all that we have perceived or have not perceived of such things, but it may so be that what we have not perceived differ from what we have perceived. Whereas our conception that a whole is greater than a part is not [formed] because we have sensuously felt every part and every whole that are so related, seeing that even such an experience will not guaranty to us that there will be no whole and no part differently related.

Likewise the dictum concerning the impossibility of two opposites (contrasts) coming together in one and the same thing, and that things which are equal to one and the same thing are equal to one another. And likewise the dictum concerning our holding proofs to be true if they be valid, for the belief in and conviction of their validity does not become valid by and through learning and effort of study; else this would draw out ad infinitum [inasmuch as each proof rests upon given presuppositions, whose validity would in its turn have to be proved]. Nor is this gained from sense, for the reason that we have mentioned. Consequently both the latter as well as the former [certainty] are gained from a godly outflow reaching unto the rational soul, and the rational soul reaching unto it; so that this mental form arises therein. Also, as to this outflow, unless it have in its own self such a generic (universal) mental form, it would not be able to engrave it within the rational soul. Hence such form is in the outflow's own self. And whatsoever Self has in it a mental form is an essence, other than a body, and not within a body, and standing of itself. Therefore this outflow unto which the soul reaches is a mental essence, not a body, not in a body, standing of itself, and one which stands towards the rational soul in the stead of light to sight; yet however with this difference, namely that light supplies unto sight the power of perceiving only, and not the perceived form, whereas this essence supplies, exclusively by and through its sole and single self, unto the rational power, the power of perceiving, and brings about therein the perceived forms also, as we have set forth above.

Now, if the rational soul's conceiving rational forms be a source of completion and perfection for it, and be effected and brought about on reaching unto this essence, and if worldly earthy labors, such as its thought, its sorrows and joy, its longings, hamper the power and withhold it from reaching thereunto, so that it will not reach thereunto save only through abandoning these powers and getting rid of them, there being nothing to stop it from continued Reaching save the living body,—then consequently if it quit the body it will not cease to be reaching unto its Perfector and attached to Him.

Again, what reaches unto its Perfector and attaches itself to Him is safe against corruption, all the more so if even during disconnection from Him it has not undergone corruption. Wherefore the soul after death shall ever remain and continue unwavering [and undying] and attached to this noble essence, which is called generic universal mind, and in the language of the lawgivers the Divine Knowledge.

As to the other powers, such as the animal and the vegetable: Whereas every one of them performs its proper peculiar action only by and through the live body, and in no other way, consequently they will never quit live bodies, but will die with their death, seeing that every thing which is, and yet has no action, is idle and useless. Yet nevertheless the rational soul does gain, by its connection with them, from them their choicest and purest lye and wash, and leaves for death the husks. And were it not so, the rational soul would not use them in consciousness. Wherefore the rational soul shall surely depart (migrate, travel) taking along the kernels of the other powers after death ensues.

We have thus made a clear statement concerning souls, and got at which souls are [ever-] lasting, and which of them will not be fitted out and armed with [ever]lastingness. It still remains for us, in connection with this research, to show how a soul exists within live bodies, and the aim and end for which it is found within the same, and what measure will be bestowed upon it, in the hereafter, of eternal delight and perpetual punishment, and of [temporary] punishment that ceases after a duration of time that shall ensue upon the decease of the live body; and to treat of the notion that is designated by the lawgivers as intercession (mediation), and of the quality (attribute) of the four angels and the throne-bearers. Were it not however that the custom prevails to isolate such research from the research whose path we have been treading, out of high esteem and reverence for it, and to make the latter research precede in order of treatment the former, to the end of levelling the road and paving it solidly, I should (would) have followed up these [ten] sections with a full and complete treatment of the subject dealt with in them. Notwithstanding all this, were it not for fear of wearying by prolixity, I would have disregarded the demands of custom herein. Thus, then whatever it may please the Prince—God prolong his highness—to command as to treating singly of such notions, I shall put forth, in humble compliance and obedience, my utmost effort, God Almighty willing; and may wisdom never cease to revive through him after fainting, to flourish after withering, so that its sway may be renewed through his sway, and through his days its days may come back again, and that through his prestige the prestige of its devotees be exalted, and the seekers after its favor abound, so God almighty will.   [33]

AXELROD, PAVEL BORISSOVICH

AXELROD, PAVEL BORISSOVICH (1850-1928). Brought up in a small provincial town in Russia, the son of a poor Jewish innkeeper, Axelrod realized that his quest for knowledge was inseparable from the struggle for human progress; that his desire for self-education was only an aspect of his desire to educate the masses of the people.

In his youth he was a disciple of Bakunin, and he remained an idealist even after adopting the Marxist concept of historical materialism. With his lifelong friend, Plekhanov, he became one of the founders of the Russian Social Democratic Party. Plekhanov was the leading theorist of the movement, and Axelrod directed its propaganda and applied the theories to practical politics. It was largely due to his efforts that the labor movement of Russia participated in the political struggle against Tsarist absolutism instead of concentrating their activities upon economic improvement. He took a leading part in directing and formulating the policies of the Menshevist Party, and was elected a member of the executive committee of the Second Internationale. One of the principal aims of his activities was to organize the Russian worker and make him as politically active as his Western European counterpart. He was often referred to as the great Westerner among the Russian Socialists. From 1903 until his death, he and Plekhanov combatted Lenin and the Bolshevists.

A MARXIST'S IDEALISM

THE motivation of my idealism, of all my public activities is that the relative progress of human nature is infinite. It may appear curious, but the more clearly I recognize the fallibility of human nature in the present time, the more passionately do I long for its future perfection, even though it may take millennia. It doesn't matter to me that the distance is nebulous and seemingly endless. For it is just that aspect, coupled with the "supermen" of the future that serve as a strong incentive and source of enthusiasm. I think this strange phenomenon is rooted in a kind of religious feeling, which I'm unable to characterize, except to say that my devoted respect for thought, conscientiousness, and spirit may be paralleled with fanaticism.

If there is no God, no creator of the universe, then may God be praised for His nonexistence. For we can behead kings, but we would be powerless against a despotic Jehovah. If there is no God, then we must prepare for the arrival of earthly gods; of beings, omnipotent because of their reason and energy of will, capable of comprehending the knowledge of the world and of their own selves, and of embracing and dominating the world by virtue of their spirit.

[34]

B

BAADER, FRANCIS XAVIER VON

BAADER, FRANCIS XAVIER VON (1765-1841). An expert on mints and mining, and consultant in both these fields, Baader was also a writer, a Catholic layman whose works were read by both Protestant and Catholic philosophers. The latter found him stimulating if unorthodox, particularly in view of the fact that he once stated that should the devil appear on earth, it would be in the garb of a professor of moral philosophy. During a five-year sojourn in England, Baader acquainted himself with the opposing ideologies of David Hartley, the sensualist, David Hume, the sceptic, and Jacob Boehme, the mystic. His writings, as a result of these influences, contained many unpredictable flashes of insight and startling affirmations. Mysticism influenced him more than did philosophies. Baader never strove for a system, but aimed at the deep and profound; he frequently appeared paradoxical. Rationalism was abhorrent to him; human knowledge required the greater wisdom of God, which he viewed as the real spontaneity in all forms of knowledge. The phrase, *con-scientia* symbolized to him man's participation in God's knowledge. He disapproved of some aspects of the papacy, but, nonetheless, elected to stay within the fold, striving, in his lectures, for a philosophic rationale of Catholicism, and making the love of God and neighbor the mainstay of his sociology, which also incorporated his ideas of liberty and equality. In 1826 he was called to assume the chair of professor of speculative dogmatics at the University of Munich, his native city. However, he was compelled in 1838 to exchange this for a chair in anthropology because he was barred from lecturing on the philosophy of religion for the reason that he was a layman.

GOD AND THE WORLD

THE only criterion of truth is the intimate consciousness of what we feel. The seed of all knowledge, of all Good and

Evil, lies in myself; all external things can only ripen it. All books can only render the service of a midwife.

The so-called sensual, material nature is a symbol, a copy of inner, spiritual nature. Every action and deed of God in both animated and inanimated nature, in nature and the Bible, are the semantic symbolic, fulfillment and revelation of the past, the germ and seal of the future.

God is universal. He is called God only in the sphere of light. The non-manifest God is only one; the divine Himself in Revelation. The ground is not undivided; it always remains the same. It is only manifestation that divides itself; unity must be laid in the ground, not in manifestations. God is the spirit of all spirits; the essence of all essences.

Theologians are correct in distinguishing the immanent revelation of God from His eminence, and asserting that the form is mediated by a generation begetting. Only begetting is true action, creation. The word is born, not made. The word is not the creature but co-substantial with it.

[35]

BAAL SHEM-TOV

BAAL SHEM-TOV (1700-1760). After seven years of solitary meditation, Israel ben Eliezer began to teach, in 1740, a mysticism which later became known as Hasidism. This earned him the title of Baal Shem-Tov (Master of the Good Name), even though in his early years he had been despised by his people as an ignorant and inefficient man.

He taught that the divine spirit is omnipresent in each man and in everything that exists. Therefore, it is possible to serve God in even the most trifling of actions. In contradistinction to other schools of mysticism and to various Jewish mystical doctrines, he declared that the pleasures of the senses are not sinful, because man must serve God with his body as well as with his soul. In his teachings, all things, including the lowest acts, had dignity. Although he did not reject learning, he put prayer above scholarship, insisting that his followers pray "with gladness" and forget, through religious concentration, all the sufferings imposed by life.

The teachings of Baal Shem-Tov gained a large number of adherents among the Jews of Eastern Europe who, at that time, were subject to frequent persecutions and whose economic situation was constantly growing worse. These people were impressed by his kind and humble personality and revered him as a saint. He received gifts of immense value, but ended each day by distributing all his wealth among the poor. He saved many co-religionists from despair, enabled them to endure extreme hardship, and imbued them with the spirit of confident piety.

THE END-ALL OF KNOWLEDGE

"Had they but abandoned Me," says God, "and kept faith with My Torah!"

This must be interpreted as follows: The end-all of knowledge is to know that we cannot know anything. But there are two sorts of not-knowing. The one is the immediate not-knowing, when a man does not even begin to examine and try to know, because it is impossible to know. Another, however, examines and seeks, until he comes to know that one cannot know. And the difference between these two—to whom may we compare them? To two men who wish to see the king. The one enters all the chambers belonging to the king. He rejoices in the king's treasure rooms and splendid halls, and then he discovers that he cannot get to know the king. The other tells himself; "Since it is not possible to get to know the king, we will not bother to enter, but put up with not knowing."

This leads us to understand what those words of God mean. They have abandoned Me, that is, they have abandoned the search to know me, because it is not possible. But oh, had they but abandoned me with searching and understanding, so keeping faith with my Torah!

Why do we say: "Our God and the God of our fathers?" There are two sorts of persons who believe in God. The one believes because his faith has been handed down to him by his fathers; and his faith is strong. The other has arrived at faith by dint of searching thought. And this is the difference between the two: The first has the advantage that his faith cannot be shaken, no matter how many objections are raised to it, for his faith is firm because he has taken it over

from his fathers. But there is a flaw in it: it is a commandment given by man, and it has been learned without thought
or reasoning. The advantage of the second man is that he has
reached faith through his own power, through much searching and thinking. But his faith too has a flaw: it is easy to
shake it by offering contrary evidence. But he who combines
both kinds of faith is invulnerable. That is why we say: "Our
God," because of our searching, and "the God of our fathers," because of our tradition.

And a like interpretation holds when we say, "The God
of Abraham, the God of Isaac, and the God of Jacob," for
this means: Isaac and Jacob did not merely take over the
tradition of Abraham, but sought out the divine for themselves.

[36]

BACON, FRANCIS

BACON, FRANCIS (1561-1626). The first philosophical work
written originally in English was Francis Bacon's *The Advancement
of Learning* (1605). Its author was a native of London, son of
Nicholas Bacon, Lord Keeper of the Great Seal. Versed, from early
age, in political and legal affairs, he advanced to the position of
Lord Chancellor. In 1621 he was accused and convicted of accepting
bribes from litigants. He subsequently retired from public life and
spent his remaining years in scientific research.

Bacon's personal character has been severely condemned by
both his contemporaries and posterity. Like many of the men of his
time, he placed his career ahead of the public welfare and his personal integrity. But despite his moral shortcomings, Bacon must be
credited with his devotion to science, with his sincere efforts to use
his power and authority for scientific promotion, and as one of the
greatest propagandists for scientific research. He earnestly endeavored to protect scientists against possible Church condemnation, a
danger inherent in the very nature of scientific conclusions. He tried
to do this by declaring his reverence for orthodox religion, by pro-
claiming and defending the secularization of science and philosophy,
and by resorting to reason and revelation wherein "double truth"
was an acceptable medieval doctrine. Bacon regarded and trusted
secularized thought as the instrument for the future improvement of
human conditions.

102

He categorized himself as the "trumpeter of the new age." Actually, he represents an age in transition. Although he emphatically stressed the importance of experiment and the inductive method, he ignored most of the real progress science had made during his lifetime. He was more interested in the effects of knowledge on human behavior than he was in knowledge for its own sake. He asserted that "human knowledge and human power meet in one"; therefore, "knowledge is power." He cautioned against the possible abuse of power. Yielding to prejudice or "idols" might result in this. His claim to have permanently established "a true and lawful marriage between the empirical and rational faculty" is a disputable one. However, it is to his incontestable merit that he saw that true philosophy is concerned with "the real business and fortunes of the human race."

IDOLS WHICH BESET MAN'S MIND

MAN, being the servant and interpreter of nature, can do and understand so much and so much only as he has observed in fact or in thought of the course of nature: beyond this he neither knows anything nor can do anything.

*   *   *

Human knowledge and human power meet in one; for where the cause is not known the effect cannot be produced. Nature to be commanded must be obeyed; and that which in contemplation is as the cause is in operation as the rule.

*   *   *

There are and can be only two ways of searching into and discovering truth. The one flies from the senses and particulars to the most general axioms, and from these principles, the truth of which it takes for settled and immovable, proceeds to judgment and to the discovery of middle axioms. And this way is now in fashion. The other derives axioms from the senses and particulars, rising by a gradual and unbroken ascent, so that it arrives at the most general axioms last of all. This is the true way, but as yet untried.

The understanding left to itself takes the same course (namely, the former) which it takes in accordance with logical order. For the mind longs to spring up to positions of higher generality, that it may find rest there; and so after a little while wearies of experiment. But this evil is increased by logic, because of the order and solemnity of its disputations.

The understanding left to itself, in a sober, patient, and grave mind, especially if it be not hindered by received doctrines, tries a little that other way, which is the right one, but with little progress; since the understanding, unless directed and assisted, is a thing unequal, and quite unfit to contend with the obscurity of things.

Both ways set out from the senses and particulars, and rest in the highest generalities; but the difference between them is infinite. For the one just glances at experiment and particulars in passing, the other dwells duly and orderly among them. The one, again, begins at once by establishing certain abstract and useless generalities, the other rises by gradual steps to that which is prior and better known in the order of nature.

*   *   *

The axioms now in use, having been suggested by a scanty and manipular experience and a few particulars of most general occurrence, are made for the most part just large enough to fit and take these in: and therefore it is no wonder if they do not lead to new particulars. And if some opposite instance, not observed or not known before, chance to come in the way, the axiom is rescued and preserved by some frivolous distinction; whereas the truer course would be to correct the axiom itself.

The conclusions of human reason as ordinarily applied in matter of nature, I call for the sake of distinction *Anticipations of Nature* (as a thing rash or premature). That reason which is elicited from facts by a just and methodical process, I call *Interpretation of Nature*.

Anticipations are a ground sufficiently firm for consent;

for even if men went mad all after the same fashion, they might agree one with another well enough.

For the winning of assent, indeed, anticipations are far more powerful than interpretations; because being collected from a few instances, and those for the most part of familiar occurrence, they straightway touch the understanding and fill the imagination; whereas interpretations on the other hand, being gathered here and there from very various and widely dispersed facts, cannot suddenly strike the understanding; and therefore they must needs, in respect of the opinions of the time, seem harsh and out of tune; much as the mysteries of faith do.

In sciences founded on opinions and dogmas, the use of anticipations and logic is good; for in them the object is to command assent to the proposition, not to master the thing.

Though all the wits of all the ages should meet together and combine and transmit their labours, yet will no great progress ever be made in science by means of anticipations; because radical errors in the first concoction of the mind are not to be cured by the excellence of functions and remedies subsequent.

It is idle to expect any great advancement in science from the superinducing and engrafting of new things upon old. We must begin anew from the very foundations, unless we would revolve forever in a circle with mean and contemptible progress.

The honour of the ancient authors, and indeed of all, remains untouched; since the comparison I challenge is not of wits or faculties, but of ways and methods, and the part I take upon myself is not that of a judge, but of a guide.

This must be plainly avowed: no judgment can be rightly formed either of my method or of the discoveries to which it leads, by means of anticipations (that is to say, of the reasoning which is now in use); since I cannot be called on to abide by the sentence of a tribunal which is itself on its trial.

Even to deliver and explain what I bring forward is no

easy matter; for things in themselves new will yet be apprehended with reference to what is old.

It was said by Borgia of the expedition of the French into Italy, that they came with chalk in their hands to mark out their lodgings, not with arms to force their way in. I in like manner would have my doctrine enter quietly into the minds that are fit and capable of receiving it; for confutations cannot be employed, when the difference is upon first principles and very notions and even upon forms of demonstration.

One method of delivery alone remains to us; which is simply this: we must lead men to the particulars themselves, and their series and order; while men on their side must force themselves for awhile to lay their notions by and begin to familiarise themselves with facts.

The doctrine of those who have denied that certainty could be attained at all, has some agreement with my way of proceeding at the first setting out; but they end in being infinitely separated and opposed. For the holders of that doctrine assert simply that nothing can be known; I also assert that not much can be known in nature by the way which is now in use. But then they go on to destroy the authority of the senses and understanding; whereas I proceed to devise and supply helps for the same.

The idols and false notions which are now in possession of the human understanding, and have taken deep root therein, not only so beset men's minds that truth can hardly find entrance, but even after entrance obtained, they will again in the very instauration of the sciences meet and trouble us, unless men being forewarned of the danger fortify themselves as far as may be against their assaults.

There are four classes of Idols which beset men's minds. To these for distinction's sake I have assigned names,—calling the first class *Idols of the Tribe;* the second, *Idols of the Cave;* the third, *Idols of the Market-place;* the fourth, *Idols of the Theatre.*

The formation of ideas and axioms by true induction is

no doubt the proper remedy to be applied for the keeping off and clearing away of idols. To point them out, however, is of great use; for the doctrine of Idols is to the Interpretation of Nature what the doctrine of the refutation of Sophisms is to common Logic.

The Idols of the Tribe have their foundation in human nature itself, and in the tribe or race of men. For it is a false assertion that the sense of man is the measure of things. On the contrary, all perceptions as well of the sense as of the mind are according to the measure of the individual and not according to the measure of the universe. And the human understanding is like a false mirror, which, receiving rays irregularly, distorts and discolours the nature of things by mingling its own nature with it.

The Idols of the Cave are the idols of the individual man. For every one (besides the errors common to human nature in general) has a cave or den of his own, which refracts and discolours the light of nature; owing either to his own proper and peculiar nature; or to his education and conversation with others; or to the reading of books, and the authority of those whom he esteems and admires; or to the differences of impressions, accordingly as they take place in a mind preoccupied and predisposed or in a mind indifferent and settled; or the like. So that the spirit of man (according as it is meted out to different individuals) is in fact a thing variable and full of perturbation, and governed as it were by chance. Whence it was well observed by Heraclitus that men look for sciences in their own lesser worlds, and not in the greater or common world.

There are also Idols formed by the intercourse and association of men with each other, which I call Idols of the Market-place, on account of the commerce and consort of men there. For it is by discourse that men associate; and words are imposed according to the apprehension of the vulgar. And therefore the ill and unfit choice of words wonderfully obstructs the understanding. Nor do the definitions or explanations wherewith in some things learned men are wont to guard and defend themselves, by any means set the matter right. But words plainly force and overrule the understanding, and throw all into confusion, and lead men away into numberless empty controversies and idle fancies.

Lastly, there are Idols which have immigrated into men's minds from the various dogmas of philosophies, and also from wrong laws of demonstration. These I call Idols of the Theatre; because in my judgment all the received systems are but so many stage-plays, representing worlds of their own creation after an unreal and scenic fashion. Nor is it only of the systems now in vogue, or only of the ancient sects and philosophies, that I speak; for many more plays of the same kind may yet be composed and in like artificial manner set forth; seeing that errors the most widely different have nevertheless causes for the most part alike. Neither again do I mean this only of entire systems, but also of many principles and axioms in science, which by tradition, credulity, and negligence have come to be received.

[37]

BACON, ROGER

BACON, ROGER (c. 1214-1294). A member of the Order of the Franciscans, Roger Bacon was educated at Oxford and Paris. He was known to some as *Doctor mirabilis,* the wonderful doctor; to others as Friar Bacon; and to still others, as a necromancer, feared and respected for the powers he presumably possessed. His ambitions to pry into the secrets of nature, to make physical calculations and experiment with chemicals roused the suspicion and envy of his Brothers who forthwith complained to the Pope. He was denounced as a "sorcerer" for any number of reasons—because he cited the Greeks and Arabs as authorities, made magnifying glasses, investigated the properties of light, discovered a powder similar to gunpowder, enumerated the errors in the Julian calendar, criticized the Schoolmen (he called St. Thomas Aquinas "a teacher yet unschooled"), and attempted to establish ethics as a basis for monastic life. Finally his opponents prevailed upon the Pope to prevent him from teaching. He was confined for ten years with neither books nor instruments. His *Opus Majus* is a defense of himself, but neither this work nor a condensed version, the *Opus Minus,* called forth

108

any notice from Rome. He made a third revision, *Opus Tertium*, with little success. In many ways the struggles of Roger Bacon parallel those of his fellow countryman, Francis Bacon.

ON THE IMPORTANCE OF EXPERIENCE

THERE are two modes of acquiring knowledge, namely, by reasoning and experience. Reasoning draws a conclusion and makes us grant the conclusion, but does not make the conclusion certain, nor does it remove doubt so that the mind may rest on the intuition of truth, unless the mind discovers it by the path of experience; since many have the arguments relating to what can be known, but because they lack experience they neglect the arguments, and neither avoid what is harmful nor follow what is good. For if a man who has never seen fire should prove by adequate reasoning that fire burns and injures things and destroys them, his mind would not be satisfied thereby, nor would he avoid fire, until he placed his hand or some combustible substance in the fire, so that he might prove by experience that which reasoning taught. But when he has had actual experience of combustion his mind is made certain and rests in the full light of truth. Therefore reasoning does not suffice, but experience does.

This is also evident in mathematics, where proof is most convincing. But the mind of one who has the most convincing proof in regard to the equilateral triangle will never cleave to the conclusion without experience, nor will he heed it, but will disregard it until experience is offered him by the intersection of two circles, from either intersection of which two lines may be drawn to the extremities of the given line; but then the man accepts the conclusion without any question. Aristotle's statement, then, that proof is reasoning that causes us to know is to be understood with the proviso that the proof is accompanied by its appropriate experience, and is not to be understood of the bare proof. His statement also in the first book of the Metaphysics that those who understand the reason and the cause are wiser than those who have empiric knowledge of a fact, is spoken of such as know only the bare truth without the cause. But I am here speaking of the man who knows the reason and the cause through experience. These men are perfect in their wisdom, as Aristotle maintains in the sixth book of the Ethics, whose simple statements must be accepted as if they offered proof, as he states in the same place.

He therefore who wishes to rejoice without doubt in regard to the truths underlying phenomena must know how to devote himself to experiment. For authors write many statements, and people believe them through reasoning which they formulate without experience. Their reasoning is wholly false. For it is generally believed that the diamond cannot be broken except by goat's blood, and philosophers and theologians misuse this idea. But fracture by means of blood of this kind has never been verified, although the effort has been made; and without that blood it can be broken easily. For I have seen this with my own eyes, and this is necessary, because gems cannot be carved except by fragments of this stone. Similarly it is generally believed that the castors employed by physicians are the testicles of the male animal. But this is not true, because the beaver has these under its breast, and both the male and female produce testicles of this kind. Besides these castors the male beaver has its testicles in their natural place; and therefore what is subjoined is a dreadful lie, namely, that when the hunters pursue the beaver, he himself knowing what they are seeking cuts out with his teeth these glands. Moreover, it is generally believed that hot water freezes more quickly than cold water in vessels, and the argument in support of this is advanced that contrary is excited by contrary, just like enemies meeting each other. But it is certain that cold water freezes more quickly for any one who makes the experiment. People attribute this to Aristotle in the second book of the Meteorologics; but he certainly does not make this statement, but he does make one like it, by which they have been deceived, namely, that if cold water and hot water are poured on a cold place, as upon ice, the hot water freezes more quickly, and this is true. But if hot water and cold are placed in two vessels, the cold will freeze more quickly. Therefore all things must be verified by experience.

But experience is of two kinds; one is gained through our external senses, and in this way we gain our experience of those things that are in the heavens by instruments made for this purpose, and of those things here below by means attested by our vision. Things that do not belong in our part of the world we know through other scientists who have had experience of them. As, for example, Aristotle on the authority of Alexander sent two thousand men through different parts of the world to gain experimental knowledge of all things that are on the surface of the earth, as Pliny bears witness in his Natural History. This experience is both human and philosophical, as far as man can act in accordance with the grace given him; but this experience does not suffice him, because it does not give full attestation in regard to things corporeal owing to its difficulty, and does not touch at all on things spiritual. It is necessary, therefore, that the intellect of man should be otherwise aided, and for this reason the holy patriarchs and prophets, who first gave sciences to the world, received illumination within and were not dependent on sense alone. The same is true of many believers since the time of Christ. For the grace of faith illuminates greatly, as also do divine inspirations, not only in things spiritual, but in things corporeal and in the sciences of philosophy; as Ptolemy states in the Centilogium, namely, that there are two roads by which we arrive at the knowledge of facts, one through the experience of philosophy, the other through divine inspiration, which is far the better way, as he says.

[38]

BAHYA IBN PAKUDA

BAHYA IBN PAKUDA (c. 1050). Little is known of the personal life of Bahya, except that he was a *dayyan* (judge at the rabbinical court) in Saragossa toward the end of the eleventh century. His book, *Hobot ha-Lebatot* (The Duties of the Heart), expressed his personal feelings more elaborately than was usual for the Middle Ages. It depicted the noble, humble soul and pure, imperturbable mind of a man ever-grateful to God, motivated by his love of God. Bahya regarded the soul elevated toward God and liberated from the shackles of earthly existence as evidence of purification, communion with God as the ultimate goal. However, his teachings neither imply nor result in neo-Platonic ecstasy. He remained faithful to the Bible and the Talmud. Unlike many other schools of mysticism, he differentiated between man and God. Although a religious moralist, he resolutely subordinated moral righteousness and lawful action to the pious contemplation of God, for the latter served as the most effective control of egoistic instincts and passions.

ADMONITIONS OF THE SOUL

Bless the Lord, O my soul; and all that is within me, bless His holy name.

O my soul, march on with strength, and bless thy Creator. Prepare a supplication for Him, and pour out thy meditation before Him. Awake from thy sleep, and consider thy place, whence thou camest, and whither thou goest.

O my soul, awake from thy slumber, and utter a song to thy Creator; sing praises unto His name, declare his wonders, and fear Him wherever thou dwellest.

O my soul, be not as the horse, or as the mule, which have no understanding; nor shouldst thou be as a drunkard that is fast asleep, or as a man that is stupefied; for out of the fountain of understanding wast thou formed, and from the spring of wisdom wast thou taken; from a holy place wast thou brought forth, and from the city of the mighty, from heaven, wast thou taken out by God.

O my soul, put on garments of prudence, and gird on a girdle of understanding, and free thyself from the vanities of thy body, in which thou dwellest. Let not thy heart beguile thee with the sweetness of its desires, and let it not allure thee with the visions of its pleasures which melt away like water that runs apace. Remember that the beginning of these pleasures is without help or profit, and their end is shame and also reproach.

O my soul, run to and fro through the streets of thy

understanding, and go about in the chambers of thy wisdom, and come unto the structure of the building of thy imagery, whose foundation is in dust; is it not a despised body and a carcass trodden under foot? It is formed out of a troubled fountain and corrupted spring, built of a fetid drop; it is burned with fire, it is cut down. It is an unformed substance resembling a worm, it is nought but terror. It is kept in a foul womb, closed up in an impure belly; it is born with pangs and sorrows to see trouble and vanities. All day long it covets pleasures, and departs from instruction and from commandments; it comes in the dark, and goes away in the dark; it is a poor, needy, and destitute wayfarer. It has no knowledge without thee, and no understanding beside thee. While alive, it is dust; and when it dies, it is ashes. As long as it lives, worms surround it, and when its end comes, vermin and clods of dust cover it. It cannot discern between its right hand and its left hand; its lot is hidden in the ground. Go thou, therefore, and reign over it, for sovereignty is meet unto the children of wisdom, and the foolish is a servant to the wise of heart. Walk not in the stubbornness of thy wicked heart, be not ensnared by its counsels, and despise the gain of its frauds; trust not in oppression, and become not vain in robbery; for oppression makes a wise man foolish, and a bribe destroys the heart.

O my soul, set thy heart toward the highway, even the way by which thou didst go; for all was made of dust, and indeed unto dust shall all return. Every thing that was created and fashioned has an end and a goal to return unto the ground, whence it was taken. Life and death are brothers that dwell together; they are joined to one another; they cling together, so that they cannot be sundered. They are joined together by the two extremes of a frail bridge over which all created beings travel: life is the entrance, and death is the exit thereof. Life builds, and death demolishes; life sows, and death reaps; life plants, and death uproots; life joins together, and death separates; life links together, and death scatters. Know, I pray thee, and see that also unto thee shall the cup pass over, and thou shalt soon go out from the lodging-place which is on the way, when time and chance befall thee, and thou returnest to thine everlasting home. On that day shalt thou delight in thy work, and take thy reward in return for thy labor wherein thou hast toiled in this world, whether it be good or bad. Therefore hearken, I pray thee, and consider, and incline thine ear; forget thy people and thy father's house. Arise, and sing unto thy King all thy day and all thy night; lift up thy hands toward Him, and bow down unto Him with thy face to the ground; let thine eyelids gush out with waters, and kneel thou upon thy knees; the King may perchance desire thy beauty, and lift up His countenance unto thee, and give thee peace. He will be gracious unto thee in the days of the affliction in this world, and also after thou hast returned to thy rest. For as long as thou didst live He dealt bountifully with thee.

O my soul, prepare provision in abundance, prepare not little, while thou art yet alive, and while thy hand has yet strength, because the journey is too great for thee. And say not: 'I shall prepare provision to-morrow'; for the day has declined, and thou knowest not what the next day may bring forth. Know likewise that yesterday shall never come back, and that whatever thou hast done therein is weighed, numbered, and counted. Nor shouldst thou say: 'I shall do it to-morrow'; for the day of death is hidden from all the living. Hasten to do thy task every day, for death may at any time send forth its arrow and lightning. Delay not to do thy daily task, for as a bird wanders from its nest, so does a man wander from his place. Think not with thyself that after thou hast gone forth from the prison of thy body thou wilt turn to correction from thy perpetual backsliding; for it will not be possible for thee then to turn away from backsliding or to repent of wickedness, guilt, and transgression. For that world has been established to render accounts—the book of the hidden and concealed deeds which every man commits is sealed—and it has been prepared to grant a good reward to them that fear the Lord and think upon His name, and to execute the vengeance of the covenant upon them that forget God, who say unto God: 'Depart from us, for we desire not the knowledge of Thy ways. What is the Almighty, that we should serve Him? and what profit should we have, if we pray unto Him?'

O my soul, if thou art wise, thou art wise for thyself; and if thou scoffest, thy error remains with thee. Hear instruction, and be wise, and refuse it not. Lay continually to thy heart the words of Koheleth the son of David: 'The end of the matter, all having been heard: fear God, and keep His commandments; for this is the whole man. For God will bring every work into judgment concerning every hidden thing, whether it be good or whether it be evil.' Forget not that He seals up the hand of every man, that all men whom He has made may know it. Remember likewise that there is no darkness and no thick darkness wherein the workers of iniquity may hide themselves. Seek the Lord thy Maker with all thy might and strength. Seek righteousness, seek meekness; it may be that thou wilt be hidden in the day of God's anger, and in the day of His fierce wrath, and that thou wilt shine as the brightness of the firmament and as the sun when it goes forth in its might. The sun of righteousness with healing in its wings shall shine upon thee. Now arise, go and make supplication unto thy Lord, and take up a melody unto thy God. Praise thou God, for it is good to sing praises to our God; for it is pleasant, and praise is comely.

[39]

BAKUNIN, MICHAEL

BAKUNIN, MICHAEL (1814-1876). For nearly thirty years, he was an active participant in all European revolutions. Neither failure nor defeat could discourage his anarchistic spirit. To him, revolution meant the destruction of a corrupt and doomed society, and the desire for destruction served as a creative outlet for him. He detested the quiet life and often reiterated: "We need a tempestuous lawlessness to secure a free world."

A lawless world seemed both possible and good to Bakunin It

would produce "the free initiative of free individuals within free groups." It would destroy the uniformity of the social order (which to him meant death) and create the variety which he considered identical with the life spirit. He was a grim adversary of all contemporary governments and of the socialism advocated by Karl Marx.

Bakunin, the prophet of destruction, who exalted radicals as the most honorable enemies of decadent institutions, was a nobleman and former officer of the Tsar's imperial guard.

SCIENCE AND LIFE

HISTORICALLY speaking, there are three fundamental principles that constitute the essential conditions for all human development. These principles apply to the individual as well as to collective humanity. They are: human animality, thought, and rebellion. The first corresponds with individual and socialized relationships; the second with science; the third with liberty.

The gradual development of the material world is one of a natural movement from the simple to the complex. Organic and animal life, the historically progressive intelligence of man, individually and socially, has been from the lowest species to the highest; from the inferior to the superior. This movement conforms with all our daily experiences, and consequently it also conforms with our natural logic; with the distinctive laws of our mind, which are formed and developed only by the aid of these same experiences; that is, the mental and cerebral reproduction or reflected summary.

Real and living individuality is perceptible only to another living individuality, not to a thinking individuality; not to the man who, by a series of abstractions, puts himself outside of and above immediate contact with life; to such a man, it can exist only as a more or less perfect example of the species—as a definite abstraction. . . .

Science is like a rabbit. Both are incapable of grasping the individuality of a man. Science is not ignorant of the principle of individuality; it conceives of it perfectly as a principle, but not as a fact.

What I preach, then, is to a certain extent, the revolt of life against science, or rather against the government of science; not to destroy science—that would be treason to humanity—but to remand it to its place so that it can never leave it again.

[40]

BARTH, KARL

BARTH, KARL (1886-   ). Barth is the first religious man since Kierkegaard violently to attack the churches. He tried to restore the theology of early Lutheran and Calvinist reform. Although a member of the Calvinist church, his "dialectical theology" and his concept of the active effect of the divine word in man is more akin to the personal spirit of Luther. He agrees and extends Calvin's belief in man's inability to know God, by emphasizing the "wholly otherness" of God. Like Luther and Calvin, he endeavors to isolate piety and salvation from knowledge. Like them, he insists that man, without the intervention of divine Grace, is helpless and forlorn. Barth consistently refutes all attempts to vindicate even the slightest autonomous values of humanity. He repudiates all idealism as an exaltation of the human mind and declines the idealist concept of the absolute as "a man-made abstraction." He does not favor optimism because its confidence is generally based upon purely human qualities. To him, the only truths are those known through revelation.

The deep earnestness and stern resoluteness of Barth's theology has attracted many adherents in almost all countries. His doctrine is one of conversion and struggle rather than one of knowledge. His ethical demands, religious convictions, and theological doctrines are manifest in his *The Word of God and the Word of Man* (1928), *Credo* (1936), *The Holy Ghost and the Christian Life* (1938), and *Dogmatics in Outline* (1949).

FAITH AS KNOWLEDGE

POSSIBLY you may be struck by the emergence of the concept of *reason*. I use it deliberately. The saying, 'Despise only reason and science, man's supremest power of all', was ut-

117

tered not by a prophet, but by Goethe's Mephisto. Christendom and the theological world were always ill-advised in thinking it their duty for some reason or other, either of enthusiasm or of theological conception, to betake themselves to the camp of an opposition to reason. Over the Christian Church, as the essence of revelation and of the work of God which constitutes its basis, stands the Word: 'The Word was made flesh.' The Logos became man. Church proclamation is language, and language not of an accidental, arbitrary, chaotic and incomprehensible kind, but language which comes forward with the claim to be true and to uphold itself as the truth against the lie. Do not let us be forced from the clarity of this position. In the Word which the Church has to proclaim the truth is involved, not in a provisional secondary sense, but in the primary sense of the Word itself—the Logos is involved, and is demonstrated and revealed in the human reason, the human *nous*, as the Logos, that is, as meaning, as truth to be learned. In the word of Christian proclamation we are concerned with *ratio* reason, in which human *ratio* may also be reflected and reproduced. Church proclamation, theology, is no talk or babbling; it is not propaganda unable to withstand the claim, Is it then true as well, that this is said? Is it really so? You have probably also suffered from a certain kind of preaching and edifying talk, from which it becomes only too clear that there is talking going on, emphatic talk with a plenteous display of rhetoric, which does not however stand up to this simple question as to the truth of what is said. The Creed of Christian faith rests upon knowledge. And where the Creed is uttered and confessed knowledge should be, is meant to be, created. Christian faith is not irrational, not anti-rational, not supra-rational, but rational in the proper sense. The Church which utters the Creed, which comes forward with the tremendous claim to preach and to proclaim the glad tidings, derives from the fact that it has apprehended something—*Vernunft* comes from *vernehmen*—and it wishes to let what it has apprehended be apprehended again. These were always unpropitious periods in the Chris-

118

tian Church, when Christian histories of dogmatics and theology separated *gnosis* and *pistis*. *Pistis* rightly understood is
gnosis; rightly understood the act of faith is also an act of
knowledge. Faith means knowledge.

But once this is established, it must also be said that
Christian faith is concerned with an illumination of the reason. Christian faith has to do with the object, with God the
Father, the Son, and the Holy Spirit, of which the Creed
speaks. Of course it is of the nature and being of this object,
of God, the Father, the Son, and the Holy Spirit that He
cannot be known by the powers of human knowledge, but is
apprehensible and apprehended solely because of His own
freedom, decision and action. What man can know by his own
power according to the measure of his natural powers, his
understanding, his feeling, will be at most something like a
supreme being, an absolute nature, the idea of an utterly
free power, of a being towering over everything. This absolute and supreme being, the ultimate and most profound, this
'thing in itself,' has nothing to do with God. It is part of the
intuitions and marginal possibilities of man's thinking, man's
contrivance. Man is able to think this being; but he has not
thereby thought God. God is thought and known when in His
own freedom God makes Himself apprehensible. We shall
have to speak later about God, His being and His nature, but
we must now say that God is always the One who has made
Himself known to man in His own revelation, and not the
one man thinks out for himself and describes as God. There
is a perfectly clear division there already, epistemologically,
between the true God and the false gods. Knowledge of God
is not a possibility which is open for discussion. God is the
essence of all reality, of that reality which reveals itself to
us. Knowledge of God takes place where there is actual experience that God speaks, that He so represents Himself to
man that he cannot fail to see and hear Him, where, in a
situation which he has not brought about, in which he becomes incomprehensible to himself, man sees himself faced
with the fact that he lives with God and God with him, be-

119

cause so it has pleased God. Knowledge of God takes place where divine revelation takes place, illumination of man by God, transmission of human knowledge, instruction of man by this incomparable Teacher.

We started from the point that Christian faith is a meeting. Christian faith and knowledge of Christian faith takes place at the point where the divine reason, the divine Logos, sets up His law in the region of man's understanding, to which law human, creaturely reason must accommodate itself. When that happens, man comes to knowledge; for when God sets up His law in man's thought, in his seeing and hearing and feeling, the revelation of the truth is also reached about man and his reason, the revelation of man is reached, who cannot bring about of himself what is brought about simply by God Himself.

Can God be known? Yes, God can be known, since it is actually true and real that He is knowable through Himself. When that happens, man becomes free, he becomes empowered, he becomes capable—a mystery to himself—of knowing God. Knowledge of God is a knowledge completely effected and determined from the side of its object, from the side of God. But for that very reason it is genuine knowledge; for that very reason it is in the deepest sense free knowledge. Of course it remains a relative knowledge, a knowledge imprisoned within the limits of the creaturely. Of course it is especially true here that we are carrying heavenly treasures in earthen vessels. Our concepts are not adequate to grasp this treasure. Precisely where this genuine knowledge of God takes place it will also be clear that there is no occasion for any pride. There always remains powerless man, creaturely reason within its limitations. But in this area of the creaturely, of the inadequate, it has pleased God to reveal Himself. And since man is foolish in this respect too, He will be wise; since man is petty, He will be great; since man is inadequate, God is adequate. 'Let my grace suffice for thee. For my strength is mighty in the weak' holds good also for the question of knowledge.

In the opening statement we said that Christian faith has to do with the illumination of the reason, in which men become free to live in the truth of Jesus Christ. For the understanding of Christian knowledge of faith it is essential to understand that the truth of Jesus Christ is living truth and the knowledge of it living knowledge. This does not mean that we are to revert once more to the idea that here knowledge is not basically involved at all. It is not that Christian faith is a dim sensation, an a-logical feeling, experiencing and learning. Faith is knowledge; it is related to God's Logos, and is therefore a thoroughly logical matter. The truth of Jesus Christ is also in the simplest sense a truth of facts. Its starting-point, the Resurrection of Jesus Christ from the dead, is a fact which occurred in space and time, as the New Testament describes it. The apostles were not satisfied to hold on to an inward fact; they spoke of what they saw and heard and what they touched with their hands. And the truth of Jesus Christ is also a matter of thoroughly clear and, in itself, ordered human thinking; free, precisely in its being bound. But—and the things must not be separated—what is involved is living truth. The concept of knowledge, or *scientia,* is insufficient to describe what Christian knowledge is. We must rather go back to what in the Old Testament is called wisdom, what the Greeks called *sophia* and the Latins *sapientia,* in order to grasp the knowledge of theology in its fullness. *Sapientia* is distinguished from the narrower concept of *scientia,* wisdom is distinguished from knowing, in that it not only contains knowledge in itself, but also that this concept speaks of a knowledge which is practical knowledge, embracing the entire existence of man. Wisdom is the knowledge by which we may actually and practically live; it is empiricism and it is the theory which is powerful in being directly practical, in being the knowledge which dominates our life, which is really a light upon our path. Not a light to wonder at and to observe, not a light to kindle all manner of fireworks at—not even the profoundest philosophical speculations—but the light on our road which may stand

121

above our action and above our talk, the light on our healthy and on our sick days, in our poverty and our wealth, the light which does not only lighten when we suppose ourselves to have moments of insight, but which accompanies us even into our folly, which is not quenched when all is quenched, when the goal of our life becomes visible in death. To live by this light, by this truth, is the meaning of Christian knowledge. Christian knowledge means living in the truth of Jesus Christ. In this light we live and move and have our being (Acts 17. 28) in order that we may be of Him, and through Him and unto Him, as it says in Romans 11. 36. So Christian knowledge, at its deepest, is one with what we termed man's trust in God's Word. Never yield when they try to teach you divisions and separations in this matter. There is no genuine trust, no really tenable, victorious trust in God's Word which is not founded in His truth; and on the other hand no knowledge, no theology, no confessing and no Scripture truth which does not at once possess the stamp of this living truth. The one must always be measured and tested and confirmed by the other.

And just because as Christians we may live in the truth of Jesus Christ and therefore in the light of the knowledge of God and therefore with an illumined reason, we shall also become sure of the meaning of our own existence and of the ground and goal of all that happens. Once more a quite tremendous extension of the field of vision is indicated by this; to know this object in its truth means in truth to know no more and no less than all things, even man, oneself, the cosmos, and the world. The truth of Jesus Christ is not one truth among others; it is *the* truth, the universal truth that creates all truth as surely as it is the truth of God, the *prima veritas* which is also the *ultima veritas*. For in Jesus Christ God has created all things, He has created all of us. We exist not apart from Him, but in Him, whether we are aware of it or not; and the whole cosmos exists not apart from Him, but in Him, borne by Him, the Almighty Word. To know Him is to know all. To be touched and gripped by the Spirit in this realm means being led into all truth. If a man believes and knows God, he can no longer ask, What is the meaning of my life? But by believing he actually lives the meaning of his life, the meaning of his creatureliness, of his individuality, in the limits of his creatureliness and individuality and in the fallibility of his existence, in the sin in which he is involved and of which daily and hourly he is guilty; yet he also lives it with the aid which is daily and hourly imparted to him through God's interceding for him, in spite of him and without his deserving it. He recognises the task assigned to him in this whole, and the hope vouchsafed to him in and with this task, because of the grace by which he may live and the praise of the glory promised him, by which he is even here and now secretly surrounded in all lowliness. The believer confesses this meaning of his existence. The Christian Creed speaks of God as the ground and goal of all that exists. The ground and goal of the entire cosmos means Jesus Christ. And the unheard-of thing may and must be said, that where Christian faith exists, there also exists, through God's being trusted, inmost familiarity with the ground and goal of all that happens, of all things; there man lives, in spite of all that is said to the contrary, in the peace that passeth all understanding, and which for that very reason is the light that lightens our understanding.

[41]

BEECHER, HENRY WARD

BEECHER, HENRY WARD (1813-1887). One of the outstanding public figures of American life and a brilliantly persuasive preacher, Henry Ward Beecher was regarded, in his youth, as unusually stupid by his parents, teachers, and playmates. He decided to study navigation and become a sailor, for he felt unsuited for other occupations. A great change took place in him during his sojourn at Mount Pleasant Classical Institute, Amherst, Massachusetts; his extraordinary vitality broke through. He became active in sports, read omnivorously, and resolved to become a preacher. He subsequently continued his studies at Lane Theological Seminary in Cincinnati. Here, he revolted against Calvinism and professed independent Presby-terianism in the name of life and the beauty of nature.

Beecher was not a man of original thought; he started no new movement, but he succeeded in attracting and educating Church people, and helped them to develop the power to withstand life's tests and conflicts. He used his sermons to advocate social reforms; he was strongly opposed to slavery despite his dislike for radical abolitionists. He taught a disbelief of hell; defended evolution, and advocated that of which he was so terribly fond, the outdoor life. Despite their great success, his sermons did not satisfy him. He carefully scrutinized and adhered to the methods of Jonathan Ed-wards, the leader of the "Great Awakening" in New England, and those of the Apostles as they are described in the book of *Acts*. His last years were troubled by a highly publicized trial in which charges of adultery were brought against him. The jury could not agree and an ecclesiastical council acquitted him. Beecher was minister, from 1847 until his death, at Plymouth Church, Brooklyn, New York. Though often ranged on the side of unpopular causes, Beecher's powers of persuasion were such that his sermons gained nation-wide hearing and swayed popular opinion.

SOME OBSERVATIONS

IT is a shiftless trick to lie about stories and groceries, argu-ing with men that you have *no time*, in a new country, for nice farming, for making good fences for smooth meadows without a stump, for draining wet patches which disfigure fine fields; to raise your own frogs in your own yard; to permit, year after year, a dirty, stinking, mantled puddle to stand before your fence in the street; to plant orchards, and allow your cattle to eat the trees up, and when gnawed down, to save your money by trying to nurse the stubs into good trees, instead of getting fresh ones from the nursery; to allow an orchard to have blank spaces, where trees have died; and when the living trees begin to bear, to wake up, and put young whips in the vacant spots. It is a filthy trick to use to-bacco at all; and it puts an end to all our affected squeamish-ness at the Chinese taste in eating rats, cats, and bird's nests. It is vile economy to lay up for remastication a half-chewed cud; to pocket a half-smoked cigar; and finally to bedrench one's self with tobacco juice; to so besmoke one's clothes that

124

a man can be scented as far off as a whaleship can be smelt at sea. It is a vile trick to borrow a choice book; to read it with unwashed hands, that have been used in the charcoal-bin; and finally to return it daubed on every leaf with nose-blood spots, tobacco-spatter, and dirty finger-marks. It is an unthrifty trick to bring in eggs from the barn in one's coat pocket, and then to sit down upon them. It is a filthy trick to borrow of or lend for others' use a tooth-brush or a toothpick; to pick one's teeth at table with a fork or a jackknife; to put your hat upon the dinner-table among the dishes; to spit generously into the fire, or at it, while the hearth is covered with food set to warm—for sometimes a man hits what he don't aim at. It is an unmannerly trick to neglect the scraper outside the door, but to be scrupulous in cleaning your feet, after you get inside, on the carpet, rug, or andiron; to bring your drenched umbrella into the entry, where a black puddle may leave to the housewife melancholy evidence that you have been there. It is a soul-trying trick for a neat dairy-woman to see her "man" watering the horse out of her milk-bucket; or filtering horse medicine through her milk-strainer; or feeding his hogs with her water-pail; or, after barn-work, to set the well-bucket outside the curb, and wash his hands out of it.

*   *   *

There is something peculiarly impressive to me in the old New England custom of announcing a death. In a village of a few hundred inhabitants all are known each to each. There are no *strangers*. The village church, the Sabbath-school, and the district-school have been channels of inter-communication; so that one is acquainted not only with the persons, but, too often, with the affairs—domestic, social, and secular—of every dweller in the town.

A thousand die in the city every month, and there is no void apparent. The vast population speedily closes over the emptied space. The hearts that were grouped about the deceased doubtless suffer alike in the country and in the city. But, outside of the special grief, there is a moment's sadness, a dash of sympathy, and then life closes over the grief, as waters fill the void made when a bucketful is drawn out of the ocean. There goes a city funeral! Well, I wonder who it is that is journeying so quietly to his last home. He was not of my house, nor of my circle; his life was not a thread woven with mine; I did not see him before, I shall not miss him now. We did not greet at the church; we did not vote at the town meeting; we had not gone together upon sleigh-rides, skatings, huskings, fishings, trainings, or elections. Therefore it is that men of might die daily about us, and we have no sense of it, any more than we perceive it when a neighbor extinguishes his lamp.

It was upon the very day that we arrived in Woodstock, upon this broad and high hill-top, in the afternoon, as we were sitting in ransomed bliss rejoicing in the boundless hemisphere above, and in the beautiful sweep of hills feathered with woods, and cultivated fields ruffled with fences; and full, here and there, of pictures of trees, single or in rounded groups; it was as we sat thus—the children, three families of them, scattered out, racing and shouting upon the village-green before us—that the church-bell swung round merrily, as if preluding, or clearing its throat for some message. It is five o'clock: What can that bell be ringing for? Is there a meeting? Perhaps a "preparatory lecture." It stops. Then one deep stroke is given, and all is still. Every one stops. Some one is dead. Another solemn stroke goes vibrating through the crystal air, and calls scores more to the doors. Who can be dead? Another solitary peal wafts its message tremulously along the air; and that long gradually dying vibration of a country bell—never heard amid the noises of the air in a city—swelling and falling, swelling and falling; aerial waves, voices of invisible spirits communing with each other as they bear aloft the ransomed one!

But now its warning voice is given. All are listening. Ten sharp, distinct strokes, and a pause. Some one is ten years old of earth's age. No; ten more follow; twenty years is it? Ten more tell us that it is an adult. Ten more, and ten more, and twice ten again, and one final stroke, count the age of *seventy-one*. Seventy-one years! Were they long, weary, sorrowful years? Was it a venerable sire, weary of waiting for the silver cord to be loosed? Seventy-one years! Shall I see as many? And if I do, the hill-top is already turned, and I am going down upon the farther side. How long to look forward to! How short to look back upon! Age and youth look upon life from opposite ends of the telescope: It is exceedingly long; it is exceedingly short! To one who muses this, the very strokes of the bell seem to emblem life. Each is like a year, and all of them roll away as in a moment, and are gone.

*　　*　　*

It is plain that Mary was imbued with the spirit of the Hebrew Scriptures. Not only was the history of her people familiar to her, but her language at the annunciation shows that the poetry of the Old Testament had filled her soul. She was fitted to receive her people's history in its most romantic and spiritual aspects. They were God's peculiar people. Their history unrolled before her as a series of wonderful providences. The path glowed with divine manifestations. Miracles blossomed out of every natural law. But to her there were no "laws of nature." Such ideas had not yet been born. "The earth was the Lord's." All its phenomena were direct manifestations of his will. Clouds and storms came on errands from God. Light and darkness were the shining or the hiding of his face. Calamities were punishments; harvests were divine gifts; famines were immediate divine penalties. To us, God acts through instruments; to the Hebrew, he acted immediately by his will. "He spake, and it was done; he commanded, and it stood fast."

To such a one as Mary there would be no incredulity as to the reality of this angelic manifestation. Her only surprise would be that *she* should be chosen for a renewal of those divine interpositions in behalf of her people of which their history was so full. The very reason which would lead us to suspect a miracle in our day, gave it credibility in other days. It is simply a question of adaptation. A miracle, as a blind appeal to the moral sense, without use of the reason, was adapted to the earlier periods of human life. Its usefulness ceases when the moral sense is so developed that it can find its own way through the ministration of the reason. A miracle is a substitute for moral demonstration, and is peculiarly adapted to the early conditions of mankind.

Of all miracles, there was none more sacred, more congruous, and grateful to a Hebrew than an angelic visitation. A devout Jew, in looking back, saw angels flying thick between the heavenly throne and the throne of his fathers. The greatest events of national history had been made illustrious by their presence. Their work began with the primitive pair. They had come at evening to Abraham's tent. They had waited upon Jacob's footsteps. They had communed with Moses, with the judges, with priests and magistrates, with prophets and holy men. All the way down from the beginning of history the pious Jew saw the shining foot-steps of these heavenly messengers. Nor had the faith died out in the long interval through which their visits had been withheld. Mary could not, therefore, be surprised at the coming of angels, but only that they should come to her.

It may seem strange that Zacharias should be struck dumb for doubting the heavenly messenger, while Mary went unrebuked. But it is plain that there was a wide difference in the nature of the relative experiences. To Zacharias was promised an event external to himself, not involving his own sensibility. But to a woman's heart there can be no other announcement possible that shall so stir every feeling and sensibility of the soul as the promise and prospect of her first child. Motherhood is the very center of womanhood. The first awakening in her soul of the reality that she bears a double life—herself within herself—brings a sweet bewilderment of wonder and joy. The more sure her faith of the fact, the more tremulous must her soul become. Such an announcement can never mean to a father's what it does to a mother's heart. And it is one of the exquisite shades of subtle truth,

and of beauty as well, that the angel who rebuked Zacharias for doubt, saw nothing in the trembling hesitancy of Mary, inconsistent with a childish faith. If the heart swells with the hope of a new life in the common lot of mortals, with what profound feeling must Mary have pondered the angel's promise to her son:
He shall be great, and shall be called the son of the Highest,
And the Lord God shall give him the throne of his father David;
And he shall reign over the house of Jacob forever.
And of his kingdom there shall be no end.

[42]

BENDA, JULIEN

BENDA, JULIEN (1867-   ). Although Benda had retired to a solitary existence prior to the collapse of France, his life was particularly endangered during the German occupation of France because he was a Jew, a defender of democracy, and an adversary of German nationalism.

Throughout his lifetime, he has consistently opposed the main currents of French spiritual life and has fought untiringly against the cult of vagueness, subjectivism, romanticism, mystic nationalism, and the blending of other arts with music. He is a successful novelist, sensitive to poetry. He maintains the superiority of science to literature; Descartes, Kant, and Darwin to Dante and Victor Hugo; and intelligence to sensibility. He has been an ardent opponent of Henri Bergson, and, although he rejected the aesthetics of Paul Valery, he has adopted his phrase, "Thought by its very nature is without style."

Benda's works proclaim his hatred of injustice, his contempt of scepticism, and his "ideal of disinterested values," those universal ideas which are independent of historical conditions. *La Trahison des Clercs* (The Treason of the Intellectuals.) (1927) accused the intellectuals of disloyalty to those concepts which, according to Benda, are the basis of individual rights and mandatory for everyone who actively participates in a spiritual life. *Uriel's Report*, written in 1926 with cruel objectivity, is a satirical picture of humanity. *Exercises of a Man Buried Alive* (1947) violently attacks almost all French celebrities, except Paul Claudel.

I SHOULD like to draw a distinction between humanitarianism as I mean it here—a sensitiveness to the abstract quality of what is human, to Montaigne's "whole form of human condition"—and the feeling which is usually called humanitarianism, by which is meant the love for human beings existing in the concrete. The former impulse (which would more accurately be called humanism) is the attachment to a concept. It is a pure passion of the intelligence, implying no terrestrial love. It is quite easy to conceive of a person plunging into the concept of what is human without having the least desire even to see a man. This is the form assumed by love of humanity in the great patricians of the mind like Erasmus, Malebranche, Spinoza, Goethe, who all were men, it appears, not very anxious to throw themselves into the arms of their neighbors. The second humanitarianism is a state of the heart and therefore the portion of plebeian souls. It occurs among moralists in periods when lofty intellectual discipline disappears among them and gives way to sentimental exaltation, I mean in the eighteenth century (chiefly with Diderot) and above all in the nineteenth century, with Michelet, Quinet, Proudhon, Romain Rolland, Georges Duhamel. This sentimental form of humanitarianism and forgetfulness of its conceptual form explain the unpopularity of this doctrine with so many distinguished minds, who discover two equally repulsive commonplaces in the arsenal of political ideology. One of them is "the patriotic bore" and the other "the universal embrace."

The humanitarianism which holds in honor the abstract quality of what is human, is the only one which allows us to love *all* men. Obviously, as soon as we look at men in the concrete, we inevitably find that this quality is distributed in different quantities, and we have to say with Renan: "In reality one is *more or less* a man, *more or less* the son of God . . . I see no reason why a Papuan should be immortal."

Modern equalitarians, by failing to understand that there can be no equality except in the abstract and that inequality is the essence of the concrete, have merely displayed the extraordinary vulgarity of their minds as well as their amazing political clumsiness.

Humanism, as I have defined it, has nothing to do with internationalism. Internationalism is a protest against national egotism, not on behalf of a spiritual passion, but on behalf of another egotism, another earthly passion. It is the impulse of a certain category of men—laborers, bankers, industrialists—who unite across frontiers in the name of private and practical interests, and who only oppose the national spirit because it thwarts them in satisfying those interests.

In comparison with such impulses, national passion appears an idealistic and disinterested impulse. In short, humanism is also something entirely different from cosmopolitanism, which is the simple desire to enjoy the advantages of all nations and all their cultures, and is generally exempt from all moral dogmatism.

[43]

BENTHAM, JEREMY

BENTHAM, JEREMY (1748-1832). Noted as an English social philosopher and sympathizer of the American and French revolutions, Bentham's ideas paralleled those of the American founding fathers more closely than those of the French Jacobins. His treatise, *Fragment on Government,* was revised and republished in 1789, the year of the French Revolution, as *An Introduction to the Principles of Morals and Legislation.*

Bentham defined the function of good government as the effort to promote the greatest happiness of the greatest number of citizens and to effect harmony between public and private interests. He declared that the American government was the only good government because it upheld these principles. According to Bentham, happiness is identical with pleasure, and serves as the underlying motivation of human behavior; thus happiness can be the only criterion of morals and legislation. Originally, Bentham called this criterion Utility, but by 1822 he felt that the word did not adequately crystallize his ideas. However, James Mill, a disciple of Bentham, revived the term, Utilitarianism, shortly afterward and henceforth Bentham has been known as the "father of the Utilitarian school."

Bentham had been nicknamed "philosopher" at the age of five.

THE FOUR SOURCES OF PLEASURE AND PAIN

THE happiness of the individuals, of whom a community is composed, that is their pleasures and their security, is the end and the sole end which the legislator ought to have in view: the sole standard, in conformity to which each individual ought, as far as depends upon the legislator, to be *made* to fashion his behaviour. But whether it be this or any thing else that is to be *done*, there is nothing by which a man can ultimately be *made* to do it, but either pain or pleasure. Having taken a general view of these two grand objects (*viz.* pleasure, and what comes to the same thing, immunity from pain) in the character of *final* causes; it will be necessary to take a view of pleasure and pain itself, in the character of efficient causes or means.

There are four distinguishable sources from which pleasure and pain are in use to flow: considered separately, they may be termed the *physical*, the *political*, the *moral*, and the *religious*: and inasmuch as the pleasures and pains belonging to each of them are capable of giving a binding force to any law or rule of conduct, they may all of them be termed *sanctions*.

If it be in the present life, and from the ordinary course of nature, not purposely modified by the interposition of the will of any human being, nor by any extraordinary interposition of any superior invisible being, that the pleasure or the pain takes place or is expected, it may be said to issue from or to belong to the *physical sanction*.

If at the hands of a *particular* person or set of persons in the community, who under names correspondent to that of *judge*, are chosen for the particular purpose of dispensing it, according to the will of the sovereign or supreme ruling power in the state, it may be said to issue from the *political sanction*.

If at the hands of such *chance* persons in the community, as the party in question may happen in the course of his life to have concerns with, according to each man's spontaneous disposition, and not according to any settled or concerted rule, it may be said to issue from the *moral* or *popular sanction*.

If from the immediate hand of a superior invisible being, either in the present life, or in a future, it may be said to issue from the *religious sanction*.

Pleasures or pains which may be expected to issue from the *physical, political,* or *moral* sanctions, must all of them be experienced, if ever, in the *present* life: those which may be expected to issue from the *religious* sanction, may be expected to be experienced either in the *present* life or in a *future*.

. . . .

Of these four sanctions the physical is altogether, we may observe, the ground-work of the political and the moral: so is it also of the religious, in as far as the latter bears relation to the present life. It is included in each of those other three. This may operate in any case, (that is, any of the pains or pleasures belonging to it may operate) independently of *them*: none of *them* can operate but by means of this. In a word, the powers of nature may operate of themselves; but neither the magistrate, nor men at large, *can* operate, nor is God in the case in question *supposed* to operate, but through the powers of nature.

[44]

BERACHYAH

BERACHYAH (c. 12th or 13th century). The literary fame of Berachyah is chiefly founded upon his *Mishle Shualim* (Fox Fables). Some of these were of his own invention; others were derived from the fables of Aesop, the Talmud, and the Hindus, but even in the adaptation of plots to his own Hebrew style, he displayed poetic originality and narrative talents. The best-known of his philosophical works, encyclopedic in quality, is *Sefer Hahibbur* (The Book of Compilation). Here, he developed the ideas of Saadia, Bahya Ibn Pakuda, and Solomon Ibn Gabirol. He was versed in the eastern and western branches of Jewish philosophy, and was well acquainted with medieval French and English literature.

The personal life of Berachyah is solely conjecture. He was called Berachyah Ben Natronai Hanakdan. His father's name indicates descent from the Jewish scholars of Babylonia, which may help to explain Berachyah's knowledge of Hindu stories. His surname means "punctuator," probably an allusion to his profession of scribe or grammarian. There is no agreement as to the time, place, or country in which he lived. Some of his biographers assume that he wrote during the twelfth century; others during the thirteenth century. Some maintain that he lived in Provence; others in Northern France, and still others in England. It is not improbable that he was an itinerant teacher, scholar, and writer.

THE COMPENDIUM

ON THE SOURCES OF KNOWLEDGE

THERE are three distinct forms of knowledge. First, the knowledge resulting from observation, *i.e.*, knowledge gained through the senses, which are the primary sources of feeling known as the five senses, viz: sight, hearing, smell, taste, and touch. Secondly the knowledge of the intellect that is, the instrument of sense, and without the association of the emotions; for instance, determining in our mind the beauty of truth and the abhorring of falsehood, without having before us any presentative images. Thirdly, intuitive knowledge, which a man is bound to believe, and the perception of which is forced upon him, his consciousness being compelled to accept it as true; for if he did not accept it as true, he would, as a natural consequence, have to deny the existence of mind altogether, and to make out knowledge to be a liar.

ON THE CLASSIFICATION OF KNOWLEDGE

All knowledge may be divided into three parts: First, the science of created matter, *i.e.*, the science of the nature of all bodies, and their accidental properties. This is required for the purposes of this world, and it is the lowest form of knowledge. Midway stands the science, which we might term the "auxiliary science," such as the science of numbers and their computations, the science of astronomy, and the science of music. These two departments of knowledge form the basis of all the secrets of the world and of the several advantages to be derived from them; inasmuch as they enlighten us with regard to the various handicrafts, and all forms of tactics, which are necessary for the development of the human body, and for worldly acquisitions. The third science is that of theology, viz: the science of the knowledge of God, and the knowledge of His Law and Commandments, such as may be grasped by the soul and the intellect. Now, every subdivision of this science, however diverse in various interests, becomes so many introductions, afforded us by God, to become acquainted with the Torah. It is the highest form of knowledge; we are bound to cultivate it for the purpose of attaining a proper understanding of our Law, and not for the purpose of attaining worldly advantages thereby.

[45]

BERDYAEV, NICHOLAS

BERDYAEV, NICHOLAS (1874-1948). Berdyaev was educated in the military school of the Tsarist cadet corps. Later he became a Marxist, was arrested in 1898 for his socialist activities, and banished to the north of Russia for three years. Around 1905 he reverted to the Christian faith, but was accused, in 1914, of insulting the Holy Synod. His trial in 1917 was ended by the Russian Revolution. The Bolshevist government had him arrested in 1920 and then again in 1922. He was expelled from the Soviet Union because of his persistent support of faithful Christians. His remaining years were spent in France.

He regarded himself as the prophet of a new world about to be born; the eventide of history whose means of research, adequate as they might appear for the sun-lit day of rationalism, would be completely inadequate for the new era. He predicted a "New Middle Ages" which would spell the end of humanism, individualism, formal liberalism, nationalism, socialism, and communism. It would be the beginning of a new religious collectivity, which would not be ruled by an ecclesiastic hierarchy, but would imbue knowledge, morality, art, and economic and political institutions with a religious spirit free from external constraint. Berdyaev's philosophy conceives of man as the conjunction of the natural and divine world. Man, created by a creator, must necessarily continue the creative process in order to prove the creative character of his cognitive faculties and use them for the perfection of true civilization. Berdyaev arrived at this point of view after considerable changes in his personal philosophy.

ON SOCIALISM

SOCIALISM cannot be fought with "bourgeois ideas"; it is useless to set over against it the middle-class, democratic, capitalist society of the nineteenth and twentieth centuries. It is precisely this bourgeois society that has bred Socialism and involved us in it. Socialism is flesh of the flesh and blood of the blood of Capitalism. They both belong to the same world; they are animated by a common spirit—or rather, by a common negation of spirit. Socialism has inherited the middle-class atheism of the capitalist nineteenth-century, which was, indeed, the most atheistical society known to history. It falsified the relation between man and man, and between man and physical nature. Its political economy corrupted the hierarchical organization of society and gave birth to economic materialism, which is an exact reflection of the actual state of that nineteenth-century civilization. The life of the spirit became almost less than an accident, a speculative adaptation to less high things. The worship of Mammon instead of God is a characteristic of Socialism as well as of Capitalism. Socialism is no longer an utopia or a dream: it is an objective threat, and a warning to Christians to show them unmistakably that they have not fulfilled the word of Christ, that they have in effect apostatized. A basis is sometimes assigned to Capitalism by the statement that human nature is sinful and that sin cannot be got rid of by force, while the essence of Socialism is in the supposition that this nature is entirely good. But it is forgotten that the moment of history can come when the evil in human nature, namely, the sin in which it is involved, will have taken on a new shape. It is the sinful part of our nature that begets Socialism. Capitalism, considered spiritually and morally, arose because human nature is prone to evil. But Socialism has arisen for exactly the same reason. Apostasy from the Christian faith, abandonment of spiritual principles and disregard of the spiritual ends of life, must of necessity lead first to the stage called Capitalism and then to the stage called Socialism. It follows clearly enough that we must begin to make our Christianity effectively real by a return to the life of the spirit, that a normal hierarchical harmony of life must be recovered, that that which is economic must be subordinated to that which is spiritual, that politics must be again confined within their proper limits.

[46]

BERGSON, HENRI

BERGSON, HENRI (1859-1941). When Bergson was asked how a philosopher should state his ideas, his reply was, "There are general problems which interest everybody and must be dealt with in language comprehensible to everybody. The solutions to these problems are frequently subordinated to those questions which interest only scholars. These may be dealt with in technical terms." While he admitted the occasional use of professional terminology, Bergson always wrote with a vocabulary easily comprehensible, inspiring, and exciting to philosophical laymen. When he used or coined technical terms, he was capable of making them popular. His mastery of language and subject matter extended his influence far beyond the realm of philosophy into such areas as the history of poetry, the social sciences, and religion. He also influenced the opinions of many contemporary philosophers.

According to Bergson, philosophy is the conscientious and reflective return to the immediate data of intuition. He classified reason as an impersonal faculty, emphasizing that every philosopher consciously proceeds from a chosen point of view. He regarded the philosopher as a man who faced the essentials of thought in order to discover the conditions for the totality of knowledge. He advocated the concept of duration as contrasted with the mechanistic concept of time. From duration, immediately felt in mental life, he

137

proceeded to the ideas of the vital impetus and creative evolution which manifest themselves in organic nature as well as in spiritual life, social processes, and individual actions. He was one of the few modern thinkers convinced of the unlimited progress of humanity.

His international fame was so great that after the collapse of France in 1940, the Vichy government offered him exemption from the Jewish laws, patterned after the Nuremberg Laws. Bergson declined the offer and resigned his professorship at the Collège de France.

ANIMAL AND HUMAN CONSCIOUSNESS

RADICAL is the difference between animal consciousness, even the most intelligent, and human consciousness. For consciousness corresponds exactly to the living being's power of choice; it is coextensive with the fringe of possible action that surrounds the real action: consciousness is synonymous with invention and with freedom. Now, in the animal, invention is never anything but a variation on the theme of routine. Shut up in the habits of the species, it succeeds, no doubt, in enlarging them by its individual initiative; but it escapes automatism only for an instant, for just the time to create a new automatism. The gates of its prison close as soon as they are opened; by pulling at its chain it succeeds only in stretching it. With man, consciousness breaks the chain. In man, and in man alone, it sets itself free. The whole history of life until man has been that of the effort of consciousness to raise matter, and of the more or less complete overwhelming of consciousness by the matter which has fallen back on it. The enterprise was paradoxical, if, indeed, we may speak here otherwise than by metaphor of enterprise and of effort. It was to create with matter, which is necessity itself, an instrument of freedom, to make a machine which should triumph over mechanism, and to use the determinism of nature to pass through the meshes of the net which this very determinism had spread. But, everywhere except in man, consciousness has let itself be caught in the net whose meshes it tried to pass through: it has remained the captive of the mechanisms it has set up. Automatism, which it tries to draw in the direction of freedom, winds about it and drags it down.

It has not the power to escape, because the energy it has provided for acts is almost all employed in maintaining the infinitely subtle and essentially unstable equilibrium into which it has brought matter. But man not only maintains his machine, he succeeds in using it as he pleases. Doubtless he owes this to the superiority of his brain, which enables him to build an unlimited number of motor mechanisms, to oppose new habits to the old ones unceasingly, and by dividing automatism against itself, to rule it. He owes it to his language, which furnishes consciousness with an immaterial body in which to incarnate itself and thus exempts itself from dwelling exclusively on material bodies, whose flux would soon drag it along and finally swallow it up. He owes it to social life, which stores and preserves efforts as language stores thought, fixes thereby a mean level to which individuals must raise themselves at the outset, and by this initial stimulation prevents the average man from slumbering and drives the superior man to mount still higher. But our brain, our society, and our language are only the external and various signs of one and the same internal superiority. They tell, each after its manner, the unique exceptional success which life has won at a given moment of its evolution. They express the difference of kind, and not only of degree, which separates man from the rest of the animal world. They let us guess that, while at the end of the vast spring-board from which life has taken its leap, all the others have stepped down, finding the cord stretched too high, man alone has cleared the obstacle.

It is in this quiet special sense that man is the "term" and the "end" of evolution. Life, we have said, transcends finality as it transcends the other categories. It is essentially a current sent through matter, drawing from it what it can. There has not, therefore, properly speaking, been any project or plan. On the other hand, it is abundantly evident that the rest of nature is not for the sake of man: we struggle like other species, we have struggled against other species. Moreover, if the evolution of life had encountered other accidents

139

in its course, if thereby, the current of life had been otherwise divided, we should have been, physically and morally, far different from what we are. For these various reasons it would be wrong to regard humanity, such as we have it before our eyes, as prefigured in the evolutionary movement. It cannot even be said to be the outcome of the world of evolution, for evolution has been accomplished on several divergent lines, and while the human species is at the end of one of them, other lines have been followed with other species at their end. It is in quite a different sense that we hold humanity to be the ground of evolution.

From our point of view, life appears in its entirety as an immense wave which, starting from a centre, spreads outwards, and which on almost the whole of its circumference is stopped and converted into oscillation: at one single point the obstacle has been forced, the impulsion has passed freely. It is this freedom that the human form registers. Everywhere but in man, consciousness has had to come to a stand; in man alone it has kept on its way. Man, then, continues the vital movement indefinitely, although he does not draw along with him all that life carries in itself. On other lines of evolution there have travelled other tendencies which life implied, and of which, since everything interpenetrates, man has, doubtless, kept something, but of which he has kept only very little. *It is as if a vague and formless being, whom we may call, as we will, man or superman, had sought to realize himself, and had succeeded only by abandoning a part of himself on the way.* The losses are represented by the rest of the animal world, and even by the vegetable world, at least in what these have that is positive and above the accidents of evolution.

From this point of view, the discordances of which nature offers us the spectacle are singularly weakened. The organized world as a whole becomes as the soil on which was to grow either man himself or a being who morally must resemble him. The animals, however distant they may be from our species, however hostile to it, have none the less been useful traveling companions, on whom consciousness has unloaded whatever encumbrances it was dragging along, and who have enabled it to rise, in man, to heights from which it sees an unlimited horizon open again before it.

It is true that it has not only abandoned cumbersome baggage on the way; it has also had to give up valuable goods. Consciousness, in man is pre-eminently intellect. It might have been, it ought, so it seems, to have been also intuition. Intuition and intellect represent two opposite directions of the work of consciousness: intuition goes in the very direction of life, intellect goes in the inverse direction, and thus finds itself naturally in accordance with the movement of matter. A complete and perfect humanity would be that in which these two forms of conscious activity should attain their full development. And, between this humanity and ours, we may conceive any number of possible stages, corresponding to all the degrees imaginable of intelligence and of intuition. In this lies the part of contingency in the mental structure of our species. A different evolution might have led to a humanity either more intellectual still or more intuitive. In the humanity of which we are a part, intuition is, in fact, almost completely sacrificed to intellect. It seems that to conquer matter, and to reconquer its own self, consciousness has had to exhaust the best part of its power. This conquest, in the particular conditions in which it has been accomplished, has required that consciousness should adapt itself to the habits of matter and concentrate all its attention on them, in fact determine itself more especially as intellect. Intuition is there, however, but vague and above all discontinuous. It is a lamp almost extinguished, which only glimmers now and then, for a few moments at most. But it glimmers wherever a vital interest is at stake. On our personality, on our liberty, on the place we occupy in the whole of nature, on our origin and perhaps also on our destiny, it throws a light feeble and vacillating, but which none the less pierces the darkness of the night in which the intellect leaves us.

These fleeting intuitions, which light up their object

only at distant intervals, philosophy ought to seize, first to sustain them, then to expand them and so unite them together. The more it advances in this work, the more will it perceive that intuition is mind itself, and, in a certain sense, life itself: the intellect has been cut out of it by a process resembling that which has generated matter. Thus is revealed the unity of the spiritual life. We recognize it only when we place ourselves in intuition in order to go from intuition to the intellect, for from the intellect we shall never pass to intuition.

Philosophy introduces us thus into the spiritual life. And it shows us at the same time the relation of the life of the spirit to that of the body. The great error of the doctrines on the spirit has been the idea that by isolating the spiritual life from all the rest, by suspending it in space as high as possible above the earth, they were placing it beyond attack, as if they were not thereby simply exposing it to be taken as an effect of mirage! Certainly they are right to listen to conscience when conscience affirms human freedom; but the intellect is there, which says that the cause determines its effect, that like conditions like, that all is repeated and that all is given. They are right to believe in the absolute reality of the person and in his independence toward matter; but science is there, which shows the interdependence of conscious life and cerebral activity. They are right to attribute to man a privileged place in nature, to hold that the distance is infinite between the animal and the man; but the history of life is there, which makes us witness the genesis of species by gradual transformation, and seems thus to reintegrate man in animality. When a strong instinct assures the probability of personal survival, they are right not to close their ears to its voice; but if there exist "souls" capable of an independent life, whence do they come? When, how and why do they enter into this body which we see arise, quite naturally, from a mixed cell derived from the bodies of its two parents? All these questions will remain unanswered, a philosophy of intuition will be a negation of science, will be sooner or later swept away by science, if it does not resolve to see the life of the body just where it really is, on the road that leads to the life of the spirit. But it will then no longer have to do with definite living beings. Life as a whole, from the initial impulsion that thrust it into the world, will appear as a wave which rises, and which is opposed by the descending movement of matter. On the greater part of its surface, at different heights, the current is converted by matter into a vortex. At one point alone it passes freely, dragging with it the obstacle which will weigh on its progress but will not stop it. At this point is humanity; it is our privileged situation. On the other hand, this rising wave is consciousness, and, like all consciousness, it includes potentialities without number which interpenetrate and to which consequently neither the category of unity nor that of multiplicity is appropriate, made as they both are for inert matter. The matter that it bears along with it, and in the interstices of which it inserts itself, alone can divide it into distinct individualities. On flows the current, running through human generations, subdividing itself into individuals. This subdivision was vaguely indicated in it, but could not have been made clear without matter. Thus souls are continually being created, which, nevertheless in a certain sense preexisted. They are nothing else than the little rills into which the great river of life divides itself, flowing through the body of humanity. The movement of the stream is distinct from the river bed, although it must adopt its winding course. Consciousness is distinct from the organism it animates, although it must undergo its vicissitudes. As the possible actions which a state of consciousness indicates are at every instant beginning to be carried out in the nervous centres, the brain underlies at every instant the motor indications of the state of consciousness; but the interdependency of consciousness and brain is limited to this; the destiny of consciousness is not bound up on that account with the destiny of cerebral matter. Finally, consciousness is essentially free; it is freedom itself; but it cannot pass through matter without settling on it, without adapting itself to it: this adaptation is what we call intellectuality; and the intellect, turning itself back toward active, that is to say free, consciousness, naturally makes it enter into the conceptual forms into which it is accustomed to see matter fit. It will therefore always perceive freedom in the form of necessity; it will always neglect the part of novelty or of creation inherent in the free act; it will always substitute for action itself an imitation artificial, approximative, obtained by compounding the old with the old and the same with the same. Thus, to the eyes of a philosophy that attempts to reabsorb intellect in intuition many difficulties vanish or become light. But such a doctrine does not only facilitate speculation; it gives us also more power to act and to live. For, with it, we feel ourselves no longer isolated in humanity, humanity no longer seems isolated in the nature that it dominates. As the smallest grain of dust is bound up with our entire solar system, drawn along with it in that undivided movement of descent which is materiality itself, so all organized beings, from the humblest to the highest, from the first origins of life to the time in which we are, and in all places as in all times, do but evidence a single impulsion, the inverse of the movement of matter, and in itself indivisible. All the living hold together, and all yield to the same tremendous push. The animal takes its stand on the plant, man bestrides animality, and the whole of humanity, in space and in time, is one immense army galloping beside and before and behind each of us in an overwhelming charge able to beat down every resistance and clear the most formidable obstacles, perhaps even death.

[47]

BERKELEY, GEORGE

BERKELEY, GEORGE (1685-1753). A keen thinker and an excellent writer, unafraid of attacking the commonplace, Berkeley's literary style persuaded many antagonistic readers. He was a champion of idealism, or rather of theistic immaterialism. His main purpose was to make evident the existence of God, and to prove that God is the true cause of all things. Proceeding from Locke's examination of the nature and range of human knowledge, Berkeley stressed the distinction between ideas and the mind itself. He conceived of the latter as an active being, distinct from the passivity of its content, and concluded that matter does not exist, that all reality is mental, and that nature is a manifestation of God. The development of his thinking shows the constant influence of Malebranche rather than Plato. In Berkeley's last philosophical works, he stated that the universe assumes a symbolic character and function. This thesis attracted the interest of Thomas de Quincey, William Blake, and Samuel Taylor Coleridge. His most important philosophical works were *A New Theory of Vision* (1709), *The Principles of Human Knowledge* (1710), and *The Dialogues of Hylas and Philonous* (1713).

Berkeley was born in Ireland. He was a militant apologist for the Anglican Church and subsequently became the Bishop of Cloyne. In 1728, he came to America and resided in Rhode Island for three years. During this period, he helped found the University of Pennsylvania, contributed land and a collection of books to Yale University, and wrote verse in praise of America. His poem, "Verses on . . . America" is chiefly remembered for the line: "westward the course of empire takes its way."

OBJECTS OF HUMAN KNOWLEDGE

1. IT is evident to any one who takes a survey of the *objects of human knowledge*, that they are either *ideas* actually imprinted on the senses; or else such as are perceived by attending to the passions and operations of the mind; or lastly, *ideas* formed by help of memory and imagination—either compounding, dividing, or barely representing those originally perceived in the aforesaid ways. By sight I have the ideas of light and colors, with their several degrees and variations. By touch I perceive hard and soft, heat and cold, motion and resistance, and of all these more and less either as to quantity or degree. Smelling furnishes me with odors; the palate with tastes; and hearing conveys sounds to the mind in all their variety of tone and composition. And as several of these are observed to accompany each other, they come to be marked by one name, and so to be reputed as one thing. Thus, for example, a certain color, taste, smell, figure and consistence having being observed to go together, are accounted one distinct thing, signified by the name *apple;* other collections of

ideas constitute a stone, a tree, a book, and the like sensible things; which as they are pleasing or disagreeable excite the passions of love, hatred, joy, grief, and so forth.

2. But, besides all that endless variety of ideas or objects of knowledge, there is likewise something which knows or perceives them, and exercises divers operations, as willing, imagining, remembering, about them. This perceiving, active being is what I call *mind, spirit, soul,* or *myself.* By which words I do not denote any one of my ideas, but a thing entirely distinct from them, wherein they exist, or, which is the same thing, whereby they are perceived—for the existence of an idea consists in being perceived.

3. That neither our thoughts, nor passions, nor ideas formed by the imagination, exist without the mind, is what everybody will allow. And to me it is no less evident that the various sensations, or ideas imprinted on the sense, however blended or combined together (that is, whatever objects they compose), cannot exist otherwise than in a mind perceiving them.—I think an intuitive knowledge may be obtained of this by any one that shall attend to what is meant by the term *exist,* when applied to sensible things. The table I write on I say exists, that is, I see and feel it; and if I were out of my study I should say it existed—meaning thereby that if I was in my study I might perceive it, or that some other spirit actually does perceive it. There was an odor, that is, it was smelt; there was a sound, that is, it was heard; a color or figure, and it was perceived by sight or touch. This is all that I can understand by these and the like expressions. For as to what is said of the absolute existence of unthinking things without any relation to their being perceived, that is to me perfectly unintelligible. Their *esse* is *percipi,* nor is it possible they should have any existence out of the minds or thinking things which perceive them.

4. It is indeed an opinion strangely prevailing amongst men, that houses, mountains, rivers, and in a word all sensible objects, have an existence, natural or real, distinct from their being perceived by the understanding. But, with how

146

great an assurance and acquiescence soever this principle may be entertained in the world, yet whoever shall find in his heart to call it in question may, if I mistake not, perceive it to involve a manifest contradiction. For, what are the forementioned objects but the things we perceive by sense? and what do we perceive besides our own ideas of sensations? and is it not plainly repugnant that any one of these, or any combination of them, should exist unperceived?

5. If we thoroughly examine this tenet, it will, perhaps, be found at bottom to depend on the doctrine of *abstract ideas*. For can there be a nicer strain of abstraction than to distinguish the existence of sensible objects from their being perceived, so as to conceive them existing unperceived? Light and colors, heat and cold, extension and figures—in a word the things we see and feel—what are they but so many sensations, notions, ideas, or impressions on the sense? and is it possible to separate, even in thought, any of these from perception? For my part, I might as easily divide a thing from itself. I may, indeed, divide in my thoughts, or conceive apart from each other, those things which, perhaps, I never perceived by sense so divided. Thus, I imagine the trunk of a human body without the limbs, or conceive the smell of a rose without thinking on the rose itself. So far, I will not deny, I can abstract—if that may properly be called *abstraction* which extends only to the conceiving separately such objects as it is possible may really exist or be actually perceived asunder. But my conceiving or imagining power does not extend beyond the possibility of real existence or perception. Hence, as it is impossible for me to see or feel anything without an actual sensation of that thing, so it is impossible for me to conceive in my thoughts any sensible thing or object distinct from the sensation or perception of it.

6. Some truths there are so near and obvious to the mind that a man need only open his eyes to see them. Such I take this important one to be, viz., that all the choir of heaven and furniture of the earth, in a word all those bodies which compose the mighty frame of the world, have not any sub-

sistence without a mind, that their *being* is to be perceived or known; that consequently so long as they are not actually perceived by me, or do not exist in my mind or that of any other created spirit, they must either have no existence at all, or else subsist in the mind of some Eternal Spirit—is being perfectly unintelligible, and involving all the absurdity of abstraction, to attribute to any single part of them an existence independent of a spirit. To be convinced of which, the reader need only reflect, and try to separate in his own thoughts the *being* of a sensible thing from its *being perceived.*

7. From what has been said it is evident there is not any other Substance than *Spirit,* or that which perceives. But, for the fuller demonstration of this point, let it be considered the sensible qualities are color, figure, motion, smell, taste, &c., i.e. the ideas perceived by sense. Now, for an idea to exist in an unperceiving thing is a manifest contradiction, for to have an idea is all one as to perceive; that therefore wherein color, figure, &c. exist must perceive them; hence it is clear there can be no unthinking substance or *substratum* of those ideas.

8. But, say you, though the ideas themselves do not exist without the mind, yet there may be things like them, whereof they are copies or resemblances, which things exist without the mind in an unthinking substance. I answer, an idea can be like nothing but an idea; a color or figure can be like nothing but another color or figure. If we look but never so little into our own thoughts, we shall find it impossible for us to conceive likeness except only between our ideas. Again, I ask whether those supposed *originals* or external things, of which our ideas are the pictures or representations, be themselves perceivable or no? If they are, then *they* are ideas and we have gained our point; but if you say they are not, I appeal to any one whether it be sense to assert a color is like something which is invisible; hard or soft, like something which is intangible; and so of the rest.

9. Some there are who make a distinction betwixt *pri-*

mary and *secondary* qualities. By the former they mean extension, figure, motion, rest, solidity or impenetrability, and number; by the latter they denote all other sensible qualities, as colors, sounds, tastes, and so forth. The ideas we have of these they acknowledge not to be the resemblances of anything existing without the mind, or unperceived, but they will have our ideas of the primary qualities to be patterns or images of things which exist without the mind, in an unthinking substance which they call *Matter*. By Matter, therefore, we are to understand an inert, senseless substance, in which extension, figure, and motion do actually subsist. But it is evident, from what we have already shewn, that extension, figure, and motion are only ideas existing in the mind, and that an idea can be like nothing but another idea, and that consequently neither they nor their archetypes can exist in an unperceiving substance. Hence, it is plain that the very notion of what is called *Matter* or *corporeal substance*, involves a contradiction in it.

10. They who assert that figure, motion, and the rest of the primary or original qualities do exist without the mind in unthinking substances, do at the same time acknowledge that colors, sounds, heat, cold, and such like secondary qualities, do not—which they tell us are sensations existing in the mind alone, that depend on and are occasioned by the different size, texture, and motion of the minute particles of matter. This they take for an undoubted truth, which they can demonstrate beyond all exception. Now, if it be certain that those original qualities are inseparably united with the other sensible qualities, and not, even in thought, capable of being abstracted from them, it plainly follows that they exist only in the mind. But I desire any one to reflect and try whether he can, by any abstraction of thought, conceive the extension and motion of a body without all other sensible qualities. For my own part, I see evidently that it is not in my power to frame an idea of a body extended and moving, but I must withal give it some color or other sensible quality which is acknowledged to exist only in the mind. In short, extension,

149

figure, and motion, abstracted from all other qualities, are inconceivable. Where therefore the other sensible qualities are, there must these be also, to wit, in the mind and nowhere else.

11. Again, *great* and *small, swift* and *slow*, are allowed to exist nowhere without the mind, being entirely relative, and changing as the frame or position of the organs of sense varies. The extension therefore which exists without the mind is neither great nor small, the motion neither swift nor slow, that is, they are nothing at all. But, say you, they are extension in general, and motion in general: thus we see how much the tenet of extended movable substances existing without the mind depends on the strange doctrines of *abstract ideas*. And here I cannot but remark how neatly the vague and indeterminate description of Matter or corporeal substance, which the modern philosophers are run into by their own principles, resembles that antiquated and so much ridiculed notion of *material prima*, to be met with in Aristotle and his followers. Without extension solidity cannot be conceived; since therefore it has been shewn that extension exists not in an unthinking substance, the same must also be true of solidity.

12. That *number* is entirely the creature of the mind, even though the other qualities be allowed to exist without, will be evident to whoever considers that the same thing bears a different denomination of number as the mind views it with different respects. Thus, the same extension is one, or three, or thirty-six, according as the mind considers it with reference to a yard, a foot, or an inch. Number is so visibly relative, and dependent on men's understanding, that it is strange to think how any one should give it an absolute existence without the mind. We say one book, one page, one line, &c.; all these are equally units, though some contain several of the others. And in each instance, it is plain, the unit relates to some particular combination of ideas arbitrarily put together by the mind.

13. Unity I know some will have to be a simple or uncompounded idea, accompanying all other ideas into the

mind. That I have any such idea answering the word *unity* I do not find; and if I had, methinks I could not miss finding it: on the contrary, it should be the most familiar to my understanding, since it is said to accompany all other ideas, and to be perceived by all the ways of sensation and reflexion. To say no more, it is an *abstract idea*.

14. I shall farther add, that, after the same manner as modern philosophers prove certain sensible qualities to have no existence in Matter, or without the mind, the same thing may be likewise proved of all other sensible qualities whatsoever. Thus, for instance, it is said that heat and cold are affections only of the mind, and not at all patterns of real beings, existing in the corporeal substances which excite them, for that the same body which appears cold to one hand seems warm to another. Now, why may we not well argue that figure and extension are not patterns or resemblances of qualities existing in Matter, because to the same eye at different stations, or eyes of a different texture at the same station, they appear various, and cannot therefore be the images of anything settled and determinate without the mind? Again, it is proved that sweetness is not really in the sapid thing, because the thing remaining unaltered the sweetness is changed into bitter, as in case of a fever or otherwise vitiated palate. Is it not as reasonable to say that motion is not without the mind, since if the succession of ideas in the mind become swifter, the motion, it is acknowledged, shall appear slower without any alternation in any external object?

15. In short, let any one consider those arguments which are thought manifestly to prove that colors and taste exist only in the mind, and he shall find they may with equal force be brought to prove the same thing of extension, figure, and motion. Though it must be confessed this method of arguing does not so much prove that there is no extension or color in an outward object, as that we do not know by sense which is the true extension or color of the object. But the arguments foregoing plainly shew it to be impossible that any color or extension at all, or other sensible quality whatsoever, should

exist in an unthinking subject without the mind, or in truth, that there should be any such thing as an outward object.

[48]

BERNARD OF CLAIRVAUX, SAINT

BERNARD OF CLAIRVAUX, SAINT (1091-1153). "The visionary of the century" was the way Bernard characterized himself, for he felt that he had been selected by God to guide Christianity along the right paths. He sincerely tried to lead the life of a saint, although he was cognizant of those temptations that led men astray. An objective observer, John of Salisbury, noticed that he often lost his temper and behaved unjustly, and Bishop Otto of Freising, a pious church member, accused him of jealousy and habitual weaknesses. Bernard asserted that his inner life was based on the stages of the ascent of his soul toward God, and upon supernatural grace. His book *De Gradibus Humilitatis et Superbiae* (published c. 1121) established him as the founder of Christian mysticism of the Middle Ages. Here, he condemned the acquisition of knowledge for merely the sake of knowledge. To him, knowledge is only justified when it promotes the purification of the soul and leads it toward union with God. Humility is the basic condition for this union, and it, in turn, engenders love. He stated that there are twelve degrees of humility—the highest constitutes the cognition of truth, and this is identical with union with God. This stage is psychologically characterized as the extinction of all sensitive life, but it does not remove the essential difference between man, a finite being, and God. With this reservation, Bernard's philosophy separates him from the monism of later mystics.

Bernard excelled as an ecclesiastical ruler, as the organizer of a monastic order, as an irresistibly persuasive orator and an experienced administrator. As abbot of the monastery at Clairvaux, he was incapable of imposing his will on popes, kings, and emperors, but his ascendency over the masses was unfailing. However, shortly before his death, the terrible disasters of the Second Crusade took place. Because he had agitated for this crusade with all his power, its failure aroused doubt and opposition. His abhorrence of knowledge for the sake of knowledge made him a grim adversary of Abailard and Gilbert de la Porrée. He succeeded in persecuting the former, but was defeated in his controversy with the latter. Bernard wrote many sermons, epistles, and hymns.

SOME EXCLAMATIONS

BERNARD'S APPEAL

I AM no longer able to veil my grief, to suppress my anxiety, to dissemble my sorrow. Therefore, contrary to the order of justice, I who have been wounded am constrained to recall him who hath wounded me; I, the despised, must seek after him who hath despised me; after suffering injury, I must offer satisfaction to him from whom the injury has come; I must, in a word, entreat him who ought rather to entreat me. But grief does not deliberate, it knows no shame, it does not consult reason, it does not fear any lowering of dignity, does not conform itself to rule, does not submit itself to sound judgment; it ignores method and rule; the mind is wholly and only occupied with this: to seek to be rid of what it pains it to have, or to gain what it grieves it to want. I am wretched because I miss thee, because I do not see thee, because I live without thee, for whom to die would be to me life, to live without whom is to die! Only come back, and all will be peace. Return, and I shall be at rest. Return, I say: return! and I shall joyfully sing, "He that was dead is alive again; he was lost, and is found." No doubt it may have been my fault that you departed. I must have appeared severe to so delicate a youth, and in my own hardness have treated thy tenderness too harshly. What I say, my son, I do not say to confound thee, but to admonish my most dear boy; for though thou mayest have many teachers in Christ, thou hast not many fathers. If thou wilt permit me to say so, I myself have brought thee forth into the life of religion, by instruction and example. How can it please thee that another should glory in thee who has in no way labored for thee?

Lectures on Bernard, R. S. Storr.

ST. BERNARD'S HYMN

Jesu, the very thought of thee
    With sweetness fills the breast;

But sweeter far Thy face to see
    And in Thy presence rest.
No voice can sing, no heart can frame,
    Nor can the memory find,
A sweeter sound than Jesus' name,
    The Saviour of mankind.
O hope of every contrite heart,
    O joy of all the meek,
To those who fall how kind Thou art!
    How good to those who seek!
But what to those who find? Ah this
    Nor tongue nor pen can show;
The love of Jesus, what it is
    None but His lov'd ones know.
Jesu our only joy be Thou,
    As Thou our prize wilt be
In Thee be all our glory now,
    And through eternity.

MY ENEMIES

The world lays close siege, and my five senses are the avenues by which it enters and attacks me. They give free passage to the fatal darts, and here death makes its approaches to my heart. My eye gazes about, and by admitting variety of engaging subjects, draws off my attention from the one thing necessary. The ear is open to pleasing sounds, and these disturb the mind in its meditations. The smell amuses, and obstructs serious thinking. The tongue is lavish in speech, and lets itself loose in flattery and falsehood. The touch kindles impure fires, takes every slight occasion to defile itself with lust, and unless the first motions be carefully guarded, and resolutely rejected, it seizes, vanquishes, and inflames the whole body: the steps by which it advances in this conquest are, first to tickle the imagination with unclean thoughts, then to pollute the mind with unlawful delight, and at last to subdue the reason by consenting to wicked inclinations. Lastly, the devil bends his bow, and makes ready his arrows within the quiver.

[49]

BOEHME, JACOB

BOEHME, JACOB (1575-1624). One day, Jacob Boehme, a shoemaker, turned from his work and stared at the cupboard, gazing at the reflection of a sunbeam on pewter. He interpreted this as the manifestation of divine truth, revealing the universe as the theater of an eternal conflict between spirit and matter. Boehme regarded matter as an embodiment of evil, but a necessary condition for the existence of all beings. Without its existence, even the divine spirit would evaporate. He thought that contemporary events reiterated and confirmed neo-Platonic and Gnostic ideas. Untiringly he contrasted his vision of the divine order with the reality he saw dominated by evil. His intrepid criticism of church and state, of economic exploitation and political oppression caused the authorities to charge him with heresy in 1612. His *Aurora* and other writings were interdicted. When Boehme tried to penetrate the mysteries of creation and salvation, his unschooled mind often appeared more confused than enlightened. He displayed a powerful originality, but became entangled in fallacies. His descriptions of the anxieties and temptations of the soul have interested many modern readers who dislike his metaphysical speculations. He exerted considerable influence among German romantics and mystics in France, Russia, England, and the United States.

GOD IS ALL

Now therefore we say (as the Scripture informs us) that God dwells in Heaven, and it is the Truth. Now mark, *Moses* writes, that God created the Heaven out of the Midst of the Waters, and the Scripture says, God dwells in Heaven; therefore we may now observe, that the water has its Original from the Longing of the eternal Nature after the eternal Light of God; but the eternal Nature is made manifest by the Longing after the Light of God, as is mentioned before;

and the Light of God is present every where, and yet remains hidden to Nature; for Nature receives only the Virtue of the Light, and the Virtue is the Heaven wherein the Light of God dwells and is hid, and so shines in the Darkness. The Water is the *Materia,* or Matter that is generated from the Heaven, and therein stands the third, which again generates a Life, and comprehensible Essence, or Substance, out of itself, *viz.* the Elements and other Creatures.

Therefore, O noble Man, let not Antichrist and the Devil befool you, who tell you that the Deity is far off from you, and direct you to a Heaven that is situated far above you; whereas there is nothing nearer to you than the Heaven is. You only stand before the Door of Heaven, and you are gone forth with *Adam* out of the paradisaical Heaven into the third Principle; yet you stand in the Gate, do but as the eternal Mother does, which by great desiring and longing after the Kingdom of God, attains the Kingdom of Heaven, wherein God dwells, wherein Paradise springs up; do you but so, set all your Desire upon the Heart of God, and so you will pass in by Force, as the eternal Mother does; and then it shall be with thee as Christ said, *The Kingdom of Heaven Suffereth Violence, and the Violent take it by Force*: So you shall make to yourself Friends in Heaven with your unrighteous *Mammon,* and so you come to be the true Similitude and Image of God, and his proper own; for all the three Principles, with the Eternity, are in you, and the holy Paradise is again generated in you, wherein God dwells. Then where will you seek for God? Seek him in your Soul only that is proceeded out of the eternal Nature, wherein the divine Birth stands.

O that I had but the Pen of Man, and were able therewith to write down the Spirit of Knowledge. I can but stammer of the great Mysteries like a Child that is beginning to speak; so very little can the earthly Tongue express what the Spirit comprehends and understands; yet I will venture to try, whether I may procure some to go about to seek the Pearl, whereby also I might labour in the Works of God in my paradisaical Garden of Roses; for the Longing of the

156

eternal Matrix drives me on to write and exercise myself in this my Knowledge.

Now if we will lift up our minds, and seek after the Heaven wherein God dwells, we cannot say that God dwells only above the Stars, and has inclosed himself with the Firmament which is made out of the Waters; in which none can enter except it be opened (like a Window) for him; with which Thoughts Men are altogether befooled [and bewildered]. Neither can we say (as some suppose) that God the Father and the Son are only with Angels in the uppermost inclosed Heaven, and rule only here in this World by the Holy Ghost, who proceeds from the Father and the Son. All these Thoughts are void of the very Knowledge of God. For then God should be divided and circumscriptive, like the Sun that moves aloft above us, and sends its Light and Virtue to us, whereby the whole Deep becomes light and active all over.

Reason is much befooled with these Thoughts; and the Kingdom of Antichrist is begotten in these Thoughts, and Antichrist has by these Opinions set himself in the Place of God, and means to be God upon Earth, and ascribes divine Power to himself, and stops the Mouth of the Spirit of God, and will not hear him speak; and so strong Delusions come upon them, that they believe the Spirit of Lies, which in Hypocrisy speaks strong Delusions, and seduces the Children of Hope, as *St. Paul* witnesses.

The true Heaven wherein God dwells, is all over, in all Places [or Corners,] even in the Midst [or Center] of the Earth. He comprehends the Hell where the Devils dwell, and there is nothing without God. For wheresoever he was before Creation of the World, there he is still, *viz.* in himself; and is himself the Essence of all Essences: All is generated from him, and is originally from him. And he is therefore called God, because he alone is the Good, the Heart, or [that which is] best; understand, he is the Light and Virtue, [or Power,] from whence Nature has its Original.

If you will meditate on God, take before you the eternal

Darkness, which is without God; for God dwells in himself, and the Darkness cannot in its own Power comprehend him; which Darkness has a great [Desire of] longing after the Light, caused by the Light's beholding itself in the Darkness, and shining in it. And in this Longing or Desiring, you find the Source, and the Source takes hold of the Power or Virtue of the Light, and the Longing makes the Virtue material, and the material Virtue is the Inclosure to God, or the Heaven; for in the Virtue stands the Paradise, wherein the Spirit which proceeds from the Father and the Son works. All this is incomprehensible to the Creation, but not impossible to be found in the Mind; for Paradise stands open in the Mind of a holy Soul.

Thus you [may] see how God created all Things out of Nothing, but only out of Himself; and yet the Out-Birth is not from his Essence, [or Substance,] but it has its Original from the Darkness. The Source of the Darkness is the first Principle, and the Virtue [or Power] of the Light is the second Principle, and the Out-Birth, [generated] out of the Darkness by the Virtue of the Light, is the third Principle; and that is not called God: God is only the Light, and the Virtue of the Light, and that which goes forth out of the Light is the Holy Ghost. [50]

BOETHIUS

BOETHIUS (475-524). It was while Boethius was rigorously confined to prison, awaiting execution, that he expressed in writing his meditations of his own fate and the destiny of mankind. For years he had served as minister to King Theodoric, the Goth. He fought corruption and, as a result, aroused the hostility of many depraved dignitaries who finally succeeded in making Theodoric believe that Boethius was a traitor in the service of the Byzantine emperor. The false accusations caused Boethius to be sentenced without trial.

The vicissitudes of his life led Boethius to consider the general problem of whether fortune or divine providence governed the world. His *De Consolatione Philosophiae*, which contains his thoughts while imprisoned, has been translated into almost every European language. It asserts that man is superior to the blind forces of nature; that the power of fortune, affecting the practical affairs of mankind, is irrelevant; and that Providence is infinite. Many persons of considerable achievement, such as Dante, Chaucer, and Queen Elizabeth, have found that the writings of Boethius enabled them to face life with courage and renewed confidence whenever they were beset by doubts or alarmed by the mystery of the future.

EVERY MAN HAS HIS CROSS

VERY narrow and very paltry is human happiness, for either it cometh not to any man, or abideth not steadily with him such as it was when it came; this I will show more clearly later on.

We know that many have worldly riches enough, but they are ashamed of their wealth if they are not as well born as they would desire. Some again are noble and famous from their high birth, but they are oppressed and saddened by their base estate and their poverty, so that they would rather be of mean birth than so poor, were it but in their power. Many are both well born and well endowed, yet are joyless, being wedded to an ill-matched or unpleasing wife. Many are happy enough in their marriage, but being childless must leave all the wealth they amass to strangers to enjoy, and therefore they are sad. Some have children enough, but these are perhaps weakly, or wicked and ignoble, or they die young, so that their parents sorrow for them all their days. Therefore no man may in this present life altogether withstand Fate; for even if he have nothing now to grieve about, yet he may grieve not to know what his future will be, whether good or evil, even as thou also didst not know; and moreover, that which he enjoys so happily while he hath it, he dreads to lose. Show me, I pray thee, the man who to thy mind is most happy, and who is most given over to self-indulgence; I will soon cause thee to see that he is often exceedingly put out by the veriest trifles if anything, however slight, thwart his will or his habits, unless he can beckon every one to run at his bidding. A very little thing may make the happiest of men in this world believe his happiness to be impaired or altogether lost. Thou art thinking now, for instance, that thou art very unhappy, and yet I know that many a man would fancy himself raised up to heaven if he had any part of the happiness which is still remaining to thee. Why, the place where thou art now imprisoned, and which thou callest exile, is a home to them that were born there, and also to them that live in it by choice. Nothing is bad, unless a man think it bad; and though it be hard to bear and adverse, yet is it happiness if a man does it cheerfully and bears it with patience. Few are so wise as not to wish in their impatience that their fortune may be changed. With the sweets of this world much bitterness is mingled; though they seem desirable, yet a man cannot keep them, once they begin to flee from him. Is it not then plain that worldly happiness is a poor thing? It is unable to satisfy poor man, who ever desireth what he hath not at the time, and even with men of patience and of sober life it will never long abide.

[51]

BOLZANO, BERNARD

BOLZANO, BERNARD (1781-1848). The personal fate of Bolzano affords a dramatic insight into the dangers to which really independent thinkers are exposed when the internal revolutions of a reactionary period are manifest. Bolzano was born shortly prior to the outbreak of the French Revolution and died during the year of multiple European revolutions. Although he was not burned at the stake, he was compelled to live in complete retirement for the last thirty years of his life. Bolzano, whose writings were forbidden publication, was a Catholic priest and professor of philosophy at the University of Prague. However, he continued to work ceaselessly, and some of his friends arranged to have his books published anonymously outside his own country. Half a century after his death, his works were discovered and read eagerly by leading modern philosophers. His consistent distinction between logic and psychology was of great importance to Husserl and his disciples. In a sense, Bolzano anticipated the modern theory of transfinite numbers. He was firmly convinced that human knowledge can be enlarged infinitely and insisted on methodical research, cautioning against wishful thinking.

ON CORRECT THINKING

IT is quite possible to know many rules of logic without previous purposeful meditation, or without having studied logic. Without knowing these rules, one can follow some of them, either through intuition, or by observing the methods of his fellow-men who are more acquainted with them. In this way, it is possible to obtain considerable skill in correct thinking, even on scientific matters. But one is more successful in avoiding mistakes, finding previously hidden new truths, and in coordinating and utilizing them, if one has completely learned the rules which must take place with all this.

The same principles that apply to careful speech also apply to careful thought, or many of the other activities where man can exercise them perfectly without having previously been taught their rules of procedure. Everyone admits that the study of the rules of language is useful; if one speaks correctly, he can follow these rules with more certainty. For the same reason, similar advantages arise from a proper study of the rules of logic and science.

The knowledge of these rules becomes particularly necessary, if one is not to be led astray by artificially invented paralogisms. One should be capable of refuting sophisms in an intelligible manner. A knowledge of the rules of logic, obtained without a proper study of logic, is insufficient if one is to disprove clearly to others the fallacious premise of a paralogism. If one is incapable of logical analysis, then he cannot guard himself or others against the dangers of manifold deceptions, especially when the senses welcome error. For it becomes difficult for rationality to disclose fallacy when one's emotions rejoice in accepting erroneous conclusions. Unfortunately there are too many ubiquitous paralogisms. Their nature is such, that they lead us astray in both our moral and religious convictions. It is therefore desirable, that each man study logic, if only to guard himself and his fellow man against seduction by paralogism.

It is impossible to treat successfully some of the more

difficult sciences, such as metaphysics, without being conscious of all the rules which must be adhered to in sequential order for a scientific demonstration. Probably the reason for the unlimited confusion in metaphysics and some of the other philosophical sciences, is the lack of a highly developed science of logic. Every useful, elaborated manual of logic is written, more or less strictly, in a scientific form; containing explanations, proofs, objections, refutations, etc. The study of such books makes for correct thinking; a training not inferior to that which may be gained through the study of many other sciences.

[52]

BONAVENTURA, SAINT

BONAVENTURA, SAINT (1221-1274). John Fidanza was born in Tuscany in 1221, and, in 1240, he entered the Order of Franciscans, where he was renamed Fra Bonaventura. He studied with Alexander of Hales in Paris, and later became a teacher of theology. In 1255 he was excluded from the University of Paris because he supported Aquinas in a dispute, but was readmitted in 1257 and elected general of the Franciscan Order. He became a cardinal in 1273, and died in 1274 at the Council of Lyons. Bonaventura, called "Doctor Seraphicus," was canonized in 1482.

A complex personality, Bonaventura was a philosopher, mystic, and dogmatic theologian. He was never a radical thinker, for he was too fond of tradition, too cautious and adverse to controversy, even though he was involved in several. He definitely formulated Franciscan doctrine, but he has been accused of having been greatly influenced by Aquinas and the Dominicans.

Bonaventura's mystical writings were of considerable influence. His central theme concerned the study of God. He stated that man possesses an imperfect but very certain knowledge of the supreme being. His path of thought proceeds from stable faith, to reason, and then to contemplation. Knowledge, derived from human science, is differentiated from mystical knowledge, which is the work of divine grace. His *Itinerarium Mentis* (Journey of the Mind) describes seven stages of ascent, three of which are the result of imagination, reason, and memory; at the fourth stage supernatural grace intervenes. The seventh stage provides knowledge of the Trinity, and is described as a psychological experience of speechless ecstasy. His doctrine of human knowledge is voluntaristic. Knowledge is a spontaneous activity which stems from God and is directed toward God. It beholds the world as a symbol which mirrors divine beauty. Knowledge for its own sake is branded as error. World opinion may consider philosophy great, but in the light of the Christian faith, it is of little value. Bonaventura established the concrete image of the world in accordance with Platonism, corrected by the idea of Biblical omnipotence. He did not consider Plato as the representative of wisdom, nor Aristotle as the representative of science. But he viewed Augustine as the manifestation of holy inspiration, and his teachings as the correct guide to human knowledge. The imagery of Bonaventura's prose creates a more lasting impression than does the originality of his thoughts.

ON FRANCIS OF ASSISI

THE grace of God our Saviour hath appeared in these our latter days in His faithful and devout servant Francis, and hath been manifested through him to all those who are truly humble and lovers of holy poverty; who honouring and devoutly adoring the superabundance of the divine mercy, which was so bountifully poured forth upon him, have been taught by his example to forsake all impiety and worldly desires, to conform their lives to the life of Christ, and with intense and burning desire to thirst after the hope of heavenly beatitude. For so graciously did God look upon this truly poor and contrite man, that He not only raised the poor and needy from the vile dust of worldly conversation, but also set him to be a light to the faithful, making him to become a true professor, leader, and herald of evangelical perfection, that, bearing witness to the light, he might prepare before the Lord a way of light and peace in the hearts of the faithful. For, shining like a morning star in the midst of a dark cloud, he enlightened by the bright rays of his pure doctrine and holy life those who lay in darkness and in the shadow of death, and thus guided them onwards by his bright shining to the perfect day. And like the glorious rainbow set in the darkness of the clouds, he came forth as the angel of true peace and the sign of the covenant between God and man, bringing glad tidings of peace and salvation: being sent by God, like the Precursor of Christ, to prepare in the desert of this world the highway of holy poverty, and by word and example to preach penance to men. Thus prevented by the gifts of heavenly grace, enriched with the merits of invincible virtue, filled with the spirit of prophecy, and ordained to the angelic office of declaring good tidings, burning with seraphic fire, and raised above all human things in the fiery chariot of divine love, it may be reasonably affirmed from the clear testimony of His whole life that he came in the spirit and power of Elias.

We may also say that he was truly shadowed forth by that other friend of Christ, the Apostle and Evangelist St. John, under the similitude of the angel whom he saw ascending from the east with the sign of the living God. Under this figure we may assuredly discern Francis, the servant, herald, and messenger of God, the beloved of Christ, the pattern for our imitation, the wonder of the world, if we carefully observe and mark the excellency of his marvellous sanctity, by which, during his life, he imitated the purity of the Angels, so that he may be set forth as an example to all the perfect followers of Christ.

[53]

BOOLE, GEORGE

BOOLE, GEORGE (1815-1864). Compared with other philosophers, it was relatively late in his lifetime that George Boole began to specialize in the field that ultimately made him famous. At the age of sixteen, he taught school in an English provincial town; by the time he was twenty, he had opened his own school; at thirty, he began to concentrate upon mathematics. In 1847 he published a pamphlet, *The Mathematical Analysis of Logic,* which contained the principal ideas he later developed in his book, *Laws of Thought* (1854). This book marks the beginning of symbolic logic, a new and efficient method of formal logic, designed to avoid the ambiguities of ordinary language. Boole recognized that the canonical forms of Aristotelian syllogism are really symbolical, but less perfect than the symbolism of mathematics. Furthermore, he realized that ordinary language is an inadequate medium for the expression of ideas. He tried to devise a symbolic language, the terms of which would express exactly what he thought. He was less interested in reducing logic to mathematics than in employing symbolic language and notation in a wide generalization of purely logical processes. He organized deductive logic as an algebra, interpretable spatially and proportionally. With this, he paved the way for Frege, Peano, Bertrand Russell, Whitehead, Hilbert, and others.

THE PLACE OF MATHEMATICS IN THE SYSTEM OF HUMAN KNOWLEDGE

THOSE who have maintained that the position of Mathematics is . . . a fundamental one, have drawn one of their strongest arguments from the actual constitution of things. The material frame is subject in all its parts to the relations of number. All dynamical, chemical, electrical, thermal actions seem not only to be measurable in themselves, but to be connected with each other, even to the extent of mutual convertibility, by numerical relations of a perfectly definite kind. But the opinion in question seems to me to rest upon a deeper basis than this. The laws of thought, in all its processes of conception and of reasoning, in all those operations of which language is the expression or the instrument, are of the same kind as are the laws of the acknowledged processes of Mathematics. It is not contended that it is necessary for us to acquaint ourselves with those laws in order to think coherently, or, in the ordinary sense of the terms, to reason well. Men draw inferences without any consciousness of those elements upon which the entire procedure depends. Still less is it desired to exalt the reasoning faculty over the faculties of observation, of reflection, and of judgment. But upon the very ground that human thought, traced to its ultimate elements, reveals itself in mathematical forms, we have a presumption that the mathematical sciences occupy, by the constitution of our nature, a fundamental place in human knowledge, and that no system of mental culture can be complete or fundamental, which altogether neglects them.

But the very same class of considerations shows with equal force the error of those who regard the study of Mathematics, and of their applications, as a sufficient basis either of knowledge or of discipline. If the constitution of the material frame is mathematical, it is not merely so. If the mind, in its capacity of formal reasoning, obeys, whether consciously or unconsciously, mathematical laws, it claims through its other capacities of sentiment and action, through its perceptions of beauty and of moral fitness, through its deep springs of emotion and affection, to hold relation to a different order of things. There is, moreover, a breadth of intellectual vision, a power of sympathy with truth in all its forms and manifestations, which is not measured by the force and subtlety of the dialectic faculty. Even the revelation of the material universe in its boundless magnitude, and pervading order, and constancy of law, is not necessarily the most fully apprehended by him who has traced with minutest accuracy the steps of the great demonstration. And if we embrace in our survey the interests and duties of life, how little do any processes of mere ratiocination enable us to comprehend the weightier questions which they present! As truly, therefore, as the cultivation of the mathematical or deductive faculty is a part of intellectual discipline, so truly is it only a part. The prejudice which would either banish or make supreme any one department of knowledge or faculty of mind, betrays not only error of judgment, but a defect of that intellectual modesty which is inseparable from a pure devotion to truth.

[54]

BOSANQUET, BERNARD

BOSANQUET, BERNARD (1848-1923). The best known (next to Bradley) of the British idealist philosophers, Bosanquet descended from an old Huguenot family. For eleven years he lectured on Greek history and philosophy at University College, Oxford. Then he left this to devote himself to charity and the study of ethics, logic, and aesthetics.

His interests, later shared by his wife, included the London Ethical Society (later known as the London School of Ethics and

166

Social Philosophy) and the Charity Organization Society. This work was not the hobby of a leisure-class gentleman, but the practical application of Bosanquet's philosophy.

His emphasis was on the importance of the individual, the fruition of a cosmoramic view which could only be realized in the individual. Accordingly, he defined the Absolute (and in this he was profoundly influenced by Hegel) not as a personality lacking coherence and unity, but as a whole being. Similarly in his logic, he defined truth as a cohering, comprehensive whole. He perceived ethics as the endeavor towards a unity of pleasure and responsibility, all the while emphasizing the importance of the individual in his relationships with others. His philosophy may be said to bear the stamp of conciliation.

His personal charm, his sympathetic attitudes, and his "critically appreciative powers" were hallmarks of his warm personality. His writings include *Knowledge and Reality, A History of Aesthetic, The Essentials of Logic, The Psychology of the Moral Self*, and *The Philosophic Theory of the State*.

ON THE STATE

THE State . . . is to the general life of the individual much as . . . the family . . . with regard to certain of his impulses. The idea is that in it, or by its help, we find at once discipline and expansion, the transfiguration of partial impulses, and something to do and to care for, such as the nature of a human self demands. If, that is to say, you start with a human being as he is in fact, and try to devise what will furnish him with an outlet and a stable purpose capable of doing justice to his capacities—a satisfying object of life— you will be driven on by the necessity of the facts at least as far as the State, and perhaps further. Two points may be insisted on to make this conception less paradoxical to the English mind.

(*a*) The State, as thus conceived, is not merely the political fabric. The term State accents indeed the political aspect of the whole, and is opposed to the notion of an anarchical society. But it includes the entire hierarchy of institutions by which life is determined, from the family to the trade, and from the trade to the Church and the University.

It includes all of them, not as the mere collection of the growths of the country, but as the structure which gives life and meaning to the political whole, while receiving from it mutual adjustment, and therefore expansion and a more liberal air. The State, it might be said, is thus conceived as the operative criticism of all institutions—the modification and adjustment by which they are capable of playing a rational part in the object of human will. And criticism, in this sense, is the life of institutions. As exclusive objects, they are a prey to stagnation and disease—think of the temper which lives solely for the family or solely for the Church; it is only as taken up into the movement and circulation of the State that they are living spiritual beings. It follows that the State, in this sense, is, above all things, not a number of persons, but a working conception of life. It is the conception by the guidance of which every living member of the commonwealth is enabled to perform his function, as Plato has taught us. If we ask whether this means that a complete conception of the aims and possibilities of the common life exists even in the minds of statesmen, not to speak of ordinary citizens, the question answers itself in the negative. And yet the State can only live and work in as far as such a conception, in however fragmentary, one-sided shapes, pervades the general mind. It is not there mostly in reflective shape; and in so far as it is in reflective shape it is according to ultimate standards contradictory and incomplete. But everyone who has a fair judgment of what his own place demands from him, has, at his own angle, so to speak, a working insight into the end of the State; and, of course, practical contradictions would be fewer if such conceptions were completer and more covered by each other. But a complete reflective conception of the end of the State, comprehensive and free from contradiction, would mean a complete idea of the realization of all human capacity, without waste or failure. Such a conception is impossible owing to the gradual character of the process by which the end of life, the nature of the good, is determined for man. The Real Will, as represented by the State, is only a partial embodiment of it.

(*b*) The State, as the operative criticism of all institutions, is necessarily force; and in the last resort, it is the only recognised and justified force. It seems important to observe that force is inherent in the State, and no true ideal points in the direction of destroying it. For the force of the State proceeds essentially from its character of being our own mind extended so to speak, beyond our immediate consciousness. Not only is the conduct of life as a whole beyond the powers of the average individual at his average level, but it is beyond the powers of all the average individuals in a society taken together at their average level. We made a great mistake in thinking of the force exercised by the State as limited to the restraint of disorderly persons by the police and the punishment of intentional lawbreakers. The State is the fly-wheel of our life. Its system is constantly reminding us of our duties, from sanitation to the incidents of trusteeship, which we have not the least desire to neglect, but which we are either too ignorant of or too indolent to carry apart from instruction and authoritative suggestion. We profit at every turn by institutions, rules, traditions, researches, made by minds at their best, which, through State action are now in a form to operate as extensions of our own minds. It is not merely the contrast between the limited activity of one individual and the greater achievement of millions put together. It is the contrast between individuals working in the order and armed with the laws, customs, writings, and institutions devised by ages, and the same individuals considered as their daily average selves, with a varying but always limited range of immediate consciousness. For at any given moment no judge knows all the law; no author knows all his own books, not to mention those of others; no official of an institution has the whole logic and meaning of the institution before his mind. All individuals are continually reinforced and carried on, beyond their average immediate consciousness, by the knowledge, resources, and energy which surround them in the social order, with its inheritance, of which the order itself

169

is the greatest part. And the return of this greater self, forming a system adjusted to unity, upon their isolated minds, as an expansion and stimulus to them, necessarily takes the shape of force, in as far as their minds are inert. And this must always be the case, not merely so long as wills are straightforwardly rebellious against the common good, but so long as the knowledge and energy of the average mind are unequal to dealing, on its own initiative and out of its own resources, with all possible conjunctions in which necessary conditions of the common good are to be maintained. In other words, there must be inertia to overcome, as long as the limitations of our animal nature exist at all. The State is, as Plato told us, the individual mind writ large, or, as we have said, our mind reinforced by capacities which are of its own nature, but which supplement its defects. And this being so, the less complete must clearly submit to find itself in the more complete, and be carried along with it so far as the latter is able to advance.

[55]

BOUTROUX, EMILE

BOUTROUX, EMILE (1845-1921). It is a rare occurrence for European scholars to hail a doctoral thesis in philosophy as a turning point in the history of thought. However, this was the case with Boutroux's thesis published in 1874, *De la Contingence des Lois de la Nature* (On the Contingency of the Laws of Nature). Subsequently he became one of the most influential teachers of philosophy at the Sorbonne in Paris; Henri Bergson was one of his many famous pupils.

He demonstrated that the concept of natural law in all branches of science (from mathematics to biology) is a result rather than a principle, for it does not prove the universal reign of necessity. According to Boutroux, generally the relatively invariable relationship between causes and effects comes about because of an inadequate grasp of such true and profound realities as life and liberty. He encountered the objection that contingency connotes hazard and disorder by stating that necessity implies immutability and death. Many of Boutroux's arguments on the problem of liberty and the extent to which necessity can be admitted have become classic. He always endeavored to strengthen the conviction that man is able to act upon nature. His adherence to the ideas advanced in his first book helped to pave the way for new progress in science. When asked what the good life involved, he replied "a thought conceived in early years and developed in maturity." His opinion was internationally revered as the expression of "Europe's conscience."

ALL BEINGS TEND TOWARD GOD

GOD is the creator of the essence and existence of beings. Moreover, it is His activity, His incessant providence, that gives the higher forms the faculty of employing the lower ones as instruments. Nor is there any reason to regard a special providence as more unworthy of Him than the creation of a manifold and changing universe.

The contingency shown in the hierarchy of the general laws and forms of the world finds its explanation in this doctrine of divine freedom. . . .

The progress of the events of life may be likened unto a sea voyage. While the main concern of the sailors is to avoid hidden reefs and come safe out of storms, their efforts do not stop there. They have a goal to reach, and, however circuitous the routes they may have to traverse, they constantly aim for this goal. To advance is not to avoid, more or less completely, the dangers along the track, it is to draw nearer the goal. But though the sailors have a mission, they also have the freedom of action necessary for its accomplishment; and those whose duty it is more especially to steer the vessel are entrusted with greater authority. Of course the power of these men is nothing compared with the might of the ocean; but then, it is an intelligent and organized power; it is put into action at the right moment. By means of a series of manoeuvres and contrivances which do not appreciably change the outer conditions, but are all calculated to make use of them in view of the goal to be attained, man succeeds in making the winds and waves obey his will.

Similarly, it is not the sole end of the beings of nature to continue in existence, amid the obstacles surrounding them, and to yield to outer conditions: they have an ideal to realize;

and this ideal consists in drawing nearer to God, in resembling Him, each after its kind. The ideal varies with the different beings, since each has a special nature and is capable of imitating God only and through its own distinctive nature.

The perfection for which creatures were born entitles them to a certain degree of spontaneity, necessary in order to transcend themselves. The higher the mission of a being, *i.e.* the more its nature admits of perfection, the wider is its liberty, the means of attaining its end.

[56]

BOWNE, BORDEN PARKER

BOWNE, BORDEN PARKER (1847-1910). For more than thirty years, Bowne was professor of philosophy at Boston University where, although the spiritual atmosphere of religious traditionalism was agreeable to him, he endeavored to and succeeded in liberalizing religious thought.

An acute critic of positivism and naturalism, he untiringly maintained the cause of theism, defending it from the viewpoints of epistemology, logic, psychology, metaphysics, and religious and social thought. He categorized his views as Kantianized Berkeleyanism, transcendental empiricism and, finally, Personalism—a term used by other philosophers, who differ from Bowne in all fundamental theses, to characterize their systems. Bowne's was chiefly influenced by Lotze.

Bowne's religious and philosophical problems conjoin in their attitude toward change and identity. Epistemologically and psychologically, Bowne regarded identity as the foundation of personality. He argued that without identity, recognition is impossible; without recognition, memory cannot be formed; that memory, the essence of the self, is the primary condition of mental life. He insisted that the mind, not the sense, gives evidence of reality; that reality is comprehended by more than the cognitive faculties; that life and aspiration are more deeply rooted in the person than logical thought; therefore, it becomes necessary to justify aesthetics, ethics, and metaphysics. Bowne stated that no fundamental antagonism exists between thought and feeling. The question of freedom intimately enters into the structure of reason. All knowledge is the result of considerable searching effort. Science is the consequence of human freedom, not of automatically functioning truth. Bowne applied his philosophy of change and identity to the experiences of daily social life, and tried to establish a balance between the claims of progress and conservatism.

THE MORAL LIFE

THAT was not first which was spiritual, but that which was natural, and afterward that which was spiritual. But the spiritual is not something apart from the natural, as a kind of detached movement; it is rather the natural itself, rising toward its ideal form through the free activity of the moral person. The natural can be understood only through the spiritual, to which it points; and the spiritual gets contents only through the natural, in which it roots.

As a consequence, the field of ethics is life itself, and, immediately, the life that now is. And our moral task is to make this life, so far as possible, an expression of rational good-will. In this work we have a double guide. Internally, we have a growing moral ideal; externally, we have a growing insight into the tendencies of conduct. Neither of these can be deduced from the other, and both are alike necessary.

For life has two poles. It demands for its perfection both outward fortune and happiness and inward worth and peace. A conditioned life like ours cannot reach an ideal form, unless it be in harmony both with its objective environment and with its subjective ideals. Either of these elements, when viewed apart from the other, is an abstraction of theory, and a source of confusion, if not a mischief. If we consider only the inner worth and peace, ethics runs to leaves. If we consider only the outer fortune and happiness, ethics runs to weeds. There is no need to ask which factor is first, as both should be first, last and always.

The moral life finds its chief field in the service of the common good. Neither virtue nor happiness is attainable as a direct abstract aim. It is a commonplace that happiness eludes direct pursuit; and it is equally true, though less generally recognized, that virtue is alike elusive. Our nature acts spontaneously and normally only when we are taken out of ourselves and our attention is directed to our normal objects. The man who is seeking to do as he would be done by, and to love his neighbor as himself, is in a much better way than the man who is engaged in self-culture and the pursuit of virtue.

The greatest need in ethics is the impartial and unselfish will to do right. With this will, most questions would settle themselves; and, without it, all theory is worthless. The selfish will is the great source not only of wars and fightings, but also of dishonest casuistry and tampering with truth and righteousness. One bent on doing wrong never lacks an excuse; and one seeking to do right can commonly find the way.

Presupposing this will to do right, the great need in ethical theory is to renounce abstractions, as virtue, pleasure, happiness, and come into contact with reality. Most of the theoretical contentions of the world would vanish if brought out of their abstraction. Mr. Mill did once suggest that two and two might make five, but he prudently located the possibility in another planet. That is, it was a purely verbal doubt, which neither he nor any one else ever dreamed of tolerating in concrete experience. Ethics, in particular, has suffered from this verbalism; and all the more because it is a practical science, which has to do with life rather than speculation. Concrete relations and duties have been overlooked in the name of various abstractions—all of them thin and bloodless, and admitting of endless verbal manipulation. It is in this region of abstractions that most ethical debate has been carried on. Hence its sterility of anything but mischief. As Mr. Mill's doubt did not touch practical arithmetic, so the doubts of the ethical schools vanish before concrete matter. The men of good will who are desirous of leading a helpful and worthy human life will generally agree in the great outlines, and also in the details, of duty, whatever their ethical philosophy. And even the tedious vaporers about the indifference of vice and virtue succeed in believing their own whims only so long as they keep clear of the concrete. A blindness more than judicial can easily be induced concerning the facts of human life by bringing in a few such terms as sin and plunging into the labyrinths of theological controversy. So great is the deceit of words! Hence the importance of rescuing ethics from its abstractions and bringing it into contact with life.

The great need of ethical practice, next to the good will, is the serious and thoughtful application of intellect to the problems of life and conduct. As error arises less from wilful lying than from indifference to truth, so misconduct and social evils in general arise less from a will to do wrong than from an indifference to doing right. As of old, the "people do not consider;" and in the ignorance thus engendered terrible things are done or ignored. There is really moral life enough to make vast and beneficent reforms, if the people would only consider. And until they do consider we must worry along in the old way, with an embryonic conscience, drugged by custom and warped into artificiality, while life is directed not by wise and serious reflection, but by conflicting passion and selfishness. We shall escape from this condition only as we control the mechanical drifting of thoughtlessness, and advance beyond the narrowness of the conventional conscience, and devote all our good will and all our intellect to the rationalization and moralization of life.

We shall also do well to remember that righteousness is nothing which can be achieved once for all, whether for the individual or for the community. The living will to do right must be ever present in both, forever reaffirming itself and adjusting itself to new conditions. The tacit dream of the half-way righteous in both fields is that some stage may be reached where the will may be relaxed, and given a vacation. But this dream also must be dismissed. Both individual and social righteousness are likely long to remain militant. As we are now constituted, righteousness cannot be so stored away in habits as to dispense with the continuous devotion of the living will. Especially is this devotion demanded in social righteousness. Here the error is perennial of thinking

175

that justice and wisdom may be so stored up in laws and constitutions as to run of themselves, while the citizens are left free to go to their farms and merchandise. This is one of the most pernicious practical errors of our time. Social righteousness may be expressed in laws, but it lives only in the moral vigilance of the people.

In a very important sense the respectable class is the dangerous class in the community. By its example it degrades the social conception of the meaning of life, and thus materializes, vulgarizes, and brutalizes the public thought. Also, by its indifference to public duties, it constitutes itself the guilty accomplice of all the enemies of society. By this same indifference, too, it becomes the great breeder of social enemies; for only where the carcass is are the vultures gathered together. The ease with which self-styled good people ignore public duties and become criminal accomplices in the worst crimes against humanity is one of the humorous features of our ethical life.

In the application of principles to life there will long be a neutral frontier on the borders of the moral life, where consequences and tendencies have not so clearly declared themselves as to exclude differences of opinion among men of good will. Here men will differ in judgment rather than in morals. It is very common to exaggerate this difference into a moral one; and then the humorous spectacle is presented of friends who ignore the common enemy and waste their strength in mutual belaborings. This is one of the great obstacles to any valuable reform.

Finally, in reducing principles to practice we must be on our guard against an abstract and impracticable idealism. Even in the personal life conscience may be a measureless calamity, unless restrained by a certain indefinable good sense. Many principles look fair and even ideal when considered in abstraction from life, which cannot, however, be applied to life without the most hideous or disastrous results. Here is the perennial oversight of off-hand reformers and socialistic quacks. Ethics when divorced from practical wisdom prevents the attainment of its own ends. The abstract ethics of the closet must be replaced by the ethics of life, if we would not see ethics lose itself in barren contentions and tedious verbal disputes.

[57]

BRADLEY, FRANCIS HERBERT

BRADLEY, FRANCIS HERBERT (1846-1924). Noted for his contribution to English philosophy, Bradley was, at first, a disciple of Hegel. He lost sympathy with Hegelian philosophy, and left it to revitalize the musty logic of Mills. Subsequently he opposed utilitarianism and supported the ethics of Kant, by insisting that good will was a universal principle, as well as a human quality. He found, by testing the relation of each claim to fundamental reality, that experience, as such, is nonrelational and contains within itself the essential features of thought which make for explicit logic. He stated that truth can only reside in judgment; that not all judgments are true; that when a subject is circumspect and sufficiently inclusive, then its judgment is true; and that truth really requires the absolute. Bradley lucidly restated the fundamental idealism and spiritual monism that form the bases for the analysis of individual experience. This analysis gradually develops into the realization of a universal coherent unity, infinite in character.

In his youth, Bradley accepted a fellowship at Merton College, Oxford, tenable for life, but terminable at marriage. He enjoyed its benefits for more than half a century. As an athlete at University College, he contracted typhoid fever and subsequently suffered from an inflammation of the kidneys. These illnesses probably resulted in his being a crochety recluse. Yet his literary efforts have polish, style, and even humor. His *Appearance and Reality* (1893) and *Essays on Truth and Reality* (1914) are philosophical classics.

THE ABSOLUTE

WE can find no province of the world so low but the Absolute inhabits it. Nowhere is there even a single fact so fragmentary and so poor that to the universe it does not matter. There is truth in every idea however false, there is reality in every existence however slight; and, where we can point to reality or truth, there is the one undivided life of the Absolute.

177

Appearance without reality would be impossible, for what then could appear? And reality without appearance would be nothing, for there certainly is nothing outside appearances. But on the other hand Reality . . . is not the sum of things. It is the unity in which all things, coming together, are transmuted, in which they are changed all alike, though not changed equally. And, as we have perceived, in this unity relations of isolation and hostility are affirmed and absorbed. These also are harmonious in the Whole, though not of course harmonious as such, and while severally confined to their natures as separate. Hence it would show blindness to urge, as an objection against our view, the opposition found in ugliness and in conscious evil. The extreme of hostility implies an intenser relation, and this relation falls within the Whole and enriches its unity. The apparent discordance and distraction is overruled into harmony, and it is but the condition of fuller and more individual development. But we can hardly speak of the Absolute itself as either ugly or evil. The Absolute is indeed evil in a sense and it is ugly and false, but the sense, in which these predicates can be applied, is too forced and unnatural. Used of the Whole each predicate would be the result of an indefensible division, and each would be a fragment isolated and by itself without consistent meaning. Ugliness, evil, and error, in their several spheres, are subordinate aspects. They imply distinctions falling, in each case, within one subject province of the Absolute's kingdom; and they involve a relation, in each case, of some struggling element to its superior, though limited, whole. Within these minor wholes the opposition draws its life from, and is overpowered by the system which supports it. The predicates evil, ugly, and false must therefore stamp, whatever they qualify, as a mere subordinate aspect, an aspect belonging to the province of beauty or goodness or truth. And to assign such a position to the sovereign Absolute would be plainly absurd. You may affirm that the Absolute *has* ugliness and error and evil, since it owns the provinces in which these features are partial elements. But to assert that it *is* one of its own fragmentary and dependent details would be inadmissible.

It is only by a license that the subject-systems, even when we regard them as wholes, can be made qualities of Reality. It is always under correction and on sufferance that we term the universe either beautiful or moral or true. And to venture further would be both useless and dangerous at once.

If you view the Absolute morally at all, then the Absolute is good. It cannot be one factor contained within and overpowered by goodness. In the same way, viewed logically or aesthetically, the Absolute can only be true or beautiful. It is merely when you have so termed it, and while you still continue to insist on these preponderant characters, that you can introduce at all the ideas of falsehood and ugliness. And, so introduced, their direct application to the Absolute is impossible. Thus to identify the supreme universe with a partial system may, for some end, be admissible. But to take it as a single character within this system, and as a feature which is already overruled, and which as such is suppressed there, would, we have seen, be quite unwarranted. Ugliness, error, and evil, all are owned by, and all essentially contribute to the wealth of the Absolute. The Absolute, we may say in general, has no assets beyond appearances; and again, with appearances alone to its credit, the Absolute would be bankrupt. All of these are worthless alike apart from transmutation. But, on the other hand once more, since the amount of change is different in each case, appearances differ widely in their degrees of truth and reality. There are predicates which, in comparison with others, are false and unreal.

To survey the field of appearances, to measure each by the idea of perfect individuality, and to arrange them in an order and in a system of reality and merit—would be the task of metaphysics.

[58]

179

BRANDEIS, LOUIS DEMBITZ

BRANDEIS, LOUIS DEMBITZ (1856-1941). Notable as a Justice of the United States Supreme Court Brandeis was a juridical heretic, who had the satisfaction of seeing his views acknowledged by orthodox jurists. Many of his dissenting opinions have since become the law of the land. He was greatly inspired by Oliver Wendell Holmes, Jr., a colleague of his on the Supreme Court bench, and he subsequently had great influence over his former teacher. Both of them stressed the historical development of law, the necessity of adapting legislation to the dynamic economic and social changes, and the social and broad cultural responsibilities of jurists and legislators. Both frequently dissented from the majority Court opinion.

Brandeis was opposed to socialism and claimed it did not increase industrial efficiency. He was favorably inclined toward labor, small businessmen, and cooperative enterprises. Although he protested that he had no general philosophy and thought only within the context of the facts that came before him, he was not only a philosopher of law, but also a social and political philosopher. His views never lost their vital contact with the facts of daily life. He distrusted those whose reasoning bounded far ahead of the facts, and considered those thinkers inadequate whose lack of imagination did not enable their ideas to withstand the test of experience and subsequent events. He always treated opponents fairly when they indicated a willingness to compromise. He firmly believed in the ultimate possibility of reconciling the varied interests of individuals, in overcoming the antagonism between the individual and society and in espousing a basic loyalty to one's fellow man and to the community. He hoped that a humanistic education would culminate in the realization of his ideas.

LAW AND DEMOCRACY

WHAT are American ideals? They are the development of the individual for his own and the common good; the development through liberty, and the attainment of the common good through democracy and social justice.

Our form of government, as well as humanity, compels us to strive for individual man. Under universal suffrage every voter is a part ruler of the state. Unless the rulers have, in the main, education and character, and are free men, our great experiment in democracy must fail. It devolves upon the state, therefore, to fit its rulers for their tasks.

Democracy must be on its toes. You cannot get democracy by doing nothing, or even by passing laws. It has to come from the people. Law is no substitute for the efforts of the citizen. We make laws for the community. We cannot make the community fit the laws. If we desire respect for the law we must first make the law respectable.

We are particularly at fault in America in making private things public and keeping public things private. There used to be a certain glamour about big things; anything big, simply because it was big, seemed to be good and great. We are now coming to see that big things may be very bad and mean.

Big business is not more efficient than small business. Within certain limits you may get through size a relatively smaller cost unit, but the size of greatest efficiency is reached at a comparatively early stage. With the growth in size comes an increasing cost of organization and administration, which is so much greater than the increase in the volume of business that the law of diminishing returns applies.

The real test of efficiency comes when success has to be struggled for; when natural or legal conditions limit the charges which may be made for the goods sold or the services rendered. Real efficiency in any business in which conditions are ever changing must ultimately depend, in large measure, upon the correctness of the judgment exercised, from day to day, on important problems as they arise.

I believe that the possibilities of human advancement are unlimited. I believe that the resources of productive enterprise are almost untouched, and that the world will see a vastly increased supply of comforts, a tremendous social surplus out of which the great masses will be apportioned a degree of well-being that is now hardly dreamed of.

[59]

181

BRENTANO, FRANZ

BRENTANO, FRANZ (1838-1917). The intellectual milieu of his early background is not manifest in Franz Brentano's writings. He was uninterested in literature and politics, and declined to exploit the influence of his relatives. He was educated by his father, Christian, a devout Catholic and religious author. Franz became a Catholic priest, but after nine years, he abandoned the Catholic Church in 1873. He then became a professor at Wuerzburg and Vienna, and spent the remaining twenty years of his life in Italy and Switzerland. He maintained friendly relations only with his brother, Lujo Brentano, who was noted as a political economist and champion of free trade.

Brentano's chief contributions were in the fields of epistemology, logic, axiology, and psychology. He declared that psychology was the basis of philosophy and the path to metaphysics. He did not believe in metaphysical systems, but believed that reliable metaphysical knowledge was possible. He thought that constant change might lead to increasing perfection. Resolutely opposed to German idealism, he stated that the natural sciences were the true method of philosophic thought. He was disdainful of the "physiological psychology" of Wilhelm Wundt and others who tried to found a psychology based upon experimental methods. Brentano revived those concepts of Scholasticism that deal with the intentional relation of the consciousness to the object. He considered this to be the essential character of psychological experience. He also made great efforts to demonstrate that psychological analysis was not the way to achieve knowledge of an object. He stressed the fundamental differences between judgment and presentation—two completely different means by which the consciousness of an object is perceived. His energetic rejection of the attempts to reduce logic to psychology were of great importance to his disciples: Husserl, Stumpf, Marty, Meinong, Kraus, and Ehrenfels.

Brentano's exemplary character and sincerity of thought enabled him to proceed courageously and independently in his defiance of religious and and secular authority. He never yielded to a need for popular approval, or paid much attention to ideas merely because they were the current vogue.

THE THREE CLASSES OF PSYCHIC PHENOMENA

IN order to adequately express the concepts concerning the

different manner of relationships to content, we have to distinguish three main classes of psychic phenomena. These
three species are not the same as those generally accepted,
and since more appropriate names are not at hand, the first
may be called "image"; the second, "judgment"; and the
third, "emotion," "interest," or "love."

We speak of image whenever something appears to us.
If we see something, we imagine its color; if we hear something, we imagine its sound; if we indulge in fancies, we
imagine fanciful creations.

By virtue of the general sense in which the word is used,
it can be said that it is impossible for the activity of the soul
to bear on some thing that cannot be imagined. Whenever I
hear and understand a name, I imagine what it stands for,
and generally speaking, it is the purpose of a name to provoke "images."

The meaning of "judgment" is in accordance with customary philosophical usage. That is, anything we accept is
true; anything we reject is false.

Unfortunately, there is no unifying expression for the
third major class: the phenomena called emotions; or the
phenomena of interests; or the phenomena of love. This class
comprises all psychic phenomena, not included in the first
two classes. Emotions are only affective phenomena which
are combined with noticeable physical excitement. Everyone
comprehends anger, fear, violence, and desire as emotions.
In the general sense in which the term "emotion" is used it
also comprises any wish, decision, or intention.

The term interest is preferably used only for certain
acts that belong to a particular sphere; those cases there is a
desire for knowledge, or where curiosity is aroused. A wish,
hope, or decision of the will is also an act of interest; similarly delight or aversion may also be categorized as interest.

Instead of calling this class by the simple name of love,
it should, strictly speaking, have been called love or hatred,
only because they are opposites. Just as when one speaks of
"judging" as an act of accepting, or when one speaks of the

phenomenon of true desire. For the sake of brevity, I have applied a simple term for the pair of names, even though the term does not embrace the meaning in every sense or sphere. One means something quite different, to be sure, when one says that one loves one's friend, as when one says that he loves wine. The former is loved by wishing him well; the latter is loved by desiring it as something good and enjoying it with pleasure. Using the sense of the word in the latter instance, each act that belongs to this third class is something that is loved, or more precisely speaking, something that is loved or hated.

In an analogous manner, each judgment takes an object as true or false; each phenomenon that belongs to the third class takes an object as good or bad.

[60]

BRIDGMAN, P. W.

BRIDGMAN, P. W. (1882-   ). A professor of mathematics and natural philosophy at Harvard University, an authority on thermodynamics, electricity, and various other physical sciences, Percy Bridgman is noted for his promulgation of the "operational" theory of meaning in his books *The Logic of Modern Physics* (1927) and *The Nature of Physical Theory* (1936). He asserts that the classical concepts of physics are inadequate. He defines concept as a set of operations comprised of mental and physical activity. Truth is identical with verifiability, and the criterion of scientific truth is the experimental method. Although Bridgman has been influenced by neither Dewey nor James, his operationalism parallels John Dewey's instrumentalism.

Bridgman enlarged his scope of observation and thought in *The Intelligent Individual and Society* (1938). His starting point is the irrationality of Man in contemporary society; Man's awareness of this makes him long for an intelligent, orderly life, even though such longing may not be directed at the perfectibility of human desires. If a perfect life is unattainable, a satisfactory life can be secured by apprehending the relations, consequences, implications of the drive, or by intelligently satisfying these drives. These drives are not subject to argument, but only to examination and modifica-

184

tion through education. Rationality does not have all the qualities requisite for this task. Emotional adjustment can complete it.

Ideally, education should provide the technique for criticism and modification of the specific drives by the individual. Thus, Bridgman seeks to secure individual freedom in society. His human ideal is a synthesis of intellectual and emotional honesty.

SCIENTIST AND SOCIAL RESPONSIBILITY

WHAT is the relation of the scientist to ideal society? It seems to me that he occupies a position of high strategic importance, a position impossible of attainment for the man who has not directly experienced the significant factors basic to this type of society. The conception of what constitutes the good life does not present itself as a primitive datum in consciousness, but is a product of cultivation and education. Furthermore, various ideals of the good life are possible, competitive with one another and to a certain extent mutually exclusive. The ideals that come to prevail will to a large extent depend on the self-conscious activities of those most concerned. It may even be that the ideals will have to be fought for. What constitutes the good life for the scientist does not at once appeal to the majority as constituting the good life. Nay, more than this, without education the majority cannot be trusted to see that it is to the advantage of the community as a whole that the scientist be allowed to lead his good life. With education, however, I believe that this can be accomplished, and that the scientist is strategically situated to impart this education. It is, of course, easy for anyone to see that the material benefits we now enjoy would not have been possible without scientific activity and to see that for this reason science should be supported. What I have in mind, however, is something less material. I think the scientist, in endeavoring to impart the vision of what this is, would do well not to take a too narrow view. The scientific life, which for him is a good life, is a special kind of a more general life which is also a good life, namely, the life of the intellect.

I think the scientist's most important educative task is to get the average man to feel that the life of the intellect not only is a good life for those who actively lead it, but that it is also good for society as a whole that the intellectual life should be made possible for those capable of it, and that it should be prized and rewarded by the entire community. It is perhaps a gamble that society as a whole can be made to feel this. But I believe it is a gamble to which the scientific man is committed. If the human race is such a sort of creature that it cannot be made to feel that intellectual activity and satisfaction of the craving for understanding are goods in themselves, then we might as well shut up shop here and now, and those of us who are made that way henceforth get the intellectual satisfactions necessary to us as best we can, surreptitiously and in spite of our fellows. Example itself can be educative. Appreciation of the element of high adventure in achieving understanding of the ways of nature should not be difficult to impart. In other fields human beings do this. There must be widespread sympathy with, and understanding of the mountain climber who, when asked why he had to climb mountains, replied, "Because the mountain is there." I believe that most men similarly can be made to feel the challenge of an external world not understood and can be made to see that the scientist has to understand nature "because nature is there." The challenge to the understanding of nature is a challenge to the utmost capacity in us. In accepting the challenge, man can dare to accept no handicaps. That is the reason that scientific freedom is essential and that artificial limitations of tools or subject matter are unthinkable. The average man, I believe, can be made to see that scientific freedom is merely freedom to be intelligent, and that the need for this freedom is born with us, and that we will practice it in the inmost recesses of our thoughts no matter what the external constraints. And I believe also that the average man can be made to see that the imposition of restraints on the freedom to be intelligent betrays fear of the unknown and of himself, and that he can be made to feel that this fear is an ignoble thing. My gamble is that the human race, once it has caught the vision, will not be willing to yield to fear of the consequences of its own intelligence.

It may appear that we have been straying rather far from our ostensible topic. I think, however, that from the broad point of view we have not. What we have been saying amounts to saying that the most intelligent way of dealing with the problems arising from scientific discoveries is to create an appropriate society. This society will be a society that recognizes that the only rational basis for its functions is to be sought in its relations to the individuals of which it is composed; a society in which the individual in his capacity as a member of society will have the integrity not to stoop to actions he would not permit himself as an individual; a society broadly tolerant and one which recognizes intellectual achievement as one of the chief glories of man; a society imaginative enough to see the high adventure in winning an understanding of the natural world about us, and a society which esteems the fear of its own intellect an ignoble thing. In a society so constituted I venture to think the problems created by scientific discoveries will pretty much solve themselves.

[61]

BRUNO, GIORDANO

BRUNO, GIORDANO (1548-1600). Poet, playwright, philosopher, Bruno is less representative of the development of the modern scientific spirit than he is of the fermentation produced by the contact of Scholastic philosophy with the natural sciences. His enthusiasm for Copernicus' astronomical discovery enabled him to enlarge his cosmic concepts. But instead of thinking empirically, he continued to think in terms of Aristotelian ideas, all the while attacking Aristotle. Bruno was convinced that true philosophy was no different than poetry, music, or painting, since the arts are bound to express divine wisdom. He believed in the infinite perfectibility of knowledge, and conceived of the universe as an imperfect mirror of God's essence in which God's infinity and unity are inadequately depicted.

Throughout his life, Bruno was beset by a restless spirit. He

187

quarreled with the Catholic Church, Calvinists, Lutherans, mathematicians, and physicists. During a fifteen-year period, he lived in
Genoa, Venice, Toulouse, Lyons, Paris, Oxford, Wittenberg, and
Prague. Wherever he lived he was first admired and then detested
for his intolerant attitudes. Like Gabirol, he was both litterateur and
philosopher. He wrote many lyrical poems, imbued with an heroic
spirit, and ribald comedies—both equally characteristic of the Ba-
roque age. After seven years of imprisonment due to his renunciation of the Dominican Order, he was burned (February 17, 1600) at
the stake during the Inquisition in Rome because of his staunch
refusal to recant.

A PHILOSOPHY OF THE INFINITE UNIVERSE

THESE are the doubts, difficulties and motives, about the solution whereof I have said enough in our dialogues to expose
the intimate and radicated errors of the common philosophy,
and to show the weight and worth of our own. Here you will
meet with the reasons why we should not fear that any part
of this Universe should fall or fly off, that the least particle
should be lost in empty space, or be truly annihilated. Here
you will perceive the reason of that vicissitude which may be
observed in the constant change of all things, whereby it
happens, that there is nothing so ill but may befall us or be
prevented, nor anything so good but may be lost or obtained
by us; since in this infinite field the parts and modes do perpetually vary, though the substance and the whole do eternally persevere the same.

From this contemplation (if we do but rightly consider),
it will follow that we ought never to be dispirited by any
strange accidents through excess of fear or pain, nor ever be
elated by any prosperous event through excess of hope or
pleasure; whence we have the way to true morality, and,
following it, we would become the magnanimous despisers
of what men of childish thoughts do fondly esteem, and the
wise judges of the history of nature which is written in our
minds, and the strict executioners of those divine laws which
are engraven in the centre of our hearts. We would know
that it is no harder thing to fly from hence up into heaven,

than to fly from heaven back again to the earth, that ascending thither and ascending hither are all one; that we are no more circumferential to the other globes than they are to us, nor they more central to us than we are to them, and that none of them is more above the stars than we, as they are no less than we covered over or comprehended by the sky. Behold us therefore free from envying them! behold us delivered from the vain anxiety and foolish care of desiring to enjoy that good afar off, which in as great a degree we may possess so near at hand, and even at home! Behold us freed from the terror that they should fall upon us, any more than we should hope that we might fall upon them; since every one as well as all of these globes are sustained by infinite ether, in which this our animal freely runs, and keeps to his prescribed course, as the rest of the planets do to theirs. . . .

We fear not, therefore, that what is accumulated in this world, should, by the malice of some wandering spirit, or by the wrath of some evil genius, be shook and scattered, as it were, into smoke or dust, out of this cupola of the sky, and beyond the starry mantle of the firmament; nor that the nature of things can otherwise come to be annihilated in substance, than, as it seems to our eyes, that the air contained in the concavity of a bubble is become nothing when that bubble is burst; because we know that in the world one thing ever succeeds another, *there being no utmost bottom*, whence, as by the hand of some artificer, things are irreparably struck into nothing. There are no ends, limits, margins, or walls, that keep back or subtract any parcel of the infinite abundance of things. Thence it is that the earth and sea are ever equally fertile, and thence the perpetual brightness of the sun, eternal fuel circulating to those devouring fires, and a supply of waters being eternally furnished to the evaporated seas, from the infinite and ever renewing magazine of matter: so that Democritus and Epicurus, who asserted the infinity of things with their perpetual variableness and restoration were so far more in the right than he who endeavored to account for the eternally same appearance of the Universe, by making homogeneous particles of matter ever and numerically to succeed one another.

Thus the excellency of God is magnified, and the grandeur of his Empire made manifest; he is not glorified in one, but in numberless suns, not in one earth nor in one world, but in ten hundred thousand, of infinite globes: so that this faculty of the intellect is not vain or arbitrary, that ever will or can add space to space, quantity to quantity, unity to unity, member to member. By this science we are loosened from the chains of a most narrow dungeon, and set at liberty to rove in a most august empire; we are removed from conceited boundaries and poverty, to the innumerable riches of an infinite space, of so worthy a field, and of such beautiful worlds: this science does not, in a word, make a horizontal circle feigned by the eye on earth, and imagined by the fancy in the spacious sky.

[62]

BRUNSCHWICG, LÉON

BRUNSCHWICG, LÉON (1869-1944). When the Germans occupied Paris in 1940, they compelled Léon Brunschwicg to leave his position as professor of philosophy at the Sorbonne, robbed him of his collection of precious books, and destroyed his manuscripts. Even though the Germans knew hardly any of his works, the fact that he was a Jew and that his wife had been an under-secretary in the Popular Front cabinet of Léon Blum was sufficient cause for his removal. Despite all the possible dangers, Brunschwicg refused to leave France and spent the remaining years of his life in complete isolation. During this period, he wrote valuable studies of Montaigne, Descartes, and Pascal which were printed in Switzerland and the United States. For his granddaughter, who was then in her teens, he composed a manual of philosophy, entitled *Héritage de Mots, Héritage d'Idées* (Legacy of Words, Legacy of Ideas) which was published posthumously in 1945 after the liberation of France.

To Brunschwicg, philosophy meant not a system of doctrines, but the expression of an attitude toward the totality of material and spiritual beings. It was essentially a reflection on the activities of the human mind in the fields of mathematics, physics, morality, the arts,

and the history of civilization. Brunschwicg energetically emphasized the creative power of the human mind and demonstrated its
function in the network of relationships that make up the framework
of the universe.

Brunschwicg made highly important contributions to the history of science and philosophy, and at the same time contributed to
the understanding and solution of practical problems. His reinter-
pretation of Descartes has become the foundation for a new idealism. He was a man of universal interests as evidenced by his lectures which criticized newspaper editorials as well as Plato or Kant.
He was a friend of Marcel Proust, the novelist, and of Marcel Denis,
the painter; a patron of the theater and modern art exhibits; an
ardent French patriot, and a fighter for human rights.

ON GOD

MODERN science, from the time of Galileo and Copernicus
to Einstein and the theorists of quantum mathematics, has
progressively revealed the true reality of the world. This
revelation reaffirms our concepts and ideas of truth. It is
characteristic for the philosopher to view this as a unified
and indivisible idea. He cannot tolerate the mind in a changing situation, to add epithet or substantive, or in any way
slacken the rigorous method of verification. Inflexibility is the
exigency of the method. Religious truth must, therefore, be
absolute truth; one need not look for the foundation or content of the religion. From the viewpoint of speculation or
rationalism, it must not be said that the basic idea of religion
is yet to be discovered. It is the *Word* which Greece received
from Egypt; which formed the center of Judaic-Christian
theology; the inner light that shines for all mankind and
whose comforting universality and unlimited productivity is
felt by all those who are able to extend and coordinate ideas.
Therefore, religion is the *Word* of God; it confirms the innermost, unparalleled certainty that there is a presence in
each of us, which makes our intelligence different from the
mere passive accumulation of images; makes our love different from the egoistic urge of instinct; keeps us from sev-
ering us from ourselves, and unites us with the community
of minds.

The very manner of attaining this proposition involves the immediate consideration of its negative. For the philosopher, there should not be any other God than the *Word*, comprehended in the immanence which secures His perfect spirituality, with no relation to external forms which would make Him dependent upon the conditions of space and time, and would, in this way, cause the relapse of the religious idea from the sphere of spirit to the inferior regions of matter or life. This new proposition broaches the problem from a negative or somewhat more restrictive aspect. Compared with the essential instincts that determine the origin of religions, the ascetic rationalism of the *Word* seems somewhat deficient and incomplete. In reality, from the viewpoint of pure philosophy, it represents the progress attained by the gradual development from the spontaneous, primitive type of religion to that of a higher type. For the sake of precision, we may call it progress from the religion of *sublimated nature* to the religion of *surmounted* nature.

The first type is derived from constant experience: the inability of the will to realize its aims with certainty; those impervious obstacles which often frustrate the most carefully prepared enterprises: sudden catastrophes, inevitable death. This leads man to form active dreams of superior striving which are at times contradictory to and at other times in accordance with his personal desires. This earthly diffuse striving becomes embodied in the psychology of a transcendent almighty being; a god who inspires fear; who for the same reason becomes the source of hope. We do anything to soften his ire and receive his grace. The supernatural powers at his disposal, secure success for us, or at least we are confident that he will compensate us for our failures and sufferings in immortal time, which according to the common creed succeeds the duration of life.

The renunciation involved in Pascal's mortification and Kant's rigorism is only an ephemeral attitude, accepted and transformed by the expectation of posthumous eternity, where the fruits of peace, denied to us on earth, will be enjoyed.

192

With this concept, God is defined according to his relations with mankind. He is the providential agent, prepared to guard the fate of our planet and the interests of its inhabitants. He is the vital source of precious comfort. Such a God is perfectly adapted to the vicissitudes and ends of human conditions.

It is needless to emphasize the difficulties secular reason, aided by logic, encounters in the analysis of those spontaneous creeds, whose echoes are transmitted to us from remote epochs, and which ethnographers again discover in contemporary primitive societies. The proof of causality *in* the world does not prove that there is a causality *of* the world. Quite the contrary. The conditions of thought which establish the relationships that shape the texture of the universe, as it is known to us, exclude extrapolation, which by pronouncing an abstract principle makes the Absolute emerge as a being that transcends the knowable reality. The more the mind becomes conscious of the proper order of its constituents, whether they belong to the realm of matter or life, the more difficult does it become to regard God as the reason that explains the animate and inanimate universe. The optimism of metaphysics was not only unsuccessful, in divining and justifying the design of creation, but in order to conceive the very idea of such a design, one had to assume first that the earth and mankind were the central interest of the Almighty. Science has considerably enlarged our speculative horizon in terms of space and time. Therefore, the former supposition must be considered a poor one, it contradicts the concept of divinity. Theology, founded upon physics or biology, projecting a supernatural vision of the world, cannot, through conjecture or speculation, solve the problem of religion.

It seems, therefore, reasonable and noble, if not easy, to understand that this speculative inability is the counterpart of moral weakness. If both are to be overcome, we must resolutely convert ourselves to the spirit of truth and change our concept of God, and remove the responsibility of our personal care from Him. God recovers all of His dignity when our concept of him is not charged with the intermediate, involuntary arrogance of terrestrial and human privilege. He does not assimilate Himself with our particular experiences or concepts that result from abstract reasoning. He is not an object of truth, detachable from itself in an unknown region of reality. He is not an object of love which enters into competition with other objects. Rather, he is the cause of our capabilities to comprehend and love without exhausting the resources of our intelligence, or limiting our affection, or reverting it solely to our personal interests. He is the reason we are able to live the life of the spirit.

[63]

BUBER, MARTIN

BUBER, MARTIN (b. 1878-   ). Martin Buber is one of the leading exponents of Hasidic philosophy. His grandfather, Solomon Buber, was the Hasidic scholar who provided impetus to the mystical movement, and the revival of some of the early tenets and practices of Judaism that resulted in a cultural renaissance among the 18th-century Jews of Eastern Europe.

Martin Buber, a student of the mystical religions of China and India, as well as that of medieval Christianity, maintains that the Judaic experience of divine immanence, as it is expressed in the Talmud and realized in prayer, has a unique importance for all peoples. He accepts the mystical concept of man's communion with God. Religious redemption is the central theme of his spirituality. He believes that the philosophies of religion and sociology have made for greater human cohesiveness.

GOD AND THE SOUL

A definition of mysticism is always open to question, if, with any other religious teaching, it is made on the basis of subject matter or chief principle; for then we only have an idea or sentence that is at the same time abstract and somewhat vague, and that fails to comprehend what makes mysticism in its historical manifestations such a singular and remarkable type of religious life. We do better if we take as our starting point that experience of the soul, which is clearly common to all mystics, for they all speak of it in one way or another and, if only in a veiled reference or even in so objective an expression that the personal foundation, that very experience, does not come within our range of vision; here too are moments when a powerful recollection suddenly pulsates through the firm notes of the objective statement. Of course that experience may be called an experience of Unity; but once again we shall only have something abstract and indefinite, if we think merely of a contemplation of Unity, in which to be sure the one contemplating recedes, his essential position however, which he still feels to some extent in the midst of his experience, is no other than the essential position of all our human contemplation, the division of Being into the contemplating and the contemplated. One of the greatest among the mystics, Plotinus, leaves much room for such a misunderstanding when, as a true Greek still in the late period of the fusion of all spiritual elements, he interprets that experience in visual language as the image of the eye contemplating the light. In Plotinus also we perceive on closer observation that this is only one, if also the thinnest, of the garments in which mystical experience cloaks itself so as to be able to reveal itself, or rather to enable the wearer to fit his experience into the framework of his inner life and then into the framework of his cognition. Indeed the crucial factor in that experience is not that the multiplicity of manifestations collapses into the one, that the interplay of colours gives place to the absoluteness of the white light, but that in the one contemplating the act of contemplation is obliterated; it is not the dissolution of phenomenal diversity but of constructive dualism, the dualism of the I experiencing and the object experienced, which is the crucial factor, the peculiarity of mysticism in the true sense. And indeed we can only speak of mysticism in the true sense where we are concerned, not with men in an early state of semi-consciousness preceding a clear distinction between subject and object, but with those to whom the fundamental position has become a matter of course: an I complete in itself and a world complete in itself facing one another.

This fundamental dualism, itself perceived only slowly by the human spirit, is at certain moments in an individual life swept aside in favor of an overwhelming experience of union; this it is which excites that deep and ever-recurring awe which, though in varying degrees of expression, we find in all mystics.

In all mysticism, however, which springs from the soil of the so-called theistic religions, there is an additional factor to which a specifically religious significance is to be attributed. Here the mystic is conscious of a close personal contact with God, and this contact has, it is true, as its goal a union with God, a union which is often felt and presented in images of the earthly Eros, but in this as in every contact between Being and Being it is the very dualism of these beings which is the primary condition of what is occurring between them. It is not the dualism of subject and object, i.e., neither is to the other merely an object of contemplation, itself having no part in the relationship, but it is the dualism of I and Thou, both entering into reciprocal relationship. However God be comprehended as an absolute Being, He is here not the whole, but the Facing, the One facing this man; He is what this man is not, and is not what this man is; it is precisely upon this that the longing for union can be based. In other words, in this close association experienced by the mystic, God, even if the mystic wants to be merged in Him, is and remains a Person. The I of the mystic seeks to lose itself in the Thou of God, but this Thou of God, or, after the I of the mystic has been merged therein, this absolute I of God cannot pass away. That man's "I am" shall perish, so that the "I am" of God remains alone. "Between me and thee," says al-Hallaj, the great martyr of Moslem mysticism, "there is an 'I am' that grieves me. Ah! through thy 'I am' take away my 'I am' from betwixt us both." The mystic never thinks of calling into question the personality of this divine "I am." "I call thee," says al-Hallaj, ". . . no, it is thou who callest me to thee! How could I have said to thee 'It is thou,' if thou hadst not whispered to me 'It is I.' " The I of the revealing God, the I of the God Who accords to the mystic the intercourse with Him, and the I of God, in Whom the human I merges itself, are identical. The mystic remains in the sphere of intercourse, as he was in the sphere of revelation, a theist.

It is otherwise when mysticism, penetrating beyond the sphere of experienced intercourse, dares to deal with God as He is in Himself, that is beyond the relation to man, and indeed beyond the relation to the created world generally. Of course it knows well that, as the greatest thinker of western mysticism, Meister Eckhart, put it, no one can really say what God is. But its conception of absolute unity, a unity therefore that nothing can face any more, is so strong that even the highest idea of the person must yield place to it. Unity which is in relationship to something other than itself is not perfect unity; and perfect unity can no more be personal. By that mysticism, sprung from the soil of a theistic religion, in no way means to deny the personal nature of the God; but it strives to raise that perfect unity, which is faced by nothing, above the God of revelation, and to differentiate between the Godhead abiding in pure being and the active God. Perfect unity merely *is*, it does not work. "Never," says Eckhart, "has the Godhead worked this or that, it is God Who creates all things." To that primal existence before the creation, to that unity transcending all dualism, the mystic strives finally to return; he wishes to become as he was before the creation.

Theistic mysticism does not always strain its conception of unity to the extreme of setting up thereby a dualism in the very being of God. Islamic mysticism avoids it by seeking to raise the attribute of work to an abstract height, where it is compatible with perfect unity. Certainly its success here is only apparent, for it transfigures as it were mystically the monotheistic tradition of the active God, without allowing any of the work of the worker to penetrate the mystical sphere itself;—the one is directed towards the world, the other is essentially acosmic; the one displays

197

God's doings in the community of mankind, the other is only acquainted with Him in His contacts with the soul; so Islamic mysticism, at the price of dividing religious life into two, achieves a questionable unity of God. Christian mysticism, in the best of its theology, proceeds here more boldly and more consistently. With unsurpassable precision it locates the tension in the divine itself. "God and Godhead," says Eckhart, "are as different as heaven and earth. . . . God becomes (wird) and vanishes (entwird)." So here "God" is the name of the Divine, in so far as from perfect unity, faced by nothing, It made Itself in creation and revelation the One facing the world, and thereby the partaker in Its becoming and vanishing. For "God" only exists for a world, by the Divine becoming its, the world's, God; when "world" becomes, God becomes; and if there is no world, God ceases to be, and again there is only Godhead.

Already here it can be seen that it would be a grave error to attribute to mysticism the view that the distinction between Godhead and God is only one of perspective, that is, one consisting not in itself but in the viewpoint of the world. Apart from all else such a view would nullify the historical revelation. Such is far from genuine theistic mysticism, which sees the distinction instead as founded in God's very being and consummated by Him.

Thus far has Christian mysticism proceeded with Eckhart, as Indian mysticism earlier in Sankara; further it has not attempted to penetrate. But by that an enigma that confronts us on the borderline of human being, at the point where it touches the Divine, has been only shifted into the Divine itself, and so for the time being withdrawn from further investigation. Not for ever; for there is in the history of later mysticism yet one more endeavour, even if only fragmentary and if apparently coming to a standstill in its very start, to penetrate still further and here again to ask "Why?" The question may be formulated provisionally thus: Why did God become Person? That Hasidism (and, so far as I can see, Hasidism alone) has ventured to attempt to answer this question—or rather, as will be shown, a related question—is indicated by the words of its greatest thinker, the Maggid of Mesritch, which we are able to extract from the notes of disciples and to some extent to put together. Here is one of the few points, in which Hasidic theology surpasses that of the later Kabbala, whose paths it follows here too, even if only gropingly.

[64]

BUDDHA, GAUTAMA

BUDDHA, GAUTAMA (c. 563-483 B.C.). The term "Buddha" means the "enlightened one who enlightens" or "the awakened who awakens the sense of truth in his fellow men." Buddhism is conceived of as the possession of perfect wisdom and supernatural powers. According to Buddhist doctrine, there is a line of Buddhas who appear in the course of human history from the time of remote antiquity to the distant future. The man who, in world history, is known as Buddha, was originally named Siddhartha (he who has accomplished his aim) or Sakyamuni (sage of the Sakya tribe). He belonged to the Gautama family, a warrior caste that ruled over the Sakya tribe. According to some scholars, the earliest reports of his life were written some two hundred to four hundred years after his death. But all these reports undoubtedly are rephrasings of verbal traditions based upon his life which appear in the detailed summaries of his original doctrines. With the exception of a few radical sceptics, most scholars agree that he married his cousin, Yasodhara, at the age of nineteen, and that a son, Rahula, was born of this union. There is no agreement as to the character of his activities.

In all probability, Buddha began to meditate upon the meaning of life in his early years, and became so disturbed by his awareness of human misfortunes and sufferings that he resolved to find the ways by which mankind could be comforted and redeemed. In India, and throughout the East, the path to knowledge that would enable him to rescue humanity, meant a nomadic life in order to obtain the advice of wise men, who themselves were wanderers, and to meditate in isolation. After six years of studying mankind, life, and doctrines, he was convinced that he had discovered Truth, and thereupon devoted the remainder of his lifetime to converting others to his ideas. He renounced his fortune and family and traveled through the valley of the Ganges as a mendicant, surrounded by an ever-increasing host of disciples, who also lived as mendicants, and finally formed an order.

Buddhism teaches four "Noble Truths," namely; Suffering; Knowledge of its cause, explained by the twelvefold Chain of Causation; Getting rid of passions as the means of deliverance from suffering; Truth, the way of removing suffering by a system of moral discipline. Buddha called his truths "noble," because he regarded nobility as moral. Whether rationalist or mystic, Buddha was a teacher of moral behavior. He avoided metaphysics and religion.

Buddhism has spread throughout Eastern Asia, and is the living faith in Ceylon, Japan, China, Indo-China, Siam, Burma, and Tibet, although it has undergone many modifications in these countries. In India the country where Buddha and Buddhism were born, Buddhism has been all but extinct since 1200 A.D. Modern Hindus are so estranged from Buddhism that Gandhi had to defend himself against the "accusation" of spreading Buddhistic teachings under the guise of Sanatana Hinduism. Gandhi did state, however, that in his "deliberate opinion, the essence of Buddha's teachings now form an integral part of Hinduism."

SOME TEACHINGS

INSIGHT into the causes of error results in the cessation of the consciousness of the self.

Phenomena, those sensuous objects that are striven for, are the cause of error.

However, the cause of error is the incorrect concept of wholeness.

Doubt arises because knowledge and ignorance are two different things.

There can be no doubt concerning the fact that the whole exists, for it has been previously demonstrated.

At the same time that we are not in doubt, other philosophers may state that it does *not* exist; that the whole or a part of the relationship is an impossible one; that there is no whole, nor are there any parts that comprise the whole; for actually there are no parts, and therefore there is no whole because there are no parts.

Moreover, continue these philosophers, there is no whole because it is not independent of its parts; nor do the parts constitute the whole.

These assertions create an unreal problem; for it does not make sense to talk of differences in the One, because it does not countenance differences.

The reason advanced by our opponents is only apparent because of the fact that the whole would not be in the parts, even if it had these parts.

To this they may object and say, that perception of the whole is like a wad of hair that dims vision.

A sense organ, like perception, whether it be keen or dull, does no more than sense its proper object. It fails to function in respect to an object that does not belong to its field.

Thus, our opponents will claim that the part-whole relationship could be continued until the dissolution of the world.

However, there is no dissolution of the world, because there are atoms.

Indeed it is said that the atom is finer than the mote in the sunbeam.

Some thinkers maintain that this is not the case, for the atom is pervaded by *akasa* (ether), and that *akasa* does not possess the quality of universal penetration.

However we say that the inner and outer parts exist only in a thing that is produced, just as one speaks of cause as something other than the thing that is produced. In anything that is not produced, there is no inner and outer.

Moreover, *akasa* has the quality of all-pervasiveness; its conjunction with sound is universally present.

Akasa has the qualities of nondispersion and nonresistance, and is omnipresent.

Some, however, do maintain that there are parts to the atom, because things possessed of form have a structure and because atoms are conjoined.

There is no valid objection to such reasoning, for that would lead to a *regressus ad infinitum,* and a *regressus ad infinitum* is not permissible.

At this point, our adversaries will say that on the basis

of intellectual analysis, one does not arrive at the nature of things, just as one does not perceive the existence of a piece of cloth except by its threads, so one does not perceive the whole except by its parts.

To this we retort, that this is not a valid reason, it confuses the issue.

The whole is not perceived as a separate entity, its parts are inherent in it.

In addition, objects are dependent upon the source of knowledge whether that source of knowledge is correct or incorrect.

Some opponents among the Buddhists tell us that this is an erroneous concept of the source and object of knowledge; just as they maintain that cognition of the image in dreams is erroneous; or that cognition is similar to the magic of the Fata Morgana of the city of Gandharvas or to the desert mirage called "thirst of the antelopes."

This is without foundation, for there is no ground for such comparison. Incorrect cognition of images in dreams is similar to the cognition involved in memory and desire. These, in turn, involve a cognition similar to our conscious existence.

Wrong perceptions disappear by virtue of knowing what is true, just as the wrong cognition of images in dreams vanishes upon waking.

Similarly, we arrive at truth by the recognition of the reality of that which is the basis of thought, as well as by the fact that there is dual knowledge: one is true, the other is false, and by the virtue of distinguishing that which is real from that which is perceived to be wrong.

Truth becomes known through special exercises for collecting one's thoughts.

Some will aver from this, because certain objects are over-powering and because one is driven by hunger and the like, thus making the collection of one's thoughts an impossibility.

Collection, by means of Yoga, should be practiced in the forest, in caves, and along river banks.

One might conclude that in the final liberation there is a disturbing influence of externals.

This is not so, because there must be a body, capable of receiving such disturbing impressions. Yet, such does not exist, nor is any longer countenanced in the liberated condition.

With this in mind, we must prepare ourselves, with physical and mental restraint, and avail ourselves of the prescriptions regarding the self in Yoga discipline.

One should practice the acquisition of insight and discuss it with those who have such wisdom.

The truth-seeker should invite discussions with students, teachers, associates, distinguished people, those who strive for the *summum bonum,* and those who have a serene disposition.

If he desires, he may seek such discussion, without antithesis, merely for the occasion to solidify his own views.

Contests and disputes should be sought out in order to establish and guard the truth; just as one surrounds the seed corn with thorns and branches to protect it as it grows.

In these two kinds of argumentation, debates engaged in accordance with the rules for winning the argument are in order.

[65]

BURCKHARDT, JAKOB

BURCKHARDT, JAKOB (1818-1897). Burckhardt taught history and lived quietly, frugally, undisturbed, and independent of the good and evil of modern civilization in his native town of Basle. His *Kultur der Renaissance* (1860) made him famous in all civilized countries, but his dislike for publicity was so great, that even though he continued to study and collect ample material to fill many more volumes, he refrained from publishing any further works during his lifetime. His skill as a teacher, his gift for narrating facts and events and integrating them with all branches of knowledge and cultural activity as part of a continuous evolutionary pattern attracted students from many countries. After his death, his lectures were edited, and those entitled *Reflections on History* have been acknowledged as a major contribution to modern historiography.

Burckhardt, the historian, was an austere judge of morality. He often condemned morally that which he admired aesthetically. He regarded history as the best means for ridding the world of its illusion, for though he saw beyond the superficial veil, nevertheless he loved and admired its fallacious charm. His sympathy was always with defeated minorities; their defeat confirmed his conviction that success had little to do with merit insofar as active life was concerned. However, he did admit that in poetry and art, greatness and success were often identical. His disapproval of results never prevented him from studying their causes.

ON WAR

It is part of the wretchedness of life on earth that even the individual believes that he can only attain a full consciousness of his own value if he compares himself with others and, in certain circumstances, actually makes others feel it. The State, law, religion and morality are hard put to it to keep this bent within bounds, that is, to prevent its finding public expression. In the individual the open indulgence of it is regarded as ridiculous, intolerable, ill-mannered, dangerous, criminal.

On a big scale, however, nations from time to time assume that it is allowable and inevitable for them to fall upon each other on some pretext or other. The main pretext is that in international relations there is no other way of arriving at a decision, and: "If we don't, others will." We shall leave aside for the moment the highly diverse internal histories of the outbreaks of wars, which are often extremely complex.

A people actually feels its full strength as a people only in war, in the comparative contest with other peoples, because it only exists at that time. It must then endeavor to sustain its power at that level. Its whole standard has been enlarged.

In philosophic form, the dictum of Heraclitus, "war is the father of all things," is quoted in proof of the benefits of war. Lasaulx accordingly explains that antagonism is the cause of all growth, that harmony is born only of the conflict of forces, the "discordant harmony" or the "harmonious conflict" of things. This means, however, that both sides are still in possession of some vital energy, and not that one triumphs while the other lies prostrate. Indeed, according to him, war is divine in character, a world law and present in all nature. Not without cause do the Indians worship Shiva, the god of destruction. The warrior, he says, is filled with the joy of destruction, wars clear the air like thunderstorms, they steel the nerves and restore the heroic virtues, upon which States were originally founded, in place of indolence, double-dealing and cowardice. We might here also recall H. Leo's reference to "fresh and cheerful war, which shall sweep away the scrofulous mob."

Our conclusion is—men are men in peace as in war, and the wretchedness of earthly things lies equally upon them both. In any case, we generally suffer from an optical illusion in favour of those parties and their members with whose interests our own are in any way connected.

Lasting peace not only leads to enervation; it permits the rise of a mass of precarious, fear-ridden, distressful lives which would not have survived without it and which nevertheless clamour for their "rights," cling somehow to existence, bar the way to genuine ability, thicken the air and as a whole degrade the nation's blood. War restores real ability to honour. As for these wretched lives, war may at least reduce them to silence.

Further, war, which is simply the subjection of all life and property to *one* momentary aim, is morally vastly superior to the mere violent egoism of the individual; it develops power in the service of a supreme general idea and under a discipline which nevertheless permits supreme heroic virtue to unfold. Indeed, war alone grants to mankind the magnificent spectacle of a general submission to a general aim.

And since, further, only real power can guarantee a

peace and security of any duration, while war reveals where real power lies, the peace of the future lies in such a war.

Yet it should, if possible, be a just and honourable war —perhaps a war of defense such as the Persian War, which developed the powers of the Hellenes gloriously in all ways, or such as the war of the Netherlands against Spain.

Further, it must be a genuine war, with existence at stake. A permanent smouldering of small feuds, for instance, may replace war but is without value as a crisis. The German feudal heroes of the fifteenth century were highly astonished when they were confronted with an elemental power like the Hussites.

Nor did the disciplined "sport of kings" of the eighteenth century lead to much more than misery.

In quite a special sense, however, the wars of today are certainly aspects of a great general crisis, but individually they lack the significance and effect of genuine crises. Civilian life remains in its rut in spite of them, and it is precisely the pitiable existences referred to above which survive. But these wars leave behind them vast debts, i.e. they bequeath the main crisis to the future. Their brevity too deprives them of their value as crises. The full forces of despair do not come into play, and hence do not remain victorious on the field of battle, and yet it is they, and they alone, which could bring about a real regeneration of life, i.e. reconciliation in the abolition of an old order by a really vital new one.

Finally, it is quite unnecessary—as unnecessary as in the case of the barbarian invasion—to prophesy of all destruction that regeneration will come of it. It may be that this globe is already aged (nor does it matter how old it is in the absolute sense, i.e. how many times it has revolved round the sun—it may be very young for all that). We cannot imagine, in great tracts of denuded country, that new forests will ever arise to replace those which have been destroyed. And so peoples may be destroyed, and not even survive as component elements of other races.

And often it is the most righteous defense that has

proved most futile, and we must be thankful that Rome went so far as to proclaim the glory of Numantia, that conquerors have a sense of the greatness of the conquered.

The thought of a higher world plan, etc., is cold comfort. Every successful act of violence is a scandal, i.e. a bad example. The only lesson to be drawn from an evil deed successfully perpetrated by the stronger party is not to set a higher value on earthly life than it deserves.

[66]

BURKE, EDMUND

BURKE, EDMUND (1729-1797). The political pamphlets, parliamentary speeches, and essays of Burke proved him to be a genuine philosopher. His contemporaries, regardless of whether they shared his opinions, admired his talent for discerning the basic principles and elucidating the philosophical issues inherent in the disputes and interests of practical matters. Some of his essays, like *The Sublime and the Beautiful*, manifest the influence of Kant, Hegel, and many aestheticians of the eighteenth century. Despite his philosophical attitude toward the events of contemporary politics, Burke was always an ardent partisan, for his theoretical insights blended with his factious spirit and his realism with his romanticism. His morality demanded a rigorous honesty and cautious regard for actual circumstances, traditions, and expediences. He was always prepared to combat imminent dangers and great evil.

For more than three decades, Burke participated in political struggles. An Irishman by birth, and master of the English language, he was one of the greatest orators in the history of the British Parliament. Basically, he was convinced that the human individual is incapable of creating newness; that all useful and legitimate innovations must result from the slow growth of the collective mind in accordance with tradition. He strongly opposed changes in the British Constitution, whose excellent form was dogma to him. He fought for the removal of administrative abuses; opposed corruption, particularly the attempts of King George III to enslave both houses of Parliament. He denounced the French Revolution as a crime because it manifested a break with the past, served as a challenge to true wisdom and experience, and was a threat to liberty and prosperity. With his derision of the theory of the "Rights of Man," Burke became the vanguard of the European counter-revolution.

ON PUBLIC DISCONTENTS

IT is an undertaking of some degree of delicacy to examine into the cause of public disorders. If a man happens not to succeed in such an inquiry, he will be thought weak and visionary; if he touches the true grievance, there is a danger that he may come near to persons of weight and consequence, who will rather be exasperated at the discovery of their errors, than thankful for the occasion of correcting them. If he should be obliged to blame favorites of the people, he will be considered as the tool of power; if he censures those in power, he will be looked on as an instrument of faction. But in all exertions of duty something is to be hazarded. In cases of tumult and disorder, our law has invested every man, in some sort, with the authority of a magistrate. When the affairs of the nation are distracted, private people are by the spirit of that law, justified in stepping a little out of their ordinary sphere. They enjoy a privilege, of somewhat more dignity and effect, than that of idle lamentation over the calamities of their country. They may look into them narrowly; they may reason upon them liberally; and if they should be so fortunate as to discover the true source of the mischief, and to suggest any probable method of removing it, though they may displease the rulers for the day, they are certainly of service to the cause of Government. Government is deeply interested in everything which, even through the medium of some temporary uneasiness, may tend finally to compose the minds of the subjects, and to conciliate their affections. I have nothing to do here with the abstract value of the voice of the people. But as long as reputation, the most precious possession of every individual, and as long as opinion, the great support of the State, depend entirely upon that voice, it can never be considered as a thing of little consequence either to individuals or to Government. Nations are not primarily ruled by laws; less by violence. Whatever original energy may be supposed either in force or regulation;

the operation of both is, in truth, merely instrumental. Nations are governed by the same methods, and on the same principles, by which an individual without authority is often able to govern those who are his equals or his superiors; by a knowledge of their temper, and by a judicious management of it; I mean—when public affairs are steadily and quietly conducted: not when the Government is nothing but a continued scuffle between the magistrate and the multitude; in which sometimes the one and sometimes the other is uppermost; in which they alternately yield and prevail, in a series of contemptible victories and scandalous submissions. The temper of the people amongst whom he presides ought therefore to be the first study of a Statesman. And the knowledge, of this temper it is by no means impossible for him to attain, if he has not an interest in being ignorant of what it is his duty to learn.

To complain of the age we live in, to murmur at the present possessors of power, to lament the past, to conceive extravagant hopes of the future, are the common dispositions of the greatest part of mankind; indeed the necessary effects of the ignorance and levity of the vulgar. Such complaints and humors have existed in all times; yet as all times have not been alike, true political sagacity manifests itself, in distinguishing that complaint which only characterizes the general infirmity of human nature, from those which are symptoms of the particular distemperature of our own air and season.

[67]

BURROUGHS, JOHN

BURROUGHS, JOHN (1837-1921). Characterized as a nature lover, friend of birds and squirrels, scientist and poet in his descriptions of animal and plant life, John Burroughs stated that his two greatest sources of inspiration were Emerson, in his youth, and Bergson, in later life. In 1882 he wrote, "With Emerson dead it seems folly to be alive." When Bergson lectured at Columbia University, Burroughs assiduously attended each lecture (although

209

he did not understand French), and hailed the French philosopher as "the prophet of the soul" who had opened new vistas to him.

Throughout his lifetime, Burroughs longed for the solitude which would allow him to enjoy the "company of one's self." He liked to live in his cabin in the woods and devote himself to "prophets of the soul" and sensory perception. He strove to attain large perspectives, but he also thought that "little things explain great things." This principle directed his observations of nature, which to him epitomized the spirit. He regarded natural objects as spiritual symbols and relished their variety, but maintained that chance does not exist in nature, but that laws dominate even the oddest singularity. He rejected materialism, but declared that "the greatest materialists I know are the spiritualists." He believed in the unity of matter and spirit. A man of action as well as of contemplation, Burroughs was an efficient bank examiner and receiver. Among his steadfast friends, he numbered Walt Whitman and Theodore Roosevelt. Whether he was leading an isolated life or a socialized existence, his spirit and actions were always forcefully compelling. His books, *Wake-Robin* (1871), *Birds and Poets* (1877), *Fresh Fields* (1884), *Ways of Nature* (1905), and *Accepting the Universe* (1920), have become favorite reading.

CONTRADICTIONS IN LIFE

LIFE and nature and philosophy are full of contradictions. The globe upon which we live presents the first great contradiction. It has no under or upper side; it is all outside. Go around it from east to west, or from north to south, and you find no bottom or top such as you see on the globe in your study, or as you apparently see on the moon and the sun in the heavens. A fly at the South Pole of the schoolroom globe is in a reversed position, but the discoverers of the South Pole on our earth did not find themselves in a reversed position on their arrival there, or in danger of falling off. The sphere is a perpetual contradiction. It is the harmonization of opposites. Our minds are adjusted to planes and to right lines, to up and down, to over and under. Our action upon things is linear. Curves and circles baffle us. My mind cannot adjust itself to the condition of free empty space.

Transport yourself in imagination away from the earth to the vacancy of the interstellar regions. Can you convince yourself that there would be no over and no under, no east and no west, no north and no south? Would one not look down to one's feet, and lift one's hand to one's head? What could one do?—No horizontal, no vertical—just the negation of all motion and direction. If one rode upon a meteorite rushing toward the earth, would one have the sensation of falling? Could one have any sensation of motion at all in absolutely vacant space—no matter at what speed with reference to the stars one might be moving? To have a sense of motion must we not have also a sense of something not in motion? In your boat on the river, carried by the tide or the current, you have no sense of motion till you look shoreward. With your eye upon the water all is at rest. The balloonist floats in an absolute calm. The wind does not buffet him because he goes with it. But he looks down and sees objects beneath him, and he looks up and sees clouds or stars above him. Fancy him continuing his journey on into space till he leaves the earth behind him—on and on till the earth appears like another moon. Would he look up or down to see it? Would he have a sense of rising or of falling? If he threw out ballast, would it drop or soar, or would it refuse to leave him?

Such speculations show how relative our sense standards are, how the law of the sphere upon which we live dominates and stamps our mental concepts. Away from the earth, in free space, and we are lost; we cannot find ourselves; we are stripped of everything but ourselves; we are stripped of night and day, of up and down, of east and west, of north and south, of time and space, of motion and rest, of weight and direction. Just what our predicament would be, who can fancy?

[68]

BUTLER, SAMUEL

BUTLER, SAMUEL (1835-1902). Butler's novel *Erewhon*, published in 1872, has been compared with Swift's *Gulliver's Travels* and Voltaire's *Candide*. Together with *The Way of All Flesh*, written

1872-1885 and published posthumously in 1903, Butler's position as a master of the English novel was firmly established. It has been a matter of considerable speculation among biographers as to what caused Butler to delay publication of his second novel and forego success as a novelist. He was a man of wide interests and abilities: he painted; composed; critically examined the evidence for the Resurrection of Christ; criticized Darwin by maintaining that the principle of natural selection deprived life of its purposiveness and "banished mind from the universe"; outlined his own theory of evolution in *Life and Habit* (1877) and *Evolution Old and New* (1879); developed his ideas in *Unconscious Memory* (1880); and advanced a new hypothesis concerning the authorship of the *Odyssey*.

Butler liked to call himself the "enfant terrible" of literature and science. He was fond of destroying the idols of his contemporaries and treating ironically those convictions generally classed as fundamentally important to the substance of civilization. He was often disturbed by his own destructive tendencies and suffered because his dissent differed from the common creed. Butler, though a diffident personality and daring humorist was incapable of liberating his emotions from the fear and hatred of his father, even after the latter's death. In his human relationships, he was alternately an attractive and repugnant personality. He disliked the past, despised the present, feared the future, and most of all, was terrified by the technological developments in engineering and machinery that he considered fatal to humanity. His acute penetration of the shortcomings of his time made him a great satirist, but he owed his deepest insights to his constant dismay at the independence of his own thoughts.

NOTES

A DEFINITION is the enclosing a wilderness of ideas within a wall of words.

To live is to love; all reason is against it, and all healthy instinct for it.

NATURE. As the word is now commonly used, it excludes nature's most interesting productions: the works of man. Nature is usually taken to mean mountains, rivers, clouds, undomesticated animals, and plants. I am not indifferent to this half of nature, but it interests me much less than the other half.

Imagination depends mainly upon memory, but there is a small percentage of creation of something out of nothing with it. We can invent a trifle more than can be got by mere combination of remembered things.

All men can do great things, if they know what great things are. So hard is this last that even where it exists the knowledge is as much unknown as known to them that have it, and is more a leaning upon the Lord than a willing of one who willeth. And yet all this leaning on the Lord in Christendom fails if there be not a will of him that willeth to back it up. God and man are powerless without one another.

GENIUS and PROVIDENCE. Among all the evidences for the existence of an overruling Providence that I can discover, I see none more convincing than the elaborate and, for the most part, effectual provision that has been made for the suppression of genius. The more I see of the world, the more necessary I see it to be, that by far the greater part of what is written or done should be of so fleeting a character as to take itself away quickly. That is the advantage in the fact that so much of our literature is journalism.

Schools and colleges are not intended to foster genius and to bring it out. Genius is a nuisance, and it is the duty of schools and colleges to abate it by setting genius-traps in its way. They are as the artificial obstructions in a hurdle race, tests of skill and endurance, but in themselves useless. Still, so necessary is it that genius and originality should be abated that, did not academies exist, we should have had to invent them.

[69]

213

C

CALKINS, MARCY WHITON

CALKINS, MARCY WHITON (1863-1930). The creed of Calkins is expressed in four principal statements which are developed in her books: *The Persistent Problems of Philosophy* (1907) and *The Good Man and The Good* (1918). She proceeded from the conviction that the universe contained distinct mental realities; that although the mind had emerged from a lower level of existence, it no longer belonged to that level, but rather to a new order of existence which had special laws of behavior. These mental realities were ultimately personal; consciousness never occurred impersonally. She defined psychology as a "science of the self as conscious." She also asserted that the universe was throughout, mental; that whatever was real was ultimately mental and therefore personal. She concluded that the universe was an all-inclusive Self; an absolute Person; a conscious being. She maintained that philosophy meant metaphysics, which she defined as "the attempt by reasoning to know what is ultimately real." To her, metaphysics did not imply a return to animism, and she stated that it was compatible with the concepts of scientific laws and that reasoning separated metaphysics from mysticism. She was considerably influenced by Royce; opposed logical atomism and instrumentalism. On several problems, she agreed with Samuel Alexander, but claimed a greater consistency.

EGOISM AND ALTRUISM

PERHAPS the most fundamental contrast between conceptions of the good is that between individualistic or (as they used to be named) egoistic theories on the one hand, and social, or altruistic, conceptions on the other. It must, however, carefully be borne in mind that there is a sense in which a

214

self is always egoistic, for, whatever else a man is conscious of, he is always (though often very vaguely) conscious of himself. Similarly, there is a sense in which a self is always altruistically, or socially, conscious, for there is no really isolated self and even such predominantly "impersonal" experiences as thinking and perceiving have a social reference. That is to say, we are aware that other people, similarly placed, see what we see and hear what we hear; and we regard the laws of thought as universal, held by everybody. The clear understanding that every man is, in this fundamental sense, both egoist and altruist and that the two attitudes are not incompatible is an important introduction to the study of ethical egoism and altruism. For when a moral system is designated as egoistic (individualistic) or altruistic (social) either term is used, in a sense far narrower than that which has just been formulated, to indicate a basal form of willing.

It will be convenient first to present in a relatively uncritical fashion both the egoistic and the altruistic theory. Egoistic willing is, as we know, self-assertion, the subordination of my environment, personal or impersonal, to myself. And, from the standpoint of ethical egoism, the good which I ought to seek is precisely my own good, not that of anybody else. The argument for ethical individualism (or egoism), is variously stated. It is sometimes urged that the supreme object of will is a man's own good since only so can his will be directed toward that part of the universe, himself, which is under his own control. A man can not, it is argued, by his willing, alter the course of the sun or the conduct of a tradesman but he can affect his own conduct and he may gain his own pleasure, advantage, enlargement. Or again, it may be argued empirically that men actually reach their highest levels of achievement, develop their utmost strength and capacity, only under the spur of ambition, only in conditions of widest freedom, only through stressing their own individual purposes. The culmination of such a view is Nietzsche's teaching (as it is usually interpreted)—the doctrine that human progress is forever impossible except as each man relentlessly seeks his own advantage in total disregard of the needs of other men so that, out of the welter of failing, defeated beings there may emerge the superman —the man strong enough to trample down all rivalry and opposition and to win against all odds. Most often, however, egoism is argued negatively by the destructive criticism (presently to be summarized) of altruistic conceptions coupled with the implication that egoism is the only alternative to altruism.

Altruistic (or social) will—sharply contrasted with egoistic self-assertion—is loyalty, or devotion, the subordination of myself to a cause, a person, an ideal—in a word, to some object other than my narrow and individual self. The altruist conceives the moral self as furthering the happiness or the perfection no longer of himself but of another self or selves. To the altruist (in the strict meaning of the term) the good man is one who lavishes and sacrifices his own possessions, health, opportunities, his very life, for others. To be good consists in turning from one's own end, in crucifying, in torturing, in annihilating one's self so that one may thereby rescue, help, or enrich others. The mother who completely subordinates herself to her children is thus the never failing embodiment of the altruist's ideal. But there are as many forms of altruism as there are types of personal and social relationship. The cavalier who gives himself, body and soul, to the king's cause, the Jesuit who yields himself to his order, the union workman who goes on a sympathetic strike—these all are (or may well be) altruists. For the altruist abjures his own good and seeks that of other self or selves. And he appeals alike to the casual observer and to the close student of biography to confirm his view that the good men are altruists and that conversely, in Spencer's words, "an unchecked satisfaction of personal desires—in absolute disregard of all other beings would cause . . . social dissolution." Clearly, the altruist repeats, men who are ever seeking others' gains—devoted physicians, tireless teachers, lavish givers—

are willing a good to which the merely individual egoistic good must be subordinate. But the egoist is never silenced by this appeal to experience. He first notes as incidental to his argument, the patent fact that many alleged altruists are really egoists in disguise, seeking, under the cloak of avowed altruism, their individual ends: reputation or material gain. And next, admitting the sincerity of genuinely altruistic ideals, the egoist emphasizes the divergence among them and the difficulty of harmonizing the objects of the personal, the domestic, and the patriotic altruist. It is, on the face of it, equally altruistic to sacrifice oneself for one's parents, one's children, one's state; but altruism contains no principle by which to decide between these conflicting objects. With greatest effect, however, the critic attacks the fundamental position of altruism strictly defined, namely, disregard of oneself. Herein, he insists, the altruistic conception is essentially irrational. The mother who wears herself out in the passionate pursuit of what she deems best for her children is purposing to defeat her own end (for she is actually choosing a course which makes her useless to the very beings whose good she is willing); and the object of her will, involving as it does disregard of an individual life, her own, can not possibly be viewed as the incontrovertibly ultimate good. With Herbert Spencer, the critic of altruism, one may go further and argue that a completely altruistic world is inherently impossible since if literally every self wills another's good, thereby giving up his own, nobody experiences good and so the end sought by each altruistically willing self is nonexistent.

[70]

CAMPANELLA, TOMMASO

CAMPANELLA, TOMMASO (1568-1639). A resident of Naples, Campanella was sentenced to lifetime imprisonment during the Spanish rule, for political plotting and heresy. During this time, he wrote a valiant and courageous vindication of Galileo, who had been tried by the Inquisition. After twenty-seven years of incarceration, Campanella succeeded in escaping to France, where he remained for the remainder of his life under the aegis of Cardinal Richelieu. His work was a source of inspiration for Mersenne and other French philosophers; as well as Leibniz. His philosophy was a blend of medieval thought combined with the methods of modern science. A Dominican and partisan of the secular power of the Pope, his communistic utopia, outlined in *City of the Sun,* was ruled by an ideal Pope. He regarded the world as the "living statue of God." Eternal truth is perceptible through the study of nature and the Bible. Many of his ideas are similar to those of modern-day existentialists; for to him, neither the reports of the senses nor the speculations of reason, but only the feelings of one's own existence offer a reliable basis for the knowledge of God, man, and nature. Preservation of existence is the aim of all human activities, and the laws that make for this preservation not only compel man to love God, but also to make him desire to return to Him.

ON STATE CONTROLLED MARRIAGE

THE race is managed for the good of the commonwealth, and not of private individuals, and the magistrates must be obeyed. They deny what we hold—viz., that it is natural to man to recognize his offspring and to educate them, and to use his wife and house and children as his own. For they say that children are bred for the preservation of the species and not for individual pleasure, as St. Thomas also asserts. Therefore the breeding of children has reference to the commonwealth, and not to individuals, except in so far as they are constituents of the commonwealth. And since individuals for the most part bring forth children wrongly and educate them wrongly, they consider that they remove destruction from the State, and therefore for this reason, with most sacred fear, they commit the education of the children, who, as it were, are the element of the republic, to the care of magistrates; for the safety of the community is not that of a few. And thus they distribute male and female breeders of the best natures according to philosophical rules. Plato thinks that this distribution ought to be made by lot, lest some men seeing that they are kept away from the beautiful women,

218

should rise up with anger and hatred against the magistrates; and he thinks further that those who do not deserve cohabitation with the more beautiful women, should be deceived while the lots are being led out of the city by the magistrates, so that at all times the women who are suitable should fall to their lot, not those whom they desire.

This shrewdness, however, is not necessary among the inhabitants of the City of the Sun. For with them deformity is unknown. When the women are exercised they get a clear complexion, and become strong of limb, tall and agile, and with them beauty consists in tallness and strength. Therefore, if any woman dyes her face, so that it may become beautiful, or uses high-heeled boots so that she may appear tall, or garments with trains to cover her wooden shoes, she is condemned to capital punishment. But if the women should even desire them, they have no facility for doing these things. For who indeed would give them this facility? Further, they assert that among us abuses of this kind arise from the leisure and sloth of women. By these means they lose their color and have pale complexions, and become feeble and small. For this reason they are without proper complexions, use high sandals, and become beautiful not from strength, but from slothful tenderness. And thus they ruin their own tempers and natures, and consequently those of their offspring. Furthermore, if at any time a man is taken captive with ardent love for a certain woman, the two are allowed to converse and joke together, and to give one another garlands of flowers or leaves, and to make verses. But if the race is endangered, by no means is further union between them permitted. Moreover, the love born of eager desire is not known among them; only that born of friendship.

[71]

CARDOZO, BENJAMIN NATHAN

CARDOZO, BENJAMIN NATHAN (1870-1938). It has been said of Justice Cardozo, that "by the magic of his pen, he transmuted law into justice." He was one of the greatest American philosophers of law; chief judge of the Supreme Court of the State of New York, for more than ten years; Justice of the Supreme Court of the United States, and recipient of many honorary degrees.

Justice, to Cardozo, was "a concept far more subtle and indefinite than any that is yielded by mere obedience to a rule. It remains, to some extent, when all is said and done, the synonym of an aspiration, a mood of exaltation, a yearning for what is fine and high."

Despite all his sensitivity to the indefinite, Cardozo was also a thinker whose profundity never excluded clear and distinct concepts and definitions. He was aware of the paradoxes and tensions of his profession, yet remained capable of viewing things with plain and simple common sense. He always tried to synthesize law and life, by comprehending the stream of historical life and the chaotic drives of social and economic forces. He was conscious of the necessity for adapting existing forms to newly emergent trends. He was not a radical, but he was imbued with the spirit of democracy. Franklin D. Roosevelt, upon the death of Cardozo, called this scholar and wise man, a "great soul." Cardozo was devoted to the welfare of the nation, defended the rights of the individual, strove for harmony between contradictory interests, staunchly opposed selfish interests, and was a courageous fighter for liberty and truth.

LAW AND LIBERTY

WHEN we speak of law and liberty, and the need of compromise between them, what is uppermost in our minds is commonly the kind of problem that is involved in the definition of the constitutional immunity. In essence, however, the problem is not different whenever a rule of law is extended into fields unoccupied before. "Shall A answer to B for the consequences of an act?" means this and nothing more, "Shall the freedom of A to work damage to B be restrained so as to preserve to B the freedom to be exempt from damage?" In determining whether it shall, we must again evaluate the social interests concerned. We have regard to the social interest of certainty. The force of precedent and analogy may lead us to refuse an extension that we would otherwise concede. If these guides are silent or inconclusive, we give heed to the prompting of justice or of expediency, which may shade down from considerations of supreme importance to those of mere convenience. "Das Recht," as Binding puts it, "ist eine Ordnung menschlicher Freiheit." The opposites, liberty and restraint, the individual and the group, are phases of those wider opposites, the one and the many, rest and motion, at the heart of all being. Dichotomy is everywhere.

One of the marks by which we recognize a social interest as worthy of protection is the spontaneity and persistence with which groups are established to conserve it. The mark, of course, is not infallible. There are groups, spontaneous and persistent enough,—camorras, secret orders, revolutionary bands—whose aims are anti-social. Even so, spontaneity and persistence are tokens not to be ignored that the associative process is moving toward a social end. A striking instance of this truth is seen in the history of trade-unions. At first the law held them anathema. They were combinations in restraint of trade, pernicious, it was thought, in so far as they were effective, and, in the long run, as futile as they were pernicious, since economic "laws," then supposed to be inexorable, would nullify the gains of victory, and restore the pre-existing level. The result belied the prophecy. The urge to associate and unify was too spontaneous and persistent for any interdict to stifle it. The courts perceived and yielded. They were helped at times by legislation. In many jurisdictions, however, they reached the same result unaided. They gave up denouncing as lawless and unsocial a form of grouping that appeared and reappeared in response to a social pressure akin in steadiness and intensity to the pressure that makes law. Whether the unions were to be classified as jural persons was another question of quite subsidiary importance. What mattered most was that they were lawful. The state would hold them in check as it would hold in check the individual and even the agencies of government, it would not repudiate or destroy them. In the struggle between liberty and restraint, a new liberty, asserting itself persistently and clamorously in the minds and hearts of men, became a liberty secured by law. Out of the psychical urge there had been born the jural right. The peace of a new compromise had been declared between the warring opposites.

[72]

CARLYLE, THOMAS

CARLYLE, THOMAS (1795-1881). The writings of Carlyle differ considerably from those of Locke, Hume, Pope, Fielding, Macaulay, and John Stuart Mill. For Carlyle wrote emotionally; his language expressed passion, love, hate, enthusiasm, or scorn; nothing left him unmoved. He was a bitter enemy of the Age of Reason, and detested cold logic, intellectual abstraction, and scientific aloofness.

Although not an orthodox Protestant, he classed himself as a Christian for whom faith was the source of wisdom and the standard of criticism for life and art. Society, as he conceived it, was the brotherhood of men and the union of souls. He categorized political constitutions, class distinctions, political parties, and trade unions as the artificial products of human arrogance. He distrusted material progress, opposed the advances of modern civilization, and scoffed at the diseases and misfortunes of modern life. He maintained that the latter were curable, provided mankind was guided by great men. He derided universal suffrage, even though he sympathized with the Chartist movement. He preferred a kind of patriarchal feudalism to the governmental regulation of wages, or the bargaining process between management and labor.

Surely he was not a misanthrope, for he sincerely desired: the improvement of human conditions, a continuing spiritual development, and increased education for the masses. He asserted that great men would serve as the instruments by which those things would be accomplished, that they were the real trustees of the common interests of human happiness and could not be judged by the moral standards of the middle and lower classes. His theories led him to exalt Frederick William I of Prussia, the soldier king, whose principles became the tenets of fascism, and to praise the regime and wars of his son, Frederick II. A great admirer of German poetry and metaphysics, he considered both to be imbued with the true Christian spirit. Until his death he remained an optimist, always hoping for those events which would lead mankind back to a true Christian way of life.

WE have undertaken to discourse here for a little on Great
Men, their manner of appearance in our world's business,
how they have shaped themselves in the world's history, what
ideas men formed of them, what work they did;—on Heroes,
namely, and on their reception and performance; what I call
Hero-worship and the Heroic in human affairs. Too evidently
this is a large topic; deserving quite other treatment than we
can expect to give it at present. A larger topic; indeed, an
illimitable one; wide as Universal History itself. For, as I
take it, Universal History, the history of what man has accomplished in this world, is at bottom the History of the
Great Men who have worked here. They were the leaders of
men, these great ones; the modellers, patterns, and in a wide
sense creators, of whatsoever the general mass of men con-
trived to do or to attain; all things that we see standing
accomplished in the world are properly the outer material
result, the practical realization and embodiment, of Thoughts
that dwelt in the Great Men sent into the world: the soul of
the whole world's history, it may justly be considered, were
the history of these. Too clearly it is a topic we shall do no
justice to in this place!

One comfort is, that Great Men, taken up in any way,
are profitable company. We cannot look, however imperfectly, upon a great man, without gaining something by him.
He is the living light-fountain, which it is good and pleasant
to be near. The light which enlightens, which has enlightened
the darkness of the world; and this not as a kindled lamp
only, but rather as a natural luminary shining by the gift of
Heaven; a flowing light-fountain, as I say, of native original
insight, of manhood and heroic nobleness;—in whose radiance all souls feel that it is well with them. On any terms
whatsoever, you will not grudge to wander in such neighbour-
hood for a while. These Six classes of Heroes, chosen out of
widely distant countries and epochs, and in mere external
figure differing altogether, ought, if we look faithfully at

them, to illustrate several things for us. Could we see *them* well, we should get some glimpses into the very marrow of the world's history.

CARNEADES

CARNEADES (c. 214-129 B.C.). Carneades was born in Cyrene, North Africa. A radical sceptic, he was the first of the philosophers to pronounce the failure of metaphysicians who endeavored to discover rational meanings in religious beliefs. By 159 B.C. he had begun to refute all dogmatic doctrines, particularly Stoicism; nor did he spare the Epicureans as previous sceptics had done. The original theory of probability that he developed was profound and of great consequence. While he attacked the efforts of the Stoics to reconcile popular religions with their philosophical convictions, he also denied the immortality of the gods, their super-human qualities, pantheism, fatalism, and providence. He refused to accept moral values as absolute, although he taught the necessity of learning how to conduct one's life in an artful manner by combining sagacity and reflective thought. In his practical ethics, he professed a moderate Platonism, devoid of all religious or metaphysical elements. He founded the third or New Academy. However, his philosophy had very little in common with Plato, the original founder of the Academy.

THE FALLACY OF THE CRITERION OF TRUTH

THERE is absolutely no criterion for truth. For reason, senses, ideas, or whatever else may exist are all deceptive.

Even if such criterion were at hand, it could not stand apart from the feelings which sense impressions produce. It is the faculty of feeling that distinguishes the living creature from inanimate things. By means of that feeling, the living creature becomes perceptive of both itself and the external world. There is no sensation or perception of anything unless the sense is irritated, agitated, or perturbed. When an object is indicated, then the senses become irritated and somewhat disturbed. It is impossible that there be an unperturbed presentation of external things.

224

The subject is more or less persuaded by the image it perceives. The strength of that persuasion depends on the disposition of the subject and on the degree of irritation produced by the image. It is not the distinctness of the image that constitutes its credibility.

The only way we can ever obtain certitude is by the difficult process of examination. We cannot be satisfied with evidence that is incomplete and only probable. Our certitude is always a precarious one. Science relies on probability, not on certitude.

[74]

CARTESIUS. See DESCARTES, RENÉ.

CARUS, PAUL

CARUS, PAUL (1852-1919). The memory of the eclectic Paul Carus is kept alive by the Carus Foundation, the Carus Lectures, and the American Philosophical Association. Carus preferred to consider himself a theologian rather than a philosopher. He referred to himself as "an atheist who loved God." The fact was that he was a pantheist who insisted that God, as a cosmic order, was a name comprising "all that which is the bread of our spiritual life." He held the concept of a personal God as untenable. Carus' monism was more frequently associated with a kind of pantheism, although it was occasionally identified with positivism. His pantheistic theology regarded every law of nature as a part of God's being. Although when he maintained that the laws of mechanics represented the action of spiritual existence, it was never quite clear whether he meant that mechanics were a part of God's being, or more simply, that the matter was identical with mind; thus he did not commit himself as to the character of divinity. He acknowledged Jesus Christ as a redeemer, but not as the only one, for he believed that Buddha and other religious founders were equally endowed with the same qualities.

Carus tried to steer a middle course between idealistic metaphysics and materialism. He disagreed with metaphysicians because they "reified" words and dealt with them as though they were realities. He objected to materialism because it ignored or overlooked the importance of form. Carus constantly emphasized form by conceiving of the divinity as a cosmic order. He also objected to any monism which sought the unity of the world not in the unity of truth but in the oneness of a logical assumption of ideas. He referred to such concepts as *henism,* not monism. He stated that truth was independent of time, human desire, and human action. Therefore, science was not a human invention, but a human revelation which needed to be apprehended; discovery meant apprehension; it was the result or manifestation of the cosmic order in which all truths were ultimately harmonious.

MONISM

THE Monism which I represent insists on the reality of form and of relations, and on the significance of ideas. The soul of man is . . . his mind. He is not a mere heap of atoms. He consists of ideas. His existence is not purely material. It is also and principally spiritual. We grant there is no ego soul. There is as little a metaphysical thing-in-itself in man as there is a thing-in-itself of a watch or a tree, or a natural law. But nevertheless, just as much as that combination called a watch is not a nonentity but a reality, in the same way man's soul, in spite of the non-existence of a metaphysical ego soul, is not a nonentity but a reality; and the mold into which we have been cast is that divinity of the world which was at the beginning and will remain forever and aye.

The term Monism is often used in the sense of one substance theory that either mind alone or matter alone exists. These views generally called materialism, idealism or spiritualism, are pseudomonisms and would better be called henism. For either view attempts to explain the world from one single concept, deriving therefrom all natural phenomena. Monism does not attempt to subsume all phenomena under one category but remains conscious of the truth that spirit and matter, soul and body, God and world are different, not entities but abstract ideas denoting certain features of reality.

Monism is a unitary conception of the world—one inseparable and indivisible entirety.

Monism stands upon the principles that all the different truths are but so many different aspects of one and the same truth.

[75]

CASSIRER, ERNST

CASSIRER, ERNST (1874-1945). Cassirer's philosophy proceeds from the basic conviction that historical investigation and systematic order do not contradict each other, but rather are conditional and mutually support one another. Their result is the demonstration of the "immanent logic of history," based upon the critical examination of abundant empirical materials. Cassirer's works contributed to historical development of epistemology. In *Philosophie der Symbolischen Formen* (1924), he dealt with the functions of linguistic and mythical thinking, coordinating the world of pure knowledge with religious, mythical, and artistic ideas. Cassirer was firmly convinced that the different approaches to reality cooperate in the formation of a totality of meaning.

During the Kaiser's reign in Germany, he was denied appointment as a professor and tolerated only as a lecturer. Under the Hitler regime, he was compelled to emigrate—first, to Sweden, where he was a professor at the University of Goetenborg, then to the United States.

MAN, AN ANIMAL SYMBOLISM

In the human world we find a new characteristic which appears to be the distinctive mark of human life. The functional circle of man is not only quantitatively enlarged; it has also undergone a qualitative change. Man has, as it were, discovered a new method of adapting himself to his environment. Between the receptor system and the effector system, which are to be found in all animal species, we find in man a third link which we may describe as the *symbolic system*. This new acquisition transforms the whole of human life. As compared with the other animals man lives not merely in a broader reality; he lives, so to speak, in a new *dimension* of reality. There is an unmistakable difference between organic reactions and human responses. In the first case a direct and immediate answer is given to an outward stimulus; in the second case the answer is delayed. It is interrupted and retarded by a slow and complicated process of thought. At first sight such a delay may appear to be a very questionable gain. Many philosophers have warned man against this pretended progress. "L'Homme qui médite," says Rousseau, "est un animal dépravé": it is not an improvement but a deterioration of human nature to exceed the boundaries of organic life.

Yet there is no remedy against this reversal of the natural order. Man cannot escape from his own achievement. He cannot but adopt the conditions of his own life. No longer in a merely physical universe, man lives in a symbolic universe. Language, myth, art, and religion are parts of this universe. They are the varied threads which weave the symbolic net, the tangled web of human experience. All human progress in thought and experience refines upon and strengthens this net. No longer can man confront reality immediately; he cannot see it, as it were, face to face. Physical reality seems to recede in proportion as man's symbolic activity advances. Instead of dealing with the things themselves man is in a sense constantly conversing with himself. He has so enveloped himself in linguistic forms, in artistic images, in mythical symbols or religious rites that he cannot see or know anything except by the interposition of this artificial medium. His situation is the same in the theoretical as in the practical sphere. Even here man does not live in a world of hard facts, or according to his immediate needs and desires. He lives rather in the midst of imaginary emotions, in hopes and fears, in illusions and disillusions, in his fantasies and dreams. "What disturbs and alarms man," said Epictetus, "are not the things, but his opinions and fancies about the things."

From the point of view at which we have just arrived we may correct and enlarge the classical definition of man. In spite of all the efforts of modern irrationalism this definition of man as an *animal rationale* has not lost its force. Rationality is indeed an inherent feature of all human activ-

ities. Mythology itself is not simply a crude mass of super-
stitions or gross delusions. It is not merely chaotic, for it
possesses a systematic or conceptual form. But, on the other
hand, it would be impossible to characterize the structure of
myth as rational. Language has often been identified with
reason, or with the very source of reason. But it is easy to
see that this definition fails to cover the whole field. It is a
pars pro toto; it offers us a part for the whole. For side by
side with logical or scientific language there is a language
of poetic imagination. Primarily language does not express
thoughts or ideas, but feelings and affections. And even a
religion "within the limits of pure reason" as conceived and
worked out by Kant is no more than a mere abstraction. It
conveys only the ideal shape, only the shadow, of what a
genuine and concrete religious life is. The great thinkers
who have defined man as an *animal rationale* were not empiricists, nor did they ever intend to give an empirical account of human nature. By this definition they were expressing rather a fundamental moral imperative. Reason is a
very inadequate term with which to comprehend the forms
of man's cultural life in all their richness and variety. But
all these forms are symbolic forms. Hence, instead of defining man as an *animal rationale,* we should define him as
an *animal symbolicum.* By so doing we can designate his
specific difference, and we can understand the new way open
to man—the way to civilization.

[76]

CHERNYSHEVSKY, NICOLAI GAVRILOVICH

CHERNYSHEVSKY, NICOLAI GAVRILOVICH (1828-1889).
After the assassination of Czar Alexander II of Russia, the secret
police, in order to avoid a similar recurrence on the occasion of the
coronation of the new Czar, affected a compromise with the revolutionary groups. The latter demanded the liberation of Chernyshevsky as the principal condition for their refraining from an attempt
on the Czar's life.

Chernyshevsky did not belong to any revolutionary organiza-

tion or party. He had been sentenced, after two years of imprisonment in a fortress, to seven years hard labor and lifelong banishment
to Siberia.

The son of an orthodox priest, educated in the spirit of Russian
orthodoxy, he adopted the views of Feuerbach, Fourier, Proudhon,
and John Stuart Mill, whose *Principles of Political Economy* he
had translated into Russian. His interpretation and critical notes
on Mill's work not only proved Chernyshevsky's independent mind,
but also pointed up the social problems of Russia. As a member
of the staff of the influential periodical, *Sovremennik* (Contemporary), he introduced the spirit of Western civilization into Russia
and defended the interests of the peasants against the great land-
owners before and after the emancipation of the serfs. He believed
that philosophical materialism was the basis for social progress,
but that ethics of self-discipline and altruism were also needed.
As prisoner in the Peter and Paul fortress, he wrote the novel,
What Is To Be Done, (1863) which was a source of inspiration
to Russian youth until the First World War.

Chernyshevsky returned to St. Petersburg in 1881, his health
undermined, forced to live in isolation, and dependent upon translating as a means of livelihood. Until the 1905 Russian revolution,
censorship did not permit any mention of his name. His works
were printed anonymously, but the Russian people recognized him
as the author, and revered him as the martyr of free thought.

THE EVOLUTION OF LANGUAGE

PHILOLOGY shows that all languages begin with that stage in
which there is no declension, no conjugation, and no change
of aspect or inflection in the word, and each case of everything assumes one and the same form. Modern Chinese serves
as an example of this.

As language becomes more developed, inflection appears with greater frequency. The composition of the word
reaches the kind of flexibility that is characteristic of the
Semitic dialects. Language acquires the extreme abundance
of grammatical suffixes that are observable in Tartarian
where the verb has seven or eight moods, a full dozen tenses,
and ten gerundial forms. In our own linguistic family, the
highest point of that evolution is marked by Sanskrit. But
evolution continues; in Latin and Old Slavic, there is less

inflection than there is in Sanskrit. The longer a language lives, and the more people develop it by speaking, the more it tends to get rid of the old richness of inflection. Modern Slavic dialects are poorer than Old Slavic. There is less inflection in Italian, French, Spanish, and other Romance languages than there is in Latin; less inflection in German, Danish, Swedish, and Dutch, than in Gothic. English is indicative of the goal towards which all European languages will march, as far as inflection is concerned.

At the onset of linguistic evolution, there are no cases; neither are there any at the end. In the grammatical evolution of language, the end corresponds to the beginning. The same fact is reproduced in all forms of intellectual and social life which have language as the common condition of their subsistence.

[77]

CHRYSIPPUS

CHRYSIPPUS (c. 280-207 B.C.). The Stoic school of philosophy, established by Zeno, would not have had as lasting an influence had not Chrysippus developed and solidified its concepts. He was born in Soli, Cilicia, Asia Minor, and went to Athens in 260 B.C. There he succeeded Cleanthes as director of the Stoic school. Chrysippus is said to have written some seven hundred books on a variety of topics. Although his literary style was far from masterful, he was a systematic thinker, logician, and psychologist. He anticipated several important propositions which were of considerable consequence in later eras. He particularly investigated sentiments and ideas, and tried to obtain through logical and dialectical disquisitions the irrefutable truths upon which his ethics and theology were based. He stated that the essential characteristic of man which distinguished him from the animals was that his judgment became active as soon as his sensations were irritated. In ethics, Chrysippus assumed that a natural impetus operated in all living creatures. This impetus was conscious in man. He did not see any dichotomy between the decision of human will and that of natural impetus. Nature, striving for virtue, made the natural impetus.

231

THE slightest thing that happens takes place in accordance with nature and its reason.

Common nature is spread throughout all things. Therefore whatever happens in the universe is in accordance with common nature and its reason, and therefore proceeds in an unhindered fashion. There is nothing outside the universe to oppose its working, nor can any of its parts be moved or conditioned in a fashion other than that which is agreeable to common nature.

Sometimes good men suffer misfortunes, not as punishment for wickedness, but in accordance with some other lines of administration.

Just as states which have a surplus population send great numbers of their people out to the colonies, and stir up wars against their neighbor, so God provides occasion for our destruction.

It is unreasonable to say that the deity is the cause of base deeds. Just as law cannot be the cause for misdemeanor, so God cannot be the cause of impiety.

Homer correctly stated: "The will of Zeus is done"; referring to the fate and nature of the universe by which all things are governed.

[78]

CHUANG CHOU

CHUANG CHOU (c. 340-280 B.C.). Modern experts on Chinese philosophy consider Chuang Chou as among the most brilliant of all the Chinese philosophers. He was a scholar, a poet, and a master of dialectic and logic. Aware of the unity of the universe, he longed for "the transcendental bliss" which brought peace of mind and enabled man to live harmoniously with nature. His ability at logic and dialectics made him appear to be a cynical debunker, fond of destroying renowned illusions, but his love of freedom was too great to allow him to deny the values of government and society; he often declined high office in order to retain his personal independence. As a formidable adversary of Confucius, he was frequently and severely criticized by Mencius. If Chuang Chou was not the founder of that which was subsequently called Taoism, certainly he was its precursor, and the extent of his soaring imagination, the profundity of his thought, and the power of his style were never matched by any of the Taoists.

EXCURSIONS INTO FREEDOM

IN THE Northern Ocean there is a fish, its name the Kun [Leviathan], its size I know not how many *li*. By metamorphosis it becomes a bird called the P'eng ['Roc'], with a back I know not how many *li* in extent. When it rouses itself and flies, its wings darken the sky like clouds. With the sea in motion this bird transports itself to the Southern Ocean, the Lake of Heaven. In the words of Ch'i Hsieh, a recorder of marvels, 'When the P'eng transports itself to the Southern Ocean, it thrashes the water for three thousand *li*, and mounts in a whirlwind to the height of ninety thousand *li*, and flies continuously for six months before it comes to rest.'

A mote in a sunbeam (that in one sense is all that this vast Roc is): flying dust which living creatures breathe in and out! And that blueness of the sky! Is it an actual color, or is it the measureless depth of the heavens which we gaze at from below and see as 'blue,' just like that and nothing more? Again take water, without the dense accumulation of which there is no power for the floating of a great ship. And (think of) a cup of water upset in a corner of the hall. A tiny mustard seed becomes a ship (afloat), but the cup which held the water will remain aground because of the shallowness of the water and the size of the cup as a ship.

So with the accumulation of wind, without sufficient density it has no power to float huge wings. Thus it is that the P'eng has to rise ninety thousand *li* and cut off the wind beneath it. Then and not before, the bird, borne up by the down-pressed wind, floats in the azure heavens with secure support. Then and not before, it can start on its journey south.

233

A cicada and a young dove giggled together over the P'eng. The cicada said, 'When we exert ourselves to fly up on to the tall elms, we sometimes fail to get there and are pulled back to the ground; and that is that. Why then should any one mount up ninety thousand *li* in order to go south?' Well, the man who goes out to the grassy country near by takes only three meals with him and comes back with his stomach well filled. But the man who has to travel a hundred *li* grinds flour for one night on the way; and the man who has to travel a thousand *li* requires food for three months. These two little creatures (the cicada and the dove), what can they know?

Small knowledge is not equal to great knowledge, just as a short life is not equal to a long one. How do we know this to be so? The mushroom with one brief morning's existence has no knowledge of the duration of a month. The chrysalis knows nothing of the spring and the autumn.

Thus it is that the knowledge of some men qualifies them for a small office and for effecting unity in one district, whilst the moral power of another man fits him to be a ruler and proves itself throughout a whole country. These men have a view of themselves which is like the quail's view of himself.

On the other hand, Master Yung of Sung State just laughs at these men. If the whole world should admire or criticize him, he would neither be encouraged nor discouraged. Having determined the difference between what is intrinsic and what extrinsic, he disputed the accepted boundaries of honor and dishonor. In this he was himself, and there are very few such men in the world. Nevertheless he was not really rooted.

Take Master Lieh. He could drive the wind as a team and go, borne aloft, away for fifteen days before returning. Such a man attains a happiness which few possess. Yet in this although he had no need to walk, there was still something on which he was dependent [viz. the wind]. Supposing, however, that he were borne on the normality of the heavens and earth, driving a team of the six elements in their changes, and thus wandered freely in infinity-eternity, would there be anything then on which he was dependent?

Thus it is that I say, 'The perfect man has no self, the spirit-endowed man no achievements, the sage no reputation.'

[79]

CICERO, MARCUS TULLIUS

CICERO, MARCUS TULLIUS (106-43 B.C.). The tremendous historical influence of Cicero's philosophical writings cannot be underestimated. It is evident in the works of the Church fathers, Petrarch, Erasmus, and Copernicus. Even Voltaire, among whose many talents the quality of admiration was the least developed, praised two of Cicero's books as "of the noblest works that were ever written." The founding fathers of the United States were equally ardent in their admiration of Cicero. Thomas Jefferson read *De Senectute* (On Old Age) every year; John Adams, the second President of the United States, declared that "all the epochs of world history combined were unable to produce statesman or philosopher as great as Cicero. His authority should have considerable weight." His son, John Quincy Adams, while lecturing at Harvard University, supported Cicero's doctrine that eloquence was the mainstay of liberty. Theodor Mommsen, in his famous *Roman History*, used all his education, ability, and authority to debunk Cicero; for it had become fashionable to abuse and sneer at Cicero as a politician and philosopher. Thadaeus Zielinski, the great Russian philologist, asserted that of all Julius Caesar's achievements none was as important to the history of human civilization as the fact that Caesar, by compelling Cicero to retire to the country, forced the latter to state his philosophy in writing.

It is somewhat difficult to define either Cicero's originality or lack of it, since the works of those Greek philosophers from whom he allegedly borrowed his ideas are lost. One idea was certainly his own: the doctrine that "no war should be undertaken, except to maintain good faith or security."

ON FRIENDSHIP

THE right course is to choose for a friend one who is frank, sociable and sympathetic—that is, one who is likely to be influenced by the same motives as yourself—since all these qualities induce to loyalty; for it is impossible for a man to be loyal whose nature is full of twists and twinings; and, indeed, one who is untouched by the same influences as yourself and is naturally unsympathetic cannot be loyal.

Since happiness is our best and highest aim we must, if we would attain it, give our attention to virtue, without which we can obtain neither friendship nor any other desirable thing; on the other hand, those who slight virtue and yet think that they have friends perceive their mistake at last when some grievous misfortune causes them to put their friends to the test. Virtue both creates the bond of friendship and preserves it. For in virtue is complete harmony, in her is permanence, in her is fidelity; and when she has raised her head and shown her own light, and recognized the same light in another, she moves towards it and in turn receives its beams; as a result love or friendship leaps into flame.

We must despair of the safety of the man whose ears are so closed to truth that he cannot hear what is true from a friend. For there is shrewdness in that well-known saying of Cato: "Some men are better served by their bitter-tongued enemies than by their sweet-smiling friends; because the former often tell the truth; the latter, never."

*　　*　　*

New friendships are not to be scorned if they offer hope of bearing fruit, like green shoots of corn that do not disappoint us at harvest time; yet the old friendships must preserve their own place, for the force of age and habit is very great.

In the intimacy existing between friends and relatives the superior should put himself on a level with his inferior, so the latter ought not to grieve that he is surpassed by the former in intellect, fortune or position. Even if you could bestow upon another any honor you chose, yet you must consider what he is able to bear.

Difference of character is attended by difference of

taste and it is this diversity of taste that severs friendships; nor is there any other cause why good men cannot be friends to wicked men, or wicked men to good men, except that there is the greatest possible difference between them in character.

We must be ever on the search for some persons whom we shall love and who will love us in return; for if good will and affection are taken away, every joy is taken from life.

[80]

ON JUSTICE

THE great foundation of justice is faithfulness, which consists in being constantly firm to your word, and a conscientious performance of all compacts and bargains. The vice that is opposite to justice is injustice, of which there are two sorts: the first consists in the actual doing an injury to another; the second, in tamely looking on while he is injured, and not helping and defending him though we are able. He that injuriously falls on another, whether prompted by rage or other violent passion, does, as it were, leap at the throat of his companion; and he that refuses to help him when injured, and to ward off the wrong if it lies in his power, is as guilty of injustice as though he had deserted his father, his friends or native country.

It is observable that the limits of justice are not fixed. Respect must be had to general rules as the ground and foundation of all justice—first, that no injury be done to another; and, secondly, that we make it our earnest endeavor to promote the good of all mankind: so that our duty is not always the same, but various, according to circumstances.

*   *   *

There are certain duties to be strictly observed, even towards those who have injured us; for we ought not to go beyond certain bounds in exacting revenge and punishment of another; in which particular it may, perhaps, be enough

237

to make him that has wronged us repent of the wrong done, so that both he himself may abstain from the like, and others may be discouraged from injuring us in the future.

There are certain peculiar laws of war, also, which are of all things most strictly to be observed in the commonwealth; for there being two sorts of disputing in the world, the one by reason, and the other by open force; and the former of these being that which is agreeable to the nature of man, and the latter to that of brutes. When we cannot obtain what is our right by the one, we must of necessity have recourse to the other. It is allowable, therefore, to undertake wars, but it must always be with the design of obtaining a secure peace; and when we have got the better of our enemies, we should rest content with the victory alone unless they are such as have been very cruel and committed inhuman barbarities in the war. In my opinion, it is always our duty to do what we can for a fair and safe peace.

Unless a man be governed by the rules of justice, and fight for the safety and good of the public, his is a sort of courage that is altogether blamable.

[80A]

CLAIRVAUX, SAINT BERNARD OF. See BERNARD OF CLAIRVAUX, SAINT.

CLEANTHES

CLEANTHES (310-232 B.C.). Noted as a director of the oldest Stoic school for thirty-one years, Cleanthes, an indigent scholar, worked mostly as a porter until finally, at the age of fifty, he was enabled to enter a philosopher's school. He became a devoted disciple of Zeno, the Stoic, studied under his master for nineteen years, and upon Zeno's death, assumed the directorship of the school. Cleanthes slightly modified Zeno's doctrine. He was also famous as a poet; of his forty works, all of them very short, many fragments are extant. A large portion of his most famous poem, *Hymn to Zeus,* has been preserved. Even as head of the school, and despite his advanced years, Cleanthes continually astonished his friends by hoisting heavy loads and earning his living by manual work.

Great Jove, most glorious of the immortal gods,
Wide known by many names, Almighty One,
King of all nature, ruling all by law,
We mortals thee adore, as duty calls;
For thou our Father art, and we thy sons,
On whom the gift of speech thou hast bestowed
Alone of all that live and move on earth.
Thee, therefore, will I praise; and ceaseless show
To all thy glory and thy mighty power.
This beauteous system circling round the earth
Obeys thy will, and, whereso'er thou leadest,
Freely submits itself to thy control.
Such is, in thine unconquerable hands,
The two-edged, fiery, deathless thunderbolt;
Thy minister of power, before whose stroke
All nature quails, and, trembling, stands aghast;
By which the common reason thou dost guide,
Pervading all things, filling radiant worlds,
The sun, the moon, and the host of stars.
So great art thou, the universal King.
Without thee naught is done on earth, O God!
Nor in the heavens above nor in the sea;
Naught save the deeds unwise of sinful men.
Which sinful men, blinded, forsake and shun,
Deceived and hapless, seeking fancied good.
Yet harmony from discord thou dost bring;
That which is hateful, thou dost render fair;
Evil and good dost so co-ordinate,
That everlasting reason shall bear sway;
The law of God they will not see nor hear;
Which if they would obey, would lead to life.
But thou, O Jove! the giver of all good,
Darting the lightning from thy home of clouds,
Permit not man to perish darkling thus;
From folly save them; bring them to the light;
Give them to know the everlasting law

By which in righteousness thou rulest all;
That we, thus honored, may return to thee
Meet honor, and with hymns declare thy deeds,
And, though we die, hand down thy deathless praise.
Since nor to men nor gods is higher meed,
Than ever to extol with righteous praise
The glorious, universal King Divine.

[81]

CLEMENCEAU, GEORGES

CLEMENCEAU, GEORGES (1841-1929). When Woodrow Wilson promulgated his famous Fourteen Points, Clemenceau remarked that "Our Father in Heaven would have been content with ten." This and others of his sayings caused Americans to regard his character as that of a cynical politician, narrow-minded French nationalist, advocate of power politics, and victim of French propaganda. The Germans did not like him. In 1871 he had protested against the peace dictated by Bismarck; he always expressed a hope for the return of Alsace to France; during World War I, he encouraged the French to resist and vanquish the German onslaught; and he was held responsible for the harsh conditions of the Treaty of Versailles. Clemenceau was feared and detested by a large group of the French people, by the majority of the deputies, and by those of the radical party, to which he himself belonged. French rightists hated him because as a defender of the Republic, he was also an opponent of clericalism; French leftists hated him because he crushed strikes and persecuted defeatists. Clemenceau was not only the most striking and vigorous of the French statesmen of his time, a formidable enemy, and genius of invective; he was also sincerely and fanatically devoted to the ideals of reason and freedom, which he regarded as compatible with his stern patriotism. He always remained a democrat. One of the last acts of his administration was the introduction of the eight-hour day for France. He had also been a resolute defender of Alfred Dreyfus. It was Clemenceau who formulated the title of Zola's famous letter, *J'Accuse*, who fully rehabilitated Dreyfus, and who appointed Colonel Picquart, (who had been persecuted because he was a witness to the innocence of Dreyfus), to the post of minister of war.

Clemenceau, a highly educated man, had lived in the United States, and intimately knew Latin America and many European countries. He was a trained art critic, a successful dramatist and novelist, and a profound thinker who meditated on the meaning of life, the charm of illusion, and the destiny of mankind. Almost all of his plays and novels are imbued with a philosophical spirit; so is his historical study, *Demosthenes* (1926). His great work, *In the Evening of My Thought* (1929), stands as proof that he overcame those temptations which make for lulled minds among many aged philosophers.

KNOWLEDGE AND EMOTION

IDEALISM is not the result of logical thinking. It grows from man's making the greatest effort of which he is capable. Since the directing principle of man cannot be the avoidance of suffering at any price, and if it is, in fact, a fine thing to accept suffering, yet scorn it, to seek it, yet despise it, as did the ancient martyrs in their generous ardor for noble achievement, then idealism can lift man to the highest pinnacle of his destiny, through supreme suffering in the service of an idea. The beauty of great causes, to which what is best in human life is attached, is revealed in the band of heroic men, known and unknown, who chose to sacrifice their lives without thought of reward for the keen joy of unselfishly doing their duty.

What then can we gain by refusing to admit scientific facts, in order to accept the hallucination of a future life beyond the confines of this world, charming only because of its unreality? Can we successfully substitute for the positive world the dream of an imaginary existence upon which to expend our energies? It is a great temptation to make promises which we have no intention of keeping. That is what is most obvious about the march to the imaginary star of eternal human felicity.

Evolution of knowledge must increase the instruments of our activity. Will it then make us happier, more powerful, longer-lived? To answer these questions with certainty would require nothing short of a precise definition of eternal happiness—than which nothing is less stable, less subject to definition, or more various for each and all of us. Experience proves that to our innermost sensibility, the fleeting happiness of each of us is in himself and in the satisfaction that lies in his power to adapt himself to his surroundings. Thus decrees the subjective character of the sensation of happiness, sometimes common and sometimes refined, to which we aspire, usually without being able to realize it except through anticipations that are found baseless as soon as they are formed. Knowledge supplies the means for momentary or durable happiness. These means we must utilize. Each person can be at least temporarily happy within his own limitations, according to how high or how low is his conception of life, and according to how great is the personal will-power which acquired knowledge and strength of character have allowed him to devote to the task.

How many will be able to understand this fact, and amid the vicissitudes of human society, such as invasions, wars, epidemics, and every other form of catastrophe, how many will have the chance even partly to act on it? The pitiless struggle for existence in time of peace has on the whole caused as much misery and death as have pitched battles. The simple-minded ideologue suggests that a remedy will be found in new social conditions which will do away with these evils, and which will automatically bring peace to men. Just so their even more simple-minded predecessors thought to alleviate earthly woe by the promise of an indefinitely adjourned happiness in an unknown, but eternal paradise—an enchanting land of inaction which, since happiness is dependent on action, is a contradiction in terms. To see what effect it has had on matters earthly one need only examine human history.

The inevitable growth of knowledge, freed through the growth of character from being dominated by emotion, could then only facilitate our achievement of that happiness which we never cease to desire, but which seems only too often to vanish when we think we have grasped it. Our ancestors of 1789 were innocent enough to believe that a mild, indulgent code would bring about a state of perfect happiness. Apt pupils of the Church, those 'liberators,' trusting at first, like

242

their masters, to the formulae of universal love, soon came to enforce them on the scaffold. To suppress the adversary in order to suppress his opinions is the dogmatic idea. The first benefit brought us by relative knowledge is the doctrine of universal tolerance. It is unfortunate that our empiricism has not progressed beyond the point of doing more than recommending its practice.

[82]

CLEMENT OF ALEXANDRIA

CLEMENT OF ALEXANDRIA (c. 150-215 A.D.). The pagan philosopher, Celsus, one of the most ardent opponents of Christianity, noticed (c. 150 A.D.) that the dispersed Christian communities were tending toward a closer organization, toward a unified doctrine and common acceptance of a canon of sacred scriptures, and toward a uniformity in their methods of interpretation. What Celsus apprehended was the early formation of a Church that claimed to be Catholic. The first spiritual representative of that Church was Clement. He was also the father of Christian apologetics based upon a faith in divine revelation, but adapted to philosophical concepts. These prevail unto modern days. He adapted the *Philo* (the general concepts of the Jews) to the aims and needs of the nascent Christian Church, although the details of his system of defense of Christianity more closely paralleled the theology of the Stoics. He is principally remembered as the creator of Christian apologetics, but the other doctrines he enunciated were not permanently accepted by the Church.

Prior to his conversion to Christianity, he traveled extensively through Egypt, Italy, Syria, and Palestine. He was initiated into the mysteries of Eleusis; imbued with the Gnostic spirit, and with the pre-Christian doctrines of salvation which were rooted in Oriental mysticism and integrated with Greek philosophy. He was well acquainted with the books of the Bible, including those which were not incorporated into the canon, and he was well versed in pagan philosophy. His books, *Protrepticus* (Exhortations), *Paidagogus*, and *Stromateis* (Carpet-Bags), were appeals to both educated Christians and pagans. He stated that the simple Christian faith was sufficient for the salvation of man and promised greater knowledge to those who were initiated with Christian philosophy. Logos, not God nor Christ, was the centrifugal point of his teachings. He defined faith as obedience to the reason of Logos. He maintained that philosophy did not make faith a verity but opened the way to complete safety from error, and strengthened the elan toward the deity. He promised pagans deification if they adopted the Christian faith.

EXHORTATION TO THE GREEKS

BUT, you say, it is not reasonable to overthrow a way of life handed down to us from our forefathers. Why then do we not continue to use our first food, milk, to which, as you will admit, our nurses accustomed us from birth? Why do we increase or diminish our family property, and not keep it for ever at the same value as when we received it? Why do we no longer sputter into our parents' bosoms, nor still behave in other respects as we did when infants in our mothers' arms, making ourselves objects of laughter? Did we not rather correct ourselves, even if we did not happen to have good attendants for this purpose? Again, in voyages by sea, deviations from the usual course may bring loss and danger, but yet they are attended by a certain charm. So, in life itself, shall we not abandon the old way, which is wicked, full of passion, and without God? And shall we not, even at the risk of displeasing our fathers bend our course towards the truth and seek after Him who is our real Father, thrusting away custom as some deadly drug? This is assuredly the noblest of all the tasks we have in hand, namely, to prove to you that it was from madness and from this thrice miserable custom that hatred of godliness sprang. For such a boon, the greatest that God has ever bestowed upon the race of men, could never have been hated or rejected, had you not been clean carried away by custom, and so had stopped your ears against us. Like stubborn horses that refuse to obey the reins, and take the bit between their teeth, you fled from our arguments. You yearned to shake yourselves free from us, the charioteers of your life; yet all the while you were being carried along by your folly towards the precipices of destruction, and supposed the holy Word of God to be accursed. Accordingly the recompense of your choice attends upon you, in the words of Sophocles,

Lost senses, useless ears, and fruitless thoughts;

and you do not know that this is true above all else, that the good and god-fearing, since they have honored that which is good, shall meet with a reward that is good; while the wicked, on the other hand, shall meet with punishment corresponding to their deeds: and torment hangs over the head of the prince of evil. At least, the prophet Zechariah threatens him: "He that hath chosen Jerusalem take vengeance upon thee! Behold, is not this a brand plucked out of the fire?" What a strange longing, then, is this for a self-chosen death which still presses upon men? Why have they fled to this death-bearing brand, with which they shall be burnt up, when they might live a noble life according to God, not according to custom? For God grants life; but wicked custom inflicts unavailing repentance together with punishment after we depart from this world. And "by suffering even a fool will learn" that daemon-worship leads to destruction, and the fear of God to salvation.

Let any of you look at those who minister in the idol temples. He will find them ruffians with filthy hair, in squalid and tattered garments, complete strangers to baths, with claws for nails like wild beasts; many are also deprived of their virility. They are an actual proof that the precincts of the idols are so many tombs or prisons. These men seem to me to mourn for the gods, not to worship them, and their condition provokes pity rather than piety. When you see sights like this, do you still remain blind and refuse to look up to the Master of all and Lord of the universe? Will you not fly from the prisons on earth, and escape to the pity which comes from heaven? For God of His great love still keeps hold of man; just as, when a nestling falls from the nest, the mother bird flutters above, and if perchance a serpent gapes for it,

Flitting around with cries, the mother mourns for her offspring.

Now God is a Father, and seeks His creature. He remedies the falling away, drives off the reptile, restores the nestling to strength again, and urges it to fly back to the nest. Once more, dogs who have lost their way discover their master's tracks by the senses of smell, and horses who have thrown their rider obey a single whistle from their own master; "the ox," it is written, "knoweth his owner, and the ass his master's crib, but Israel doth not know Me." What then does the Lord do? He bears no grudge; He still pities, still requires repentance of us. I would ask you, whether you do not think it absurd that you men who are God's last creation, who have received your soul from Him, and are entirely His, should serve another master; aye, and more than that, should pay homage to the tyrant instead of to the rightful king, to the wicked one instead of to the good? For, in the name of truth, what man in his senses forsakes that which is good to keep company with evil? Who is there that flees from God to live with daemons? Who is pleased with slavery, when he might be a son of God? Or who hastens to a region of darkness, when he might be a citizen of heaven; when it is in his power to till the fields of paradise, and traverse the spaces of heaven, when he can partake of the pure and life-giving spring, treading the air in the track of that bright cloud, like Elijah, with his eyes fixed on the rain that brings salvation? But there are some who, after the manner of worms, wallow in marshes and mud, which are the streams of pleasure, and feed on profitless and senseless delights. These are swinish men; for swine, says one, "take pleasure in mud" more than in pure water; and they "are greedy for offal," according to Democritus. Let us not then, let us not be made slaves, nor become swinish, but as true "children of the light," direct our gaze steadily upward towards the light, lest the Lord prove us bastards as the sun does the eagles.

Let us therefore repent, and pass from ignorance to knowledge, from senselessness to sense, from intemperance

to temperance, from unrighteousness to righteousness, from
godlessness to God.

[83]

COHEN, HERMANN

COHEN, HERMANN (1842-1918). The basis of Cohen's philosophy
was that God made truth possible. His system of critical idealism
dealt with the logic of pure knowledge, the ethics of pure will,
and the aesthetics of pure feeling. He emphasized that basically
his ethical philosophy was connected with the teachings of Judaism.

For many years, he was a professor at the University of Mar-
burg. Upon his retirement at the age of seventy, he spent his last
years as a teacher of Jewish philosophy at the Institute for the
Science of Judaism in Berlin. In addition to educating rabbinical
students, he directed discussions each Friday for the benefit of the
general public. Many non-Jewish scholars attended these, eager to
profit by Cohen's answers to questions concerning the whole range
of science and philosophy. His method for teaching the rudiments of
philosophy to beginners was greatly admired. He listened patiently
to his students, helped them articulate their thoughts and express
themselves methodically. He regarded this technique of discussion
with beginners a test of his doctrine wherein thought was "pure
creation," not the result but the condition of experience. His interpretations of the critiques of Kant, in his early years, gave
new direction to the Neo-Kantian movement.

KANT AS THE FOUNDER OF THE
PHILOSOPHY OF SCIENCE

THE mere title, *Prolegomena to Every Future Metaphysic
Which May Present Itself As Science,* by Kant is indicative
of his historical influence. It was neither Kant's intention to
end all philosophical endeavors, nor to confine the spirit of
future thought to the terms of his literary language; but he
did claim to have written the most methodical introduction
(the prolegomena) of both past and future metaphysics.
His claim was founded upon the limitations of metaphysics
in presenting itself "as a science." The words "as a science"
signify the peculiarity of Kant's system and method; for
no inspirational frenzy shall supersede the genius of wisdom

247

in the future, nor shall proud resignation (*scio me veram intellegere philosophiam*) make the feeling of truth the ultimate fundament of certainty; for metaphysics will become science and coordinate itself with the "steady pace of science." That is the historical meaning of Kant's eminent fundamental thought. From it we may also derive the direction and manner in which Kant's historical influence may be pursued.

The mathematical science of nature had been accepted as real science about one hundred and fifty years before Kant. That earlier period witnessed the publication of Newton's *Philosophiae Naturalis Principia* (1687) and Galileo's *Discorsi* (1638). Scientific abstraction was prevalent in both these works. Galileo formulated the fundamental idea of modern science, according to which all things consisted of motions determinable by laws, and explorable only as such. Newton's theories that all motions belonged to a coherent system whose center was the astronomical system was fundamentally related to Galileo's concepts. They form the historical basis for Kant's thesis that the system of the universe is the disposition of the system of reason.

The general attitude of philosophy toward science is similar to that of Kant's attitude toward science. It is similar to that of poetry toward myth; the myth creates its images in a naive fashion as a means of conceiving things; poetry utilizes such images as symbols and metaphors, and the poet reflects upon the material of the myths. Science, in parallel ways, unsophisticatedly uses the natural power of the mind "rightly conscious of an obscure impulse." Philosophy must clarify the obscure impulse in order that science may proceed, without necessarily being led, along the right path. The obscure impulse presents a problem; it is a natural phenomenon undeterminable by psychological laws, even if psychology were in perfect accordance with the standards of natural science. Humanity, in general, like each child, begins by thinking mythically. Civilization, through poetry and art, obtains its freedom of the soul. Human reason and science acquire their free self-consciousness, their certainty of spontaneous action, the awareness of their purposes, and the knowledge of their limits through philosophy. In this sense, science is to philosophy what nature is to art.

Thus, philosophy, itself, becomes a science when it verifies the mentioned metaphor. Its object cannot be nature as such, but the science of nature. Newton systematized nature and those who accept his theories must also accept that as his underlying purpose. One may well question: How is the science of nature possible? What epistemological conditions does it presuppose? Upon which principles is it founded? According to Kant, the answers to all these questions make philosophy a science. Philosophy becomes science by recognizing the realities of science, and by inquiring into the conditions that make science possible. The title, *Prolegomena to Every Future Metaphysics Which May Present Itself As Science,* means the aforementioned. In fact the theoretical aspects of Kant's philosophy are nothing but proof of their physical examples; the demonstration of their epistemological value within the bounds of the science of nature based upon mathematies. Such demonstration is the performance of philosophical genius. Throughout the history of philosophy, whether it be Plato, Descartes, Leibniz, or Kant, the philosophical genius becomes evident whenever the question: "What is science?" is raised.

[84]

COHEN, MORRIS RAPHAEL

COHEN, MORRIS RAPHAEL (1880-1947). When Cohen was a boy in Minsk, Russia, he was called Kallyeleh, the Yiddish equivalent of moron. At the age of twelve, he emigrated to the United States. People from Cohen's native town were considerably astonished to hear, in later years, that the so-called moron was generally acknowledged as one of the strongest intellectual forces in American education and philosophy. Many of the greatest contemporary minds—Einstein, Woodbridge, Dewey, Russell, Oliver Wendell Holmes, Jr., and Cardozo—considered Cohen their equal. His disciples admired his wisdom and his teaching methods. His cardinal virtue was his integrity of mind and conscience. He was outstanding as a logician and mathematician, and was chiefly responsible for the renaissance of philosophy in American law.

Cohen's interest in the philosophy of law and religion dated back to his "moronic" boyhood, when he was educated in Biblical and Talmudic law and read Maimonides and Judah Halevi's *Kuzari*. As a young man, he was attracted to Marxian socialism, but his strong belief in democracy helped him to discover other ways of serving the common good and acting in accordance with his social conscience. Felix Adler influenced his approach to ethics; but Cohen was essentially a logician, devoted to mathematical logic and to the investigation of the relationships between science and philosophy. He characterized himself as a realistic rationalist who conceived of reason as "the use of both deductive and inductive inferences working upon the material of experience." He regarded reality as a category that belonged to science not religion.

PHILOSOPHY AND LITERATURE

UNLIKE SCIENCE, philosophy has never been able entirely to dispense with pure speculation, nor has it been able entirely to eliminate the bias of temperament, and in these respects philosophy resembles a certain art, viz., the art of poetry and of reflective literature generally. Actual scientific knowledge is too fragmentary to enable us to so form a complete picture of the world to which we must react, and so imagination must be called in. Sometimes imagination and science work together, but often imagination does all the work and science is a silent spectator, as in the case of Fechner's "Zend-Avesta."

It has generally been assumed that of two opposing systems of philosophy, *e. g.*, realism and idealism, one only *can* be true and one *must* be false; and so philosophers have been hopelessly divided on the question, which is the true one. The assumption back of this attitude is that philosophy is determinate knowledge which will not admit of variation. But is this assumption necessary? Can not two pictures of the same object both be true, in spite of radical differences? The picture which the philosopher draws of the world is surely not one in which every stroke is necessitated by pure logic. A creative element is surely present in all great systems, and it does not seem possible that all sympathy or fundamental attitudes of will can be entirely eliminated from any human philosophy. The method of exposition which philosophers have adopted leads many to suppose that they are simply inquiries, that they have no interest in the conclusions at which they arrive, and that their primary concern is to follow their premises to their logical conclusions. But it is not impossible to think that the minds of philosophers sometimes act like those of other mortals, and that, having once been determined by diverse circumstances to adopt certain views, they then look for and naturally find reasons to justify these views.

There are a number of points in which the method of philosophers is precisely that of literary essayists of the type of St. Benre, Matthew Arnold, Stevenson, or Lowell. Both use examples to suggest or illustrate rather than to demonstrate. In science this would be called the fallacy of one example. In both literature and philosophy the temper of the lesser Napoleon, *aut Caesar aut nullus,* is very prominent. In science this might be called the "all or nothing" fallacy. Constant reservations and numerous qualifications destroy literary sweep, and take away the air of profundity from philosophic discussion. Some philosophers, notably Aristotle and St. Thomas, might perhaps be excepted from the last statement, but in spite of all our hankering after the epithet science, I can not see that we have been making much progress in this habit of self-control against the extravagance of generalization. Again, both literature and philosophy work by appealing to certain reigning idols. These idols came into vogue in different ways. They are seldom refuted or directly overthrown. Generally they are simply outlived, or they do not survive the change of fashion. In the latter eighties or in the earlier nineties the term *relation* was a magic word to conjure with. It was brought into mode by Thomas Hill Green, and died a natural death with the eclipse of his influence. To-day if anything is characterized as *experimental, functional,* or *dynamic,* that is enough to allow it to pass all the watch-dogs of philosophic criticism, and to characterize anything as *static* is to consign it to the lowermost depths from which no power can rescue it. I am not anxious to bring down the wrath of the gods by questioning the all-sufficient potency of such terms as *experience, evolution,* etc.; but may I ask what progress would mathematical physics have made if every time one approached a problem of stresses, he were frightened off by the warning that he must not for a moment entertain that most heinous criminal, the static point of view? I humbly agree with those who claim that the static point of view is mechanical and lifeless and, therefore, inapplicable to the entire universe, but I am quite sure that the dynamic point of view itself may be mechanical and lifeless.

Lastly, literature and philosophy both allow past idols to be resurrected with a frequency which would be truly distressing to a sober scientist. If a philosophic theory is once ruled out of court, no one can tell when it will appear again.

In thus pointing out certain respects in which philosophy resembles literature more than science, I do not mean, of course, to imply that it would be well for philosophy if it ceased to aim at scientific rigor. Let philosophy resolutely aim to be as scientific as possible, but let her not forget her strong kinship with literature.

[85]

COLERIDGE, SAMUEL TAYLOR

COLERIDGE, SAMUEL TAYLOR (1772-1834). A gifted poet and leader of the English romantic movement, Coleridge found life a continuous struggle against passion and physical suffering. His unhappy marriage and his love for another married woman caused him grave psychological disturbance and his addiction to opium undermined his physical health. Coleridge did not do justice to his philosophical expositions and often said that he found no comfort "except in the driest speculations." His psychological observations of the activities of the mind under abnormal and morbid conditions are invaluable. The results of his keen self-examination anticipate many of the researches of modern psychopathology. From 1816 to 1834 Coleridge lived in the house of a physician who finally succeeded in curing him, and the last years of the poet were spent in relative psychological security.

Coleridge's philosophy was largely the result of his changing political sentiments. At first an ardent supporter of the French Revolution, he turned to fanatical conservatism and traditionalism. He staunchly opposed almost all of the eighteenth century British philosophers—particularly Locke, Hartley, Hume, and Bentham— and subsequently was converted to German idealism. His *Biographia Literaria*, which developed a theory of literary criticism, influenced British and American aesthetics and philosophy.

PRECISION IN THE USE OF TERMS

I ADVERTISE to the prevailing laxity in the use of terms: this is the principal complaint to which the moderns are exposed; but it is a grievous one in as much as it inevitably tends to the misapplication of words, and to the corruption of language. . . . The word 'taste' . . . applies not merely to substantives and adjectives, to things and their epithets, but to verbs: thus, how frequently is the verb 'indorsed' strained from its true signification, as given by Milton in the expression, 'And elephants endorsed with towers.' Again, 'virtue' has been equally perverted: originally it signified merely strength; then it became strength of mind and valor, and it has now been changed to the class term for moral excellence in all its various species. I only introduce these as instances by the way, and nothing could be easier than to multiply them.

At the same time, while I recommend precision both of thought and expression, I am far from advocating a pedantic niceness in the choice of language: such a course would only render conversation stiff and stilted. Dr. Johnson used to say that in the most unrestrained discourse he always sought for the properest word—that which best and most exactly conveyed his meaning: to a certain point he was right, but because he carried it too far, he was often laborious where he ought to have been light, and formal where he ought to have been familiar. Men ought to endeavor to distinguish subtly, that they may be able afterwards to assimilate truly.

[86]

INWARD BLINDNESS

TALK to a blind man—he knows he wants the sense of sight, and willingly makes the proper allowances. But there are certain internal senses which a man may want, and yet be wholly ignorant that he wants them. It is most unpleasant to converse with such persons on subjects of taste, philosophy, or religion. Of course, there is no *reasoning* with them, for they do not possess the facts, on which the reasoning must be grounded. Nothing is possible but a naked dissent, which implies a sort of unsocial contempt; or—what a man of kind disposition is very likely to fall into—a heartless tacit acquiescence, which borders too nearly on duplicity.

[86A]

TYPES OF READERS

READERS may be divided into four classes:

1. Sponges, who absorb all they read and return it nearly in the same state, only a little dirtied.

2. Sand-glasses, who retain nothing and are content to get through a book for the sake of getting through the time.

3. Strain-bags, who retain merely the dregs of what they read.

4. Mogul diamonds, equally rare and valuable, who profit by what they read, and enable others to profit by it also.

[86B]

THE LOVE OF NATURE

THE love of nature is ever returned double to us, not only (as) the delighter in our delight, but by linking our sweetest, but of themselves perishable feelings to distinct and vivid images, which we ourselves, at times, and which a thousand casual recollections recall to our memory. She is the preserver, the treasurer, of our joys. Even in sickness and nervous diseases she has peopled our imagination with lovely forms, which have sometimes overpowered the inward pain and brought with them their old sensations. And even when all men have seemed to desert us, and the friend of our heart has passed on with one glance from his "cold disliking eye—" yet even then the blue heaven spreads itself out and bends over us, and the little tree still shelters us under its plumage as a second cope, a domestic firmament, and the low creeping gale will sigh in the heath plant and soothe us by sound of sympathy, till the lulled grief lose itself in fixed gaze on the purple heath-blossom, till the present beauty becomes a vision of memory.

[86C]

THE WORTH AND PRICE OF KNOWLEDGE

IT IS not true that ignorant persons have no notion of the advantages of truth and knowledge. They see and confess those advantages in the conduct, the immunities, and the superior powers of the possessors. Were these attainable by pilgrimages the most toilsome, or penances the most painful, we should assuredly have as many pilgrims and self-tormentors in the service of true religion and virtue as now exist under the tyranny of Papal and Brahman superstition. This inefficacy of legitimate reason, from the want of fit objects—this its relative weakness, and how narrow at all times its immediate sphere of action must be—is proved to us by the impostors of all professions. What, I pray you, is their fortress, the rock which is both their quarry and their foundation, from which and on which they are built?—the desire of arriving at the end without the effort of thought and will which are the appointed means.

Let us look back three or four centuries. Then, as now, the great mass of mankind were governed by the three main wishes: the wish for vigor of body, including the absence of painful feelings; for wealth, or the power of procuring the external conditions of bodily enjoyment—these during life; and security from pain and continuance of happiness here-

255

after. Then, as now, men were desirous to attain them by some easier means than those of temperance, industry, and strict justice. They gladly therefore applied to the Priest, who could ensure them happiness hereafter without the performance of their duties here; to the Lawyer, who could make money a substitute for a right cause; to the Physician, whose medicines promised to take the sting out of the tail of their sensual indulgences, and let them fondle and play with vice, as with a charmed serpent; to the Alchemist, whose gold-tincture would enrich them without toil or economy; and to the Astrologer, from whom they could purchase foresight without knowledge or reflection.

[86D]

INTRODUCTORY APHORISMS

In philosophy, equally as in poetry, it is the highest and most useful prerogative of genius to produce the strongest impressions of novelty, while it rescues admitted truths from the neglect caused by the very circumstance of their universal admission. Extremes meet. Truths of all others the most awful and interesting are often considered as so true that they lose all the power of truth, and lie bed-ridden in the dormitory of the soul, side by side with the most despised and exploded errors.

*   *   *

As a fruit-tree is more valuable than any one of its fruits singly, or even than all its fruits of a single season, so the noblest object of reflection is the mind itself, by which we reflect. And as the blossoms, the green and ripe fruit of an orange-tree are more beautiful to behold when on the tree, and seen as one with it, than the same growth detached and seen successively, after their importation into another country and different climate; so it is with the manifold objects of reflection, when they are considered principally in reference to the reflective power, and as part and parcel of the same. No object, of whatsoever value our passions may represent it, but becomes foreign to us as soon as it is altogether unconnected with our intellectual, moral, and spiritual life. To be ours, it must be referred to the mind, either as a motive, or consequence, or symptom.

*   *   *

Life is the one universal soul, which, by virtue of the enlivening Breath and the informing Word, all organized bodies have in common, each after its kind. This, therefore, all animals possess—and Man, as an animal. But, in addition to this, God transfused into man a higher gift, and specially imbreathed:—even a Living (that is, self-subsisting) Soul; a Soul having its life in itself:—"And Man became a Living Soul." He did not merely possess it—he *became* it. It was his proper being, his truest self—the Man in the man. None, then, not one of human kind, so poor and destitute but there is provided for him, even in his present state, "a house not built with hands;" aye, and in spite of the philosophy (falsely so-called) which mistakes the causes, the conditions, and the occasions of our becoming conscious of certain truths and realities for the truths and realities themselves—a house gloriously furnished. Nothing is wanted but the eye, which is the light of this house, the light which is the eye of the soul. This very light, this enlightening eye, is Reflection. It is more, indeed, than is ordinarily meant by that word; but it is what a Christian ought to mean by it, and to know, too, whence it first came, and still continues to come:—of what Light even this light is but a reflection. This, too, is Thought; and all thought is but unthinking that does not flow out of this or tend toward it.

*   *   *

It may be an additional aid to reflection to distinguish the three kinds severally, according to the faculty to which each corresponds—the part of our human nature which is more particularly its organ. Thus: the *prudential* corresponds to the sense and the understanding; the *moral* to the heart and conscience; the *spiritual* to the will and the reason; that is, to the finite will reduced to harmony with, and in subordination to the reason, as a ray from that true light which is both reason and will absolute.

COMENIUS, JOHANN AMOS

COMENIUS, JOHANN AMOS (1592-1670). A bishop of the Bohemian Brethren and the first great democrat among Christian educational philosophers, Comenius fled from Czechoslovakia in 1628 when that country lost its liberty and its national culture was threatened with extinction by the Hapsburg emperor. He roamed throughout Europe working untiringly for the salvation of his nation and the realization of his educational, political, and scientific projects. Despite his misfortunes and precarious existence, Comenius never lost confidence in the rational mind or in human progress.

His ultimate aim was universal peace. He recognized that the necessary steps, preliminary to the attainment of this goal involved the unification of rival Christian denominations, fundamental reforms in education, and a new approach to natural science. It was largely the result of his initiative that scientific societies promoting research were founded throughout Europe during the seventeenth century. He insisted that education should be free, universally available, and compulsory for every child; that automatic memorization should be replaced by teaching words with perceptual objects; and that the sensual faculties of school children should be taken into consideration. Comenius stands as a transitional figure in the area of science—halfway between the medieval Aristotelianism and modern empiricism. He believed that independent study and observation offered greater intellectual rewards than did constant reliance upon Aristotle or Pliny. His textboks, translated into more than seventeen languages, were used in the early years of Harvard University, and throughout the seventeenth century schools of New England, Asia, and Europe. His principal works were: *The Gates of Unlocked Tongues* (1631); *The Way of Light* (1642); *Patterns of Universal Knowledge* (1651); and *The Great Didactic* (1657).

LAST DECLARATION

WHERE shall I now begin, after so many labyrinths and Sisyphian stones, with which I have been plagued all my life? Shall I say with Elias: "Now, O Lord, take away my life from me, since I am no better than my fathers;" or with

258

David: "Forsake me not, O Lord, in my age, until I have prophesied all that thine arm shall bring to pass." Neither; that I may not be unhappy with painful longing for the one or the other; but I will have my life and death, my rest and my labor, according to the will of God; and with closed eyes will follow wherever He leads me, full of confidence and humility, praying, with David: "Lead me in thy wisdom, and at last receive me into glory." And what I shall do hereafter, shall happen no otherwise than as if directed by Christ, so that the longer I live the more I may be contented with what is needful for me, and may burn up or cast away all that is unnecessary. Would that I were soon to depart to the heavenly country, and leave behind me all earthly things! Yea, I will cast away all the earthly cares which I yet have, and will rather burn them in the fire, than to encumber myself further with them.

To explain this, my last declaration, more clearly, I say that a little hut, wherever it be, shall serve me instead of a palace; or if I have no place whereto lay my head, I will be contented after the example of my Master, though none receive me under his roof. Or I will remain under the roof of the sky, as did He during that last night upon the Mount of Olives, until, like the beggar Lazarus, the angels shall receive me into their company. Instead of a costly robe, I will be contented, like John, with a coarse garment. Bread and water shall be to me instead of a costly table, and if I have therewith a few vegetables, I will thank God for them. My library shall consist of the threefold book of God; my philosophy shall be, with David, to consider the heavens and the works of God, and to wonder that He, the Lord of so great a kingdom, should condescend to look upon a poor worm like me. My medicine shall be, a little eating and frequent fasting. My jurisprudence, to do unto others as I would that they do unto me. If any ask after my theology, I will, like the dying Thomas Aquinas—for I, too, shall die soon—take my Bible, and say with tongue and heart, "I believe what is written in this book." If he ask further about my creed, I will repeat

259

to him the apostolic one, for I know none shorter, simpler, or more expressive, or that cuts off all controversy. If he ask for my form of prayer, I will show him the Lord's Prayer; since no one can give a better key to open the heart of the father than the son, his own off-spring. If any ask after my rule of life, there are the ten commandments; for I believe no one can better tell what will please God than God Himself. If any seek to know my system of casuistry, I will answer, everything pertaining to myself is suspicious to me; therefore I fear even when I do well, and say humbly, "I am an unprofitable servant, have patience with me!"

[87]

COMTE, AUGUSTE

COMTE, AUGUSTE (1798-1857). The Utopian socialist, Saint-Simon influenced Comte in his youth. Comte had little use either for logic or psychology, but instead advocated the study of phrenology. His object was to show that philosophy was in the stage of being absorbed by science. Theology was the first stage of philosophy, wherein nature was explained by the supernatural; metaphysics constituted the second stage, and philosophy was concerned with such abstractions as purpose, life, and the *a priori*; the third and last stage was positivism, which Comte said implied experiment, observation, and the consequences derived from the laws of phenomena. His best known work, *Cours de Philosophie Positive* was published (1830-42) in six volumes. He maintained that science had always been experimental and observational, and therefore positivistic; that it never required metaphysics either to help determine its course or its limits. His ethics was based on the factor of egotism. This, he said, would lead to a consideration of others, or altruism, and thence to mankind as the guarantor of a social order that would be beneficial to the individual. In order to insure the effectiveness of this, he formalized this attitude into a religion with saints, holy days, sacraments and prayers, and made himself the high priest of the cult. Although he died in 1857, there still are remnants of sects that uphold the religion he founded.

The personal life of Comte had many unhappy aspects. He was twice committed to an insane asylum: the first time, as a result of his unhappy marriage to a woman of the streets; the second, after the death of Clotilde de Vaux, the wife of a man imprisoned for life. It was Clotilde, who served as liaison between the *grand être* (that is, mankind) and its high priest. John Stuart Mill was one of Comte's principal sponsors, helping him to remain solvent, write, and spread his cult. The positivist philosophy was a reaction to the speculative phase that developed in philosophy after Kant.

POSITIVE PHILOSOPHY

IN order to explain properly the true nature and peculiar character of the Positive Philosophy, it is indispensable that we should first take a brief survey of the progressive growth of the human mind, viewed as a whole; for no idea can be properly understood apart from its history.

In thus studying the total development of human intelligence in its different spheres of activity, from its first and simplest beginning up to our own time, I believe that I have discovered a great fundamental Law, to which the mind is subjected by an invariable necessity. The truth of this Law can, I think, be demonstrated both by reasoned proofs furnished by a knowledge of our mental organization, and by historical verification due to an attentive study of the past. This Law consists in the fact that each of our principal conceptions, each branch of our knowledge, passes in succession through three different theoretical states: the Theological or fictitious state, the Metaphysical or abstract state, and the Scientific or positive state. In other words, the human mind —by its very nature—makes use successively in each of its researches of three methods of philosophising, whose characters are essentially different, and even radically opposed to each other. We have first the Theological method, then the Metaphysical method, and finally the Positive method. Hence there are three kinds of philosophy or general systems of conceptions on the aggregate of phenomena, which are mutually exclusive of each other. The first is the necessary starting-point of human intelligence: the third represents its fixed and definite state: the second is only destined to serve as a transitional method.

In the Theological state, the human mind directs its researches mainly towards the inner nature of beings, and towards the first and final causes of all the phenomena which it observes—in a word, towards Absolute knowledge. It therefore represents these phenomena as being produced by the direct and continuous action of more or less numerous supernatural agents, whose arbitrary intervention explains all the apparent anomalies of the universe.

In the Metaphysical state, which is in reality only a simple general modification of the first state, the supernatural agents are replaced by abstract forces, real entities or personified abstractions, inherent in the different beings of the world. These entities are looked upon as capable of giving rise by themselves to all the phenomena observed, each phenomenon being explained by assigning it to its corresponding entity.

Finally, in the Positive state, the human mind, recognizing the impossibility of obtaining absolute truth, gives up the search after the origin and destination of the universe and a knowledge of the final causes of phenomena. It only endeavors now to discover, by a well-combined use of reasoning and observation, the actual *laws* of phenomena— that is to say, their invariable relations of succession and likeness. The explanation of facts, thus reduced to its real terms, consists henceforth only in the connection established between different particular phenomena and some general facts, the number of which the progress of science tends more and more to diminish.

The Theological system arrived at its highest form of perfection, when it substituted the providential action of a single being, for the varied play of the numerous independent gods which had been imagined by the primitive mind. In the same way, the last stage of the Metaphysical system consisted in replacing the different special entities by the idea of a single great general entity—Nature—looked upon as the sole source of all phenomena. Similarly, the ideal of the Positive system, towards which it constantly tends, although in all probability it will never attain such a stage, would be reached if we could look upon all the different phenomena observable as so many particular cases of a single general fact, such as that of Gravitation, for example.

This is not the place to give a special demonstration of this fundamental Law of Mental Development, and to deduce from it its most important consequences. We shall make a direct study of it, with all the necessary details, in the part of this work relating to social phenomena. I am only considering it now in order to determine precisely the true character of the Positive Philosophy, as opposed to the two other philosophies which have successively dominated our whole intellectual system up to these latter centuries. For the present, to avoid leaving entirely undemonstrated so important a law, the applications of which will frequently occur throughout this work, I must confine myself to a rapid enumeration of the most evident general reasons which prove its exactitude.

In the first place, it is, I think, sufficient merely to enumerate such a law for its accuracy to be immediately verified, by all those who are fairly well acquainted with the general history of the sciences. For there is not a single science which has to-day reached the Positive stage, which was not in the past—as each can easily see for himself—composed mainly of metaphysical abstractions, and, going back further still, it was altogether under the sway of theological conceptions. Unfortunately, we shall have to recognize on more than one occasion in the different parts of this course, that even the most perfect sciences still retain to-day some very evident traces of these two primitive states.

This general revolution of the human mind can, moreover, be easily verified to-day, in a very obvious, although indirect, manner, if we consider the development of the individual intelligence. The starting-point being necessarily the same in the education of the individual as in that of the race, the various principal phases of the former must reproduce the fundamental epochs of the latter. Now, does not each of us in contemplating his own history recollect that he has been successively—as regards the most important ideas—a *theo-*

logian in childhood, a *metaphysician* in youth, and a *natural philosopher* in manhood? This verification of the law can easily be made by all who are on a level with their age.

But, in addition to the proofs of the truth of this law furnished by direct observation of the race or the individual, I must, above all, mention in this brief summary the theoretical considerations which show its necessity.

The most important of these considerations arises from the very nature of the subject itself. It consists in the need at every epoch of having some theory to connect the facts, while, on the other hand, it was clearly impossible for the primitive human mind to form theories based on observation.

All competent thinkers agree with Bacon that there can be no real knowledge except that which rests upon observed facts. This fundamental maxim is evidently indisputable if it is applied, as it ought to be, to the mature state of our intelligence. But, if we consider the origin of our knowledge, it is no less certain that the primitive human mind could not, and indeed ought not to, have thought in that way. For if, on the one hand, every Positive theory must necessarily be founded upon observations, it is, on the other hand, no less true that, in order to observe, our mind has need of some theory or other. If in contemplating phenomena we did not immediately connect them with some principles, not only would it be impossible for us to combine these isolated observations, and therefore to derive any profit from them, but we should even be entirely incapable of remembering the facts, which would for the most part remain unnoted by us.

Thus there were two difficulties to be overcome: the human mind had to observe in order to form real theories, and yet had to form theories of some sort before it could apply itself to a connected series of observations. The primitive human mind, therefore, found itself involved in a vicious circle, from which it would never have had any means of escaping, if a natural way out of the difficulty had not fortunately been found by the spontaneous development of

Theological conceptions. These presented a rallying-point for the efforts of the mind, and furnished materials for its activity. This is the fundamental motive which demonstrated the logical necessity for the purely Theological character of Primitive Philosophy, apart from those important social considerations relating to the matter which I cannot even indicate now.

This necessity becomes still more evident, when we have regard to the perfect congruity of Theological Philosophy, with the peculiar nature of the researches on which the human mind, in its infancy, concentrated to so high a degree all its powers. It is, indeed, very noticeable how the most insoluble questions—such as the inner nature of objects, or the origin and purpose of all phenomena—are precisely those which the human mind proposes to itself, in preference to all others, in its primitive state; all really soluble problems being looked upon as hardly worthy of serious thought. The reason for this is very obvious, since it is experience alone which has enabled us to estimate our abilities rightly, and if man had not commenced by over-estimating his forces, these would never have been able to acquire all the development of which they are capable. This fact is a necessity of our organization. But, be that as it may, let us picture to ourselves as far as we can this early mental disposition, so universal and so prominent, and let us ask ourselves what kind of reception would have been accorded at such an epoch to the Positive Philosophy, supposing it to have been then formed. The highest ambition of this Philosophy is to discover the *laws* of phenomena, and its main characteristic is precisely that of regarding as necessarily interdicted to the human reason, all those sublime mysteries which Theological Philosophy, on the contrary, explains with such admirable facility, even to the smallest detail. Under such circumstances, it is easy to see what the choice of primitive man would be.

The same thing is true, when we consider from a practical standpoint the nature of the pursuits which the human mind first occupies itself with. Under that aspect, they offer to man the strong attraction of an unlimited control over the exterior world, which is regarded as being entirely destined for our use, while all its phenomena seem to have close and continuous relations with our existence. These chimerical hopes, these exaggerated ideas of man's importance in the universe, to which the Theological Philosophy gives rise, are destroyed irrevocably by the first-fruits of the Positive Philosophy. But, at the commencement, they afforded an indispensable stimulus without the aid of which we cannot, indeed, conceive how the primitive human mind would have been induced to undertake any arduous labours.

We are at the present time so far removed from that early state of mind—at least as regards the majority of phenomena—that it is difficult for us to appreciate properly the force and necessity of such considerations. Human reason is now so mature that we are able to undertake laborious scientific researches, without having in view any extraneous goal capable of strongly exciting the imagination, such as that which the astrologers or alchemists proposed to themselves. Our intellectual activity is sufficiently excited by the mere hope of discovering the laws of phenomena, by the simple desire of verifying or disproving a theory. This, however, could not be the case in the infancy of the human mind. Without the attractive chimeras of Astrology, or the example, where should we have found the perseverance and ardour necessary for collecting the long series of observations and experiments which, later on, served as a basis for the first Positive theories of these two classes of phenomena?

The need of such stimulus to our intellectual development was keenly felt long ago by Kepler in the case of astronomy, and has been justly appreciated in our own time by Berthollet in chemistry.

The above considerations show us that, although the Positive Philosophy represents the true final state of human intelligence—that to which it has always tended more and more—it was none the less necessary to employ the Theological Philosophy at first and during many centuries, both as a method and as furnishing provisional doctrines. Since the Theological Philosophy is spontaneous in its character, it is, for that reason, the only one possible in the beginning; it is also the only one which can offer a sufficient interest to our budding intelligence. It is now very easy to see that, in order to pass from this provisional form of philosophy to the final stage, the human mind was naturally obliged to adopt Metaphysical methods and doctrines as a transitional form of philosophy. This last consideration is indispensable, in order to complete the general sketch of the great law which I have pointed out.

It is easily seen that our understanding, which was compelled to progress by almost insensible steps, could not pass suddenly, and without any intermediate stages, from Theological to Positive philosophy. Theology and Physics are so profoundly incompatible, their conceptions are so radically opposed in character, that, before giving up the one in order to employ the other exclusively, the human intelligence had to make use of intermediate conceptions, which, being of a hybrid character, were eminently fitted to bring about a gradual transition. That is the part played by Metaphysical conceptions, and they have no other real use. By substituting, in the study of phenomena, a corresponding inseparable entity for a direct supernatural agency—although, at first, the former was only held to be an offshoot of the latter— Man gradually accustomed himself to consider only the facts themselves. In that way, the ideas of these metaphysical agents gradually became so dim that all right-minded persons only considered them to be the abstract names of the phenomena in question. It is impossible to imagine by what other method our understanding could have passed from frankly supernatural to purely natural considerations, or, in other words, from the Theological to the Positive *régime*.

[88]

CONDILLAC, ETIENNE BONNOT DE

CONDILLAC, ETIENNE BONNOT DE (1715-1780). Often referred to as the "philosophers' philosopher," historically, the influence of Condillac is still important, although his prestige has waned. He was an eighteenth century abbot, whose ecclesiastical garment neither hampered his enjoyment of life, nor interfered with his secular thinking.

Condillac professed spiritualism in the area of metaphysics; metaphysics was only loosely connected with his principal interests and occupied a very small part of his writings. In his chief works, *Essai Sur L'Origine des Connaissances Humaines* (An Essay on the Origin of Human Knowledge) (1746) and *Traité des Sensations* (1754) Condillac, like Locke and some of the Cartesians who in some respects deviated from Descartes, denied the usefulness of speculating about the metaphysical nature of the mind. He preferred to study the human mind as a psychologist in order to understand its operations. He thought that the analysis of sensation contained the elements of any judgment connected with the sensation. He regarded the human individual as composed of two egos, that of habit and that of reflection. The ego of habit acted unconsciously: it was capable of the senses of sight, hearing and smell. The ego of reflection was conscious of its acts while performing them. Instinct was derived from the ego of habit, and reason from the habit of reflection. Many of his solutions were considered rash; today, it is recognized that his critics, Kant and Helmholtz among others, were wrong. Condillac was also interested in the psychology of animals, logic and mathematics. His work in economics, *Le Commerce et Le Gouvernement*, deals with ideas and problems very similar to those treated by Adam Smith in his *Wealth of Nations*, both published simultaneously (1776).

TREATISE ON SENSATIONS

NOTIONS OF A MAN POSSESSING THE SENSE OF SMELL ONLY

THE notions of our statue being limited to the sense of smell, can include odors only. It cannot have any conception of extent, of form, of anything external to itself, or to its sensations, any more than it can have of color, sound or taste.

If we offer the statue a rose, it will be, in its relation to us, a statue which smells a rose; but in relation to itself, it will be merely the scent itself of the flower.

Therefore, according to the objects which act upon its organ, it will be scent of rose, of carnation, of jasmine, of violet. In a word, odors are, in this respect merely modifications of the statue itself or modes of being; and it is not capable of believing itself aught else, since these are the only sensations it can feel.

Let those philosophers to whom it is so evident that everything is material, put themselves for a moment in the place of the statue, and let them reflect how they could suspect that there exists anything resembling what we call *matter*.

We may then already be convinced that it is sufficient to increase or to diminish the number of the senses to cause us to come to conclusions wholly different from those which are at present so natural to us, and our statue, limited to the sense of smell, may thus enable us to comprehend somewhat the class of beings whose notions are the most restricted.

THE SLEEP AND DREAMS OF A MAN LIMITED TO THE SENSE OF SMELL

Our statue may be reduced to the condition of being merely the remembrance of an odor; then the sense of its existence appears to be lost to it. It feels less that it is existing than that it has existed, and in proportion as memory recalls ideas to it with less intensity, this remnant of feeling becomes weaker yet. Like a light which goes out gradually, the feeling ceases wholly when the faculty of memory becomes entirely inactive.

Now, our own experience compels us to believe that exercise must in the end fatigue the memory and the imagination of the statue. Let us therefore consider these faculties at rest, and refrain from exciting them by any sensation: the resultant condition will be that of sleep.

If the repose of these faculties be such that they are completely inactive, there is nothing to note, save that the sleep is the soundest possible. If, on the contrary, these faculties continue to act, they will act upon a part only of the notions acquired. A number of links in the chain will be cut out, and the succession of ideas, during sleep, will necessarily differ from the order in a waking state. Pleasure will no longer be the sole cause determining the action of the imagination. This faculty will awaken those ideas only over which it still exercises a measure of power, and it will tend just as frequently to make the statue unhappy as to make it happy.

This is the dreaming state: it differs from the waking state only in that the ideas do not preserve the same order and that pleasure is not always the law which governs the imagination. Every dream, therefore, involves the interception of a number of ideas, on which the faculties of the soul are unable to act.

Since the statue is unacquainted with any difference between imagining intensely and having sensations, it cannot distinguish any difference between dreaming and waking. Whatever, therefore, it experiences while asleep is as real, so far as it is concerned, as what it has experienced before falling asleep.

OF THE EGO, OR PERSONALITY OF A MAN — LIMITED TO THE SENSE OF SMELL

Our statue being capable of remembering, it is no sooner one odor than it remembers that it has been another. That is its personality, for if it could say *I*, it would say it at every instant of its own duration, and each time its *I* would comprise all the moments it remembered.

True, it would not say it at the first odor. What is meant by that term seems to me to suit only a being which notes in the present moment, that it is no longer what it has been. So long as it does not change, it exists without thought of itself; but as soon as it changes, it concludes that it is the selfsame which was formerly in such another state, and it says *I*.

This observation confirms the fact that in the first instant of its existence the statue cannot form desires, for before being able to say *I wish*, one must have said *I*.

The odors which the statue does not remember do not therefore enter into the notion it has of its own person. Being as foreign to its *Ego* as are colors and sounds, of which it has no knowledge, they are, in respect of the statue, as if the statue had never smelled them. Its *Ego* is but the sum of the sensations it experiences and of those which memory recalls to it. In a word, it is at once the consciousness of what it is and the remembrance of what it has been.

CONCLUSIONS

Having proved that the statue is capable of being attentive, of remembering, of comparing, of judging, of discerning, of imagining; that it possesses abstract notions, notions of number and duration; that it is acquainted with general and particular truths; that desires are formed by it, that it has the power of passions, loves, hates, wills; and finally that it contracts habits, we must conclude that the mind is endowed with as many faculties when it has but a single organ as when it has five. We shall see that the faculties which appear to be peculiar to us are nothing else than the same faculties which, applied to a greater number of objects, develop more fully.

If we consider that to remember, compare, judge, discern, imagine, be astonished, have abstract notions, have notions of duration and number, know general and particular truths, are but different modes of attention; that to have passions, to love, to hate, to hope, to fear and to will are but different modes of desire, and that, finally, attention and desire are in their essence but sensation, we shall conclude that sensation calls out all the faculties of the soul.

If we consider that there are no absolutely indifferent sensations, we shall further conclude that the different degrees of pleasure and of pain constitute the law according to which the germ of all that we are has developed in order to produce all our faculties.

This principle may be called want, astonishment, or otherwise, but it remains ever the same, for we are always moved by pleasure or by pain in whatever we are led to do by need or astonishment.

The fact is that our earliest notions are pain or pleasure only. Many others soon follow these, and give rise to comparisons, whence spring our earliest needs and our earliest desires. Our researches, undertaken for the purpose of satisfying these needs and desires, cause us to acquire additional notions which in their turn produce new desires. The surprise which makes us feel intensely any extraordinary thing happening to us, increases from time to time the activity of our faculties, and there is formed a chain the links of which are alternately notions and desires, and it is sufficient to follow up this chain to discover the progress of the enlightening of man.

Nearly all that I have said about the faculties of the soul, while treating of the sense of smell, I might have said if I had taken any other sense; it is easy to apply all to each of the senses.

[89]

CONFUCIUS

CONFUCIUS (556-479 B.C.). Kung Fu Tse, the Grand Master or Confucius, was officially worshipped from 195 B.C. to 1912, but the traditional cult still continues in almost every district of China. Kung lived during a period of cultural decadence, but his teachings and exemplary personal conduct effected a moral and spiritual recovery and cultural renaissance among the people of China. Despite the many foreign influences and internal political conflicts, the stamp of Confucius on Chinese civilization has been more or less permanent.

Kung, a contemporary of Pythagoras and some of the later Hebrew prophets, roamed for some fourteen years throughout China, observing, teaching, and acquiring a steadily increasing number of disciples about him. He taught poetry, history, music, and adherence to tradition. He promulgated an ideal conduct of life, the basis of which was learning, wisdom, moral perfection, and decency in behavior. His doctrine of reciprocity in man's relations with his fellow man paralleled, with almost the same words, the concept of the Golden Rule. He demanded that his followers practice the virtues of sincerity, justice, benevolence, courtesy, respect for older people, and ancestor reverence. He urged them to live in harmony with themselves because that was a requisite condition for harmony between the individual and the universe. He sometimes referred to "Heaven," without, however, expressing belief in a supreme deity. He constantly exhorted that all intellectual and moral energies be channeled for self-perfection, the common good, and social and universal peace.

For a short time he held high office, using his power for reforms, and for the punishment of evil-doers, even when they were mandarins. His services, however, were not adequately appreciated by the ruler.

THE GREAT LEARNING

1. WHAT the Great Learning teaches, is—To illustrate illustrious virtue; to renovate the people; and to rest in the highest excellence.—2. The point where to rest being known, the object of pursuit is then determined; and, that being determined, a calm unperturbedness may be attained. To that calmness there will succeed a tranquil repose. In that repose there may be careful deliberation, and that deliberation will be followed by the attainment [of the desired end].—3. Things have their root and their completion. Affairs have their end and their beginning. To know what is first and what is last will lead near to what is taught [in the Great Learning].—4. The ancients who wished to illustrate illustrious virtue throughout the empire, first ordered well their own States. Wishing to order well their States, they first regulated their families. Wishing to regulate their families, they first cultivated their persons. Wishing to cultivate their persons, they first rectified their hearts. Wishing to rectify their hearts, they first sought to be sincere in their thoughts. Wishing to be sincere in their thoughts, they first extended to the utmost their knowledge. Such extension of knowledge lay in the investigation of things.—5. Things being investigated, knowl-

edge became complete. Their knowledge being complete, their thoughts were sincere. Their thoughts being sincere, their hearts were then rectified. Their hearts being rectified, their persons were cultivated. Their persons being cultivated, their families were regulated. Their families being regulated, their States were rightly governed. Their States being rightly governed, the whole empire was made tranquil and happy. —6. From the emperor down to the mass of the people, all must consider the cultivation of the person the root [of everything besides].—7. It cannot be, when the root is neglected, that what should spring from it will be well ordered. It never has been the case that what was of great importance has been slightly cared for, and, at the same time, that what was of slight importance has been greatly cared for.

[90]

THE DOCTRINE OF THE MEAN

1. WHAT heaven has conferred is called *The Nature;* an accordance with this nature is called *The Path* of duty; the regulation of this path is called *Instruction.*—2. The path may not be left for an instant. If it could be left, it would not be the path. On this account, the superior man does not wait till he sees things, to be cautious, nor till he hears things, to be apprehensive—3. There is nothing more visible than what is secret, and nothing more manifest than what is minute. Therefore the superior man is watchful over himself, when he is alone.—4. While there are no stirrings of pleasure, anger, sorrow, or joy, the mind may be said to be in the state of *Equilibrium.* When those feelings have been stirred, and they act in their due degree, there ensues what may be called the state of *Harmony.* This *Equilibrium* is the great root from which grow all the human actings in the world, and this Harmony is the universal path which they all should pursue.—5. Let the states of Equilibrium and Harmony exist in perfection, and a happy order will prevail throughout heaven and earth, and all things will be nourished and flourish.

[90A]

274

COOK, JOSEPHUS FLAVIUS

COOK, JOSEPHUS FLAVIUS (1838-1901). A descendant of the Pilgrim fathers, Josephus Cook achieved his fame as a lecturer. His direction of the Monday noon prayer meeting in Tremont Temple, Boston, received considerable public attention, and for more than twenty years the meetings were among Boston's greatest attractions. So popular were they that he was invited to repeat them throughout the United States, England, and many other countries, and their printed editions were translated into several languages.

He was extremely popular as a lecturer because he awakened and confirmed in his audience the conviction that modern science could not disrupt faith in Christianity. Though he was orthodox in his sympathies, he advised his listeners to follow him in a friendly understanding of the sciences. He attempted to prove that where science was not harmonious with Christian religion, it was easily refutable. He frequently used colorful descriptions and quotations to illustrate his points and drew upon his fund of diverse reading and his travels in Germany, Southern Europe, Palestine, Egypt, India, Japan, and Australia. Many of his friends admitted, however, that he often pretended to know that which he had not understood and lacked real erudition.

THE UNITY OF CONSCIOUSNESS

THERE is a great fact known to us more certainly than the existence of matter: it is the unity of consciousness. I know that I exist, and that I am One. Hermann Lotze's supreme argument against materialism is the unity of consciousness. I know that I am *I*, and not *you;* and I know *this* to my very finger-tips. That finger is part of my organism, not of yours. To the last extremity of every nerve, I know that I am One. The unity of consciousness is a fact known to us by much better evidence than the existence of matter. I am a natural realist in philosophy, if I may use a technical term: I believe in the existence of both matter and mind. There are two things in the universe; but I know the existence of mind better than I know the existence of matter. Sometimes in dreams we fall down precipices and awake, and find that the gnarled savage rocks had no existence. But we touched them; we felt them; we were bruised by them. Who knows but that some day we may awake, and find that all matter is merely a dream? Even if we do that, it will yet remain true that I am *I*. There is more support for idealism than for materialism; but there is no sufficient support for either. If we are to reverence all, and not merely a fraction, of the list of axiomatic or self-evident truths, if we are not to play fast and loose with the intuitions which are the eternal tests of verity, we shall believe in the existence of both tests of verity, we shall believe in the existence of both matter and mind. Hermann Lotze holds that the unity of consciousness is a fact absolutely incontrovertible and absolutely inexplicable on the theory that our bodies are woven by a complex of physical arrangements and physical forces, having no co-ordinating presiding power over them all. I know that there is a co-ordinating presiding power somewhere in me. I am *I*. I am One. Whence the sense of a unity of consciousness, if we are made up according to Spencer's idea, or Huxley's, of infinitely multiplex molecular mechanisms? We have the idea of a presiding power that makes each man one individuality from top to toe. How do we get it? It must have a sufficient cause. To this hour, no man has explained the unity of consciousness in consistency with the mechanical theory of life.

[91]

COURNOT, ANTOINE AUGUSTINE

COURNOT, ANTOINE AUGUSTINE (1801-1877). Modesty and resignation are the repetitious themes of Cournot's philosophy. His concept of truth was founded upon probability rather than certainty. He renounced those inquiries into what other philosophers termed the essence of truth. He was satisfied with investigating the role of truth in the development of the sciences and determined to find the most adequate expression for that kind of truth instrumental in the promotion of scientific research. His efforts to determine the foundation of human knowledge were not directed to an analysis of general human faculties, but to a study of those principles which make for progress in the positive sciences. The major conclusions of Cournot's reflections were that chance is a positive factor in the sum total of reality; that contingency maintained its position beside order; and that the total continuity of evolution could not be proved. He believed that man could approach truth even though he might not be able to attain it and elaborated this point of view in his books: *Considérations sur la Marche des Idées* (1872) and *Traité de L'Enchanement des Idées Fondamentales dans les Sciences et dans L'Histoire* (A Treatise on the Relationships of the Fundamental Concepts in the Sciences and History, 1881). In his early years, Cournot was a tutor in the house of Marshalie Gouvion St. Cyr; later, he became an important dignitary, but regardless of his position, he always led a modest and unpretentious existence. He declined to head a school, and for that reason, his philosophy was neglected for a long time.

EXAMPLES OF THE CREATION AND
DESTRUCTION OF WEALTH

THE abstract idea of *wealth* or of *value in exchange,* a definite idea, and consequently susceptible of rigorous treatment in combinations, must be carefully distinguished from the accessory ideas of utility, scarcity, and suitability to the needs and enjoyments of mankind, which the word *wealth* still suggests in common speech. These ideas are variable, and by nature indeterminate, and consequently ill suited for the foundation of a scientific theory. The division of economists into schools, and the war waged between practical men and theorists, have arisen in large measure from the ambiguity of the word *wealth* in ordinary speech, and the confusion which has continued to obtain between the fixed, definite idea of *value in exchange,* and the ideas of utility which every one estimates in his own way, because there is no fixed standard for the utility of things.

It has sometimes happened that a publisher, having in store an unsalable stock of some work, useful and sought after by connoisseurs, but of which too many copies were originally printed in view of the class of readers for whom it was intended, has sacrificed and destroyed two-thirds of the number, expecting to derive more profit from the remainder than from the entire edition.

There is no doubt that there might be a book of which it would be easier to sell a thousand copies at sixty francs, than three thousand at twenty francs. Calculating in this way, the Dutch Company is said to have caused the destruction in the islands of the Sound of a part of the precious spices of which it had a monopoly. Here is a complete destruction of objects to which the word *wealth* is applied because they are both sought after, and not easily obtainable. Here is a miserly, selfish act, evidently opposed to the interests of society; and yet it is nevertheless evident that this sordid act, this actual destruction, is a real creaion of *wealth* in the commercial sense of the word. The publisher's inventory will rightly show a greater value for his assets; and after the copies have left his hands, either wholly or in part, if each individual should draw up his inventory in commercial fashion, and if all these partial inventories could be collated to form a general inventory or balance sheet of the wealth in circulation, an increase would be found in the sum of these items of wealth.

On the contrary, suppose that only fifty copies exist of a curious book, and that this scarcity carries up the price at auction to three hundred francs a copy. A publisher reprints this book in an edition of a thousand copies, of which each will be worth five francs, and which will bring down the other copies to the same price from the exaggerated value which their extreme scarcity had caused. The 1050 copies will therefore only enter for 5250 francs into the sum of wealth which can be inventoried, and this sum will thus have suffered a loss of 9750 francs. The decrease will be even more considerable if (as should be the case) the value of the raw materials is considered, from which the reprints were made, and which existed prior to the reprinting. Here is an industrial operation, a material production, useful to the publisher who undertook it, useful to those whose products and labor it employed, useful even to the public if the book contains valuable information, and which is nevertheless a real destruction of wealth, in the abstract and commercial meaning of the term.

[92]

COUSIN, VICTOR

COUSIN, VICTOR (1792-1867). The disrespect largely prevalent for the philosophy of Victor Cousin is based upon his emphasis of *eclecticism,* a term he used to characterize his method, disregarding·the pejorative meaning of the word which implied shallowness and dependence. Although Cousin does not belong to that small nucleus of great philosophers, many of his ideas influenced American transcendentalism while others parallel modern American views, and continue to inspire European philosophers.

Cousin was attracted by that which is common to humanity. He was convinced that mankind could not be sceptical; that it needed a common faith, (not necessarily a religious faith, but certainty). He maintained that the mission of philosophy was to explain faith, not destroy it. His philosophical studies were principally aimed at the elevation of the soul, not at insight into the mystery of things. His cardinal principle asserted that truth was contained in each of the philosophical systems known throughout historical time; that every major philosopher had made a contribution to the knowledge of truth, and that their composite contributions comprised the whole truth, even though they contained some errors. Modifications of Cousin's concepts are manifest in Wilhelm Dilthey's "doctrine of philosophical types," and Benedetto Croce's identification of philosophy with its history. Cousin believed that he had discovered a method of intellectual distillation whereby the method of essential truth could be extrapolated from the various historical systems. He called this method of critical choice *eclecticism.* It was based upon his belief that spontaneous reason, freed from the control of the will, became pure in its contemplation, and thereby was able to behold essential truth.

As a young man, Cousin adhered to the Scottish school of Thomas Reid; in the period from 1815 to 1833 he was seized by a "metaphysical fever," and studied Hegel and Schelling, both of whom he later came to know personally. In 1840 he returned to the Scottish school of philosophy, and severely criticized his earlier writings. However, it was the writings of his "metaphysical fever"

279

that had the greatest influence on American thought. Cousin was the intermediary whereby the transcendentalists acquainted themselves with German idealism, for his was a more lucid, if not altogether correct, presentation. For a time, James Marsh (the founder of Transcendentalism), Theodore Parker, Charles Sumner, and George Bancroft were his devoted adherents; James Walker and Caleb Henry maintained his views somewhat later. Emerson, too, was indebted to Cousin, although he rightly declared that Cousin's method of "distillation" was the result of optical delusion. Cousin became a peer of France, royal councillor, and minister of public education during the régime of Louis Philippe. He was attacked by the clergy for his defense of the liberty of science, and later by the radical leftists. He became politically obscure after the coup d'état of Napoleon III.

WHAT IS ECLECTICISM

PHILOSOPHY, at the present day, can do only one of these three things:

Either abdicate, renounce its independence, submit again to the ancient authority, return to the Middle Ages;

Or continue its troubled motion in the circle of worn-out systems which mutually destroy each other;

Or finally disengage what is true in each of these systems, and thus construct a philosophy superior to all systems, which shall be no longer this or that philosophy, but philosophy itself in its essence and in its unity.

*   *   *

The third course remains. In the absence of fanaticism for this or that specific system, which a tendency to enthusiasm and an incomplete view of things would perhaps produce, and of which we must almost despair with our present characteristics, both good and bad, I see no resource left to philosophy, if it is unwilling to pass under the yoke of theocracy, but equity, moderation, impartiality, wisdom. It is, I confess, somewhat of a desperate resource but for myself, I see no other. It would be strange if there were no longer any thing but common sense which could produce an effect on the imagination of men. But it is certain that every other charm appears to be worn out. All the parts of fanaticism in philosophy, all the parts which have been performed at once by injustice and by folly, that is to say again, all the inferior parts have been taken from the nineteenth century by the preceding centuries; it is condemned to a new part, the most humble in appearance, but the most elevated and important in reality—that of being just towards all systems, and the dupe of none of them; of making them all the object of study, and instead of following in the train of any one, whatever it may be, of enrolling them all under its own banner, and thus marching at their head to the discovery and the conquest of truth. This procedure—to reject no system and to accept none entirely, to neglect this element and to take that, to select in all what appears to be true and good, and consequently everlasting—this, in a single word, is ECLECTICISM.

[93]

ANALYSIS OF FREE ACTION

FREE action is a phenomenon which contains several different elements combined together. To act freely, is to perform an action with the consciousness of being able not to perform it; now, to perform an action with the consciousness of being able not to perform it, supposes that we have preferred performing it to not performing it; to commence an action when we are able not to commence it, is to have preferred commencing it; to continue it when we are able to suspend it, is to have preferred continuing it; to carry it through when we are able to abandon it, is to have preferred accomplishing it. Now, to prefer supposes that we had motives for preferring, motives for performing this action, and motives for not performing it; that we were acquainted with these motives, and that we have preferred a part of them to the rest; in a word, preference supposes the knowledge of motives for and against. Whether these motives are passions or ideas, errors or truths, this or that, is of no consequence; it is important only to ascertain what faculty is here in operation; that is to say, what it is that recognizes these motives, which prefers one to the other, which judges that one is preferable to the other; for this is precisely what we mean by preferring. Now what is it that knows, that judges, but intelligence? Intelligence therefore is the faculty which prefers. But in order to prefer certain motives to others, to judge that some are preferable to others, it is not sufficient to know these different motives, we must moreover have weighed and compared them; we must have deliberated on these motives in order to form a conclusion; in fact, to prefer, is to judge definitively, to conclude. What, then, is it to deliberate? It is nothing else than to examine with doubt, to estimate the relative value of different motives without yet perceiving it with the clear evidence that commands judgment, conviction, preference.

Now, what is it that examines, what is it that doubts, what is it that judges that we should not yet judge in order to judge better? Evidently it is intelligence—the same intelligence which, at a subsequent period, after having passed many provisional judgments, will abrogate them all, will judge that they are less true, less reasonable than a certain other; will pass this latter judgment, will conclude and prefer after having deliberated. It is in intelligence that the phenomenon of preference takes place, as well as the other phenomena which it supposes. Thus far, then, we are still in the sphere of intelligence, and not in that of action. Assuredly intelligence is subjected to conditions; no one examines who does not wish to examine; and the will intervenes in deliberation; but this is the simple condition, not the foundation, of the phenomena; for, if it be true, that without the faculty of willing, all examination and all deliberation would be impossible, it is also true that the faculty itself which examines and which deliberates—the faculty which is the peculiar subject of examination, of deliberation, and of all judgment, provisional or definitive, is intelligence. Deliberation and conclusion, or preference, are therefore facts purely intellectual. Let us continue our analysis.

We have conceived different motives for performing or

not performing an action; we have deliberated on these motives, and we have preferred some of them to others; we have
concluded that we ought to perform it rather than not to
perform it; but to conclude that we ought to perform, and to
perform, are not the same thing. When intelligence has
judged that we ought to do this or that, for such or such
motives, it remains to proceed to action; in the first place to
resolve to assume our part, to say to ourselves, not I *ought*
to do, but I *will* to do. Now, the faculty which says I ought
to do, is not and cannot be the faculty which says I will
to do, I resolve to do. The office of intelligence here closes
entirely. I ought to do is a judgment; I will to do is not a
judgment, nor consequently an intellectual phenomenon. In
fact, at the moment when we form the resolution of doing
a particular action, we form it with the consciousness of being
able to form the contrary resolution. Here then is a new
element which should not be confounded with the preceding;
this element is will; just before it was our business to judge
and to know; now it is our business to will. To will, I say,
and not to do; for precisely as to judge that we ought to do
is not to will to do, so to will to do is not in itself to do.
To will is an act, not a judgment; but an act altogether internal. It is evident that this act is not action properly so
called; in order to arrive at action we must pass from the internal sphere of will to the sphere of the external world, in
which is definitively accomplished the action which you had
at first conceived, deliberated on, and preferred; which you
then willed; and which it was necessary to execute. If there
were no external world, there would be no consummated action; and there must not only be an external world; the
power of will also, which we have recognized after the power
of comprehending and of judging, must be connected with
another power, a physical power, which serves it as an
instrument with which to attain the external world. Suppose
that the will were not connected with organization, there
would be no bridge between the will and the external world;
no external action would be possible. The physical power,

necessary to action, is organization; and in this organization it is acknowledged that the muscular system is the special instrument of the will. Take away the muscular system, no effort would any longer be possible, consequently, no locomotion, no movement whatever would be possible; and if no movement were possible, no external action would be possible. Thus, to recapitulate, the whole action which we undertook to analyze is resolved into three elements perfectly distinct: (1) the intellectual element, which is composed of the knowledge of the motives for and against, of deliberation, of preference, of choice; (2) the voluntary element, which consists entirely in an internal act, namely the resolution to do; (3) the physical element, or the external action.

[93A]

CREIGHTON, JAMES EDWIN

CREIGHTON, JAMES EDWIN (1861-1924). To have his own philosophical system would have been contrary to Creighton's fundamental conviction that human thoughts are never completely the work of an isolated mind. He was an ardent advocate of social cooperation in philosophy, repeatedly pointing to the successes that resulted from cooperation in science. He regarded intellectual life as a form of experience which can be realized only in common with others through participation in a social community. With this point of view, Creighton concluded first, that the philosopher must participate intimately in the mental activities and interests of other people; and second, that he must define the task of philosophy as that of determining the real, stressing the importance of a precise concept of experience. He regarded "concept of experience" as an ambiguous term which was generally appealed to in a very uncritical and too confident fashion. Though he endeavored to define experience as strictly as possible, he was influenced in his earlier years by Kant, Bradley, and Bosanquet. Later, he accepted some views of Windelband and Rickert, without sharing all of their opinions. Creighton differentiated between that which is intelligible in philosophy and that which is intelligible in the natural sciences.

INDIVIDUAL AND SOCIETY

IN our theories as to the practical relations of men in society, we have at length come to see that it is necessary to

284

read the facts in a new way. If it is true that the individual, as a moral, political, or religious being, includes as an essential element within himself relations to his fellow-men that involve some form of organized society, then it is evidently a wrong scientific procedure to assume as the fundamental reality a self-centered individual whose activities are all concerned with the promotion of his own happiness. The older theories of politics and ethics accepted unquestioningly the notion of the individual as a self-contained given entity, endowed with certain properties and principles, *e.g.*, "self-love to move and reason to direct." Guided by a similar logic, the older physical theories assumed as their unquestioned datum of fact the self-enclosed atom with its properties of attraction and repulsion. From these isolated atoms, physical and social alike, the nature of the physical world and of human society had to be explained. But the same logic that overthrew the notion of the hard atom led in the social field to a truer view of the nature of the human individual. In both cases alike, a dynamic and relative view came to displace the older static and external set of conceptions. This new doctrine teaches that nothing is isolated and nothing fixed: that the parts live in and through their relation to the whole; and that change finds its way to the very heart of things.

I do not feel competent to speak of the results which the application of these new categories have brought about in the physical sciences. We know, however, that the older hypotheses have been revolutionized, and that much has happened and is happening in these departments of knowledge that was wholly undreamed of in the old philosophy. Similarly, the abandonment of atomistic conceptions of man and of society has brought about consequences that seem in many respects even more strikingly revolutionary. In order to give an account of these changes, it would be necessary to undertake to write the history of recent thought in these fields. We have only to consider the older political philosophy which was based on the conception of a social contract, the hedonistic or intuitional theories of morality, or the classical forms of political economy, in order to realize how great is the gulf that separates our thought from the individualism of the eighteenth and early nineteenth centuries. Even those of us who still call ourselves individualists no longer base our arguments upon a conception of the rights, duties, or interests of the formal or nominal individual; we have been forced to abandon the notion of *exclusive* individuality, and to recognize that individuals have reality and significance, not in themselves and by natural or divine right; but in so far as they embody and express the life and purpose of a larger social whole of which they are members. It is as *members of society*, not as self-subsistent entities, that individuals must be interpreted. Individuality involves partnership with others, coöperation in a common cause, loyalty to interests that carry the individual out beyond the limits of his merely private life. This conception of concrete individuality, as deriving its positive content from social relationships, is leading at the present day to new methods of inquiry and to new problems in the fields of social and political life. Even in religion, which has never been entirely deprived of social significance, emphasis has in recent times been laid less upon the individual's so-called inner life, and more upon his relations to his fellows. It must, of course, be added that this whole process of reconstruction is still going on, and that many questions as to the lines of its detail are still under debate. For our present purpose, however, it is not necessary to give an account of the results so far achieved, or to attempt a criticism or justification of the doctrines of any particular writer. These references are intended only to introduce the question whether the adoption of a similar standpoint is not necessary in order to understand the significance of the individual's thinking, and the influences which go toward the development of the intellectual life.

It might seem that this view would require only to be stated in order to find assent. For it is impossible to separate the concrete life of the mind into separate departments. The mind is a whole, and if its social nature is demonstrated in certain forms of experience, we should hardly expect to find it, in any one of its aspects, remaining isolated and self-centered. Nevertheless, both in popular thinking and in psychological analysis there is a tendency to regard the thinking mind as a particular form of existence, somehow enclosed within a body, and expressing the functioning of a brain. Just as one body keeps another body out of the same space, so the thinking mind of the individual is regarded as isolated, repellent, exclusive. The thinker is taken to be a solitary being, wrestling with his own problems alone and unassisted. By the power of his mind he is supposed to create truth through his own analysis and meditations. And, again, as an independent thinker, *Athanasius contra mundum*, he is supposed to be capable of bearing witness to this truth, and of making it prevail. As opposed to this contention, I wish to suggest that the process of verification always involves, either directly or indirectly, the coöperation and interplay of a plurality of thoughts of other men so that the individual is able to free himself from subjective fancies and hasty generalizations, and so to attain to universal truth. The result is not original in the sense that it has sprung wholly from his brain, but it is the product of many minds working together. In short, I am expressing again the doctrine that I have already suggested: thinking is the outcome of the functioning of a society of minds, not of an abstract individual mind, just as morality, and political institutions, and religion spring from and belong to such an organic unity of individuals. "Without society no individual," is a statement that applies to man as a thinker no less than to man as a moral or political being.

[94]

CRESCAS, HASDAI

CRESCAS, HASDAI (1340-1410). Like almost all Jewish philosophers of the Middle Ages, Crescas developed his philosophy in the face of persecution and imminent personal danger. He was born in Barcelona and was denounced and victimized there, imprisoned and fined, despite the recognition of his innocence. He moved and settled in Saragossa, where he declined appointment as rabbi of the congregation. He then became an authority on Jewish law and ritual tradition, and often intervened diplomatically on behalf of his co-religionists in Aragon and neighboring kingdoms. In a letter from him to the Jews of Avignon, he described the personal pain he and other Jews endured during the persecution of Jews in Spain. It was during this Inquisition period (1391), that he lost his only son.

Crescas did not content himself with bemoaning the fate of the Jews. He endeavored to defend the spirit and doctrines of Judaism against its religious and philosophical opponents. His criticism of Christianity, written in Spanish, is lost, except for those fragments which were translated into Hebrew by Joseph ibn Shemtob in 1451. Crescas' principal work, *Or Adonai* (The Light of God), completed in 1410, the year of his death, was of great consequence. It refuted Neo-Platonism and Aristotle, and implied a sharp criticism of Gersonides and Maimonides because of their efforts to reconcile Judaism with Greek philosophy. Crescas rejected Aristotle's physics, metaphysics, and axiology. He defended the cause of Judaism with a spiritual originality, radicalism, and courage, uncommon in the history of the Middle Ages. The importance of his thinking was by no means confined to the history of Jewish philosophy. His rejection of Aristotle, by stating that "there are no other worlds" than the one system in which the earth is situated, inspired such Christian thinkers as Nicholas Cusanus, Giordano Bruno, Marsilio Ficino, and Pico della Mirandola. There is little doubt that Spinoza was indebted to Crescas for his concept of the universe.

ON TIME AND CHANGE

THE correct definition of time is that it is the measure of the duration of motion or of rest between two instants. It is, moreover, evident that the genus most essentially appropriate of time is magnitude, for time belongs to continuous quantity and number to discrete. If we describe time as number, we describe it by a genus which is not essential nor primary. It is indeed measured by both motion and rest because it is our supposition of the measure of duration that is time. It seems therefore that the existence of time is only in the soul. . . .

Time may exist without motion . . . what we may reasonably maintain is that, since rest is the privation of motion, when we measure time by rest, we inevitably conceive of motion; but to say that the idea of time cannot be conceived except if it be connected with motion, must be denied.

Every change has two aspects. First it may be regarded with respect to the substratum, in which case change means the transition of that which underlies the change from one accident to another. In this respect, change exists in the other categories, and is in no-time. Second, change may also be regarded with respect to the matter of the change, the matter being, e.g., quantity, quality and place. In this respect it exists in that category in which the matter of the change is to be found.

Aristotle's statement that every motion is a change is evident. The proposition, however, is not convertible, for not every change is motion, inasmuch as there is a kind of change that takes place in no-time, as, e.g., generation and corruption and the transition of the substratum from one accident to another, in which latter respect, change is to be included under the category of action and passion.

While indeed the division of numbers into odd and even is true and unavoidable, still infinite number, not being limited, is not to be described by either evenness or oddness. And so an infinite number is not impossible in the case of intellects and souls.

That the possibility of infinite increase is not incompatible with being actually limited, may appear from the case of infinite decrease, for the examination into contraries is by one and the same science. . . . It is possible for a distance infinitely to decrease and still never completely to disappear. It is possible to assume, for instance, two lines which, by how much farther they are extended, are brought by so much nearer to each other and still will never meet, even if they are produced to infinity. If, in the case of decrease, there is always a certain residual distance which does not disappear, *a fortiori* in the case of increase it should be possible for a distance, though infinitely increased, always to remain limited.

[95]

CROCE, BENEDETTO

CROCE, BENEDETTO (1866-1952). The changing relations between the various forms of the human mind interested Croce far more than the solution of metaphysical problems. According to him, there is nothing that does not represent a manifestation of spirit either in nature or in the realm of science. He is opposed to materialism, naturalism, and the dualism of Kant, and often resorts to a renewal of Scholastic concepts. He considers himself to be a disciple of Plato and De Sanctis in aesthetics; of Herbart in ethics. To read Hegel, is to Croce "a debate within my own consciousness." He never intended to construct a system of philosophy, but, rather, a series of systematizations. He regards all philosophical thoughts as transitional steps, "because philosophy is the history of philosophy."

Croce began with historical studies, became engrossed with records and deeds, and astonished his colleagues with his keen critical faculties. He turned to philosophy around 1893, because his method of examining documents and interpreting historical facts involved an inquiry into the relations between history and the sciences, and an examination of those general concepts from which historical ideas may be derived or with which they may be integrated. The first result of these studies was *Aesthetics* (1902), conceived as the science of expression. Together with three volumes dealing with logic, ethics, and the theory of history, it is a part of his *Philosophy of Spirit* which was completed in 1917.

Croce lost his parents and sister in the earthquake of 1883, and was severely injured himself. However, it was not this experience that made him broach philosophical questions. The news of such events had made Voltaire and Goethe think about metaphysics. Under the Fascist regime of Mussolini, Croce was neither arrested nor compelled to emigrate; he continued to defy the Duce's claims of infallibility within his own country. He was neither intimidated by threats nor lured by promises; continuing to profess idealistic liberalism before, during, and after the reign of terror.

THE HUMANITY OF HISTORY

ENFRANCHISING itself from servitude to extra-mundane ca-

290

price and to blind natural necessity, freeing itself from transcendency and from false immanence (which is in its turn transcendency), thought conceives history as the work of man, as the product of human will and intellect, and in this manner enters that form of history which we shall call *humanistic*.

This humanism first appears as in simple contrast to nature or to extra-mundane powers, and posits dualism. On the one side is man, with his strength, his intelligence, his reason, his prudence, his will for the good; on the other there is something that resists him, strives against him, upsets his wisest plans, breaks the web that he has been weaving and obliges him to weave it all over again. History, envisaged from the viewpoint of this conception, is developed entirely from the first of these two sides, because the other does not afford a dialectical element which can be continually met and superseded by the first, giving rise to a sort of interior collaboration, but represents the absolutely extraneous, the capricious, the accidental, the meddler, the ghost at the feast. Only in the former do we find rationality combined with human endeavor, and thus the possibility of a rational explication of history. What comes from the other side is announced, but not explained: it is not material for history, but at the most for chronicle.

This first form of humanistic history is known under the various names of *rationalistic, intellectualistic, abstractistic, individualistic, psychological* history, and especially under that of *pragmatic* history. It is a form generally condemned by the consciousness of our times, which has employed these designations, especially *rationalism* and *pragmatism*, to represent a particular sort of historiographical insufficiency and inferiority, and has made proverbial the most characteristic pragmatic explanations of institutions and events, as types of misrepresentation into which one must beware of falling if one wishes to think history seriously. But as happens in the progress of culture and science, even if the condemnation be of culture and science, even if the condemnation be cordially accepted and no hesitation entertained as to drawing practical consequences from it in the field of actuality, there is not an equally clear consciousness of the reasons for this, or of the thought process by means of which it has been attained. This process we may briefly describe as follows.

Pragmatic finds the reasons for historical facts in man, but in man *in so far as he is an individual made abstract*, and thus opposed as such not only to the universe, but to other men, who have also been made abstract. History thus appears to consist of the mechanical action and reaction of beings, each one of whom is shut up in himself. Now no historical process is intelligible under such an arrangement, for the sum of the addition is always superior to the numbers added. To such an extent is this true that, not knowing which way to turn in order to make the sum come out right, it became necessary to excogitate the doctrine of 'little causes,' which were supposed to produce 'great effects.' This doctrine is absurd, for it is clear that great effects can only have real causes (if the illegitimate conceptions of great and small, of cause and effect, be applicable here). Such a formula, then, far from expressing the law of historical facts, unconsciously expresses the defects of the doctrine, which is inadequate for its purpose. And since the rational explanation fails, there arise crowds of fancies to take its place, which are all conceived upon the fundamental motive of the abstract individual. The pragmatic explanation of religious is characteristic of this; these are supposed to have been produced and maintained in the world by the economic cunning of the priests, taking advantage of the ignorance and credulity of the masses. But historical pragmatic does not always present itself in the guise of this egoistic and pessimistic inspiration. It is not fair to accuse it of egoism and utilitarianism, when the true accusation should, as we have already said, be levelled at its abstract individualism. This abstract individualism could be and sometimes was conceived even as highly moral, for we certainly find among the pragmatics sage legislators, good kings, and great men, who benefit humanity by means of science, inventions, and well-organized institutions. And if the greedy priest arranged the deceit of religions, if the cruel despot oppressed weak and innocent people, and if error was prolific and engendered the strangest and most foolish customs, yet the goodness of the enlightened monarch and legislator created the happy epochs, caused the arts to flourish, encouraged poets, aided discoveries, encouraged industries. From these pragmatic conceptions is derived the verbal usage whereby we speak of the age of Pericles, of that of Augustus, of that of Leo X, or of that of Louis XIV. And since fanciful explanations do not limit themselves merely to individuals physically existing, but also employ facts and small details, which are also made abstract and shut up in themselves, being thus also turned into what Vico describes as 'imaginative universals,' in like manner all these modes of explanation known as 'catastrophic' and making hinge the salvation or the ruin of a whole society upon the virtue of some single fact are also derived from pragmatic. Examples of this, which have also become proverbial, because they refer to concepts that have been persistently criticized by the historians of our time, are the fall of the Roman Empire, explained as the result of barbarian invasions, European civilization of the twelfth and thirteenth centuries, as the result of the Crusades, the renascence of classical literatures, as the result of the Turkish conquest of Constantinople and of the immigration of the learned Byzantines into Italy—and the like. And in just the same way as when the conception of the single individual did not furnish a sufficient explanation recourse was for that reason had to a multiplicity of individuals, to their co-operation and conflicting action, so here, when the sole cause adduced soon proved itself too narrow, an attempt was made to make up for the insufficiency of the method by the search for and enumeration of multiple historical causes. This enumeration threatened to proceed to the infinite, but, finite or infinite as it might be, it never explained the process to be explained, for the obvious reason that the continuous is never made out of the discontinuous, however much the latter may be multiplied and solidified. The so-called theory of the causes or factors of history, which survives in modern consciousness, together with several other mental habits of pragmatic, although generally inclined to follow other paths, is rather a confession of powerlessness to dominate history by means of individual causes, or causes individually conceived, than a theory; far from being a solution, it is but a reopening of the problem.

[96]

CUDWORTH, RALPH

CUDWORTH, RALPH (1617-1688). A theologian, Cudworth constantly warned against the over-estimation of dogmatic differences. He was Regius professor of Hebrew at Cambridge University, England, from 1645 to 1688 and while there became known as the leader of the Cambridge Platonists. In his *True Intellectual System of the World* (1678), he concentrated upon the refutation of all the atheistic schools, particularly those of Democritus, Lucretius, and Hobbes. However, he did consider it incumbent upon him to present fairly the disputed doctrines. This caused many critics, among them Dryden, to express apprehension lest readers of these presentations become converts to atheism, and stop reading before perusing Cudworth's refutation. Cudworth maintained that a primitive monotheistic creed could be found even in ancient paganism. In his explanation of the universe, he tried to avoid both the assumption of chance and the hypothesis of a steady interference of God. Therefore, he introduced the concept of "plastic nature" which was to act in a creative manner in accordance with its own laws. This concept, very likely, influenced Spinoza, and the nineteenth century French philosopher, Paul Janet, whose work was based on the idea of "plastic nature."

When the Stuarts resumed their reign of England in 1660, Cudworth encountered some governmental difficulties. They hesitated to reappoint him because he had been an intimate friend of Thurloe, Cromwell's secretary, and Cromwell had consulted Cudworth in 1655 on the question of the readmission of the Jews to England.

FOR, first, *Sense* only Suffering and receiving from without, and having no *Active Principle* of its own, to take Acquaintance with what it receives, it must needs be a Stranger to that which is altogether adventitious to it, and therefore cannot know or understand it. For to *Know* or *Understand* a thing, is nothing else but by some Inward Anticipation of the Mind, that is Native and Domestic, and so familiar to it, to take Acquaintance with it; of which I shall speak more afterward.

Sense is but the Offering or Presenting of some Object to the Mind, to give it an Occasion to exercise its own Inward *Activity* upon. Which two things being many times nearly conjoined together in Time, though they be very different in Nature from one another, yet they are vulgarly mistaken for one and the same thing, as if it were all nothing but mere Sensation or Passion from the Body. Whereas *Sense* itself is but the *Passive Perception* of some Individual Material Forms, but to *Know* or *Understand*, is Actively to Comprehend a thing by some Abstract, Free and Universal *Reasonings, from whence the Mind as it were looking down* (*as Boetius expresseth it*) *upon the individuals below it, views and understands them.* But *Sense* which lies Flat and Grovelling in the Individuals, and is stupidly fixed in the Material Form, is not able to rise up or ascend to an Abstract Universal Notion; For which Cause it never *Affirms* or *Denies* any thing of its Object, because (as *Aristotle* observes) in all Affirmation, and Negation at least, the Predicate is always Universal. The Eye which is placed in a Level with the sea, and touches the Surface of it, cannot take any large Prospect upon the Sea, much less see the whole Amplitude of it. But an Eye Elevated to a higher Station, and from thence looking down, may comprehensively view the whole Sea at once, or at least so much of it as is within our Horizon. The Abstract Universal *Reasons* are that higher Station of the Mind, from whence looking down upon

Individual things, it hath a Commanding view of them, and as it were *a priori* comprehends or Knows them.

But Sense, which either lies in the same Level with that Particular Material Object which it perceives, or rather under it and beneath it, cannot emerge to any Knowledge or Truth concerning it.

[97]

CUSA, NICHOLAS OF

CUSA, NICHOLAS OF (1401-1464). Nicholas Krebs, the son of a poor boatman, was born in Cues à Moselle, France. He rose to become bishop and cardinal, and distinguished himself as a mystical theologian, jurist, and diplomat. He was educated by the Brethren of the Common Life at Deventer, Holland and studied law, mathematics, astronomy, and theology at the Universities of Heidelberg, Padua, Rome and Cologne. He achieved great repute as a scholar and bibliophile, and was especially famous for his large collection of the manuscripts of Augustine and other authors of that period.

Although he was highly respected by the early Italian humanists, he remained, essentially, a scholastic Platonist. To some extent he was also influenced by Arabic and Jewish philosophy. His attempts to integrate metaphysics and mathematics were the result of numerous influences: the theosophical arithmetic of the Jewish Cabala; the *Zohar* or *Book of Splendor;* and the writings of Bonaventura (from whom he borrowed the term *"docta ignorantia"*). Although he was interested in astronomy, he maintained that God, not the sun, was the center of the universe. He upheld the Ptolemaic system, even though he had adopted the views of Jewish and Arabic thinkers that the earth really did move.

Cusanus said that there were two directions which enabled the human spirit to arrive at the truth. The first was reason, whose realm was measureable; the second, intellect, whose objectives were infinite. Reason was solely a human activity wherein God could only be expressed by antinomies, that is by the coincidence of opposites, so that pure reason was compelled to conceive God, at one and the same time, as both a being and one who was not a being, or as an infinite circle. Intellect was understanding illuminated by faith. This activity had supernatural qualities which enabled God to be viewed as an absolute unity without finite proportions. Since God was infinite, he remained undefinable by the concepts of reason, and therefore generally remained ignored by reason; he was conceived without being comprehended. Cusanus conceived of God as the concentrated unity of all essences; the world as the multiple explications of Divine essences. He used the theory of emanation as the basis for this concept. The essence of God comprised not only all existing creation but all possible creation. Cusanus deviated from one of the principal tenets of Christianity by adopting a statement of William of Ockham that the earth was the peculiar place of death and corruption.

THE VISION OF GOD

APART from Thee, Lord, naught can exist. If, then, Thine essence pervade all things, so also doth Thy sight, which is Thine essence. For even as no created thing can escape from its own proper essence, so neither can it from Thine essence, which giveth essential being to all beings. Wherefore, neither can it from Thy sight. Accordingly, Thou, Lord, seest all things and each thing at one and the same time, and movest with all that move, and standest with them that stand. And because there be some that move while others stand, Thou, Lord, dost stand and move at the same time, at the same time Thou dost proceed and rest. For if both motion and rest be individuated at the same time in divers beings, and if naught can exist apart from Thee, and no motion be apart from Thee, nor any rest; then Thou, Lord, art wholly present to all these things, and to each, at one and the same time. And yet Thou dost not move nor rest, since Thou art exalted above all, and freed from all that can be conceived or named. Wherefore, Thou standest and proceedest, and yet at the same time dost not stand or proceed, and that this painted face showeth me. For, if I move, its glance seemeth to move because it quitteth me not; if, while I am moving, another look on the face while standing still, its glance in like manner quitteth not him, but standeth still as he doth. Howbeit, the condition of motion or standing cannot rightly suit with a face that is freed from such conditions, for it is above all standing or motion, in simplest and absolute infinity; and 'tis on the hither side of this infinity that are found motion, and rest, and their opposition, and whatever may be uttered or conceived.

Hence I observe how needful it is for me to enter into the darkness, and to admit the coincidence of opposites, beyond all the grasp of reason, and there to seek the truth where impossibility meeteth me. And beyond that, beyond even the highest ascent of intellect, where I shall have attained unto that which is unknown to every intellect, and which every intellect judgeth to be most far removed from truth, there, my God, art Thou, who art Absolute Necessity. And the more that dark impossibility is recognised as dark and impossible, the more truly doth His Necessity shine forth and is more unveiledly present, and draweth nigh.

Wherefore I give Thee thanks, my God, because Thou makest plain to me that there is none other way of approaching Thee than that which to all men, even the most learned philosophers, seemeth utterly inaccessible and impossible. For Thou hast shown me that Thou canst not be seen elsewhere than where impossibility meeteth and faceth me. Thou hast inspired me, Lord, who art the Food of the strong, to do violence to myself, because impossibility coincideth with necessity, and I have learnt that the place wherein Thou art found unveiled is girt round with the coincidence of contradictories, and this is the wall of Paradise wherein Thou dost abide. The door whereof is guarded by the most proud spirit of Reason, and, unless he be vanquished, the way in will not lie open. Thus 'tis beyond the coincidence of contradictories that Thou mayest be seen, and nowhere this side thereof. If, then, in Thy sight, Lord, impossibility be necessity, there is naught that Thy sight seeth not.

[98]

$\mathcal{D}$

D'ALEMBERT, JEAN BAPTISTE LE ROND

D'ALEMBERT, JEAN BAPTISTE LE ROND (1717-1783). Considered the father of positivism, and in many ways the progenitor of pragmatism, D'Alembert maintained that truth is hypothetical but useful. In his introduction to the famous encyclopedia that he and Diderot edited, D'Alembert outlined the psychological genesis of knowledge, and the logical order and historical sequence of the sciences. He classed mathematics with natural philosophy, stating that it could be developed into a science of general dimensions contrary to the mathematical theories of Plato and Descartes. One of the most eminent mathematicians of his century, his theory of mathematics was consistent with his perceptual empiricism. He also made valuable contributions to physics, meteorology, and astronomy. In his literary works, he violently opposed all religious organization.

Abandoned as an infant, he was found on November 16, 1717, near the entrance to the Church St. Jean-Le-Rond by a glazier's wife. Brilliant and talented as a child, he achieved membership in the Academy of Science at the age of twenty-four. When he had become famous, his real mother, Madame de Tencin, socially important in Paris, recognized him, but he remained attached to his foster mother. He declined the presidency of the Prussian Academy of Sciences, offered him by Frederick II of Prussia, and the offer of Catherine II of Russia who wanted him to become a tutor for her grandson, who later became Czar Paul I.

ANECDOTES OF BOSSUET

BOSSUET's talents for the pulpit disclosed themselves almost from his infancy. He was announced as a phenomenon of early oratory at the hotel de Rambouillet, where merit of all kinds was summoned to appear, and was judged of, well or ill. He there, before a numerous and chosen assembly, made a sermon on a given subject, almost without preparation, and with the highest applause. The preacher was only sixteen years old, and the hour was eleven at night; which gave occasion to Voiture, who abounded in plays on words, to say that he had never heard so early or so late a sermon.

One of those persons who make a parade of their unbelief, wished to hear, or rather to brave him. Too proud to confess himself conquered, but too just to refuse the homage due to a great man, he exclaimed, on leaving the place, "This man to me is the first of preachers; for I feel it is by him I should be converted, if I were ever to be so."

He one day presented to Louis XIV Father Mabillon, as "the most learned Religieux of his Kingdom."— "And the humblest too," said le Tellier, Archbishop of Rheims, who thereby thought to epigrammatise adroitly the modesty of the prelate. The famed Archbishop, however, humiliated as he felt himself by the elevated genius of Bossuet, was too just to suffer it to be slighted. Some young court chaplains, one of whom has since occupied high stations, talking one day in his presence, with French levity, of the works and abilities of the Bishop of Meaux, whom they ventured to ridicule; "Be silent," said le Tellier, "respect your master and ours."

[99]

DARWIN, CHARLES

DARWIN, CHARLES (1809-1882). The age-old dispute between Biblical cosmology and modern natural science was completely overshadowed by Darwin's *Origin of Species* (1859) which resulted in innumerable arguments on evolution. Darwin's earlier book and his *Descent of Man* (1871) revolutionized biology and deeply affected philosophy, historical perspectives, religious controversies, and political, social, and economic criteria.

Darwin, humble, of delicate health, and adverse to publicity, upheld Christian behavior, though he had abandoned theism. He had never intended to provoke religious or philosophical debates. The aim of his special studies, which occupied him for more than twenty-five years, was to show that higher species had come into existence as a result of the gradual transformation of lower species; that the process of transformation could be explained through the selective effects of the natural environment upon organisms. His theory was based upon the propositions that all organisms and instincts are variable, that the gradual perfection of any organism or instinct is the result of an adaptation to the environment, and that the general struggle for existence (which Darwin considered to be the powerful method of selection) allowed only those organisms which were fit for adaptation to survive. Heredity continued this survival and reproduction of parental and ancestral qualities for many epochs. Darwin stated that although natural selection was the essential factor, it was not the sole factor in transformation. He admitted the possibility of inheriting acquired characteristics; this was denied by later Darwinists. Darwin did not exclude man from his theory that the higher organisms are the result of long processes of transformation which began with the lowest on the scale.

His work was based upon painstaking observation. His principle of the struggle for existence was not based upon his primary studies of nature. For years, he had sought for a principle by means of which he could arrange the collected facts. Neither his thoughts as a natural scientist nor his observations of nature led him to this. Malthus' *Essay on Population* which Darwin read (1838) clarified for him the entire problem of variation in plants and animals. Malthus maintained that more individuals are born than are able to survive and that the capability of adaptation to the environment is the reason for the survival of the fittest. This principle, borrowed by Darwin from a political economist, has become one of the most disputed portions of his theory.

Since the appearance of the *Origin of Species*, Darwinism and evolutionism have become synonymous. It was Herbert Spencer, to whom Darwin fondly referred as "our philosopher," who characterized Darwin's theory as evolutionism, and to which Darwin agreed. Darwin's concept of evolution is entirely different from other evolutionary theories which assumed a metaphysical entity as the evolving or directing power. Natural selection, regardless of whether it is valid, was conceived and kept by Darwin, free from any metaphysics. Darwin's hypothesis that transformation or evolution proceeds by minute gradations, has been disputed by Thomas Huxley, who, despite this dissension, was an important champion of Darwinism. Most modern biologists share Huxley's views on this question.

"EVERYONE believing, as I do, that all the corporeal and mental organs (excepting those which are neither advantageous nor disadvantageous to the possessor) of all beings have been developed through natural selection, or the survival of the fittest, together with use or habit, will admit that these organs have been formed so that their possessors may compete successfully with other beings, and thus increase in number. Now an animal may be led to pursue that course of action which is most beneficial to the species by suffering, such as pain, hunger, thirst, and fear; or by pleasure, as in eating and drinking, and in the propagation of the species, &c.; or by both means combined, as in the search for food. But pain or suffering of any kind, if long continued, causes depression and lessens the power of action, yet is well adapted to make a creature guard itself against any great or sudden evil. Pleasurable sensations, on the other hand, may be long continued without any depressing effect; on the contrary, they stimulate the whole system to increased action. Hence it has come to pass that most or all sentient beings have been developed in such a manner, through natural selection, that pleasurable sensations serve as their habitual guides. We see this in the pleasure from exertion, even occasionally from great exertion of the body or mind,— in the pleasure of our daily meals, and especially in the pleasure derived from sociability, and from our loving families. The sum of such pleasures as these, which are habitual or frequently recurrent, give, as I can hardly doubt, to most sentient beings an excess of happiness over misery, although many occasionally suffer much. Such suffering is quite compatible with the belief in Natural Selection, which is not perfect in its action, but tends only to render each species as successful as possible in the battle for life with other species, in wonderfully complex and changing circumstances.

"That there is much suffering in the world no one disputes. Some have attempted to explain this with reference to man by imagining that it serves for his moral improvement. But the number of men in the world is as nothing compared with that of all other sentient beings, and they often suffer greatly without any moral improvement. This very old argument from the existence of suffering against the existence of an intelligent First Cause seems to me a strong one; whereas, as just remarked, the presence of much suffering agrees well with the view that all organic beings have been developed through variation and natural selection.

"At the present day the most unusual argument for the existence of an intelligent God is drawn from the deep inward conviction and feelings which are experienced by most persons.

"Formerly I was led by feelings such as those just referred to (although I do not think that the religious sentiment was ever strongly developed in me), to the firm conviction of the existence of God and of the immortality of the soul. In my Journal I wrote that whilst standing in the midst of the grandeur of a Brazilian forest, 'it is not possible to give an adequate idea of the higher feelings of wonder, admiration, and devotion which fill and elevate the mind.' I well remember my conviction that there is more in man than the mere breath of his body; but now the grandest scenes would not cause any such convictions and feelings to rise in my mind. It may be truly said that I am like a man who has become color-blind, and the universal belief by men of the existence of redness makes my present loss of perception of not the least value as evidence. This argument would be a valid one if all men of all races had the same inward conviction of the existence of one God; but we know that this is very far from being the case. Therefore I cannot see that such inward convictions and feelings are of any weight as evidence of what really exists. The state of mind which grand scenes formerly excited in me, and which was intimately connected with a belief in God, did not essentially differ from that which is often called the sense of sublimity; and however difficult it may be to explain the genesis of this sense, it can hardly be advanced as an argument for the existence of God, any more than the powerful though vague and similar feelings excited by music.

"With respect to immortality, nothing shows me [so clearly] how strong and almost instinctive a belief it is as the consideration of the view now held by most physicists, namely, that the sun with all the planets will in time grow too cold for life, unless indeed some great body dashes into the sun and thus gives it fresh life. Believing as I do that man in the distant future will be a far more perfect creature than he now is, it is an intolerable thought that he and all other sentient beings are doomed to complete annihilation after such long-continued slow progress. To those who fully admit the immortality of the human soul, the destruction of our world will not appear so dreadful."

[100]

DE BROGLIE, LOUIS

DE BROGLIE, LOUIS (1892-   ). Albert Einstein evaluated De Broglie's genius and achievements as something which "happens only in large intervals of history." He also expressed great satisfaction with the decision of the Nobel Prize Committee to award the 1929 Nobel Prize to De Broglie.

De Broglie's principal achievement is his formulation of "undulatory mechanics" or "wave mechanics." He overcame the constant antagonism between the theories of emission and undulation by showing the interaction between radiation and matter. The almost-forgotten wave principle of optics was discussed during the seventeenth and eighteenth centuries, and applications of this principle to physics were considered to be completely out of the question. De Broglie's theory assimilates the photons as particulars of light, and the electrons as particulars of matter. These have been confirmed experimentally by noted British and American physicists. De Broglie has always acknowledged that Einstein's theory of relativity was his constant inspiration. He established a relativist mechanics of a more physical character; whereas Einstein's physics is of a more mathematical nature. De Broglie's theory has been stated to be of equal importance with those of Einstein and Planck. It allows for a more rigorous approximation of measurement and

304

a more concrete objectivity of scientific symbolism. It makes for progress in the exactitude of theoretical physics and increasingly reconciles the principles of continuity and discontinuity.

THE MARCH OF SCIENCE

In the history of thought, particularly scientific thought, there are moments when great, earth-shaking evolutions are produced, and decisive distances that formerly existed, disappear. These mutations are slowly and secretly prepared during anterior periods and occur with the same abruptness, frequency, and similarity that contemporary biologists have demonstrated in the evolution of living organisms.

The progressive formation and coincidence of individual efforts converging toward the same end often takes place without knowledge of those engaged in the work. Powerful currents of thought emerge simultaneously. The exact form of whole branches of science whose great features had only been vaguely seen by precursors is suddenly illumined by the work of superior minds. It is as though the chisel of an inspired artist sculpts a statue that is admired for centuries. Sometimes the effect of pre-established harmony is the discovery of more than one exceptional mind; it becomes the simultaneous flowering of ingenious savants; an ensemble of imperishable discoveries whose production a privileged generation is witness to in its lifetime. It becomes a glorious epoch of scientific thought from which all progress issues forth in ensuing years.

[101]

DEDEKIND, RICHARD

DEDEKIND, RICHARD (1831-1916). When Dedekind was seventy-three years old, he read in a mathematical annual, an obituary that stated he had died on September 4, 1899. As a cautious mathematician, he wrote to the editor of the annual, pointing out that as far as he could see, September 4 might be proved to be correct in the future, but that the year, 1899, as the year of his death was certainly not correct. The incident was characteristic of Dedekind's modesty and aversion to publicity, which resulted in his remaining unknown even to mathematical experts, who daily utilized his findings and studies.

Dedekind's principal works: *Continuity and Irrational Numbers* (1871) and *The Nature and Meaning of Numbers* (1888) are highly important contributions to the theory of numbers. Dedekind's "cut," in the first book, is considered to be the foundation of irrational numbers. In the second, the concept and the fundamental qualities of natural numbers are developed by the pure theory of quantity, beginning with the idea of imaged systems. A system (totality or quantity) is called infinite if it cannot be imaged homologously.

THE NATURE AND MEANING OF NUMBERS

IN science nothing capable of proof ought to be accepted without proof. Though this demand seems so reasonable yet I cannot regard it as having been met even in the most recent methods of laying the foundations of the simplest science; viz., that part of logic which deals with the theory of numbers. In speaking of arithmetic (algebra, analysis) as a part of logic I mean to imply that I consider the number-concept entirely independent of the notions or intuitions of space and time, that I consider it an immediate result from the laws of thought. My answer to the problems propounded in the title of this paper is, then, briefly this: numbers are free creations of the human mind; they serve as a means of apprehending more easily and more sharply the difference of things. It is only through the purely logical process of building up the science of numbers and by thus acquiring the continuous number-domain that we are prepared accurately to investigate our notions of space and time by bringing them into relation with this number-domain created in our mind. If we scrutinise closely what is done in counting an aggregate or number of things, we are led to consider the ability of the mind to relate things to things, to let a thing correspond to a thing, or to represent a thing by a thing, an ability without which no thinking is possible.

I like to compare this action of thought, so difficult to trace on account of the rapidity of its performance, with the action which an accomplished reader performs in reading; this reading always remains a more or less complete repetition of the individual steps which the beginner has to take in his wearisome spelling-out; a very small part of the same, and therefore a very small effort or exertion of the mind, is sufficient for the practiced reader to recognize the correct, true word, only with very great probability, to be sure; for, as is well known, it occasionally happens that even the most practiced proof-reader allows a typographical error to escape him, i.e., reads falsely, a thing which would be impossible if the chain of thoughts associated with spelling were fully repeated. So from the time of birth, continually and in increasing measure we are led to relate things to things and thus to use that faculty of the mind on which the creation of numbers depends; by this practice continually occurring, though without definite purpose, in our earliest years and by the attending formation of judgments and chains of reasoning we acquire a store of real arithmetic truths to which our first teachers later refer as to something simple, self-evident, given in the inner consciousness; and so it happens that many very complicated notions (as for example that of the number [*Anzahl*] of things) are erroneously regarded as simple.

[102]

DELMEDIGO, JOSEPH SOLOMON

DELMEDIGO, JOSEPH SOLOMON (1591-1655). A restless spirit made Delmedigo the prototype of the wandering Jew. He peregrinated from Candia, Crete, his native town, to Padua, Italy; thence to Egypt, Turkey, Poland, Hamburg, Amsterdam, Frankfort, Worms, and then finally died in Prague. He earned his living either as physician or teacher but wherever he sojourned, he remembered to study the natural sciences. He was a disciple of Galileo and a keen critic of the medieval philosophy of nature; but he had to be careful, lest the ecclesiastical and secular authorities were offended by his ideas. He was shrewd enough to avoid such disturbances. His only known works are: *Elim* (Palms) dealing with mathematics, the natural sciences, and metaphysics, and some of letters and essays.

GOOD AND BAD BOOKS

PEOPLE say that the art of printing has brought us great advantages, whereas it has in fact been detrimental to us. For in former days authors were handsomely paid and people would buy from them only the good, pleasing, useful books, while the useless, vain books would of themselves disappear. Not so, however, in our days, when many ignorant people assume airs, and, though benighted and smaller than the least throughout their lives, seek to set themselves up as shining lights to another generation that has not learned to know them. And everyone who possibly can, and whose wealth is greater than his understanding, connives to publish books in which he is arbitrarily referred to as a great and worthy man, whereas he is no more an authority than is a carpenter's apprentice.

The only concern for the publishers is for new books. No one pays any attention to the writings of the early authors, or makes effort to preserve them and to shake the dust from them. Because of the art of printing you find a topsy-turvy world—the native below and the stranger on top.

It seems to me that books are subject to the same process as souls: they migrate from one body to another. Not by chance are son and book designated in Latin by the same term, *liber*. And so it is in the case of scholarly books that are translated from one language into another, in a different style, in other words, and in changed order. The language becomes different but the content is the same. And the book is given a new title—for example, a book originally entitled *Precious Vessel* will be called *Costly Vessel*. The matter remains exactly the same except that it has been poured from one receptacle into another. Ecclesiastes has taught us all this in these his words: "That which hath been is that which shall be, and that which hath been done is that which shall be done; and there is nothing new under the sun. Is there a thing whereof it is said: 'See, this is new'?—it hath been already, in the ages which were before us. There is no remembrance of them of former times; neither shall there be any remembrance of them of latter times that are to come, among those that shall come after." He also said: "Seeing that in the days to come all will long ago have been forgotten."

It is true indeed that there is no cause for concern about the good, useful, pleasing authors, for under any circumstances their names will live for many days, perhaps they will even shine forever, like stars. But not so in the case of those who pen spurious writings, who have consumed their time and their money to no advantage. When their ignorance is laid bare and their mischief gives offense, their shortcomings are recognized and their hope turns to despair. For their eye is dimmed. Even if they were to offer their books as gifts, no one would accept them. They become like thorns in their eyes, they are piled high in their houses, heaps upon heaps, and the rats feed upon and glut themselves with them. And the rain falls, drips down upon them drop upon drop, and the birds, pigeons, and chickens nest among them. The sun sets at noon for the authors of these books, before their very eyes, and their books die in their lifetime.

But if the authors were only wise enough to realize all this, they would recoil from "much study that is a weariness of the flesh." But their love for themselves is great, and they shut their minds to the fact that the ultimate end of their books is but a vain one, for no one would ever commit the folly of publishing them anew. Thus one who writes a number of inferior books will live unto all generations just as little as the name of one who begets many illegitimate children.

[103]

DEMOCRITUS OF ABDERA

DEMOCRITUS OF ABDERA (460-c. 360 B.C.). Although only scarce fragments of the numerous works of Democritus are extant, sufficient pieces have remained to prove that he was one of the greatest of the Greek thinkers; equally outstanding as a scientist and philosopher; a peer of Plato and Aristotle; and a man whose thoughts and feelings were close to the common people. Many legends have been formed about his life. He is said to have traveled from Ethiopia and Egypt to Persia and India. He certainly visited Athens, but no one there took notice of him. Plato, his contemporary, never mentioned Democritus, but Aristotle and Hippocrates quoted him frequently. The legends depicted Democritus as a man easily disposed to laughter; an incurable optimist; moderate, serene, and always prepared to understand the errors and failures of his fellow men.

Democritus conceived the universe to be composed of essential transitory combinations of an infinite number of atoms and their separations as the necessary condition for eternal change; that atomic theory was a working hypothesis which would help explain the experiences of mind and nature; his concepts were comparable to idealistic metaphysics. He was not only an important systematizer of Greek atomism, anticipating the underlying principle of modern physics, but also an acute psychologist; a sage moralist, inspired by humanitarian ideals, without illusions about human nature. He taught that equanimity and fortitude must prevail in all life situations, and that there must be resistance to evil and temptations. He contributed to epistemology, physics, mathematics, and technics. He dealt with logical and musical problems; avoided politics in his writings.

THE SYMMETRY OF LIFE

In truth we know nothing about anything, but every man shares the generally prevailing opinion.

In fact we do not know anything infallibly, but only that which changes according to the condition of our body and of the [influences] that reach and impinge upon it.

There are two forms of knowledge, one genuine, one obscure. To the obscure belong all of the following: sight, hearing, smell, taste, feeling. The other form is the genuine, and is quite distinct from this. (And then distinguishing the genuine from the obscure, he continues:) Whenever the obscure [way of knowing] has reached the *minimum sensible* of hearing, smell, taste, and touch, and when the investigation must be carried farther into that which is still finer, then arises the genuine way of knowing, which has a finer organ of thought.

310

By convention sweet is sweet, by convention bitter is bitter, by convention hot is hot, by convention cold is cold, by convention color is color. But in reality there are atoms and the void. That is, the objects of sense are supposed to be real and it is customary to regard them as such, but in truth they are not. Only the atoms and the void are real.

Of practical wisdom these are the three fruits: to deliberate well, to speak to the point, to do what is right.

If one choose the goods of the soul, he chooses the diviner [portion]; if the goods of the body, the merely mortal.

'Tis not in strength of body nor in gold that men find happiness, but in uprightness and in fullness of understanding.

Not from fear but from sense of duty refrain from your sins.

He who does wrong is more unhappy than he who suffers wrong.

Many who have not learned wisdom live wisely, and many who do the basest deeds can make most learned speeches.

Fools learn wisdom through misfortune.

One should emulate works and deeds of virtue, not arguments about it.

Strength of body is nobility in beasts of burden, strength of character is nobility in men.

The hopes of the right-minded may be realized, those of fools are impossible.

Neither art nor wisdom may be attained without learning.

It is better to correct your own faults than those of another.

Those who have a well-ordered character lead also a well-ordered life.

Good means not [merely] not to do wrong, but rather not to desire to do wrong.

There are many who know many things, yet are lacking in wisdom.

Fame and wealth without wisdom are unsafe possessions.

You can tell the man who rings true from the man
who rings false, not by his deeds alone, but also by his desires.

False men and shams talk big and do nothing.

My enemy is not the man who wrongs me, but the man
who means to wrong me.

The enmity of one's kindred is far more bitter than the
enmity of strangers.

The friendship of one wise man is better than the
friendship of a host of fools.

No one deserves to live who has not at least one good-
man-and-true for a friend.

Seek after the good, and with much toil shall ye find
it; the evil turns up of itself without your seeking it.

In the weightiest matters we must go to school to the
animals, and learn spinning and weaving from the spider,
building from the swallow, singing from the birds,—from
the swan and the nightingale, imitating their art.

An evil and foolish and intemperate and irreligious life
should not be called a bad life, but rather, dying long drawn
out.

Fortune is lavish with her favors, but not to be depended
on. Nature on the other hand is self-sufficing and therefore
with her feebler but trustworthy [resources] she wins the
greater [meed] of hope.

The right-minded man, ever inclined to righteous and
lawful deeds, is joyous day and night, and strong, and free
from care. But if a man take no heed of the right, and leave
undone the things he ought to do, then will the recollection
of no one of all his transgressions bring him any joy, but only
anxiety and self-reproaching.

Now as of old the gods give men all good things, excepting only those that are baneful and injurious and useless.
These, now as of old, are not gifts of the gods: men stumble
into them themselves because of their own blindness and
folly.

A sensible man takes pleasure in what he has instead of pining for what he has not.

The pleasures that give most joy are the ones that most rarely come.

Throw moderation to the winds, and the greatest pleasures bring the greatest pains.

Men achieve tranquility through moderation in pleasure and through the symmetry of life. Want and superfluity are apt to upset them and to cause great perturbations in the soul. The souls that are rent by violent conflicts are neither stable nor tranquil. One should therefore set his mind upon the things that are within his power, and be content with his opportunities, nor let his memory dwell very long on the envied and admired of men, nor idly sit and dream of them. Rather, he should contemplate the lives of those who suffer hardship, and vividly bring to mind their sufferings, so that your own present situation may appear to you important and to be envied, and so that it may no longer be your portion to suffer torture in your soul by your longing for more. For he who admires those who have, and whom other men deem blest of fortune, and who spends all his time idly dreaming of them, will be forced to be always contriving some new device because of his [insatiable] desire, until he ends by doing some desperate deed forbidden by the laws. And therefore one ought not to desire other men's blessings, and one ought not to envy those who have more, but rather, comparing his life with that of those who fare worse, and laying to heart their sufferings, deem himself blest of fortune in that he lives and fares so much better than they. Holding fast to this saying you will pass your life in greater tranquillity and will avert not a few of the plagues of life—envy and jealousy and bitterness of mind.

[104]

DE MORGAN, AUGUSTUS

DE MORGAN, AUGUSTUS (1806-1871). De Morgan made a number of important contributions to an algebra of logic, and his laws of the propositional calculus have been widely discussed. He is also acknowledged as the founder of the logic of relations. However, the author of *Formal Logic* (1847) never renounced his claims of promoting metaphysics in no lesser degree than he did mathematics and logic. For more than thirty years, De Morgan, as professor at University College in London, acted and taught in accordance with his principle that positive theism must be made the basis of psychological explanation and that, in elucidating mathematical principles, it is necessary to refer to an intelligent and disposed Creator when mental organization is to be dealt with as effect of a cause.

Although a convinced theist, De Morgan never joined a religious congregation. He was a staunch adversary of religious discrimination and was fond of his nonconformism. He renounced his professorship in 1866, when James Martineau was denied a chair at University College because he was a Unitarian. De Morgan, who was admired for his "reading algebra like a novel," was an intimate friend of George Boole who shared his views on mathematics as well as those on religion and ethics.

IDEAS

THE word *idea*, as here used, does not enter in that vague sense in which it is generally used, as if it were an opinion that might be right or wrong. It is that which the object gives to the mind, or the state of the mind produced by the object. Thus the idea of a horse is *the horse in the mind*: and we know no other horse. We admit that there is an external *object,* a horse, which may give a *horse in the mind* to twenty different persons: but no one of these twenty knows the object; each one only knows his *idea*. There is an object, because each of the twenty persons receives an idea without communicating with the others: so that there is something external to give it them. But when they talk about it, under the name of a horse, they talk about their ideas. They all refer to the object, as being the thing they are talking about, until the moment they begin to differ: and then they begin to speak, not of external horses, but of impressions on their minds; at least this is the case with those who know what knowledge is; the positive and the unthinking part of them still talk of the *horse*. And the latter have a great advantage over the former with those who are like themselves.

Why then do we introduce the term *object* at all, since all our knowledge lies in ideas? For the same reason as we introduce the term *matter* into natural philosophy, when all we know is form, size, color, weight, &c., no one of which is matter, nor even all together. It is convenient to have a word for that external source from which *sensible* ideas are produced: and it is just as convenient to have a word for the external source, material or not, from which *any* idea is produced. Again, why do we speak of our power of considering things ideally or objectively, when as we can know nothing but ideas, we can have no right to speak of any thing else? The answer is that, just as in other things, when we speak of an object, we speak of the *idea of an object*. We learn to speak of the external world, because there are others like ourselves who evidently draw ideas from the same sources as ourselves: hence we come to have the idea of those sources, the idea of external objects, as we call them. But we do not know those sources; we know only our ideas of them.

We can even use the terms ideal and objective in what may appear a metaphorical sense. When we speak of ourselves in the manner of this chapter, we put ourselves, as it were, in the position of spectators of our own minds: we speak and think of our own minds objectively. And it must be remembered that by the word object, we do not mean *material* object only. The mind of another, any one of its thoughts or feelings, any relation of minds to one another, a treaty of peace, a battle, a discussion upon a controverted question, the right of conveying a freehold,—are all objects, independently of the persons or things engaged in them. They are things external to our minds, of which we have ideas.

An object communicates an idea: but it does not follow that every idea is communicated by an object. The mind can create ideas in various ways; or at least can derive, by combinations which are not found in external existence, new collections of ideas. We have a perfectly distinct idea of unicorn, or a flying dragon: when we say there are no such things, we speak objectively only: ideally, they have as much existence as a horse or a sheep; to a herald, more. Add to this, that the mind can separate ideas into parts, in such manner that the parts alone are not ideas of any existing separate material objects, any more than the letters of a word are constituent parts of the meaning of the whole. Hence we get what are called *qualities* and *relations*. A ball may be hard and round, or may have hardness and roundness: but we cannot say that hardness and roundness are separate external material objects, though they are objects the ideas of which necessarily accompany our perception of certain objects. These ideas are called *abstract* as being removed or abstracted from the complex idea which gives them: the abstraction is made by comparison or observation of resemblances. If a person had never seen any thing round except an apple, he would perhaps never think of roundness as a distinct object of thought. When he saw another round body, which was evidently not an apple, he would immediately, by perception of the resemblance, acquire a separate idea of the thing in which they resemble one another.

[105]

DE SANCTIS, FRANCESCO

DE SANCTIS, FRANCESCO (1817-1883). In the 1848 revolution in Naples, when the revolutionaries struggled against the king's troops, one barricade, in particular, attracted wide attention. It was led by De Sanctis, then the director of a boys' school, who commanded and organized his pupils as a company of trained soldiers. When the revolution was defeated, De Sanctis was imprisoned for more than four years. He utilized this period of enforced idleness to study the philosophy of Hegel and to translate several German works into Italian. Upon his release, he earned his living as a private tutor and free-lance writer; he later became a professor at Zurich, Switzerland, with the German Hegelian, Friederich Theodor Vischer, and the historian, Jacob Burckhardt, as his colleagues. When the unified kingdom of Italy was achieved, King Victor Emmanuel II appointed De Sanctis minister of public education (1861),

316

and he was later made professor of comparative literature at the University of Naples (1871). There, De Sanctis had many faithful disciples, among whom Benedetto Croce was the most outstanding.

De Sanctis' chief contribution was to aesthetics. Although he remained a Hegelian, he did not found his aesthetic views upon ideas; instead he concentrated upon form. He stated that living form was the essence of art, rather than the ideal or beauty. He opposed all psychological approaches to the arts, especially poetry, and insisted upon formal analysis. His influence upon Italian literary criticism remained strong up to the present time.

THE INTELLECTUAL FUTURE

ITALY, compelled to struggle for a whole century to win independence and liberal institutions, kept by that struggle in a circle of ideas too general, too uniform, subordinated to political ends, is witnessing the falling to pieces of that whole theological-metaphysical-political system, which has nothing left to give her. The positive tendencies were vanquished by ontology with its brilliant synthesis; and now ontology is failing too, is stale and repetitive. It has sunk into the Arcadian and academic, as happens inevitably to systems that have ceased to progress. Ontology's heir is criticism, a criticism bearing on its face the stamp of the fantastic and dogmatic it received at its birth; but visibly inclined to investigate, rather than to postulate and demonstrate. Philosophical and literary synthesis are declining; their place is being taken by the humble and patient monograph. Systems are suspect, laws are received with diffidence, principles until now regarded as absolute are being tested in the crucible. Nothing is admitted that has not been proved by a series of ascertained facts—the verification of a fact is an event of greater importance than the establishment of a law. That whole collection of ideas, maxims, and formulae that once gave rise to such struggles and excitements, has sunk into a conventional repertory no longer representative of opinion as it really is: Giacomo Leopardi has left his touch on them. It would seem that at this very moment when Italy at last has formed herself, that the intellectual and political world which made her formation possible, was dissolving. That Italy herself is alive we know from the new horizon that has dawned—vague as yet and shadowy, but unmistakable. A never-flagging force is driving her onward; no sooner is one aspiration appeased than another appears.

Italy till now has been dazzled by her brilliant sphere —the sphere of nationality and liberty. Her philosophy has sprung from a thing outside of her, even if around her. Now she must look into her heart, must seek for her very self. The sphere must develop and become concrete as her inner life. The religious hypocrisies, the academic habits, the political necessities, the long periods of lying fallow, the foreign motives superimposed on her liberal development, the memories of a servitude that lasted for centuries—all these have led to an artificial and vacillating consciousness, preventing absorption and intimacy. Her life, even today, is external and artificial. Let her look into her heart with clear eyes, unhindered by veil or obstacle; let her look for the "effectual thing" with the spirit of Galileo and Machiavelli. In this search for the elements of the real in her life the Italian spirit will create its culture once more, will restore her moral world, will refresh her impressions, will find in her own inner life new sources of inspiration—woman, the family, love, nature, liberty, science, and virtue—and not as brilliant ideas revolving in space around and about her but as concrete, definite things, become her content.

[106]

DESCARTES, RENÉ

DESCARTES, RENÉ (1595-1650). Descartes represented the spirit of the age which rid itself of ancient authority and conventions. His personal life manifested a change from bon vivant to that of recluse. The life-loving, teeming existence of Paris did not deter him. He had been a soldier of fortune with different armies during the Thirty Years' War, a scholar, traveler, pilgrim, and firm adherent to the Catholic faith.

On November 10, 1619 a dream revealed to him the synthetic

318

and analytic method which he was to follow. He never published it in the form he had originally intended because news of the persecution of Galileo, with whom he had sympathized, reached him. Like everyone in that age, he doubted everything; even his own existence. The more he doubted, the more certain he became of himself as a thinking being. He tersely couched this insight with the phrase: "I think, therefore I am." His constant intellectual search led him to the idea of an infinite God, which fact he then took as proof that God exists. He argued thus: nothing so great as a divine being could be without a real basis in fact. He stated that the existence of a perfect being was comprised in the idea of it, just as the equality of the three angles to two right ones is comprised in the idea of a triangle. Since God was truthful, he could not be thought of as wishing to deceive man. Hence God guaranteed the truth of whatever is clear and distinct to man's reason and perception.

Thus Descartes, or Cartesius—the Latin form of his name—became the father of modern rationalism. He was also a mechanist, explaining matter by differently shaped corpuscles interacting mechanically. He and his disciples maintained that even animals are living automata; that man is also a machine, except for his spirit which represents thinking substance, as distinct from extended substance. Descartes died unhappily in the service of Queen Christina of Sweden who meant to make full use of his talents for philosophy, mathematics, and natural science.

THE NATURE OF THE HUMAN MIND

I SUPPOSE . . . that all the things which I see are fictitious; I believe that none of those objects which my fallacious memory represents ever existed; I suppose that I possess no senses; I believe that body, figure, extension, motion, and place are merely fictions of my mind. What is there, then, that can be esteemed true? Perhaps this only, that there is absolutely nothing certain.

But how do I know that there is not something different altogether from the objects I have now enumerated, of which it is impossible to entertain the slightest doubt? Is there not a God, or some being, by whatever name I may designate him, who causes these thoughts to arise in my mind? But why suppose such a being, for it may be I myself am capable of producing them? Am I, then, at least not something? But

I before denied that I possessed senses or a body; I hesitate, however, for what follows from that? Am I so dependent on the body and the senses that without these I cannot exist? But I had the persuasion that there was absolutely nothing in the world, that there was no sky and no earth, neither minds nor bodies; was I not, therefore, at the same time, persuaded that I did not exist? Far from it; I assuredly existed, since I was persuaded. But there is I know not what being, who is possessed at once of the highest power and the deepest cunning, who is constantly employing all his ingenuity in deceiving me. Doubtless, then, I exist, since I am deceived; and, let him deceive me as he may, he can never bring it about that I am nothing, so long as I shall be conscious that I am something. So that it must, in fine, be maintained, all things being maturely and carefully considered, that this proposition I am, I exist, is necessarily true each time it is expressed by me, or conceived in my mind.

But I do not yet know with sufficient clearness what I am, though assured that I am; and hence, in the next place, I must take care, lest perchance I inconsiderately substitute some other object in room of what is properly myself, and thus wander from the truth, even in that knowledge which I hold to be of all others the most certain and evident. For this reason, I will now consider anew what I formerly believed myself to be, before I entered on the present train of thought; and of my previous opinion I will retrench all that can in the least be invalidated by the grounds of doubt I have adduced, in order that there may at length remain nothing but what is certain and indubitable. What then did I formerly think I was? Undoubtedly I judged that I was a man. But what is a man? Shall I say a rational animal? Assuredly not; for it would be necessary forthwith to inquire into what is meant by animal, and what by rational, and thus, from a single question, I should insensibly glide into others, and these more difficult than the first; nor do I now possess enough of leisure to warrant me in wasting my time amid subtleties of this sort. I prefer here to attend to the thoughts

320

that sprung up of themselves in my mind, and were inspired by my own nature alone, when I applied myself to the consideration of what I was. In the first place, then, I thought that I possessed a countenance, hands, arms, and all the fabric of members that appears in a corpse, and which I called by the name of body. It further occurred to me that I was nourished, that I walked, perceived, and thought, and all those actions I referred to the soul; but what the soul itself was I either did not stay to consider, or, if I did, I imagined that it was something extremely rare and subtile, like wind, or flame, or ether, spread through my grosser parts. As regarded the body, I did not even doubt of its nature, but thought I distinctly knew it, and if I had wished to describe it according to the notions I then entertained, I should have explained myself in this manner: By body I understand all that can be terminated by a certain figure: that can be comprised in a certain place, and so fill a certain space as therefrom to exclude every other body; that can be perceived either by touch, sight, hearing, taste, or smell; that can be moved in different ways, not indeed of itself, but by something foreign to it by which it is touched [and from which it receives the impression]; for the power of self-motion as likewise that of perceiving and thinking, I held as by no means pertaining to the nature of body; on the contrary, I was somewhat astonished to find such faculties existing in some bodies.

But [as to myself, what can I now say that I am], since I suppose there exists an extremely powerful, and, if I may so speak, malignant being, whose whole endeavors are directed towards deceiving me? Can I affirm that I possess any one of all those attributes of which I have lately spoken as belonging to the nature of body? After attentively considering them in my own mind, I find none of them that can properly be said to belong to myself. To recount them were idle and tedious. Let us pass, then, to the attributes of the soul. The first mentioned were the powers of nutrition and walking; but, if it be true that I have no body, it is true likewise that I am capable neither of walking nor of being nourished. Perception is another attribute of the soul; but perception too is impossible without the body: besides, I have frequently, during sleep, believed that I perceived objects which I afterwards observed I did not in reality perceive. Thinking is another attribute of the soul; and here I discover what properly belongs to myself. This alone is inseparable from me. I am—I exist: this is certain; but how often? As often as I think; for perhaps it would even happen, if I should wholly cease to think, that I should at the same time altogether cease to be. I now admit nothing that is not necessarily true: I am therefore, precisely speaking, only a thinking thing, that is, a mind, understanding, or reason,—terms whose signification was before unknown to me. I am, however, a real thing, and really existent; but what thing? The answer was, a thinking thing. The question now arises, am I aught besides? I will stimulate my imagination with a view to discover whether I am not still something more than a thinking being. Now it is plain I am not the assemblage of members called the human body; I am not a thin and penetrating air diffused through all these members, or wind, or flame, or vapour, or breath, or any of all the things I can imagine; for I supposed that all these were not, and, without changing the supposition, I find that I still feel assured of my existence.

But it is true, perhaps, that those very things which I suppose to be non-existent, because they are unknown to me, are not in truth different from myself whom I know. This is a point I cannot determine, and do not now enter into any dispute regarding it. I can only judge of things that are known to me: I am conscious that I exist, and I who know that I exist inquire into what I am. It is, however, perfectly certain that the knowledge of my existence, thus precisely taken, is not dependent on things, the existence of which is as yet unknown to me: and consequently it is not dependent on any of the things I can feign in imagination. Moreover, the phrase itself, I frame an image, reminds me of my error; for I should in truth frame one if I were to imagine myself to be anything, since to imagine is nothing more than to contemplate the figure or image or a corporeal thing; but I already know that I exist, and that it is possible at the same time that all those images, and in general all that relates to the nature of body, are merely dreams [or chimeras]. From this I discover that it is not more reasonable to say, I will excite my imagination that I may know more distinctly what I am, than to express myself as follows: I am now awake, and perceive something real; but because my perception is not sufficiently clear, I will of express purpose go to sleep that my dreams may represent to me the object of my perception with more truth and clearness. And, therefore, I know that nothing of all that I can embrace in imagination belongs to the knowledge which I have of myself, and that there is need to recall with the utmost care the mind from this mode of thinking, that it may be able to know its own nature with perfect distinctness.

But what, then, am I? A thinking thing, it has been said. But what is a thinking thing? It is a thing that doubts, understands, [conceives], affirms, denies, wills, refuses, that imagines also, and perceives. Assuredly it is not little, if all these properties belong to my nature. But why should they not belong to it? Am I not that very being who now doubts of almost everything; who, for all that, understands and conceives certain things; who affirms one alone as true, and denies the others; who desires to know more of them, and does not wish to be deceived; who imagines many things, sometimes even despite his will; and is likewise percipient of many, as if through the medium of the senses. Is there nothing of all this as true as that I am, even although I should be always dreaming, and although he who gave me being employed all his ingenuity to deceive me? Is there also any one of these attributes that can be properly distinguished from my thought, or that can be said to be separate from myself? For it is of itself so evident that it is I who doubt, I who understand, and I who desire, that it is here unnecessary to add anything by way of rendering it more clear. And I am as certainly the same being who imagines; for, although it may be (as I before supposed) that nothing I imagine is true, still the power of imagination does not cease really to exist in me and to form part of my thought. In fine, I am the same being who perceives, that is, who apprehends certain objects as by the organs of sense, since, in truth, I see light, hear a noise, and feel heat. But it will be said that these presentations are false, and that I am dreaming. Let it be so. At all events it is certain that I seem to see light, hear a noise, and feel heat; this cannot be false, and this is what in me is properly called perceiving, which is nothing else than thinking. From this I begin to know what I am with somewhat greater clearness and distinctness than heretofore.

But, nevertheless, it still seems to me, and I cannot help believing, that corporeal things, whose images are formed by thought, [which fall under the senses], and are examined by the same, are known with much greater distinctness than that I know not what part of myself which is not imaginable; although, in truth, it may seem strange to say that I know and comprehend with greater distinctness things whose existence appears to me doubtful, that are unknown, and do not belong to me, than others of whose reality I am persuaded, that are known to me, and appertain to my proper nature; in a word, than myself. But I see clearly what is the state of the case. My mind is apt to wander, and will not yet submit to be restrained within the limits of truth. Let us therefore leave the mind to itself once more, and, according to it every kind of liberty, [permit it to consider the objects that appear to it from without], in order that, having afterwards withdrawn it from these gently and opportunely, [and fixed it on the consideration of its being and the properties it finds in itself], it may then be the more easily controlled.

Let us now accordingly consider the objects that are commonly thought to be [the most easily, and likewise] the most distinctly known, viz., the bodies we touch and see; not, indeed, bodies in general, for these general notions are usually somewhat more confused, but one body in particular. Take, for example, this piece of wax; it is quite fresh, having been but recently taken from the bee-hive; it has not yet lost the sweetness of the honey contained; it still retains somewhat of the odor of the flowers from which it was gathered; its color, figure, size, are apparent (to the sight); it is hard, cold, easily handled; and sounds when struck upon with the finger. In fine, all that contributes to make a body as distinctly known as possible, is found in the one before us. But, while I am speaking, let it be placed near the fire—what remained of the taste exhales, the smell evaporates, the color changes, its figure is destroyed, its size increases, it becomes liquid, it grows hot, it can hardly be handled, and, although struck upon, it emits no sound. Does the same wax still remain after this change? It must be admitted that it does remain; no one doubts it, or judges otherwise. What, then, was it I knew with so much distinctness in the piece of wax? Assuredly, it could be nothing of all that I observed by means of the senses, since all the things that fell under taste, smell, sight, touch, and hearing are changed, and yet the same wax remains. It was perhaps what I now think, viz., that this wax was neither the sweetness of honey, the pleasant odor of flowers, the whiteness, the figure, nor the sound, but only a body that a little before appeared to me conspicuous under these forms, and which is now perceived under others. But, to speak precisely, what is it that I imagine when I think of it in this way? Let it be attentively considered, and, retrenching all that does not belong to the wax, let us see what remains. There certainly remains nothing, except something extended, flexible, and movable. But what is meant by flexible and movable? Is it not that I imagine that the piece of wax, being round, is capable of becoming square, or of passing from a square into a triangular figure? Assuredly such is not the case, because I conceive that it admits of an infinity of similar changes; and I am, moreover, unable to compass this infinity by imagination, and consequently this conception which I have of the wax is not the product of the faculty of imagination. But what now is this extension? Is it not also unknown? for it becomes greater when the wax is melted, greater when it is boiled, and greater still when the heat increases; and I should not conceive [clearly and] according to truth, the wax as it is, if I did not suppose that the piece we are considering admitted even of a wider variety of extension than I ever imagined. I must, therefore, admit that I cannot even comprehend by imagination what the piece of wax is, and that it is the mind alone which perceives it. I speak of one piece in particular; for, as to wax in general, this is still more evident. But what is the piece of wax that can be perceived only by the [understanding or] mind? It is certainly the same which I see, touch, imagine; and, in fine, it is the same which, from the beginning, I believed it to be. But (and this it is of moment to observe) the perception of it is neither an act of sight, of touch, nor of imagination, and never was either of these, though it might formerly seem so, but is simply an intuition of the mind, which may be imperfect and confused, as it formerly was, or very clear and distinct, as it is at present, according as the attention is more or less directed to the elements which it contains, and of which it is composed.

But, meanwhile, I feel greatly astonished when I observe [the weakness of my mind, and] its proneness to error. For although, without at all giving expression to what I think, I consider all this in my own mind, words yet occasionally impede my progress, and I am almost led into error by the terms of ordinary language. We say, for example, that we see the same wax when it is before us, and not that we judge it to be the same from its retaining the same color and figure: whence I should forthwith be disposed to conclude that the wax is known by the act of sight, and not by the intuition of the mind alone, were it not for the analogous instance of human beings passing on in the street below, as observed from a window. In this case I do not fail to say that I see the men themselves, just as I say that I see the wax; and yet what do I see from the window beyond hats and cloaks that might cover artificial machines, whose motions might be determined by springs? But I judge that there are human beings from these appearances, and thus I comprehend, by the faculty of judgment alone which is in the mind, what I believed I saw with my eyes.

The man who makes it his aim to rise to knowledge superior to the common, ought to be ashamed to seek occasions of doubting from the vulgar forms of speech: instead, therefore, of doing this, I shall proceed with the matter in hand, and inquire whether I had a clearer and more perfect perception of the piece of wax when I first saw it, and when I thought I knew it by means of the external sense itself, or, at all events, by the common sense, as it is called, that is, by the imaginative faculty; or whether I rather apprehend it more clearly at present, after having examined with greater care, both what it is, and in what way it can be known. It would certainly be ridiculous to entertain any doubt on this point. For what, in that first perception, was there distinct? What did I perceive which any animal might not have perceived? But when I distinguish the wax from its exterior forms, and when, as if I had stripped it of its vestments, I consider it quite naked, it is certain, although some error may still be found in my judgment, that I cannot, nevertheless, thus apprehend it without possessing a human mind.

But, finally, what shall I say of the mind itself, that is, of myself? for as yet I do not admit that I am anything but mind. What, then! I who seem to possess so distinct an apprehension of the piece of wax,—do I not know myself, both with greater truth and certitude, and also much more distinctly and clearly? For if I judge that the wax exists because I see it, it assuredly follows, much more evidently, that I myself am or exist, for the same reason: for it is possible that what I see may not in truth be wax, and that I do not even possess eyes with which to see anything; but it cannot be that when I see, or, which comes to the same thing, when I think I see, I myself who think am nothing. So likewise, if I judge that the wax exists because I touch it, it will also follow that I am; and if I determine that my imagination, or any other cause, whatever it be, persuades me of the existence of the wax, I will still draw the same conclusion. And what is here remarked of the piece of wax, is applicable to all the other things that are external to me. And further, if the [notion or] perception of wax appeared to me more precise and distinct, after that not only sight and touch, but many other causes besides, rendered it manifest to my apprehension, with how much greater distinctness must I now know myself, since all the reasons that contribute to the knowledge of the nature of wax, or of any body whatever, manifest still better the nature of my mind? And there are besides so many other things in the mind itself that contribute to the illustration of its nature, that those dependent on the body, to which I have here referred, scarcely merit to be taken into account.

But, in conclusion, I find I have insensibly reverted to the point I desired; for, since it is now manifest to me that bodies themselves are not properly perceived by the senses nor by the faculty of imagination, but by the intellect alone; and since they are not perceived because they are seen and touched, but only because they are understood [or rightly comprehended by thought], I readily discover that there is nothing more easily or clearly apprehended than my own mind. But because it is difficult to rid one's self so promptly of an opinion to which one has been long accustomed, it will be desirable to tarry for some time at this stage, that, by long continued meditation, I may more deeply impress upon my memory this new knowledge.

[107]

DEWEY, JOHN

DEWEY, JOHN (1859-1952). At the celebration of his ninetieth anniversary, John Dewey declared that losing faith in our fellow men means losing faith in ourselves, "and that is the unforgivable

328

sin." Dewey is generally recognized as America's leading philosopher, and the foremost apostle of the faith in the essential union of the democratic and philosophical spirit. Since his revolt against German philosophy, he repudiated the separation of the individual and the social, both of which, according to him, are concrete traits and capacities of human beings. He always regarded reason, not as something existing timelessly in the nature of things, but simply as a fortunate and complex development of human behavior. His criticism of the traditional notions of truth is embodied in his theory of *instrumentalism,* which he defines as "an attempt to constitute a precise logical theory of concepts, judgments and inferences in their various forms, by primarily considering how thought functions in the experimental determinations of future consequences." Dewey made inquiry, rather than truth or knowledge, the essence of logic.

He regarded philosophy as the criticism of those socially important beliefs which are part and parcel of the social and cultural life of human communities. This criticism involves an examination of the way in which ideas, taken as solutions of specific problems, function within a wider context. It is in this way that a theory of knowledge—logic, ethics, psychology, aesthetics, and metaphysics becomes necessary and explainable. These are not to be derived from the assumption of an abstract truth, that is, a higher reality or a reality different from that within which we live and act, nor from everlasting values. Dewey objects to transcendental philosophers, because they ignore the kind of empirical situations to which their themes pertain; even the most transcendental philosophers use empirical subject matter, if they philosophize at all. But they become nonempirical because they fail to supply directions for experimentation. The supply of such directions is the core of Dewey's philosophy. His standard of belief and conduct claims to lie within, rather than outside of, a situation of life, that can be shared. Idealists, in contradistinction to Dewey's search for a guide to the beliefs of a shareable situation, deny to common life the faculty of forming its own regulative methods; they claim to have private access to truth. In Dewey's democratic philosophy, common life is the reality of a dignity equivalent to that of nature or the individual.

Dewey devoted his studies not only to the conditions but also to the consequences of knowledge. He never made philosophy subservient to the vested interests of any class or nation; nor was he afraid to hurt any sensibility. He insisted that philosophy, in contrast to all other human activities, must be allowed to remain outside and above the public domain in order to maintain sound relations with these other human activities and to whose progress it must contribute. Dewey was opposed to any isolation of cognitive experience and its subject matter from other modes of experience and their subject matter, because he attempted to integrate spiritual life into the precise framework of natural phenomena, and, for the sake of all-embracing experience, tried to do away with the distinction between the objective and the subjective, and the psychical and the physical. He denied that the characteristic object of knowledge has a privileged position of correspondence with an allegedly ultimate reality; he insisted that action is involved in knowledge and that knowledge is not subordinate to action or practice; that it is in experimental knowing that genuine intellectual integrity is found.

Dewey did not accept any alternative between knowledge or intelligence and action. To him it is "intelligent action" that matters. The failure of human intelligence in social areas has made Dewey strongly emphasize the social aspects of his philosophy. Throughout his long life he tried not only to apply his experimental methods to social philosophy, but he also actively participated in disputes and struggles of political, social, and cultural relevance. Political, social, cultural, and theoretical motives have enhanced Dewey's interest in education. He recognized the important role education plays in the survival of democrary, and the importance of democratic thought and action in the improvement of education. For more than forty years, Dewey maintained a leadership in American education, bringing increased human interest into school life and work, making for the increased encouragement of pupil initiative and responsibility. Dewey's instrumentalism was first expressed in his *Studies in Logical Theory* (1903) where he acknowledged his obligation to William James. His other principal works are: *Democracy and Education* (1916); *Essays in Experimental Logic* (1917); *Reconstruction in Philosophy* (1920); *Human Nature and Conduct* (1922); *The Quest for Certainty* (1929), and *Logic: The Theory of Inquiry* (1938).

ON THE USE OF THE WORD "OBJECT"

IT is not a new discovery that the word "object" is highly ambiguous, being used for the sticks and the stones, the cats and the dogs, the chairs and tables of ordinary experiences, for the atoms and electrons of physics, and for any kind of "entity" that has logical subsistence—as in mathematics. In spite of the recognized ambiguity, one whole branch of modern epistemology is derived from the assumption that in the case of at least the first two cases, the word "object" has the same general meaning. For otherwise the subject matter of physics and the things of everyday experience would not have presented themselves as rivals, and philosophy would not have felt an obligation to decide which is "real" and which is "appearance," or at least an obligation to set up a scheme in which they are "reconciled." The place occupied in modern philosophy by the problem of the relation of the so-called, "scientific objects" and "common-sense objects" is proof, in any case, of the dominating presence of a distinction between the "objective" and the "subjective" which was unknown in ancient philosophy. It indicates that at least in the sense of awareness of an ever-present problem, modern philosophy is "objective-subjective," not just subjective. I suggest that if we give up calling the distinctive material of the physical sciences by the name "objects" and employ instead the neutral term "scientific subject matter," the genuine nature of the problem would be greatly clarified. It would not of itself be solved. But at least we should be rid of the implication which now prevents reaching a solution. We should be prepared to consider on its merits the hypothesis here advanced: namely, that scientific subject matter represents the *conditions* for having and not-having things of direct experience.

Genuinely complete empirical philosophy requires that there be a determination *in terms of experience* of the relation that exists between physical subject-matter and the things of direct perception, use, and enjoyment. It would seem clear that historic empiricism, because of its commitment to sensationalism, failed to meet this need. The obvious way of meeting the requirement is through explicit acknowledgement that direct experience contains, as a highly important direct ingredient of itself, a wealth of *possible* objects. There is no inconsistency between the idea of direct experience and the idea of objects of that experience which are as yet unrealized. For these latter objects are directly experienced as possibilities. Every plan, every protection, yes, every forecast and anticipation, is an experience in which some non-directly experienced object is directly experienced *as a possibility*. And, as previously suggested, modern experience is marked by the extent to which directly perceived, enjoyed, and suffered objects are treated as signs, indications, of what has *not* been experienced in and of itself, or/and are treated as means for the realization of these things of possible experience. Because historic empirical philosophy failed to take cognizance of this fact, it was not able to account for one of the most striking features of scientific method and scientific conclusions—preoccupation with generality as such.

For scientific methods and scientific subject matter combine highly abstract or "theoretical" considerations with directly present concrete sensible material, and the generality of conclusions reached is directly dependent upon the presence of the first-named type of considerations. Now in modern philosophy, just as scientific "objects" have been set over against objects in direct experience, thereby occasioning the *ontological* problem of modern philosophy (the problem of where "reality" is to be found) so identification of the experimental with but one of the two factors of the method of knowing has created the *epistemological* problem of modern philosophy; the relation of the "conceptual" and "perceptual"; of sense and understanding. In terms of our hypothesis, the distinction and the connection of the distinguished aspects rests upon the fact that what *is* (has been) experienced is of cognitive importance in connection with what *can* be experienced: that is, as evidence, sign, test, of forecast, anticipation, etc. while, on the other hand, there is no way of valid determination of objects of possible experiences save by employing what *has* been experienced, and hence is sensible. Anticipation, foresight, prediction, depend upon taking what is "given" (what has indubitably been experienced) as ominous, or of prospective reference. This is a speculative operation, a wager about the future. But the wager is subject to certain techniques of control. Although every projection of a possible object of experience goes beyond what has been experienced and is in so far risky, this fact does not signify that every idea or projected possibility has an equal claim. Techniques of observation on one side and of calculation (in its broad sense) on the other side have been developed with a view to effective cooperation. Interactivity *of the two factors* constitutes the method of science. Were it not for the influence of the inertia of habit it would be fairly incredible that empiricists did not long ago perceive that material provided by direct sense perception is limited and remains substantially the same from person to person and from generation to generation. Even when we take into account the additional sense data furnished by artificial instruments, the addition bears no proportionate ratio to the expansion of the subject matter of the sciences that is constantly taking place. Were it not that "rationalist" theories are in no better case with respect to accounting for increase in scientific knowledge (which is its most striking trait in modern times), the marked impotency of sensationalist empiricism would long ago have effected its disappearance.

[108]

DIDEROT, DENIS

DIDEROT, DENIS (1713-1784). As a philosopher, Diderot has often been underestimated. His unique versatility of mind was amazing. The journalistic vein (characteristic of his mentality) enabled him to enlarge, rectify, and communicate his philosophical knowledge and his personal concepts of man, nature, life, and moral and cultural values. His arguments were founded upon those recent scientific discoveries whose philosophical consequences he grasped with extraordinary agility.

Diderot, in addition to being the editor of the most influential and famous encyclopedia, was himself a living encyclopedia; well versed in the natural and social sciences, in the history of literature and the arts; in philosophy and religion. He never confined his achievements to the mere summarization of the knowledge of his

333

time; he was an innovator in many fields. He was the first modern art critic. He rebelled against the authority of classicism in the literary and artistic life of continental Europe. He criticised the civil and religious institutions of his time and demonstrated the necessity for change. As a dramatist, he pioneered in dealing with social problems and in representing modern middle-class life on the stage.

All of these activities were compatible with his philosophical outlook which conceived of life and spirit as eternal and eternally changing. He stated that the formation of moral values could be traced back to the experiences of early childhood of both the individual and mankind. He made many studies of the blind, mute, and deaf, and proceeded to epistemological, psychological, aesthetic, and sociological points of view that have since had great consequence. His daring spirit caused Diderot to incur royal and papal interdictions and imprisonment.

ON REASON

DOUBTS in religious matters, far from being blamable—far from being acts of impiety, ought to be regarded as praiseworthy, when they proceed from a man who humbly acknowledges his ignorance, and arise from the fear of offending God by the abuse of reason.

To admit any conformity between the reason of man, and the eternal reason of God, and to pretend that God demands the sacrifice of human reason, is to maintain that God wills one thing, and intends another thing at the same time.

When God, of whom I hold my reason, demands of me to sacrifice it, he becomes a mere juggler that snatches from me what he pretended to give.

If I renounce my reason, I have no longer a guide—I must then blindly adopt a *secondary principle,* and the matter in question becomes a supposition.

If *reason* be a gift of Heaven, and we can say as much of *faith,* Heaven has certainly made us two presents not only incompatible, but in direct contradiction to each other. In order to solve the difficulty, we are compelled to say either that *faith* is a chimera, or that reason is useless.

Pascal, Nicole and others have said, that God will punish with eternal torments the faults of a guilty father upon all his innocent offspring; and that this is a proposition *superior* to reason, and not in *contradiction* to it; but what shall we propose as being contradictory to reason if such blasphemy as this is not so?

Bewildered in an immense forest during the night, and having only one small torch for my guide, a stranger approaches and thus addresses me:—*"Friend, blow out thy light if thou wouldst make sure of the right path."* This stranger was a priest.

If my reason be the gift of Heaven, it is the voice of Heaven that speaks; shall I hearken to it?

Neither merit nor demerit is applicable to the judgment of our rational faculties, for all the submission and good will imaginable could not assist the blind man in the perception of colors.

I am compelled to perceive evidence where it is, or the want of evidence where it is not, so long as I retain my senses; and if my judgment fail me, it becomes a *misfortune,* not a *sin.*

The Author of Nature would not reward me for having been a *wit,* surely, then, he will not *damn* me for having been a *fool.* Nay, more; he will not *damn* me even for being wicked. Is not my own conscience a sufficient punishment for me?

[109]

DILTHEY, WILHELM

DILTHEY, WILHELM (1833-1911). Wilhelm Dilthey was born two years after Hegel's death. He devoted much of his energy to the task of investigating the structure of the human mind and in writing its history. This had been Hegel's purpose, but Dilthey was strongly opposed to the Hegelian system, as well as to any metaphysical inquiry into the realm of the supernatural.

Hegel regarded the human mind as one of the manifestations of the cosmic spirit, and when he wrote the history of the human mind, he believed that he had recognized and defined the essence of mind. Dilthey, on the other hand, relied upon empiricism: historical facts, biographies, the extant works of great personalities, documents on the currents of cultural life, religious traditions, and social institutions supplied the answer to the question of what man really is. Dilthey, the historian of the human mind, stated that philosophical definitions were the historical documents which informed him about the mental situation of an epoch; poems, laws, and customs of that epoch did the same.

He saw history as a means of comprehending man as a thinking, feeling, willing, creating being who lived in the historical stream of life. His total activities were designed to elaborate "a critique of historical reason," as necessary for the completion of Kant's three critiques. It was to be founded upon an "understanding and analyzing psychology" whose starting point was the analysis of consciousness, and whose development was necessary for understanding the way of civilization and its functional relation to the totality of spontaneous impulses, which he considered to be the stream of life.

Dilthey left great and important fragments of his projected work. His academic career was extremely brilliant, but his real influence was felt only after he died.

STRUCTURAL COHERENCE OF THE PSYCHE

THE psychical sciences form a cognitive whole which strives to achieve a factual and objective knowledge of the chain of human experiences in the human-historical-social world. The history of the sciences of the mind reveals a constant struggle with the difficulties which confront us here. These are gradually overcome to a certain degree, and the inquiry approaches, though remotely, this goal which hovers incessantly before each and every true scholar. The inquiry into the possibility of factual and objective knowledge forms the foundation of the mental sciences. I submit the following contributions toward this end.

The mental sciences are confronted by the human-historical world; this world is often an inexact picture of the reality that exists outside these sciences. Such a thing cannot produce knowledge. It is and remains bound up with the means of intuition, understanding, and conceptual thinking. The mental sciences do not desire to produce the exact picture; rather they refer to that which has occurred and occurs: this unique, accidental, and momentary happening back to a sensible and value-giving coherence. Progressive cognition seeks to penetrate ever deeper into this. It becomes ever more objective in its understanding of it, without ever being able to reveal its fundamental nature; so that, in fact, it discovers that which is always a mere after-feeling, constructing, uniting, and separating in abstract connections of a conceptual nexus. Thus the historical description of what has once happened can approximate these events only upon the foundations of the analytic sciences whose only common purpose is to attain an objective grasp of their object within the bounds of the medium of understanding and conceptual comprehension.

A knowledge of those events in which the mental sciences specialize is a condition for an understanding of their history. It clarifies the relationship of the individual mental sciences to the coexistence and succession of experience on which they are based.

PLAN FOR A CRITIQUE OF HISTORICAL REASON

THE current of life is composed of parts and experiences which bear an inner relation to each other. Each single experience refers to a self, of which it is a part; it is united structurally with other parts in a coherence. Coherence is found in all mind, so that coherence is a category which springs from life. We comprehend coherence by virtue of the unity of consciousness. This is the condition under which all comprehension stands; but it is clear that the appearance of cohesion will not follow from this mere fact, or that a manifoldness of experiences is granted to the unity of consciousness. Only because life itself is a structural coherence to which experiences (i.e. relations of experience) inhere, is it possible for us to have a coherence of life. This coherence is included in a more comprehensive category which is a mode

337

of predication regarding all reality; the relation of the whole
to the parts.

[110]

DRIESCH, HANS

DRIESCH, HANS (1867-1941). A discovery made in 1895 by Hans
Driesch attracted international attention and firmly placed him
among the important figures in the history of biology. Driesch,
by experiment, demonstrated that it was possible to remove large
pieces from eggs; shuffle the blastomeres at will; take several blastomeres away; interfere in many ways, and yet not affect the resulting embryo. The fact that despite such operations, a normal,
though small-sized embryo emerged was taken as proof that any
single monad in the original egg cell was capable of forming any
part of the completed embryo. This discovery made Driesch internationally famous as a zoologist. Until then he had been a disciple
and adherent of Ernest Haeckel, but the success of the experiments
led him to abandon the mechanistic point of view and to profess a
renovated vitalism. At this time, he turned from biology to philosophy.

His system was comprised of three parts: the first dealt with
causality and consciousness; the second with logic, which he called
"a doctrine of order"; the third was a doctrine of reality. Driesch
was converted to vitalism because he believed that physical laws
were insufficient to explain his discovery, which he declared to be
beyond the powers of any machine ever constructed by man. Thus
far, he encountered no objections. When he tried to prove the
autonomy of life by introducing a nonphysical cause: entelechy
(using Aristotle), he met with violent opposition. This opposition
held for all other arguments that he advanced. Until his death,
Driesch energetically continued to defend his views. Though he was
an unscholarly thinker, his style was animated and colorful.

CAUSALITY

CAUSALITY, in the proper sense of the word, is the determination of events within the natural stream of things expressly
so that the effects of events are determined by earlier causes.
Here we deal with fairly new matter as compared with mere
functionality, namely the concept of "temporal," expressed
by such words as "cause" and "effect" and concatenated with

the meaning of "because." The effects of events do not only follow the cause, but it is because of the cause that the events have occurred.

Just as substance is the objectivated concept of identity, that is to say a concept "thrown out" into nature, so causality is consequence "thrown out." A judgment is valid *because* one or more judgments are valid. A concept subsists *because* it is a component of earlier concepts; its attributes make it a partial totality of other concepts. Thus in the pure sense of words, meanings deal with proper consequences; that is, they are "posited together." Events happen *because* under certain constant "conditions" the causes of the event happened. Thus we say: this is causality.

Events have a sequential relationship to time. The aspect of consequence is that means of partial identity which makes for a "positing together." This makes for the transmission of events.

Mathematical physics is essentially incapable of coming close to causality. It cannot even approach such temporal sequence as *post hoc*, let alone the *propter* in *post*.

Those who question the aforementioned statement should consider the well-known fact that mathematical physics uses equations. Equations can be read from left to right *and* from right to left. They are indifferent to direction. But causality, even temporal sequence is *not* indifferent to direction. If a cigar is thrown into a powder keg it causes an explosion; the explosion is not the cause of the throwing.

Mathematical physics can only extract from the totality a part of the true cause, the quantitative equivalences, or more precisely those *coupled* quantities which are expressed by the equal sign. It takes out something that accompanies causality or is in it. It never meets causality itself. This is typically illustrated by the principle of the conservation of energy: a given amount lost in one area is gained in another. The two areas may be infinitely close together; however, one can never state that the cause of the loss makes for the effect of the gain; or that gain takes place *because*, in the course of time, there is loss.

Although mathematical physics cannot come close to causality, the concept of causality is quite indispensable to the true science of nature. In fact that "I can push" might psychologically evoke the concept of causality in an individual; its proper basis is logical, the application of the meaning of *because* to temporal succession.

Suffice it to say, that I do not consider "causality" a true category which can be analyzed, a "pure principle of understanding," as Kant did. Rather, it is a concept composed of true original meanings. The meanings of "because" and "events" are here joined.

It goes without saying that causality is only a postulate; a logical desire. It is one that up to now has always been demonstrated empirically. Up to now, we have always found or invented successful causes when or where changes, referred to as effects, have taken place.

[111]

DÜHRING, EUGEN

DÜHRING, EUGEN (1833-1921). "Heroic materialism" characterized Dühring's philosophy. The only reality he acknowledged was the world of the natural sciences. He regarded thinking and feeling as "states of irritation of matter." He substituted ethical education for religion in the "direction of the mind." He asserted that the universe was spatially finite, and that the beginning of the formation of the world was fixable in time. He attacked capitalism, Marxism, organized Christianity and Judaism, and the faculties of the German universities. Had it not been for his blindness, he probably would have played a much more important role in German political life.

PESSIMISM

PESSIMISM is itself the peak of moral evil, in the sense that it adores nothing and condemns nature. Scepticism tries to do that with regard to reason. It is the theoretical supplement to practical corruption. It is incompatible with the trust of healthy knowledge, and is opposed to real logical knowledge as a final possibility. When it remains faithful to its essence (or rather its nuisance), it implies that there can be deviation for personal contingencies; therefore it assists wickedness.

Since everything is basically bad, people consider it only right for them not to consider some of their own base acts. If they resign themselves to demoralization and thereby adjust themselves to the character of the world, they're merely following the pattern of all things. If they commit an evil act and extend it further; or even approve of it (in a particular case), they contribute their share to the moral evil. They try to protect themselves with the hypocritical excuse that they are redeeming the world with their demoralized behavior; that they help make for that saintly order which tends toward the adoration of *nil.*

Even with better people, there is some demoralization too; it takes the form of discouragement, or the reduction of confidence in the state of things, and makes for a sapping of strength. That kind of demoralization parallels the circumstances involved in the demoralization of troops. In the struggle for existence, the opinion that the good have no chance in the sphere of the knowledge of things, or the possibility of doing good, must certainly produce a demoralizing effect. A philosophy hostile to life, which professes the total evilness of nature and explains the world as a single and great evil is in itself the greatest thing that makes for demoralization, because of necessity it eradicates the courage for life and good will.

[112]

DUNS SCOTUS, JOHN

DUNS SCOTUS, JOHN (1270-1308). The popular identification of the words "dunce" and "blockhead," which were sanctioned by Alexander Pope's satiric poem, signifies the age-old contempt in which posterity has held the man who probably was born in the

Scottish village of Duns. Although he was so famous and success-ful as a professor at Oxford that the numerous foreign students could not be accommodated in the town, and although he taught at Paris with even greater success, his name was disparaged by his opponents who, after his premature death, publicly burned his books and distorted the meaning of his doctrine. For Duns Scotus had dared to criticize Augustine and Aquinas, and had attempted to destroy their notions of matter, form and potency, the indispen-sable resources of Peripatetic philosophers. Victorious Thomism did not pardon this challenge, and imposed its prejudice against Duns Scotus on its opponents, namely, enlightenment.

But, since Charles S. Peirce adopted Duns Scotus' realism, more and more historians have become convinced that Duns Scotus is to be ranked among the great constructive thinkers. In the Middle Ages, Duns Scotus, the inveterate antagonist of Aquinas was called "Doctor Subtilis." Now he is acknowledged to be not only subtle but vigorous. His insistence on demonstrative proof led him to a de-marcation between rationalism and empiricism that has followers among recent philosophers. Instead of matter and form, he estab-lished the extremely modern concept of "haecceity," or principle of individuation, which is explained as ontological independence, singularity, or the undefinable quality of ultimate reality, anticipat-ing ways of *Gestalt psychology, Gegenstands theory* and existenti-alism. Duns Scotus admitted that there is no science of the singular, but he maintained that this indicates only a limit of the human intellect, not of reality. His psychology is essentially voluntaristic. In several of his views, Duns Scotus was inspired by Solomon ibn Gabirol's *Fons Vitae* (Source of Life) which influenced many Fran-ciscans, to whose order Duns Scotus belonged; however he shows strong originality in their elaboration.

UNDERSTANDING AND EXPERIENCE

WHEN the evidence or the certitude of first principles has been had, it is evident how certitude may be had of conclu-sions inferred from them, because of the evidence of the perfect forms of the syllogism, since the certitude of the conclusions depends only on the certitude of the principles and inference.

But will not the understanding err in this knowledge of principles and conclusions, if the senses are deceived con-cerning all the terms? I reply that, with respect to the knowledge, the understanding does not have the senses for cause, but only for occasion, for the understanding cannot have knowledge of simples unless it has received that knowledge from the senses: still, having received it, it can compound simples with each other by its own power; and if, from the relation of such simples, there is a combination which is evidently true, the understanding will assent to that combination by its own power and by the power of the terms, not by the power of the senses by which it receives the terms from without. . . .

Concerning things known by experience, I say that although experience is not had of all singulars, but of a large number, and that although it is not always had but in a great many cases, still one who knows by experience knows infallibly that it is thus, and that it is always thus, and that it is thus in all, and he knows that by the following proposition reposing in the soul: whatever occurs as in a great many things from some cause which is not free, is the natural effect of that cause, which proposition is known to the understanding, even though it has accepted the terms of it from erring senses; for a cause which is not free cannot produce as in a great many things an effect to the opposite of which it is ordered, or to which it is not ordered by its form; but a casual cause is ordered to the producing of the opposite of the casual effect or to not producing it: therefore nothing is the casual cause in respect to an effect produced frequently by it, and if it is not free, it is a natural cause.

That, however, this effect occurs by such a cause producing as in a great many cases, this must be learned by experience.

[113]

DURKHEIM, DAVID EMILE

DURKHEIM, DAVID EMILE (1858-1917). A founder of the science of sociology, Durkheim regarded sociology neither as a branch of philosophy, psychology, nor biology, though he always stressed the importance of psychological and biological knowledge. Similarly, he was well versed in ethnology and utilized many of its results; but he carefully defined the method and object of sociology as distinct from the former.

Even as a sociologist, Durkheim retained his belief in moral values. He stated that these could not be explained without taking into account the existence of society; that society formed and enlightened the individual; that it was impossible to separate the individual from society, or to regard society as the mere totality of individuals. He conceived of the group mind as a reality distinct from the minds of the individuals who comprised the group.

Durkheim's real starting point was his study of the division of labor. He regarded the division of labor not only as an important social and economic phenomenon but as a proof that the individual was incapable of controlling his life. From this he proceeded to demonstrate that the concepts of causality, space, and time had to be derived from collective sources. He was a man of wide perspectives. His inquiries embraced religion (particularly its elementary forms), law, criminology, ethics, moral data, economics, aesthetics, and the histories of language and the arts. He was particularly interested in education which he viewed as the birth of social man from the embryo of the individual.

All who met Durkheim were deeply impressed by his ascetic appearance. He seemed to be the embodiment of the scientific spirit. His disciples, among whom Lucien Lévy-Bruhl was the outstanding, never forgot the inspiration engendered by Durkheim for methodical investigation. Even his opponents respected the austerity of his devotion to the cause of truth.

THE HEALTHY AND MORBID

PAIN is commonly regarded by the layman as the index of morbidity; and in general it is true that there is a relation between these two conditions, but a relation which lacks uniformity and precision. There are serious but painless maladies; while less serious afflictions, such as those resulting from a speck of coal dust in the eye, may cause real torture. In certain cases the very absence of pain, or even actual pleasure, are symptoms of morbidity. There is an insensibility to pain which is pathological. Circumstances causing suffering to a healthy man may give to a neurasthenic a sensation of enjoyment of an incontestably morbid nature. Conversely, pain accompanies many states belonging to normal physiology, such as hunger, fatigue, and parturition.

Shall we say that health, consisting in successful development of the vital forces, is recognizable by the perfect adaptation of the organism to its environment; and shall we, on the contrary, term "morbidity" whatever disturbs this adaptation? But first . . . it has by no means been proved that every state of the organism corresponds to some external state of the environment. And, further, even if this criterion of adaptation were truly distinctive of the state of health, another criterion would be needed in order to recognize it. We must be able to distinguish varying degrees of completeness of adaptation.

Or shall we take as this criterion the effect health and morbidity may have on our probabilities of survival? Health would then be the state of an organism in which these probabilities are at a maximum; and morbidity, on the contrary, would include everything which reduces them. Unquestionably, morbidity weakens the organism. But it is not alone in producing this result. The functions of reproduction inevitably cause death in certain lower species, and they are accompanied by risks even in the higher orders. They are, however, normal. Senility and infancy have the same effects, for both the old and the very young are peculiarly susceptible to the causes of destruction. Are infancy and old age morbid types then? And can only the adult be healthy? How strangely would the domain of health and physiology then be restricted!

If, moreover, old age is already synonymous with morbidity, how distinguish the healthy from the diseased old person? From the same point of view, one is obliged to place menstruation among the morbid phenomena, for the disturbances it causes increase female susceptibility to disease. But would we then be justified in designating as "morbid" a state whose absence or premature disappearance constitutes an incontestably pathological phenomenon? People argue about this question as if, in a healthy organism, each element played a useful role, as if each internal state corresponded exactly to some external condition and, consequently, helped to maintain vital equilibrium and to diminish the chance of death. But it is, on the contrary, legitimate to suppose that some anatomical or functional arrangements are of no direct use, but are merely the products of the general conditions of life. We cannot, however, call them morbid, for morbidity is, above all, something escapable, something not essential to the constitution of the organism. It may even be true that, instead of strengthening the organism, these anatomical and functional arrangements diminish its resistance and, consequently, increase the risks of death.

[114]

E

ECKHART, JOHANNES

ECKHART, JOHANNES (c. 1260-1327). "Wouldst thou be perfect, do not yelp about God." This sentence, uttered by Johannes Eckhart, characterized him as a man of deepest spirituality whose sermons utilized the Bible as an opportunity to lead his listeners to the oneness of God, to make them realize that the approach to God was through the self and silence. A Dominican monk, he rose to high office in the service of the Church. He was prior at Erfurt; vicar-provincial of Thuringia; provincial of Saxony; and vicar-general of Bohemia. A Master of Sacred Theology and Doctor of Divinity, he preached his "sweet doctrine" at the College of St. James, Paris, and in the nunneries of Strassburg and Cologne. Always welcome, he was reverently referred to as the "Holy Master Eckhart."

A "Brother of the Free Spirit," he differed markedly from the schoolmen and their arid teachings. His message paralleled the best of Hindu teachings in *Sankara Acharya*: that God is in every human being; nothing is apart from God, and the complete dissolution of all opposites and self-abandonment to Him constitutes salvation. In the early stages of the Inquisition his mystic teachings and symbolic interpretations were not opposed, but charges were preferred against him in 1327. He was unwilling to recant all his teachings and appealed to Rome. Pope John XXII issued a bull condemning the majority of his propositions as heretical and the rest as "ill-sounding, rash, and probably heretic." It was during that year that Eckhart died; however, official condemnation did not prevent his followers from clinging to his teachings.

SECLUSION

I HAVE read many writings of both Pagan masters and the Prophets of the old and new Covenant, and have investigated seriously and with great zeal which would be the best and highest virtue by which Man could best become similar to God, and how he could resemble again the archetype such as he was in God when there was no difference between him and God until God made the creatures. If I go down to the bottom of all that is written as far as my reason with its testimony and its judgment can reach, I find nothing but mere seclusion of all that is created. In this sense our Lord says to Martha: "One thing is needed," this means: He who wants to be pure and untroubled has to have one thing, Seclusion.

Many teachers praise Love as the highest virtue, like Saint Paul when he says: "Whatever exercises I undergo, if I have no Love I have nothing." I however place seclusion higher than love. First: The best about love is that it forces me to love God. But it is much more important that I force God down to me than that I force myself up to God. For my eternal bliss rests upon my being united with God. For God is more able to penetrate into me and to become united with me, than I with Him. That seclusion forces God down to me, I can prove in the following way: Every creature likes to be in its natural abode, the abode that is appropriate for it is the most natural, the most appropriate abode of God, unity and purity. Both rest upon seclusion. That is why God cannot help abandoning himself to a secluded heart.

The second reason why I place seclusion above love is: If love induces me to suffer anything for God, seclusion induces me to be receptive only to God. This however is superior. For while suffering, Man is still aiming at the creature through which he is suffering, though seclusion is free from all other creatures so that seclusion is receptive only for God I can prove by the following: What shall be received has to be received somewhere. Seclusion is so near to sheer nothing that there is nothing that would be fine enough that it could find space in it, but God. He is so simple and so fine that he finds room in the secluded heart.

[115]

348

EDWARDS, JONATHAN

EDWARDS, JONATHAN (1703-1758). Until the very end of the nineteenth century, Jonathan Edwards was considered America's greatest philosopher. Only in later manuals of philosophy published in the United States were men like Charles Peirce and William James hesitantly acknowledged as his equals. Outside of the United States Edwards' philosophy remains virtually unknown; his name is mentioned only in the histories of American religious life.

Edwards, who, in his early years, admired Locke and adopted the ideas of Cudworth and other Cambridge Platonists, lost interest in theoretical philosophy after he was ordained minister (1726) in the church of Northampton. A persuasive preacher and devoted spiritual leader of his congregation, he was also very influential as the author of religious and theological treatises. His sermon *Justification by Faith* (1734) marked the beginning of "New England Theology" which dominated the congregationalism of New England until 1880. Edwards had revolted against Calvinism in his youth and initiated what has been called "Consistent Calvinism," "Strict Calvinism," or the "New Divinity." He defended its fundamental doctrines against Arminians and deists, and preached the doctrine of divine immanence and divine initiative. He denied the freedom of human will and affirmed election by predestination. His congregation was the starting point of the "Great Awakening" of New England. Edwards was not only the theologian of this movement, but also its historian and psychologist. His *Treatise Concerning Religious Affections* (1746) tried to distinguish between sincere religious emotion, genuine conversion, hysteria, false sentimentality, and enthusiastic exaggeration. William James praised Edwards' descriptions as "admirably rich and delicate."

Unfortunately, the life of piety and purity to which Edwards tried to convert his people was beyond their comprehension. He was dismissed in 1750 by his parishioners when he excluded from full communion those members of the congregation who did not correspond to his ideal. He turned to missionary work among the Indians and wrote voluminous works on topics he had previously dealt with in shorter form. In 1757 he was elected president of the College of New Jersey, later to become Princeton University.

GOD AND THE EVIL IN THE WORLD

THAT there is a great difference between God's being concerned thus, by his *permission*, in an event and act, which, in the inherent subject and agent of it, is sin, (though the event will certainly follow on his permission) and his being concerned in it by *producing* it and exerting the act of sin; or between his being the *orderer* of its certain existence, by *not hindering* it, under certain circumstances, and his being the proper *actor* or *author* of it, by a *positive agency* or *efficiency*. And this, notwithstanding what Dr. Whitby offers about a saying of philosophers, that *causa deficiens, in rebus necessariis, ad causam per se efficientem reducenda est.* As there is a vast difference between the sun's being the cause of the lightsomeness and warmth of the atmosphere, and brightness of gold and diamonds, by its presence and positive influence; and its being the occasion of darkness and frost in the night, by its motion, whereby it descends below the horizon. The motion of the sun is the occasion of the latter kind of events; but it is not the proper cause, efficient, or producer of them; though they are necessarily consequent on that motion under such circumstances: no more is any action of the Divine Being the cause of the evil of men's wills. If the sun were the proper *cause* of cold and darkness, it would be the *fountain* of these things, as it is the fountain of light and heat; and then something might be argued from the nature of cold and darkness, to a likeness of nature in the sun; and it might be justly inferred, that the sun itself is dark and cold, and that his beams are black and frosty. But from its being the cause no otherwise than by its departure, no such thing can be inferred, but the contrary: it may justly be argued, that the sun is a bright and hot body, if cold and darkness are found to be the consequence of its withdrawment; and the more constantly and necessarily these effects are connected with and confined to its absence, the more strongly does it argue the sun to be the fountain of light and heat. So, inasmuch as sin is not the fruit of any positive agency or influence of the Most High, but, on the contrary, arises from the withholding of his action and energy, and, under certain circumstances, necessarily follows on the want of his influence; this is no argument that he is sinful, or his operation evil, or has anything of the nature of evil; but on the contrary, that he, and his agency, are altogether good and holy, and that he is the fountain of all holiness. It would be strange arguing, indeed, because men never commit sin, but only when God leaves them *to themselves*, and necessarily sin when he does so, that therefore their sin is not *from themselves*, but from God; and so that God must be a sinful being: as strange as it would be to argue, because it is always dark when the sun is gone, and never dark when the sun is present, that therefore all darkness is from the sun, and that his disc and beams must needs be black.

It properly belongs to the supreme and absolute Governor of the universe to order all important events within his dominion by his wisdom: but the events in the moral world are of the most important kind; such as the moral actions of intelligent creatures, and their consequences.

These events will be ordered by something. They will either be disposed by wisdom, or they will be disposed by chance; that is, they will be disposed by blind and undesigning causes, if that were possible, and could be called a disposal. Is it not better that the good and evil which happen in God's world, should be ordered, regulated, bounded, and determined, by the good pleasure of an infinitely wise Being, —who perfectly comprehends within his understanding and constant view the universality of things, in all their extent and duration, and sees all the influence of every event, with respect to every individual thing and circumstance throughout the grand system, and the whole of the eternal series of consequences,—than to leave these things to fall out by chance, and to be determined by those causes which have no understanding or aim? Doubtless, in these important events there is a better and a worse, as to the time, subject, place, manner, and circumstances of their coming to pass, with regard to their influence on the state and course of things.

And if there be, it is certainly best that they should be determined to that time, place, etc. which is best. And therefore it is in its own nature fit, that wisdom, and not chance, should order these things. So that it belongs to the Being who is the Possessor of infinite wisdom, and is the Creator and Owner of the whole system of created existences, and has the care of all; I say it belongs to him to take care of this matter; and he would not do what is proper for him if he should neglect it. And it is so far from being unholy in him to undertake this affair, that it would rather have been unholy to neglect it; as it would have been a neglecting what fitly appertains to him; and so it would have been a very unfit and unsuitable neglect.

Therefore the sovereignty of God doubtless extends to this matter; especially considering, that if it should be supposed to be otherwise, and God should leave men's volitions, and all moral events, to the determination and disposition of blind unmeaning causes, or they should be left to happen perfectly without a cause; this would be no more consistent with liberty, in any notion of it, and particularly not in the Arminian notion of it, than if these events were subject to the disposal of Divine Providence, and the will of man were disposed by Divine wisdom, as appears by what has been already observed. But it is evident, that such a providential disposing and determining men's moral actions, though it infers a moral necessity of those actions, yet it does not in the least infringe the real liberty of mankind; the only liberty that common sense teaches to be necessary to moral agency, which, as has been demonstrated, is not inconsistent with such necessity.

On the whole it is manifest, that God may be, in the manner which has been described, the orderer and disposer of that event, which, in the inherent subject and agent is moral evil; and yet his so doing may be no moral evil. He may will the disposal of such an event, and its coming to pass, for good ends, and his will not be an immoral or sinful will, but a perfectly holy will. And he may actually, in his providence, so dispose and permit things, that the event may be certainly and infallibly connected with such disposal and permission, and his act therein not be an immoral or unholy,

352

but a perfectly holy act. Sin may be an evil thing; and yet that there should be such a disposal and permission as that it should come to pass, may be a good thing. This is no contradiction or inconsistence. Joseph's brethren selling him into Egypt, consider it only as it was acted by them, and with respect to their views and aims, which were evil, was a very bad thing; but it was a good thing, as it was an event of God's ordering, and considered with respect to his views and aims, which were good. Gen. 1.20. "As for you, ye thought evil against me; but God meant it unto good." So the crucifixion of Christ, if we consider only those things which belong to the event as it proceeded from his murderers, and are comprehended within the compass of the affair considered as their act, their principles, dispositions, views, and aims; so it was one of the most heinous things that ever was done, in many respects the most horrid of all acts: but consider it as it was willed and ordered of God, in the extent of his designs and views, it was the most admirable and glorious of all events; and God's willing the event was the most holy volition of God that ever was made known to men; and God's act in ordering it was a divine act, which, above all others, manifests the moral excellency of the Divine Being.

*　　　*　　　*

There is no inconsistency in supposing, that God may hate a thing as it is in itself, and considered simply as evil, and yet that it may be his will it should come to pass, considering all consequences. I believe there is no person of good understanding, who will venture to say, he is certain that it is impossible it should be best, taking in the whole compass and extent of existence, and all consequences in the endless series of events, that there should be such a thing as moral evil in the world. And if so, it will certainly follow, that an infinitely wise Being who always chooses what is best, must choose that there should be such a thing. And if so, then such a choice is not an evil, but a wise and holy choice. And if so, then that providence which is agreeable to such a choice, is a wise and holy providence. Men do *will* sin as sin, and so are the authors and actors of it: they love it as sin, and for evil ends and purposes. God does not will sin as sin, or for the sake of anything evil; though it be his pleasure so to order things, that, he permitting, sin will come to pass; for the sake of the great good that by his disposal shall be the consequence. His willing to order things so that evil should come to pass, for the sake of the contrary good, is no argument that he does not hate evil as evil: and if so, then it is no reason why he may not reasonably forbid evil as evil, and punish it as such.

[116]

EINSTEIN, ALBERT

EINSTEIN, ALBERT (1879-   ). The overwhelming majority of scientists continually testify that Einstein has accomplished "one of the greatest generalizations of all time" and "has revolutionized our nineteenth century concepts not only of astronomy, but also of the nature of time, space, and of the fundamental ideas of science." Modern humanity reveres Einstein as one of its profoundest thinkers, as well as a man of the highest intellectual integrity, free of personal ambition, an intrepid fighter for human rights, social justice, and social responsibility. In the few decades that have passed between the time that Einstein made his theory of relativity known to the public and his seventieth birthday, more than five thousand books and pamphlets in every language have been published about him and his work. Although Einstein himself did nothing to popularize his ideas, his fame spread internationally after he predicted that the deflection of light in a gravitational field would occur in 1916 and 1919. He had and still has opponents, some of whom are prejudiced against him because he remains conscious of his Jewish origin. But humble people throughout the world are comforted by the knowledge that Einstein, whose thoughts pervade the universe, feels with all who suffer from oppression and persecution. Seldom has it happened that any man has become so popular, even though his theory is largely beyond popular imagination and common-sense thought. While the achievements of Copernicus, Galileo, Newton, and Darwin have been, at least in broad outline, explicable to the public, it has been impossible up to the present time to translate Einstein's theory of relativity adequately

354

into the non-technical language of popular literature.

The most important consequence of Einstein's special theory of relativity for scientific and philosophical thought has been the change in the concepts of time and space. Einstein destroyed the assumption that there is a single all-embracing time in which all events in the universe have their place. He has shown that "it is impossible to determine absolute motion by any experiment whatever." As long as time and space are measured separately, there always remains a kind of subjectivity which affects not only human observers but all other things. Time and space, which for classical physics are absolute constituents of the world, are conceived by Einsteinian physics as dependent upon each other, forming a relationship which can be analyzed in many different ways into what is referred to as spatial distance or lapse of time. Time which previously had been regarded as a cosmic measure is presented by Einstein as "local time" connected with the motion of the earth. He conceives of time as so completely analogous to the three dimensions of space that physics can be transformed into a kind of four-dimensional geometry. On the other hand, the special theory of relativity confers an absolute meaning on a magnitude, namely the velocity of light, which had only a relative significance in classical physics.

After this special theory, Einstein formulated his general theory of relativity which offers new explanations of the size of the universe, of gravitation and inertia. Einstein's achievements are by no means limited to the special and general theories of relativity. He was awarded the Nobel Prize in 1922 for his studies in photochemical equivalents. Later, he took a leading part in the investigation of atomic energy. On many occasions, he has expressed his personal views on problems of daily life, contemporary history, war, peace, education, religion, science and the fate of the Jews.

RELIGION AND SCIENCE

EVERYTHING that the human race has done and thought is concerned with the satisfaction of felt needs and the assuagement of pain. One has to keep this constantly in mind if one wishes to understand spiritual movements and their development. Feeling and desire are the motive forces behind all human endeavor and human creation, in however exalted a guise the latter may present itself to us. Now what are the feelings and needs that have led men to religious thought and belief in the widest sense of the words? A little consideration will suffice to show us that the most varying emotions preside over the birth of religious thought and experience. With primitive man it is above all fear that evokes religious notions—fear of hunger, wild beasts, sickness, death. Since at this stage of existence understanding of causal connections is usually poorly developed, the human mind creates for itself more or less analogous beings on whose wills and actions these fearful happenings depend. One's object now is to secure the favor of these beings by carrying out actions and offering sacrifices which, according to the tradition handed down from generation to generation, propitiate them or make them well disposed towards a mortal. I am speaking now of the religion of fear. This, though not created, is in an important degree stabilized by the formation of a special priestly caste which sets up as a mediator between the people and the beings they fear, and erects a hegemony on this basis. In many cases the leader or ruler whose position depends on other factors, or a privileged class, combines priestly functions with its secular authority in order to make the latter more secure; or the political rulers and the priestly caste make common cause in their own interests.

The social feelings are another source of the crystallization of religion. Fathers and mothers and the leaders of larger human communities are mortal and fallible. The desire for guidance, love, and support prompts men to form the social or moral conception of God. This is the God of Providence who protects, disposes, rewards, and punishes, the God who, according to the width of the believer's outlook, loves and cherishes the life of the tribe or of the human race, or even life as such, the comforter in sorrow and unsatisfied longing, who preserves the souls of the dead. This is the social or moral conception of God.

The Jewish scriptures admirably illustrate the development from the religion of fear to moral religion, which is continued in the New Testament. The religions of all civilized peoples, especially the peoples of the Orient, are primarily moral religions. The development from a religion of fear to moral religion is a great step in a nation's life. That primitive religions are based entirely on fear and the religions of civilized peoples purely on morality is a prejudice against which we must be on our guard. The truth is that they are all intermediate types, with this reservation, that on the higher levels of social life the religion of morality predominates.

Common to all these types is the anthropomorphic character of their conception of God. Only individuals of exceptional endowments and exceptionally high-minded communities, as a general rule, get in any real sense beyond this level. But there is a third state of religious experience which belongs to all of them, even though it is rarely found in a pure form and which I will call cosmic religious feeling. It is very difficult to explain this religious feeling to anyone who is entirely without it, especially as there is no anthropomorphic conception of God corresponding to it.

The individual feels the nothingness of human desires and aims, and the sublimity and marvellous order which reveal themselves both in nature and in the world of thought. He looks upon individual existence as a prison of the spirit and wants to experience the universe as a single significant whole. The beginnings of cosmic religious feeling already appear in earlier stages of development—e.g., in many of the Psalms of David and in some of the Prophets. Buddhism, as we have learnt from the wonderful writings of Schopenhauer especially, contains a much stronger element of it.

The religious geniuses of all ages have been distinguished by this kind of religious feeling, which knows no dogma and no God conceived in man's image; so that there can be no Church whose central teachings are based on it. Hence, it is precisely among the heretics of every age that we find men who are filled with the highest kind of religious feeling and were in many cases regarded by their contemporaries as Atheists, sometimes also as saints. Looked at in this light, men like Democritus, Francis of Assisi, and Spinoza are closely akin to one another.

How can cosmic religious feeling be communicated

from one person to another, if it can give rise to no definite notion of a God and no theology? In my view, it is the most important function of art and science to awaken this feeling and keep it alive in those who are capable of it.

We thus arrive at a conception of the relation of science to religion very different from the usual one. When one views the matter historically one is inclined to look upon science and religion as irreconcilable antagonists, and for a very obvious reason. The man who is thoroughly convinced of the universal operation of the law of causation cannot for a moment entertain the idea of a being who interferes in the course of events—that is, if he takes the hypothesis of causality really seriously. He has not use for the religion of fear and equally little for social or moral religion. A God who rewards and punishes is inconceivable to him for the simple reason that a man's actions are determined by necessity, external and internal, so that in God's eyes he cannot be responsible, any more than an inanimate object is responsible for the motions it goes through. Hence science has been charged with undermining morality, but the charge is unjust. A man's ethical behavior should be based effectually on sympathy, education, and social ties; no religious basis is necessary. Man would indeed be in a poor way if he had to be restrained by fear and punishment and hope of reward after death.

It is therefore easy to see why the Churches have always fought science and persecuted its devotees. On the other hand, I maintain that cosmic religious feeling is the strongest and noblest incitement to scientific research. Only those who realize the immense efforts and, above all, the devotion which pioneer work in theoretical science demands, can grasp the strength of the emotion out of which alone such work, remote as it is from the immediate realities of life, can issue. What a deep conviction of the rationality of the universe and what a yearning to understand, were it but a feeble reflection of the mind revealed in this world, Kepler and Newton must have had to enable them to spend years of solitary labor in disentangling the principles of celestial mechanics! Those whose acquaintance with scientific research is derived chiefly from its practical results easily develop a completely false notion of the mentality of the men, who, surrounded by a skeptical world, have shown the way to those like-minded with themselves, scattered through the earth and the centuries. Only one who has devoted his life to similar ends can have a vivid realization of what has inspired these men and given them the strength to remain true to their purpose in spite of countless failures. It is cosmic religious feeling that gives a man strength of this sort. A contemporary has said, not unjustly, that in this materialistic age of ours the serious scientific workers are the only profoundly religious people.

[117]

ELIEZER, ISRAEL BEN. See BAAL SHEM-TOV.

ELIOT, GEORGE

ELIOT, GEORGE (1819-1880). Mary Ann Evans is best known by her pseudonym of George Eliot. Her novels are regarded, today, as classics. She was educated by her father in a spirit of rigorous evangelism, but she broke with Christian orthodoxy after studying the writings of David Friederich Strauss and Ludwig Feuerbach. She translated some of their works into English. Her novels attempt to illustrate that character is a process of mental and moral unfolding, that each individual must face his own nemesis and that departure from orthodoxy does not corrupt moral standards. They also contain many comments on moral and philosophical questions. Many critics have thought that she placed too much emphasis on ethical problems. Inclined as she was to meditation, her observations of life were very keen. She excelled in painting rural life, in presenting the tragic and comic aspects of ordinary people, and in characterizing them with the utmost detail. She also depicted great historical figures sympathetically. In *Daniel Deronda* (1876), Eliot dealt with the question of Jewish national survival in such manner that, according to Nahum Sokolow (a Zionist leader), it significantly prepared the way for Theodor Herzl's work.

For many years, Eliot lived together with G. H. Lewes in a

common-law relationship. Though she was a conscientious non-conformist, she never scorned tradition light-heartedly. Her best known works are *Scenes of Clerical Life* (1858), *Middlemarch* (1872), *Silas Marner* (1861), *Adam Bede* (1859), and *The Mill on The Floss* (1860).

VALUE IN ORIGINALITY

THE supremacy given in European cultures to the literature of Greece and Rome has had an effect almost equal to that of a religion in binding the Western nations together. It is foolish to be forever complaining of the consequent uniformity, as if there were an endless power of originality in the human mind. Great and precious origination must always be comparatively rare, and can only exist on condition of a wide and massive uniformity. When a multitude of men have learned to use the same language in speech and writing, then, and then only can the greatest masters of language arise.

For in what does their mastery consist? They use words which are already a familiar medium of understanding and sympathy in such a way as greatly to enlarge understanding and sympathy. Origination of this order changes the wild grasses into world-feeding grain. Idiosyncrasies are pepper and spices of questionable aroma.

[118]

EMERSON, RALPH WALDO

EMERSON, RALPH WALDO (1803-1882). William James pointed out that there were two Emersons: one was the instinctive New Englander whose sharp eyes penetrated the defects of the American republic without despairing of it; the other was the Plotinizing Emerson who exalted the Over-Soul, and before whom revelations of time, space, and nature shrank away. Emerson was often aware of the fact that his readiness to perceive various phenomena and to expand his spiritual interests could lead his mind in disparate directions. The elder Henry James asserted that Emerson "had no conscience, in fact he lived by perception." Emerson looked upon consistency as the hob-goblin of little minds. In *Self-Reliance*, he stated: "With consistency a great soul has simply nothing to do."

In *History,* he declared: "It is the fault of our rhetoric that we cannot state one fact without seeming to belie some other."

When Emerson spoke of the realm of the soul which embraced the mind and the spirit, it was with certainty and strong conviction, not theoretical knowledge. He distinguished between philosophers like Spinoza, Kant, and Coleridge and others like Locke, Paley, Mackintosh, and Stewart. He held that the former spoke from within or from experience as parties to or possessors of the fact; while the others spoke from without, as spectators whose acquaintance with the fact came from the evidence of third persons. He treated the latter and their doctrines contemptuously, and characterized them as coarse translators of things into conscience, ignorant of the relationship of the soul to the divine spirit. The latter relationship was the only thing that mattered to Emerson, for him no facts as such were sacred; none unworthy but which became instantly important when they indicated or symbolized the history of the living soul, regardless of whether they voiced a mythical imagination, history, law, customs, proverbial wisdom, the creative spirit of artists and poets, the contemplation of a saint, the decision of a hero, or the conversation of ordinary persons. He believed that the worth of any individual man was derived from the universe which contained all human life and was therefore mysterious. He regarded every man as the entrance to the universal mind, capable of feeling and comprehending that which at any time befell any man

SELF-RELIANCE

I READ the other day some verses written by an eminent painter which were original and not conventional. The soul always hears an admonition in such lines, let the subject be what it may. The sentiment they instill is of more value than any thought they may contain. To believe your own thought, to believe that what is true for you in your private heart is true for all men,—that is genius. Speak your latent conviction, and it shall be the universal sense; for the inmost in due time becomes the outmost, and our first thought is rendered back to us by the trumpets of the Last Judgment. Familiar as the voice of the mind is to each, the highest merit we ascribe to Moses, Plato and Milton is that they set at naught books and traditions, and spoke not what men, but what *they* thought. A man should learn to detect and watch that gleam of light which flashes across his mind from within, more than the luster of the firmament of bards and sages. Yet he dismisses without notice his thought, because it is his. In every work of genius we recognize our own rejected thoughts; they come back to us with a certain alienated majesty. Great works of art have no more affecting lesson for us than this. They teach us to abide by our spontaneous impression with good-humored inflexibility then most when the whole cry of voices is on the other side. Else tomorrow a stranger will say with masterly good sense precisely what we have thought and felt all the time, and we shall be forced to take with shame our own opinion from another.

There is a time in every man's education when he arrives at the conviction that envy is ignorance; that imitation is suicide; that he must take himself for better for worse as his portion; that though the wide universe is full of good, no kernel of nourishing corn can come to him through his toil bestowed on that plot of ground which is given to him to till. The power which resides in him is new in nature, and none but he knows what that is which he can do, nor does he know until he has tried. Not for nothing one face, one character, one fact, makes much impression on him, and another none. This sculpture in the memory is not without pre-established harmony. The eye was placed where one ray should fall, that it might testify of that particular ray. We but half express ourselves, and are ashamed of that divine idea which each of us represents. It may be safely trusted as proportionate and of good issues, so it be faithfully imparted, but God will not have his work made manifest by cowards. A man is relieved and gay when he has put his heart into his work and done his best; but what he has said or done otherwise shall give him no peace. It is a deliverance which does not deliver. In the attempt his genius deserts him; no muse befriends; no invention, no hope.

Trust thyself: every heart vibrates to that iron string. Accept the place the divine providence has found for you, the society of your contemporaries, the connection of events.

Great men have always done so, and confided themselves childlike to the genius of their age, betraying their perception that the absolutely trustworthy was seated at their heart, working through their hands, predominating in all their being. And we are now men, and must accept in the highest mind the same transcendent destiny; and not minors and invalids in a protected corner, not cowards fleeing before a revolution, but guides, redeemers and benefactors, obeying the Almighty effort and advancing on Chaos and the Dark.

What pretty oracles nature yields us on this text in the face and behavior of children, babes, and even brutes! That divided and rebel mind, that distrust of a sentiment because our arithmetic has computed the strength and means opposed to our purpose, these have not. Their mind being whole, their eye is as yet unconquered, and when we look in their faces we are disconcerted. Infancy conforms to nobody; all conform to it; so that one babe commonly makes four or five out of the adults who prattle and play to it. So God has armed youth and puberty and manhood no less with its own piquancy and charm, and made it enviable and gracious and its claims not to be put by, if it will stand by itself. Do not think the youth has no force, because he cannot speak to you and me. Hark! in the next room his voice is sufficiently clear and emphatic. It seems he knows how to speak to his contemporaries. Bashful or bold then, he will know how to make us seniors very unnecessary.

The nonchalance of boys who are sure of a dinner, and would disdain as much as a lord to do or say aught to conciliate one, is the healthy attitude of human nature. A boy is in the parlor what the pit is in the playhouse; independent, irresponsible, looking out from his corner on such people and facts as pass by, he tries and sentences them on their merits, in the swift, summary way of boys, as good, bad, interesting, silly, eloquent, troublesome. He cumbers himself never about consequences, about interests; he gives an independent, genuine verdict. You must court him; he does not court you. But the man is as it were clapped into jail by his consciousness. As soon as he has once acted or spoken with *éclat* he is a committed person, watched by the sympathy or the hatred of hundreds, whose affections must now enter into his account. There is no Lethe for this. Ah, that he could pass again into his neutrality! Who can thus avoid all pledges and, having observed, observe again from the same unaffected, unbiased, unbribable, unaffrighted innocence,—must always be formidable. He would utter opinions on all passing affairs, which being seen to be not private but necessary, would sink like darts into the ear of men and put them in fear.

These are the voices which we hear in solitude, but they grow faint and inaudible as we enter into the world. Society everywhere is in conspiracy against the manhood of every one of its members. Society is a joint-stock company, in which the members agree, for the better securing of his bread to each shareholder, to surrender the liberty and culture of the eater. The virtue in most request is conformity. Self-reliance is its aversion. It loves not realities and creators, but names and customs.

Whoso would be a man, must be a nonconformist. He who would gather immortal palms must not be hindered by the name of goodness, but must explore if it be goodness. Nothing is at last sacred but the integrity of your own mind. Absolve you to yourself, and you shall have the suffrage of the world. I remember an answer which when quite young I was prompted to make to a valued adviser who was wont to importune me with the dear old doctrines of the church. On my saying, "What have I to do with the sacredness of traditions, if I live wholly from within?" my friend suggested,—"But these impulses may be from below, not from above." I replied, "They do not seem to me to be such; but if I am the Devil's child, I will live then from the Devil." No law can be sacred to me but that of my nature. Good and bad are but names very readily transferable to that or this; the only right is what is after my constitution; the only wrong what is against it. A man is to carry himself in the presence of all opposition as if everything were titular and

ephemeral but he. I am ashamed to think how easily we capit-
ulate to badges and names, to large societies and dead institutions. Every decent and well-spoken individual affects and
sways me more than is right. I ought to go upright and vital,
and speak the rude truth in all ways.

*   *   *

The other terror that scares us from self-trust is our consistency; a reverence for our past act or word because the
eyes of others have no other data for computing our orbit
than our past acts, and we are loth to disappoint them.

But why should you keep your head over your shoulder?
Why drag about this corpse of your memory, lest you contradict somewhat you have stated in this or that public place?
Suppose you should contradict yourself; what then? It seems
to be a rule of wisdom never to rely on your memory alone,
scarcely even in acts of pure memory, but to bring the past
for judgment into the thousand-eyed present, and live ever
in a new day. In your metaphysics you have denied personality to the Deity, yet when the devout motions of the soul
come, yield to them heart and life, though they should clothe
God with shape and color. Leave your theory, as Joseph his
coat in the hand of the harlot, and flee.

A foolish consistency is the hobgoblin of little minds,
adored by little statesmen and philosophers and divines. With
consistency a great soul has simply nothing to do. He may as
well concern himself with his shadow on the wall. Speak
what you think now in hard words and tomorrow speak what
tomorrow thinks in hard words again, though it contradict
every thing you said today.—"Ah, so you shall be sure to be
misunderstood."—Is it so bad then to be misunderstood?
Pythagoras was misunderstood, and Socrates, and Jesus, and
Luther, and Copernicus, and Galileo, and Newton and every
pure and wise spirit that ever took flesh. To be great is to be
misunderstood.

[119]

EMPEDOCLES

EMPEDOCLES (c. 490-435 B.C.). Born in Acragas (Agrigentum)
on the south coast of Sicily, Empedocles, like his teacher Parmenides, was bred in the Pythagorean tradition. He tried to combine this
with the more naturalistic philosophy and science of the Milesians.
He did not share Parmenides' distrust of the senses, and like him,
composed his philosophy in verse. Fragments of two treatises, one
entitled *On Nature* and the other *Purification,* are extant. The term
catharsis, which became highly important in poetry and aesthetics,
was first used in *Purification.* The doctrine of the four elements,
water, fire, air, and earth, which dominated the popular thinking
about nature for more than two thousand years, was probably
originated by Empedocles. According to him, change was produced
by the two fundamental forces, love and strife. The first was the
cause of combination; the other of separation. He explained cosmic
nature, the functions of the human body, and the activities of the
soul as the result of conflicting forces. His philosophy was a blend
of mythological imagination and scientific observation. He was an
opponent of tyranny and a miracle-worker who claimed to be a
God. Hundreds of stories abounded about him throughout ancient
Greece and Italy. He was credited with founding the first great
medical school. His legendary death is supposed to have taken place
by jumping into the crater of Mount Etna; this has been a source
of inspiration for many poets, among them: Matthew Arnold and
Friedrich Hoelderlin.

FRAGMENTS

BUT, O ye Gods, turn aside from my tongue the madness of
those men. Hallow my lips and make a pure stream flow from
them! And thee, much-wooed, white-armed Virgin Muse, do
I beseech, that I may hear what is lawful for the children of
a day! Speed me on my way from the abode of Holiness
and drive my willing car! Constrain me not to win garlands
of honor and glory at the hands of mortals on condition of
speaking in my pride beyond that which is lawful and right,
and only so to gain a seat upon the heights of wisdom.

Go to now, consider with all thy powers in what way
each thing is clear. Hold nothing that thou seest in greater

credit than what thou hearest, nor value thy resounding ear above the clear instructions of thy tongue; and do not with-hold thy confidence in any of thy other bodily parts by which there is an opening for understanding, but consider every-thing in the way it is clear.

*　　*　　*

And thou shalt learn all the drugs that are a defense against ills and old age, since for thee alone shall I accomp-lish all this. Thou shalt arrest the violence of the weariless winds that arise and sweep the earth, laying waste the corn-fields with their breath; and again, when thou so desirest, thou shalt bring their blasts back again with a rush. Thou shalt cause for men a seasonable drought after the dark rains, and again after the summer drought thou shalt produce the streams that feed the trees as they pour down from the sky. Thou shalt bring back from Hades the life of a dead man.

*　　*　　*

And I shall tell thee another thing. There is no coming into being of aught that perishes, nor any end for it in bane-ful death; but only mingling and separation of what has been mingled. Coming into being is but a name given to these by men.

*　　*　　*

But, when the elements have been mingled in the fashion of a man and come to the light of day, or in the fashion of the race of wild beasts or plants or birds, then men say that these come into being; and when they are separated, they call that, as is the custom, woeful death. I too follow the custom, and call it so myself.

*　　*　　*

Fools!—for they have no far-reaching thoughts—who deem that what before was not comes into being, or that aught can perish and be utterly destroyed. For it cannot be that aught arise from what it no way is, and it is impossible and unheard of that what is should perish; for it will always be, wherever one may keep putting it.

A man who is wise in such matters would never surmise in his heart that, so long as mortals live what men choose to call their life, they are, and suffer good and ill; while, before they were formed and after they have been dissolved they are, it seems, nothing at all.

I shall tell thee a twofold tale. At one time things grew to be one only out of many; at another, that divided up to be many instead of one. There is a double becoming of perishable things and a double passing away. The coming together of all things brings one generation into being and destroys it; the other grows up and is scattered as things become divided. And these things never cease, continually changing places, at one time all uniting in one through Love, at another each borne in different directions by the repulsion of Strife. Thus, as far as it is their nature to grow into one out of many, and to become many once more when the one is parted as-under, so far they come into being and their life abides not. But, inasmuch as they never cease changing their places continually, so far they are immovable as they go round the circle of existence.

*　　*　　*

Nor is any part of the whole empty. Whence, then, could aught come to increase it? Where, too, could these things perish, since no place is empty of them? They are what they are; but, running through one another, different things continually come into being from different sources, yet ever alike.

*　　*　　*

Come now, look at the things that bear virtues. Behold the sun, everywhere bright and warm, and all the immortal things that are bathed in its heat and bright radiance. Behold the rain, everywhere dark and cold; and from the earth issue forth things close-pressed and solid. When they are in strife all these things are different in form, and sep-arated; but they come together in love, and are desired by one another.

For out of these have sprung all things that were and are and shall be,—trees and men and women, beasts and birds and the fishes that dwell in the waters, yea, and the gods that live long lives and are exalted in honor.

For these things are what they are; but, running through one another, they take different shapes—so much does mixture change them.

*   *   *

For, of a truth, they (i.e. Love and Strife) were aforementioned and shall be; nor ever, methinks, will boundless time be emptied of that pair. And they prevail in turn as the circle comes round, and pass away before one another, and increase in their appointed turn.

*   *   *

For all of them—sun, earth, sky, and sea,—fit in with all the parts of themselves, the friendly parts which are separated off in perishable things. In the same way, all those things that are more adapted for mixture, are united to one another in Love, made like by the power of Aphrodite. But they themselves (i.e. the elements) differ as far as possible in their origin and mixture and the forms imprinted on each, being altogether unaccustomed to come together, and very hostile, under the influence of Strife, since it has wrought their birth.

Thus all things have thought by the will of fortune. . . . And, inasmuch as the rarest things come together in their fall. . . .

Fire is increased by Fire, Earth increases its own mass, and Air swells the bulk of Air.

And the kindly earth in its well-wrought ovens received two parts of shining Nestis out of the eight, and four of Hephaistos; and they became white bones, divinely fitted together by the cements of Harmony.

And the earth meets with these in nearly equal proportions, with Hephaistos and Water and shining Air, anchoring

in the perfect haven of Kypris,—either a little more of it, or
less of it and more of them. From these did blood arise
and the various forms of flesh.

[120]

ENGELS, FRIEDRICH

ENGELS, FRIEDRICH (1820-1895). As long as Karl Marx lived,
Engels was his intimate friend, collaborator, and supporter. Though
he remained in the background, were it not for Engels' money,
moral encouragement, and innumerable other services, Marx would
have perished. Several of the writings were the collaboration of
both; Engels was always ready to recognize Marx as his superior.
After Marx died, Engels edited the second and third volumes of
Marx's *Capital;* when socialists disagreed about the meaning of the
work, or adversaries distorted it, Engels untiringly interpreted his
late friend's meaning.

Engels was the descendant of a dynasty of German industrialists
who adhered to religious orthodoxy and political conservatism. He
had planned, in his youth, to become a poet, for he was an enthusiast of German romanticism, the historical past and beauty and
nature in art. When a new Oriental crisis threatened to cause war
between France and Germany (1840), Engels, still an excited nationalist, dreamed of German military victories. A sojourn in
London and military service in the Prussian army made him revise
his beliefs. He abandoned German nationalism, and all prospects
of succeeding his father in his well-to-do business. Thereafter, he
devoted his life to the fight for the rights of the working class
and for the realization of Marx's plans. In 1845 Engels published
his pamphlet, *On The Situation of The Working Class*, in England.
He was greatly indebted for this to Constantin Pecqueur, who also
wrote a pamphlet dealing with the same subject. Engels' subsequent
collaboration with Marx was so close that it is impossible to define
his part in it with exactness. In his later years, Engels blended
dialectical materialism (as Marx had conceived of it) with philosophical materialism. He also tried to expand the meaning of
Marx's terminology. He developed a great interest in ethnology in
order to attack social conventions with arguments that demonstrated
the relativity of social values. Until his death, he remained the
executor of Marx's will.

MORALITY IS CLASS MORALITY

THE conceptions of good and bad have varied so much from
nation to nation and from age to age that they have often

been in direct contradiction to each other. But all the same, someone may object, good is not bad and bad is not good; if good is confused with bad there is an end to all morality, and everyone can do and leave undone whatever he cares. This is also, stripped of his oracular phrases, Herr Dühring's opinion. But the matter cannot be so simply disposed of. If it was such an easy business there would certainly be no dispute at all over good and bad; everyone would know what was good and what was bad. But how do things stand today? What morality is preached to us today? There is first Christian-feudal morality, inherited from past centuries of faith; and this again has two main sub-divisions, Catholic and Protestant moralities, each of which in turn has no lack of further subdivisions from the Jesuit-Catholic and Orthodox-Protestant to loose "advanced" moralities. Alongside of these we find the modern bourgeois morality and with it too the proletarian morality of the future, so that in the most advanced European countries alone the past, present and future provide three great groups of moral theories which are in force simultaneously and alongside of each other. Which is then the true one? Not one of them, in the sense of having absolute validity; but certainly that morality which contains the maximum of durable elements is the one which, in the present, represents the overthrow of the present, represents the future: that is, the proletarian.

But when we see that the three classes of modern society, the feudal aristocracy, the bourgeoisie and the proletariat, each have their special morality, we can only draw the one conclusion, that men, consciously or unconsciously, derive their moral ideas in the last resort from the practical relations on which they carry on production and exchange.

But nevertheless there is much that is common to the three moral theories mentioned above—is this not at least a portion of a morality which is externally fixed? These moral theories represent three different stages of the same historical development, and have therefore a common historical background, and for that reason alone they necessarily have much in common. Even more. In similar or approximately similar stages of economic development moral theories must of necessity be more or less in agreement. From the moment when private property in movable objects developed, in all societies in which this private property existed there must be this moral law in common: Thou shalt not steal. Does this law thereby become an eternal moral law? By no means. In a society in which the motive for stealing has been done away with, in which therefore at the very most only lunatics would ever steal, how the teacher of morals would be laughed at who tried solemnly to proclaim the eternal truth: Thou shalt not steal!

We therefore reject every attempt to impose on us any moral dogma whatsoever as an eternal, ultimate and forever immutable moral law on the pretext that the moral world has its permanent principles which transcend history and the differences between nations. We maintain on the contrary that all former moral theories are the product, in the last analysis, of the economic stage which society had reached at that particular epoch. And as society has hitherto moved in class antagonisms, morality was always a class morality; it has either justified the domination and the interests of the ruling class, or, as soon as the oppressed class has become powerful enough, it has represented the revolt against this domination and the future interests of the oppressed.

[121]

EPICTETUS

EPICTETUS (c. 60-110). The son of a slave, himself crippled by a brutal master, Epictetus was legally emancipated and became the example of an upright, independent, free man. Often, when men were afflicted by misfortune, they declined religious consolation and read the *Encheiridion* (Manual) to regain peace of mind. The manual was not written by the Stoic philosopher, Epictetus, but by his faithful disciple Arrian (a military commander and important dignitary of the Roman Empire) who had made notes on his teacher's psychological observations, moral meditations, lectures, and conversations. About half the original manual is extant.

Epictetus was born in Phrygia, Asia Minor. He was sold to one of the retinue of Emperor Nero. He was allowed to attend the lectures of the Stoic philosopher Caius Musonius Rufus whom he greatly admired. From Musonius he learned how to make theoretical discussions personal confessions. When Musonius died (81), Epictetus, who by this time had been freed from slavery, held philosophical lectures in Rome. Emperor Domitian, who disliked freedom of expression, banished Epictetus (90) and all other philosophers from the capital. Epictetus went to Nicopolis, in Epirus, Greece, where among the members of his large audience was the future Emperor Hadrian. He also exerted considerable influence over Emperor Marcus Aurelius; the latter's views almost consistently agreed with those of Epictetus. Epictetus taught that reason governed the world and was identical with God. Sometimes he paralleled Christian doctrines. He mentioned the "Galileans"; praised their courage, but maintained that they were devoid of reason. His work, expressed in simple and frank language, attracted many thinkers of later centuries, notably Montaigne and Kant.

TO THOSE WHO FEAR WANT

ARE you not ashamed of being more cowardly and more mean than fugitive slaves? How do they when they run away leave their masters? on what estates do they depend, and what domestics do they rely on? Do they not after stealing a little which is enough for the first days, then afterwards move on through land or through sea, contriving one method after another for maintaining their lives? And what fugitive slave ever died of hunger? But you are afraid lest necessary things should fail you, and are sleepless by night. Wretch, are you so blind, and don't you see the road to which the want of necessaries leads?—Well, where does it lead?—To the same place to which a fever leads, or a stone that falls on you, to death. Have you not often said this yourself to your companions? have you not read much of this kind, and written much? and how often have you boasted that you were easy as to death?

Yes: but my wife and children also suffer hunger.— Well then does their hunger lead to any other place? Is there not the same descent to some place for them also? Is not there not the same state below for them? Do you not choose then to look at that place full of boldness against every want and deficiency, to that place to which both the richest and those who have held the highest offices, and kings themselves and tyrants must descend? or to which you will descend hungry, if it should so happen, but they burst by indigestion and drunkenness. What beggar did you hardly ever see who was not an old man, and even of extreme age? But chilled with cold and night, and lying on the ground, and eating only what is absolutely necessary they approach near to the impossibility of dying. Cannot you write? Cannot you teach (take care of) children? Cannot you be a watchman of another person's door?—But it is shameful to come to such a necessity.—Learn then first what are the things which are shameful, and then tell us that you are a philosopher: but at present do not, even if any other man call you so, allow it. Is that shameful to you which is not your own act, that of which you are not the cause, that which has come to you by accident, as a headache, as a fever? If your parents were poor, and left their property to others, and if while they live they do not help you at all, is this shameful to you? Is this what you learned with the philosophers? Did you ever hear that the thing which is shameful ought to be blamed, and that which is blamable is worthy of blame? Whom do you blame for an act which is not his own, which he did not do himself? Did you then make your father such as he is, or is it in your power to improve him? Is this power given to you? Well then, ought you to wish the things which are not given to you, or to be ashamed if you do not obtain them? And have you also been accustomed while you were studying philosophy to look to others and to hope for nothing from yourself? Lament then and groan and eat with fear that you may not have food to-morrow. Tremble about your poor slaves lest they steal, lest they run away, lest they die. So live and continue to live, you who in name only have approached philosophy, and have disgraced its theorems as far as you can by showing them to be useless and unprofitable to those who take them up; you who have never sought

374

constancy, freedom from perturbation, and from passions: you who have not sought any person for the sake of this object, but many for the sake of syllogisms; you who have never thoroughly examined any of these appearances by yourself, Am I able to bear, or am I not able to bear? What remains for me to do? But as if all your affairs were well and secure, you have been resting on the third topic, that of things being unchanged, in order that you may possess unchanged —what? cowardice, mean spirit, the admiration of the rich, desire without attaining any end, and avoidance which fails in the attempt? About security in these things you have been anxious.

Ought you not to have gained something in addition from reason, and then to have protected this with security? And whom did you ever see building a battlement all round and not encircling it with a wall? And what door-keeper is placed with no door to watch? But you practice in order to be able to prove—what? You practice that you may not be tossed as on the sea through sophisms, and tossed about from what? Shew me first what you hold, what you measure, or what you weigh; and shew me the scales or the mediums (the measure); or how long will you go on measuring the dust? Ought you not to demonstrate those things which make men happy, which make things go on for them in the way as they wish, and why we ought to blame no man, accuse no man, and acquiesce in the administration of the universe? Shew me these. 'See, I shew them; I will resolve syllogisms for you.'—This is the measure, slave; but it is not the thing measured. Therefore you are now paying the penalty for what you neglected, philosophy: you tremble, you lie awake, you advise with all persons; and if your deliberations are not likely to please all, you think that you have deliberated ill. Then you fear hunger, as you suppose: but it is not hunger that you fear, but you are afraid that you will not have a cook, that you will not have another to purchase provisions for the table, a third to take off your shoes, a fourth to dress you, others to rub you, and to follow you, in order that in the bath, when you have taken off your clothes and stretched yourself out like those who are crucified you may be rubbed on this side and on that, and then the aliptes (rubber) may say (to the slave), Change his position, present the side, take hold of his head, shew the shoulder; and then when you have left the bath and gone home, you may call out, Does no one bring something to eat? And then, Take away the tables, sponge them: you are afraid of this, that you may not be able to lead the life of a sick man. But learn the life of those who are in health, how slaves live, how laborers, how those live who are genuine philosophers; how Socrates lived, who had a wife and children; how Diogenes lived, and how Cleanthes who attended to the school and drew water. If you choose to have these things, you will have them everywhere, and you will live in full confidence. Confiding in what? In that alone in which a man can confide, in that which is secure, in that which is not subject to hindrance, in that which cannot be taken away, that is in your own will. And why have you made yourself so useless and good for nothing that no man will choose to receive you into his house, no man to take care of you?: but if a utensil entire and useful were cast abroad, every man who found it, would take it up and think it a gain; but no man will take you up, and every man will consider you a loss. So cannot you discharge the office even of a dog, or of a cock? Why then do you choose to live any longer, when you are what you are?

Does any good man fear that he shall fail to have food? To the blind it does not fail, to the lame it does not; shall it fail to a good man? And to a good soldier there does not fail to be one who gives him pay, nor to a laborer, nor to a shoemaker: and to the good man shall there be wanting such a person? Does God thus neglect the things he has established, his ministers, his witnesses, whom alone he employs as examples to the uninstructed, both that he exists, and administers well the whole, and does not neglect human affairs, and that to a good man there is no evil either when he is living or when he is dead? What then when he does not supply him with food? What else does he do than like a good general he has given me the signal to retreat? I obey, I follow, assenting to the words of the commander, praising his acts: for I came when it pleased him, and I will also go when it pleases him; and while I lived, it was my duty to praise God both by myself, and to each person severally and to many. He does not supply me with many things, nor with abundance, he does not will me to live luxuriously; for neither did he supply Hercules who was his own son; but another (Eurystheus) was king of Argos and Mycenae, and Hercules obeyed orders, and labored, and exercised. And Eurystheus was what he was, neither king of Argos nor of Mycenae, for he was not even king of himself; but Hercules was ruler and leader of the whole earth and sea, who purged away lawlessness, and introduced justice and holiness; and he did these things both naked and alone. And when Ulysses was cast out shipwrecked, did want humiliate him, did it break his spirit? but how did he go off to the virgins to ask for necessaries, to beg which is considered most shameful?

As a lion bred in the mountains trusting in his strength.

Relying on what? Not on reputation nor on wealth nor on the power of a magistrate, but on his own strength, that is, on his opinions about the things which are in our power and those which are not. For these are the only things which make men free, which make them escape from hindrance, which raise the head (neck) of those who are depressed, which make them look with steady eyes on the rich and on tyrants. And this was the gift given to the philosopher. But you will not come forth bold, but trembling about your trifling garments and silver vessels. Unhappy man, have you thus wasted your time till now?

What then, if I shall be sick? You will be sick in such

a way as you ought to be.—Who will take care of me?—
God; your friends—I shall lie down on a hard bed—But
you will lie down like a man—I shall not have a convenient
chamber—You will be sick in an inconvenient chamber—
Who will provide for me the necessary food?—Those who
provide for others also. You will be sick like Manes.—
And what also will be the end of the sickness? Any other
than death?—Do you then consider this the chief of all
evils to man and the chief mark of mean spirit and of
cowardice is not death, but rather the fear of death? Against
this fear then I advise you to exercise yourself: to this let
all your reasoning tend, your exercises, and reading; and
you will know that thus only are men made free.

[122]

EPICURUS

EPICURUS (341-270 B.C.). According to Epicurus, philosophy
must be a cure for the mind and soul; it must be a guide to happiness. He taught that pleasure was the beginning and end of the
blessed life; that wisdom and culture must be directed toward this
end. Contrary to other hedonists, Epicurus regarded the permanent
absence of pain as the only true pleasure, rather than joy or debauchery. The pleasure he conceived of demanded self-control; prudence was necessary for the pursuit of happiness. He recommended
an extremely frugal life; he himself was ordinarily satisfied with
bread and water. The essential part of his philosophy was devoted
to ethics and teaching a wise conduct of life. Logic, epistemology,
physics, and metaphysics were regarded as helpful toward securing
tranquility of soul or disturbing it. He thus concluded that fear
of death and religion were the main sources of psychic disorder.
He staunchly opposed superstition or any belief in supernatural
interference. His concept of nature mainly followed that of Democritus. Although he adopted atomism, he disaffirmed determinism,
and established the doctrine of cosmic chance. The latter doctrine
has been revived in contemporary times.

In 310 B.C. he founded the oldest sanatorium, in Mytilene,
for persons suffering from psychic or nervous disorders, depressions,
or the consequences of failure or disappointment. Four years later
the sanatorium was removed to Athens. Epicurus, himself, always
suffered from diseases of the stomach, bladder, or kidneys. His

378

philosophy enabled him to endure pain and he was able to cure many of the patients in his sanatorium by teaching them his philosophy. Many were indebted to his knowledge whereby psychic disorders could be avoided. Persons of all origins, professions, and social stature were admitted to his sanatorium or school. Neither slaves nor hetaerae were excluded. His teachings, though often distorted, were spread throughout the ancient world. They have had considerable influence through all of history, up to the present time.

ON PLEASURE

WE must consider that of desires some are natural, others vain, and of the natural some are necessary and others merely natural; and of the necessary some are necessary for happiness, others for the repose of the body, and others for very life. The right understanding of these facts enables us to refer all choice and avoidance to the health of the body and (the soul's) freedom from disturbance, since this is the aim of the life of blessedness. For it is to obtain this end that we always act, namely, to avoid pain and fear. And when this is once secured for us, all the tempest of the soul is dispersed, since the living creature has not to wander as though in search of something that is missing, and to look for some other thing by which he can fulfill the good of the soul and the good of the body. For it is then that we have need of pleasure, when we feel pain owing to the absence of pleasure; (but when we do not feel pain), we no longer need pleasure. And for this cause we call pleasure the beginning and end of the blessed life. For we recognize pleasure as the first good innate in us, and from pleasure we begin every act of choice and avoidance, and to pleasure we return again, using the feeling as the standard by which we judge every good.

And since pleasure is the first good and natural to us, for this very reason we do not choose every pleasure, but sometimes we pass over many pleasures, when greater discomfort accrues to us as the result of them: and similarly we think many pains better than pleasures, since a greater pleasure comes to us when we have endured pains for a long time. Every pleasure then because of its natural kinship to us is good, yet not every pleasure is to be chosen: even as every pain also is an evil, yet not all are always of a nature to be avoided. Yet by a scale of comparison and by the consideration of advantages and disadvantages we must form our judgment on all these matters. For the good on certain occasions we treat as bad, and conversely the bad as good.

And again independence of desire we think a great good—not that we may at all times enjoy but a few things, but that, if we do not possess many, we may enjoy the few in the genuine persuasion that those have the sweetest pleasure in luxury who least need it, and that all that is natural is easy to be obtained, but that which is superfluous is hard. And so plain savors bring us a pleasure equal to a luxurious diet, when all the pain due to want is removed; and bread and water produce the highest pleasure, when one who needs them puts them to his lips. To grow accustomed therefore to simple and not luxurious diet gives us health to the full, and makes a man alert for the needful employments of life, and when after long intervals we approach luxuries disposes us better towards them, and fits us to be fearless of fortune.

When, therefore, we maintain that pleasure is the end, we do not mean the pleasures of profligates and those that consist in sensuality, as is supposed by some who are either ignorant or disagree with us or do not understand, but freedom from pain in the body and from trouble in the mind. For it is not continuous drinkings and revellings, nor the satisfaction of lusts, nor the enjoyment of fish and other luxuries of the wealthy table, which produce a pleasant life, but sober reasoning, searching out the motives for all choice and avoidance, and banishing mere opinions, to which are due the greatest disturbance of the spirit.

Of all this the beginning and the greatest good is prudence. Wherefore prudence is a more precious thing even than philosophy: for from prudence are sprung all the other virtues, and it teaches us that it is not possible to live pleasantly without living prudently and honorably and justly, (nor again, to live a life of prudence, honor, and justice) without living pleasantly. For the virtues are by nature bound up with the pleasant life, and the pleasant life is inseparable from them.

[123]

ERASMUS, DESIDERIUS

ERASMUS, DESIDERIUS (1466-1536). Born in Rotterdam, Erasmus was brought up in the tradition of the Brethren of the Common Life. He believed in Christ and His mission and regarded Christianity not only as a religion and doctrine of salvation, but also as a guide to moral life. He held that philosophy and the arts could also show the right way. In his later years, he conceived of Christianity more as a religion of the spirit based upon confidence in human reason. He stated that all human evils were rooted in ignorance and infatuation and therefore education of humanity was the essential task of his life.

Although he suffered from living in "a century of fury," he endeavored to stem the tide of fanaticism, by complaining and despising religious exaltation and partisanship, thereby exposing himself to the fury of all religious parties. Sometimes referred to as the Voltaire of the Age of Reformation, he was essentially a man of deep religious feeling and conviction; an independent thinker; the greatest philologist of his time and one of the greatest of all times; a staunch defender of human reason, opposed Luther's teachings; a fearless critic of clerical abuses; and a religious reformer who tried to avoid schisms.

Though he disapproved of Luther's theology, of his doctrine of predestination, and his derogation of human reason, he defended Luther only for the sake of freedom of conscience and because he approved of Luther's criticisms of the existing Church, which he himself had severely criticized. In fact, it was Erasmus' courageous intervention that saved Luther's life at the very beginning of the latter's reforming activities. Luther essentially relied on St. Paul; Erasmus maintained that the *Sermon on the Mount* was the principal basis of the Christian religion. He refused to give dogma primary importance, placed piety above tenets, moral righteousness above orthodoxy, and nothing above "true and perfect friendship, dying and living with Christ." Erasmus exerted considerable influence in the spiritual life of England. He died in Basle in 1536.

IF the ancient teachers of children are commended for alluring them with wafers that they might be willing to learn their first rudiments, I think it ought not to be charged as a fault upon me that, by the like regard, I allure youth either to the elegance of Latin or to piety. Besides, it is a good part of prudence to know the foolish affections of the common people and their absurd opinions. I judge it to be much better to instruct those out of my little book than by experience, the mistress of fools. The rules of grammar are crabbed things to many persons. Aristotle's *Moral Philosophy* is not fit for children. Scotus' *Divinity* is less fit, nor is it, indeed, of great use to men to give them understanding. And it is a matter of great moment to disseminate a taste of the best things into the tender minds of children. I cannot tell that anything is learned with greater success than what is learned by playing, and this is in truth a very harmless fraud to trick a person into his own profit. . . .

There is nothing more base than to find fault with that which thou dost not understand. That view vilifies everything; it produces but bitterness and discord. Therefore, let us candidly interpret other men's work and not esteem our own as oracles, nor look upon the judgments of those men who do not understand what they read. Where there is hatred in judgment, judgment is blind.

[124]

ERIUGENA, JOHANNES SCOTUS

ERIUGENA, JOHANNES SCOTUS (c. 815-877). The translator of Pseudo-Dionysius from Greek to Latin adopted Neo-Platonism and tried to reconcile this with Christianity. He regarded Church doctrine as dynamic and therefore attempted an original approach to religion and philosophy. For this heresy, he narrowly escaped persecution.

He asserted that there was only one reality, namely God, who created all things by emanation and to whom all creatures return.

In his principal work, *On the Division of Nature,* he stated that God emanates nature in four forms: the highest is God himself, who creates but is not created; then there are those which are created and create; those which are created but do not create, and finally God again, who rests neither created nor creating. Eriugena declined to speculate on God's attributes. He declared: "God is not a what but a that." True religion and true philosophy are identical. Both of them rest upon the unity of God who is not subject to necessity but creates by his own free will. Man is a microcosmos with his own unique soul, but in the last analysis "all our souls are but one soul." His concept of the dogma of Trinity is more similar to Plotinus' triad than it is to the doctrine of the Church. Eriugena also wrote about predestination, reducing this concept to a vagueness which makes it little different from free will. Although he never claimed that he was an independent thinker, he actually was. At any rate, he succeeded in fitting what were apparently his personal thoughts within the framework of accepted doctrines. His influence was greater with the mystics than it was with the logicians of the later Middle Ages. An Irish monk, he had mastered Greek and Latin, and was responsible for the revival of philosophical thought which had remained dormant in Western Europe after the death of Boethius. He taught at the royal palace school of Charles the Bald of France and was often entrusted by him to settle theolog-ical disputes.

THE HUMAN MIND

IT would suffice for me to answer you briefly when you ask why God should have created man, whom he proposed to make in his own image, in the genus of animals. He wished so to fashion him, that there would be a certain animal in which he manifested his own express image. But whoever asks why He wished that, asks the cause of the divine will; to ask that is too presumptuous and arrogant. . . .

I should not, therefore, say why He willed, because that is beyond all understanding, but I shall say, as He has permitted, what He has willed to do. He has made all creation, visible and invisible, in man since the whole spread of created nature is understood to be in him. For although it is still unknown how much the first creation of man, after the transgression, is in defect of the eternal light, nevertheless there is nothing naturally present in the celestial essences which does not subsist essentially in man. For there is understanding and reason, and there is naturally implanted the sound reason of possessing a celestial and angelic body, which after the resurrection will appear more clearly than light both in the good and the evil. For it will be common to all human nature to rise again in eternal incorruptible spiritual bodies. . . .

Man is a certain intellectual idea, formed eternally in the divine mind. . . . The human mind, its idea by which it knows itself, and the discipline by which it learns itself that it knows itself, subsists as one and the same essence. . . . Reason teaches us . . . that the human mind assuredly knows itself and does not know itself. For it knows that it is, but it does not know what it is. . . . The divine likeness in the human mind . . . is recognized most clearly in that it is known only to be, but what it is, is not known.

[125]

EUCKEN, RUDOLF

EUCKEN, RUDOLF (1846-1926). The core of Eucken's philosophy was that the concept of life manifests its mere existence through sensual experience, activity, and in a world of relationships comprehensible to the spirit. He explained the history of the world as a blending of reason and blind necessity. Throughout the course of history, spiritual life was evolved as a new level of reality. It was not the human individual, nor the sum of individuals, who created the new order of things and relationships, but the motion of the universe. Eucken thought that his concept corresponded more to the nature of man than that of Fichte, Schelling, or Hegel who overestimated the range of the human mind. Eucken accused positivism, materialism, and naturalism of ignoring the faculties of the mind.

His colleagues, professors of philosophy at the German universities, were surprised when he was awarded the Nobel Prize (1908); they felt that the selection of candidates for the prize should be made more carefully. Eucken, however, maintained that German philosophers were indifferent to his writings; that he was popular in England, America, and China before he even began to attract attention in Germany. During World War I, Eucken pro-

fessed aggressive German nationalism, and this new attitude in
creased the number of his German adherents.

THE PROBLEM OF HAPPINESS

OUR age has particularly urgent cause to occupy itself with
the problem of happiness, for we are confronted by a remarkable contrast between the greatness of the outward
achievements of the age and the insecurity of its sense of
happiness. In successful devotion to the work of civilization
we surpass all other periods; how far are we in advance
of them in the knowledge of nature, in the mastery and
utilization of its forces, in the humane ordering of society!
But it cannot be denied that all these achievements do not
help us to attain a joyous and assured sense of life, that a
pessimistic tone has become very widespread and continually
extends further. How is it that with us work and happiness
refuse to associate?

When such a dislocation compels us to consider the nature and conditions of happiness, we immediately encounter
a grave misgiving. May man as a general rule make happiness the goal of his efforts, is it not a sign of a narrow and
petty character that in every effort man should think principally of what gain he is to receive in happiness? Experience, too, seems to show plainly that not only individual men
but whole nations and religions have been able to renounce
happiness: we know, further, that thinkers of the very first
rank have called for something higher than the struggle for
happiness. But if we look more closely we find that their
opposition has been directed not so much against happiness
as against lower conceptions of happiness: even in the sub-
stitutes which have been offered in its place a craving after
happiness can always finally be recognized. Men have wanted
something different from the majority, but they have always
opposed to the existing condition of life another which was
higher and better, and have sought to enlist human feelings
and faculties in the task of attaining it: but is this not a
craving after happiness? Thus even the Indian sage strives

for happiness when he tries as far as possible to negate his life, to bring it into a condition of absolute repose and indeed indifference. For then absorption in the universe or even complete annihilation appears to him a better state than his previous life with its labors and cares, its excitements and disappointments. And the struggle for happiness need by no means remain bound to the narrowness and poverty of the natural ego, but rather the very aim of the struggle may be to find a new, purer, nobler being, a life which is freed from this ego and yet remains active and vigorous. Thus we see that the conception of happiness is itself by no means simple, and that the opposition does not apply to happiness so much as to lower and inadequate conceptions of happiness. Indeed, it is a thing to be insisted upon that man should let the thought of happiness control his efforts, for it is only by doing so that he can put all the vigor of his life and strength of his emotions into his action: he cannot devote all his energy to the struggle after anything in which he does not expect to find satisfaction for his own nature. Fundamentally different conceptions are included in the term happiness, but it is only dullness of thought which can agree to a general renunciation of happiness: all real life is strictly individual life, and to this happiness is indispensable.

[126]

EUCLID

EUCLID (c. 335-275 B.C.). Hippocrates and Euclid were regarded as the most popular scientists of classical antiquity, but no ancient author made note of even the slightest biographical detail of the latter. From Euclid's own statements and from the earliest allusions to his writings by Greek scholars, it may be concluded that he lived during the reign of Ptolemy I of Egypt (305-285 B.C.).

Euclid's *Stoicheia* (Elements) are the basis of the mathematical sciences of both ancient and modern times. He did not perform all, and perhaps not even a large portion of the discoveries he systematized in his book. But certainly he corrected, amplified, and developed many of the propositions made by predecessors. He gave to mathematics the form which was maintained until the nineteenth century, and he established a standard of scientific exactitude retained by scholars active in all branches of science, even though entirely new concepts of mathematics were current. Philosophers have tried to imitate Euclid's methods of demonstration. The philosophy of Spinoza is the most famous example of the application of Euclid's manner. Euclid was well acquainted with Greek philosophy. His fundamental views were derived from Plato, but he also studied the works of Aristotle and his disciples.

THE FIRST ELEMENTS

DEFINITIONS

A POINT is that which has no part.

A line is breadthless length.

The extremities of a line are points.

A straight line is a line which lies evenly with the points on itself.

A surface is that which has length and breadth only.

The extremities of a surface are lines.

A plane surface is a surface which lies evenly with the straight lines on itself.

A plane angle is the inclination to one another of two lines in a plane which meet one another and do not lie in a straight line.

And when the lines containing the angle are straight, the angle is called rectilineal.

When a straight line set up on a straight line makes the adjacent angles to one another, each of the equal angles is right, and the straight line standing on the other is called a perpendicular to that on which it stands.

An obtuse angle is an angle greater than a right angle.

An acute angle is an angle less than a right angle.

A boundary is that which is an extremity of anything.

A figure is that which is contained by any boundary or boundaries.

A circle is a plane figure contained by one line such that all the straight lines falling upon it from one point among those lying within the figure are equal to one another.

AND the point is called the center of the circle.

A diameter of the circle is any straight line drawn through the center and terminated in both directions by the circumference of the circle, and such a straight line also bisects the circle.

A semicircle is the figure contained by the diameter and the circumference cut off by it. And the center of the semicircle is the same as that of the circle.

Rectilineal figures are those which are contained by straight lines, trilateral figures being those contained by three, quadrilateral those contained by four, and multilateral those contained by more than four straight lines.

Of trilateral figures, an equilateral triangle is that which has its three sides equal, an isosceles triangle that which has two of its sides alone equal, and a scalene triangle that which has its three sides unequal.

Further, of trilateral figures, a right-angled triangle is that which has a right angle, an obtuse-angled triangle that which has an obtuse angle, and an acute-angled triangle that which has its three angles acute.

Of quadrilateral figures, a square is that which is both equilateral and right-angled; an oblong that which is right-angled but not equilateral; a rhombus that which is equilateral but not right-angled; and a rhomboid that which has its opposite sides and angles equal to one another but is neither equilateral nor right-angled. And let quadrilaterals other than these be called trapezia.

Parallel straight lines are straight lines which, being in the same plane and being produced indefinitely in both directions, do not meet one another in either direction.

POSTULATES

Let the following be postulated:
To draw a straight line from any point to any point.

To produce a finite straight line continuously in a straight line.

To describe a circle with any center and distance.

That all right angles are equal to one another.

That, if a straight line falling on two straight lines make the interior angles on the same side less than two right angles, the two straight lines, if produced indefinitely, meet on that side on which are the angles less than the two right angles.

COMMON NOTIONS

Things which are equal to the same thing are also equal to one another.

If equals be added to equals, the wholes are equal.

If equals be subtracted from equals, the remainders are equal.

Things which coincide with one another are equal to one another.

The whole is greater than the part.

[127]

EVANS, MARY ANN. See ELIOT, GEORGE.

_F_

FECHNER, GUSTAV THEODOR

FECHNER, GUSTAV THEODOR (1801-1887). When Fechner studied medicine, he regarded the world from a mechanistic point of view and almost became an atheist. Then he read Lorenz Oken's _Philosophy of Nature_. This disciple of Schelling influenced him to become a firm theist. Fechner called his philosophy an "offshoot from the tree of Schelling, though growing far away from the mother tree." He ignored Kant completely. As a professor of physics and chemistry, he contended that the natural sciences can only offer partial knowledge and demand completion by a metaphysical-idealistic interpretation of nature. But he also proved to be a staunch empiricist by founding psycho-physics and experimental aesthetics. He was a native of Lusatia, whose population was largely composed of Slavs, who were inclined toward mysticism. Fechner himself turned for a while from empiricism to speculations about the supernatural, but then returned again to empiricism.

THE SPIRITS OF MAN

MAN uses many means to one end; God one means to many ends.

The plant thinks it is in its place for its own purpose, to grow, to toss in the wind, to drink in light and air, to prepare fragrance and color for its own adornment, to play with beetles and bees. It is indeed there for itself, but at the same time it is only one pore of the earth, in which light, air, and water meet and mingle in processes important to the whole earthly life; it is there in order that the earth may exhale, breathe, weave for itself a green garment and provide nourishment, raiment and warmth for men and animals. Man thinks that he is in his place for himself alone, for

390

amusement, for work, and getting his bodily and mental growth; he, too, is indeed there for himself; but his body and mind are also but a dwelling place into which new and higher impulses enter, mingle, and develop, and engage in all sorts of processes together, which both constitute the feeling and thinking of the man, and have their higher meaning for the third stage of life.

The mind of man is alike indistinguishably his own possession and that of the higher intelligences, and what proceeds from it belongs equally to both always, but in different ways. Just as in this figure, which is intended not for a representation but only a symbol, the central, colored, six-rayed star (looking black here) can be considered as independent and having unity in itself; its rays proceeding from the middle point are all thereby dependently and harmoniously bound together; on the other hand, it appears again mingled together from the concatenation of the six single colored circles, each one of which has its own individuality. And as each of its rays belongs as well to it as to the circles, through the overlapping of which it is formed, so is it with the human soul.

Man does not often know from whence his thoughts come to him: he is seized with a longing, a foreboding, or a joy, which he is quite unable to account for; he is urged to a force of activity, or a voice warns him away from it, without his being conscious of any special cause. These are the visitations of spirits, which think and act in him from another center than his own. Their influence is even more manifest in us, when, in abnormal conditions (clairvoyance or mental disorder) the really mutual relation of dependence between them and us is determined in their favor, so that we only passively receive what flows into us from them, without return on our part.

But so long as the human soul is awake and healthy, it is not the weak plaything or product of the spirits which grow into it or of which it appears to be made up, but precisely that which unites these spirits, the invisible center, possessing primitive living energy, full of spiritual power of attraction, in which all unite, intersect, and through mutual communication engender thoughts in each other. This is not brought into being by the mingling of the spirits, but is inborn in man at his birth; and free will, self-determination, consciousness, reason, and the foundation of all spiritual power are contained herein. But at birth all this lies still latent within, like an unopened seed, awaiting development into an organism full of vital individual activity.

So when man has entered into life other spirits perceive it and press forward from all sides and seek to add his strength to theirs in order to reinforce their own power, but while this is successful, their power becomes at the same time the possession of the human soul itself, is incorporated with it and assists its development.

The outside spirits established within a man are quite as much subjected to the influence of the human will, though in a different way, as man is dependent upon them; he can, from the center of his spiritual being, equally well produce new growth in the spirits united to him within, as these can definitely influence his deepest life; but in harmoniously developed spiritual life no will has the mastery over another. As every outside spirit has only a part of itself in common with a single human being, so can the will of the single man have a suggestive influence alone upon a spirit which with its whole remaining part lies outside the man; and since every human mind contains within itself something in common with widely differing outside spirits, so too can the will of a single one among them have only a quickening influence upon the whole man, and only when he, with free choice, wholly denies himself to single spirits is he deprived of the capacity to master them.

All spirits cannot be united indiscriminately in the same soul; therefore the good and bad, the true and false spirits contend together for possession of it, and the one who conquers in the struggle holds the ground.

The interior discord which so often finds place in men

is nothing but this conflict of outside spirits who wish to get possession of his will, his reason, in short, his whole innermost being. As the man feels the agreement of spirits within him as rest, clearness, harmony, and safety, he is also conscious of their discord as unrest, doubt, vacillation, confusion, enmity, in his heart. But not as a prize won without effort, or as a willing victim, does he fall to the stronger spirits in this contest, but, with a source of self-active strength in the center of his being, he stands between the contending forces within which wish to draw him to themselves and fights on whichever side he chooses; and so he can carry the day even for the weaker impulses, when he joins his strength to theirs against the stronger. The Self of the man remains unendangered so long as he preserves the inborn freedom of his power and does not become tired of using it. As often, however, as he becomes subject to evil spirits, is it because the development of his interior strength is hindered by discouragement, and so, to become bad, it is often only necessary to be careless and lazy.

The better the man already is, the easier it is for him to become still better; and the worse he is, so much the more easily is he quite ruined. For the good man has already harbored many good spirits, which are now associated with him against the evil ones remaining and those freshly pressing for entrance, and are saving for him his interior strength. The good man does good without weariness, his spirits do it for him; but the bad man must first overcome and subdue by his own will all the evil spirits which have striven against him. Moreover, kin seeks and unites itself to kin, and flees from its opposites when not forced. Good spirits in us attract good spirits outside us, and the evil spirits in us the evil spirits outside. Pure spirits turn gladly to enter a pure soul, and evil without fastens upon the evil within. If only the good spirits in our souls have gained the upper hand, so of itself the last devil still remaining behind in us flees away, he is not secure in good society; and so the soul of a good man becomes a pure and heavenly abiding place for happy indwelling spirits. But even good spirits, if they despair of winning a soul from the final mastery of evil, desert it, and so it becomes at last a hell, a place fit only for the torments of the damned. For the agony of conscience and the inner desolation and unrest in the soul of the wicked are sorrows which, not they alone, but the condemned spirits within them also, feel in still deeper woe.

[128]

FEUERBACH, LUDWIG

FEUERBACH, LUDWIG (1804-1872). Modern existentialists ought to recognize Feuerbach as well as Kierkegaard as their forerunners, instead of regarding the former as a mere materialist. It is true that Feuerbach, while opposing Hegel's idealism, professed materialistic views, but materialism, to him, meant only a part of the truth, not its entirety. He defined philosophy as "the science of reality in its truth and totality." To find the total truth, he resorted to a concept of anthropology which included theology. He did not deny the existence of God, but explained the formation of the idea of God as the result of the longing of sensual man to reconcile the apparent contradictions of life. He accused the idealist philosophers of having deprived man of his feelings of immediateness and existence. According to Feuerbach, man was nothing without the world of objects with which he was connected: existence was defined as the abundance of relations; sensuality was the criterion of existence, but not its only characteristic. He maintained that the cooperation of physical and psychic elements made for the unity of man. He denied the possibility of reducing mental phenomena to the physical level or deriving God from nature. The antinomy between mind and nature was described by Feuerbach with ironic humor. He enjoined his fellow men not to ignore the contradictions of life, and to concentrate upon the tasks of the present day.

ABOVE RELIGION

OUR relation to religion is not a merely negative, but a critical one; we only separate the true from the false;—though we grant that the truth thus separated from falsehood is a new truth, essentially different from the old. Religion is the first form of self-consciousness. Religions are sacred because they are the traditions of the primitive self-consciousness. But that which in religion holds the first place,—namely, God,—is, as we have shown, in itself and according to truth, the second, for it is only the the nature of man regarded objectively; and that which to religion is the second,—namely, man,—must therefore be constituted and declared the first. Love to man must be no derivative love; it must be original. If human nature is the highest nature to man, then practically also the highest and first law must be the love of man to man. *Homo homini Deus est*:—this is the great practical principle:—this is the axis on which revolves the history of the world. The relations of child and parent, of husband and wife, of brother and friend,—in general of man to man,—in short, all the moral relations are *per se* religious. Life as a whole is, in its essential, substantial relations, throughout of a divine nature. Its religious consecration is not first conferred by the blessing of the priest. But the pretension of religion is that it can hallow an object by its essentially external cooperation; it thereby assumes to be itself the only holy power; besides itself it knows only earthly, ungodly relations; hence it comes forward in order to consecrate them and make them holy.

But marriage—we mean, of course, marriage as the free bond of love—is sacred in itself, by the very nature of the union which is therein effected. That alone is a religious marriage, which is a true marriage, which corresponds to the essence of marriage—of love. And so it is with all moral relations. Then only are they moral,—then only are they enjoyed in a moral spirit, when they are regarded as sacred in themselves. True friendship exists only when the boundaries of friendship are preserved with religious conscientiousness, with the same conscientiousness with which the believer watches over the dignity of his God. Let friendship be sacred to thee, property sacred, marriage sacred,—sacred the well-being of every man; but let them be sacred *in and by themselves*.

In Christianity the moral laws are regarded as the commandments of God; morality is even made the criterion of piety; but ethics have nevertheless a subordinate rank, they have not in themselves a religious significance. This belongs only to faith. Above morality hovers God, as a being distinct from man, a being to whom the best is due, while the remnants only fall to the share of man. All those dispositions which ought to be devoted to life, to man,—all the best powers of humanity, are lavished on the being who wants nothing. The real cause is converted into an impersonal means, a merely conceptional, imaginary cause usurps the place of the true one. Man thanks God for those benefits which have been rendered to him even at the cost of sacrifice by his fellow man. The gratitude which he expresses to his benefactor is only ostensible; it is paid, not to him, but to God. He is thankful, grateful to God, but unthankful to man. Thus is the moral sentiment subverted in religion! Thus does man sacrifice man to God! The bloody human sacrifice is in fact only a rude, material expression of the innermost secret of religion. Where bloody human sacrifices are offered to God, such sacrifices are regarded as the highest thing, physical existence as the chief good. For this reason life is sacrificed to God, and it is so on extraordinary occasions; the supposition being that this is the way to show him the greatest honor. If Christianity no longer, at least in our day, offers bloody sacrifices to its God, this arises, to say nothing of other reasons, from the fact that physical existence is no longer regarded as the highest good. Hence the soul, the emotions are now offered to God, because these are held to be something higher. But the common case is, that in religion man sacrifices some duty towards man—such as that of respecting the life of his fellow, of being grateful to him— to a religious obligation,—sacrifices his relation to man to his relation to God. The Christians, by the idea that God is without wants, and that he is only an object of pure adoration, have certainly done away with many pernicious conceptions. But this freedom from wants is only a metaphysical idea, which is by no means part of the peculiar nature of religion. When the need for worship is supposed to exist only on one side, the subjective side, this has the invariable effect of one-sidedness, and leaves the religious emotions cold; hence, if not in express words, yet in fact, there must be attributed to God a condition corresponding to the subjective need, the need of the worshipper, in order to establish reciprocity. All the positive definitions of religion are based on reciprocity. The religious man thinks of God, because God thinks of him; he loves God, because God has first loved him. God is jealous of man; religion is jealous of morality; it sucks away the best forces of morality; it renders to man only the things that are man's, but to God the things that are God's; and to Him is rendered true, living emotion,—the heart.

When in times in which peculiar sanctity was attached to religion, we find marriage, property, and civil law respected, this has not its foundation in religion, but in the original, natural sense of morality and right, to which the true social relations are sacred *as such*. He to whom the Right is not holy for its own sake, will never be made to feel it sacred by religion. Property did not become sacred because it was regarded as a divine institution; but it was regarded as a divine institution because it was felt to be in itself sacred. Love is not holy, because it is a predicate of God, but it is a predicate of God because it is in itself divine. The heathens do not worship the light or the fountain, because it is a gift of God, but because it has of itself a beneficial influence on man, because it refreshes the sufferer; on account of this excellent quality they pay it divine honors.

Wherever morality is based on theology, wherever the right is made dependent on divine authority, the most immoral, unjust, infamous things can be justified and established. I can found morality on theology only when I myself have already defined the divine being by means of morality. In the contrary case, I have no criterion of the moral and immoral, but merely an *un*moral, arbitrary basis, from which I may deduce anything I please. Thus, if I would found

397

morality on God, I must first of all place it in God: for Morality, Right, in short, all substantial relations, have their only basis in themselves, can only have a real foundation—such as truth demands—when they are thus based. To place anything in God, or to derive anything from God, is nothing more than to withdraw it from the test of reason, to institute it as indubitable, unassailable, sacred, without rendering an account *why*. Hence self-delusion, if not wicked, insidious design, is at the root of all efforts to establish morality, right, on theology. Where we are in earnest about the right we need no incitement or support from above. We need no Christian rule of political right; we need only one which is rational, just, human. The right, the true, the good, has always its ground of sacredness in itself, in its quality. Where man is in earnest about ethics, they have in themselves the validity of a divine power. If morality has no foundation in itself, there is no inherent necessity for morality; morality is then surrendered to the groundless arbitrariness of religion.

Thus the work of the self-conscious reason in relation to religion is simply to destroy an illusion:—an illusion, however, which is by no means indifferent, but which, on the contrary, is profoundly injurious in its effects on mankind; which deprives man as well of the power of real life, as of the genuine sense of truth and virtue; for even love, in itself the deepest, truest emotion, becomes by means of religiousness merely ostensible, illusory, since religious love gives itself to man only for God's sake, so that it is given only in appearance to man, but in reality to God.

And we need only, as we have shown, invert the religious relations—regard that as an end which religion supposes to be a means—exalt that into the primary which in religion is subordinate, the accessory, the condition,—at once we have destroyed the illusion, and the unclouded light of truth streams in upon us. The sacraments of Baptism and the Lord's Supper, which are the characteristic symbols of the Christian religion, may serve to confirm and exhibit this truth.

The water of Baptism is to religion only the means by which the Holy Spirit imparts itself to man. But by this conception it is placed in contradiction with reason, with the truth of things. On the one hand, there is virtue in the objective, natural quality of water; on the other, there is none, but it is a merely arbitrary medium of divine grace and omnipotence. We free ourselves from these and other irreconcilable contradictions, we give a true significance to Baptism, only by regarding it as a symbol of the value of water itself. Baptism should represent to us the wonderful but natural effect of water on man. Water has in fact not merely physical effects, but also, and as a result of these, moral and intellectual effects on man. Water not only cleanses man from bodily impurities, but in water the scales fall from his eyes: he sees, he thinks, more clearly; he feels himself freer; water extinguishes the fire of appetite. How many saints have had recourse to the natural qualities of water, in order to overcome the assaults of the devil! What was denied by Grace has been granted by Nature. Water plays a part not only in dietetics, but also in moral and mental discipline. To purify oneself, to bathe, is the first, though the lowest of virtues. In the stream of water the fever of selfishness is allayed. Water is the readiest means of making friends with Nature. The bath is a sort of chemical process, in which our individuality is resolved into the objective life of Nature. The man rising from the water is a new, a regenerate man. The doctrine that morality can do nothing without means of grace, has a valid meaning if, in place of imaginary, supernatural means of grace, we substitute natural means. Moral feeling can effect nothing without Nature; it must ally itself with the simplest natural means. The profoundest secrets lie in common every-day things, such as supranaturalistic religion and speculation ignore, thus sacrificing real mysteries to imaginary, illusory ones; as here, for example, the real power of water is sacrificed to an imaginary one. Water is the simplest means of grace or healing for the maladies of the soul as well as of the body. But water is effectual only where its use is constant and regular. Baptism, as a single act, is either an altogether useless and unmeaning institution, or, if real effects are attributed to it, a superstitious one. But it is a rational, a venerable institution, if it is understood to typify and celebrate the moral and physical curative virtues of water.

But the sacrament of water required a supplement. Water, as a universal element of life, reminds us of our origin from Nature, an origin which we have in common with plants and animals. In Baptism we bow to the power of a pure Nature-force; water is the element of natural equality and freedom, the mirror of the golden age. But we men are distinguished from the plants and animals, which together with the inorganic kingdom we comprehend under the common name of Nature;—we are distinguished from Nature. Hence we must celebrate our distinction, our specific difference. The symbols of this our difference are bread and wine. Bread and wine are, as to their materials, products of nature; as to their form, products of man. If in water we declare: man can do nothing without Nature; by bread and wine we declare: Nature needs man, as man needs Nature. In water, human, mental activity is nullified; in bread and wine it attains self-satisfaction. Bread and wine are supernatural products,—in the only valid and true sense, the sense which is not in contradiction with reason and Nature. If in water we adore the pure force of Nature, in bread and wine we adore the supernatural power of mind, of consciousness, of man. Hence this sacrament is only for man matured into consciousness; while baptism is imparted to infants. But we at the same time celebrate here the true relation of mind to Nature: Nature gives the material, mind gives the form. The sacrament of Baptism inspires us with thankfulness towards Nature, the sacrament of bread and wine with thankfulness towards man. Bread and wine typify to us the truth that Man is the true God and Saviour of man.

Eating and drinking is the mystery of the Lord's Supper;—eating and drinking is in fact in itself a religious act; at least, ought to be so. Think, therefore, with every morsel of bread which relieves thee from the pain of hunger, with every draught of wine which cheers thy cheer, of the God, who confers these beneficent gifts upon thee,—think of Man! But in thy gratitude towards man forget not gratitude towards holy Nature! Forget not that wine is the blood of plants, and flour the flesh of plants, which are sacrificed for thy well-being! Forget not that the plant typifies to thee the essence of nature, which lovingly surrenders itself for thy enjoyment! Therefore forget not the gratitude which thou owest to the natural qualities of bread and wine! And if thou art inclined to smile that I call eating and drinking religious acts, because they are common every day acts, and are therefore performed by multitudes without thought, without emotion; reflect, that the Lord's Supper is to multitudes a thoughtless, emotionless act, because it takes place often; and, for the sake of comprehending the religious significance of bread and wine, place thyself in a position where the daily act is unnaturally, violently interrupted. Hunger and thirst destroy not only the physical but also the mental and moral powers of man; they rob him of his humanity—of understanding, of consciousness. Oh! if thou shouldst ever experience such want, how wouldst thou bless and praise the natural qualities of bread and wine, which restore to thee thy humanity, thy intellect! It needs only that the ordinary course of things be interrupted in order to vindicate to common things an uncommon significance, *to life, as such, a religious import.* Therefore let bread be sacred for us, let wine be sacred, and also let water be sacred! Amen.

[129]

FICHTE, JOHANN GOTTLIEB

FICHTE, JOHANN GOTTLIEB (1762-1814). Fichte, a German philosopher, studied at Meissen, Pforta, Jena and Leipzig to be a theologian. Shortly thereafter, he accepted a tutoring position in

Switzerland, but dissatisfied with it, he intended to accept one in Poland. En route there he met Kant whose moral and religious doctrines attracted him and caused him to change all his plans. Forthwith he wrote *An Essay Towards A Critique of All Revelation.* For some unaccountable reason, the publisher neglected to place Fichte's name on the title page; everyone hailed the essay as a new work of Kant. When the real author became known, Fichte, overnight, was recognized as a first-rate philosopher and was called to Jena to lecture on the vocation of the scholar.

Fichte lost his position because he regarded God as the moral order of the universe; he went to Berlin, and lectured on occasion at the University of Erlangen. When the French occupied Berlin, (1806) Fichte left. He returned the following year and devoted himself wholeheartedly to freeing Prussia of foreign domination. As rector of the new Berlin university, he fired his listeners with enthusiasm. His addresses to the German nation are still famous. His view of the state was socialistic, and he had visions of a league of peoples united in a moral endeavor and in true culture.

As a philosopher, he was a transcendental subjective idealist; his system reversed the idea of I, the non-I or the world, and their synthesis in experience. In his *Science of Knowledge,* he sought a complete system of reason. His life was devoted to ideals and he exemplified his thesis that the world is but the occasion for man to exercise his moral duty. "The system of freedom satisfies my heart; the opposite system destroys and annihilates it. To stand cold and unmoved, amid the current of events, a passive mirror of fugitive and passing phenomena—this existence is impossible for me. I scorn and detest it. I will love; I will lose myself in sympathy; I will know the joy and grief of life."

THE EGO

WE have to search for the absolute, first, and unconditioned fundamental principle of human knowledge. It cannot be proven, nor determined if it is to be absolute first principle.

This principle is to express that *deed-act* which does not occur among the empirical determinations of our consciousness, nor can so occur, since it is rather the basis of all consciousness, and first and alone makes consciousness possible. In representing this deed-act it is not so much to be feared that my readers will *not* think what they ought to think, as that they will think what they ought not to think. This renders necessary a *reflection* on what may perhaps for the present be taken for that deed-act, and an *abstraction* from all that does not really belong to it.

Even by means of this abstracting reflection, that deed-act, which is not empirical *fact* of consciousness, cannot become fact of consciousness: but by means of this abstracting reflection we may recognize so much; that this deed-act must necessarily be *thought* as the basis of all consciousness.

The laws according to which this deed-act must necessarily be thought as basis of human knowledge, or, which is the same, the rules according to which that abstracting reflection proceeds, have not yet been proven as valid, but are for the present tacitly presupposed as well known and agreed upon. As we proceed we shall deduce them from that fundamental principle, the establishment whereof is correct only if they are correct. This is a circle, but an unavoidable circle. And since it is unavoidable and freely admitted, it is also allowable to appeal to all the laws of general logic in establishing this highest fundamental principle.

In undertaking this abstracting reflection, we must start from some proposition which every one will admit without dispute. Doubtless there are many such. We choose the one which seems to us to open the shortest road to our purpose. In admitting this proposition, the deed-act, which we intend to make the basis of our whole science of knowledge, must be admitted; and the reflection must show *that* this deed-act is admitted the moment that proposition is admitted.

Our course of proceeding in this reflection is as follows: Any fact of empirical consciousness, admitted as such valid proposition, is taken hold of, and from it we separate one of its empirical determinations after the other, until only that remains, which can no longer be separated and abstracted from.

As such admitted proposition we take this one: A is A.

Every one admits this proposition, and without the least hesitation. It is recognized by all as completely certain and evident.

If any one should ask a proof of its certainty, no one would enter upon such a proof, but would say: This proposition is *absolutely* (*that is, without any further ground*) *certain;* and by saying this would ascribe to himself the power of *absolutely positing something.*

In insisting on the in-itself certainty of the above proposition, you posit *not* that A *is.* The proposition A is A is by no means equivalent to A *is. Being* when posited without predicate is something quite different from being when posited with a predicate. Let us suppose A to signify a space enclosed within two straight lines, then the proposition A is A would still be correct; although the proposition A *is* would be false, since such a space is impossible.

But you posit by that proposition: *If* A is, *then* A is. The question *whether* A is at all or not, does not, therefore, occur in it. The *content* of the proposition is not regarded at all: merely its *form.* The question is not whereof you know, but *what* you know of any given subject. The only thing posited, therefore, by that proposition is the *absolutely* necessary connection between the two A's. This connection we shall call X.

In regard to A itself nothing has as yet been posited. The question, therefore, arises: Under what condition *is* A?

X at least is in the Ego, and posited *through* the Ego, for it is the Ego, which asserts the above proposition, and so asserts it by virtue of X as a law, which X or law must, therefore, be given to the Ego; and, since it is asserted absolutely, and without further ground, must be given to the Ego through itself.

Whether and *how* A is posited we do not know; but since X is to designate a connection between an unknown positing of A (of the first A in the proposition A is A) and a positing of the same A, which latter positing is absolute on condition of the first positing, it follows that A, *at least in so far as that connection is posited,* is posited *in* and *through* the Ego, like X. Proof: X is only possible in relation to an A; now X is really posited in the Ego; hence, also, A must be posited in the Ego, in so far as X is related to it.

X is related to that A, in the above proposition, which occupies the logical position of subject, and also to that A which is the predicate, for both are united by X. Both, therefore, are posited in the Ego, in so far as they are posited; and the A of the predicate is posited *absolutely* if the first one is posited. Hence the above proposition may be also expressed: If A is posited *in the Ego,* then *it is posited,* or then it *is.*

Hence, by means of X, the Ego posits; that A *is* absolutely for the asserting Ego, and *is* simply because it is posited in the Ego: or that there is something in the Ego which always remains the same, and is thus able to connect or posit: and hence the absolutely posited X may also be expressed, Ego=Ego, or I am I.

Thus we have already arrived at the proposition I *am;* not as expression of a deed-act, it is true, but, at least, as expression of a *fact.*

For X is absolutely posited; this is a fact of empirical consciousness, as shown by the admitted proposition. Now X signifies the same as I am I; hence, this proposition is also absolutely posited.

But Ego is Ego, or I am I, has quite another significance than A is A. For the latter proposition had content only on a certain condition, namely, *if* A is posited. But the proposition I am I is unconditionally and absolutely valid, since it is the same as X; it is valid not only in form but also in content. In it the Ego is posited not on condition, but absolutely, with the predicate of self-equality; hence, it is posited, and the proposition may also be expressed, I *am.*

This proposition, *I am,* is as yet only founded upon a fact, and has no other validity than that of a fact. If "A= A" (or X) is to be certain, then "I am" must also be certain. Now, it is fact of empirical consciousness that we are compelled to regard X as absolutely certain; hence, also "I am" is certain, since it is the ground of the X. It follows from this, that the *ground of explanation of all facts of em-*

pirical consciousness is this: *before all positing, the Ego must oe posited through itself.*

I say of *all* facts; and to prove this I must show that X is the highest fact of empirical consciousness, is the basis of all others, and contained in all other facts; which, perhaps, would be admitted by all men, without proof, although the whole science of knowledge busies itself to prove it.

The proposition A is A is *asserted.* But all asserting is an act of the human mind; for it has all the conditions of such an act in empirical consciousness, which must be pre-supposed as well known and admitted in order to advance our reflection. Now, this act is based on something which has no higher ground, namely X or I am.

Hence, that which is *absolutely posited and in itself grounded* is the ground of *a certain* (we shall see hereafter of *all*) acting of the human mind; hence its pure character; the pure character of activity in itself, altogether abstracting from its particular empirical conditions.

The positing of the Ego through itself is, therefore, the pure activity of the Ego. The Ego *posits* itself; and the Ego is by virtue of this mere self-positing. Again, *vice versa*: the Ego *is* and *posits* its being, by virtue of its mere being. It is both the acting and the product of the act; the active and the result of the activity; deed and act in one; and hence the *I am* is expressive of a deed-act; and of the *only possible* deed-act, as our science of knowledge must show.

Let us again consider the proposition *I am I.* The Ego is absolutely posited. Let us assume that the first Ego of this proposition (which has the position of formal subject) is the *absolutely posited* Ego, and that the second Ego (that of the predicate) is the *being* Ego; then the absolutely valid as-sertion that both are one signifies: the Ego is, *because* it has posited itself.

This is, indeed, the case according to the logical form of the proposition. In A═A the first A is that which is posited in the Ego, (either absolutely, like the Ego itself, or conditionally, like any non-Ego) and in this positing of A the Ego is absolutely subject; and hence the first A is also called the subject. But the second A designates that which the Ego, in now making itself the object of its own reflection discovers thus *as* posited in itself, (since it has just before itself posited the Λ in itself). The Ego, in asserting that proposition A=A, predicates in truth not something of A, but of itself, namely, that it has found an A posited in itself; and hence the second A is called predicate.

The Ego in the former and the Ego in the latter significance are to be absolutely Equal. Hence, the above proposition may be turned around, and then it reads: The Ego posits itself simply *because* it is. It posits itself through its mere being, and *is* through its mere being posited.

This, then, will explain clearly in what significance we here use the word Ego (I), and will lead us to a definite explanation of the Ego as absolute subject. The Ego as absolute subject is *that, the being, essence, whereof consists merely in positing itself as being*. As soon as it posits itself, it is; and as soon as it is, it posits itself; and hence the Ego is for the Ego absolute and necessary. Whatsoever is not for itself is not an Ego.

The question has been asked, What *was* I before I became self-conscious? The answer is, *I* was not at all, for I was not I. The Ego is only, in so far as it is conscious of itself. The possibility of that question is grounded upon mixing up of the Ego as *subject*, and the Ego as *object* of the reflection of the absolute subject; and is in itself altogether improper. The Ego represents itself, and in so far takes itself up in the form of representation, and now first becomes a *somewhat*, that is, an object. Consciousness receives in this form of representation a substrate, which *is*, even without the real consciousness, and which, moreover, is thought bodily. Such a condition is thought, and the question asked, *What was the Ego at that time?* that is, what is the substrate of consciousness? But even in this thought you unconsciously *add in thinking* the *absolute subject* as looking at that substrate; and hence you unconsciously add in thought the very thing whereof you wanted to abstract, and thus you contradict yourself. The truth is, you cannot think anything at all without adding in thought your Ego as self-conscious; you cannot abstract from your self-consciousness; and all questions of the above kind are not to be answered, since maturely considered, they cannot be asked.

If the Ego *is* only so far as it posits itself, then it also is only *for* the positing, and posits only for the being Ego. *The Ego is for the Ego;* but if it posits itself absolutely, as it is, then it posits itself necessarily, and is necessary for the Ego. *I am only for me; but for me I am necessarily.* (By saying *for me,* I already posit my being.) *To posit itself* and *to be* is, applied to the Ego, the same. Hence, the proposition I am because I have posited myself, can also be expressed; *I am absolutely because I am.*

Again, the Ego as positing itself and the Ego as being are one and the same. The Ego is as *what* it posits itself and posits itself as *what* it is. Hence, *I am absolutely what I am.*

The immediate expression of the thus developed deed-act may be given in the following formula: *I am absolutely because I am, and I am absolutely what I am for myself.*

If this narration of the original deed-act is to be placed at the head of a science of knowledge as its highest fundamental principle, it may perhaps be best expressed thus:

The Ego posits originally its own being.

(In other words, the Ego is necessarily identity of subject and object; is itself subject-object; and it is this without further meditation.)

We started from the proposition A=A, not as if the proposition, I am, could be proven by it, but because we had to start from some one certain proposition given in empirical consciousness. And our development, also, has shown that A=A does not contain the ground of "I am," but, on the contrary, that the latter proposition is the ground of the former.

By abstracting from the content of the proposition I am, and looking merely to its form, namely, the form of drawing a conclusion from the being posited of something to its being, as we must abstract for the sake of logic, we thus obtain as *fundamental principle of logic* the proposition A=A, which can only be proven and determined through the science of knowledge. *Proven*: for A is A because the Ego which has posited A is the same as the Ego in which A is posited. *Determined*: for whatever is, is only in so far as it is posited in the Ego, and there is nothing outside of the Ego. No possible A (no *thing*) can be any thing else but an A posited in the Ego.

By abstracting, moreover, from all asserting as a determined acting, and looking merely to the general *manner* of acting, of the human mind, which is given through that form, we obtain the *category of reality*. Every thing to which the proposition A=A is applicable has reality, *in so far as that proposition is applicable to it*. That which is posited through the mere positing of any thing (in the Ego)is its reality, its essence.

[130]

FRANKLIN, BENJAMIN

FRANKLIN, BENJAMIN (1706-1790). At the beginning of his *Autobiography*, Franklin states that if Providence allowed him the choice, "he should have no objection to go over the same life from beginning to the end, requesting only the advantage authors from of correcting, in a second edition, the faults of the first." Franklin was always fond of such harmless and shrewd remarks which prevented his earnestness from being pathetic. This inclination resulted in the legend that he was not entrusted with writing the *Declaration of Independence*, because the Founding Fathers feared he might include a joke in the writing of the solemn proclamation.

Franklin, throughout his lifetime, made strenuous efforts to perfect his mind and character. He regarded a lack of moderation as incompatible with human perfection, human dignity, efficiency, and success. The story of his love and courtship of his wife proved his talents for tempering his passion. He read poetry for amusement and for the improvement of his literary style, but he did not allow himself to become absorbed in its charms. He always reacted to life zestfully, and with humorous detachment. He regarded reason as the means by which life could be conducted intelligently. In his youth, he was greatly interested in metaphysics, but he later disavowed this branch of philosophy; the problem of absolute and consistent truth left him unmoved.

He was a famous inventor and philanthropist; a skillful politician and diplomat. He always accomplished his tasks and fulfilled his duties because his moral conscience directed him to take care of the common good. Though very busy, he was always ready to obey the demands of his community and country, for he was never that completely absorbed in his own affairs. It was only to science that he was deeply devoted. In science he sought for laws that govern nature and point toward the orderliness of cosmic and human relations, though he was aware that the moral sciences of his time lagged far behind the standards of the natural sciences.

Franklin summarized his experiences by eliminating the words "certainly" and "undoubtedly" from his vocabulary. In place of them, he adopted: "I conceive; I apprehend; I imagine a thing to be so; or so it appears to me at present." Other thinkers, before and after Franklin, have gone the same way. To him, it was not only the result of reasoning, but a means of success. He especially appreciated the "advantage of change," whether it concerned his own manners, or his relations to his fellow men. Truth that is not useful was not truth to him. He formulated his creed by the words: "truth; sincerity, and integrity" as "of the utmost importance for the felicity of life." Franklin was not absorbed in utilitarianism; he enjoyed truth and integrity, "a naïve lustre," independently and successfully.

WISE SAYINGS

THE eyes of Christendom are upon us, and our honor as a people is becoming a matter of the utmost consequence to be taken care of. If we give up our rights in this contest, a century to come will not restore us to the opinion of the world; we shall be stamped with the character of . . . poltroons and fools . . . Present inconveniences are, therefore, to be borne with fortitude, and better times expected.

We make daily great improvement in *natural* [philosophy], but there is one I wish to see in *moral* philosophy; the discovery of a plan, that would induce and oblige nations to settle their disputes without first cutting one another's throats. When will human reason be sufficiently improved to see the advantage of this! When will we be convinced that even successful wars at length become misfortunes to those who unjustly commenced them and who triumphed blindly in their success, not seeing all its consequences.

I think with you, that nothing is of more importance for the public weal, than to form and train up youth in wisdom and virtue. Wise and good men are, in my opinion, the strength of a state far more so than riches or arms, which, under the management of ignorance and wickedness, often draw on destruction, instead of providing for the safety of a people. Though the culture bestowed on *many* should be successful only with a *few,* yet the influence of those few and the service in their power may be very great. . . . General virtue is more probably to be expected and obtained from the *education* of youth, than from the *exhortation* of adult persons; bad habits, and vices of the mind being, like diseases of the body, more easily prevented than cured . . .

Commerce among nations, as well as between private persons, should be fair and equitable, by equivalent exchanges and mutual supplies. Taking unfair advantages of a neighbor's necessities tho' attended with temporary success, always breeds bad blood.

The rapid progress *true* science now makes occasions my regretting sometimes that I was born so soon. It is impossible to imagine the height to which may be carried, in a thousand years, the power of man over matter. We may perhaps learn to deprive large masses of their gravity, and give them absolute levity, for the sake of easy transport. Agriculture may diminish its labor and double its produce; all diseases may by sure means be prevented or cured, not excepting even that of old age, and our lives lengthened even beyond the antediluvian standard.

Righteousness, or *justice*, is, undoubtedly of all the virtues, the surest foundation on which to create and establish a new state. But there are two nobler virtues, *industry* and *frugality,* which tend more to increase the wealth, power and grandeur of the community, than all the others without them.

Lost time is never found again; and what we call time enough, always proves little enough.

Diligence overcomes difficulties, sloth makes them.

The busy man has few idle visitors; to the boiling pot, the flies come not.

Laziness travels so slowly that poverty soon overtakes him.

Beware of little expenses; a small leak will sink a great ship.

Industry pays debts, despair increases them.

Mad kings and mad bulls are not to be held by treaties and packthread.

But dost thou love life, then do not squander Time, for that's the stuff Life is made of.

Glass, china, and reputation, are easily cracked, and never well mended.

Three may keep a secret, if two of them are dead.

[131]

G

GANDHI, MOHANDAS KARAMCHAND

GANDHI, MOHANDAS KARAMCHAND (1869-1948). Not only the vast majority of Hindus but also many Westerners have accorded to Gandhi the title of "Mahatma," the "great soul," and have revered him as a master of wisdom and saintliness, while also recognizing his political skill and steadfastness. At least in modern times, Gandhi has had no equal in his ability to use spiritual weapons for political aims, in his power to make the resistance of the powerless irresistible. He has been adored as the father of the new State of India. But shortly after he had realized the ideal of a free India, for which he had struggled for nearly half a century, he was assassinated by a fanatical son of his own people.

Gandhi restored the self-reliance of Hinduism after he had been imbued with the spirit of Western civilization and had rejected it. In 1889 he was called to the bar in London. Then, for seventeen years, he was a lawyer in South Africa before becoming the champion of the cause of the Indian settlers in that country. In 1914 he returned to India and in 1919 started the Satyagraha (Truth-seeking movement). From 1920 on he campaigned for non-cooperation with the British government. Devoted to Hinduism as Gandhi was, he was also inspired by Tolstoy's doctrine of non-violence which became his principal battle-cry in the struggle against British domination and was considered by him the panacea for every evil. Non-violence was conceived by him as "conscious suffering," not as meek submission to the will of the evil-doer, but "the putting of one's whole soul against the will of the tyrant." It means the restitution of the ancient Indian law of self-sacrifice. He repeatedly protested against being regarded as a visionary. Instead, he described himself as a "practical idealist" and rightly claimed "to know my millions" and to "recognize no God except the God that is to be found in the hearts of the dumb millions." But he also claimed that he recognized God's presence while the millions could not see it.

LET me for a few moments consider what Hinduism consists of, and what it is that has fired so many saints about whom we have historical record. Why has it contributed so many philosophers to the world? What is it in Hinduism that has so enthused its devotees for centuries? Did they see untouchability in Hinduism and still enthuse over it? In the midst of my struggle against untouchability I have been asked by several workers as to the essence of Hinduism. We have no simple *Kalema,* they said, that we find in Islam, nor have we *John,* Chapters 3-16 of the *Bible.* Have we or have we not something that will answer the demands of the most philosophic among the Hindus or the most matter-of-fact among them? Some have said, and not without good reason, the *Gayatri* answers that purpose. I have perhaps recited the *Gayatri Mantra* a thousand times, having understood the meaning of it. But still it seems to me that it did not answer the whole of my inspirations. Then as you are aware I have, for years past, been swearing by the *Bhagavad Gita,* and have said that it answers all my difficulties and has been my *Kamadhenu,* my guide, my open sesame, on hundreds of moments of doubts and difficulty. I cannot recall a single occasion when it has failed me. But it is not a book that I can place before the whole of this audience. It requires a prayerful study before the *Kamadhenu* yields rich milk she holds in her udders.

But I have fixed upon one *Mantra* that I am going to recite to you as containing the whole essence of Hinduism. Many of you I think, know the *Ishopanishad.* I learnt it by heart in Yervada Jail. But it did not then captivate me, as it has done during the past few months, and I have now come to the final conclusion that if all the *Upanishads* and all the other scriptures happened all of a sudden to be reduced to ashes, and if only the first verse in the *Ishopanishad* were left intact in the memory of Hindus, Hinduism would live for ever.

Now this *Mantra* divides itself in four parts. The first part is:

All this that we see in this great Universe is pervaded by God. Then come the second and third parts which read together, as I read them:

I divide these into two and translate them thus: *Renounce it and enjoy it.* There is another rendering which means the same thing: *Enjoy what He gives you.* Even so you can divide it into two parts. Then follows the final and most important part, which means: *Do not covet anybody's wealth or possession.* All the other *Mantras* of that ancient *Upanishad* are a commentary or an attempt to give us the full meaning of the first *Mantra.* As I read the *Mantra* in the light of the *Gita* or the *Gita* in the light of the *Mantra* I find that the *Gita* is a commentary on the *Mantra.* It seems to me to satisfy the craving of the socialist and the communist. I venture to suggest to all who do not belong to the Hindu faith that it satisfies their cravings also. And if it is true—and I hold it to be true—you need not take anything in Hinduism which is inconsistent with or contrary to the meaning of this *Mantra.* What more can a man in the street want to learn than this that the one God and Creator and Master of all that lives pervades the Universe? The three other parts of the *Mantra* follow directly from the first. If you believe that God pervades everything that He has created you must believe that you cannot enjoy anything that is not given by Him. And seeing that He is the Creator of His numberless children, it follows that you cannot covet anybody's possession. If you think that you are one of His numerous creatures, it behooves you to renounce everything and lay it at His feet. That means the act of renunciation of everything is not a mere physical renunciation but represents a second or new birth. It is a deliberate act, not done in ignorance. It is therefore a regeneration. And then since he who holds the body must eat and drink and clothe himself, he must naturally seek all that he needs from Him. And he gets it as a natural reward of that renunciation. As if this

415

was not enough the *Mantra* closes with this magnificent thought: *Do not covet anybody's possession.* The moment you carry out these precepts, you become a wise citizen of the world, living at peace with all that lives. It satisfies one's highest aspirations on this earth and hereafter. No doubt it will not satisfy the aspirations of him who does not believe in God and His undisputed sovereignty. It is no idle thing that the Maharaja of Travancore is called *Padmabhadas.* It is a great thought we know that God himself has taken the title of *Dasanudas* Servant of servants. If all the princes would call themselves servants of God, they would be correctly describing themselves, but they cannot be servants of God unless they are servants of the people. And if *zamndars* and moneyed men and all who have possessions would treat themselves as trustees and perform the act of renunciation that I have described, this world would indeed be a blessed world to live in.

[133]

GASSENDI, PIERRE

GASSENDI, PIERRE (1592-1655). When, in 1633, Galileo was tormented by his condemnation and was watched narrowly by the Inquisition, many scholars were terrified, and not a few denied any connection with him. But Gassendi, a Catholic priest, known by his writings on astronomy, physics and mathematics, wrote a letter to Galileo that had to pass the censorship of the Inquisition, as Gassendi knew. He comforted Galileo by protesting that the ecclesiastical sentence had nothing to do with the conscience of a scientist, and Galileo had no reason to accuse himself of any moral failure. There were not many savants who acted as frankly as Gassendi did.

Gassendi himself was wise, or at least cautious enough to avoid persecution on the part of the Church, although he professed materialism and criticized Descartes' idealistic views. For Gassendi combined his atomistic materialism with the belief in the Biblical God, and asserted that the atoms, conceived in accordance with the doctrines of Democritus and Epicurus, were created by the Christian God. Gassendi therefore was called the "Christianized Epicurus." Also in his personal life, Gassendi knew how to be a dignified priest, a learned theologian, and how to enjoy the society of witty

416

and gay men, no matter whether they were faithful Christians or libertines.

ACTIVE HAPPINESS

SUPPOSING that there are two kinds of life and thus two sorts of happiness, the philosophers have always preferred the contemplative to the active life. Nevertheless, that does not prevent those whom birth or genius, hazard or necessity has pushed into any business from keeping a laudable and convenient tranquility. For he who undertakes it not at random but after mature consideration, looks at human things not from the midst of the crowd but from an elevated point. He knows that in the actual course of affairs a hundred things might happen which human sagacity might not foresee. He provides not specifically, but generally for all the difficulties that might happen. He is prepared to be ready often to make up his mind on the spot. He recognizes that he is the master of what is within him, but not of the things that are not depending on his free will. He performs as much as is possible for him, the duties of an honest man. He thinks that finally he shall be happy and satisfied whatever might occur. He is never too sure about the good outcome of his enterprises as not to think that they might turn out to be different from what he wished and he adjusts his mind in such a manner that although he might have to stand bad luck he would nevertheless bear it constantly and patiently. This one, I say, who is endowed and disposed in such a manner, will be engaged in any business, will be able to act in the outside world in such a way that in the middle of all agitation and troubles of his affairs he will keep inwardly and within himself a sweet and calm tranquillity.

[134]

GENTILE, GIOVANNI

GENTILE, GIOVANNI (1875-1944). Gentile was the official philosopher of Italian fascism. After having been a professor of philosophy at the University of Palermo from 1907 to 1914, and later at the University of Pisa, he was Mussolini's minister of Public Education from 1922 to 1924. Then he became senator of the kingdom, and was entrusted with what Mussolini called "reform of the educational system." In this position, he dismissed all teachers who were suspected of being liberals or democrats; but, since he was not a member of the Fascist Party, Gentile did not satisfy all demands concerning the curriculum. Benedetto Croce protested against Gentile's purge with vigor but without result.

According to Gentile, as he explained it in his principal works *General Theory of the Spirit as Pure Act* (1916) and *Logic as Theory of Knowledge* (1917), philosophy isolated from life and life isolated from philosophy are equally symptoms of cultural bankruptcy. Philosophy must penetrate into human life, govern and mould it. Thought is all-embracing. No one can go out of the sphere of thinking or exceed thought. Reality is not thinkable but in relation to an activity by means of which it becomes thinkable. Every experience occurs between a subject which is one, a center, and of spiritual nature, and a multitude of phenomena which lack such a center. The Real can be thought of only as posing itself, not as being. Reality therefore is spiritual. The spirit is both unity and multitude, and is recognized in the pure act. Gentile added that the "one-multiple" spirit is the same as the ineffable one of the mystics. By this remark, Gentile deviated from Hermann Cohen who characterized thinking as pure creation. Benedetto Croce objected that Gentile's "pure act" is nothing other than Schopenhauer's will. While Gentile followed Hegel, in general he tried to combine the Hegelian phenomenology of the spirit with Berkeley's ideas on perception.

SCIENCE AND PHILOSOPHY

WE not only distinguish philosophy from art and religion, we also distinguish it from science. Although science has the cognitive character of philosophy yet *stricto sensu* it is not philosophy. It has not the universality of its object which philosophy has, and therefore it has not the *critical and systematic* character of philosophy. Every science is one among others and is therefore particular. When a particular science transcends the limits of its own special subject matter it tends to be transformed into philosophy. As particular, that is, concerned with an object which itself is particular and can have its own meaning apart from other objects which co-exist with it, science rests on the naturalistic presupposition. For it is only when we think of reality as nature that it presents itself to us as composed of many elements, any one of which can be made the object of a particular investigation. A naturalistic view is the basis, then, of the analytical character of every science. Thence the logically necessary tendency of science in every period towards mechanism and materialism.

Again, every science presupposes its object. The science arises from the presupposition that the object exists before it is thought, and independently altogether of being known. Had science to apprehend the object as a creation of the subject, it would have first to propound the problem of the position of the real in all its universality, and then it would no longer be science, but philosophy. In presupposing the object as a datum to be accepted not proved, a natural datum, a fact, every particular science is necessarily empirical, unable to conceive knowledge otherwise than as a relation of the object to the subject extrinsic to the nature of both. This relation is sensation or a knowing which is a pure fact on which the mind can then work by abstraction and generalization. Science, therefore, is *dogmatic*. It does not prove and it cannot prove its two fundamental presuppositions: (1) that its object exists; (2) that the sensation, the initial and substantial fact of knowledge, which is the immediate relation with the object, is valid.

Philosophy, on the other hand, proposes to prove the value of the object, and of every form of the object, in the system of the real, and its why and how. It gives, or seeks to give, an account not only of the existence of the objects which the particular sciences dogmatically presuppose, but even of the knowing (which itself also is at least a form of reality) whereby every science is constituted. And therefore philosophy, in being systematic, is critical.

[135]

419

GEORGE, HENRY

GEORGE, HENRY (1839-1897). John Dewey called Henry George "one of the world's great social philosophers, certainly the greatest which our country has produced." Dewey's appraisal of George has not been shared by many Americans. The great majority of American economists have severely criticized George's insistence on nationalization of land and on the "single tax," the two principal tenets of his system. In 1941, George R. Geiger stated that Henry George was neglected and even ignored in liberal and progressive circles and that he had been forgotten by his conservative critics. But the statement is true for America only. In England and Germany the doctrine of Henry George always had greater influence than in his homeland, and it still has many adherents there. His *Progress and Poverty* (1880) became of special consequence for British socialism, as well as for the *Socialist League,* led by William Morris, and the *Fabian Society,* the great training school for labor leaders.

George regarded political economy as justified only when directed by moral principles and social consciousness. He founded his movement for abolition of private landed property upon both religious and political grounds. Land, he said, is the creation of God; it therefore must be common property of all people. Land, he also argued, is the physical foundation of the entire economic process. Therefore, he concluded, no democracy is secure as long as it is in private hands.

George repudiated materialism and evolutionism. He vigorously attacked Herbert Spencer because he had, in 1850, declared that property in land was wrong and in 1882 recanted what George considered the fundamental truth.

DEMOCRACY'S DANGER

To turn a republican government into a despotism the basest and most brutal, it is not necessary formally to change its constitution or abandon popular elections. It was centuries after Caesar before the absolute master of the Roman world pretended to rule other than by authority of a Senate that trembled before him.

But forms are nothing when substance is gone, and the forms of popular government are those from which the substance of freedom may most easily go. Extremes meet, and a government of universal suffrage and theoretical equality may, under conditions which impel the change, most readily become a despotism. For there despotism advances in the name and with the might of the people. The single source of power once secured, everything is secured. There is no unfranchised class to whom appeal may be made, no privileged orders who in defending their rights may defend those of all. No bulwark remains to stay the flood, no eminence to rise above it. They were belted barons led by a mitered archbishop who curbed the Plantagenet with Magna Charta; it was the middle classes who broke the pride of the Stuarts; but a mere aristocracy of wealth will never struggle while it can hope to bribe a tyrant.

And when the disparity of condition increases, so does universal suffrage make it easy to seize the source of power. . . . Given a community with republican institutions, in which one class is too rich to be shorn of its luxuries, no matter how public affairs are administered, and another so poor that a few dollars on election day will seem more than any abstract consideration; in which the few roll in wealth and the many seethe with discontent as a condition of things they know not how to remedy, and power must pass into the hands of jobbers who will buy and sell it as the Praetorians sold the Roman purple, or into the hands of demagogues who will seize and wield it for a time, only to be displaced by worse demagogues.

[136]

GERSONIDES

GERSONIDES (1288-1344). Levi ben Gershom, called Gersonides, was the greatest astronomer of his time. His writings attracted the interest of Kepler and his inventions, the "Jacob's staff" to measure visual angles and the *camera obscura*, became of great use. He also wrote on physics, physiology, mathematics, logic, ethics, psychology, metaphysics, the Bible and Talmud. Whatever he dealt with, he did so in a new manner. In some regards he was a precursor of

421

Galileo, in others even of modern thinkers like Bertrand Russell, for Gersonides' principal problem in general philosophy was the relation between individual experience and the body of scientific knowledge, or the way science can be developed and subsist in the course of history. As a philosopher of religion, Gersonides, in his principal work *Milhamoth Adonai* (The Wars of the Lord), made a vigorous effort to integrate the historical experience of the Jewish people into a conception of the universe that rests upon the secular sciences of astronomy, physics and the other branches with which he was acquainted. He insisted that scientific research must be conducted independently of the Torah, which, he said, does not compel men to believe what is not true. But he was convinced that truth, in accordance with modern science, is contained in the Torah, though not explicitly, and that the history of the Jewish people reflects and confirms the universal truth, in whose discovery time plays an important part.

A large part of Gersonides' writings is either lost or still unpublished.

IS THE UNIVERSE CREATED OR EXTERNAL?

It behooves us first of all to point out the great difficulty of this investigation, as this will lead us to some extent to make the investigation into this problem more complete. For by being aware of the difficulty of a problem, we are guided to the way which leads us to the attainment of the truth thereof.

The fact that the philosophers who have hitherto investigated it greatly differ from one another in their opinions concerning it points to its difficulty; for this proves that arguments may be derived from the nature of existing things, wherewith each of the conflicting views can be either established or refuted. And it is very difficult to investigate a problem with such a peculiarity.

What undoubtedly points to the great difficulty inherent in this enquiry is the fact that we have to investigate whether all existing things were created by God, who is blessed, after a period of non-existence, or were never created at all. Now it is manifest that if we desire to fathom one of the attributes of an object, by the way of speculative investigation, whether that object possesses that attribute or not, it is first of all necessary that we should know the essence of the object and its attributes. For it is only through them that we may attain to that which we seek to know. It is thus evident that one who desires to investigate this problem thoroughly must first of all know the essence and attributes of the thing under examination as far as it is possible for man to perceive. This would necessitate that a man desirous of thoroughly investigating this subject should know the nature and the attributes of all existing things, so that he may be able to explain whether there is among them a thing or an attribute which would lead us to the conclusion that the universe was not created; or whether there is among them a thing or an attribute which would lead us to the conclusion that the universe was created; or whether there is not among them a thing or an attribute from which it could be concluded either that the universe was created, or that it was not created. The matter being so, a man, to whom the knowledge of one of the existing things or of the attributes thereof, so far as a human being can possibly know, is inaccessible, is unable to make as thorough an investigation of this problem as is humanly possible. Now it is evident that to obtain as thorough a knowledge of all existing things and of their attributes as is humanly possible is extremely difficult.

What makes this investigation more difficult is the fact that the investigator must necessarily have some knowledge of the First Cause as far as it is possible. For this enquiry leads him to investigate whether God, who is blessed, could possibly have existed at first without this world, which He afterwards brought into existence and created, or it is necessary that the world should have always existed with Him. It is, however, evident from the preceding argument itself that it is necessary for a man, desirous of making this investigation as perfect as possible, to know of the essence of God, who is blessed, all that can be attained, so that he may be able to decide accurately whether God, who is blessed, can possibly be active at one time, and cease to be active at another time, or whether this is impossible. This greatly adds to the difficulty of this investigation, since our knowledge of the essence of the First Cause is necessarily slight, as has become manifest from the preceding.

Another point which makes this investigation still more difficult is the circumstance that it is hard to know from which essences or attributes of existing things it is possible for us to attain to the truth of this problem. For it is necessary that a man, desirous of making this investigation perfect, should know this at the very outset, otherwise he can only attain to the truth thereof by accident.

The statement of the philosopher, as recorded by the author of the *Guide*, points to the difficulty of this investigation. It is as follows: 'As for the things concerning which we have no argument, and which are too high for us, our statement about them is, according to this, as difficult as our statement whether the world is eternal or not.' This shows that this question was considered extremely difficult by the philosopher, so that he was perplexed and doubtful about it, despite the numerous arguments he mentioned to prove that the universe is eternal. The reason for that is undoubtedly because the philosopher assumed that there were numerous arguments likewise to prove that the universe was created, and that his own arguments did not in any way establish the truth in this matter; and this is the very truth, as will be explained further on. Now if this question was considered difficult by the philosopher, despite his high rank of wisdom, how much more difficult would it be to other men who are lower than he on the ladder of knowledge.

And indeed we find that the opinions of the ancients concerning this investigation are diametrically opposed to one another. Some maintain that the universe was created and destroyed an endless number of times. Others hold that it was created only once; these are divided into two opinions: some of them think that the universe was created out of something, as, for instance, Plato and the later philosophers who follow his doctrine; while others think that the universe was created out of absolute non-existence, as for instance the early Mutakallimites, like Yahya the grammarian, according to what Ibn Roshd recorded of him in his commentary on the *Metaphysics*. In this theory they were followed by the Mutakallimites. This view was also adopted by the great philosopher, the author of the *Guide*, and by many of the sages of our religion. But there are still others who maintain that the universe is eternal. This is the theory of the philosopher and his followers. It is evident that the cause of their disagreement concerning these doctrines is the variety of objects from which they derived their proofs with regards to the nature of existing things, or because they were compelled by the Torah, or because of these two causes combined.

[137]

GEULINCX, ARNOLD

GEULINCX, ARNOLD (1624-1669). For twelve years, Geulincx was professor at the University of Louvain, Belgium, a stronghold of Catholic orthodoxy. Then he was converted to Calvinism, and became professor at the University of Leyden, Holland, at that time the center of learning, and an asylum for scholars who had been persecuted in their native country. He wrote all of his works in Latin, and died before his principal books, namely *Ethica* and *Metaphysica* could be published.

Although Geulincx often and intensely dealt with metaphysical questions, he was even more interested in ethics, but did not separate one from another. On the contrary, his ethics is founded upon metaphysics, though he also used psychological experience for his argumentation. He summed up his doctrine in the words: *Ita est, ergo ita sit* (So it is, therefore be it so). His view on life is colored with optimistic resignation. His steady confidence in God does not shut his eyes to the shortcomings of the existing world; if he expressed the idea of what Leibniz, about twenty-five years after Geulincx' death, has called the "pre-established harmony," he did not intend to assert that the existing world was good or the best of all possible but rather that it were good enough for Man who is morally and intellectually far from perfection.

Geulincx was a man of moderation, opposite to any kind of extremism. Following Descartes, he regarded doubt as the force that makes Man ask for truth. He appreciated the educational value of provisional scepticism, but demanded that mature men must believe in God whom he regarded as the first cause of all things, without denying second causes. Geulincx therefore, while adopting the Scholastic term of occasional cause, held that occasionalism was an indispensable hypothesis, apt to explain natural and mental facts, but was far from the radical standpoint of Malebranche who published his views only five years after Geulincx' death.

THE PHILOSOPHER'S VIEW ON PASSION

AFTER philosophers noticed that the activities of the mob are directed by passion, they resolved to insist on a contrary conduct of life and tried to act against their own passions. But, in doing so, they became not wiser than the mob, though, in a different, maybe more brilliant, manner, insane. Thus they came to the same state of mind as the mob, although sometimes by a sideways or roundabout route.

Some of these philosophers endeavored to extinguish all of their passions, as did the Cynics and Stoics. That is evidently madness, for we cannot extinguish passion without destroying our whole body.

If there really is something that is permanently certain, it is the certainty that passion cannot be eliminated because it is a constituent of what is good in human conditions. Passions are not bad. Some of them are morally neutral, others are good by nature, and we are obliged to tolerate them.

Just a little wiser are those philosophers who are not prepared to extinguish all passions—what would be insane, impossible, inadmissible—but to omit or to suspend all actions which they consider caused by passion. Plato belongs to this group.

In this regard we can discern four strata of philosophers —namely, first, Cynics and Stoics; second, Platonists; and finally two schools of mortification.

They all are acting against reason. They, therefore, are themselves directed by passion. For, whenever we act, we act deliberately, and our impulse is either reason or any kind of passion.

[138]

GILSON, ETIENNE

GILSON, ETIENNE (1884-   ). While Jacques Maritain is the outstanding militant exponent of the philosophy of Aquinas in our time, Gilson is its outstanding historian. But, in analyzing Thomism historically, Gilson does not lack the fighting spirit. He defends his master by attacking what is called modern philosophy, and he does so both by special studies and by outlining large aspects, in order to prove that Thomism has not the ambition of achieving philosophy once and for all but rather of keeping philosophical thought alive, and that Thomism is able to offer a basis for relating reality as we know it to the permanent principles in whose light all the changing problems of science, of ethics or of the arts must be solved. To Gilson, Thomism is by no means identical with Scholasticism, but rather a revolt against it. Gilson does not believe in systems of philosophy. He believes firmly in the guidance of such principles which, in the course of the history of philosophy, have become evident as an impersonal necessity for philosophical inquiry and orientation. History of philosophy, therefore, is, for him, by far more a part of philosophy itself than history of science is a part of science. It is possible, he says, to become a competent scientist without knowing much about history of science, but no man can carry very far his own philosophical reflections, unless he first studies the history of philosophy. For Gilson, there have been only three really great metaphysicians, viz., Plato, Aristotle and Aquinas, and none of them had a philosophical system, which would have meant the abolition of philosophy. From the Middle Ages until the present time three great experiments for founding a system have been attempted, and all of them have failed. The medieval, the Cartesian and the modern experiment, represented by Immanuel Kant and Auguste Comte have broken down. The result, as Gilson sees it, is the reduction of philosophy to science. Its consequences would be the abdication of the right to judge and rule nature, the conception of Man as a mere part of nature, and the green light for the most reckless social adventures to play havoc with human lives and institutions. Gilson is convinced that the revival of the philosophy of Aquinas opens the way out of that zone of danger.

THE only way to ascertain what the free will can do is to define what it is. Knowing its nature, you will find in that knowledge a safe rule to define the power of the will as well as its limitations. If, on the contrary, you start on the assumption that it is safer to keep a little below the line, where are you going to stop? Why, indeed, should you stop at all? Since it is pious to lessen the efficacy of free will, it is more pious to lessen it a little more, and to make it utterly powerless should be the highest mark of piety. In fact, there will be mediaeval theologians who come very close to that conclusion, and even reach it a long time before the age of Luther and Calvin. Nothing, of course, would have been more repellent to St. Bonaventura than such a doctrine; the only question here is: was St. Bonaventura protected against it? If we allow pious feelings to decree what nature should be, we are bound to wrong nature, for how could we find in piety a principle of self-restriction? In theology, as in any other science, the main question is not to be pious, but to be right. For there is nothing pious in being wrong about God!

If piety is not theology, still less is it philosophy. Yet it cannot be denied that, as a philosopher, St. Bonaventura sometimes allowed himself to be carried away by his religious feelings. In dealing with the nature of causality, for instance, two different courses were open to him. First, he could favor the view that where there is efficient causality, something new, which we call effect, is brought into existence by the efficacy of its cause; in this case, every effect can be rightly considered as a positive addition to the already existing order of reality. Or St. Bonaventura could maintain, with St. Augustine, that God has created all things present and future at the very instant of creation. From this second point of view, any particular being, taken at any time of world history, should be considered, so to speak, as the seed of all those other beings, or events, that are to flow from it according to the laws of divine providence. It is typical of St. Bonaventura's theologism that he always clung to this second interpretation of causality. He never could bring himself to think that efficient causality is attended by the springing up of new existences. To him, such a view practically amounted to crediting creatures with a creative power that belongs only to God. An effect, says Bonaventura, is to its cause as the rose is to the rosebud. It is permissible to appreciate the poetic quality of his comparison and the religious purity of his intention, without overlooking its philosophical implications.

[139]

GINZBERG, ASHER

GINZBERG, ASHER (1856-1927). Best known under his pseudonym, Ahad Haam, (one of the people), Ginzberg became noted as a philosopher and contributor to the revival of the Hebrew language and Hebrew literature. He also played a significant role in the modern Jewish nationalist movement.

Although his writings deal principally with Jewish affairs, his fundamental ideas are of general interest. Dissatisfied with material evolution, he emphasized the importance of spiritual evolution. He concentrated upon the moral aspects of all problems, rejecting that relationship between ethics and religion where the role of ethics is limited only to the confines of a sociological frame of reference. He regarded ethics as the most important determinant in national character and, for that reason, insisted that the national development of ethical views precedes all political activity. His aim was to harmonize nationalistic sentiments with the necessary sense of responsibility for the future of human civilization. The success of that aim will depend on one's devotion to the ideals of justice enunciated by the prophets of the Old Testament.

His concept of Zionism established him as a genuine philosopher. It is founded upon an original explanation of reality and ideals. For many years he was opposed to political Zionism, advocating, instead, the establishment of a Jewish cultural center in Palestine. This, he hoped, would become a "center of emulation" for Jews dispersed all over the world, effectively raising their cultural standards, and inspiring them to produce a genuine Jewish culture.

EVEN when the world as a whole is at peace, there is no rest or peace for its inhabitants. Penetrate to the real life, be it of worms or of men, and beneath the veil of peace you will find an incessant struggle for existence, a constant round of aggression and spoliation, in which every victory involves a defeat and a death.

Yet we do distinguish between time of war and time of peace. We reserve the term "war" for a visible struggle between two camps, such as occurs but seldom—a struggle that we can observe, whose causes and effects we can trace, from beginning to end. But to all the continual petty wars between man and man, of which we know in a general way that they are in progress, but of which we cannot envisage all the details and particulars, we give the name of "peace," because such is the normal condition of things.

In the spiritual world also there is war and peace; and here also "peace" means nothing but a number of continual petty wars that we cannot see—wars of idea against idea, of demand against demand, of custom against custom. The very slightest change in any department of life—as, for instance, the substitution of one letter for another in the spelling of a word—can only be brought about by a battle and a victory; but these tiny events happen silently, and escape observation at the time. It is only afterwards, when the sum total of all the changes has become a considerable quantity, that men of intelligence look backwards, and find to their astonishment that everything—opinions, modes of life, speech, pronunciation—has undergone vast changes. These changes appear to have taken place automatically; we do not know in detail when they came about, or through whose agency.

Peace, then, is the name that we give to a continuous, gradual development. But in the spiritual world, as in the material, there is sometimes a state of war; that is, a visible struggle between two spiritual camps, two complete systems, the one new, the other old. The preparations for such a war are made under cover, deep down in the process of continuous development. It is only when all is in readiness that the war breaks out openly, with all its drums and tramplings; and then a short space of time sees the most far-reaching changes.

The character of these changes, as well as the general course of the war, depends chiefly on the character of the new system of thought that raises the storm. They differ according as the system is wholly positive, wholly negative, or partly positive and partly negative.

A new *positive* system comes into existence when the process of continuous development produces in the minds of a select few some new positive concept. This may be either a belief in some new truth not hitherto accepted by society, or the consciousness of some new need not hitherto felt by society; generally the two go together. This new conception, in accordance with a well-known psychological law, gives rise to other conceptions of a like nature, all of which strengthen one another, and become knit together, till at last they form a complete system. The center point of the system is the new positive principle; and round this center are grouped a number of different beliefs, feelings, impulses, needs, and so forth, which depend on it and derive their unity from it.

A new system such as this, though essentially and originally it is wholly positive, cannot help including unconsciously some element of negation. That is to say, it cannot help coming into contact, on one side or another, with some existing system that covers the same ground. It may not damage the essential feature, the center, of the old system; but it will certainly damage one of the conceptions on its circumference, or, at the very least, it will lessen the strength of men's attachment to the old principles. When, therefore, the reformers begin to put their system into practice, to strive for the attainment of what they need by the methods in which they believe, their action necessarily arouses opposition on the part of the more devoted adherents of the old system, with which the reformers have unwittingly come into conflict. The result of this opposition is that the new system spreads, and attracts to its ranks all those who are adapted to receive it. As their number increases, the animosity of their opponents grows in intensity; and so the opposition waxes stronger and stronger, until it becomes war to the knife.

At first the disciples of the new teaching are astounded at the accusations hurled at them. They find themselves charged with attempting to overthrow established principles; and they protest bitterly that no such thought ever entered their minds. They protest with truth: for, indeed, their whole aim is to add, not to take away. Intent on their task of addition, they overlook the negation that follows at its heels; even when the negation has been made plain by their opponents, they strive to keep it hidden from others, and to ignore its existence themselves, and they do not recognize the artificiality of the means by which they attain this end.

The older school, on the other hand, who derive all their inspiration from the old doctrine, are quick to see or feel the danger threatened by the new teaching; and they strive, therefore, to uproot the young plant while it is still tender. But as a rule they do not succeed. Despite their efforts, the new system finds its proper place; gradually the two systems, the new and the old, lose some of their more sharply opposed characteristics, share the forces of society between them in proportion to their relative strength, and ultimately come to terms and live at peace. By this process society has been enriched; its tree of life has gained a new branch; its spiritual equipment has received a positive addition.

[140]

GIOBERTI, VINCENZO

GIOBERTI, VINCENZO (1801-1852). The part Gioberti acted in the history of the Italian struggle for national unity is more important than the consequence of his philosophical thoughts. Gioberti was a faithful son of the Catholic Church and a convinced liberal in the sense of early nineteenth-century liberalism. An ordained priest in 1825, he sympathized with the revolutionaries who endeavored to liberate Italy from Austrian domination but differed from them because he intended to entrust the Pope with the task of organizing the country politically. Popes Leo XII, and Pius VIII and Gregory XVI were opposed to any change of both the political and the cultural order, and Gioberti was exiled to France in 1833. When Pius IX was elected Pope in 1846, Gioberti built his hopes upon him, and for a short time, the new Pope seemed to justify Gioberti's expectations. After the outbreak of the revolution in 1848, Gioberti returned to Italy but he was soon disappointed, for the revolution was crushed and Pius IX denied his early liberalism. Gioberti continued in his efforts to reconcile the papacy and political liberalism and to defend the holy see against reproaches on the part of the liberals. But his strength was broken by his painful experiences, and he died soon after the end of the revolution.

In Gioberti's philosophy there is a conspicuous difference between his fundamental concepts and his method. While his method relied upon immediate intuition of the Absolute, his system was concerned with the dialectical relations between essence and existence. He stated that there is a permanent processus by virtue of which essence creates existence, and existence returns to essence. The individual, whose source is divine, is subject to the same processus. The universal spirit returns to universality after having passed the stages from sensibility to intelligibility. Gioberti's last years were all the more unhappy since, in addition to his political failure, he became aware of the severe opposition of Italian philosophers to his doctrine.

THE TWO HUMANITIES

ONE can distinguish two orders of humanities: One of nature and one of grace. Stemming both from one man they grew successively. But the natural order, having lost any moral unity, propagates by generation, while the predestined order propagates by election and maintains the spiritual unity which confers on it its privilege. The former is a material society consisting more of bodies than of souls, lacking as it does the integrity of the ideal principle. The latter is a spiritual society, a council of intelligences that

433

originate in the Idea and that are strictly united within only one body. Both proceed from one Individual and pass successively through the threefold ring of the family, the nation and the assemblage of nations. Both are tending toward a great universality of the future from which both are still far off. Both are progressive and move from the individual unity in order to reach the universal unity. Unity is their beginning and their end. Divided in their march toward the future type, they are imperfect; for one is lacking the unity characteristic of the elected race, the other, embracing only one part of humanity, does not possess all the variety characteristic of the natural race. But when each of them will have completed its course, they will merge again and will complete each other naturally. The natural species will become, still in the order of time, the elected species and the restored primitive unity of our species will be led to its ultimate perfection. At the present moment, the Church through election and spiritual generation represents the human race set up in a superhuman fashion. It can be defined, in this respect, as the reorganization of the human generation divided and reunited by grace by means of the ideal unity.

[141]

GOBINEAU, JOSEPH ARTHUR, COMTE DE

GOBINEAU, JOSEPH ARTHUR, COMTE DE (1816-1882). Not only in his youth but in later years, Gobineau was enthralled by dreams of his miraculous greatness. He felt that he was the descendant of Vikings and condottieri, and in the midst of the plain 19th century he planned to astonish humanity by his leadership in war on sea and land. Reality forced him to acquiesce in a more modest conduct of life. But, after a short period of difficulty, he did not reject nepotism on his behalf, and, due to the protection of high-ranking relatives, he became a diplomat who could afford to visit, or stay in, many countries, from Germany to Persia, from Sweden to Brazil.

All these favors could not overcome Gobineau's feelings of tediousness, his disdain of modern civilization which he regarded as decadent and doomed. In his book *The Inequality of Human Races* (1855-57), which was ignored in his native country, France, but hailed in Germany, Gobineau expressed his longing for and admiration of the Teutons who had once conquered Europe, shaped its civilization, and surpassed all other peoples in beauty, physical strength and spiritual creativeness. The restitution of Teutonic supremacy was considered by Gobineau as the only way to salvation. Although he carefully declined to identify modern Germans with his ideal Teutons, Gobineau's doctrine became favorite reading in Pan-German circles, above all in Richard Wagner's Bayreuth and at the court of Emperor William II who was initiated into Gobineau's doctrine by Prince Philip Eulenburg, an intimate friend of Gobineau's. A "Gobineau-Society," founded in Germany, continued to propagate his ideas until Hitler's accession. Gobineau also wrote novels and dramatic scenes in which he displayed artistic skill.

THE MEANING OF DEGENERATION

THE word *degenerate,* when applied to a people, means (as it ought to mean) that the people has no longer the same intrinsic value as it had before, because it has no longer the same blood in its veins, continual adulterations having gradually affected the quality of that blood. In other words, though the nation bears the name given by its founders, the name no longer connotes the same race; in fact, the man of a decadent time, the *degenerate* man properly so called, is a different being, from the racial point of view, from the heroes of the great ages. I agree that he still keeps something of their essence; but the more he degenerates the more attenuated does this "something" become. The heterogeneous elements that henceforth prevail in him give him quite a different nationality—a very original one, no doubt, but such originality is not to be envied. He is only a very distant kinsman of those he still calls his ancestors. He, and his civilization with him, will certainly die on the day when the primordial race unit is so broken up and swamped by the influx of foreign elements, that its effective qualities have no longer a sufficient freedom of action. It will not, of course, absolutely disappear, but it will in practice be so beaten down and enfeebled, that its power will be felt less and less as time goes on. It is at this point that all the results of degeneration will appear, and the process may be considered complete.

If I manage to prove this proposition, I shall have given a meaning to the word "degeneration." By showing how the essential quality of a nation gradually alters, I shift the responsibility for its decadence, which thus becomes, in a way, less shameful, for it weighs no longer on the sons but on the nephews, then on the cousins, then on collaterals more or less removed. And when I have shown by examples that great peoples, at the moment of their death, have only a very small and insignificant share in the blood of the founders, into whose inheritance they come, I shall thereby have explained clearly enough how it is possible for civilizations to fall—the reason being that they are no longer in the same hands. At the same time I shall be touching on a problem which is much more dangerous than that which I have tried to solve in the preceding chapters. This problem is: "Are there serious and ultimate differences of value between human races; and can these differences be estimated?"

[142]

GOEDEL, KURT

GOEDEL, KURT (1906-   ). Goedel's important discovery of the existence of nondemonstrable mathematical theorems which can neither be proved nor refuted has been considered as proof of the essential incompleteness and incompletability of mathematics.

Examining the two most comprehensive formal systems of our time, namely the *Principia Mathematica* (by Alfred N. Whitehead and Bertrand Russell) and Fraenckel's and Zermelo's system of axioms of quantity, Goedel shows that in both of these systems there are even relatively simple problems of the theory of ordinary whole numbers which cannot be decided on the ground of the axiom, and that this is not the fault of the two systems but is valid for all formal systems. Goedel holds that if we submit mathematical demonstrations to certain limitations, there certainly are undecidable formulas. But he also shows that the truth or falsehood of these formulas can be found out by methods using the metalanguage. He

436

has prepared the proof of his own theorems by his device of arith-metization of syntax, a way of attacking syntactical problems by means of a mathematical algorism. In his lecture on *The Consistency of the Continuum Hypothesis* (1941), Goedel proves that the axiom of choice and Cantor's continuum hypothesis are consistent with the other axioms of set theory, if these axioms are consistent. His purpose is to show how the proof for theorems of a certain kind can be accomplished by a general method.

A P H O R I S M S

THE true reason for the incompleteness inherent to all formal systems of mathematics lies in the fact that the formation of more and more higher types can be continued to the trans-finite.

THE general existence theorem is a *metatheorem*, that is a theorem about the system, not in the system, and merely in-dicates, once and for all, how the formal derivation would proceed in the system for any given proof.

[142 A]

GOETHE, JOHANN WOLFGANG VON

GOETHE, JOHANN WOLFGANG VON (1749-1832). Goethe often expressed his resentment when he was hailed and exalted as the au-thor of *Faust, Werther* and so many other dramatic, epic and lyrical poems but ignored as a scientist. In his later years, he constantly declared that no adequate appraisal of his work was possible with-out taking into account the importance of his contributions to anatomy, mineralogy, meteorology, botany, zoology, optics, and most modern scientists agree with his biographers that Goethe was right. It is true, Goethe's theory of colors is disputed, but in all the other fields, his scientific activities, especially concerning com-parative morphology, are acknowledged as of high value. Moreover, there is today an almost general agreement that Goethe's life and personality cannot be comprehensively understood and appreciated without due regard to his studies on natural sciences. It was science to which Goethe devoted most of his time during many years, even decades, and it was his scientific activities that formed a conspic-uous strain in his character and mind.

437

To Goethe, science meant exact observation of the phenomena, inquiry into their conditions, effects, coherence and variety. His methods were both analytical and synthetical, study of the characteristics of the individual and of general laws of formation. But, as far as science is concerned with measuring and counting, with mathematical methods, Goethe did not like it. The instrument he regarded as the most sure and precious was the human eye, and he passionately protested confidence in sensory experience.

Goethe's science and poetry were founded upon general views of philosophical character, although he remained distrustful of any technical philosophy. The only philosopher he admired without reserve, was Spinoza. He adopted his pantheism but not his determinism. Or, more precisely, he adopted his determinism to a certain extent but did not believe that life and the universe are totally determined. He even did not believe in the general validity of causality. Goethe repeatedly declared that freedom is blended, in a mysterious manner, with necessity, and that law and arbitrary forces rule the universe, working side by side. It was for these reasons that Goethe regarded man as both subject to necessity and capable of free will. In his autobiography *Fiction and Truth,* in his studies on French literature and on oriental poetry, he tried to penetrate into the realm of necessity, by inquiring into historical factors that condition the existence of the individual, but he felt himself obliged to state that all knowable factors of historical development are not sufficient to explain the peculiarity of the human individual. On the other hand, he repeatedly warned against miscalculation or neglect of historical, social and natural conditions which limit the freedom of the individual.

Goethe's philosophy spells serene resignation. But it does not mean easy acquiescence in the fact that human knowledge is limited. He constantly admonished mankind to inquire as far as possible and not to give up too quickly. It is quite another thing, said Goethe, to resign near the boundaries of human thought, than to rest within one's narrow-minded ego. What he regarded as the greatest happiness of thinking man was "to have explored whatever is explorable, and to revere silently what is inexplorable."

ACTIONS AND WORDS

ART is long, life short, judgment difficult, opportunity transient. To act is easy, to think is hard; to act according to our thought is troublesome. Every beginning is cheerful; the threshold is the place of expectation. The boy stands astonished, his impressions guide him; he learns sportfully, seriousness comes on him by surprise. Imitation is born with us; what should be imitated is not easy to discover. The excellent is rarely found, more rarely valued. The height charms us, the steps to it do not; with the summit in our eye, we love to walk along the plain. It is but a part of art that can be taught; the artist needs it all. Who knows it half, speaks much and is always wrong; who knows it wholly, inclines to act and speaks seldom or late. The former have no secrets and no force; the instruction they can give is like baked bread, savoury and satisfying for a single day; but flour cannot be sown, and seed corn ought not to be ground. Words are good, but they are not the best. The best is not to be explained by words. The spirit in which we act is the highest matter. Action can be understood and again represented by the spirit alone. No one knows what he is doing while he acts aright; but of what is wrong we are always conscious. Whoever works with symbols only is a pedant, a hypocrite, or a bungler. There are many such, and they like to be together. Their babbling detains the scholar; their obstinate mediocrity vexes even the best. The instruction which the true artist gives us opens the mind; for where words fail him, deeds speak. The true scholar learns from the known to unfold the unknown, and approaches more and more to being a master.

[143]

GORGIAS

GORGIAS (About 483-375 B.C.). Next to Protagoras, the most important and respected sophist was Gorgias, born in Leontini in Sicily, who, as leader of an embassy which was sent by his native city to Athens in order to ask for help against Syracusan aggression, succeeded in persuading the Athenians who were deeply impressed by his powerful eloquence.

Gorgias has often been mentioned as an example of longevity, and this has been attributed to his great egoism. He did not marry, and was always indifferent to both the sufferings and the happiness

439

of other people. He developed rhetoric as an art whose possibilities are not restricted by anything, least of all by philosophy. To prove this thesis, Gorgias proceeded from Empedocles' theory of perception. He wrote a treatise *On Nature*, a *Technic of Rhetorics*, and several eulogies. Only two small fragments, probably from the treatise *On Nature*, are extant.

FRAGMENTS

NOTHING exists.

If ever anything did exist, it would be unknowable. If anything existed and would be knowable, the knowledge of it could not be conveyed to other people. For he who knows it, would be incapable to describe it to his fellow-men.

Every sign is different from what it signifies. How can anyone communicate the idea of color by means of words, since the ear does not hear colors but only sounds? And how can two persons, different one from another, have the same idea?

[144]

GREEN, THOMAS HILL

GREEN, THOMAS HILL (1836-1882). "Shut up your Mill and Spencer," Green, professor of moral philosophy at Oxford, admonished his audience, "and open your Kant and Hegel." Green repudiated the whole tradition of British philosophy, especially Locke and Hume, and became the leader of the opposition against positivism and utilitarianism in England. His oratoric power enabled him to convert many British students of philosophy to German idealism. He praised Kant's categories as "the connective tissue of the known world," derived from Kant his conception of self-distinguishing consciousness as a combining agency, and, although he did not adopt Hegel's dialectical method, he did agree with him regarding history and organized society as embodiments of divine will. He flatly rejected Locke's and Hume's assumption that sensations are the raw material of knowledge. According to Green, every experience takes place by forming relations which, consequently, are the real elements of that which is regarded as sensation. Since relations are the work of human mind, reality is characterized as essentially spiritual.

Bitterly opposed as Green was to Darwin, his mind was nevertheless influenced by biological as well as Hegelian evolutionism. He held that an animal organism which has its history in time, gradually becomes the vehicle of an eternally complete consciousness, which, in itself, can have a history of the process by which the animal organism becomes its vehicle. Green even described mystical union as an evolutionary process. He exposed the foundations of his metaphysics and ethics in *Prolegomena to Ethics* (1883).

UTILITARIANISM EVALUATED

On the whole there is no doubt that the theory of an ideal good, consisting in the greatest happiness of the greatest number, as the end by reference to which the claim of all laws and powers and rules of action on our obedience is to be tested, has tended to improve human conduct and character. This admission may be made quite as readily by those who consider such conduct and character an end in itself, as by those who hold that its improvement can only be measured by reference to an extraneous end, consisting in the quantity of pleasure produced by it; perhaps, when due account has been taken of the difficulty of deciding whether quantity of pleasure is really increased by "social progress," *more* readily by the former than by the latter. It is not indeed to be supposed that the Utilitarian theory, any more than any other theory of morals, has brought about the recognition or practice of any virtues that were not recognized and practised independently of it; or that any one, for being a theoretic Utilitarian, has been a better man—i.e. one more habitually governed by desire for human perfection in some of its forms—than he otherwise would have been. But it has helped men, acting under the influence of ideals of conduct and rules of virtuous living, to fill up those ideals and apply those rules in a manner beneficial to a wider range of persons—beneficial to them in the sense of tending to remove certain obstacles to good living in their favor. It has not given men a more lively sense of their

441

duty to others—no theory can do that—but it has led those in whom that sense has already been awakened to be less partial in judging who the "others" are, to consider all men as the "others," and, on the ground of the claim of all men to an equal chance of "happiness," to secure their political and promote their social equality. To do this is not indeed directly to advance the highest living among men, but it is to remove obstacles to such living, which in the name of principle and authority have often been maintained.

*   *   *

Those who are glad of a topic for denunciation may, if they like, treat the prevalence of such opinions among educated men as encouraging the tendency to vicious self-indulgence in practice. No such unfairness will here be committed. There is no good reason to apprehend that there is relatively more—we may even hope that there is less—of self-indulgence than in previous generations; though, for reasons just indicated, it has a wider scope for itself, talks more of itself and is more talked about, than at times when men were more tied down by the necessities of their position. We are no more justified in treating what we take to be untrue theories of morals as positive promoters of vice, than in treating what we deem truer theories as positive promoters of virtue. Only those in whom the tendencies to vicious self-indulgence have been so far overcome as to allow the aspirations after perfection of life to take effect, are in a state to be affected either for better or for worse by theories of the good. The worst that can truly be objected against the prevalence of Hedonistic theory, just noticed, is that it may retard and mislead those who are already good, according to the ordinary sense of goodness as equivalent to immunity to vice, in their effort to be better; and the most that can be claimed for the theory which we deem truer, is that it keeps the way clearer of speculative impediments to the operation of motives, which it seeks to interpret but does not pretend to supply.

*   *   *

We should accept the view, then, that to think of ultimate good is to think of an intrinsically desirable form of conscious life; but we should seek further to define it. We should take it in the sense that to think of such good is to think of a state of self-conscious life as intrinsically desirable for oneself, and for that reason is to think of it as something else than pleasure—the thought of an object as pleasure for oneself, and the thought of it as intrinsically desirable for oneself, being thoughts which exclude each other. The pleasure anticipated in the life is not that which renders it desirable; but so far as desire is excited by the thought of it as desirable, and so far as that desire is reflected on, pleasure comes to be anticipated in the satisfaction of that desire. The thought of the intrinsically desirable life, then, is the thought of something else than pleasure, but the thought of what? The thought, we answer, of the full realization of the capacities of the human soul, of the fulfilment of man's vocation, as of that in which alone he can satisfy himself—a thought of which the content is never final and complete, which is always by its creative energy further determining its own conduct, but which for practical purposes, as the mover and guide of our highest moral effort, may be taken to be the thought of such a social life as that described. The thought of such a life, again, when applied as a criterion for the valuation of the probable effects of action, may be taken to be represented by the question . . . "Does this or that law or usage, this or that course of action—directly or indirectly, positively or as preventive of the opposite—contribute to the better being of society, as measured by the more general establishment of conditions favorable to the attainment of the recognized virtues and excellencies, by the more general attainment of those excellencies in some degree, or by their attainment on the part of some persons in higher degree without detraction from the opportunities of others?"

The reader, however, will be weary of hearing of this ideal, and he will be waiting to know in what particular way it can afford guidance in cases of the kind supposed, where conventional morality and Utilitarian theory alike fail to do so. We have argued that no man could tell whether, by denying himself according to the examples given, he would in the whole result increase the amount of pleasant living in the world, present and to come. Can he tell any better whether he will further that realization of the ideal just described, in regard to which we admit the impossibility of saying positively what in its completeness it would be?

We answer as follows. The whole question of sacrificing one's own pleasure assumes a different aspect, when the end for which it is to be sacrificed is not an addition to a general aggregate of pleasures, but the harmonious exercise of man's proper activities in some life resting on a self-sacrificing will. According to the latter view, the individual's sacrifice of pleasure does not—as so much loss of pleasure—come into the reckoning at all; nor has any balance to be attempted of unascertainable pains and pleasures spreading over an indefinite range of sentient life. The good to be sought is not made up of pleasures, nor the evil to be avoided made up of pains. The end for which the sacrifice is demanded is one which in the sacrifice itself is in some measure attained,—in some measure only, not fully, yet so that the sacrifice is related to the complete end, not as a means in itself valueless, but as a constituent to a whole which it helps to form. That realization of the powers of the human spirit, which we deem the true end, is not to be thought of merely as something in a remote distance, towards which we may take steps now, but in which there is no present participation. It is continuously going on, though in varying and progressive degrees of completeness; and the individual's sacrifice of an inclination, harmless or even in its way laudable, for the sake of a higher good, is itself already in some measure an attainment of the higher good.

[145]

444

GROTIUS, HUGO (Hugues De Groot)

GROTIUS, HUGO (HUGUES DE GROOT) (1583-1645). At the age of sixteen, Grotius was already a highly successful lawyer in Leyden. He excelled as a jurist, theologian, historian, philologist, poet and diplomat. In 1619, after the defeat of the Dutch republicans, he was tried by the victorious monarchists and sentenced to prison for life, but, in 1621, he escaped to France. Thereafter he lived as an exile, internationally respected as a scholar, and later was recognized by his own country as one of the greatest Dutchmen of all times. For about fifteen years, Grotius was Swedish minister to Paris and accomplished a number of difficult tasks while negotiating with Richelieu.

Grotius was not the first to expound natural law, but he was first to construct a system of international jurisprudence in which the distinction between natural and historical law was essential. According to Grotius, the principle of natural morality is written by God in the hearts and minds of mankind. It is to be ascertained by reason. On the other hand, the existing institutions and laws of the nations are products of human will. The ultimate end of legal development must be the establishment of the supreme command of natural law. For the time being, some minimum demands must be formulated in order to eliminate license in making and conducting war. Grotius' significant work *On the Law of Peace and War* (1625) was directed against arbitrary power policy and radical pacifists, although just wars were admitted. Previously, Grotius, in his *Mare Liberum* (Free Sea, 1609), had tried to secure the rights of neutral ships against ruthless force on the parts of Portugal, Spain and England.

Grotius also had a great effect on Old Testament exegesis by his cold lucidity which secured his independence of Christian traditions and enabled him to recognize the historical uniqueness of the Hebrew Bible.

THE RATIONAL BASIS OF INTERNATIONAL LAW

THE civil law, both that of Rome and that of each nation in particular, has been treated of by many, with a view either to elucidate it, through commentaries, or to present it in a compendious form. But that law which regards the relations between peoples, or between rulers of peoples, whether it proceed from nature or be instituted by divine commands or introduced by custom and tacit agreement, has been touched on by few, and has by no one been treated as a whole and in an orderly manner. And yet that this be done is of concern to the human race.

And such a work is the more necessary because of the fact that persons in our time, as well as in former ages, have held in contempt what has been done in this province of jurisprudence, as if no such thing existed, as a mere name. Every one is familiar with the saying of Euphemius in Thucydides, that for a king or city who has authority to maintain, nothing is unjust which is useful; and to the same effect is the saying that with good fortune equity is where strength is, and that the commonwealth cannot be administered without doing some wrong. To this we add that the controversies which arise between peoples and between kings commonly have war as their arbiter. But that war has nothing to do with laws is not only the opinion of the ignorant; even wise and learned men often let fall expressions which support such an opinion. For nothing is more common than to place laws and arms in opposition to each other. . . .

Since our discussion of law is undertaken in vain if there is no law, it will serve both to commend and fortify our work if we refute briefly this very grave error. And that we may not have to deal with a mob of opponents, let us appoint an advocate to speak for them. And whom can we select fitter than Carneades, who had arrived at the point— the supreme aim of his academic philosophy—where he could use the strength of his eloquence for falsehood as easily as for truth? When he undertook to argue against justice—especially, the justice of which we here treat, he found no argument stronger than this: that men had, as utility prompted, established laws, differing among different peoples as manners differed, and, among the same people, often changing with the change of times; but that there is no natural law, since all men, as well as other animals, are impelled by nature to seek their own advantage; and that either there is no justice, or if it exist, it is the highest folly since through it one harms oneself in consulting the interests of others.

But what this philosopher says, and, following him, the poet—"Nature cannot distinguish the just from the unjust," must by no means be admitted. For though man is indeed an animal, he is an uncommon animal, differing much more from all other animals than they differ from one another; this is evidenced in many actions peculiar to the human species. Among the attributes peculiar to man is the desire for society—that is for communion with his fellow-men, and not for communion simply, but for a tranquil association and one suited to the quality of his intellect; this the Stoics called *Oykeiosin*. Therefore, the statement that by nature every animal is impelled to seek only its own advantage cannot be conceded in this general form.

Even in other animals their desires for their own good are tempered by regard for their offspring and for others of their species; this we believe to proceed from some intelligence outside of themselves; for with regard to other acts not at all more difficult than these an equal degree of intelligence does not appear. The same is to be said of infants, in whom, previous to all teaching, there is manifested a certain disposition to do good to others, as is sagaciously remarked by Plutarch; for example, at that age compassion breaks forth spontaneously. A man of full age knows how to act similarly in similar cases, and he has exceptional craving for society, whose peculiar instrument, language, he alone among all animals possesses; accordingly, he has the faculty of knowing and acting according to general principles; the tendencies which agree with this faculty do not belong to all animals, but are the peculiar properties of human nature.

This concern for society, which we have now stated in a rude manner, and which is in agreement with the nature of the human intellect, is the source of law, properly so called, of which we are speaking. It is law that determines the abstention from another's property; the restitution of another's goods which we have in our possession and of any gain we have derived from such possession; the obligation to fulfill promises; the reparation for damage wrongfully done; and the retribution of punishments.

From this signification of law there has flowed another larger meaning. For man is superior to other animals not only in the social impulse, of which we have spoken, but also in his judgment in estimating what is pleasant and what is injurious—not only for the present but for the future also, and the things which may lead to good or to ill. We know, therefore, that, in accordance with the quality of the human intellect, it is congruous to human nature to follow, in such matters, a judgment rightly formed and not to be misled by fear or by the enticement of present pleasure, or to be carried away by heedless impulse; and that what is plainly repugnant to such judgment is likewise contrary to natural law, that is, to natural human law.

And here comes the question of a wise assignment in bestowing upon each individual and each body of men the things which peculiarly belong to them; this disposition will sometimes prefer the wiser man to the less wise, the neighbor to a stranger, the poor man to the rich man, according as the nature of each act and each matter requires. This question some have made a part of law, strictly and properly so called; though law, properly speaking, has a very different nature; for it consists in this—that each should leave to another what is his and give to him what is his due.

What we have said would still be in point even if we should grant, what we cannot without great wickedness, that there is no God, or that He bestows no regard upon human affairs. Since we are assured of the contrary, partly by our reason and partly by constant tradition, confirmed by many arguments and by miracles attested by all ages, it follows that God, as our creator to whom we owe our being and all that we have, is to be obeyed by us without exception, especially since He has in many ways shown himself to be supremely good and supremely powerful. Wherefore, He is able to bestow upon those who obey Him the highest rewards, even eternal rewards, since He himself is eternal; and He must be believed to be willing to do this, particularly if He has promised to do so in plain words; and this we as Christians believe, convinced by the indubitable faith of testimonies.

And here we find another origin of law, besides that natural source of which we have spoken; it is the free will of God, to which our reason indisputably tells us we must submit ourselves. But even natural law—whether it be the natural social law, or law in the looser meaning of which we have spoken—may yet be rightfully ascribed to God, though it proceed from the principles of man's inner nature; for it was in accordance with His will that such principles came to exist within us. In this sense Chrysippus and the Stoics said that the origin of law was not to be sought in any other source than Jove himself; and it may be conjectured that the Latins took the word *jus* from the name *Jove.*

It may be added that God has made these principles more manifest by the commandments which He has given in order that they might be understood by those whose minds have weaker powers of reasoning. And He has controlled the aberrations of our impulses, which drive us this way and that, to the injury of ourselves and of others; bridling our more vehement passions, and restraining them within due limits.

In the next place, since it is conformable to natural law to observe compacts (for some mode of obliging themselves was necessary among men, and no other natural mode can be imagined) civil rights were derived from that very source. For those who joined any community, or put themselves in subjection to any man or men, either expressly promised or from the nature of the case must have been understood to promise tacitly, that they would conform to that which either the majority of the community, or those whom power was assigned, should determine.

And therefore what Carneades said, and what has been said by others—that utility is the mother of justice and right —is, if we are to speak accurately, not true. For the mother of natural law is human nature itself, which would lead us to desire mutual society even though we were driven thereto by other wants. The mother of civil law is obligation by compact; and since compacts derive their force from natural law, nature may be said to be the great-grandmother of civil law. But utility supplements (*accedit*) natural law. For the Author of nature ordained that we, as individuals, should be weak and in need of many things for living well, in order that we might be the more impelled to cherish society. But utility furnished the occasion for civil law; for that association or subjection of which we have spoken, was at the first instituted for the sake of some utility. Accordingly, those who prescribe for others ordinarily design, or should design, some utility in their laws.

But just as the laws of each state regard the utility of that state, so also between all states, or, at least, between most of them, certain laws could be established by consent—and it appears that laws have been established—which regard the utility, not of particular communities but of the great aggregate of communities. And this is what is called the law of nations (*jus gentium*), in so far as we distinguish it from natural law. This part of law is omitted by Carneades, who divides all law into natural law and the civil law of particular peoples; although as he was about to treat of that law which obtains between one people and another (for he subjoins a discussion upon war and acquisitions by war), he was especially called upon to make mention of law of this kind.

Moreover, Carneades improperly traduces justice when he calls it folly. For since, as he himself acknowledges, the citizen is not foolish who in a state obeys the civil law, although in consequence of such respect for the law he may lose some things which are useful to him, so too a people is not to be deemed foolish which does not estimate its interests so highly as to disregard the common laws between peoples for the sake of its own advantage. The reason is the same in both cases. For as a citizen who disobeys the civil law for the sake of present utility destroys that in which the perpetual utility of himself and his posterity is bound up, so too a people which violates the laws of nature and of nations breaks down the bulwark of its own tranquillity for future time. Even though no utility were to be looked on from the observation of law, such a course would be one not of folly but of wisdom, to which we feel ourselves drawn by nature.

Wherefore, that saying that we were compelled to establish laws from fear of wrong, is not universally true; this opinion is explained by a speaker in Plato's dialogues, who says that laws were introduced because of the fear of receiving wrong, and that men are driven to respect justice by a certain compulsion. But this applies only to those institutions and statutes which were devised for the more easy enforcement of law; as when many, individually weak, fearing oppression by those who were stronger, combined to establish judicial authorities and to protect them by their common strength, so that those whom they could not resist singly, they might, united, control. Only in this sense may we properly accept the statement that law is that which pleases the stronger party: namely, that we are to undersand that law does not attain its external end unless it has force as its servant. Thus Solon accomplished great things, as he himself said, *by linking together force and law.*

But even law that is unsupported by force is not destitute of all effect; for justice brings serenity to the conscience, while injustice brings torments and remorse such as Plato describes as afflicting the hearts of tyrants. The common feeling of upright men approves justice and condemns injustice. The important point is that justice has for its friend, God, while injustice has Him as an enemy; He reserves his judgments for another life, yet in such manner that He often exhibits their power in this life; we have many examples of this in history.

The error which many commit who, while they require justice in citizens, hold it to be superfluous in a people or the ruler of a people, is caused primarily by this fact: they are regarding only the utility which arises from the law. This utility is evident in the case of citizens, who individually are too weak to secure their own protection. Great states, on the other hand, which seem to embrace within themselves all that is necessary to support life, do not appear to have need of that virtue which regards extraneous parties and is called justice.

But—not to repeat what I have already said, that law is not established for the sake of utility alone—there is no state so strong that it may not at some time need the aid of others external to itself, either in the way of commerce or in order to repel the force of many nations combined against it. Hence we see that alliances are sought even by the most powerful peoples and kings; the force of such alliances is entirely destroyed by those who confine law within the boundaries of a state. It is most true that everything becomes uncertain if we withdraw from law.

Since, for the reasons which I have stated, I hold it to be completely proved that there is between nations a common law which is of force with respect to war and in war, I have had many and grave reasons why I should write a work on that subject. For I saw prevailing throughout the Christian world a license in making war of which even barbarous nations would have been ashamed, recourse being had to arms for slight reasons or for no reason; and when arms were once taken up, all reverence for divine and human law was lost, just as men were henceforth authorized to commit all crimes without restraint.

It remains now that I briefly explain with what aids

and with what care I have undertaken this work. In the first place, it was my object to refer to the truth of the things which belong to natural law to certain notions so certain that no one can deny them without doing violence to his own nature. For the principles of that law, if you attend to them rightly, are of themselves patent and evident almost in the same way as things which we perceive by our external senses; for these do not deceive us, if the organs are rightly disposed and other necessary things are not wanting.

For the demonstration of natural law I have used the testimonies of philosophers, historians, poets, and finally orators. Not that these are to be trusted indiscriminately; for they are ordinarily writing to serve their sect, their argument, or their cause. But when many, writing in different times and places, affirm the same thing as true, their unanimity must be referred to some universal cause, which, in the questions with which we are here concerned, can be no other than either a right deduction proceeding from principles of nature, or some common agreement. The former cause points to the law of nature, the latter to the law of nations; the difference between these two is to be discerned not in the testimonies themselves (for writers everywhere confound the law of nature and the law of nations), but in the quality of the matter. For what can not be deduced from certain principles by unerring reasoning, and yet is seen to be observed everywhere, must have its origin in free consent.

Passages of history have a two-fold use in our argument: they supply both examples and judgments. In proportion as examples belong to better times and better nations, they have greater authority; we have therefore preferred the examples from ancient Greece and Rome. Nor are judgments to be despised, especially when many of them agree; for natural law is, as we have said, to be proved by such concord; and the law of nations can be proved in no other manner.

The opinions of poets and orators have not so much weight; and these we often use not so much to gain confirmation from them as to give to what we are trying to say some ornamentation from their modes of expression.

The books written by men inspired by God, or approved by them, I often use as authority, with a distinction between the Old and the New Testament.

[146]

454

H

HAEBERLIN, PAUL

HAEBERLIN, PAUL (1878-   ). The evolution of Haeberlin's thinking has proceeded from the religious belief of a Protestant minister
to idealism, returned to a prevalently religious attitude, then approached a purely theoretical standpoint, and returned again to the
view that religious experience, and not philosophical knowledge,
is able to master the problems of life and to. comprehend the
meaning of existence. Haeberlin assigns a very important task
to philosophy but he does not give it the last word. Haeberlin
maintains that life, and existence are essentially problematical,
and concludes that knowledge also is necessarily problematical.
The human mind is characterized by him as the constant protest
against this inevitable fact which remains a mystery to man but
is not a mystery to God. Man is capable of becoming aware of his
real situation only by assuming a religious attitude. Philosophy,
provided it recognizes its true function, can help man to obtain
knowledge of his real situation.

Haeberlin has made valuable contributions to psychology,
characterology, pedagogics and psychotherapeutics. He was especially successful in treating psychopathic children and young people in their teens. Since 1922 he has been a full professor of philosophy, psychology and pedagogics at the University of Basel. His
principal works are: *The Object of Psychology* (1921), *Aesthetics*
(1929), *The Essence of Philosophy* (1934) and *Possibilities and
Limits of Education* (1936).

THE PRINCIPLES OF SCIENTIFIC KNOWLEDGE

KNOWLEDGE supposes correct thinking. Correct thinking lies
in correct judgment. The essence of knowledge is the absolute correctness of judgment. The task of knowledge is to
make correct judgment. Its object is the content of this judgment. Judgment does not mean any single judgment or the

judgment of a definite judging subject, e.g., a human subject, but judgment altogether, and therewith judgment independent of the kind of the subject. The absolute judging subject corresponds to the absolute judgment. This is, however, of lesser importance than the fact that knowledge is correct thinking and therefore can be found only in correct judgment. In this connection, "correctness" means absolute correctness or objective correctness. But when is judgment in this sense correct? There is only one possible answer to this question. It can only be found if one considers that all judging is acting, that every judgment is an action. An action is correct in this object sense if it corresponds to an absolutely valid objective demand, or, as we also can say, if it is the realization of a norm. The concept of correctness of acting supposes the concept of an objective norm. The norm of acting corresponds to absolutely correct acting. Furthermore, if judging is a modification of acting, the concept of correctness of judgment supposes the concept of norm of judgment as a definite modification of the norm of acting altogether. The absolute norm of judgment corresponds to the correct judgment, and is the modification of the norm altogether. Correct judgment is the realization of this norm of judgment. A judgment is correct if it fulfils its norm of judgment and therewith fulfils, on its part and in its way, the norm of judgment. Knowledge, as totality of correct judgment, consequently, means the realization of the absolute norm of judgment.

Every judgment has a content, or, as we also could say, a result. That means what is "made" by the judgment, in the sense of a position or statement. For every judgment does notify something, and this something is just its content. But such a statement is an action by means of which that something is formed; in as far the content is a formation. The content of a correct judgment is correctly formed. It is a correct formation. In general, we characterize the correctness of a formation made by judgment, in contradistinction to a formation by action altogether, as truth. Correct judgments have true contents. The content of correct judgment altogether is the very truth. Truth, therefore, is the content of knowledge. The correct judgment, consequently, can also be defined from the viewpoint of the content. A judgment is correct if its content is true. This definition is quite as valid as the inverse: the content of a judgment is true if the judgment is correct. Both of them mean realization of the norm of judgment.

[147]

HALEVI, JUDAH

HALEVI, JUDAH (About 1080-1140). As a "flaming pillar of song," Judah Halevi, the greatest Jewish poet of the Middle Ages, was exalted by Heinrich Heine, who, himself an undeniable expert, sensed through the medium of a translation Halevi's mastership of versification and his fervent soul. Halevi sang of love and friendship, of virtue and beauty, and most passionately of the fate of the Jewish people, of Zion and God. Several of his sacred poems form part of Jewish prayer-books in every country where Jewish congregations exist.

But Halevi was also an important philosopher of religion. His *Kitab Al Khazari*, written in Arabic and translated into Hebrew under the title *Sefer Ha-Kuzari* (Book of the Khazar), referring to the conversion to Judaism of the Khazar King Bulan II (about 740), is a defense of the Jewish faith against Christian and Islamic attacks and at the same time, a profound meditation on Jewish history and an acute demarcation between philosophy and religion. The close connection between the revealed religion and the history of the Jewish people is characteristic of Halevi's position. He maintained that Judaism does not center in the person of its founder as the religions of Christ and Mohammed do but in the people to whom the Torah has been given, and he goes so far as to declare: "If there were no Jews there would be no Torah." But he by no means idolizes his people in the way modern nationalists do. Jewish history is the work of Divine Providence which he regarded as the continuation of the Divine creative activity. Halevi was opposed to Aristotelianism which he reproached for subjecting the Deity to necessity and for being incompatible with the idea of a personal God. Platonic tradition seemed more fitting to him, for he was inclined to regard God as the principle of form that moulds the eternal material principle. Fundamentally, however, Halevi re-

457

mained reluctant to use philosophical categories in matters that concern religion, and he often expressed his dislike of philosophy and philosophers, although he proved to be one of them.

ON REVELATION

OUR intellect which, a priori, is only theoretical, being sunk in matter, cannot penetrate to the true knowledge of things, except by the grace of God, by special faculties which He has placed in the senses. There is no difference between my perception and thine that this circumscribed disc, giving forth light and heat is the sun. Should even these characteristics be denied by reason, this does no harm, because we can derive it from argument for our purposes. Thus also a sharp-eyed person, looking for a camel, can be assisted by a weak-eyed and squinting one who tells him that he has seen two cranes at a certain place. The sharp-eyed person then knows that the other has only seen a camel, and the weakness of his eyes made him believe that it was a crane, and his squint that there were two cranes. In this way the sharp-eyed person can make use of the evidence of the weak-eyed one, whilst he excuses his faulty description by his faulty sight. A similar relation prevails between senses and imagination on one side and reason on the other. The Creator was as wise in arranging this relation between the exterior senses and the things perceived, as He was in fixing the relation between the abstract sense and the uncorporeal substratum. To the chosen among His creatures He has given an inner eye which sees things as they really are, without any alteration. Reason is thus in a position to come to a conclusion regarding the true spirit of these things. He to whom this eye has been given is clear-sighted indeed. Other people, who appear to him as blind, he guides on their way. It is possible that this eye is the power of imagination as long as it is under the control of the intellect. It beholds, then, a grand and awful sight which reveals unmistakable truths among the whole of this species and those sights. By this I mean all the prophets. For they witnessed things which are described to the other in the same manner as we do with things we have seen. We testify to the sweetness of honey and the bitterness of the colocynth; and if any one contradicts us, we say that he has failed to grasp a fact of natural history. Those prophets without doubt saw the divine world with the inner eye; they beheld a sight which harmonized with their natural imagination. Whatever they wrote down, they endowed with attributes as if they had seen them in corporeal form. Those attributes are true as far as regards what is sought by inspiration, imagination, and feeling; they are untrue as regards the reality sought by reason.

[148]

HAMANN, JOHANN GEORG

HAMANN, JOHANN GEORG (1730-1788). During a stay in London, where he was bound to become acquainted with British business methods, Hamann, a native of Königsberg, Prussia, had a mystical experience which made him a grim adversary of rationalism and the spirit of enlightenment that fascinated most of his contemporaries. With the aid of allegorical interpretation, Hamann regarded the Bible as the fundamental book of all possible knowledge, including that of nature. Allegory and symbol gave Hamann truer knowledge than notions. Myths and poetry were to him of greater validity than scientific research and logical conclusions. Language was the key that opens the door to reality. Hamann was a past master in sensing the unconscious tendencies of speech. But in his style there are no consequences, no development of ideas. He tried to grasp the flux of life, but, according to his own avowal, often forgot the meaning of the similes he had used and to which he alluded in later pages of the same treatise. His fugitive associations, therefore, are of greater value than his efforts to express his intentions elaborately. Devout and coquettish, excessive in his piety and repentance of transgressions with which his imagination remained fascinated, Hamann tried to embrace spirit and sensuality, sometimes illuminating their relations, sometimes becoming hopelessly confused. His writings were inspired by sublime earnestness and brilliant irony. He accused the rationalistic spirit of his age of ignoring God and nature, human genius, creative action and the enjoyment of real life. His views deeply impressed Herder, Goethe, Friedrich Heinrich Jacobi, Hegel and Kierkegaard.

459

NATURE is a book, a letter, a fairy tale (in the philosophical sense) or whatever you want to call it. Suppose we know all the letters in this book as well as possible, suppose we know how to spell the words and how to pronounce them, suppose we know even the language in which it is written—is that enough to understand the book, to judge it, to give an account of it or to make an excerpt of it? You need more physics in order to interpret nature. Physics is nothing but the ABC's. Nature is an equation with an unknown, a Hebrew word which is written only with consonants to which reason has to add the dots. I stick to the letters, to the visible and to the natural, like the hands of the watch. But what is behind the dial plate? That is where you find the art of the master, wheels and springs which like the mosaic serpent need an Apocalypse. The entire visible nature is nothing but a dial and the hand; the wheels and the right weight are stones, winds and flames of fire. . . .

Reason discovers in us nothing more than what Hiob saw . . . the misfortune of our birth, the advantage of the grave and the uselessness and the shortcomings of the human life, since we have no insight and feel passion and urges in us whose purposes are unknown to us. All human wisdom works and has worries and grief as reward. The farther reason looks the greater is the haze in which it loses itself. Everything is vain and tortures the spirit instead of calming and satisfying it. It is with reason, as with eyes with lenses, whereby the most tender skin becomes nauseating, whereby the most delicate dish becomes a heap of worms and the most refined work of art becomes a bungling work. We see the impossibility of remedying all inequalities in human society and we see an overwhelming number of deficiencies and flaws in it. The weakness of ourselves and of our reason makes us see flaws in beauties by making us consider everything piece by piece.

[149]

HAMILTON, ALEXANDER

HAMILTON, ALEXANDER (1757-1804). "A great man, but not a great American," "a great Englishman bred in America"—so Hamilton was called by Woodrow Wilson. Other historians have equally assumed that Hamilton threw himself into the American Revolution as much out of ambition as through adherence to the principle of popular government. However, Hamilton's services to the cause of America's independence and to the formation of the republic cannot be questioned. He stormed the redoubt at Yorktown; his activities were instrumental in the ratification of the Constitution; as Washington's Secretary of the Treasury, he secured the credit of the national government, and some historians call him the greatest finance minister in American history. His efficiency, his talents for organization were of inestimable value to the establishment of public order in the young republic. In addition to his brilliancy and his personal charm, some defects of his character, however, must not be overlooked. He was quarrelsome and excitable, and, although he was undeniably a great statesman, there was also in his personality a quixotic strain, and he not only favored a strong, centralized government but also avowedly admired the British monarchy and the institution of the House of Lords.

Even as a youth of eighteen, Hamilton showed his great literary talents. He was well acquainted with Locke, Montesquieu and Hume, and was always eager to read and to learn. His most important contribution to American political philosophy was his articles in the *Federalist Papers*. It was their aim to explain the Constitution and to recommend its acceptance by the people of the thirteen colonies. "No constitution," said Chancellor Kent, "ever received a more masterly and successful vindication."

ON A JUST PARTITION OF POWER

IT is of great importance in a republic not only to guard the society against the oppression of its rulers, but to guard one part of the society against the injustice of the other part. Different interests necessarily exist in different classes of citizens. If a majority be united by a common interest, the rights of the minority will be insecure. There are but two methods of providing against this evil: the one by creating a will in the community independent of the majority, that is, of the society itself; the other by comprehending in the society so many separate descriptions of citizens as will render an unjust combination of a majority of the whole very improbable, if not impracticable. The first method prevails in all governments possessing a hereditary or self-appointed authority. This at best is but a precarious security; because a power independent of the society may as well espouse the unjust views of the major as the rightful interests of the minor party, and may possibly be turned against both parties. The second method will be exemplified in the federal republic of the United States. While all authority in it will be derived from and dependent on the society, the society itself will be broken into so many parts, interests, and classes of citizens that the rights of individuals or of the minority will be in little danger from interested combinations of the majority. In a free government the security for civil rights must be the same as that for religious rights. It consists in the one case in the multiplicity of interests, and in the other in the multiplicity of sects. The degree of security in both cases will depend on the number of interests and sects; and this may be presumed to depend on the extent of country and number of people comprehended under the same government. This view of the subject must particularly recommend a proper federal system to all the sincere and considerate friends of republican government; since it shows that in exact proportion as the territory of the Union may be formed into more circumscribed confederacies, or States, oppressive combinations of a majority will be facilitated; the best security under republican forms, for the rights of every class of citizens, will be diminished; and, consequently, the stability and independence of some member of the government, the only other security, must be proportionally increased. Justice is the end of government. It is the end of civil society. It ever has been and ever will be pursued until it be obtained or until liberty be lost in the pursuit. In a society, under the forms of which the stronger faction can readily unite and oppress the weaker, anarchy may as truly be said to reign, as in a state of nature, where the weaker individual is not secured against the violence of the stronger; and as in the latter state even the stronger individuals are prompted by the uncertainty of their condition to submit to a government which may protect the weak as well as themselves, so in the former state will the more powerful factions or parties be gradually induced by a like motive to wish for a government which will protect all parties, the weaker as well as the more powerful. It can be little doubted that if the State of Rhode Island was separated from the confederacy, and left to itself, the insecurity of rights under the popular form of government within such narrow limits would be displayed by such reiterated oppressions of factious majorities that some power altogether independent of the people would soon be called for by the voice of the very factions whose misrule had proved the necessity of it. In the extended republic of the United States, and among the great variety of interests, parties, and sects which it embraces, a coalition of a majority of the whole society could seldom take place on any other principles than those of justice and the general good; while there being thus less danger to a minor from the will of a major party, there must be less pretext, also, to provide for the security of the former, by introducing into the government a will not dependent on the latter; or, in other words, a will independent of the society itself. It is no less certain than it is important, notwithstanding the contrary opinions which have been entertained, that the larger the society, provided it lie within a practical sphere, the more duly capable it will be of self-government. And happily for the republican cause, the practical sphere may be carried to a very great extent, by a judicious modification and mixture of the federal principle.

[150]

HAN FEI

HAN FEI (died 233 B.C.). Han Fei, a disciple of Hsun Ching and the greatest Chinese philosopher of law, committed suicide because he, as an unofficial adviser of a ruler, had aroused the jealousy of the latter's responsible minister.

Han Fei concentrated upon the problems of government, state-craft, authority and public welfare, and advanced views similar to those of Jeremy Bentham and other British utilitarians. But he also adopted Taoist ideas on essential truth.

E S S A Y S

NOTHING is more valuable than the royal person, more honorable than the throne, more powerful than the authority of the sovereign, and more august than the position of the ruler. These four excellences are not obtained from outside, nor secured from anybody else, but are deliberated in the ruler's own mind and acquired thereby. . . . This the ruler of men must keep firmly in mind.

Master Shen [i.e. Shen Tao, fourth century] said, 'A flying dragon rides the winds, a floating serpent wanders through the mist on the water; but when the clouds disperse and the mist is gone, a dragon and a serpent are no different from a cricket or an ant. They have lost what they depended on. Thus the reason why a man of worth may be overpowered by a worthless one is that the able man's power is weak and his position humble. And the reason why a worthless man submits to a man of worth is that the able man's power is strong and his position high. Yao [the Sage-king] as a common man could not have governed three people, whilst Chieh [the villain-king] as Son of Heaven could bring the whole of society into confusion. Thus I know that authority and position are to be trusted, ability and wisdom are not particularly desirable. . . . It was when Yao ascended the throne and was king over the Great Society that what he commanded was done, what he banned was not done. From this angle I see that worth and wisdom are not enough to subdue a population whilst authority and position are enough to overpower men of worth.'

To this the reply is made, 'In the case of a dragon . . . riding the clouds, I do not regard the dragon as not depending on the clouds. . . . None the less, if worth is discarded and reliance put solely on authority, is it enough to produce good government? If it is, I have never seen it. There is something which goes along with the particular prestige of clouds and makes the dragon able to ride them . . .; and this something is the dragon's or the serpent's, special quality. . . . However thick the clouds and mist might be, the quality of the cricket or the ants is not up to the mark. In the case of a Chieh, seated on the throne and using the majesty of the son of Heaven as clouds and mist, society nevertheless cannot escape great confusion; and this because a Chieh's quality is inadequate. What is more, supposing a sovereign using the authority of a Yao to govern the Great Society, how different that authority is from the kind which makes confusion! . . . The sovereigns who use their authority to make confusion are many, those who use their authority to make order are few. . . .'

*　　　*　　　*

No country is permanently strong, nor is any country permanently weak. If conformers to law are strong, the country is strong; if conformers to law are weak, the country is weak. . . . Any ruler able to expel private crookedness and uphold public law finds the people become law-abiding and the state ordered; and any ruler able to eradicate individualistic action and act on public law finds his army become strong and his enemy weak. So, find out men who follow the discipline of laws and regulations, and place them above the body of officials. Then the sovereign cannot be deceived by anybody with fraud and falsehood. . . .

Now supposing promotions were made because of mere reputation, then ministers would be estranged from the sovereign and all officials would associate for treasonable purposes. Supposing officials were appointed on account of their partisanship, then the people would strive to cultivate friendships and never seek employment in accordance with the law. Thus, with the government lacking able men, the state will fall into confusion. If rewards are bestowed according to mere reputation, and punishments are inflicted according to mere defamation, then men who love rewards and hate punishments will discard public law and practice self-seeking tricks and associate for rebellious purposes. . . . Therefore, the intelligent sovereign makes the law select men, and makes no arbitrary regulation himself. In consequence able men cannot be obscured, bad characters cannot be disguised, falsely praised fellows cannot be advanced, wrongly defamed people cannot be degraded. In consequence the distinction between the ruler and minister becomes clear and order is attained. . . .

Hence to govern the state by law is to praise the right and blame the wrong. The law does not fawn on the noble, (just as) an inked string does not follow a crooked line. Whatever the law applies to, the wise cannot reject it nor the brave defy it. Punishment for fault never skips ministers, and reward for good never misses commoners. Therefore for correcting the faults of the high, for rebuking the vices of the low, for suppressing disorders, for deciding against mistakes, for subduing the arrogant, for straightening the crooked, and for unifying the folk-ways of the masses, nothing can match with the law: for warning officials and overaweing the people, for rebuking obscenity and danger and for forbidding falsehood and decit, nothing can match with penalties. If they are strictly administered, no discrimination is made between noble and commoner. If the law is definite, superiors are esteemed and not flouted. If superiors are not flouted, the sovereign will become strong and able to maintain the proper course of government. This was the reason why the early kings esteemed legalism and handed it down to posterity.

[151]

HARRIS, WILLIAM TORREY

HARRIS, WILLIAM TORREY (1835-1909). When passions ran high at the beginning of the Civil War, a group met together in St. Louis and calmly interpreted the events as part of a universal

466

plan, the working out of an eternal dialectic which Hegel had explained in all his works, particularly his *Philosophy of History.* One of the key men of that philosophical society was Harris who rose from teacher in the public schools to the superintendency and the United States Commissionership of Education, which post he held for 17 years, longer than any other incumbent. He might be termed the idealist in education in that he organized all phases of it on the principles of a philosophical pedagogy in which the German idealists Hegel, Kant, Fichte and Goethe were his principal teachers, apart from Froebel, Pestalozzi and the rest.

Harris founded and edited the first philosophical periodical in America, the *Journal of Speculative Philosophy,* in which men like William James, Josiah Royce and John Dewey first spread their wings. He initiated, with Brokmeyer, the St. Louis Movement in Philosophy which had far-reaching influence. Together with Amos Bronson Alcott and with the support of Emerson, he revived New England transcendentalism but gave it a more logical, metaphysical twist. Lecturing from coast to coast as one of America's most popular educators, he made his hearers realize the importance of philosophy, of having objectives in an education for democracy, and of viewing things in their whole.

Far from being a dreamer, he was practical in his activities. As editor-in-chief of Webster's, he originated the divided page. He expanded the functions of the Bureau of Education; presented the United States in graphic exhibits at many an international exposition; incorporated the first kindergarten into an American public school system, and was responsible for introducing the reindeer into Alaska as a condition for educating the natives who were thus supplied with an industry and a livelihood which the whalers and trappers had brought to the verge of extinction.

THE LAST JUDGMENT

MICHELANGELO passes by all subordinate scenes and seizes at once the supreme moment of all history—of the very world itself and all it contains. This is the vastest attempt that the artist can make, and is the same that Dante had ventured upon in the *Divina Commedia.* In religion we seize the absolute truth as a process going on in time: the deeds of humanity are judged "after the end of the world." After death Dives goes to torments, and Lazarus to the realm of the blest. In this supreme moment all wordly distinctions fall away, and the naked soul stands before eternity with naught save the pure essence of its deeds to rely upon. All souls are equal before God, so far as mere worldly eminence is concerned. Their inequality rests solely upon the degree that they have realized the eternal will by their own choice.

But this dogma, as it is held in the christian religion, is not merely a dogma; it is the deepest of speculative truths. As such it is seized by Dante and Michelangelo, and in this universal form every one must recognize it if he would free it from all narrowness and sectarianism. The point of view is this:—The whole world is seized at once under the form of eternity; all things are reduced to their lowest terms. Every deed is seen through the perspective of its own consequences. Hence every human being under the influence of any one of the deadly sins—anger, lust, avarice, intemperance, pride, envy, and indolence—is being dragged down into the inferno just as Michelangelo has depicted. On the other hand any one who practises the cardinal virtues—prudence, justice, temperance, and fortitude—is elevating himself toward celestial clearness.

If any one will study Dante carefully, he will find that the punishments of the inferno are emblematical of the very states of the mind one experiences when under the influence of the passion there punished. To find the punishment for any given sin, Dante looks at the state of mind which it causes in the sinner, and gives it its appropriate emblem. . . .

So Michelangelo in this picture has seized things in their essential nature; he has pierced through the shadows of time, and exhibited to us at one view the world of humanity as it is in the sight of God, or as it is in its ultimate analysis. Mortals are there, not as they seem to themselves or to their companions, but as they are when measured by the absolute standard—the final destiny of spirit. This must recommend the work to all men of all times, whether one holds to this or that theological creed; for it is the last judgment in the sense that it is the ultimate or absolute estimate to be pronounced upon each deed, and the question of the eternal punishment of any individual is not necessarily brought into account. Everlasting punishment is the true state of all who persist in the commission of those sins. The sins are indissolubly bound up in pain. Through all times anger shall bring with it the "putrid mud" condition of the soul; the indulgence of lustful passions, the stormy tempest and spiritual night; intemperance, the pitiless rain of hail and snow and foul water. The wicked sinner—shall be tormented forever; for we are now and always in eternity. . . . Just as we strive in our human laws to establish justice by turning back upon the criminal effects of his deeds, so *in fact* when placed "under the form of Eternity," all deeds do return to the doer; and this is the final adjustment, the "end of all things"—it is *the last judgment.* And this judgment is always the only actual fact in the world.

[152]

HARTMANN, EDUARD VON

HARTMANN, EDUARD VON (1842-1906). An officer in the Prussian army, Eduard von Hartmann became disabled, suffering from a nervous disease that forced him to lie on his back. After quitting military service, he studied philosophy, and soon became famous because of the great success of his *Philosophie des Unbewussten* (Philosophy of the Unconscious, 1869). Later, he published many other books, none of which attracted as much attention as his first work.

By no means was Hartmann a precursor of modern investigation of unconscious or subconscious activities. He is rather to be regarded as one of the last constructors of systems, each of whom was immediately inspired by Schelling. Avowedly Hartmann tried to form a synthesis of Leibniz, Schelling, Hegel, Schopenhauer and the results of modern natural sciences. What he called the Unconscious combines the qualities of Hegel's absolute spirit and Schopenhauer's blind will. It is proclaimed as the "thing in itself," the origin of the cosmic order and the mental life of the human individual. Hartmann called his system "transcendental realism" and claimed to have constructed the reliable bridge to metaphysics and, at the same time "the only possible bridge to natural science."

469

I SHOULD like to . . . call every original philosopher a mystic, so far as he is truly original; for in the history of philosophy no high thought has ever been brought to light by laborious conscious trial and induction, but has always been apprehended by the glance of genius, and then elaborated by the understanding. Add to that, that philosophy essentially deals with a theme which is most intimately connected with the one feeling *only* to be *mystically* apprehended, namely, the *relation of the individual to the Absolute.* All that has gone before only concerned such matter of consciousness as can or could arise in no other way, thus is here only called mystical, because the *form of its origin* is mystical; but now we come to an item of consciousness, which, in its inmost character, is *only* to be apprehended mystically, which thus also, *materially,* may be called mystical; and a human being who can produce this mystical content will have to be called pre-eminently a mystic.

To wit, *conscious thought* can comprehend the identity of the individual with the Absolute by a rational method, as we too have found ourselves on the way to this goal on our inquiry; but the Ego and the Absolute and their identity stand before it as three *abstractions,* whose *union* in the *judgment* is made probable, it is true, through the preceding proofs, yet an *immediate feeling of this identity* is not attained by it. The *authoritative belief* in an external revelation may credulously repeat the dogma of such a unity—the living feeling of the same cannot be engrafted or thrust on the mind from without, it can only spring up in the mind of the believer himself; in a word, it is to be attained neither by philosophy nor external revelation, but only mystically, by one with equal mystical proclivities, the more easily, indeed, the more perfect and pure are the philosophical notions or religious ideas already possessed. Therefore this feeling is the content of mysticism, *Kat exochen,* because it finds its existence *only* in it, and, at the same time, the *highest* and *ultimate,* if also, as we have seen before, by no means the only aim of all those who have devoted their lives to mysticism. Nay, we may even go so far as to assert that the production of a certain degree of this mystical feeling, and the enjoyment lurking in it, is the sole *inner* aim of all religion, and that it is, therefore, not incorrect, if less significative, to apply the name *religious* feeling to it.

Further, if the highest blessedness lurks in this feeling for its possessor, as is confirmed by the experience of all mystics, the transition is manifestly easy to the endeavor to heighten this feeling in degree, by seeking to make the union between the Ego and the Absolute ever closer and more intimate. But it is also not difficult to see that we have here arrived at the point previously indicated, where mysticism spontaneously degenerates into the morbid, by overshooting its mark. Undoubtedly we must elevate ourselves for this purpose a little above the standpoint hitherto attained in our investigations. The unity, namely of the Absolute and the individual, whose individuality or egoity is given through consciousness, thus, in other words, the unity of the unconscious and conscious, is once for all given, inseparable and indestructible, except by destruction of the individual; wherefore, however, every attempt to make this unity more close than it is, is so absurd and useless. The way which, historically, has almost always been taken, is that of the annihilation of consciousness—the endeavor to let the individual perish in the Absolute. This, however, contains a great error, as if, when the goal of annihilation of consciousness was reached, the individual still existed; the Ego at once desires to be annihilated, and to subsist in order to enjoy this annihilation. Consequently this goal has hitherto been always imperfectly attained on both sides, although the accounts of the mystics enable us to perceive that many on this path have attained an admirable height, or rather depth.

[153]

471

HARTMANN, NICOLAI

HARTMANN, NICOLAI (1882-1950). Born and educated in Tsarist Russia, Hartmann, shortly after 1900, emigrated to Germany where he became naturalized. During World War I, he fought in the German army. In his adopted country, Hartmann was at first a follower of Hermann Cohen, but later became an adversary of Neo-Kantianism. Since this change, Hartmann has developed his philosophical views with progressive consistency.

Hartmann emphasizes the necessity that the philosopher must take into account the fact that no one begins with his own thinking, but rather meets a historically conditioned situation in which ideas and problems, already developed by previous thinkers, or expressed in various spiritual creations of the time direct the way a beginner selects the questions which interest him, and formulate his problems and principles. From this standpoint, Hartmann proceeds to the establishment of the science of ontology, which, to him, is at least equally as important as epistemology. According to Hartmann, the realm of reason covers only a sector of reality. It is impossible to solve the metaphysical problem because irrational remainders always defy reason. But, if metaphysics is impossible in the form of any system, it remains the principal business of the philosopher to mark the boundary between the rational and the irrational and to recognize the metaphysical elements in all branches of philosophy. His inquiry results in the statement that epistemology, ethics, and aesthetics can offer partial solutions only, and that the notions of logic are subject to historical change, although their ideal structure remains unalterable. The history of the notions forms the center of the history of philosophy and science. As to ethics and axiology, Hartmann tries to harmonize the absolute character of the moral duty with the historical variety of evaluations.

VALUE AND VALIDITY

THE so-called "relativity of values" is nothing but the historical instability of their actuality which results in the instability of validity. That solves the puzzle why it is so often asserted that the values themselves are relative. For validity has always been considered the sort of being of the values themselves. But that has been recognized as an error, and therefore the relativity of the "being valuable" is untenable.

Notwithstanding all regarding the change of the real, there remains a definite kind of independence of the value-character itself, or of the "being valuable" (for instance the being valuable of a certain manner of acting in certain circumstances). This absoluteness is very evident in the fact of the super-temporariness of the being valuable, even if the valuable real is only ephemeral. It is an error to think that only the eternal could have eternal value. Just the transient has eternal value. Its value-character is the eternal in it. The value of a thing is as little dependent on its duration as the truth of a proposition is dependent on the flash or disappearance of the insight in human minds.

Upon this footing, a synthesis of the right value relativism and the right value-absolutism is possible. If both of them limit themselves strictly to the phenomena and refrain from constructing theories, they can complete one another harmoniously. Relativism may be satisfied with the historical conditionality of actuality and "validity," which is conceded by the adversary. Absolutism, on its part, may be satisfied with the continuance of the "being valuable," even when it is not actual and not "valid," and that does not affect the facts of historical relativity.

Both of these theories not only contain a truth but are indispensable to each other. For only the relativity of validity demonstrates the meaning of independent continuance, and only that meaning can make evident what relativity really is. Moreover, only these two theories together can clarify the mystery of the value-consciousness.

If the perception of values is dependent on historical circumstances, it seems to be unreliable for that reason. Since, however, we have no other knowledge about values, that would mean that any kind of comprehending values is uncertain. It therefore is important to recognize that it really does matter that certain values are at certain times non-valid while they are valid at other times. This phenomenon is clarified entirely by the historical conditionality of actuality. This explanation is completed by Scheler's notion of "value-blindness" and the notion of "narrowness of the value-consciousness" introduced by myself. To understand this phenomenon, we do not need the assumption of a deceivableness of the valuing feelings. It is sufficient to think that all valuing feelings are limited as far as their contents are concerned, incapable of comprehending all of the values, and may become seeing only in accordance with the degree of their maturing, though conditional upon the historical change of the shape of life. However, the valuing feeling can grasp values only in accordance with the laws of its own development.

The notion of "narrowness of the value-consciousness" needs as its complementary notion that of the "wandering of the valuing glance" whose horizon is inside the plane of the values. Seen from the realm of the values this wandering means just the same as the historical conditionality of "validity." For it is moving in the course of time, and is dependent on the changing conditions of life. For at any time the consciousness is in touch with only a sector of the realm of values. This sector is another one at any time. The values themselves, however, remain motionless.

[154]

HEGEL, GEORG WILHELM FRIEDRICH

HEGEL, GEORG WILHELM FRIEDRICH (1770-1831). Long after Hegel lost his once immense authority, many of his intellectual formulas continued to attract the philosophers of various schools in various countries. Hegel's philosophy is often regarded as typically German, and certainly some of its main features represent the very characteristics of the German way of reacting to reality. Numerous great philosophers in England and America, in Italy and France, and in other countries have testified that they owed to Hegel not only an increase of knowledge but the fundamental principles of their own thinking. Outstanding Hegelians in England were T. H. Green, Edward and John Caird, J. H. Bradley and Bernard Bosanquet, and in America, W. T. Harris, Royce, Creighton and

474

Calkins. John Dewey said that "acquaintance with Hegel has left a permanent deposit in my thinking."

Hegel's philosophy has often been despised as abstract speculation. Yet soon after his death it became evident that his thoughts could offer an ideological basis to political parties which were radically opposed to each other. Bismarck and the Prussian Junkers adopted Hegel's view on the state. So did Fascism and National Socialism, while Marx, and after him, Lenin, adapted Hegel's dialectical method to give reasons for the doctrine of the dictatorship of the proletariat. And even staunch defenders of liberalism and democracy have appealed to Hegel's philosophy of history.

In a similar way, the champions of religious orthodoxy and liberalism have used Hegel's ideas to justify their respective positions. King Frederick William III of Prussia and his minister of public education favored Hegelianism as the firmest bulwark of Christianity, while King Frederick William IV of Prussia and his minister of public education persecuted the Hegelians whom they accused of undermining the Christian faith.

Hegel has been glorified and vilified as the protector of reactionary conservatism and as the prophet of revolutionary change because his system tries to synthesize antagonistic tendencies. On the one hand, he put becoming above being, and conceived of the world as an eternally evolutionary process; on the other hand, he claimed to have laid the groundwork for definite knowledge and for the understanding of timeless perfection.

In a lecture on the history of philosophy, Hegel, from his chair at the University of Berlin, called to his audience: "Man cannot over-estimate the greatness and power of his mind." For he regarded human mind as one of the manifestations of the Absolute which he defined as spirit. The world, Hegel stated, is penetrable to thought which is, on its part, a description of the Absolute. Cosmic reason operates within the soul of man, whose consciousness is the area of the subjective spirit, while the objective spirit becomes manifest in cultural and social institutions like law and morality, and the absolute spirit can be grasped in the arts, in religion and philosophy. Human history and social life, culminating in the state, represent the highest level of a gradation that rises from inorganic nature to human genius, from "mere existence" to consciousness, knowledge of truth and action in accordance with recognized duties. The history of the world means the progressive realization of freedom which can be demonstrated by purely logical development. For Hegel does not acknowledge any other cause of historical change than the movement of thought by integrating a thesis and its antithesis into a synthesis which, on its part, provokes a new antithesis with which it becomes integrated into a new synthesis. These succeeding syntheses will bring the world to reason. Hegel thought that he had found the pattern for both human and cosmic reason in this conflict of thesis and antithesis which he called the dialectics. For becoming was regarded by Hegel as the modification of a being by factors which he defined as the negation of the being to be modified. In this way, evolution was conceived by Hegel as a purely logical procedure for which he claimed the acknowledgment of real necessity.

ON THE NATURE OF SPIRIT

THE nature of spirit may be understood by a glance at its direct opposite—*Matter*. As the essence of matter is gravity, so, on the other hand, we may affirm that the substance, the essence, of spirit is freedom. All will readily assent to the doctrine that spirit, among other properties, is also endowed with freedom; but philosophy teaches that all the qualities of spirit exist only through freedom; that all are but means for attaining freedom; that all seek and produce this and this alone. It is a result of speculative philosophy, that freedom is the sole truth of spirit. Matter possesses gravity in virtue of its tendency towards a central point. It is essentially composite; consisting of parts that *exclude* each other. It seeks its unity; and therefore exhibits itself as self-destructive, as verging towards its opposite [an indivisible point]. If it could attain this, it would be matter no longer, it would have perished. It strives after the realization of its idea; for in unit it exists *ideally*. Spirit, on the contrary, may be defined as that which has its center in itself. It has not a unity outside itself, but has already found it; it exists *in* and *with* itself. Matter has its essence out of itself; spirit is *self-contained existence*. Now this is freedom, exactly. For if I am dependent, my being is referred to something else which I am not; I cannot exist independently of anything external. I am free, on the contrary, when my existence depends upon myself. This self-contained existence of spirit is none other than self-consciousness—consciousness of one's own being. Two things must be distinguished in consciousness; first, the fact

476

that I know; secondly *what I know.* In *self*-consciousness these are merged in one; for spirit knows itself. It involves an appreciation of its own nature, as also an energy enabling it to realize itself; to make itself *actually* that which it is *potentially.* According to this abstract definition it may be said of universal history, that it is the exhibition of spirit in the process of working out the knowledge of that which it is potentially. . . .

This vast congeries of volitions, interests, and activities, constitutes the instruments and means of the world-spirit for attaining its object; bringing it to consciousness, and realizing it. And this aim is none other than finding itself— coming to itself—and contemplating itself in concrete actuality. But that those manifestations of vitality on the part of individuals and peoples, in which they seek and satisfy their own purposes, are, at the same time, the means and instruments of a higher and broader purpose of which they know nothing,—which they realize unconsciously,—might be made a matter of question; rather has been questioned, and in every variety of form negatived, decried, and contemned as mere dreaming and "Philosophy." But on this point I announced my view at the very outset, and asserted our hypothesis,—which, however, will appear in the sequel, in the form of a legitimate inference, and our belief that reason governs the world, and has consequently governed its history. In relation to this independently universal and substantial existence—all else is subordinate, subservient to it, and the means for its development. The union of universal abstract existence generally with the individual, the subjective, that this alone is truth, belongs to the department of speculation, and is treated in this general form in logic. But in the process of the world's history itself—as still incomplete,—the abstract final aim of history is not yet made the distinct object of desire and interest. While these limited sentiments are still unconscious of the purpose they are fulfilling, the universal principle is implicit in them and is realizing itself through them. The question also assumes the form of the union of *freedom* and *necessity;* the latent abstract process of spirit being regarded as *necessity,* while that which exhibits itself in the conscious will of men, as their interest, belongs to the domain of *freedom.* As the metaphysical connection (*i.e.* the connection in the idea) of these forms of thought, belongs to logic, it would be out of place to analyze it here. The chief and cardinal points only shall be mentioned.

Philosophy shows that the idea advances to an infinite antithesis; that, viz. between the idea in its free, universal form—in which it exists for itself—and the contrasted form of abstract introversion, reflection on itself, which is formal existence-for-self, personality, formal freedom, such as belongs to spirit only. The universal idea exists thus as the substantial essence of free volition on the other side. This reflection of the mind on itself is individual self-consciousness—the polar opposite of the idea in its general form, and therefore existing in absolute limitation. This polar opposite is consequently limitation, particularization for the universal absolute thing; it is the side of its *definite existence;* the sphere of its formal reality, the sphere of the reverence paid to God. To comprehend the absolute connection of this antithesis, is the profound task of metaphysics. This limitation originates all forms of particularity of whatever kind. The formal volition (of which we have spoken) wills itself; desires to make its own personality valid in all that it purposes and does; even the pious individual wishes to be saved and happy. This pole of the antithesis, existing for itself, is—in contrast with the absolute universal being— a special separate existence, taking cognizance of specialty only, and willing that alone. In short it plays its part in the region of mere phenomena. This is the sphere of particular purposes, in effecting which individuals exert themselves on behalf of their individuality—give it full play and objective realization. This is also the sphere of happiness and its opposite. He is happy who finds his condition suited to his special character, will, and fancy, and so enjoys himself in that condition.

The history of the world is not the theater of happiness. Periods of happiness are blank pages in it, for they are periods of harmony,—periods when the antithesis is in abeyance. Reflection on self,—the freedom above described—is abstractly defined as the formal element of the activity of the absolute idea. The realizing *activity* of which we have spoken is the middle term of the syllogism, one of whose extremes is the universal essence, the *idea*, which reposes in the penetralia of spirit; and the other, the complex of external things,—objective matter. That activity is the medium by which the universal latent principle is translated into the domain of objectivity.

*   *   *

What is the material in which the ideal of reason is wrought out? The primary answer would be,—personality itself—human desires—subjectivity, generally. In human knowledge and volition, as its material element, reason attains positive existence. We have considered subjective volition where it has an object which is the truth and essence of a reality, viz. where it constitutes a great world-historical passion. As a subjective will, occupied with limited passions, it is dependent, and can gratify its desires only within the limits of this dependence. But the subjective will has also a substantial life—a reality,—in which it moves in the region of *essential* being, and has the essential itself as the object of its existence. This essential being is the union of the *subjective* with the *rational* will: it is the moral whole, the *state*, which is that form of reality in which the individual has and enjoys his freedom; but on the condition of his recognizing, believing in and willing that which is common to the whole. And this must not be understood as if the subjective will of the social unit attained its gratification and enjoyment through that common will; as if this were a means provided for its benefit; as if the individual, in his relations to other individuals, thus limited his freedom, in order that this universal limitation—the mutual constraint of all—

might secure a small space of liberty for each. Rather, we affirm, are law, morality, government, and they alone, the positive reality and completion of freedom. Freedom of a low and limited order, is mere caprice; which finds its exercise in the sphere of particular and limited desires.

Subjective volition—passion—is that which sets men in activity, that which effects "practical" realization. The idea is the inner spring of action; the state is the actually existing, realized moral life. For it is the unity of the universal, essential will, with that of the individual; and this is "morality." The individual living in this unity has a moral life; possesses a value that consists in this substantiality alone. Sophocles in his Antigone says, "The divine commands are not of yesterday, nor of to-day; no, they have an infinite existence, and no one could say whence they came." The laws of morality are not accidental, but are the essentially rational. It is the very object of the state, that what is essential in the practical activity of men, and in their dispositions, should be duly recognized; that it should have a manifest existence, and maintain its position. It is the absolute interest of reason that this moral whole should exist; and herein lies the justification and merit of heroes who have founded states, —however rude these may have been. In the history of the world, only those peoples can come under our notice which form a state. For it must be understood that this latter is the realization of freedom, *i.e.* of the absolute final aim, and that it exists for its own sake. It must further be understood that all the worth which the human being possesses—all spiritual reality, he possesses only through the state. For his spiritual reality consists in this, that his own essence— reason—is objectively present to him, that it possesses objective immediate existence for him. Thus only is he fully conscious; thus only is he a partaker of morality—of a just and moral social and political life. For truth is the unity of the universal and subjective will; and the universal is to be found in the state, in its laws, its universal and rational arrangements. The state is the divine idea as it exists on earth. We have in it, therefore, the object of history in a more definite shape than before; that in which freedom obtains objectivity, and lives in the enjoyment of this objectivity. For law is the objectivity of spirit; volition in its true form. Only that will which obeys law is free; for it obeys itself—it is independent and so free. When the state or our country constitutes a community of existence; when the subjective will of man submits to laws,—the contradiction between liberty and necessity vanishes. The rational has necessary existence, as being the reality and substance of things, and we are free in recognizing it as law, and following it as the substance of our own being. The objective and the subjective will are then reconciled, and present one identical homogeneous whole. For the morality of the state is not of that ethical reflective kind, in which one's conviction bears sway; this latter is rather the peculiarity of the modern time, while the true antique morality is based on the principle of abiding by one's duty (to the State at large). An Athenian citizen did what was required of him, as it were from instinct: but if I reflect on the object of my activity, I must have the consciousness that my will has been called into exercise. But morality is duly—substantial right—a "second nature" as it has been justly called; for the *first* nature of man is his primary merely animal existence.

*   *   *

Summing up what has been said of the state, we find that we have been led to call its vital principle, as actuating the individuals who compose it,—morality. The state, its laws, its arrangements, constitute the rights of its members; its natural features, its mountains, air, and waters are *their* country, their fatherland, their outward material property; the history of this state, *their* deeds; what their ancestors have produced belongs to them and lives in their memory. All is their possession, just as they are possessed by it; for it constitutes their existence, their being.

Their imagination is occupied with the ideas thus presented, while the adoption of these laws, and of a fatherland so conditioned is the expression of their will. It is this matured totality which thus constitutes *one* being, the spirit of *one* people. To it the individual members belong; each unit is the son of his nation, and at the same time—in so far as the state to which he belongs is undergoing development—the son of his age. None remains behind it, still less advances beyond it. This spiritual being (the spirit of his time) is his; he is a representative of it; it is that in which he originated, and in which he lives. Among the Athenians the word Athens had a double import; suggesting primarily, a complex of political institutions, but no less, in the second place, that goddess who represented the spirit of the people and its unity.

This spirit of a people is a *determinate* and particular spirit, and is, as just stated, further modified by the degree of its historical development. This spirit, then, constitutes the basis and substance of those other forms of a nation's consciousness, which have been noticed. For spirit in its self-consciousness must become an object of contemplation to itself, and objectivity involves, in the first instance, the rise of differences which make up a total of distinct spheres of objective spirit, in the same way as the soul exists only as the complex of its faculties, which in their form of concentration in a simple unity produce that soul. It is thus *one individuality* which, presented in its essence as God, is honored and enjoyed in *religion;* which is exhibited as an object of sensuous contemplation in *art;* and is apprehended as an intellectual conception in *philosophy.* In virtue of the original identity of their essence, purport, and object, these various forms are inseparably united with the spirit of the state. Only in connection with this particular religion, can this particular political constitution exist; just as in such or such a state, such or such a philosophy or order of art.

The remark next in order is, that each particular national genius is to be treated as only one individual in the process of universal history. For that history is the exhibition of the divine, absolute development of spirit in its highest forms,—that gradation by which it attains its truth and consciousness of itself. The forms which these grades of progress assume are the characteristic "national spirits" of history, the peculiar tenor of their moral life, of their Government, their art, religion, and science. To realize these grades is the boundless impulse of the world-spirit—the goal of its irresistible urging; for this division into organic members, and the full development of each, is its idea. Universal history is exclusively occupied with showing how spirit comes to a recognition and adoption of the truth: the dawn of knowledge appears; it begins to discover salient principles, and at last it arrives at full consciousness.

Having, therefore, learned the abstract characteristics of the nature of spirit, the means which it uses to realize its idea, and the shape assumed by it in its complete realization in phenomenal existence,— namely, the state, nothing further remains for this introductory section to contemplate, but— *the course of the world's history.*

[155]

HEHASID, JUDAH BEN SAMUEL OF REGENSBURG

HEHASID, JUDAH BEN SAMUEL OF REGENSBURG (12th and 13th centuries). The Hebrew word *Hehasid* means "the Saint." Judah's co-religionists revered him because he was an extremely pious man, absorbed in mystical contemplation, a great teacher, scholar and a careful leader of the Jewish community of Regensburg where he settled in 1195. He was the initiator of Jewish mysticism in Germany, a way of thinking and feeling that is different from cabalistic mysticism because it insists more on prayer and moral conduct. Judah denied all possibility of human understanding of God. Man must fulfill his religious duties, as they are prescribed in the Bible, without reasonable knowledge of the Almighty, but, by purification, obedience to ceremonial life and asceticism, he may obtain union with God that is beyond reasoning. In this way, Judah tried to reconcile the demands of orthodox Judaism with enjoyment of mystical ecstasy.

Judah's biography is adorned with many legends which testify to the admiration of his contemporaries and succeeding generations. He wrote *Sefer Hasidim* (Book of the Pious), and *Sefer Hakahod* (Book of Glory). The second book has been lost. It is known only by quotations other authors have made from it.

CERTAIN FORMS OF VIRTUE LEAD TO SIN

THERE is a kind of humility which inherits Gehenna, and causes the heirs of the humble to inherit a burning fire in Gehenna. In what manner is it? If a man sees that his children, relatives, or pupils are of bad behavior, and it lies within his power to correct them, by reprimanding or by beating them, but he says to himself: 'I shall rather be agreeable to them and not reprimand or beat them,' he causes them to inherit Gehenna. For they will corrupt their way, and will even do mischief to their father and their mother, so that they will despise them, and curse the day wherein they were born. It is in connection with such a case that it is written: 'He that spareth the rod hateth his son.' It is also said that he who smites his grown-up son transgresses the injunction: 'Put not a stumbling-block before the blind.' But a son that is accustomed to reproofs of instruction, and is beaten while small, will not resent if his father beats him when he is grown up. It is also written: 'Unless I had believed to see the goodness of the Lord;' there are some dots on the word *Unless*, for David said: 'Peradventure I caused my sons to sin, and am not able to make amends by repenting'; for it is written: 'And his father had not grieved him all his life in saying: "Why hast thou done so?"'

There is another kind of humility which likewise brings a man down to Gehenna. For instance, a man sits in a court of justice, and knows that the judges are in error; or a private man knows that the court is in error, but says: 'How shall I go and put them to shame?' or a man knows that the judges are not well-versed in law, while he is well-versed, and when they say to him: 'Sit with us that we may not go astray', he replies: 'I shall not take a seat, for ye are well-versed.' It is obvious that if they go astray, the sin is to be attached to him. Another instance is, when a man hears that the congregation speak falsely, and he says: 'Who am I that I should speak before them?' Behold, it is written: 'And in thy majesty prosper, ride on, in behalf of truth and humility of righteousness'; from this we infer that there is a kind of humility which is not righteousness, as the above and similar cases show. It is also said: 'An untutored priest should not say the benedictions in the presence of scholars.'

There is a kind of charity which is pernicious. In what manner is it? One who gives alms to adulterers or to a glutton or a drunkard. For it is written: 'She shall not fall into harlotry,' and thou mayest read: 'She shall not cause to fall into harlotry;' 'Thou shall not commit adultery,' and thou mayest read: 'Thou shall not cause to commit adultery.' 'Thou shalt not murder,' and it may be read: 'Thou shalt not cause to murder.' He who supplies weapons of destruction to murderers is regarded as if he himself had committed murder. For it is written: 'He hath also prepared for him the weapons of death.' He who gives food to robbers is like their accomplice. Similarly, he who gives alms to adulterers is regarded as though he had aided them and brought them together, for they take the money that is given to them, and offer it as hire to harlots. It is also said that a man should give no alms at all rather than give it publicly. In a similar sense it is also said that if a man who cannot pay his debts gives alms, it is obvious that his charity is robbery.

There is a kind of piety which is bad. For instance, a man whose hands are unclean sees a holy book fall into the fire, and says: 'It is better that it should be burned,' and does not touch the book. Another instance has also been cited: a man sees a woman drown in the river, and says: 'It is better that she should drown than that I should touch her.'

There is also false piety. For instance: a man brings out a Scroll of the Law into the public thoroughfare on the Sabbath on account of a fire; or when a man says: 'How shall I save a man's life and profane the Sabbath?' Another instance is: a question about declaring a thing forbidden or unlawful is referred to a man who knows that he is well-versed in the Law, though there are others like him in the city, and he says: 'Address the question to others;' behold, his meekness may lead to sin: peradventure if he had given his decision, he would have forbidden that which others had declared lawful.

There is sometimes a righteous judge that perishes in his righteousness. For instance: he sees two litigants, one being a swindler, and the other a simpleton; the swindler knows how to plead, but the simpleton, who does not know how to plead, is right; concerning him it is written: 'Open thy mouth for the dumb.' Likewise, if he knows that the verdict is unjust, one of the litigants having hired false witnesses, he should say: 'Let the sin be attached to the witnesses.'

A favor sometimes turns out to be harmful, and is regarded as an evil for its author and his offspring. In what manner is it? For instance: a man causes that sinners and they that lead others astray should dwell in the city. Now since it is bad for the people of the city, it is evident that he and his offspring will stumble over them, and they will do mischief to his offspring. It is in connection with such a case that it is written: 'And he did that which is not good among his people.' (Another explanation: *And he did that which is not good among his people* refers to him who disgraces his family; he is punished, because he sinned by inflicting shame and injury upon his people). Another instance: he who does a good deed in order to be honored and to praise himself thereby.

[156]

HEIDEGGER, MARTIN

HEIDEGGER, MARTIN (1889-   ). Heidegger is a modern German philosopher who has a considerable French following despite the fact that he had leanings toward the socio-political views of the Third Reich. As a keen analyst of being, Being, existence being present and thus-being (even the French speak of *le Sosein* and *le*

Desein) he has no equal and the fine distinctions which he draws have earned him derision and the charge of mental acrobatics among those incapable of following him. Yet he is no more abstruse than his teacher Husserl, and in his philosophy he is continually reaching down into the very core of personality in which he discovers grave guilt, anxiety and fear which make our existence one for death. Man is lost in utter loneliness, he is totally isolated. Only against the background of historical fate does his present existence attain value.

Heidegger himself is conscious of the difficult style in which his main work *Sein und Zeit* and all the others are written, and he is now clarifying his position, controversial on that account, by occupying himself with the problem of language and communication. Spending his summers in a tiny cottage deep in the Black Forest (but not deep enough to exclude philosophical and journalistic pilgrims), his winters in Freiburg (where he accepted the rectorship at the University in 1933, but resigned it the following year to continue as professor of philosophy), he has a number of significant works on his desk ready for publication if history so decrees.

NOTHINGNESS

From ancient times, metaphysics has spoken about nothingness in an ambiguous sentence. *Ex nihilo nihil fit.* Nothing becomes out of nothing. Although "nothing" has never been a problem in the discussion of that sentence, the leading and fundamental concept of being is expressed in it.

Ancient metaphysics conceives nothingness in the sense of not being, of unshaped matter that is incapable of shaping itself into a formed being. Formed being offers an aspect, appearance (*eidos*). Being is form that represents something in an image. Origin, right and limit of that concept of being are as little discussed as nothingness itself.

But Christian dogmatics denies the truth of the sentence *Ex nihilo nihil fit* and gives nothingness a changed meaning, in the sense of absolute absence of non-godly being. *Ex nihilo ens creatum.* Being has been created out of nothing. Now nothingness has become the contradiction of the true being, of the *summum ens*, of God as the *ens increatum*, the uncreated being. Here, too, the interpretation of nothingness indicates a fundamental concept of the Being. The metaphysical discussion of the Being maintains itself on the same level as the question concerning nothingness. It, therefore, does not care about the difficulty that, if God creates out of nothing, He just must have an attitude toward nothingness. If, however, God is God, then He cannot know nothingness, provided that the "Absolute" excludes from itself all nothingness.

This sketchy historical survey shows nothingness as the counter-concept of the true Being, as its negation. But if nothingness becomes a problem anyhow, then this counter-relation is not only more distinctly determined, but then the very metaphysical question of the "being of being" is broached. Nothingness does not remain the indefinite contrary to Being, but is revealed as belonging to the "Being of Being."

"Pure Being and pure non-being are the same thing"— this sentence of Hegel is true. Being and nothing belong together, but not because, as from Hegel's point of view, both agree in their indefiniteness and immediateness, but because Being is essentially finite and becomes manifest only in the transcendence of Being taken into the realm of nothingness.

[157]

HELMHOLTZ, HERMANN VON

HELMHOLTZ, HERMANN VON (1821-1894). When Helmholtz, in 1847, delivered his lecture on the conservation of energy, he was prepared to be reproached by the authorities of his time for talking about old stuff. Instead he was hailed by some as a discoverer, and blamed by others as a fanciful speculative philosopher. Most of the physicists had ignored the principle of persistence of energy. Helmholtz knew better. He did not claim to have discovered it. His intention was rather to demonstrate what it means to physical phenomena and to what numerical consequences it leads everywhere.

The universality of Helmholtz' mind is proved by the mere fact that he was successively appointed full professor of physiology, anatomy and physics at the greatest universities of Germany. He promoted optics and acoustics, mechanics, the general theory of electricity, thermodynamics, hydrodynamics, electrodynamics, geometry and the theory of numbers. In 1850 he invented the ophthalmoscope, and received no other material profit from his invention than about fifteen dollars as honorarium for the treatise in which he communicated it.

Helmholtz was also interested in philosophy which, according to him, is concerned with the inquiry into the cognitive faculties and performances of man. He characterized sensation as a symbol, not an image of the external world, and the world of these symbols as the mirror of the real world. If man learns to read the symbols correctly, he becomes able to arrange his actions in a way that the effects correspond to the aims. Helmholtz conceded the theoretical possibility of interpreting the facts in terms of subjective idealism but held that the realist interpretation is the simpler one. Helmholtz, one of whose maternal ancestors was William Penn, was respected internationally not only because of his scientific performances but as the very incarnation of the dignity and probity of science.

THE INTERDEPENDENCE OF THE SCIENCES

MEN of science form, as it were, an organized army, laboring on behalf of the whole nation, and generally under its direction, and at its expense, to augment the stock of such knowledge as may serve to promote industrial enterprise, to increase wealth, to adorn life, to improve political and social relations, and to further the moral development of individual citizens. After the immediate practical results of their work we forbear to inquire; that we leave to the instructed. We are convinced that whatever contributes to the knowledge of the forces of nature or the powers of the human mind is worth cherishing, and may, in its own due time, bear practical fruit, very often where we should least have expected it. Who, when Galvani touched the muscles of a frog with different metals, and noticed their contraction, could have dreamt that eighty years afterward, in virtue of the self-same process, whose earliest manifestations attracted his attention in his anatomical researches, all Europe would be traversed with wires, flashing intelligence from Madrid to St. Petersburg with the speed of lightning? In the hands of Galvani, and at first even in Volta's, electrical currents were phenomena capable of exerting only the feeblest forces, and could not be detected except by the most delicate apparatus. Had they been neglected, on the ground that the investigation of them promised no immediate practical result, we should now be ignorant of the most important and most interesting of the links between the various sources of nature. When young Galileo, then a student at Pisa, noticed one day during divine service a chandelier swinging backward and forward, and convinced himself, by counting his pulse, that the duration of the oscillations was independent of the arc through which it moved, who could know that this discovery would eventually put it in our power, by means of the pendulum, to attain an accuracy in the measurement of time till then deemed impossible, and would enable the storm-tossed seaman in the most distant oceans to determine in what degree of longitude he was sailing?

Whoever, in the pursuit of science, seeks after immediate practical utility, may generally rest assured that he will seek in vain. All that science can achieve is a perfect knowledge and a perfect understanding of the action of natural and moral forces. Each individual student must be content to find his reward in rejoicing over new discoveries, enjoying the aesthetic beauty of a well-ordered field of knowledge, where the connection and the filiation of every detail is clear to the mind, and where all denotes the presence of a ruling intellect; he must rest satisfied with the consciousness that he too has contributed something to the increasing fund of knowledge on which the dominion of man over all the forces hostile to intelligence reposes. . . .

The sciences have, in this respect, all one common aim, to establish the supremacy of intelligence over the world: while the moral sciences aim directly at making the resources of intellectual life more abundant and more interesting, and seek to separate the pure gold of Truth from alloy, the physical sciences are striving indirectly toward the same goal, inasmuch as they labor to make mankind more and more independent of the material restraints that fetter their activity. Each student works in his own department, he chooses for himself those tasks for which he is best fitted by his abilities and his training. But each one must be convinced that it is only in connection with others that he can further the great work, and that therefore he is bound, not only to investigate, but to do his utmost to make the results of his investigation completely and easily accessible. If he does this, he will derive assistance from others, and will in his turn be able to render them his aid. The annals of science abound in evidence of how such mutual services have been exchanged, even between departments of science apparently most remote. Historical chronology is essentially based on astronomical calculations of eclipses, accounts of which are preserved in ancient histories. Conversely, many of the important data of astronomy—for instance, the invariability of the length of the day, and the periods of several comets, rest upon ancient historical notices. Of late years, physiologists, especially Brücke, have actually undertaken to draw up a complete system of all the vocables that can be produced by the organs of speech, and to base upon it propositions for a universal alphabet, adapted to all human languages. Thus physiology has entered the service of comparative philology, and has already succeeded in accounting for many apparently anomalous substitutions, on the ground that they are governed, not as hitherto supposed, by the laws of euphony, but by similarity between the movements of the mouth that produce them. Again, comparative philology gives us information about the relationships, the separations, and the migrations of tribes in prehistoric times, and of the degree of civilization which they had reached at the time when they parted. For the names of objects to which they had already learnt to give distinctive appellations reappear as words common to their later languages. So that the study of languages actually gives us historical data for periods respecting which no other historical evidence exists. Yet again I may notice the help which not only the sculptor, but the archaeologist, concerned with the investigation of ancient statues, derives from anatomy. And if I may be permitted to refer to my own most recent studies, I would mention that it is possible, by reference to physical acoustics and to the physiological theory of the sensation of hearing, to account for the elementary principles on which our musical system is constructed, a problem essentially within the sphere of aesthetics. In fact, it is a general principle that the physiology of the organs of sense is most intimately connected with psychology, inasmuch as physiology traces in our sensations the results of mental processes which do not fall within the sphere of consciousness, and must therefore have remained inaccessible to us.

I have been able to quote only some of the most striking instances of this interdependence of different sciences, and such as could be explained in a few words. Naturally, too, I have tried to choose them from the most widely separated sciences. But far wider is of course the influence which allied sciences exert upon each other.

[158]

HELVÉTIUS, CLAUDE ADRIEN

HELVÉTIUS, CLAUDE ADRIEN (1715-1771). Many moralists of many ages have complained that personal interest in the pursuit of happiness is the only efficient principle of human actions. The awareness of this fact has made some of them melancholy, others resigned to that fate, and still others fundamentally pessimistic, or indignant, or hypocritical. There has been no lack of efforts to deny such statements or to change the character of man if the statement were true. Helvétius, contrary to all of these critics of egoism, was the first to draw an optimistic conclusion from the conviction that personal interest was the real rule of human behavior. His book De l'Esprit (On the Mind, 1758), in which Helvétius explained his views and founded them upon Condillac's sensualism, was condemned by the Sorbonne and burned in Paris after the judges had declared it dangerous to state and society.

Helvétius was a clever financier by profession. He used his

large income for the promotion of literature, philosophy and social welfare. He was one of the first to insist on taking the social
environment and economic conditions into consideration before sen-
tencing a defendant. Not this demand but other suggestions advanced by Helvétius were later realized by the legislation of the
First French Republic and by Napoleon.

Helvétius' book *On the Mind* was studied by Bentham and,
through him, influenced British utilitarianism.

OF THE ERRORS OCCASIONED BY PASSION

THE passions lead us into error because they fix our attention to that particular part of the object they present to us,
not allowing us to view it on every side. A king passionately
affects the title of Conqueror. Victory, says he, calls me to
the remotest part of the earth: I shall fight; I shall gain the
victory; I shall load mine enemy with chains, and the terror
of my name, like an impenetrable rampart, will defend the
entrance of my empire. Inebriated with this hope, he forgets
that fortune is inconstant; and, that the victor shares the
load of misery almost equally with the vanquished. He does
not perceive, that the welfare of his subjects is only a pretence for his martial frenzy; and that pride alone forges
his arms, and displays his ensigns: his whole attention is
fixed on the pomp of the triumph.

Fear, equally powerful with pride, will produce the
same effect; it will raise ghosts and phantoms, and disperse
them among the tombs, and in the darkness of the woods,
present them to the eyes of the affrighted traveler, seize on
all the faculties of his soul, without leaving any one at liberty to reflect on the absurdity of the motives for such a
ridiculous terror.

The passions not only fix the attention on the particular
sides of the objects they present to us; but they also deceive
us, by exhibiting the same objects, when they do not really exist. The story of a country clergyman and an amorous lady is
well known. They had heard, and concluded, that the moon
was peopled, and were looking for the inhabitants through
their telescopes. If I am not mistaken, said the lady, I per-

ceive two shadows; they mutually incline towards each other: doubtless they are two happy lovers.—O fie! madam, replied the clergyman, these two shadows are the two steeples of a cathedral. This tale is our history, it being common for us to see in things what we are desirous of finding there: on the earth, as in the moon, different passions will cause us to see either lovers or steeples. Illusion is a necessary effect of the passions, the strength of force of which is generally measured by the degree of obscurity into which they lead us. This was well known to a certain lady, who being caught by her lover in the arms of his rival, obstinately denied the fact of which he had been a witness. How! said he, have you the assurance—Ah! perfidious creature, cried the lady, it is plain you no longer love me; for you believe your eyes, before all I can say. This is equally applicable to all the passions, as well as to love. All strike us with the most perfect blindness. When ambition has kindled a war between two nations, and the anxious citizens ask one another the news, what readiness appears, on one side, to give credit to the good; and, on the other, what incredulity with regard to the bad? How often have christians, from placing a ridiculous confidence in monks, denied the possibility of the antipodes. There is no century which has not, by some ridiculous affirmation or negation, afforded matter of laughter to the following age. A past folly is seldom sufficient to show mankind their present folly.

The same passions, however, which are the germ of an infinity of errors, are also the sources of our knowledge. If they mislead us, they, at the same time, impart to us the strength necessary for walking. It is they alone that can rouse us from that sluggishness and torpor always ready to seize on the faculties of our soul.

[159]

HERACLITUS

HERACLITUS (about 540-480 B.C.). One of the most vigorous thinkers of Greek antiquity, proud and independent, Heraclitus

494

stated with utter candor his opinion of his fellow citizens of Ephesus: They ought to go and hang themselves and hand over the city to juveniles, having expelled Hermodoros, the best among them. So disgusted was he with political intrigue and the wrangles of small minds, that he left the city and sought solace and inspiration in the beauty and grandeur of nature. But for the Ephesians he had a strange wish: Would that their wealth never decline so that their worthlessness might appear to even better advantage!

Himself of noble birth, he disdained the masses. His admirer, Nietzsche, would have concurred in this: "One man to me is worth as much as 10,000, provided he be the best." The masses, he believed, cannot comprehend the divine nature. Indeed, they could not follow Heraclitus in the flight of his spirit, and thus they called him the Dark Philosopher.

From his spiritual height he flayed their idolatry and base thinking, and aligned himself with fate and a divine being for whom all is beautiful, good and just. The world, not created in time but existing from all eternity, he considered as ever in flux, and war as the father of all things. There is a cycle, however, from the eternal fire through want to the manifold of things, and back again through satedness, harmony and peace. Everything is relative—the most beautiful ape is ugly compared to man; illness makes health sweet, evil the good . . . Contentment is achieved by submission to order, reason and wisdom. The soul, a spark of the substance of the stars, is immortal and returns upon death to the all-soul to which it is related.

FRAGMENTS

IT is wise to hearken not to me but my argument, and to confess that all things are one.

Though this discourse is true evermore, yet men are as unable to understand it when they hear it for the first time as before they have heard it at all. For, although all things happen in accordance with the account I give, men seem as if they had no experience of them, when they make trial of words and works such as I set forth, dividing each thing according to its nature and explaining how it truly is. But other men know not what they are doing when you wake them up, just as they forget what they do when asleep.

Fools when they do hear are like the deaf; of them

does the proverb bear witness that they are absent when present.

Eyes and ears are bad witnesses to men, if they have souls that understand not their language.

The many have not as many thoughts as the things they meet with; nor, if they do remark them, do they understand them, though they believe they do.

Knowing not how to listen nor how to speak.

If you do not expect the unexpected, you will not find it; for it is hard to be sought out and difficult.

Those who seek for gold dig up much earth and find a little.

Nature loves to hide.

The lord whose is the oracle at Delphi neither utters nor hides his meaning, but shows it by a sign.

And the Sibyl, with raving lips uttering things solemn, unadorned, and unembellished, reaches over a thousand years with her voice because of the god in her.

Am I to prize these things above what can be seen, heard, and learned?

. . . bringing untrustworthy witnesses in support of disputed points.

The eyes are more exact witnesses than the ears.

The learning of many things teacheth not understanding, else would it have taught Hesiod and Pythagoras, and again Xenophanes and Hekataios.

Pythagoras, son of Mnesarchos, practised inquiry beyond all other men, and made himself a wisdom of his own, which was but a knowledge of many things and an art of mischief.

Of all whose discourses I have heard, there is not one who attains to understanding that wisdom is apart from other things.

Wisdom is one thing. It is to know the thought by which all things are steered through all things.

This order, which is the same in all things, no one of gods or men has made; but it was ever, is now, and ever shall be everliving Fire, fixed measures of it kindling and fixed measures going out.

The transformations of Fire are, first of all, sea (and half of the sea is earth, half fiery storm-cloud). . . .

All things are exchanged for Fire, and Fire for all things, as wares are exchanged for gold and gold for wares.

(The earth) is liquified, and the sea is measured by the same tale as before it became earth.

Fire is want and satiety.

Fire lives the death of earth, and air lives the death of fire; water lives the death of air, earth that of water.

Fire will come upon and lay hold of all things.

How can one hide from that which never sinks to rest?

It is the thunderbolt that steers the course of all things.

The sun will not exceed his measures; if he does, the Erinyes, the avenging handmaids of Justice, will find him out.

The limit of East and West is the Bear; and opposite the Bear is the boundary of bright Zeus.

If there were no sun, it would be night.

The sun is new every day.

The seasons that bring all things.

Hesiod is most men's teacher. Men think he knew very many things, a man who did not know day or night! They are one.

God is day and night, winter and summer, war and peace, satiety and hunger; but He takes various shapes, just as fire, when it is mingled with different incenses, is named according to the savour of each.

If all things were turned to smoke, the nostrils would distinguish them.

Souls smell in Hades.

It is cold things that become warm, and what is warm that cools; what is wet dries, and the parched is moistened.

It scatters things and brings them together; it approaches and departs.

You cannot step twice into the same rivers; for fresh waters are ever flowing in upon you.

Homer was wrong in saying: "Would that strife might perish from among gods and men!" He did not see that he was praying for the destruction of the universe; for, if his prayer were heard, all things would pass away.

War is the father of all and the king of all; and some he has made gods and some men, some bond and some free.

Men do not know how that which is drawn in different directions harmonises with itself. The harmonious structure of the world depends upon opposite tension, like that of the bow and the lyre.

It is opposition that brings things together.

The hidden harmony is better than the open.

Let us not conjecture at random about the greatest things.

Men who love wisdom must be acquainted with very many things indeed.

The straight and the crooked path of the fuller's comb is one and the same.

Asses would rather have straw than gold.

Oxen are happy when they find bitter vetches to eat.

The sea is the purest and the impurest water. Fish can drink it, and it is good for them; to men it is undrinkable and destructive.

Swine like to wash in the mire rather than in clean water, and barnyard fowls in dust.

Every beast is tended with blows.

Good and ill are the same.

Physicians who cut, burn, stab, and rack the sick, then complain that they do not get any adequate recompense for it.

You must couple together things whole and things not whole, what is drawn together and what is drawn asunder, the harmonious and the discordant. The one is made up of all things, and all things issue from the one.

Men would not have known the name of justice if there were no injustice.

Men themselves have made a law for themselves, not knowing what they made it about; but the gods have ordered the nature of all things. Now the arrangements which men have made are never constant, neither when they are right nor when they are wrong; but all the arrangements which the gods have made are always right, both when they are right and when they are wrong; so great is the difference.

We must know that war is the common and justice is strife, and that all things come into being and pass away(?) through strife.

... for they are undoubtedly allotted by destiny.

All the things we see when awake are death, even as the things we see in slumber are sleep.

Wisdom is one only. It is willing and unwilling to be called by the name of Zeus.

The bow (bios') is called life (bi'os), but its work is death.

Mortals are immortals and immortals are mortals, the one living the other's death and dying the other's life.

For it is death to souls to become water, and death to water to become earth. But water comes from earth; and from water, soul.

The way up and the way down is one and the same.

The beginning and the end are common (to both paths).

You will not find the boundaries of soul by travelling in any direction.

It is pleasure to souls to become moist.

A man, when he gets drunk, is led by a beardless lad, knowing not where he steps, having his soul moist.

The dry soul is the wisest and best.

Man is kindled and put out like a light in the night-time.

The quick and the dead, the waking and the sleeping, the young and the old are the same; the former are changed and become the latter, and the latter in turn are changed into the former.

Time is a child playing draughts, the kingly power is a child's.

I have sought to know myself.

We step and do not step into the same rivers; we are and are not.

It is a weariness to labor at the same things and to be always beginning afresh.

It finds rest in change.

Even the ingredients of a posset separate if it is not stirred.

Corpses are more fit to be cast out than dung.

When they are born, they wish to live and to meet with their dooms—or rather to rest, and they leave children behind them to meet with dooms in turn.

A man may be a grandfather in thirty years.

Those who are asleep are fellow-workers. . . .

Wisdom is common to all things. Those who speak with intelligence must hold fast to the common as a city holds fast to its law, and even more strongly. For all human laws are fed by one thing, the divine. It prevails as much as it will, and suffices for all things with something to spare.

Though wisdom is common, yet the many live as if they had a wisdom of their own.

They are estranged from that with which they have most constant intercourse.

It is not meet to eat and speak like men asleep.

The waking have one and the same world, but the sleeping turn aside each into a world of his own.

The way of man has no wisdom, but that of the gods has.

Man is called a baby by God, even as a child by a man.

The wisest man is an ape compared to God, just as the most beautiful ape is ugly compared to man.

The people must fight for its law as for its walls.

Greater deaths win greater portions.

Gods and men honor those who are slain in battle.

Wantonness needs to be extinguished even more than a conflagration.

It is not good for men to get all they wish to get. It is disease that makes health pleasant and good; hunger, plenty; and weariness, rest.

It is hard to fight with desire. Whatever it wishes to get, it purchases at the cost of soul.

It is best to hide folly; but it is a hard task in times of relaxation, over our cups.

And it is the law, too, that we obey the counsel of one.

For what thought or wisdom have they? They follow the poets and take the crowd as their teacher, knowing not that there are many bad and few good. For even the best of them choose one thing above all others, immortal glory among mortals, while most of them fill their bellies like beasts.

In Priene lived Bias, son of Teutamas, who is of more account than the rest. (He said, "Most men are bad.")

One is as ten thousand to me, if he be the best.

The Ephesians would do well to hang themselves, every grown man of them, and leave the city to beardless youths; for they have cast out Hermodoros, the best man among them, saying: "We will have none who is best among us; if there be any such, let him be so elsewhere and among others."

Dogs bark at every one they do not know.

. . . (The wise man) is not known because of men's want of belief.

The fool is fluttered at every word.

The most esteemed of those in estimation knows how to feign; yet of a truth justice shall overtake the artificers of lies and the false witnesses.

Homer should be turned out of the lists and whipped, and Archilochos likewise.

One day is equal to another.

Man's character is his fate.

There await men when they die such things as they look not for nor dream of.

. . . that they rise up and become the guardians of the hosts of the quick and dead.

Night-walkers, Magians, priests of Bakchos and priestesses of the wine-vat, mystery-mongers. . . .

The mysteries into which men are initiated are unholy.

And they pray to these images, as if one were to talk with a man's house, knowing not what gods or heroes are.

For if it were not to Dionysos that they made a procession and sang the shameful phallic hymn, they would be acting most shamelessly. But Hades is the same as Dionysos in whose honor they go mad and keep the feast of the wine-vat.

They purify themselves by defiling themselves with blood, just as if one who had stepped into the mud were to go and wash his feet in mud.

[160]

HERBART, JOHANN FRIEDRICH

HERBART, JOHANN FRIEDRICH (1776-1841). American thinking was influenced by Herbart during the two decades which preceded the First World War. But even those who declined to follow him thereafter could not but acknowledge that Herbart was a pioneer in psychological research and pedagogics.

Herbart, who occupied Immanuel Kant's chair at the University of Königsberg for many years, was regarded by Fichte, Schelling and Hegel as their most formidable adversary. In some regards, Herbart maintained the Kantian tradition but more often he relied upon Leibniz, Hume and British associationism. He was an excellent musician, a master of the piano, the violin, the violoncello and the harp, and liked to explain psychological laws by examples taken from the theory of harmony.

Contrary to Fichte, Schelling and Hegel, Herbart always took great care to tally his thoughts with the results of the empirical sciences. To him, philosophy was the reflection upon the conceptions which are commonly used in experience, both daily and scientific. The philosopher must ask what is it that in reality corresponds to the empirical conceptions which are called substance and causality. While German idealists proceeded from the individual knower, the subject, to the metaphysics of nature and mind, Herbart regarded the subject as the highest metaphysical problem. At the same time, the subject was known to him as the changing product of ideas, and, therefore, was explorable by means of psychological research. Psychology, to Herbart, was founded upon experience, metaphysics and mathematics. He followed Locke and Hume by trying to conceive complex psychic phenomena in terms of simple ideas, each of which was supposed to have a certain degree of strength. His great dream was a future psychodynamics determined by mathematical laws.

CHIEF CLASSES OF INTEREST

INSTRUCTION must be joined to the knowledge furnished by experience, and to the disposition which is nourished by intercourse. Experience corresponds immediately with empirical, intercourse with sympathetic, interest. Progressive thought about the objects of experience develops speculative interest,—thought about the more complex relationships of intercourse develops social interest. To these we add on the one side aesthetic, on the other religious, interest. Both have their origin not so much in progressive thought, as in a quiet contemplation of things and their destiny.

It must not be expected that all these various kinds of interest will develop equally in each individual, but on the other hand we may expect to find them all more or less amongst a number of pupils. The required many-sidedness will be more perfectly attained, the more closely each individual approaches the standard of mental culture in which all these interests are aroused with equal energy.

That these six classes of interest naturally fall into two groups, has been already indicated when pointing out the historical and scientific divisions. This tallies with what has been generally observed in the Gymnasia (classical schools), that the pupils generally show a leaning either to the one side or the other. But it would be a great mistake to put for this reason, the historic interest in opposition to the scientific, or even to substitute in the place of these two the philological and mathematical, as is often done. This confusion of ideas must not be continued, otherwise entirely wrong views on instruction will be the result. This erroneousness will be most easily demonstrated, by a consideration of the many varieties of one-sidedness already occurring even *within* the two classes mentioned. In this way, at least, the many varieties it is necessary to distinguish here, will become more clearly separated. For the possible one-sided varieties of interest are much more widely differentiated from each other, than could be indicated by the previous six-fold classification.

Empirical interest will be in its way one-sided, if a certain class of objects of experience are dwelt on to the exclusion of others. So it will be, for instance, if a man desires to be a botanist only, or a mineralogist, or zoologist; or if he only cares for languages, perhaps only dead or only modern languages, or even but for one; or again, if a traveller (like many so-called tourists) only wishes to see certain celebrated districts during his journey, in order to be able to say he has seen them; or again, if as a collector he has only this or that particular hobby; or if as an historian he only cares for the annals of one country and one parish, and so on.

Speculative interest will be in its way one-sided, if it deals only with logic or mathematics, possibly with merely a branch of the latter, such as the geometry of the ancients,— or with metaphysics only, which again may be limited to the views of one school,—or with physics only, perhaps limited to the establishment of one hypothesis,—or finally, with pragmatic history alone.

Aesthetic interest tends to confine itself exclusively to painting or sculpture or poetry—perhaps the latter only of a lyric or dramatic class; or to music, or even only to a variety thereof, etc., etc.

Sympathetic interest will become one-sided, if an individual only cares to live with people of his own class, or with his compatriots, or only with members of his own family, and has no feeling for any others.

Social interest becomes one-sided, when a man is entirely devoted to his own political party, and measures all weal and woe by its interests alone.

Religious interest becomes one-sided, when it leads a man to adhere to certain sects and dogmas, and to despise those who think otherwise.

Many of these species of one-sidedness are brought about in later life, by the individual's vocation, but it ought not to isolate the man. It would certainly do so if such narrowness ruled him in earlier years.

It would be possible to analyze one-sided tendencies still further, but this is not necessary in order to determine what place the studies in the Gymnasia referred to, occupy amongst the subjects that serve to animate interest. Languages are the first on the list, as we know from experience, but why is the preference among so many given to Latin and Greek? Clearly because of their literature and history. Literature with the poets and orators belongs to aesthetic interest, history awakens sympathy for excellent men and for social weal and woe; through both channels it has a direct influence in developing religious interest. No better centre of unity for so many various stimuli can be found. Even speculative interest is not neglected, when the grammatical construction of these languages is added. But history does not stand still with the ancients; literary knowledge also widens, and aids in animating still more completely the interests before mentioned. The pragmatic treatment of history assists speculative interest from another side. In this respect however, mathematics have the preference, only, in order to gain a firmer footing and permanent influence, they must be combined with the natural sciences which arouse both empiric and speculative interest.

Now if these studies *co-operate* thoroughly, they achieve, conjoined with religious instruction, a good deal towards guiding the young mind in the direction conducive to many-sided interest. But were philology and mathematics to be separated, the connecting links removed, and every individual be left the choice of one or the other according to his own preference, the result would then show specimens of pure one-sidedness such as have been sufficiently characterized in the preceding remarks.

It is generally admitted now that the higher citizens' schools ought to introduce just this same many-sided education,—that is to say, they should make use of the very same main classes of interest as the Gymnasia, etc. The only difference is, that the pupils of the Gymnasia begin the exercise of their future calling later than do those of the citizens' schools. Consequently modern literature and history receive more consideration in the latter, and to those who are capable of going beyond these subjects, the higher ones necessary to complex mental activity can be given, but not *quite so fully* as in the Gymnasia. The same applies to all those lower schools which give a general education. It is different with technical schools and polytechnics, in short with such as presuppose that education is already finished, at least in so far as circumstances will allow.

Accordingly when a higher citizens' school has a correct curriculum, it will be seen from it, just as from that of a Gymnasium, that an attempt has been made, through that curriculum, to avoid the *extreme* one-sidedness which results if one only of the *six main classes of interest* be disregarded.

But no instruction whatever is able to avoid those special one-sidednesses which occur within each main class. When once observation, reflection, taste for the beautiful, sympathy, social instincts, and religious feeling have been called into activity, though but in a narrow circle of subjects, it is chiefly left to the individual and opportunity to initiate further expansion, including a greater number and variety of subjects. To talented individuals, still more to geniuses, sufficient breadth of view may be given by instruction, to show them what has been done before by others of talent and genius; their idiosyncrasies however they must retain, and be responsible for themselves.

Nor are all these subordinate one-sided tendencies equally disadvantageous, for not all assert themselves exclusively to the same extent. Although all of them may be-

506

come arrogant, yet they are not all equally liable to do so.

Under favorable conditions as regards time and opportunity, such as Gymnasia and higher citizens' schools have, the aim of instruction is not as is well known restricted to merely first efforts. The question then comes up, in what sequence should the interests which have been aroused be cultivated further? There is no lack of teaching matter; it is necessary to choose and systematize. For this purpose we must apply in general what has been said regarding the conditions of manysidedness and of interest. These conditions are, to proceed from the simple to the complex, and to provide suitable opportunities for the exercise of involuntary apperceptive attention. It is useless however to deceive ourselves about the difficulties and all that is required to carry this out.

Empirical subject-matter (in languages, history, geography, etc.) requires certain complications and series of presentations, together with their interconnections. To start with, the mere words consist of roots and those particles that pertain to modification and derivation, and these again of single articulate sounds. History has its periods in time, and geography its interconnections in space. The psychological laws of reproduction determine the acts of learning by memory, and of memory itself.

The mother-tongue serves as medium for the comprehension of foreign languages, but at the same time the child's mind struggles against foreign sounds and idioms. Besides this, a younger boy takes a long while to get accustomed to the idea, that at a remote time and place there were, and still are, human beings who speak and have spoken differently to himself—human beings who concern us here and now. The illusion also of many masters is very common and injurious, that because their expression (language) is clear, it must therefore be comprehended by the boy, whose child's language only grows slowly. These clogging influences can be overcome. Geography helps with respect to spatial distances, though the visible presentation of mountains is wanting to the inhabitants of a flat country, and that of plains to one who lives in a valley, and again of the sea to the majority of people. That the earth is a ball and turns on its axis, and revolves round the sun, sounds to children for a long time like a fairy-tale, and there are cultivated youths who doubt the theory of the planetary system, because they do not comprehend how it can be known. Such obstructions must be got rid of, and not multiplied unnecessarily. Old ruins might be made use of as a starting point for history, if they were not far too meagre and too near in time, when the young are to be introduced to Jewish, Greek and Roman antiquities. Recourse can only be had to stories to arouse a lively interest; these become the fulcrum of thought about a long vanished past, but the estimation of chronological distances leading up to our own time is still wanting, and can only be gradually realized by subsequent insertions.

Practice in thinking, and together with it, the animation of speculative interest, is stimulated by everything which reveals or even only suggests connection by general laws in nature, in human affairs, in the structure of languages, in religious teaching. But everywhere, even in the things most commonly used, in general arithmetic and grammar, the pupil is confronted by general concepts, judgments and conclusions. He remains however attached to the single, familiar, sensuous. The abstract is strange to him; even geometrical figures drawn for the eye are but individual concrete things to him, and he only recognizes their general import with difficulty. The general notion ought to drive the special example out of his thoughts, but *vice versa* the special instance comes to the front in the usual series of presentations, and of the generalization, little remains to the boy but the words with which it is designated. If he is to draw a conclusion, he loses sight of one premise in dealing with the other, and the teacher must continually begin again, and illustrate the concepts and connect them, and gradually bring the premises together. When the middle terms in the premises have at last been correctly united, the union is still at first incomplete; the very same syllogisms are often forgotten, and afterwards too frequently repetitions have to be avoided, lest interest be extinguished instead of animated.

It is advisable to allow much of what has already been arrived at through conclusions to be for a time forgotten, as this cannot be prevented, and to return to the principal points later *by different routes*. The first preliminary exercises attain their purpose, if they give a glimpse of the general as revealed in the particular, before the concepts become the subjects of formulae, and before the propositions are formed into series of conclusions. Association must be made between the first demonstrations of the generalization and the systematic teaching of its interconnection.

Manifold external interests and also excited emotions may be the causes of aesthetic contemplation. But it only takes place spontaneously, when the spirit is sufficiently tranquil, to enable it to perfectly comprehend the simultaneously beautiful, and to follow the successively beautiful with answering rhythm. Comprehensible objects must be offered, contemplation must not be forced; but inappropriate remarks and, still more, damage done to objects of aesthetic value to which respect is due must certainly be forbidden. Frequently imitation, even if at first but roughly done, in drawing, singing, and reading aloud, and later on in translating, is a sign of attracted attention; such imitation may be encouraged, but certainly not praised. The true enthusiasm which grows spontaneously in aesthetic culture, is easily spoiled by being over-stimulated. To overburden is injurious; works of art that belong to a higher stage of culture must not be drawn down to a lower, and opinions and art criticisms should not be forced upon pupils.

The interests of sympathy are still more dependent on intercourse and home life than the former interests are on experience. If children are frequently moved from place to place, their attachment cannot take root anywhere. Even the change of masters and school is injurious. The pupils make comparisons of their own; an authority which is not permanent counts for little; on the contrary, efforts to obtain freedom act against it. Instruction cannot do away with such evils, the less because it is itself constantly obliged to change its form, which causes the master to appear different. It is consequently all the more necessary that in giving historical instruction, such warmth and sympathy should be expressed as is due to the personalities and events in question. For this reason, which is so important for the whole of education, we should carefully avoid making history a mere chronological skeleton. Specially should this be observed in the earlier instruction in history, as on it mainly depends what impression history as a whole will make later on.

It is needless to add, how much religious instruction should make the children feel their dependence, and how just are our expectations that it will not leave their souls untouched. In all this, historical must be combined with religious instruction, otherwise religious doctrine will occupy an isolated position, and will run the danger of not duly influencing the teaching and learning in all other subjects.

[161]

HERDER, JOHANN GOTTFRIED

HERDER, JOHANN GOTTFRIED (1744-1803). It would not be incorrect to derive the growth, if not the origin, of modern German nationalism from Herder's writings. But it would not do justice to him to ignore his humanitarian cosmopolitanism. In fact, Slavic national feelings have been equally strengthened by Herder who spoke and wrote German but was a descendant from Germanized Lithuanians. More than once, Herder not only expressed his fondness of Slavic literature but protested against German oppression of the Baltic Slavs. He attributed a high value to nationality as a medium of human civilization. But he denied any claim to superiority.

To Herder, love of the historical past was a cultural force, a way to psychic renovation. He believed that acquaintance with the poetry of the Bible, with Homer, Shakespeare and medieval folk songs would refresh and enhance the sentiments of modern humanity. But he was an enthusiast of history because he was no less

510

an enthusiast of the future of civilization, and he was firmly convinced that humanitarian ideals were the manifestations of God's will. In his *Ideen zur Philosophie der Geschichte der Menschheit* (Ideas on the Philosophy of History of Humanity, 1784-91), Herder combined biological, ethnological and literary studies with the ideas of Spinoza, Leibniz, Shaftesbury, Montesquieu and Voltaire. His work began with the stars, among which earth is one of many others, and described the influence of climate, geography, customs and individual fates on the history of mankind. Change, growth, and development were of basic importance to Herder's image of the world.

Originally a disciple of Kant, Herder, in his later years, opposed his teacher, especially his ideas concerning the "depraved nature" of man, as a consequence of original sin. He also tried to refute Kant's Critiques.

MAN, A LINK BETWEEN TWO WORLDS

EVERY thing in nature is connected: one state pushes forward and prepares another. If then man be the last and highest link, closing the chain of terrestrial organization, he must begin the chain of a higher order of creatures as its lowest link, and is probably, therefore, the middle ring between two adjoining systems of the creation. He cannot pass into any other organization upon earth, without turning backwards, and wandering in a circle: for him to stand still is impossible; since no living power in the dominions of the most active goodness is at rest; thus there must be a step before him, close to him, yet as exalted above him, as he is preeminent over the brute, to whom he is at the same time nearly allied. This view of things, which is supported by all the laws of nature, alone gives us the key to the wonderful phenomenon of man, and at the same time to the only *philosophy* of his *history*. For thus,

I. The singular *inconsistency* of man's condition becomes clear. As an animal he tends to the earth, and is attached to it as his habitation: as a man he has within him the seeds of immortality, which require to be planted in another soil. As an animal he can satisfy his wants; and men that are contented with this feel themselves sufficiently happy here below: but they who seek a nobler destination find every thing around them imperfect and incomplete; what is most noble is never accomplished upon earth, what is most pure is seldom firm and durable: this theatre is but a place of exercise and trial for the powers of our hearts and minds. The history of the human species, with what it has attempted, and what has befallen it, the exertions it has made, and the revolutions it has undergone sufficiently proves this. Now and then a philosopher, a good man, arose, and scattered opinions, precepts, and actions on the flood of time: a few waves played in circles around them, but these the stream soon carried away and obliterated: the jewel of their noble purposes sunk to the bottom. Fools overpowered the councils of the wise; and spendthrifts inherited the treasures of wisdom collected by their forefathers. Far as the life of man here below is from being calculated for eternity, equally far is this incessantly revolving sphere from being a repository of permanent works of art, a garden of never-fading plants, a seat to be eternally inhabited. We come and go: every moment brings thousands into the world, and takes thousands out of it. The earth is an inn for travellers; a planet, on which birds of passage rest themselves, and from which they hasten away. The brute lives out his life; and, if his years be too few to attain higher ends, his inmost purpose is accomplished: his capacities exist, and he is what he was intended to be. Man alone is in contradiction with himself, and with the earth: for, being the most perfect of all creatures, his capacities are the farthest from being perfected, even when he attains the longest term of life before he quits the world. But the reason is evident: his state, being the last upon this earth, is the first in another sphere of existence, with respect to which he appears here as a child making his first essays. Thus he is the representative of two worlds at once; and hence the apparent duplicity of his essence.

II. Thus it becomes clear, what part must predominate in most men here below. The greater part of man is of the animal kind: he has brought into the world only a capacity for humanity, which must be first formed in him by diligence and labor. In how few is it rightly formed! and how slender and delicate is the divine plant even in the best! Throughout life the brute prevails over the man, and most permit it to sway them at pleasure. This incessantly drags man down, while the spirit ascends, while the heart pants after a freer sphere: and as the present appears more lively to a sensual creature than the remote, as the visible operates upon him more powerfully than the invisible, it is not difficult to conjecture, which way the balance will incline. Of how little pure delight, of how little pure knowledge and virtue, is man capable! And were he capable of more, to how little is he accustomed! The noblest compositions here below are debased by inferior propensities, as the voyage of life is perplexed by contrary winds; and the creator, mercifully strict, has mixed the two causes of disorder together, that one might correct the other, and that the germ of immortality might be more effectually fostered by tempests, than by gentle gales. A man who has experienced much has learned much: the careless and indolent knows not what is within him; and still less does he feel with conscious satisfaction how far his powers extend. Thus life is a conflict, and the garland of pure immortal humanity is with difficulty obtained. The goal is before the runner: by him who fights for virtue, in death the palm will be obtained.

III. Thus, if superior creatures look down upon us, they may view us in the same light as we do the *middle species*, with which nature makes a transition from one element to another. The ostrich flaps his feeble wings to assist himself in running, but they cannot enable him to fly: his heavy body confines him to the ground. Yet the organizing parent has taken care of him, as well as of every middle creature; for they are all perfect in themselves, and only appear defective to our eyes. It is the same with man here below: his defects are perplexing to an earthly mind; but a superior spirit, that inspects the internal structure, and sees more links of the chain, may indeed pity, but cannot despise him. He perceives why man must quit the world in so many different states, young and old, wise and foolish, grown gray in second childhood, or an embryo yet unborn. Omnipotent goodness embraces madness and deformity, all the degrees of cultivation, and all the errors of man, and wants not balsams to heal the wounds that death alone could mitigate. Since probably the future state springs out of the present, as our organization from inferior ones, its business is no doubt more closely connected with our existence here than we imagine. The garden above blooms only with plants, of which the seeds have been sown here, and put forth their first germs from a coarser husk. If, then, as we have seen, sociality, friendship, or active participation in the pains and pleasures of others, be the principal end, to which humanity is directed; this finest flower of human life must necessarily there attain the vivifying form, the overshadowing height, for which our heart thirsts in vain in any earthly situation. Our brethren above, therefore, assuredly love us with more warmth and purity of affection, than we can bear to them: for they see our state more clearly, to them the moment of time is no more, all discrepancies are harmonized, and in us they are probably educating, unseen, partners of their happiness and companions of their labors. But one step farther, and the oppressed spirit can breathe more freely, the wounded heart recovers: they see the passenger approach and stay his sliding feet with a powerful hand.

[162]

HESS, MOSES

HESS, MOSES (1812-1875). Hess, who assumed the first name Moses instead of Moritz in order to show his adherence to Judaism, provoked the indignation of his relatives by marrying a prostitute in order to show his contempt of the existing moral standards. He lived with her in happiness until his death. He was, however, a man who willingly obeyed those ethical demands that his thinking recognized as right. He was an early apostle of socialism, and a precursor of Zionism. Because of his participation in the revolution

514

of 1848, Hess was sentenced to death and on escaping had to wander through many countries of Europe before he found refuge in Paris.

In his youth, Hess abounded in ideas. His influence with Karl Marx was considerable. For a time they were closely associated. Later Marx felt himself superior to Hess, and made him smart for his previous ascendancy. Although Hess recognized the importance of economic and social forces, he conceived socialism as a prevalently humanitarian ideal, dissenting from Marx who regarded it as the inevitable result of economic evolution. It was also for the sake of humanity that Hess agitated for the establishment of a Jewish commonwealth in Palestine by publishing his book *Rome and Jerusalem* (1862) and numerous essays in which he expresses Messianic hopes. According to Hess, Judaism has no other dogma but "the teaching of the unity." As already shown by his *Holy Story of Humanity* (1837), he deviated from the Jewish conception of God and called the history of humanity holy because, in his opinion, it is really the history of God, then conceived by him partly in accordance with Spinoza, partly with the Christian doctrine of Trinity. In *European Triarchy* (1841) he outlined a new order of Europe which he claimed was in accordance with "human nature." His socialism is not strictly egalitarian but an effort to satisfy the wants of "human nature," which remained his principal standard of judging human institutions. In his later years he came closer to the views developed in Jewish traditions, but he built his hopes for the settlement of the Jews in the Holy Land upon France, which he regarded as the champion of liberty. After France's defeat in the war of 1870, he admonished the nations of Europe to ally with one another against German militarism.

ORGANIC LIFE

EVERY transformation of matter on behalf of the life of humanity means working, creating, producing, acting—in short, living. For, in reality, whatever is living is working. Concerning human life, not only head and hands but also all the other members and organs of the body work to transform the matter received from outside. The mouth works up the matter for the stomach, which, on its part, digests it for the blood, and so on. That means that every organ of the human body and every member of human society is producing, on behalf of the whole. Every man is working while apparently only consuming or enjoying, and he enjoys his life, while apparently working or producing for the whole. But the harmony between work and enjoyment takes place only in organic or organized life, not in a life that lacks organization.

[163]

HIYYA, ABRAHAM BAR

HIYYA, ABRAHAM BAR (About 1065-1136). While Christianity and Islam met each other on the battlefield, Abraham bar Hiyya, called by his fellow Jews "the prince," and by non-Jews "Savasorda" (Latinization of his Arabic title Sahib al Shurta, governor of a city), took a leading part in promoting spiritual interchange between the representatives of the Christian and Arabic civilizations, without neglecting his principal task, namely the vindication of the Jewish faith and its harmonization with science and philosophy.

His treatise on areas and measurements which introduced new scientific terms and new methods for the measurement of surfaces, was translated into Latin under the title *Liber Embadorum*, and, for centuries, it remained a standard work. His contributions to mathematics, astronomy, music and optics were highly appreciated by Jewish, Christian and Moslem scholars. In his *Hegyon Hanefesh* (Reflection on the Soul), Abraham bar Hiyya, while exposing his ideas on creation and the destiny and conduct of Man, showed a strong inclination to an ascetic conception of life.

THE LIFE OF THE PIOUS

THOSE people of the law who do not uphold the faith are not helped much by their learning.

Those separated unto God eat food they have, not to satisfy a desire for its good taste but to silence the pain of hunger, and they wrap themselves with any garment to protect the body against the cold without being concerned as to whether it is of wool or flax.

Any potentiality the actualization of which wisdom affirms must have already changed to actuality.

[164]

HOBBES, THOMAS

HOBBES, THOMAS (1588-1679). Born prematurely due to his mother's anxiety over the approach of the Spanish Armada, Hobbes had a streak of timidity in him which did not jibe with the philosophy propounded in his *Leviathan* and *Behemoth*. Influenced by the greatest thinkers of the times—among them Descartes, Gassendi and Galileo, whom he met on the Continent as tutor to Charles II and during an 11-year self-imposed, needless exile—Hobbes professed materialism, seeking to explain everything on mechanical principles. All knowledge comes by way of the senses, he held, and the objects of knowledge are material bodies obeying physical forces. Man too, in his natural state is "brutish and nasty." Realizing, that if man were to continue as wolf to man, chaos and destruction would result, men have, therefore, entered into a social contract, delegating the control of their fellow men to the state, which is governed and thus insures them a measure of security. In essence, therefore, the state and the kingship is a thing bargained for.

Uninfluenced by Francis Bacon, whose secretary he was for a time, "gaping on mappes" while supposed to be studying at Oxford, reading few books, getting himself into trouble with every publication because either conceptions or Parliament had changed, absorbed in mathematics for which he did not have the talent to make original contributions, and translating Homer and other Greeks, he attained the age of 89 complaining of having trouble keeping the flies "from pitching on the baldness" of his head. With consistency he had resisted the gains of the Renaissance as well as the resuscitation of scholasticism. His books were condemned by Parliament. Although the clergy hated him as an atheist, he nevertheless played safe by affiliating himself with a church and showing devoutness in the face of death.

STATE AND SOVEREIGNTY

THE final cause, end, or design of men, who naturally love liberty, and dominion over others, in the introduction of that restraint upon themselves, in which we see them live in commonwealths, is the foresight of their own preservation, and of a more contented life thereby; that is to say, of getting themselves out from that miserable condition of war, which is necessarily consequent . . . to the natural passions of men, when there is no visible power to keep them in awe, and tie them by fear of punishment to the performance of their covenants, and observation of those laws of nature set down in the fourteenth and fifteenth chapters.

For the laws of nature, as "justice," "equity," "modesty," "mercy," and, in sum, "doing to others as we would be done to," of themselves, without the terror of some power to cause them to be observed, are contrary to our natural passions, that carry us to partiality, pride, revenge, and the like. And covenants, without the sword, are but words and of no strength to secure a man at all. Therefore notwithstanding the laws of nature which every one hath then kept, when he has the will to keep them, when he can do it safely, if there be no power erected, or not great enough for our security, every man will and may lawfully rely on his own strength and art, for caution against all other men. And in all places where men have lived by small families, to rob and spoil one another has been a trade, and so far from being reputed against the law of nature, that the greater spoils they gained, the greater was their honor; and men observed no other laws, therein, but the laws of honor; that is, to abstain from cruelty, leaving to men their lives, and instruments of husbandry. And as small families did then, so now do cities and kingdoms, which are but greater families, for their own security, enlarge their dominions, upon all pretences of danger, and fear of invasion, or assistance that may be given to invaders, and endeavor as much as they can to subdue or weaken their neighbors, by open force and secret arts, for want of other caution, justly; and are remembered for it in after ages with honor.

Nor is it the joining together of a small number of men that gives them this security; because in small numbers, small additions on the one side or the other make the advantage of strength so great as is sufficient to carry the victory; and therefore gives encouragement to an invasion. The multitude sufficient to confide in for our security is not determined by any certain number, but by comparison with the enemy we fear; and is then sufficient, when the odds of the enemy is not of so visible and conspicuous moment to determine the event of war, as to move him to attempt.

And be there never so great a multitude; yet if their actions be directed according to their particular judgments and particular appetites, they can expect thereby no defence, nor protection, neither against a common enemy, nor against the injuries of one another. For being distracted in opinions concerning the best use and application of their strength, they do not help but hinder one another; and reduce their strength by mutual opposition to nothing: whereby they are easily, not only subdued by a very few that agree together; but also when there is no common enemy, they make war upon each other, for their particular interests. For if we could suppose a great multitude of men to consent in the observation of justice, and other laws of nature, without a common power to keep them all in awe, we might as well suppose all mankind to do the same; and then there neither would be nor need to be any civil government or commonwealth at all; because there would be peace without subjection.

Nor is it enough for the security, which men desire should last all the time of their life, that they be governed and directed by one judgment, for a limited time: as in one battle, or one war. For though they obtain a victory by their unanimous endeavor against a foreign enemy; yet afterwards, when either they have no common enemy, or he that by one part is held for an enemy is by another part held for a friend, they must needs by the difference of their interests dissolve, and fall again into a war amongst themselves.

It is true that certain living creatures, as bees and ants, live sociably one with another, which are therefore by Aristotle numbered amongst political creatures; and yet have no other direction than their particular judgments and appetites; nor speech, whereby one of them can signify to another what he thinks expedient for the common benefit: and therefore some man may perhaps desire to know why mankind cannot do the same. To which I answer,

First, that men are continually in competition for honor and dignity, which these creatures are not; and consequently amongst men there ariseth on that ground, envy and hatred, and finally war; but amongst these not so.

Secondly, that amongst these creatures, the common good differeth not from the private; and being by nature inclined to their private, they procure thereby the common benefit. But man, whose joy consisteth in comparing himself with other men, can relish nothing but what is eminent.

Thirdly, that these creatures, having not, as man, the use of reason, do not see, nor think they see any fault in the administration of their common business; whereas amongst men there are very many that think themselves wiser and abler to govern the public better than the rest; and these strive to reform and innovate, one this way, another that way, and thereby bring it into distraction and civil war.

Fourthly, that these creatures, though they have some use of voice, in making known to one another their desires and other affections; yet they want that art of words by which some men can represent to others that which is good in the likeness of evil, and evil in the likeness of good, and augment or diminish the apparent greatness of good and evil; discontenting men, and troubling their peace at their pleasure.

Fifthly, irrational creatures cannot distinguish between injury and damage; and therefore as long as they be at ease, they are not offended with their fellows: whereas man is then most troublesome when he is most at ease; for then it is that he loves to show his wisdom, and control the actions of them that govern the commonwealth.

Lastly, the agreement of these creatures is natural; that of men is by covenant only, which is artificial: and therefore it is no wonder if there be somewhat else required, besides covenant, to make their agreement constant and lasting; which is a common power, to keep them in awe, and to direct their actions to the common benefit.

The only way to erect such a common power as may be able to defend them from the invasion of foreigners and the injuries of one another, and thereby to secure them in such sort as that by their own industry, and by the fruits of the earth, they may nourish themselves and live contentedly, is to confer all their power and strength upon one man, or upon one assembly of men, that may reduce all their wills, by plurality of voices, unto one will: which is as much as to say, to appoint one man, or assembly of men, to bear their person; and every one to own and acknowledge himself to be author of whatsoever he that so beareth their person shall act, or cause to be acted, in those things which concern the common peace and safety; and therein to submit their wills, every one to his will, and their judgments to his judgment. This is more than consent, or concord; it is a real unity of them all in one and the same person, made by covenant of every man with every man, in such manner as if every man should say to every man, "I authorize and give up my right of governing myself, to this man or to this assembly of men, on this condition, that thou give up thy right to him and authorize all his actions in like manner." This done, the multitude so united in one person is called a "common-wealth," in Latin *civitas*. This is the generation of that great leviathan, or rather, to speak more reverently, of that mortal god, to which we owe under the immortal God, our peace and defence. For by this authority, given him by every particular man in the commonwealth, he hath the use of so much power and strength conferred on him, that by terror thereof, he is enabled to perform the wills of them all, to peace at home, and mutual aid against their enemies abroad. And in him consisteth the essence of the commonwealth; which, to define it, is "one person, of whose acts a great multitude, by mutual covenants one with another, have made themselves every one the author, to the end he may use the strength and means of them all, as he shall think expedient, for their peace and common defence."

And he that carrieth this person is called sovereign, and

said to have sovereign power; and every one besides, his subject.

The attaining to this sovereign power is by two ways. One, by natural force; as when a man maketh his children to submit themselves, and their children, to his government, as being able to destroy them if they refuse; or by war subdueth his enemies to his will, giving them their lives on that condition. The other is when men agree amongst themselves to submit to some man, or assembly of men, voluntarily, on confidence to be protected by him against all others. This latter may be called a political commonwealth, or commonwealth by institution; and the former, a commonwealth by acquisition.

*   *   *

A commonwealth is said to be instituted when a multitude of men do agree and covenant, every one with every one, that to whatsoever man or assembly of men shall be given by the major part the right to present the person of them all, that is to say, to be their representative; every one, as well he that voted for it as he that voted against it, shall authorize all the actions and judgments of that man or assembly of men in the same manner as if they were his own, to the end to live peaceably amongst themselves and be protected against other men.

From this institution of a commonwealth are derived all the rights and faculties of him, or them, on whom sovereign power is conferred by the consent of the people assembled.

First, because they covenant, it is to be understood, they are not obliged by former covenant to anything repugnant hereunto. And consequently that they have already instituted a commonwealth, being thereby bound by covenant to own the actions and judgments of one, cannot lawfully make a new covenant amongst themselves, to be obedient to any other in any thing whatsoever, without his permission. And therefore, they that are subjects to a monarch, cannot without his

leave cast off monarchy, and return to the confusion of a
disunited multitude; nor transfer their person from him that
beareth it, to another man, or other assembly of men: for
they are bound, every man to every man, to own and be
reputed author of all that he that already is their sovereign
shall do, and judge fit to be done: so that any one man dissenting, all the rest should break their covenant made to that
man, which is injustice: and they have also every man given
the sovereignty to him that beareth their person; and therefore if they depose him, they take from him that which is his
own, and so again it is injustice. Besides, if he that attempteth
to depose his sovereign be killed, or punished by him for
such attempt, he is author of his own punishment, as being
by the institution author of all his sovereign shall do: and
because it is injustice for a man to do anything for which he
may be punished by his own authority, he is also upon that
title unjust. And whereas some men have pretended for
their disobedience to their sovereign, a new covenant, made
not with men, but with God, this also is unjust: for there
is no covenant with God but by meditation of somebody that
representeth God's person; which none doth but God's lieuten-
ant, who hath the sovereignty under God. But this pretence
of covenant with God is so evident a lie, even in the pre-
tenders' own consciences, that it is not only an act of an
unjust, but also of a vile and unmanly disposition.

Secondly, because the right of bearing the person of
them all is given to him they make sovereign, by covenant
only of one to another, and not of him to any of them, there
can happen no breach of covenant on the part of the sovereign: and consequently none of his subjects, by any pretence of forfeiture, can be freed from his subjection. That he
which is made sovereign maketh no covenant with his subjects beforehand, is manifest; because either he must make
it with the whole multitude, as one party to the covenant,
or he must make a several covenant with every man. With
the whole, as one party, it is impossible; because as yet
they are not one person; and if he make so many several

covenants as there be men, those covenants after he hath the sovereignty are void; because what act soever can be pretended by any one of them for breach thereof, is the act both of himself and of all the rest, because done in the person and by the right of every one of them in particular. Besides, if any one or more of them pretend a breach of the covenant made by the sovereign at his institution; and others, or one other of his subjects, or himself alone, pretend there was no such breach, there is in this case no judge to decide the controversy; it returns therefore to the sword again, and every man recovereth the right of protecting himself by his own strength, contrary to the design they had in the institution. It is therefore in vain to grant sovereignty by way of precedent covenant. The opinion that any monarch receiveth his power by covenant, that is to say, on condition, proceedeth from want of understanding this easy truth, that covenants being but words and breath, have no force to oblige, contain, constrain, or protect any man, but what they have from the public sword; that is, from the united hands of that man or assembly of men that hath the sovereignty, and whose actions are avouched by them all, and performed by the strength of them all, in him united. But when an assembly of men is made sovereign, then no man imagineth any such covenant to have passed in the institution; for no man is so dull as to say, for example, the people of Rome made a covenant with the Romans to hold the sovereignty on such or such conditions; which not performed, the Romans might lawfully depose the Roman people. That men see not the reason to be alike in a monarchy and in a popular government, proceedeth from the ambition of some that are kinder to the government of an assembly, whereof they may hope to participate, than of monarchy, which they despair to enjoy.

Thirdly, because the major part hath by consenting voices declared a sovereign, he that dissented must now consent with the rest, that is, be contented to avow all the actions he shall do, or else justly be destroyed by the rest.

For if he voluntarily entered into the congregation of them that were assembled, he sufficiently declared thereby his will, and therefore tacitly covenanted to stand to what the major part should ordain: and therefore if he refuse to stand thereto, or make protestation against any of their decrees, he does contrary to his covenant, and therefore unjustly. And whether he be of the congregation or not, and whether his consent be asked or not, he must either submit to their decrees, or be left in the condition of war he was in before; wherein he might without injustice be destroyed by any man whatsoever.

Fourthly, because every subject is by this institution author of all the actions and judgments of the sovereign instituted, it follows that whatsoever he doth it can be no injury to any of his subjects, nor ought he to be by any of them accused of injustice. For he that doth anything by authority from another doth therein no injury to him by whose authority he acteth: but by this institution of a commonwealth every particular man is author of all the sovereign doth; and consequently, he that complaineth of injury from his sovereign complaineth of that whereof he himself is author and therefore ought not to accuse any man but himself; no, nor himself of injury, because to do injury to one's self is impossible. It is true that they that have sovereign power may commit iniquity, but not injustice or injury in the proper signification.

Fifthly, and consequently to that which was said last, no man that hath sovereign power can justly be put to death, or otherwise in any manner by his subjects punished. For seeing every subject is author of the actions of his sovereign, he punisheth another for the actions committed by himself.

And because the end of this institution is the peace and defence of them all, and, whosoever has right to the end has right to the means, it belongeth of right to whatsoever man or assembly that hath the sovereignty to be judge both of the means of peace and defence, and also of the hindrances and disturbances of the same, and to do whatsoever he shall think necessary to be done, both beforehand, for the preserving of peace and security, by prevention of discord at home and hostility from abroad; and, when peace and security are lost, for the recovery of the same.

Sixthly, it is annexed to the sovereignty to be judge of what opinions and doctrines are averse and what conducting to peace; and consequently, on what occasions, how far, and what men are to be trusted withal, in speaking to, multitudes of people, and who shall examine the doctrines of all books before they be published. For the actions of men proceed from their opinions, and in the well governing of opinions consisteth the well governing of men's actions, in order to their peace and concord. And though in matter of doctrine nothing ought to be regarded but the truth; yet this is not repugnant to regulating the same by peace. For doctrine repugnant to peace can be no more true than peace and concord can be against the law of nature. It is true that in a commonwealth, where, by the negligence or unskilfulness of governors and teachers, false doctrines are by time generally received, the contrary truths may be generally offensive. Yet the most sudden and rough bursting in of a new truth that can be, does never break the peace, but only sometimes awake the war. For those men that are so remissly governed, that they dare take up arms to defend or introduce an opinion, are still in war; and their condition not peace, but only a cessation of arms for fear of one another; and they live, as it were, in the precincts of battle continually. It belongeth therefore to him that hath the sovereign power to be judge, or constitute all judges, of opinions and doctrines, as a thing necessary to peace, thereby to prevent discord and civil war.

Seventhly, is annexed to the sovereignty, the whole power of prescribing the rules whereby every man may know what goods he may enjoy and what actions he may do, without being molested by any of his fellow-subjects; and this is it men call "propriety." For before constitution of sovereign power, as hath already been shown, all men had right to all things, which necessarily causeth war: and therefore this propriety, being necessary to peace, and depending on sovereign power, is the act of that power, in order to the public peace. These rules of propriety, or *meum* and *tuum*, and of good, evil, lawful, and unlawful in the actions of subjects, are the civil laws; that is to say, the laws of each commonwealth in particular; though the name of civil law be now restrained to the ancient civil laws of the city of Rome, which being the head of a great part of the world, her laws at that time were in these parts the civil law.

Eighthly, is annexed to the sovereignty, the right of judicature, that is to say, of hearing and deciding all controversies which may arise concerning law, either civil or natural, or concerning fact. For without the decision of controversies, there is no protection of one subject against the injuries of another; the laws concerning *meum* and *tuum* are in vain, and to every man remaineth, from the natural and necessary appetite of his own conservation, the right of protecting himself by his private strength, which is the condition of war, and contrary to the end for which every commonwealth is instituted.

Ninthly, is annexed to the sovereignty, the right of making war and peace with other nations and commonwealths, that is to say, of judging when it is for the public good, and how great forces are to be assembled, armed, and paid for that end, and to levy money upon the subjects to defray the expenses thereof. For the power by which the people are to be defended consisteth in their armies, and the strength of an army, in the union of their strength under one command, which command the sovereign instituted, therefore hath; because the command of the "militia," without other institution, maketh him that hath it sovereign. And therefore whosoever is made general of an army, he that hath the sovereign power is always generalissimo.

Tenthly, is annexed to the sovereignty, the choosing of all counsellors, ministers, magistrates, and officers, both in peace and war. For seeing the sovereign is charged with the end, which is the common peace and defence, he is understood to have power to use such means as he shall think most fit for his discharge.

Eleventhly, to the sovereign is committed the power of rewarding with riches or honor, and of punishing with corporal or pecuniary punishment, or with ignominy, every subject according to the law he hath formerly made; or if there be no law made, according as he shall judge most to conduce to the encouraging of men to serve the commonwealth, or deterring of them from doing disservice to the same.

Lastly, considering what value men are naturally apt to set upon themselves, what respect they look for from others, and how little they value other men, from whence continually arise amongst them, emulation, quarrels, factions, and at last war, to the destroying of one another and diminution of their strength against a common enemy, it is necessary that there be laws of honor, and a public rate of the worth of such men as have deserved or are able to deserve well of the commonwealth; and that there be force in the hands of some or other, to put these laws in execution. But it hath already been shown that not only the whole "militia," or forces of the commonwealth, but also the judicature of all controversies, is annexed to the sovereignty. To the sovereign therefore it belongeth also to give titles of honor; and to appoint what order of place and dignity each man shall hold; and what signs of respect, in public or private meetings, they shall give to one another.

These are the rights which make the essence of sovereignty, and which are the marks whereby a man may discern in what man, or assembly of men, the sovereign power is placed and resideth. For these are incommunicable, and inseparable. The power to coin money, to dispose of the estate and persons of infant heirs, to have preemption in markets, and all other statute prerogatives, may be transferred by the sovereign, and yet the power to protect his subjects be retained. But if he transfer the "militia," he retains the judicature in vain, for want of execution of the laws: or if he grant away the power of raising money, the "militia" is in vain; or if he give away the government of doctrines, men will be frighted into rebellion with the fear of spirits. And so if we consider any one of the said rights, we shall presently see that the holding of all the rest will produce no effect in the conservation of peace and justice, the end for which all commonwealths are instituted. And this division is it whereof it is said, "a kingdom divided in itself cannot stand:" for unless this division precede, division into opposite armies can never happen. If there had not first been an opinion received of the greatest part of England that these powers were divided between the King, and the Lords, and the House of Commons, the people had never been divided and fallen into this civil war, first between those that disagreed in politics, and after between the dissenters about the liberty of religion; which have so instructed men in this point of sovereign right, that there be few now in England that do not see that these rights are inseparable, and will be so generally acknowledged at the next return of peace, and so continue, till their miseries are forgotten; and no longer, except the vulgar be better taught than they have hitherto been.

And because they are essential and inseparable rights, it follows necessarily that in whatsoever words any of them seem to be granted away, yet if the sovereign power itself be not in direct terms renounced, and the name of sovereign no more given by the grantees to him that grants them, the grant is void: for when he has granted all he can, if we grant back the sovereignty, all is restored, as inseparably annexed thereunto.

This great authority being indivisible and inseparably annexed to the sovereignty, there is little ground for the opinion of them that say of sovereign kings, though they be *singulis majores*, of greater power than every one of their subjects, yet they be *universis minores*, of less power than

529

them all together. For if by "all together" they mean not the collective body as one person, then "all together" and "every one" signify the same; and the speech is absurd. But if by "all together," they understand them as one person, which person the sovereign bears, then the power of all together is the same with the sovereign's power; and so again the speech is absurd: which absurdity they see well enough, when the sovereignty is in an assembly of the people; but in a monarch they see it not; and yet the power of sovereignty is the same in whomsoever it be placed.

And as the power, so also the honor of the sovereign, ought to be greater than that of any or all the subjects. For in the sovereignty is the fountain of honor. The dignities of lord, earl, duke, and prince are his creatures. As in the presence of the master the servants are equal, and without any honor at all; so are the subjects in the presence of the sovereign. And though they shine some more, some less, when they are out of his sight; yet in his presence, they shine no more than the stars in the presence of the sun.

But a man may here object that the condition of subjects is very miserable; as being obnoxious to the lusts, and other irregular passions of him or them that have so unlimited a power in their hands. And commonly they that live under a monarch, think it the fault of monarchy; and they that live under the government of democracy, or other sovereign assembly, attribute all the inconvenience to that form of commonwealth; whereas the power in all forms, if they be perfect enough to protect them, is the same: not considering that the state of man can never be without some incommodity or other; and that the greatest, that in any form of government can possibly happen to the people in general, is scarce sensible, in respect of the miseries and horrible calamities that accompany a civil war, or that dissolute condition of masterless men, without subjection to laws and a coercive power to tie their hands from rapine and revenge: nor considering that the greatest pressure of sovereign governors proceedeth not from any delight or profit they can expect in the damage or weakening of their subjects, in whose vigor consisteth their own strength and glory; but in the restiveness of themselves, that unwillingly contributing to their own defence, make it necessary for their governors to draw from them what they can in time of peace, that they may have means on any emergent occasion, or sudden need, to resist, or take advantage on their enemies. For all men are by nature provided of notable multiplying glasses, that is their passions and self-love, through which every little payment appeareth a great grievance; but are destitute of those prospective glasses, namely, moral and civil science, to see afar off the miseries that hang over them, and cannot without such payments be avoided.

[165]

HOCKING, WILLIAM ERNEST

HOCKING, WILLIAM ERNEST (1873-   ). The strength of Hocking's religious and philosophical convictions is rooted not only in his actual belief but also in the memory of his childhood. He grew up in a home where, according to him, "religious life was concrete, vivid and regulatory." If he has not really been influenced by such recollections, he nevertheless has reason to be satisfied with the fact that the development of his thinking has not involved conflict with his family traditions.

At first, Hocking intended to become a civil engineer. It was not an incident of external nature that prevented him from choosing this profession definitely, but rather his spiritual interests which were attracted at first by Herbert Spencer, then by Royce, and, decisively, by the study of German idealism. Hocking went to Germany, and attended lectures of almost all important philosophers in that country at that time, particularly Dilthey, Natorp, Husserl, Windelband and Rickert.

Hocking must be considered the outstanding recent defender of idealism in America. His allegiance to this way of thinking is strong enough to allow him occasional concessions to pragmatism, although he declares that it cannot supply idealism whatever the latter's deficiencies may be. Furthermore, Hocking is very critical toward the actual performances of idealism, which he has accused of having been incapable of finding the way "to worship, to the particular and historical in religion, to the authoritative and super-

531

personal." In many regards, Hocking seems to agree with Wilhelm Luetgert, a German critic of idealism; however, he does not abandon its cause. To him, idealism means "in name and truth the unlimited right of Idea in a world where nothing is ultimately irrational." While declaring that there is no inaccessible truth, no "unknowable," contrary to Spencer, he agrees with Santayana, but his idea of the possibility of perceiving and experiencing God is more intensively colored by mysticism even though he far from ignores the dangers and aberrations of mysticism.

AN ART PECULIAR TO MAN

USING the word art in the widest sense, as including all conscious efforts to remake the world, we may say that all animal behavior includes some degree of outwardly directed art. While life permits its world to shape it, it promotes thereby the artisanship by which it shapes the world.

There is but one exception, presumably, to the rule that the arts of animals are directed to the environment. The human being does deliberately undertake, while reshaping his outer world, to reshape himself also. In meeting unsatisfactory conditions,—scarcity of food, danger, etc.,—the simpler animal does what it can to change those conditions. The human being does likewise; but there sometimes occurs to him the additional reflection, "perhaps there should be some change in myself also." Scarcity of food may become to him an argument for greater foresight or industry, danger for more caution. If a beast is threatened, it may either fight or retreat: if a man is threatened, he may (while dealing with the facts) become a critic also of his own fear or anger.

Man thus becomes for himself an object of artful reconstruction, and this is an art peculiar to man. Whatever is done in the world by way of producing better human individuals, whether for the benefit of the species or for the ends of individuals themselves, man is an agent in it: it is done not merely to him but by him. He has become judge of his own nature and its possibilities. "Evolution" leaves its work in his hands—so far as he is concerned.

I do not say that man is the only creature that has a part in its own making. Every organism may be said (with due interpretation of terms) to build itself, to regenerate itself when injured, to recreate itself and, in striving for its numerous ends, to develop itself—to grow. It may be, as we were saying, an agent in evolution. But in all likelihood, it is only the human being that does these things with conscious intention, that examines and revises his mental as well as his physical self, and that proceeds according to a preformed idea of what this self should be. To be human is to be self-conscious; and to be self-conscious is to bring one's self into the sphere of art, as an object to be judged, altered, improved.

Human beings as we find them are accordingly artificial products; and for better or for worse they must always be such. Nature has made us: social action and our own efforts must continually remake us. Any attempt to reject art for "nature" can only result in an artificial naturalness which is far less genuine and less pleasing than the natural work of art.

[166]

HODGSON, SHADWORTH HOLLWAY

HODGSON, SHADWORTH HOLLWAY (1832-1912). Hodgson neither held any post as a University teacher nor did he ever seek one. He lived a retired, happy life, devoted to philosophy. He regarded the poets Wordsworth and Coleridge as his principal teachers, especially the latter from whom he adopted the idea of intimate union of intellectual and emotional elements in human nature, although not his identification of religious experience with theological dogma.

In his principal work *The Metaphysic of Experience* (1898) Hodgson, by his criticism of Kant, prepared the way for New Realism. His method was to analyze the content of consciousness without any assumption concerning its origin or nature. Contrary to Kant, he did not take the existence of the ego for granted. While Kant proceeded from consciousness as a synthetic agency, Hodgson held that this agency is also part of experience and must be analyzed. He objected to empiricism in its postulating of things and persons. Against both Kant and empiricism, Hodgson insisted that neither subject nor object are warranted as initial assumptions of philosophy. From this depth of experience, Hodgson ascended to the metaphysical heights of speculation on God and the Universe, but maintained that thinking about invisible reality is not a matter of knowledge but rather the consequence of moral drives.

FAITH

THE faith of the man lies in his conscious and volitional reciprocation of the love of God, but the ultimate source of its efficacy, that which calls it into existence as a redeeming agency, lies not in the belief, but in the thing believed, the fact that it is *love* which is believed in, and that love the love of God, man's response to which is love and faith at once, a response whereby he places himself in conscious union and harmony with the Divine Object of his faith.

From the twofold fact, that this ultimate source both lies wholly beyond the man, and also, as the love of God, is unchanging and eternal, and therefore demands a response at every moment and in all circumstances, it follows, that the act of response, which is the initial act of faith, must be constantly sustained or perpetually repeated. Consequently it involves an immanent and permanent change in the dominant principle of life, a change from seeking the realization of the ideals of the Self to bringing the Self and its ideals into conformity with the will of God; a change of heart, *metanoia*, repentance, self-surrender. Love to God then becomes the *sine qua non* condition of the man's whole conduct.

From this the love of mankind also follows. For how can anyone, whose life is centered in the primal source of love and righteousness, indulge in enmity or even indifference to those who are objects of the divine love equally with himself? Love is the great subduing, transforming, and harmonizing emotion in human nature. And it is love alone by which responsive love is awakened, or on account of which love is felt in return. Ultimately, therefore, it is the love of

God for man, and that alone, which redeems the man; because that love alone calls forth in return that love of man for God, by which the man's whole nature is transformed. But to be efficacious in man, it must be appropriated by man, that is, believed in and reciprocated by conscious acts of will.

It would appear, that there is no human consciousness so depraved, that the thought of the love of God cannot occur to it, and consequently no kind of degree of abjectness from which the redeeming faith, founded on that thought, cannot uplift a man. Even at its first arising, and in moments at which (provided it be genuine) it is accompanied by the deepest sense of shame, humility, and unworthiness, it gives a certain sense of security, of dignity, and of hopefulness. It ennobles, even while it humbles. In repentance the man begins, or begins again so often as repentance is renewed, to feel himself in communion and fellowship with the sole almighty Power, and the sole righteous Judge. His state in this respect has nothing to do with the estimation in which he may be held by his fellow-men. This was no doubt the hidden reason of Christianity spreading so rapidly as it did throughout the mixed and struggling populations of the great cities of the ancient world. A new life was laid open before every soul of them. For though founded in the strictest individualism, it was for that very reason universal, the same kernel of human nature being the one thing common to all individuals alike.

This is the true source and meaning of the universality of Christianity. It is not confined to men of a particular race (Jews), or of a particular degree of intellectual enlightenment (philosophers), or of a particular standard of moral attainment (the "ninety and nine just persons who need no repentance" of the parable); but is capable of arising independently from the emotional and volitional endowment of all men as men by nature, apart from circumstances of every other kind, whether of the organism or of the environment.

[167]

535

HÖFFDING, HARALD

HÖFFDING, HARALD (1843-1931). After a long, difficult struggle, Höffding resolved to renounce theology and to devote his life
to philosophy. It was his great esteem for Kierkegaard, the adversary of the established church and inquirer into the mystery of personal faith, that fortified Höffding in his decision. He became Den-
mark's most important modern philosopher, and his works have
also been read and highly appreciated in France, England and
Germany.

Höffding was more interested in philosophical problems than
in systems. Asked which philosopher was his personal ideal, Höffding answered Spinoza. But he rejected Spinoza's system. He only
loved and revered his personality. Höffding called himself a critical
positivist. He held that experience is of decisive importance to all a
philosopher might think, but declared that experience is a problem
that defies the efforts of all philosophers. To Höffding, philosophy
alone frees human mind from habits, prejudices and traditions. It
enlarges the spiritual horizon in such a manner as no special science
can.

PLURALISM AND MONISM

THE importance of pluralism, *i.e.*, of the tendency to accen-
tuate the multiplicity and the difference of phenomena, depends on its power to raise problems. Both thought and sensations suppose difference, contrast, variation. Already
Thomas Hobbes saw that, when he said that to have always
one single sensation would be the same as to have no sensation at all. The psychology of our time has, generally speaking, confirmed this view. Fechner's law on the relation
between physical impression and psychical sensation points in
this direction. And our thought starts with greatest energy
when two judgments contradict one another, *i.e.*, when a
problem arises.

I believe there is reason for accentuating this point in
the actual state of philosophy. There seems to be too much
metaphysics in the air, and it is important not to forget
what we have learnt from positivism and criticism. The old

English school had the mission to keep the attention of philosophers on experience, and it started the great movement against dogmatism in the last three centuries. It is no accident that the greatest setter of problems, David Hume, belonged to this school. In evolutionism this school has said its last word—the widening of the concept of experience to connote not only the experience of the single individual, but the organized experience of the whole species. We may hope that a new, refreshing start will be made.

Pluralism makes the world new for us and necessitates a revision of our categories, our principles and our methods. A dogmatic sleep is too tempting for the human mind. We are inclined to suppose that we can develop—or perhaps already have developed—thoughts in which all existence can be expressed. But, as a Danish thinker, Sören Kierkegaard, has said we live forward, but we understand backward. Understanding comes after experience. Only when life is closed can it be thoroughly understood. This is our tragicocomical situation. Even a divine thinker could only understand the world when the life of the world was finished.

But pluralism as such brings no understanding, no intelligence. To understand is to connect one fact with other facts, to find a uniting principle. Multiplicity as such would only make description and classification possible, and even this only under the condition that the manifold phenomena were not only different, but also similar. The only meaning of 'understanding' which a consistent pluralism can acknowledge is understanding as mere recognition, not as explanation.

. . . Now, it is a fact that we in many cases have found such connection of continuity in nature. It is the ideal of knowledge to find it in all domains of observation. Our mind can only understand by synthesis, and the principle of continuity is therefore the presupposition, the working hypothesis, of all science. But we must also acknowledge continuity as a characteristic of reality. We have no right to suppose that the fact that we can not understand phenomena, if we can find no connection or continuity, should be without ground in reality itself. If we will build our philosophy on experience, we ought to give full importance to connection, unity and continuity, as well as to difference and multiplicity. Experience shows us both, and pluralism can, therefore, not be the sole or the last word of the philosopher. And there is an inner connection between continuity and multiplicity. All qualities, powers and characters which we ascribe to the single elements or beings which pluralism acknowledges are only known through the connection of these elements or beings with a whole order of things. We can, for example, only ascribe energy to a being because we experience that it actually does a certain work, that alterations in it or out of it have their cause in it. If it were absolutely isolated, we could not ascribe any predicate to it, we could not know it at all.

Perhaps it is impossible to develop a metaphysical theory which shall give both facts their full right. But this ought not to lead us to forget the urgency of the problem.

I, for my part, call myself a monist, because connection and continuity seem to me to be more important facts than multiplicity; it is, as I have shown, only through their connection one with another and with us, that things can be understood.

[168]

HOLBACH, PAUL HENRI THIRY BARON D'

HOLBACH, PAUL HENRI THIRY BARON D' (1723-1789). Friends and foes of the French Revolution used to regard Holbach, who died some months before its outbreak, as one of its most important prophets. His writings were deemed responsible for the anti-clerical and anti-Christian excesses which took place. This may be true. But Holbach's atheism was detested by such influential leaders as Robespierre just as by the priests who had been attacked constantly in Holbach's pamphlets and books.

All who knew Holbach personally liked him. He was gentle, generous, ready to help poor writers and scholars, and a brilliant host. Only priests, the Church and religions were hated fanatically by him. His criticism of deism and theism challenged even Voltaire.

Holbach was a German nobleman who settled in Paris and adopted French nationality. He wrote many treatises on political, social and religious questions, generally hiding himself behind a pseudonym. His principal work *The System of Nature* (1770) has been called "the Bible of the atheists." It is something more. Holbach, while dealing with "the laws of the physical and moral world," represented nature not as a creation but as an immense workshop that provides man with tools by means of which he is enabled to give his life a better shape. He developed a philosophy of eternal change, and energetically rejected the assumption that all species have existed all the time or must exist in the future. He sneered at those philosophers or scientists who think nature incapable of giving rise to new organisms hitherto unknown. Man is not exempt from the law of change. Nature is indispensable to man, but man is not indispensable to nature which can continue her eternal course without man. Holbach must be credited for having, in 1770, pronounced evolutionism, declaring "Nature contains no constant forms."

THE ATHEIST

An atheist is a man who knoweth nature and its laws, who knoweth his own nature, who knoweth what it imposes upon him: An atheist hath experience, and this experience, proveth to him, every moment, that vice can injure him, that his most concealed faults, that his most secret dispositions may be detected and display him in open day: this experience proveth to him that society is useful to his happiness; that his interest demands, that he should attach himself to the country which protects him, and which enables him to enjoy in security the benefits of nature; every thing shows him, that in order to be happy, he must make himself beloved; that his father is for him the most certain of friends; that ingratitude would remove from him his benefactor; that justice is necessary to the maintenance of every association; and that no man, whatever may be his power, can be content with himself, when he knoweth he is an object of public hatred.

He who hath maturely reflected upon himself, upon his own nature, and upon that of his associates, upon his own wants, and upon the means of procuring them, cannot prevent himself from knowing his duties, from discovering that which he oweth to himself, and that he hath morality, he hath real motives to conform himself to its dictates; he is obliged to feel, that these duties are necessary; and if his reason be not disturbed by blind passions, or by vicious habits, he will feel that virtue is for all men the surest road to felicity. The atheists, or the fatalists, found all their systems upon necessity; thus, their moral speculations, founded upon the necessity of things, are, at least, much more permanent and more invariable, than those which only rest upon a god who changes his aspect, according to the dispositions and the passions of all those who contemplate him. The nature of things, and its immutable laws, are not subject to vary; the atheist is always obliged to call that which injures him, vice and folly; to call that which injures others crime; to call that which is advantageous to society, or which contributes to its permanent happiness, virtue.

[169]

HOLMES, OLIVER WENDELL

HOLMES, OLIVER WENDELL (1809-1894). Oliver Wendell Holmes, professor of anatomy and physiology at Harvard Medical School and a popular figure in Boston, had become an American celebrity by 1860, due to the publication of his *Autocrat of the Breakfast Table*, a book of conversational charm, abundant in satirical glances at mankind and its good and bad customs, sharp and jovial judgments on life, the expression of common sense, love of nature, knowledge of nature, and a treasury of puns and anecdotes. The book became extremely popular in England too and was translated into French and German. Holmes' poems have sometimes been severely criticized, but among them there are many attractive creations of a sometimes robust, sometimes gracious humor, as well as witty and serious articulations of feelings which are shared by people of various levels of education. Some of them are representative of American sentiments of that time. Others surprise by their artful play with allusions and their skill in turning from joke to tender sensibility.

Holmes' mind was less profound than that of his son, Justice

540

Oliver Wendell Holmes. He was a successful teacher, admired and loved by his students, relying more on routine than on research. As a natural scientist, he was an independent yet not a creative thinker. As a physician, he was devoted to the welfare of his patients and eager to support medical progress. He introduced the term anaesthesia into medical practice by suggesting it to the dentist Morton, who was the first to use ether for making his patients insensible during operation.

WORKING OF THE UNCONSCIOUS

THERE are thoughts that never emerge into consciousness, which yet make their influence felt among the perceptible mental currents, just as the unseen planets sway the movements of those which are watched and mapped by the astronomer. Old prejudices, that are ashamed to confess themselves, nudge our talking thought to utter their magisterial veto. In hours of languor, as Mr. Lecky has remarked, the beliefs and fancies of obsolete conditions are apt to take advantage of us. We know very little of the contents of our minds until some sudden jar brings them to light, as an earthquake that shakes down a miser's house brings out the old stockings full of gold, and all the hoards that have hid away in holes and crannies.

We not rarely find our personality doubled in our dreams, and do battle with ourselves, unconscious that we are our own antagonists. Dr. Johnson dreamed that he had a contest of wit with an opponent, and got the worst of it: of course, he furnished the wit for both. Tartini heard the Devil play a wonderful sonata, and set it down on awaking. Who was the Devil but Tartini himself? I remember, in my youth, reading verses in a dream, written, as I thought, by a rival fledgling of the Muse. They were so far beyond my powers, that I despaired of equalling them; yet I must have made them unconsciously as I read them. Could I only have remembered them waking!

But I must here add another personal experience, of which I will say beforehand,—somewhat as honest Izaak Walton said of his pike, "This dish of meat is too good for any but anglers or very honest men,"—this story is good only for philosophers and very small children. I will merely hint to the former class of thinkers, that its moral bears on two points: first, the value of our self-estimate, sleeping,—possibly, also, waking; secondly, the significance of general formulae when looked at in certain exalted mental conditions.

I once inhaled a pretty full dose of ether, with the determination to put on record, at the earliest moment of regaining consciousness, the thought I should find uppermost in my mind. The mighty music of the triumphal march into nothingness reverberated through my brain, and filled me with a sense of infinite possibilities which made me an archangel for the moment. The veil of eternity was lifted. The one great truth which underlies all human experience, and is the key to all the mysteries that philosophy has sought in vain to solve, flashed upon me in a sudden revelation. Henceforth all was clear: a few words had lifted my intelligence to the level of the knowledge of the cherubim. As my natural condition returned, I remembered my resolution; and, staggering to my desk, I wrote in ill-shaped, straggling characters, the all-embracing truth still glimmering in my consciousness. The words were these (children may smile; the wise will ponder): "A strong smell of turpentine prevails throughout."

[170]

HOLMES, OLIVER WENDELL

HOLMES, OLIVER WENDELL (1841-1935). One day, when Justice Holmes was eighty-seven, a reporter, walking round Capitol Square in Washington, D. C., asked passers-by if they knew who Justice Holmes was. One of them answered "Holmes? Oh sure, that's the young judge on the Supreme Court that is always dissenting with the old guys."

Holmes has been called "the great dissenter." He often dissented from the majority of the United States Supreme Court because he thought that the law cannot be dealt with "as if it contains only the axioms and corollaries of a book of mathematics."

Holmes repeatedly emphasized that the life of the law is not logic, not logical cohesion of part with part, but experience, the history of the nation, the "felt necessities" of the present, and the endeavor of men, conscious of their national and human responsibilities, to shape the future development in harmony with the ideals of the common good. These views have been expounded by Holmes in his *Common Law* (1881), in numerous lectures, essays, addresses and, above all, in his written dissents. He regarded the Constitution of the United States not as the embodiment of any particular economic theory, but as "an experiment, as all life is an experiment." However, even though he admitted that the Constitution could be interpreted in various senses, he insisted that one of its principles "more imperatively calls for attachment than any other," namely, the principle of free thought. In accordance with Lord Acton, the British liberal historian, Holmes demanded "free thought not for those who agree with us but freedom for the thoughts that we hate."

When Holmes insisted that jurisdiction had to rest upon the "felt necessities" rather than upon logical conclusions he was not prepared to identify these "felt necessities" with the pressure of public opinion or vested interests. He was always remote from party politics. The philosophical foundation of his legal theory relied on John Stuart Mill, whose utilitarianism he found more acceptable than Kant's idealism, on Peirce and William James, his admired and admiring friend, and also upon a comprehensive study of history, of the causes of formation and dissolution of cultural patterns.

Holmes regarded his remoteness from political struggles as the essential condition of his judicial impartiality. But impartiality and scholarship were not to him the highest degree of human value. Scholars, men of letters, Holmes said, "give up half of their life" in order to be allowed to work in undisturbed detachment. But "the place for a man who is complete in all his powers is in the fight." Scholarship and freedom from prejudices did not prevent Holmes from making up his mind at his peril upon living questions, and to take his place in the fight, no matter how mighty his adversaries were.

THE OUGHT OF NATURAL LAW

THE jurists who believe in natural law seem to me to be in that naive state of mind that accepts what has been familiar and accepted by them and their neighbors as something that must be accepted by all men everywhere. No doubt it is true that, so far as we can see ahead, some arrangements and the rudiments of familiar institutions seem to be necessary elements in any society that may spring from our own and that would seem to us to be civilized—some form of permanent association between the sexes—some residue of property individually owned—some mode of binding oneself to specified future conduct—at the bottom of all, some protection for the person. But without speculating whether a group is imaginable in which all but the last of these might disappear and the last be subject to qualifications that most of us would abhor, the question remains as to the *Ought* of natural law.

It is true that beliefs and wishes have a transcendental basis in the sense that their foundation is arbitrary. You can not help entertaining and feeling them, and there is an end of it. As an arbitrary fact people wish to live, and we say with various degrees of certainty that they can do so only on certain conditions. To do it they must eat and drink. That necessity is absolute. It is a necessity of less degree but practically general that they should live in society. If they live in society, so far as we can see, there are further conditions. Reason working on experience does tell us, no doubt, that if our wish to live continues, we can do it only on those terms. But that seems to me the whole of the matter. I see no *a priori* duty to live with others and in that way, but simply a statement of what I must do if I wish to remain alive. If I do live with others they tell me that I must do and abstain from doing various things or they will put the screws on to me. I believe that they will, and being of the same mind as to their conduct I not only accept the rules but come in time to accept them with sympathy and emotional affirmation and begin to talk about duties and rights. But for legal purposes a right is only the hypostasis of a prophecy—the imagination of a substance supporting the fact that the public force will be brought to bear upon those who do things said to contravene it—just as we talk of the force of gravitation accounting for the conduct of bodies in space. One phrase adds no more than the other to what we know without it. No doubt behind these legal rights is the fighting will of the subject to maintain them, and the spread of his emotions to the general rules by which they are maintained; but that does not seem to me the same thing as the supposed *a priori* discernment of a duty or the assertion of a pre-existing right. A dog will fight for his bone.

The most fundamental of the supposed pre-existing rights—the right to life—is sacrificed without a scruple not only in war, but whenever the interest of society, that is, of the predominant power in the community, is thought to demand it. Whether that interest is the interest of mankind in the long run no one can tell, and as, in any event, to those who do not think with Kant and Hegel it is only an interest, the sanctity. disappears. I remember a very tender-hearted judge being of opinion that closing a hatch to stop a fire and the destruction of a cargo was justified even if it was known that doing so would stifle a man below. It is idle to illustrate further, because to those who agree with me I am uttering commonplaces and to those who disagree I am ignoring the necessary foundations of thought. The *a priori* men generally call the dissentients superficial. But I do agree with them in believing that one's attitude on these matters is closely connected with one's general attitude toward the universe. Proximately, as has been suggested, it is determined largely by early associations and temperament, coupled with the desire to have an absolute guide. Men to a great extent believe what they want to—although I see in that no basis for a philosophy that tells us what we should want to want.

[171]

HSUN CHING

HSUN CHING (About 298-238 B.C.). The purely philosophical strain in Confucianism was developed to its highest point by Hsun Ching who, however, was also a great poet and a master of lyrical reflection, penetrating into the secrets of the human soul, inspired by the beauty of nature. Although he adopted views of Mo-Ti and some Taoists, he remained faithful to Confucianism, believing firmly in the necessity of moral order and individual self-perfection, and strongly opposing the belief in fate.

HEAVEN'S way of acting is unchanging. It did not act specially to make Yao [the Sage-Emperor] survive nor to bring Ch'ieh [the arch-criminal] to destruction. Respond to Heaven by governing well, then there will be good fortune: respond to it by governing badly, and then there will be bad fortune. If the basic industries [i.e. those in connection with agriculture] are in a flourishing state and economy is being practiced in public expenditure, Heaven cannot make the country poor; and if the supply of foodstuffs is complete and energy is exercised at the right times, Heaven cannot make the people sick; and if the Right Way is being cultivated, Heaven cannot send down calamities. The fact is that (by themselves) flood and drought cannot cause famine, extremes of cold and heat cannot cause distress, nor malicious spirits bring bad fortune. If, however, the basic industries are neglected, and expenditure is extravagant, then Heaven cannot make the country rich. . . . The fact is that famine is there before flood and drought, sickness arrives before the rigors of cold and heat. . . . Observance of the seasons and good government go together, whilst calamities and good government are incompatible; and it is wrong to inveigh against Heaven because its Way is so. Thus it is that only if a man be clear as to the relative spheres of Heaven and man may he be called a man of consummate understanding.

To carry to completion by actionless activity [*wu wei*], to accomplish without trying to, is to be described as Heaven's function. Deep though that function is, great though it is and of vital import, the man of consummate understanding nevertheless does not consider it to any extent, nor does he get additional ability through it, nor does he probe into it. This means that he does not try to complete Heaven. (For) Heaven has its times and seasons, Earth its wealth, and Man his work of making order: a blending into a trinity of powers, as it should be described.

Now the man who neglected the condition on which this

blending of powers depended, hoping to be the blender himself, would be on the wrong track altogether. The serried ranks of stars follow their courses: the sun and the moon take turns in shining: the four seasons successively take charge: the Yin and Yang make their great transformations: the wind and the rain exercise their all-pervading influence. Thus the myriad creatures come within the scope of this life-giving harmony (of forces) and in every case get the nourishment which brings them to completion. This we call a miraculous work, for we cannot see it going on, although we see the final accomplishment. We call it Heaven's accomplishment, for in every case we know that something has brought completion, although we have no knowledge of this something in its intangibility. The true sage does not try to know Heaven.

Heaven's function has been established once for all, its accomplishment brought to completion once for all. Thus man's body was prepared and the spirit of man came to life, and with loving and hating, delight and annoyance, sorrow and joy: that is, the 'Heaven-given emotions' were stored up within. Man has eyes, ears, nose, mouth, and limbs, 'the Heaven-given (natural) pipes,' each of them in contact with the others but not able to interchange its aptitude for the others. In the central emptiness dwells the mind [*hsin*], that is 'the Heaven-given (natural) sovereign,' controller of the five senses. The mind makes the arrangements by which the other species are used to nourish the human species: that is 'Heaven-given (natural) nourishing'; for to protect one's own species is what is called 'happiness,' to go against it is 'calamity.' This is 'the Heaven-given (natural) system of government.'

Now to darken man's Heaven-given sovereign, to throw his Heaven-given senses into confusion, to let go his Heaven-given nourishment, to disobey his Heaven-given system of governing, and to do violence to his Heaven-given emotions, this is the supreme evil fortune. The sage purifies his Heaven-given sovereign, rectifies his Heaven-given senses, prepares his Heaven-given nourishment [i.e. by attention to agricultural pursuits], protects his Heaven-given government, nourishes his Heaven-given emotions in order to bring to perfection his Heaven-given merit of accomplishment. If this be done, then he knows what he can do and what he cannot do, and with Heaven and Earth discharging their responsibilities the myriad creatures are at man's command. . . .

The high-minded man [*chun tzu*] is concerned about the matters in his own sphere and does not hanker after the matters in Heaven's sphere of action; whilst the low-minded man does the reverse. Because the former is so, his affairs daily go forward, and because the latter is so, his affairs daily go backward. There is a single reason for the one going forward and the other going backward. In this lies the difference between the two.

If a star falls or a tree groans, the people of the country are all in a panic. The question is, why (this state of panic)? The answer is, for no reason. There is some change in Heaven or in Earth, some Yin and Yang transformation, something which rarely happens in the material sphere. It is right to wonder at it; it is not right to fear it. In every generation there are these occurrences from time to time, eclipses of the sun or the moon, wind and rain at unseasonable times, strange stars appearing in groups. If those in authority are intelligent and their government is equable, then in spite of these occurrences in one generation after another there is no harm done. If they are unintelligent and their government leads in dangerous paths, in spite of there being no such occurrence they are not better off.

It follows that 'human omens' are the things to be feared, the scamped ploughing which affects the final crop, the sketchy hoeing which misses the weeds, the foolhardiness in government which saps the confidence of the people. When the fields are overgrown with weeds and the harvest is bad, the price of corn high and the people short of food and their dead bodies found on the roads, these are what I call human omens. When the official orders are stupid ones, when public undertakings are put in hand at the wrong times and the basic industries are not properly organized, these are what I call 'human omens.' If the (sense of) ritual-and-righteousness is not cultivated, if the women's and men's apartments are not kept separate and there is sex license, then father and son are suspicious of each other, rulers and ruled are at cross purposes, tyranny and distress go hand in hand. These I call human omens. They are born of disorder, and when these three kinds come together, peace is dead in that country. . . .

The question is put: What about the special sacrifices for rain and then the rain coming? The answer is that there is nothing to it. It would rain all the same if there were no sacrifices. When people 'save' the sun and moon from being devoured, or when they pray for rain at a time of drought, or when they divine the omens before taking an important decision, these prayers are not to be taken as being answered. They are superfluous embellishments, for that is how enlightened men regard them, although the people generally take them to be signs of the supernatural. (Rather) it is good fortune to see them as embellishments, bad fortune to see them as supernatural. . . . Which is better, to magnify Heaven and meditate on it or to have your goods properly cared for and systematically controlled; to submit to Heaven and sing its praises or to systematize its commissions and make good use of them; to rely on things multiplying of themselves or to exercise all one's ability in developing them? . . .

[172]

HUI SHIH

HUI SHIH (4th century B.C.). Documents of the teachings of Hui Shih are preserved only in the book of Chuang Chou, the brilliant precursor of Taoism, who considered him the worthiest of his adversaries, and evidently esteemed him higher than Confucius. Hui Shih probably was some years older than Chuang Chou and died before the latter had finished his book *Chuang Tzu.* In the aphorisms quoted by Chuang Chou, Hui Shih appears to be a disciple of Confucius' grandson Tzu Ssu, deeply impressed by his awareness of eternal change and fond of pointing out the paradoxical.

THE APHORISMS

Hui Shih explored the significance of things . . . and said:

1. That beyond which there is nothing greater should be called the great unit. That beyond which there is nothing smaller should be called the small unit.

2. That which has no thickness cannot be increased in thickness, (but) its size can be a thousand miles (long).

3. The heavens are as low as the earth, mountains on the same level as marshes.

4. The sun exactly at noon is exactly (beginning to) go down. And a creature exactly when he is born is exactly (beginning to) die.

5. A great similarity compared with a small similarity is very different. This state of affairs should be described as a small similarity-in-dissimilarity. The myriad things in Nature are both completely similar and completely dissimilar. This state of affairs should be described as a great similarity-in-dissimilarity.

6. The Southern region (beyond the borders of China and not fully explored) has no limit and yet has a limit.

7. To-day I go to Yueh State and I arrive there in the past.

8. Linked rings can be sundered.

9. I know that the hub of the world is north of Yen State and south of Yueh State.

10. Love all things equally: the heavens and the earth are one composite body.

[173]

HUIZINGA, JOHAN

HUIZINGA, JOHAN (1872-1945). After Huizinga had become internationally renowned as a historian of the civilization of the later Middle Ages, the Renaissance and Humanism, he began to develop his own philosophy of civilization. His books which deal with problems of contemporary culture, especially his *Shadow of Tomorrow* (1936), show clearly that the historical phenomenon of the *Waning of the Middle Ages,* as his most popular work is entitled, deeply influenced his thoughts about the present and future state of humanity. Although Huizinga regarded history as an irreversible process, he protested his belief in absolute principles of ethics and in eternal truth, which subsist "above the stream of change and evolution," and he regretted the loss of an universal authority, as was represented by the Medieval Church, bound to guide mankind in accordance with unchanging principles.

Culture was defined by Huizinga as cooperation of social life with spiritual productivity. He later abandoned this definition as too narrow, and, while retaining the emphasis on cooperation, tried to introduce the concept of human vocation into it. As the principal symptoms of the present cultural crisis, Huizinga recognized lack of mental concentration, weakening of judgment, renunciation of rationality, worship of life and lack of charity. The last-mentioned symptom became of increasing importance to Huizinga who was induced by the events of contemporary history to lean more and more upon Catholic moral theology. In a letter to Julien Benda he declared that the doctrine of the seven mortal sins is a better direction for human life than all modern psychology.

BARBARISM

JUST as barbarism can prevail in a society with a high degree of technical perfection, it may equally coincide with that other positive characteristic of modern society, universal education. To determine the level of culture from the degree of illiteracy is to deceive oneself with an outworn belief. A certain modicum of school knowledge in no way guarantees the possession of culture. It can hardly be called undue pessimism when, looking at the general state of mind of our time, one feels bound to speak in the following terms.

Delusion and misconception flourish everywhere. More than ever men seem to be slaves to a word, a motto, to kill one another with, to silence one another in the most literal sense. The world is filled with hate and misunderstanding. There is no way of measuring how great the percentage of the deluded is and whether it is greater than formerly, but delusion and folly have more power to harm and speak with

551

greater authority. For the shallow, semi-educated person the beneficial restraints of respect for tradition, form and cult are gradually falling away. Worst of all is that widely prevalent indifference to truth which reaches its peak in the open advocacy of the political lie.

Barbarisation sets in when, in an old culture which once, in the course of many centuries, had raised itself to purity and clarity of thought and understanding, the vapours of the magic and fantastic rise up again from the seething brew of passions to cloud the understanding: when the *muthos* supplants the *logos*.

Again and again the new creed of the heroic will to power, with its exaltation of life over understanding, is seen to embody the very tendencies which to the believer in the Spirit spell the drift towards barbarism. For the "life-philosophy" does exactly this: it extols *muthos* over *logos*. To the prophets of the life-philosophy barbarism has no deprecatory implications. The term itself loses its meaning. The new rulers desire nothing else.

The gods of our time, mechanization and organization, have brought life and death. They have wired up the whole world, established contact throughout, created everywhere the possibility of co-operation, concentration of strength and mutual understanding. At the same time they have trapped the spirit, fettered it, stifled it. They have led man from individualism to collectivism. But with his unguided insight man has so far succeeded only in realizing the evil that is in every collectivism, the negation of the deepest personal values, the slavery of the spirit. Will the future be one of ever greater mechanization of society solely governed by the demands of utility and power?

[174]

HUMBOLDT, WILHELM VON

HUMBOLDT, WILHELM VON (1767-1835). As a contemporary observer remarked, Humboldt was not young at the age of sixteen and not old at the age of sixty. Although Humboldt did not disagree with that statement, he claimed that his independence from change was the result of his self-education and striving and of the organization and economy of his living energies. Even if this assumption was incorrect, it is true that Humboldt endeavored, from his early years till his death, to construct his character in accordance with his ideals of human perfection and, although he persisted in wearing such a mask, his behavior was considered natural by men like Goethe and Schiller, his friends. This mask helped him, sensitive and sensual as he actually was, to appear serene and imperturbable. But he was by no means a hypocrite. He was deeply convinced that character was not a natural human quality but the result of will.

Humboldt was a man of highest culture and wide interests. He was a great linguist, a pioneer in studying the languages of American aborigines, of Sanskrit and Basque; in philosophy, an independent disciple of Kant and Schelling, not abandoning, however, the ideas of enlightenment; a historian; and a statesman who was an excellent minister of public education in Prussia, but was defeated when he struggled against routine and reaction and for a moderate liberalism.

In his early writings, Humboldt was an extreme individualist. Later he was interested in investigating the relations between the individual and the great movements of history, but he maintained, in opposition to Hegel, that the individual and the so-called spirit of the epoch or nation are incommensurable. He became convinced of the coherence of the spiritual life of all times and nations but his principal interest remained devoted to the individual. To him the diversity of men, times and nations constituted no objection to the establishment of a universal ideal of human education and perfection, and he constantly endeavored to give this ideal a telling, characteristic, concrete content.

SENSES AND REASON

THE impressions, inclinations, and passions which have their immediate source in the senses, are those which first and most violently manifest themselves in human nature. Wherever, before the refining influences of culture have imparted a new direction to the soul's energies, these impressions, etc., do not show themselves, all seeds of power have perished, and nothing either good or great can take root and flourish. They constitute the great original source of all spontaneous activity, and first inspire a glowing, genial warmth in human nature. They infuse life and elastic vigor into the soul: when unsatisfied, they render it active, buoyant, ingenious in the invention of schemes, and courageous in their execution; when satisfied, they promote an easy and unhindered play of ideas. In general, they animate and quicken all conceptions with a greater and more varied activity, suggest new views, point out hitherto unnoticed aspects, and, according to the manner in which they are satisfied, intimately react on the physical organization, which in its turn acts upon the soul, although we only notice how from the results.

The influence, however, of these impressions and inclinations differs, not only in its intensity, but in the manner of its operation. This is, to a certain extent, owing to their strength or weakness; but it is also partly to be attributed to their degree of affinity with the spiritual element in human nature, or from the difficulty or facility of raising them from mere animal gratifications to human pleasures. Thus, for instance, the eye imparts to the substance of its impressions that outline of form which is so full of enjoyment and fertile in ideas; while the ear lends to sound the proportionate succession of tones in the order of time. The nature of these impressions readily suggests many interesting reflections, if this were the proper place for such a topic, but I will only pause to notice their different importance as regards the culture of the soul.

The eye supplies the reason, so to speak, with a more prepared substance; and the inner part of our nature, with its own form and that of other things which stand in a relation to it, is thus presented to us in a single and distinct situation. If we conceive of the ear merely as an organ of sense, and in so far as it does not receive and communicate words, it conveys far less distinctness of impression. And it is for this reason that Kant assigns the preference to the plastic arts when compared with music. But he observes that the culture secured to the soul by the several arts, (and I would add, directly secured), is presupposed as a scale for determining this preference.

The question, however, presents itself whether this scale of previous culture is the just standard of appreciation. Energy appears to me to be the first and chiefest of human virtues. Whatever exalts our energy is of greater worth than anything that merely puts material into our hands for its exercise. . . .

But the sensual and spiritual are linked together by a mysterious bond, of which our hearts are distinctly conscious, though it remains hidden from our eyes. To this double nature of the visible and invisible world, and to the deep-implanted longing for the latter, coupled with the feeling of the sweet necessity of the former, we owe all sound and logical systems of philosophy, truly based on the immutable principles of our nature, just as to the same source we are able to trace the most visionary and incoherent reveries.

[175]

HUME, DAVID

HUME, DAVID (1711-1776). "If one reads Hume's books," Albert Einstein declared, "one is amazed that many sometimes highly esteemed philosophers after him have been able to write so much obscure stuff and even to find grateful readers for it. Hume has permanently influenced the development of the best of philosophers who came after him."

Sometimes, this influence had the very character of a revelation. Immanuel Kant "openly confessed" that Hume awakened him "from my dogmatic slumber and gave my investigation in the field of speculative philosophy quite a new direction." Jeremy Bentham described how, while reading Hume, "I felt as if scales had fallen from my eyes." In modern times, thinkers differing so widely from each other as William James, G. E. Moore, George Santayana and Bertrand Russell, agree in their devotion to Hume, although they have criticized and modified many of his statements.

Hume concentrated upon philosophy in his early years only. Later on he was a soldier, a diplomat, a politician, a member of the Tory party, Under-Secretary of State, and a librarian. He wrote on history, social sciences and religion. But he remained a philosopher, and part of his philosophy must be read out of his later works. Hume called himself a sceptic. Modern philosophers characterize him more rightly as the precursor of positivism. His scepticism was mainly confined to his rejection of the principles of induction. From this position, Hume proceeded to the statement that the concept of causality cannot be gained from material given by the senses. To connect one occurrence with some other by the notions of cause and effect, is, according to Hume, not the result of rational knowledge but of a habit of expecting the perception of the second after having perceived the first, because that sequence has previously taken place in innumerable cases. This habit is founded upon a belief which can be explained psychologically but cannot be derived by abstraction from either the ideas of the two objects or the impressions of the senses. Hume did not deny that causality works. He only denied that reason is capable of understanding it. Neither did Hume deny the possibility of true knowledge by comprehending resemblance, contrariety, proportions in quantity or degrees in quality. Modern physicists, whose causal laws are elaborated inferences from the observed course of nature, have supported Hume's challenge to the traditional causal connection. Hume has often emphasized that the propensity to believe in the existence of the world and in man's faculty to think and judge is stronger than the awareness of the limits of human reason. Occasionally Hume was depressed by doubts. But his enjoyment of life overcame his melancholy as soon as he recognized that the inadequacy of his reason was natural and common to all men. This insight was to him a cure. By critical examination of facts Hume pioneered in the sciences of political and cultural history, economics, comparative history of religion and sociology.

ON THE ORIGIN OF OUR IDEAS

ALL the perceptions of the human mind resolve themselves into two distinct kinds, which I shall call *impressions* and *ideas*. The difference betwixt these consists in the degrees of force and liveliness with which they strike upon the mind and make their way into our thought or consciousness. Those perceptions which enter with most force and violence we may name *impressions*; and under this name I comprehend all our sensations, passions, and emotions, as they make their first appearance in the soul. By *ideas* I mean the faint images of these in thinking and reasoning; such as, for instance, are all the perceptions excited by the present discourse, excepting only those which arise from the sight and touch, and excepting the immediate pleasure or uneasiness it may occasion. I believe it will not be very necessary to employ many words in explaining this distinction. Every one of himself will readily perceive the difference betwixt feeling and thinking. The common degrees of these are easily distinguished, though it is not impossible but in particular instances they may very nearly approach to each other. Thus in sleep, in a fever, in madness, or in any very violent emotions of soul, our ideas may approach to our impressions; as on the other hand it sometimes happens that our impressions are so faint and low, that we cannot distinguish them from our ideas. But notwithstanding this near resemblance in a few instances, they are in general so very different that no one can make a scruple to rank them under distinct heads, and assign to each a peculiar name to mark the difference.

There is another division of our perceptions which it will be convenient to observe, and which extends itself both to our impressions and ideas. This division is into *simple* and *complex*. Simple perceptions or impressions and ideas are such as admit of no distinction nor separation. The complex are the contrary to these, and may be distinguished into parts. Though a particular color, taste, and smell are qualities all united together in this apple, 'tis easy to perceive they are not the same but are at least distinguishable from each other.

Having by these divisions given an order and arrangement to our objects, we may now apply ourselves to consider with the more accuracy their qualities and relations. The first circumstance that strikes my eye is the great resemblance betwixt our impressions and ideas in every other particular except their degree of force and vivacity. The one seem to be in a manner of the reflection of the other; so that all the perceptions of the mind are double, and appear both as impressions and ideas. When I shut my eyes and think of my chamber, the ideas I form are exact representations of the impressions I felt; nor is there any circumstance of the one which is not to be found in the other. In running over my other perceptions I find still the same resemblance and representation. Ideas and impressions appear always to correspond to each other. This circumstance seems to me remarkable, and engages my attention for a moment.

Upon a more accurate survey I find I have been carried away too far by the first appearance, and that I must make use of the distinction of perceptions into simple and complex, to limit this general decision *that all our ideas and impressions are resembling.* I observe that many of our complex ideas never had impressions that corresponded to them, and that many of our complex impressions never are exactly copied in ideas. I can imagine to myself such a city as the New Jerusalem, whose pavement is gold and walls are rubies, though I never saw any such. I have seen Paris; but shall I affirm I can form such an idea of that city as will perfectly represent all its streets and houses in their real and just proportions?

I perceive, therefore, that though there is in general a great resemblance betwixt our *complex* impressions and ideas, yet the rule is not universally true that they are exact copies of each other. We may next consider how the case stands with our *simple* perceptions. After the most accurate examination of which I am capable, I venture to affirm that the rule here holds without any exception, and that every simple idea has a simple impression which resembles it, and every simple impression a correspondent idea. That idea of red which we form in the dark and that impression which strikes our eyes in sunshine differ only in degree, not in nature. That the case is the same with all our simple impressions and ideas 'tis impossible to prove by a particular enumeration of them. Everyone may satisfy himself in this point by running over as many as he pleases. But if anyone should deny this universal resemblance, I know no way of convincing him but by desiring him to show a simple impression that has not a correspondent idea, or a simple idea that has not a correspondent impression. If he does not answer this challenge, as 'tis certain he cannot, we may from his silence and our own observation establish our conclusion.

Thus we find that all simple ideas and impressions resemble each other; and as the complex are formed from them, we may affirm in general that these two species of perception are exactly correspondent. Having discovered this relation, which requires no farther examination, I am curious to find some other of their qualities. Let us consider how they stand with regard to their existence, and which of the impressions and ideas are causes and which effects.

The *full* examination of this question is the subject of the present treatise; and therefore we shall here content ourselves with establishing one general proposition, *that all our simple ideas in their first appearance are derived from simple impressions, which are correspondent to them, and which they exactly represent.*

In seeking for phenomena to prove this proposition I find only those of two kinds, but in each kind the phenomena are obvious, numerous, and conclusive. I first make myself certain, by a new review, of what I have already asserted, that every simple impression is attended with a correspondent idea and every simple idea with a correspondent impression. From this constant conjunction of resembling perceptions I immediately conclude that there is a great connection betwixt our correspondent impressions and ideas, and that the existence of the one has a considerable influence upon that of the other. Such a constant conjunction, in such an infinite number of instances, can never arise from chance; but clearly proves a dependence of the impressions on the ideas, or of the ideas on the impressions. That I may know on which side this dependence lies I consider the order of their *first appearance,* and find by constant experience that the simple impressions always take the precedence of their correspondent ideas, but never appear in the contrary order. To give a child an idea of scarlet or orange, of sweet or bitter, I present the objects, or in other words, convey to him these impressions; but proceed not so absurdly as to endeavor to produce the impressions by exciting the ideas. Our ideas upon their appearance produce not their correspondent impressions, nor do we perceive any color or feel any sensation merely upon thinking of them. On the other hand we find that any impression either of the mind or body is constantly followed by an idea which resembles it and is only different in the degrees of force and liveliness. The constant conjunction of our resembling perceptions is a convincing proof that the one are the causes of the other; and this priority of the impression is an equal proof that our impressions are the causes of our ideas, not our ideas of our impressions.

To confirm this I consider another plain and convincing phenomenon; which is, that wherever by any accident the faculties which give rise to any impressions are obstructed in their operations, as when one is born blind or deaf, not only the impressions are lost but also their correspondent ideas; so that there never appear in the mind the least traces of either of them. Nor is this only true where the organs of sensation are entirely destroyed, but likewise where they have never been put in action to produce a particular impression. We cannot form to ourselves a just idea of the taste of a pineapple without having actually tasted it.

There is however one contradictory phenomenon which may prove that 'tis not absolutely impossible for ideas to go before their correspondent impressions. I believe it will readily be allowed that the several distinct ideas of colors which enter by the eyes, or those of sounds which are conveyed by the hearing, are really different from each other, though at the same time resembling. Now if this be true of different colors, it must be no less so of the different shades of the same color, that each of them produces a distinct idea, independent of the rest. For if this should be denied, 'tis possible, by the continual gradation of shades, to run a color insensibly into what is most remote from it; and if you will not allow any of the means to be different, you cannot without absurdity deny the extremes to be the same. Suppose therefore a person to have enjoyed his sight for thirty years, and to have become perfectly well acquainted with colors of all kinds excepting one particular shade of blue, for instance, which it never has been his fortune to meet with. Let all the different shades of that color, except that single one, be placed before him, descending gradually from the deepest to the lightest, 'tis plain that he will perceive a blank where that shade is wanting, and will be sensible that there is a greater distance in that place betwixt the contiguous colors than in any other. Now I ask whether 'tis possible for him, from his own imagination, to supply this deficiency, and raise up to himself the idea of that particular shade, though it had never been conveyed to him by his senses? I believe there are few but will be of opinion that he can; and this may serve as a proof that the simple ideas are not always derived from the correspondent impressions; though the instance is so particular and singular that 'tis scarce worth our observing, and does not merit that for it alone we should alter our general maxim.

But besides this exception, it may be amiss to remark on this head that the principle of the priority of impressions to ideas must be understood with another limitation, *viz.*, that as our ideas are images of our impressions, so we can form secondary ideas which are images of the primary; as appears from this very reasoning concerning them. This is not, properly speaking, an exception to the rule so much as an explanation of it. Ideas produce the images of themselves in new ideas; but as the first ideas are supposed to be derived from impressions, it still remains true that all our simple ideas proceed either mediately or immediately from their correspondent impressions.

This then is the first principle I establish in the science of human nature; nor ought we to despise it because of the simplicity of its appearance. For 'tis remarkable that the present question concerning the precedency of our impressions or ideas is the same with what has made so much noise in other terms, when it has been disputed whether there be any *innate ideas,* or whether all ideas be derived from sensation and reflection. We may observe that in order to prove the ideas of extension and color not to be innate, philosophers do nothing but show that they are conveyed by our senses. To prove the ideas of passion and desire not to be innate, they observe that we have a preceding experience of these emotions in ourselves. Now if we carefully examine these arguments. we shall find that they prove nothing but that ideas are preceded by other more lively perceptions, from which they are derived, and which they represent. I hope this clear stating of the question will remove all disputes concerning it, and will render this principle of more use in our reasonings than it seems hitherto to have been.

[176]

HUNEIN IBN ISHAK

HUNEIN IBN ISHAK (809-873). The *Sayings of the Philosophers,* written by Hunein Ibn Ishak, a Nestorian Christian who was born in Syria and wrote in Syriac and Arabic, has been translated into Hebrew, Spanish and other languages, and became a very popular book among the intellectuals of the early Middle Ages in Europe and the Middle East. This book, however, is highly significant of the deformation of Greek philosophy in the sixth and seventh centuries. Hunein was a learned man. He wrote an *Introduction into the Science of Medicine,* a Syriac-Arabic dictionary and grammar, and many other books. He traveled a great deal and collected Greek manuscripts, which he either translated into Syriac or Arabic, or used as sources for his own books. Without any doubt, Hunein was a careful writer and faithful translator, but the texts of the manuscripts he had at hand were spoiled, because the copyists had been incapable of understanding what they copied, and each succeeding scribe had added new errors to those of his predecessors. Thus Hunein confounded Socrates with Diogenes, or Plato with Bias. Even his own philosophy, whether it consisted of original thoughts or of quotations, is more characteristic of the fate of certain Greek thoughts in a time of spiritual decay.

A PHILOSOPHICAL COLLOQUY

At a Greek holiday, four philosophers met in a temple which was adorned with golden pictures. These philosophers were

562

the pillars of wisdom. They talked about the objects of wisdom, and discussed the philosophical principles of wisdom, while mentioning sayings of the old thinkers.

One of them said: This meeting shall not be forgotten. For the friends of wisdom will always like to learn wisdom. Now, we will utter wise sentences to be remembered by late generations so that posterity may learn from them. They shall be a moral school for those who come next, and established wisdom for those who come long after us.

The first said: Through noble souls and pure thoughts the spirits soar up to the air of spiritual understanding in the realm of light and power which are hidden to those who glance at the real world. There, they walk about celestial flower-beds, free from any misfortune. After the spirit has become pure, they will live an eternal life that cannot perish nor vanish into nothing. Then, ultimate ground will be united with ultimate ground, the pure will be united with the pure, and the obscure will be drowned into the obscure. Then the spirit will behold hidden mysteries, and will have sure possession of the knowledge that is obtained by the force of thought and by the union of ideas and concepts.

The second said: How can the spirit strive to grasp what is hidden, since the essence of truth is hidden to it? How can the pure be separated from the impure if the spirit is not imbued with the knowledge of pure thought? How can thought reach the depth of hiddenness since it is abiding in the darkness of foolishness, and since greed is spoiling the origin?

The third said: While grasping eternal truth, ideas get into the whirlpool of consideration, and thus are raised to the sphere of pure spirit, and strive with all their forces for grasping the hidden. Thus they arrive at the realm of high sublimity where the souls are resting in the shadow of Divine Majesty.

The fourth said: Contradictions can be reconciled, and the hidden can be recognized only if the spirit becomes allied with the other spirits; goes along the path of understanding;

becomes purified from obscure stupidity, and if it becomes separated from the abode of darkness in order to arrive at the free square of understanding. That is the highest happiness, the most magnificent and noble.

[177]

HUSSERL, EDMUND

HUSSERL, EDMUND (1859-1938). More than fifty years of strenuous work had to pass between the beginning and the accomplishment of Husserl's philosophy. At its completion he expressed his confidence in having established philosophy as a "rigorous science," as an "absolute discipline," and he classified all precedent philosophies as either superficial or poor, vague or sterile. In his early days, however, Husserl was tormented by doubts that his own talents were adequate to his aspirations, and that philosophy in itself could satisfy them. It was his teacher, Franz Brentano, who not only encouraged Husserl to devote his life to philosophy but gave him certainty that philosophy could clear up any doubt. Husserl did not find the way to Brentano spontaneously. He was brought into contact with him by his friend Thomas G. Masaryk, who was to become the founder and first president of the Czechoslovakian republic.

Brentano taught Husserl the importance of three points which remained characteristic of Husserl's own thinking, notwithstanding the modifications or even radical changes his philosophy underwent in the course of time. At first, he taught him to distinguish between logical laws and the laws of psychic facts which involved opposition to "psychologism," to any concept of logical notions as psychic formations apt to be explained by their genesis. Secondly, Husserl took from Brentano the Scholastic distinction between essence and existence, and, furthermore, the term of "intentionality" of thought, which means that thought is always directed toward things different from itself.

From this basis, Husserl proceeded to the foundation of phenomenology, which, before him, had been used as a theory of appearances, and, through him, became a full-fledged philosophy. It deals with insight into essences without regard to the empirical conditions of their perceptibility, even without regard to existence. Intuitive evidence is the criterion of truth. It is not to be confounded with certainty or proof of reality. Husserl would not deal with metaphysical considerations of any kind but he was convinced

564

that his phenomenology could provide answers to any "legitimate" metaphysical question, and he maintained that recognition and pursuit of phenomenological analysis, as developed by him, would produce true knowledge quite independently of the adherence of the analyzer to any philosopher in other regard. Husserl claimed to have established a doctrine of ideal conditions of the possibility of science, and to have served truth in a safer way than any philosophical system.

CONSCIOUSNESS AND NATURAL REALITY
THE VIEW OF THE "MAN IN THE STREET"

ALL THE ESSENTIAL characteristics of experience and consciousness which we have reached are for us necessary steps towards the attainment of the end which is unceasingly drawing us on, the discovery, namely, of the essence of that *"pure" consciousness* which is to fix the limits of the phenomenological field. Our inquiries were eidetic; but the individual instances of the essences we have referred to as experience, stream of experience, "consciousness" in all its senses, belonged as real events to the natural world. To that extent we have not abandoned the ground of the natural standpoint. Individual consciousness is interwoven with the *natural world* in a *twofold* way: it is some *man's* consciousness, or that of some *man* or *beast,* and in a large number at least of its particularizations it is a consciousness of this world. *In respect now of this intimate attachment with the real world, what is meant by saying that consciousness has an essence "of its own",* that with other consciousness it constitutes a self-contained *connexion determined purely through this, its own essence,* the connexion, namely, of the stream of consciousness? Moreover, since we can interpret consciousness in the widest sense to cover eventually whatever the concept of experience includes, the question concerns the experience-stream's own essential nature and that of all its components. To what extent, in the first place, must the *material world* be fundamentally different in kind, *excluded from the experience's own essential nature?* And if it is this, if over against all consciousness and the essential being proper to it, it is that which is *"foreign"* and *"other"*, how can consciousness be *interwoven* with it, and consequently with the whole world that is alien to consciousness? For it is easy to convince oneself that the material world is not just any portion of the natural world, but its fundamental stratum to which all other real being is *essentially* related. It still fails to include the souls of men and animals; and the new factor which these introduce is first and foremost their "experiencing" together with their conscious relationship to the world surrounding them. *But here consciousness and thinghood form a connected whole,* connected within the particular psychological unities which we call *animalia,* and in the last resort within the *real unity of the world as a whole.* Can the unity of a whole be other than made one through the essential proper nature of its parts, which must therefore have some *community of essence* instead of a fundamental heterogeneity?

To be clear, let us seek out the ultimate sources whence the general thesis of the world which I adopt when taking up the natural standpoint draws its nourishment, thereby enabling me as a conscious being to discover over against me an existing world of things, to ascribe to myself in this world a body, and to find for myself within this world a proper place. This ultimate source is obviously *sensory experience.* For our purpose, however, it is sufficient to consider *sensory perception,* which in a certain proper sense plays among experiencing acts the part of an original experience, whence all other experiencing acts draw a chief part of their power to serve as a ground. Every perceiving consciousness has this peculiarity, that it is the consciousness of *the embodied (leibhaftigen) self-presence of an individual object,* which on its own side and in a pure logical sense of the term is an individual or some logico-categorical modification of the same. In our own instance, that of sensory perception, or, in distincter terms, perception of a world of things, the logical individual is the Thing; and it is sufficient for us to treat the perception of things as representing all other perception (of properties, processes, and the like).

The natural wakeful life of our Ego is a continuous perceiving, actual or potential. The world of things and our body within it are continuously present to our perception. How then does and can *Consciousness itself* separate out as a *concrete thing in itself*, from that within it, of which we are conscious, namely, the *perceived being*, *"standing over against"* consciousness *"in and for itself"*?

I meditate first as would the man "in the street." I see and grasp the thing itself in its bodily reality. It is true that I sometimes deceive myself, and not only in respect of the perceived constitution of the thing, but also in respect of its being there at all. I am subject to an illusion or hallucination. The perception is not the "genuine." But if it is, if, that is, we can "confirm" its presence in the actual context of experience, eventually with the help of correct empirical thinking, then the perceived thing *is real* and itself really given, and that bodily in perception. Here perceiving considered simply as consciousness, and apart from the body and the bodily organs, appears as something in itself essenceless, an empty looking of an empty "Ego" towards the object itself which comes into contact with it in some astonishing way.

[177A]

HUXLEY, THOMAS HENRY

HUXLEY, THOMAS HENRY (1825-1895). Huxley, the son of a poor schoolmaster, attended a regular school for only two years. He described that education as "a pandemonium." Thereafter, from his tenth year on, he had to pursue his studies by himself, which he did with such energy and clear-sightedness that he easily passed the examination for admission to the University. As a surgeon in the British Navy, Huxley was able to study tropical fauna and flora, and he became a pioneer in biology. His contributions to the anatomy of vertebrate and invertebrate animals are regarded as of lasting value. As a professor at London University, Lord Rector of the University of Aberdeen, president of the Royal Society and member of the Privy Council, Huxley used his authority and influence for the promotion of all sciences and the defense of science against detractors of any kind. Not the least of his accomplishments, Huxley was successful in popularizing science and making the working classes acquainted with its principal results. Full of energy and initiative, daring and circumspect in his way of thinking, Huxley was a pugnacious but always courteous critic who was fond of disputing with great authorities in science, in State and Church.

Although Huxley, in his early years, was convinced of the immutability of species, he became, immediately after the publication of Darwin's *Origin of Species,* a brilliant champion of evolutionism. He did not share Darwin's faith in the absolute rule of small variations, and insisted on cases of sudden change observed by himself. But this and other objections did not prevent him from defending and continuously explaining Darwin's theory. As a philosophical thinker, Huxley, a great admirer of Hume, defined his standpoint as *agnosticism,* a strict insistence on the impossibility of knowing anything beyond observation of the senses, indifferent to any theory of reality. Huxley's attitude was not a negative scepticism but rather a plea for sceptical caution in the matter of belief. He was as radically opposed to materialism as to the faith of the Church.

THE RELATIONS OF MAN TO THE LOWER ANIMALS

THE question of questions to mankind—the problem which underlies all others, and is more deeply interesting than any other—is the ascertainment of the place which man occupies in nature, and of his relations to the universe of things. Whence has our race come? what are the limits of our power over nature, and of nature's power over us? To what good are we tending?—these are the problems which present themselves anew and with undiminished interest to every man born into the world.

Most of us, shrinking from the difficulties and dangers which beset the seeker after original answers to these riddles, are contented to ignore them altogether, or to smother the investigating spirit under the feather-bed of respected and respectable tradition. But in every age one or two restless spirits, blest with that constructive genius which can build a secure foundation, or cursed with the mere spirit of scepticism, are unable to follow in the well-worn and comfortable track of their forefathers and contemporaries; and, unmindful of thorns and stumbling-blocks, strike out into paths of their own. The sceptics end in the infidelity which asserts the problem to be insoluble, or in the atheism which denies the existence of any orderly progress and governance of things. The men of genius propound solutions which grow into systems of theology or philosophy; or, veiled in musical language which suggests more than it asserts, take the shape of the poetry of an epoch.

Each such answer to the great question—invariably asserted by the followers of its propounder, if not by himself, to be complete and final—remains in high authority and esteem, it may be for one century, or it may be for twenty; but, as invariably, time proves each reply to have been a mere approximation to the truth—tolerable chiefly on account of the ignorance of those by whom it was accepted, and wholly intolerable when tested by the larger knowledge of their successors.

In a well-worn metaphor a parallel is drawn between the life of man and the metamorphosis of the caterpillar into the butterfly; but the comparison may be more just, as well as more novel, if for its former term we take the mental progress of the race. History shows that the human mind, fed by constant accessions of knowledge, periodically grows too large for its theoretical coverings, and bursts them asunder to appear in new habiliments, as the feeding and growing grub at intervals casts its too narrow skin and assumes another, itself but temporary. Truly the *imago* state of man seems to be terribly distant; but every moult is a step gained, and of such there have been many.

It will be admitted that some knowledge of man's position in the animated world is an indispensable preliminary to the proper understanding of his position in the universe; and this again resolves itself, in the long run, into an inquiry into the nature and the closeness of the ties which connect him with those singular creatures which have been styled the man-like apes. The importance of such an inquiry is indeed intuitively manifest. Brought face to face with these blurred copies of himself, the least thoughtful of men is conscious of a certain shock, due, perhaps, not so much to disgust at the aspect of what looks like an insulting caricature, as to the awakening of a sudden and profound mistrust of time-honored theories and strongly rooted prejudices regarding his own position in nature, and his relations to the Under-world of life; while that which remains a dim suspicion for the unthinking becomes a vast argument, fraught with the deepest consequences, for all who are acquainted with the recent progress of anatomical and physiological sciences.

I now propose briefly to unfold that argument, and to set forth, in a form intelligible to those who possess no special acquaintance with anatomical science, the chief facts upon which all conclusions respecting the nature and the extent of the bonds which connect man with the brute world must be based. I shall then indicate the one immediate conclusion which, in my judgment, is justified by those facts; and I shall finally discuss the bearing of that conclusion upon the hypotheses which have been entertained respecting the origin of man.

*   *   *

Leaving Mr. Darwin's views aside, the whole analogy of natural operations furnishes so complete and crushing an argument against the intervention of any but what are termed secondary causes in the production of all the phenomena of the universe that, in view of the intimate relations between man and the rest of the living world, and between the forces exerted by the latter and all other forces, I can see no excuse for doubting that all are coordinated terms of nature's progression, from the formless to the formed—from the inorganic to the organic—from blind force to conscious intellect and will. Science has fulfilled her mission when she has ascertained and enunciated truth; and were these pages addressed to men of science only, I should now close this essay, knowing that my colleagues have learned to respect nothing but evidence, and to believe that their highest duty lies in submitting to it, however much it may jar against their inclinations.

But desiring, as I do, to reach the wider circle of the intelligent public, it would be unworthy cowardice were I to ignore the repugnance with which the majority of my readers are likely to meet the conclusions to which the most careful and conscientious study I have been able to give to this matter has led me. On all sides I shall hear the cry— "We are men and women, and not a mere better sort of ape—a little longer in the leg, more compact in the foot, and bigger in the brain, than your brutal chimpanzees and gorillas. The power of knowledge—the consciousness of good and evil—the pitiful tenderness of human affections—raise us out of all real fellowship with the brutes, however closely they may seem to approximate us."

To this I can only reply that the exclamation would be most just, and would have my own entire sympathy, if it were only relevant. But it is not I who seek to base man's dignity upon his great-toe, or insinuate that we are lost if an ape has a *hippocampus minor*. On the contrary, I have done my best to sweep away this vanity. I have endeavored to show that no absolute structural line of demarcation, wider than that between the animals which immediately succeed us in the scale, can be drawn between the animal world and ourselves. And I may add the expression of my belief that the attempt to draw a physical distinction is equally futile, and that even the highest faculties of feeling and intellect begin to germinate in the lower forms of life. At the same time, no one is more thoroughly convinced than I am of the vastness of the gulf between civilized man and the brutes; or is more certain that whether *from* them or not, he is assuredly not *of* them. No one is less disposed to think lightly of the present dignity, or despairingly of the future hopes, of the only consciously intelligent denizen of the world.

We are indeed told by those who assume authority in these matters that the two sets of opinions are incompatible, and that the belief of the unity of origin of man and brutes involves the brutalization and degradation of the former. But is this really so? Could not a sensible child confute, by obvious arguments, the shallow rhetoricians who would force this conclusion upon us? Is it indeed true that the poet, or the philosopher, or the artist, whose genius is the glory of his age, is degraded from his high estate by the undoubted historical probability—not to say certainty—that he is the direct lineal descendant of some naked and bestial savage, whose intelligence was just sufficient to make him a little more cunning than the fox, and by so much more dangerous than the tiger? Or is he bound to howl and grovel on all fours because of the wholly unquestionable fact that he was once an egg, which no ordinary power of discrimination could distinguish from that of the dog? Or is the philanthropist or the saint to give up his endeavors to lead a noble life because the simplest study of man's nature reveals, at its foundations, all the selfish passions and fierce appetites of the quadruped? Is the mother-love vile because the hen shows it; or fidelity base because dogs possess it?

The common-sense of the mass of mankind will answer these questions without a moment's hesitation. Healthy humanity, finding itself hard-pressed to escape from real sin and degradation, will leave the brooding over speculative pollution to the cynics and the "righteous overmuch," who, disagreeing in everything else, unite in blind insensibility to the nobleness of the visible world and inability to appreciate the grandeur of the place man occupies therein. Nay, more thoughtful men, once escaped from the blinding influences of traditional prejudice, will find in the lowly stock whence man has sprung the best evidence of the splendor of his capacities, and will discern in his long progress through the past a reasonable ground of faith in his attainment of a nobler future.

They will remember that in comparing civilized man with the animal world one is as the Alpine traveler who sees the mountains soaring into the sky, and can hardly discern where the deep-shadowed crags and roseate peaks end, and where the clouds of heaven begin. Surely the awe-struck voyager may be excused if he at first refuses to believe the geologist, who tells him that these glorious masses are, after all, the hardest mud of primeval seas, or the cooled slag of subterranean furnaces—of one substance with the dullest clay, but raised by inward forces to that place of proud and seemingly inaccessible glory. But the geologist is right; and the due reflection on his teachings, instead of diminishing our reverence and our wonder, adds all the force of intellectual sublimity to the more aesthetic intuition of the uninstructed beholder.

And after passion and prejudice have died away, the same result will attend the teachings of the naturalist respecting that great Alps and Andes of the living world—man. Our reverence for the nobility of manhood will not be lessened by the knowledge that man is, in substance and structure, one with the brutes; for he alone possesses the marvellous endowment of intelligible and rational speech, whereby, in the secular period of his existence, he has slowly accumulated and organized the experience which is almost wholly lost with the cessation of every individual life in other animals; so that he now stands on the mountain-top, far above the level of his humble fellows, and transfigured from the grosser nature by reflecting, here and there, a ray from the Infinite source of truth.

PROTOPLASM IN ANIMALS AND PLANTS

NOTWITHSTANDING all the fundamental resemblances which exist between the power of the protoplasm in plants and animals, they present one striking difference, in the fact that plants can manufacture fresh protoplasm out of mineral compounds, whereas animals are obliged to procure it ready-made; and hence, in the long run, depend upon plants. Upon what condition this difference in the powers of the two great divisions of the world of life depends, nothing at present is known. With such qualification as arises out of this fact, it may be truly said that all the acts of all living things are fundamentally one. Is any such unity predicable of their forms? Let us seek in easily verified facts for a reply to this question.

If a drop of blood be drawn by pricking one's finger, and viewed with proper precautions, and under a sufficiently high microscopic power, there will be seen, among the innumerable multitude of little, circular, discloidal bodies, or corpuscles, which float in it and give it its color, a comparatively small number of colorless corpuscles, of somewhat large size and irregular shape. If the drop of blood be kept at the temperature of the body, these colorless corpuscles will seem to exhibit marvellous activity, changing their forms with great rapidity, drawing in and thrusting out prolongations of their substance, and creeping about as if they were independent organisms.

The substance which is thus active is a mass of protoplasm, and its activity differs in detail rather than in principle from that of the protoplasm of the nettle. Under sundry circumstances the corpuscle dies, and becomes distended into a round mass, in the midst of which is seen a smaller spherical body, which existed, but was more or less hidden, in the living corpuscle, and is called its *nucleus*. Corpuscles of essentially similar structure are to be found in the skin, in the lining of the mouth, and scattered through the whole framework of the body. Nay, more; in the earliest condition of the human organism—in that state in which it has just become distinguishable from the egg in which it arises —it is nothing but an aggregation of such corpuscles; and every organ of the body was once no more than an aggregation of such corpuscles. Thus a nucleated mass of protoplasm turns out to be what may be termed the structural unit of the human body. As a matter of fact, the body, in its earliest state, is a mere multiple of such units, variously modified.

But does the formula which expresses the essential structural character of the highest animal cover all the rest, as the statement of its powers and faculties covered that of all others? Very nearly. Beast and fowl, reptile and fish, mollusk, worm, and polype, are all composed of structural units of the same character—namely, masses of protoplasm with a nucleus. There are sundry very low animals each of which, structurally, is a mere colorless blood-corpuscle, leading an independent life. But at the very bottom of the animal scale even this simplicity becomes simplified, and all the phenomena of life are manifested by a particle of protoplasm without a nucleus. Nor are such organisms insignificant by reason of their want of complexity. It is a fair question whether the protoplasms of those simplest forms of life which people an immense extent of the bottom of the sea would not outweigh that of all the higher living beings which inhabit the land put together. And in ancient times, no less than at the present day, such living beings as these have been the greatest of rock-builders.

What has been said of the animal world is no less true of plants. Imbedded in the protoplasm at the broad or attached end of the nettle-hair there lies a spherical nucleus. Careful examination further proves that the whole substance of the nettle is made up of a repetition of such masses of nucleated protoplasm, each contained in a wooden case, which is modified in form, sometimes into a woody fibre, sometimes into a duct or spiral vessel, sometimes into a pollen-grain or an ovule. Traced back to its earliest state, the nettle arises, as a man does, in a particle of nucleated protoplasm. And in the lowest plants, as in the lowest animals, a single mass of such protoplasm may constitute the whole plant, or the protoplasm may exist without a nucleus.

Under these circumstances, it may well be asked, How is one mass of non-nucleated protoplasm to be distinguished from another? Why call one plant and the other animal?

The only reply is that, so far as form is concerned, plants and animals are not separable; and that, in many cases, it is a mere matter of convention whether we call a given organism an animal or a plant.

There is a living body called *Aethalium septicum*, which appears upon decaying vegetable substances, and, in one of its forms, is common upon the surface of tanpits. In this condition, it is, to all intents and purposes, a fungus, and formerly was always regarded as such. But the remarkable investigations of De Bary have shown that in another condition, that *Aethalium* is an actively locomotive creature, and takes in solid matters upon which, apparently, it feeds, thus exhibiting the most characteristic features of animality. Is this a plant? or is it an animal? Is it both? or is it neither? Some decide in favor of the last supposition, and establish an intermediate kingdom— a sort of no man's land—for all these intermediate forms. But as it is admittedly impossible to draw any distinct boundary line between this no man's land and the vegetable world, on the one hand, or the animal, on the other, it appears to me that this proceeding merely doubles the difficulty, which before was single.

Protoplasm—simple or nucleated—is the formal basis of all life. It is the clay of the potter, which—bake it and paint it as he will—remains clay, separated by artifice, and not by nature, from the commonest brick or sun-dried clod. Thus it becomes clear that all living powers are cognate; and that all living forms are fundamentally of one character. The researches of the chemist have revealed a no less striking uniformity of material composition in living matter.

[178]

576

I

IBN BADJDJA. See AVENPACE.

IBN GABIROL, SOLOMON

IBN GABIROL, SOLOMON (About 1021-about 1058). From the middle of the 12th to the end of the 14th century, Dominicans and Franciscans struggled with great bitterness over the ideas expressed in the book *Fons Vitae,* which the monk Dominicus Gundisalvi, assisted by the baptized Jew John Hispalensis, had translated from the Arabic. Its author was called Avicebron. The Franciscans, among them famous philosophers like Alexander of Hales and Duns Scotus, accepted its ideas and used it as a source for their own work, while the majority of the Dominicans, including Thomas Aquinas, opposed them. The importance of *Fons Vitae* as a source of medieval Neo-Platonism can hardly be exaggerated. It was not until 1840 that the great orientalist Salomon Munk discovered the real author of the book—namely, Solomon Ibn Gabirol who, up to then, was known only as one of the greatest Spanish-Jewish poets. The Hebrew title of Ibn Gabirol's book is *Mekor Hayim* (Fountain of Life). It deals with the total subject matter from the point of view of the antagonism of form and matter, and establishes a hierarchy of all beings, a graduation which, on each higher level, shows a more perfect relation between form and matter. Gabirol, who continued to express his Jewish convictions in his poetry, dealt with the philosophical problems of his metaphysical work without any relation to Judaism.

SEEK WISDOM

A SOUL whose raging tempests wildly rise, whither shall she send her meditations? She rages, and is like a flame of fire, whose smoke constantly ascends. This time her meditations are like a wheel that turns around on the earth and the multitudes thereof, or like the seas wherein the earth's foundations were fastened: "How canst thou be so strong and filled with courage, that thou disdainest a place upon the stars? From the path of wisdom turn thou away thy heart; the world shall then smooth thy path for thee."

Oh comfort ye my soul for that, my friends, and likewise for her sorrows comfort her; she thirsts for a man of prudence, but finds not a man to slake her thirst. Seek ye amongst the men of fame, perchance there may be one to grant her desires. If this world sins against me, my heart will regard it disdainfully. If it cannot see my light with its eye, let the world then be contented with its blindness. But afterwards, if it appeases me, I shall turn round, and forgive its sins. The earthly sphere would then be good; the hand of Time would place no yoke upon the wise.

Oh too much wrong didst thou commit; long have the gourds been as cedars of the earth. Despise the vile ones of the people, for stones are less burdensome to me than they. Cut off the tail of them that say to me: "Where is then wisdom and her votaries?" Oh that the world would judge them aright! oh that it would give food unto her sons! They would then rest, not toil, and would attain their goal, without knowing worldly joys. Some took the sun's daughters, and begot folly, but they were not its sons-in-law.

Why do ye chide me for my understanding, O ye thorns and briers of the earth? If wisdom is of light esteem to you, vile and despised are ye in her sight. Though she is closed, and reaches not your heart, lo, I shall open her chests. How shall I now abandon wisdom, since God's spirit made a covenant between us? or how shall she forsake me, since she is like a mother to me and I am the child of her old age? or like an ornament which adorns the soul, or like a necklace on her neck. How can ye say to me: "Take off thy ornaments, and remove the precious chain from her neck?" In her my heart rejoices, and is glad, because her rivers of delights are pure. Throughout my life I shall make my soul ascend until her abode is beyond the clouds. For she adjured me not to rest, until I find the knowledge of her Master.

[179]

578

IBN TUFAIL

IBN TUFAIL (About 1105-1185). The author of "Robinson Crusoe" certainly must have read the English version of Ibn Tufail's book *Hai Ebn Yokdhan* (Alive, Son of Awaken), the imaginary and allegorical story of a man 'who, living alone on an island, without any intercourse with human beings, discovered truth and conquered nature by reasonable thinking. This book became favorite reading in Europe. It was translated into French, Spanish, German and Dutch, and into English in 1674 and 1708. Its English title is *The Improvement of Human Reason.*

The full name of its author is Abu Bekr Mohammed ben Abd'el Malik ben Mohammed ben Mohemmed ben Tufail el-Quaici. His contemporaries also called him El Andaloci, which, at that time, meant Spaniard, or the man of Cordova, or the man of Seville. He was a physician in Granada who then became secretary to the governor and finally the vizier of Sultan Abu Yakub Yusuf, who ruled over Islamic Spain and Morocco. Ibn Tufail distinguished himself in medicine, poetry and astronomy. He criticized the Ptolemaic system as did other Arabic and Jewish thinkers of that period. He was highly respected as a scholar whose wisdom attracted men of all countries. The chronicles of his time also praise him as a Maecenas. Ibn Tufail especially protected Averroës and recommended him to his ruler as his successor when, in 1182, he retired from office. According to contemporary reports, Averroës was inspired to his commentaries on Aristotle by a conversation with Ibn Tufail and the Sultan, who complained that Aristotle was too obscure to him.

THE IMPROVEMENT OF HUMAN REASON

HE observed that if a star arose at any time in a great circle and another star at the same in a lesser circle, yet nevertheless, as they arose together, so they set together; and he observed it of all the stars, and at all times. From whence he concluded that the heaven was of a spherical figure; in which opinion he was confirmed by observing the return of the sun, moon and stars to the east after their setting; and also because they always appeared to him of the same bigness, both when they rose, and when they were in the midst of heaven, and at the time of their setting; whereas, if their motions had not been circular, they must have been nearer to sight, at some times than others; and consequently their dimensions would have appeared proportionably greater or lesser; but since there was no such appearance, he concluded that their motions were circular. Then he considered the motion of the moon and the planets from west to east, till at last he understood a great part of astronomy. Besides, he apprehended that their motions were in different spheres, all which were comprehended in another which was above them all, and which turned about all the rest in the space of a day and a night. But it would be too tedious to explain particularly how he advanced in this science; besides, 'tis taught in other books; and what we have already said is as much as is requisite for our present purpose.

When he had attained to this degree of knowledge, he found that the whole orb of the heavens, and whatsoever was contained in it was as one thing compacted and joined together; and that all those bodies which he used to consider before as earth, water, air, plants, animals and the like, were all of them so contained in it as never to go out of its bounds, and that the whole was like one animal, in which the luminaries represented the senses; the spheres so joined and compacted together answered to the limbs; and the sublunary world to the belly, in which the excrements and humors are contained, and which oftentimes breeds animals, as the greater world.

Now when it appeared to him that the whole world was only one substance, depending upon a voluntary agent, and he had united all the parts of it, by the same way of thinking which he had before made use of in considering the sublunary world; he proposed to his consideration the world in general, and debated with himself whether it did exist in *time*, after it had been; and came to *be* out of nothing; or whether it had been from eternity, without any privation preceding it. Concerning this matter, he had very many and great doubts; so that neither of these two opinions did prevail over the other. For when he proposed to himself the belief of its eternity, there arose a great many objections in his mind; because he thought that the notion of infinite existence was pressed with no less difficulties than that of infinite extension. And that such a being as was not free from accidents produced anew, must also itself be produced anew, because it cannot be said to be more ancient than those accidents. And that which cannot exist before accidents produced in time, must needs itself be produced in time. Then on the other hand, when he proposed to himself the belief of its being produced anew, other objections occurred to him; for he perceived that it was impossible to conceive any notion of its being produced anew, unless it was supposed that there was time before it; whereas time was one of those things which belonged to the world, and was inseparable from it; and therefore the world could not be supposed to be later than time. Then he considered that a thing created must needs have a Creator. And, if so, why did this Creator make the world now and not, as well before? Was it because of any new chance which happened to Him? That could not be, for there was nothing existent besides Himself? Was it then upon the account of any change in His own nature? But what should cause that change? Thus he continued for several years, arguing pro and con about this matter; and a great many arguments offered themselves on both sides so that neither of these two opinions in his judgment overbalanced the other.

This put him to a great deal of trouble, which made him begin to consider with himself what were the consequences which did follow from each of these opinions, and that perhaps they might be both alike. And he perceived that if he held the world was created in time and existed after a total privation, it would necessarily follow from thence that it could not exist of itself, without the help of some Agent to produce it. And that this Agent must needs be such an one as cannot be apprehended by our senses; for if He should be the object of sense, He must be *body*, and if *body*, then a part of the world, and consequently a created being; such an one as would have stood in need of some other cause to create Him. And if that second creator was *body*, He would depend upon a third, and that third upon a fourth, and so *ad infinitum*, which is absurd. Since therefore the world stands in need of an incorporeal Creator, and since the Creator thereof is really incorporeal, 'tis impossible for us to apprehend Him by any of our senses; for we perceive nothing by the help of them but *body*, or such accidents as adhere to bodies. And because He cannot be perceived by the senses, it is impossible He should be apprehended by the imagination; for the imagination does only represent to us the forms of things in their absence, which we have before learned by our senses. And since He is not *body*, we must not attribute to Him any of the properties of *body*; the first of which is extension, from which He is free, as also from all those properties of bodies which flow from it. And seeing that He is the maker of the world, doubtless He has the sovereign command over it. *Shall not he know it, that created it? He is wise, omniscient!*

On the other side, he saw that if he held the eternity of the world, and that it always was as it is, without any privation before it; then it would follow, that its motion must be eternal too; because there could be no rest before it, from whence it might commence its motion. Now all motion necessarily requires a mover; and this mover must be either a power diffused through the body, or else through some other body without it, or else a certain power, not diffused or dispersed through any body at all. Now every power which passeth or is diffused through any body is divided or doubled. For instance, the gravity in a stone, by which it tends downwards, if you divide the stone into two parts, is divided into two parts also; and if you add to it another like it, the gravity is doubled. And if it were possible to add stones *in infinitum*, the gravity would increase *in infinitum* too. And if it were possible, that stone should grow still bigger till it reached to an infinite extension, the weight would increase also in the same proportion; and if, on the other side, a stone should grow to a certain size, and stop there, the gravity would also increase to such a pitch, and no farther. Now it is demonstrated that all body must necessarily be finite; and consequently, that' power which is in body is finite too. If therefore we can find any power, which produces an infinite effect, 'tis plain that it is not in body. Now we find that the heaven is moved about with a perpetual motion without any cessation. Therefore if we affirm the eternity of the world, it necessarily follows that the power which moves it is not in its own body, nor in the other exterior body; but proceeds from something altogether abstracted from body, and which cannot be described by corporeal adjuncts or properties. Now he had learned from his first contemplation of the sublunary world, that the true essence of body consisted in its *form*, which is its disposition to several sorts of motion; but that part of its essence which consisted in *matter* was very mean, and scarce possible to be conceived; therefore, the existence of the whole world consists in its disposition to be moved by this mover. Who is free from matter and the properties of body; abstracted from everything which we can perceive by our senses, or reach by our imagination. And since He is the efficient cause of the motion of the heavens, in which (notwithstanding their several kinds) there is no difference, no confusion, no cessation; without doubt He has power over it, and a perfect knowledge of it.

Thus his contemplation this way brought him to the same conclusion it did the other way. So that doubting concerning the eternity of the world and its existence *de novo*, did him no harm at all. For it was plain to him both ways, that there was a being, which was not body, nor joined to body, nor separated from it; nor within it, nor without it; because conjunction and separation, and being within any thing, or without it, are all properties of body, from which that being is altogether abstracted. And because all bodies stand in need of a form to be added to their matter, as not being able to subsist without it, nor exist really; and the form itself cannot exist, but by this Voluntary Agent, it appeared to him that all things owed their existence to this Agent; and that none of them could subsist but through Him, and, consequently, that He was the cause, and they the effects (whether they were newly created after a privation, or whether they had no beginning in respect of Him, 'twas all one), and creatures whose existence depended upon that Being; and that without His continuance they could not continue, nor exist without His existing, nor have been eternal without His being eternal; but that He was essentially independent of them and free from them. And how should it be otherwise when it is demonstrated that His power and might are infinite, and that all bodies, and whatsoever belongs to them are finite? Consequently, that the whole world and whatsoever was in it, the heavens, the earth, the stars, and whatsoever was between them, above them, or beneath them, was all His work and creation and posterior to Him in nature, if not in time. As, if you take any body whatsoever in your hand, and then move your hand, the body will without doubt follow the motion of your hand with such a motion as shall be posterior to it in nature, though not in time, because they both began together. So all this world is caused and created by this Agent out of time, *Whose command is, when he would have anything done, BE, and it is.*

And when he perceived that all things which did exist were His workmanship, he looked them over again, considering attentively the power of the efficient, and admiring the wonderfulness of the workmanship, and such accurate wisdom and subtile knowledge. And there appeared to him in the most minute creatures (much more in the greater) such footsteps of wisdom and wonders of the work of creation that he was swallowed up with admiration, and fully assured that these things could not proceed from any other than a Voluntary Agent of infinite perfection, nay, that as above all perfection; such an one, to Whom the weight of the least atom was not unknown, whether in heaven or earth; no, nor any other thing, whether lesser or greater than it.

Then he considered all the kinds of animals and how this Agent had given such a fabric of body to every one of them, and then taught them how to use it. For if He had not directed them to apply those limbs which He had given them, to those respective uses for which they were designed, they would have been so far from being of any service that they would rather have been a burden. From whence he knew that the Creator of the world was supereminently bountiful and exceedingly gracious. And then when he perceived among the creatures any that had beauty, perfection, strength, or excellency of any kind whatever, he considered with himself, and knew that it all flowed from that Voluntary Agent (Whose name be praised) and from His essence and operation. And he knew that what the Agent had in His own nature was greater than that (which he saw in the creatures), more perfect and complete, more beautiful and glorious, and more lasting; and that there was no proportion between the one and the other. Neither did he cease to prosecute this search, till he had run through all the attributes of perfection, and found that they were all in this Agent, and all flowed from Him; and that He was most worthy to have them all ascribed to Him, above all the creatures which were described by them.

In like manner he enquired into all the attributes of imperfection and perceived that the Maker of the world was free from them all. And how was it possible for Him to be otherwise, since the notion of *imperfection* is nothing but *mere privation* or what depends upon it? And how can He any way partake of *privation* Who is *very essence*, and cannot but exist; Who gives being to everything that exists and besides Whom there is no existence? But HE is the Being, HE is the Absoluteness, HE is the Beauty, HE the Glory, HE the Power, HE the Knowledge. HE is HE, and besides Him all things are subject to perishing.

Thus far his knowledge had brought him towards the

end of the fifth septenary from his birth, viz., when he was 35 years old. And the consideration of this Supreme Agent was then so rooted in his heart that it diverted him from thinking upon anything else, and he so far forgot the consideration of the creatures and the enquiring into their natures, that as soon as e'er he cast his eyes upon anything of what kind soever, he immediately perceived in it the footsteps of this Agent; and in an instant his thoughts were taken off from the creature and transferred to the Creator. So that he was inflamed with the desire of Him, and his heart was altogether withdrawn from thinking upon this inferior world, which contains the objects of sense, and wholly taken up with the contemplation of the upper, intellectual world.   [180]

IMITATION OF CHRIST. See AUTHOR OF THE IMITATION OF CHRIST.

INGE, WILLIAM RALPH

INGE, WILLIAM RALPH (1860-1954). Dean Inge is one of the most popular figures in Britain's public life, and his interpretation of English peculiarities has been heeded outside the kingdom. He has spoken about questions of the day quite as often as G. B. Shaw, and some people have grumbled that in England a playwright and a dean always fancy they know everything better than anybody else. In matters of public opinion, if not in those of religion, Inge is, in his own way, as heretic as was Shaw.

Inge has searched for a philosophy by which he could live. He found it in those Christian mystics who were steeped in the Platonic tradition, and it was Plotinus whose work he regarded as the summit of Platonism. Inge's *Philosophy of Plotinus* (1918) has been recognized as a work of penetrating scholarship, even by those who do not share Inge's appraisal of that thinker.

To Inge, Christianity is a religion of spiritual redemption, not one of social reform, and he has protested, "I am unable to distinguish between philosophy and religion." He holds that mythology, which rightly claims a large place in all religions, cannot be kept out of philosophy, provided that the thinker tries to "live by the rule of his thought." The real world is regarded by Inge neither as the material universe, assumed as existent independently of mind, nor as the thought of the universe in the mind of man, but rather as the unity of the thought and its object. Values are defined as the attributes of the ultimate real. According to Inge, the founder of Christianity made the greatest contribution to the science or art of living by teaching that wisdom, knowledge and judgment of value are the result of love and sympathy. These ideas are explained in Inge's *Faith and Knowledge* (1904) and *Speculum Animae* (Mirror of the Soul, 1911).

MATTER AND MIND

My own belief is that whatever is born in time must perish for time, and this must be true of world systems no less than of individual lives. Time and space are not part of the framework of the real or spiritual world; they are as real as the lives of those who live in them, while they live in them, but they are not—neither of them, nor the two rolled into one—the stuff of which reality is made. If the present world order had a beginning, "with time, not in time," as Augustine says, it will have an end, "not in time but with time," that is to say, with its own time framework. We are not obliged to believe that ours is the only world order. It is more natural to suppose that as God is eternal, so His creative activity is perpetual. The different world orders may be entirely independent of each other. But here we are guessing about what we neither know nor can ever hope to know.

It has been necessary to argue at length against the prevalent pantheistic theory that the world is as necessary to God as God is to the world. This error, as we regard it, comes from metaphysics, not from natural science. But though Christianity asserts the transcendence of God, it is equally emphatic in maintaining His immanence. On this subject a little more must be said.

However we regard matter and mind, and the relation between them, they are as a fact given to us in combination. We do not perceive matter by itself, but as it affects our minds through the senses. Colors and musical sounds come, as we know, from vibrations which have no sound and no color. To this extent we may claim that the immanence of mind in matter is given to us in experience. External nature has always had a religious influence upon mankind; we think we can find in the external world traces of divine working. Of course the interpretations differ widely. One man finds evidence for a good God; another for two warring principles; another for polytheism; another for pantheism. But the belief that there is a spiritual reality behind phenomena is itself, by its general prevalence, a very impressive phenomenon. I have emphasized . . . the great importance for philosophy of this apprehension of values, which though they are immanent in visible things plainly belong to a higher order. It is also worth saying that this spiritual vision is neither simply emotional nor moral nor intellectual; it is an affirmation of the undivided personality. If we may trust our own impressions, we are equally sure that we are in touch with the divine in our contact with these values, and that our knowledge of the divine mind is fitful and incomplete. From this we infer that though we live and move and have our being in God, He is immeasurably above us while we live here.

[181]

INGERSOLL, ROBERT GREEN

INGERSOLL, ROBERT GREEN (1833-1899). As soon as Thomas Henry Huxley coined the term "agnosticism" in 1869, Ingersoll enthusiastically adopted it because it gave adequate expression to what he had felt and tried to formulate himself for many years. Ingersoll, who tried untiringly to enlighten the American people by his speeches, lectures and books, was subsequently called "America's great agnostic." He was a gifted and powerful orator, a formidable debater who, in public discussions, was almost always victorious. Before he began his career as a lecturer on philosophical and religious questions, he had refined his oratorical techniques as a successful lawyer, and, for two years, he had been attorney general of Illinois. Of his publications, *Some Mistakes of Moses* (1879) and *Why I Am an Agnostic* (1896) became the most popular. But the effect of his lectures and speeches was incomparably greater. The enthusiasm of his audiences compensated him for the many setbacks in his professional and political career which were due to his provoking heresy.

Before the Civil War, Ingersoll adhered to the Democratic Party, but thereafter he was a Republican. His nomination speech in favor of James G. Blaine at the Republican Convention in Cincinnati, 1876, made him a national figure. Following that, he was recognized as one of America's greatest orators even by those who were strongly opposed to his utterances concerning religion.

THE DAMAGE RELIGION CAUSES

RELIGION makes enemies instead of friends. That one word, "religion," covers all the horizon of memory with visions of war, of outrage, of persecution, of tyranny, and death. That one word brings to the mind every instrument with which man has tortured man. In that one word are all the fagots and flames and dungeons of the past, and in that word is the infinite and eternal hell of the future.

In the name of universal benevolence Christians have hated their fellow-men. Although they have been preaching universal love, the Christian nations are the warlike nations of the world. The most destructive weapons of war have been invented by Christians. The musket, the revolver, the rifle, cannon, the bombshell, the torpedo, the explosive bullet, have been invented by Christian brains. Above all other arts, the Christian world has placed the art of war.

A Christian nation has never had the slightest respect for the rights of barbarians; neither has any Christian sect any respect for the rights of other sects. Anciently, the sects discussed with fire and sword, and even now, something happens almost every day to show that the old spirit that was in the Inquisition still slumbers in the Christian breast.

Whoever imagines himself a favorite with God, holds other people in contempt.

Whenever a man believes that he has the exact truth from God, there is in that man no spirit of compromise. He has not the modesty born of the imperfections of human nature; he has the arrogance of theological certainty and the tyranny born of ignorant assurance. Believing himself to be the slave of God, he imitates his master, and of all tyrants, the worst is a slave in power.

When a man really believes that it is necessary to do a certain thing to be happy forever, or that a certain belief is necessary to ensure eternal joy, there is in that man no spirit of concession. He divides the whole world into saints and sinners, into believers and unbelievers, into God's sheep and Devil's goats, into people who will be glorified and people who will be damned.

A Christian nation can make no compromise with one not Christian; it will either compel that nation to accept its doctrine, or it will wage war. If Christ, in fact, said "I came not to bring peace but a sword," it is the only prophecy in the New Testament that has been literally fulfilled.

[182]

ISOCRATES

ISOCRATES (436-338 B.C.). Isocrates, who, despite his delicate health and many misfortunes, lived to be nearly a hundred years old, was considered by the Greeks to be not the most powerful but the most skilled of all orators. After political events had ruined him financially, he established himself as a dealer in speeches and pamphlets which he wrote and sold or prepared on order. He was acquainted with Socrates, though not his disciple. Isocrates attacked the Sophists, as Socrates did, but not for the same reasons. Occasionally, he also attacked, or counter-attacked, Plato and Antisthenes.

Isocrates frequently dealt with political questions. His standpoint was very close to that of Aristotle. Both of them condemned the policy which was inaugurated by Themistocles and developed by Pericles, namely, Athens' claim to naval supremacy which, as Isocrates saw it, would provoke an overwhelming alliance of other powers against Athens' ambitions. Isocrates steadily advocated peace among all Greek states. He declared that all Greeks were united, less by blood than by common education and ideals.

PANEGYRIC OF ATHENS

THE inhabitants of Greece anciently led a wandering, unsettled life, uncultivated by laws, and unrestrained by any regular form of government. While one part fell a sacrifice to unbridled anarchy and sedition, another was oppressed

590

by the wanton insolence of tyrants. But Athens delivered them from these calamities, either by receiving them under her immediate protection, or by exhibiting herself as a model of a more equitable system of policy: for of all the states of Greece she was the first who established a government of laws, and rendered the voice of equity superior to the arm of violence. This is evident from the first criminal prosecutions, where the punishment was sought for in a legal manner and not by the decision of the sword. The parties, though strangers, came to Athens, and received the benefit of our laws.

Our ancestors bestowed their attention not merely on the useful arts, but likewise on those which are agreeable. Many of these they invented, others they carried to perfection, and all of them they communicated and diffused. Both their public institutions and the whole system of their private economics were founded on the most liberal and extensive principles. They were adapted to the enjoyments of the rich and the necessities of the poor. The prosperous and the unfortunate found themselves equally accommodated; to the one we offered an elegant retreat; to the other a comfortable asylum.

The commodities of the different states of Greece were different. No one sufficed for itself; but, while it could spare of its own productions, it stood in need of those of its neighbors. This occasioned everywhere a double inconveniency; for they could neither sell what was superfluous, nor purchase what they had occasion for. Athens erects the Piraeus: the evil immediately disappears. A trading town is established in the middle of Greece, where the merchandise of all the different countries is brought to market, and purchased at a cheaper rate than on the spot which produced them.

*　　　*　　　*

But I begin to think differently from what I did in the beginning of this discourse. I then imagined that it was possible to speak suitably to the grandeur of the subject; but

I am sensible how far I have fallen short of it. Several things have escaped my memory. But do you yourselves consider the advantages of carrying the war into the continent, and of returning into Europe with all the wealth and happiness of Asia. Think it not sufficient for you to hear and to approve of what I have here advanced. Those who possess active talents must vie with one another in effecting a reconciliation between Athens and Lacedaemon. Those who court literary fame must abandon the study of deposits, and others equally uninteresting; they must pursue the career which I have followed, and endeavor to outstrip me in the race. Let them consider that such as make great professions ought not to stoop to mean objects; that they ought not to employ themselves on inferior matters, which even to prove, would be attended with small advantage; but that, making a proper distinction between the subjects of eloquence, they should select and cultivate those only which, if they succeed in, will establish their own fame, and extend the glory of their country.

[183]

ISRAELI, ISAAC

ISRAELI, ISAAC (About 850-950). Israeli, who, during the one hundred years of his life, was a famous physician and founder of an influential medical school, did not escape the fate of many other philosophers whose renown was founded upon their nonphilosophical activities. But it is just that objection made by some leaders of philosophical schools that he has written his philosophical books from the medical point of view, which should attract the interest of modern scholars. For his description of the faculty of cogitation and his distinction between the impressions received by "the five senses" and the post-sensatory perceptions show him to have been an acute psychologist whose hints at anthropology anticipated modern discoveries. His principal work *Kitab al Istiksat*, written in Arabic, was translated into Hebrew under the title *Sefer Hayesodoth* and into Latin under the title *De Elementis*. He also wrote a treatise on definitions and commentaries on *Genesis* and the mystical *Sefer Yetzirah*, the oldest Cabalistic work which is extant.

Israeli practiced medicine at Cairo, Egypt, and later at Kair-

wan, Tunisia. The Christian monk Constantine of Carthage translated several of Israeli's medical treatises into Latin in 1087, and
used them as textbooks at the University of Salerno, the earliest
university in Western Europe, but he omitted the real author's
name, which was finally made known to the European public only
in 1515 when *Opera Omnia Isaci* was printed at Lyons, France.

MAN AND GOD

MEN cannot obtain knowledge of the divine will except
through God's envoys. For truth itself cannot have intercourse with everyone, since there are some people dominated
by their animal soul, while others are dominated by their
vegetative soul, and only a few have a cogitative soul.

Only a man who is exclusively dominated by his cogitative soul can be chosen by God as His envoy.

God cannot be known or grasped by human thought.
He is exempt from change or alteration since He has no
form which might turn from one state to another. We can
only say that God is the Creator, but we must not think that
we can conceive His attributes.

[184]

ISVARAKRSNA

ISVARAKRSNA (Fifth Century A.D.). The name of Isvarakrsna is
connected with the *Samkya Karika,* composed about the middle of
the fifth century, and probably the oldest of the six traditional
systems of Indian philosophy. Its foundation is attributed to the
sage Kapila. Samkya philosophy inspired Buddha who lived about
a century later.

The Samkya school shares with other systems the belief in the
Indian gods, demi-gods and demons, but it conceives them as
mortal and subject to transmigration. Contrary to the Brahman
concept, there is no place for a universal God in the Samkya system, which expressly denies the existence of such a god. The
Samkya philosophy is pessimistic, regarding all existence as suffering, and dualistic, insisting on the fundamental difference between
soul and matter. Salvation from suffering can be reached by cognitive grasping of the absolute difference between the soul and
everything material. It is probable that the Samkya doctrine influenced Gnosticism and Neo-Platonism.

THE [present] inquiry is into the [problem] of how to obviate the three kinds of pain [arising within the individual, outside him, or from more remote causes, all presenting a person with the not too cheerful prospect of being reborn again and again]. Now, even though there are obvious means for getting rid of these difficulties, this enquiry is not superfluous, for conclusiveness and permanency is not theirs.

What rests on [sacred Vedic] tradition is like what is [ordinarily] experienced, for it is not pure, being at once deficient or too ornate. Something different from either is more worth-while, consisting in an analytical knowledge of the phenomenal (*vyakta*), the noumenal (*avyakta*), and the knower.

The root creative principle (*prakrti*) is not a modification [or development]. Seven, intelligence (*mahat*) and the rest [self-consciousness (*ahamkara*) and five principles (*tanmatras*)] are creative principles and modifications. Sixteen [or five powers of perception, five of action, mind and five elements] are modifications [merely]. The self (*purusa*) is neither a creative principle nor a modification.

Perception, inference and authority, in that they comprise all sources of knowledge, are respected as the threefold source of knowledge. By virtue of a source of knowledge, the object of knowledge is obtained.

Perception is ascertaining particular sense-objects. Inference is of three sorts, [antecedent, subsequent and by analogy, and] premises a predicate and [deduces] what it is predicated of. Authority is trustworthy tradition.

By inference, that is, reasoning by analogy, are things lying beyond the grasp of the senses ascertained; but what cannot be ascertained thus must be received by revelation.

Things may be imperceptible due to various reasons, such as distance, proximity, deficiency in the sense organ, inattention, minuteness, blocking out, ascendency and intermixture with identical things.

[The creative principle] is not apprehended in perception, not because it does not exist, but because of its subtlety; it is [properly] apprehended in its effects. Intelligence and the rest [of the principles named above] are effects which are [in one respect] identical with, [and in another] different from the creative principle.

The effect is existent [as a specific effect], for, [1.] a cause does not produce what is not; [2.] [one] appropriate cause may be assigned [to anything]; [3.] it is impossible that anything particular could connect up with anything and everything else; [4.] a cause operates only within its own competency; and [5.] there is a specificity of cause.

The phenomenal is causally conditioned, not eternal, specifically disperse, mutable, pluralistic, grounded in something, conjugial, tending to enter relationships, dependent on something else. The noumenal has just the opposite characteristics.

The phenomenal as well as matter (*pradhana*) have three moods (*gunas*), are undifferentiated, are an object of sense, public, unintelligible, full of urges. Soul (*pums*) has, like [the noumenal mentioned in the previous *sutra*], characteristics to these.

The moods consist of pleasure, pain and indifference, have as purpose manifestation, activity and restraint, and dominate, depend on and produce one another mutually, join up with one another and are interchangeable. . . .

In order to attain the intelligent comprehension of the self and the unity of matter, the two cooperate like the halt and the blind. This accomplished, there is creation.

From the creative principle comes forth intelligence, from thence self-consciousness, and from that the group of sixteen [mentioned above]. From five among the sixteen proceed five elements. . . .

The evolution of the creative principle from intelligence to the different elements is for the liberation of the individual selves, done for self as much as for the other.

Just as it is the function of milk, an unconscious [sub-

595

stance], to nourish the calf, so it is the function of matter to accomplish the liberation of the self.

Just as people engage in acts for the purpose of allaying anxiety, so the noumenal acts in order to liberate the self.

Just as a dancer, having exhibited herself to the spectator, desists from the dance, so the creative principle desists, having manifested itself to the self.

Without deriving benefits, the versatile servant serves unselfishly in multifarious ways the purposes of the selfish master (*pums*) who has no qualities whatever.

Nothing, in my opinion, is more delicate than the creative principle. Having once become aware of having been beheld, she does not again expose herself to the view of the self.

Indeed, nothing is bound, nor freed, nor is migrating. The creative principle alone is bound, freed and migrates in the various vehicles. . . .

[185]

J

JACOBI, FRIEDRICH HEINRICH

JACOBI, FRIEDRICH HEINRICH (1743-1819). As far as Jacobi's philosophy enjoyed any authority during his lifetime, it seemed to be definitely destroyed by the devastating criticism of Kant, Fichte, Schelling and Hegel. Jacobi died a defeated man. Today, however, he is regarded as a precursor of existentialism.

Jacobi called himself an aphoristic thinker. He was aware of his incapability to overcome all the contradictions which prevented him from being consistent. His principal propositions are presented in the form of novels. The first *Allwill* (1775) was intended as an encomium of Goethe, who was his friend, but it finally became a warning against the man of genius. Jacobi blamed contemporary civilization for its lack of original and immediate feelings, of natural behavior, for the decay of heart and intellect, and he exalted the morals of the man of genius who is independent of traditional ethical standards, whose life is dominated by passion which means confidence in life. Nevertheless, he recognized that surrendering to passion entails individual and social dangers. The second novel *Woldemar* (1777) is essentially the author's self-criticism.

It was Jacobi's principal intention to present "humanity as it is," no matter whether it be conceivable or inconceivable. He was inclined to attribute to life an absolute value but he was also aware of the ambiguity of life. He insisted that feeling, not knowledge, constitutes the contact between the ego and the external world, and that what cannot be proved by reason, can be comprehended by feeling; but he did not question traditional logic which secures experience by creating steadiness. Only when steadiness degenerates into rigidity does it become a danger. According to Jacobi, the only philosophical system that is logically irrefutable is that of Spinoza which, however, he rejected as metaphysically wrong. Jacobi's God, different from the pantheistic deity, is also different from the Christian God. But, personally, Jacobi sympathized with Christian piety, and his conception of man is essentially Christian. Faith is, he said, intellectual evidence of logical principles as well as divination of Truth, imperfect knowledge as well as immediateness of feeling. The faithful disposition is the condition of any knowledge of truth and secures permanent certainty and peace of mind.

From this position, Jacobi proceeded to a severe criticism of the German idealists who replied with a roughness unheard of until then in the history of German controversies.

CHRISTIANITY AND PAGANISM

EVERY man has some kind of religion: that is, a supreme Truth by which he measures all his judgments— a supreme Will by which he measures all his endeavors. These everyone has who is at one with himself, who is everywhere decidedly the same. But the worth of such a religion and the honor due to it, and to him who has become one with it, cannot be determined by its *amount*. Its *quality* alone decides friendship, a higher value than to another. At bottom every religion is anti-Christian which makes the form the thing, the letter, the substance. Such a materialistic religion, in order to be consistent, ought to maintain a material infallibility.

There are but two religions—Christianity and Paganism—the worship of God and Idolatry. A third, between the two, is not possible. Where Idolatry ends, there Christianity begins; and where Idolatry begins, there Christianity ends. Thus the apparent contradiction is done away with between the two propositions— "Whoso is not against me is for me," and "Whoso is not for me is against me."

As all men are by nature liars, so all men are by nature idolators—drawn to the visible and averse to the invisible. Hamann called the body the first-born, because God first made a clod of earth, and then breathed into it a breath of life. The formation of the earth-clod and the spirit are both *of God*, but only the spirit is *from* God; and only on account of the spirit is man said to be made after the likeness of God. . . . Since man cannot do without the letter—

598

images and parables—no more than he can dispense with time, which is incidental to the finite, though both shall cease—I honor the letter, so long as there is a breath of life in it, for that breath's sake.

[186]

JAMBLICUS

JAMBLICUS (About 270-330 A.D.). So far as modern theosophy does not go back to Hindu mysticism, its adherents are using doctrines formulated mostly by Jamblicus, a Syrian and a disciple of Porphyry who tried to systematize the philosophy of Plotinus, wrote commentaries on Plato and about the Greek gods, the doctrines of the Egyptians, Chaldeans and Assyrians. Until the 19th century, Jamblicus was considered one of the great philosophers. In late antiquity his renown was enormous. He was glorified as "posterior to Plato only in time, not in genius," and his devoted disciples did not refrain from forging letters allegedly written by Emperor Julianus, in which Jamblicus was hailed as "Savior of Greece," "Treasury of the Hellenes" or "healer of the souls." For a long time these forgeries enjoyed full credit. For, in fact, Julianus did esteem Jamblicus highly and quoted him frequently in his genuine writings. Jamblicus was revered as a divine being, and many miracles were attributed to him. He attracted many adherents because he promised that the initiation into his philosophy would endow the adept with superhuman powers. Besides, he also promised success in practical life. His thoughts will not impress modern readers except by the eloquence with which they are displayed.

THE PROMISES OF PHILOSOPHY

THOSE things which are subject to us in our life, as the body, and those things about or connected with the body, were given to us as certain instruments. The use of these can be dangerous, causing much injury, to those who do not use them rightly. It is necessary, therefore, to seek and acquire scientific knowledge and to use it rightly so that we may use all these instruments properly and without detriment. We must philosophize, accordingly, if we wish to become good citizens and to pass through life usefully. . . .

If we pursue the heavenly way and live in our kindred

599

star, then we will philosophize, living truly, busied with the most profound and marvelous speculations, beholding the beauty in the soul immutably related to Truth, viewing the rules of the gods with joy, gaining perpetual delight and additional insight from contemplating and experiencing pure pleasure absolutely unmingled with any pain or sorrow. Turning this way, therefore, we will find that philosophy leads us to total felicity.

[187]

JAMES, HENRY, SR.

JAMES, HENRY, SR. (1811-1882). What made Henry James, Sr., the father of the great philosopher William and the great novelist Henry James, critical of the existing order was not the accident which caused amputation of one of his legs and impaired him permanently, but the wealth of his family which seemed to grant him undue favor. His revolt against the existing social system led him to enthusiastic adherence to the views of the French socialist Fourier. His opposition to Presbyterian orthodoxy made him a radical religious individualist who combined ideas of enlightenment with Swedenborg's mysticism. James never ceased to fight for his ideals, but during the last thirty years of his life the care of the education and progress of his sons became his dominant interest. He published *The Church of Christ Not an Ecclesiasticism* (1854) and other works on religion and morality.

GOOD AND EVIL RELATIVE

ALL natural existence may be classified into forms of use; all spiritual existence into forms of power. Every real existence, whatsoever we rightly denominate a *thing* as addressing any of our senses, is a form of use to superior existence. Every spiritual existence, whatsoever we rightfully denominate a *person* as addressing our interior perception, is a form of power over inferior existence. Thus the vegetable on its material side is a form of use to the animal kingdom, as giving it sustenance; while on its spiritual side it is a form of power over the mineral kingdom, as compelling it into the service of its own distinctive individuality. The animal, again, on its visible or corporeal side is a purely subjective implication of the human form, while on its spiritual or invisible side it furnishes the creative unity or objectivity of the vegetable world. So man, on his natural side, furnishes a helpful platform or basis to the manifestation of God's perfection, while to the power of his spiritual or individual aptitudes the animal and all the lower kingdoms of nature bear resistless testimony.

But in thus classifying all natural existence into forms of use, and all spiritual existence into forms of power, we must not forget to observe that the use promoted by the one class is never absolutely but only relatively good, nor the power exerted by the other class absolutely but only relatively benignant. That is to say, it is good and benignant not in itself, but in opposition to something else. Thus every natural form is a form of use, but some of these uses are relatively to others good, and some evil. And when we contemplate human nature we find some of its forms relatively accordant with the Divine perfection, others relatively to these prior ones again most discordant; the former exerting a decidedly benignant influence upon whatever is subject to them, the latter exerting a decidedly malignant influence.

This contrarious aspect both of nature and man has given rise, as the reader well knows, to a great amount of unsatisfactory speculation, because men have scarcely known how, apart from the light of Revelation, to shape their speculations into accordance with the demands of the Divine unity. The demand of unity in the Creator is so peremptory and inflexible that the mind utterly refuses in the long run to acquiesce in any scheme of creation which leaves creation divided, or puts the Creator in permanent hostility with any of His works. More than this: The mind not only rejects these puerile cosmologies which leave the Creator at war with His own creature, but it goes further, and insists, by an inevitable presentment of the great philosophic verity, that wherever we find a sphere of life antagonistic with itself, the antagonism is pure phenomenal; *i.e.*, is not final, does not exist for its own sake but only in the interest of some higher unity.

The same rule holds in regard to moral existence, though the nonsensical pride we feel in ourselves habitually blinds us to the fact. I am not a bad man by virtue of any absolute or essential difference between us but altogether by virtue of the difference in our relation to that great unitary life of God in our nature which we call society, fraternity, fellowship, equality, and which from the beginning of human history has been struggling to work itself, by means of this strictly subjective antagonism, into final perfect and objective recognition; you as a morally good man being positively related to that life; I as a morally evil one being negatively related to it. The needs of this great life—which alone manifests God's spiritual presence in our nature—require the utmost conceivable intensity of human freedom; require, in other words, that man should be spontaneously good of himself, good without any antagonism of evil, infinitely good even as God is good. But clearly if we had had no preliminary acquaintance with imperfect or finite good, good as related to evil, we should be destitute of power to appreciate or even apprehend this higher and perfect good. If we had not first suffered, and suffered, too, most poignantly, from the experience of evil in ourselves as *morally, i.e.,* finitely, constituted, constituted in reciprocal independency each of every other, we should have been utterly unable even to discern that ineffable Divine and infinite good which is yet to be revealed in us as *socially, i.e.,* infinitely constituted, constituted in the closest reciprocal unity of all with each and each with all.

[188]

JAMES, WILLIAM

JAMES, WILLIAM (1842-1910). William James is generally considered not only the most influential of all American philosophers but the very representative of American thought. However, the results of his thinking are by no means confined to his native country, and his background is anything but exclusively American. Very few American families maintained such intimate contact with Europe as did Henry James, Senior, a theologian and philosophical writer, and a great amateur of wide culture, and his sons William and Henry, the great novelist, who, on his part, was more at home in France and England than in the land of his birth. William James often visited Europe where he became acquainted with Alexander Bain, Herbert Spencer, Wilhelm Wundt and Hermann von Helmholtz, whose works he appreciated as sources of information but whose principles he rejected. He became an intimate friend of James Ward and Carl Stumpf and felt himself much indebted to Charles Renouvier whose personality he revered.

In his youth, William James desired to become known as a painter. But, while living with art, he learned that he could live without art, and turned to medicine and the natural sciences. However, his early study of painting was no labor lost. On the contrary, James derived from it his pictorial manner of philosophizing, which does not involve picturesqueness of style but rather his talents for conveying the present aspect of a situation, for finding immediate joy in the variety of appearances from which he proceeded to enjoy the various psychic experiences, while being capable of describing them in scientific terms, coined afresh, without much regard to traditional terminology. Such blending of scientific sagacity with artistic sensibility, such psychological perspicacity, enriched and refined by his previous study of art, and disciplined by scientific training, are characteristic of James' brilliant lectures and writing, and the cause of his great success. His gifts became known to the public in 1890 when his *Principles of Psychology* appeared, marking a new period in this special branch of science and foreshadowing his turn to philosophy.

It was the latent artist in James that made his treatment of moral, epistemological, and metaphysical problems a revolt of the spirit of immediate concrete experience against the intellectualistic idealism. James' radical empiricism maintains the plurality of the real units of which, according to him, experience consists, against any harmonizing or simplifying monism. Pragmatism, as James defines his empiricism, has become of immense consequence in modern thinking. James surpasses Hume by denying consciousness. He acknowledges a stream of experiences but not a stream of conscious experiences. Therewith he denies that in knowledge the relation between the knowing subject and the object to be known is fundamental, which almost all modern philosophers had taken for

603

granted. This denial has induced many contemporary philosophers, though opposed to James' views, to reconsider the bases and starting points of their own thoughts.

PRAGMATISM

TRUTH, as any dictionary will tell you, is a property of certain of our ideas. It means their "agreement," as falsity means their disagreement, with "reality." Pragmatists and intellectualists both accept this definition as a matter of course. They begin to quarrel only after the question is raised as to what may precisely be meant by the term "agreement," and what by the term "reality," when reality is taken as something for our ideas to agree with.

In answering these questions the pragmatists are more analytic and painstaking, the intellectualists more offhand and irreflective. The popular notion is that a true idea must copy its reality. Like other popular views, this one follows the analogy of the most usual experience. Our true ideas of sensible things do indeed copy them. Shut your eyes and think of yonder clock on the wall, and you get just such a true picture or copy of its dial. But your idea of its "works" (unless you are a clockmaker) is much less of a copy, yet it passes muster, for it in no way clashes with the reality. Even though it should shrink to the mere word "works," that word still serves you truly; and when you speak of the "time-keeping function" of the clock, or of its spring's "elasticity," it is hard to see exactly what your ideas can copy.

You perceive that there is a problem here. Where our ideas cannot copy definitely their object, what does agreement with that object mean? Some idealists seem to say that they are true whenever they are what God means that we ought to think about that object. Others hold the copy-view all through, and speak as if our ideas possessed truth just in proportion as they approach to being copies of the Absolute's eternal way of thinking.

These views, you see, invite pragmatistic discussion. But the great assumption of the intellectualists is that truth means essentially an inert static relation. When you've got your true idea of anything, there's an end of the matter. You're in possession; you *know;* you have fulfilled your thinking destiny. You are where you ought to be mentally; you have obeyed your categorical imperative; and nothing more need follow on that climax of your rational destiny. Epistemologically you are in stable equilibrium.

Pragmatism, on the other hand, asks its usual question. "Grant an idea or belief to be true," it says, "what concrete difference will its being true make in any one's actual life? How will the truth be realized? What experiences will be different from those which would obtain if the belief were false? What, in short, is the truth's cash-value in experiential terms?"

The moment pragmatism asks this question, it sees the answer: *True ideas are those that we can assimilate, validate, corroborate and verify. False ideas are those that we can not.* That is the practical difference it makes to us to have true ideas; that, therefore, is the meaning of truth, for it is all that truth is known as.

This thesis is what I have to defend. The truth of an idea is not a stagnant property inherent in it. Truth *happens* to an idea. It *becomes* true, is *made* true by events. Its verity *is* in fact an event, a process: the process namely of its verifying itself, its veri-*fication*. Its validity is the process of its validation.

But what do the words verification and validation themselves pragmatically mean? They again signify certain practical consequences of the verified and validated idea. It is hard to find any one phrase that characterizes these consequences better than the ordinary agreement-formula—just such consequences being what we have in mind whenever we say that our ideas "agree" with reality. They lead us, namely, through the acts and other ideas which they instigate, into or up to, or towards, other parts of experience with which we feel all the while—such feeling being among our potentialities—that the original ideas remain in agreement. The connections and transitions come to us from point to point as being progressive, harmonious, satisfactory. This function of agreeable leading is what we mean by an idea's verification. Such an account is vague and it sounds at first quite trivial, but it has results which it will take the rest of my hour to explain.

Let me begin by reminding you of the fact that the possession of true thoughts means everywhere the possession of invaluable instruments of action; and that our duty to gain truth, so far from being a blank command from out of the blue, or a "stunt" self-imposed by our intellect, can account for itself by excellent practical reasons.

The importance to human life of having true beliefs about matters of fact is a thing too notorious. We live in a world of realities that can be infinitely useful or infinitely harmful. Ideas that tell us which of them to expect count as the true ideas in all this primary sphere of verification, and the pursuit of such ideas is a primary human duty. The possession of truth, so far from being here an end in itself, is only a preliminary means toward other vital satisfactions. If I am lost in the woods and starved, and find what looks like a cow path, it is of the utmost importance that I should think of a human habitation at the end of it, for if I do so and follow it, I save myself. The true thought is useful here because the house which is its object is useful. The practical value of true ideas is thus primarily derived from the practical importance of their objects to us. Their objects are, indeed, not important at all times. I may on another occasion have no use for the house; and then my idea of it, however verifiable, will be practically irrelevant, and had better remain latent. Yet since almost any object may some day become temporarily important, the advantage of having a general stock of *extra* truths, of ideas that shall be true of merely possible situations, is obvious. We store such extra truths away in our memories, and with the overflow we fill our books of reference. Whenever such an extra truth becomes practically relevant to one of our emergencies, it passes from cold storage to do work in the world and our belief in it grows active. You can say of it then either that "it is useful because it is true" or that "it is true because it is useful." Both these phrases mean exactly the same thing, namely that here is an idea that gets fulfilled and can be verified. True is the name for whatever idea starts the verification process, useful is the name for its completed function in experience. True ideas would never have been singled out as such, would never have acquired a class-name, least of all a name suggesting value, unless they had been useful from the outset in this way.

From this simple cue pragmatism gets her general notion of truth as something essentially bound up with the way in which one moment in our experience may lead us towards other moments which it will be worth while to have been led to. Primarily, and on the common sense level, the truth of a state of mind means this function of *a leading that is worth while*. When a moment in our experience, of any kind whatever, inspires us with a thought that is true, that means that sooner or later we dip by that thought's guidance into the particulars of experience again and make advantageous connection with them. This is a vague enough statement, but I beg you to retain it, for it is essential.

"The true," to put it briefly, is only the expedient in the way of our thinking, just as "the right" is only the expedient in the way of our behaving. Expedient in almost any fashion; and expedient in the long run and on the whole of course; for what meets expediently all the experience in sight won't necessarily meet all farther experiences equally satisfactorily. Experience, as we know, has ways of *boiling over*, and making us correct our present formulas.

The "absolutely" true, meaning what no farther experience will ever alter, is that ideal vanishing-point towards which we imagine that all our temporary truths will some day converge. It runs on all fours with the perfectly wise man, and with the absolutely complete experience; and, if these ideals are ever realized, they will all be realized together. Meanwhile we have to live to-day by what truth we can get to-day, and be ready to-morrow to call it falsehood. Ptolemaic astronomy, euclidean space, aristotelian logic, scholastic metaphysics, were expedient for centuries, but human experience has boiled over those limits, and we now call these things only relatively true, or true within those borders of experience. "Absolutely" they are false; for we know that those limits were casual, and might have been transcended by past theorists just as they are by present thinkers.

When new experiences lead to retrospective judgments, using the past tense, what these judgments utter *was* true, even though no past thinker had been led there. We live forwards, a Danish thinker has said, but we understand backwards. The present sheds a backward light on the world's previous processes. They may have been truth-processes for the actors in them. They are not so for one who knows the later revelations of the story.

This regulative notion of a potential better truth to be established later, possibly to be established some day absolutely, and having powers of retroactive legislation, turns its face, like all pragmatist notions, towards concreteness of fact, and towards the future. Like the half-truths, the absolute truth will have to be *made*, made as a relation incidental to the growth of a mass of verification-experience, to which the half true ideas are all along contributing their quota.

I have already insisted on the fact that truth is made largely out of previous truths. Men's beliefs at any time are so much experience *funded*. But the beliefs are themselves parts of the sum total of the world's experience, and become matter, therefore, for the next day's funding operations. So far as reality means experienceable reality, both it and the truths men gain about it are everlastingly in process of mutation towards a definite goal—it may be—but still mutation.

Mathematicians can solve problems with two variables. On the Newtonian theory, for instance, acceleration varies with distance, but distance also varies with acceleration. In the realm of truth-processes facts come independently and determine our beliefs provisionally. But these beliefs make us act, and as fast as they do so, they bring into sight or into existence new facts which re-determine the beliefs accordingly. So the whole coil and ball of truth, as it rolls up, is the product of a double influence. Truths emerge from facts; but they dip forward into facts again and add to them; which facts again create or reveal new truth (the word is indifferent) and so on indefinitely. The "facts" themselves meanwhile are not *true*. They simply *are*. Truth is the function of the beliefs that start and terminate among them.

The case is like a snowball's growth, due as it is to the distribution of the snow on the one hand, and to the successive pushes of the boys on the other, with these factors codetermining each other incessantly.

[189]

JASPERS, KARL

JASPERS, KARL (1883-   ). Since Germany's unconditional surrender, Jaspers has been the most respected, if not the most influential philosopher in that country. His prestige had already been great during the time of the Weimar Republic. He disliked Nazism and did not abandon his Jewish wife, but neither had he felt a predilection for the pre-Hitlerian republic and he cannot be considered a convert to parliamentarian democracy. Jaspers began his career as a psychiatrist. His *General Psychopathology* (1913), in which he offered a new classification of mental illnesses, has been of great consequence for the diagnosis of psychoses and neuroses. It was from the viewpoint of a psychiatrist that Jaspers first studied the philosophy of Friedrich Nietzsche and then the works of Kierkegaard, whose habits interested the student of abnormalities. As his *Psychology of Weltanschauungen* (1919) shows, Jaspers became more and more interested in inquiring into the relations between a philosopher's personality and his doctrine. The results of these studies remained valid to him when he exposed his own philosophy in *Principles of Philosophy* (1932), *Existenzphilosophie* (1938) and *The Perennial Scope of Philosophy* (1949). Despite all changes, Jaspers maintained the principle that philosophy is more than cogent intellectual knowledge and fundamentally different from, yet not opposite to science. The distinguishing feature of the philosophical mind, in contradistinction to the scientific mind, is characterized as personal faith. Though always allied with knowledge, philosophical faith transcends object cognition. Philosophical faith is neither grounded in any concept of anything objective or finite in the world nor subordinated to it. The truth of philosophical faith is not universal but both eternal and historical, a dynamism acting in time and longing for transcending time. The true value of man is seen by Jaspers not in the species or type but in the historical individual, and the situation of this individual—the conditions of his existence—is one of the principal problems of Jaspers' disquisitions.

Jaspers is one of the earliest contemporary existentialists. He belongs neither to the Christian nor to the atheistic group, and differs from most of them because he adopts Kant's idea of the phenomenality with its division into subject and object, and because he regards reason an indispensable element of philosophical faith, bluntly declining irrationalism.

The religious trend and the theistic conviction have become most conspicuous in Jaspers' latest works. He praises the values of the Old and New Testament but thinks that Judaism and Christianity are wrong in claiming absolute truth. According to Jaspers, the aim of philosophy is at all times to achieve the independence of man as an individual. To him independence is attachment to transcendence, and awareness of true being is identical with certainty of God. In his earlier works Jaspers stated that philosophy and religion will be in constant struggle with each other. Now he says that in all philosophical efforts lies a tendency to aid religious institutions whose practical values are affirmed by philosophy although philosophers cannot participate directly in them.

REASON

REASON is the comprehensive in us; it does not flow from the primal source of being, but is an instrument of existence. It is the existential absolute that serves to actualize the primal source and bring it to the widest manifestation.

There is something like a climate of reason. The passion for the open works in cool clarity. The rational man lives resolutely out of the root of his own historical soil, and at the same time he gives himself to every mode of historicity which he encounters, in order to penetrate to the depths of the world's historicity, through which alone a sympathetic understanding of everything becomes possible. From this develops what was also the motive force from the outset—the love of being, of everything existent as existent in its transparency, thanks to which its relation to the primal source becomes visible. Reason enriches man by sharpening his hearing, increases his capacity for communication, makes him capable of change through new experience, but while doing all this it remains essentially one, unswerving in its faith, living in actually efficacious memory of everything that was once real to it.

He who engages in philosophy cannot sufficiently praise reason, to which he owes all his achievements. Reason is the bond that unites all the modes of the comprehensive. It allows no existent to separate itself absolutely, to sink into isolation, to be reduced to nothingness by fragmentation. Nothing must be lost. Where reason is effective, that which is strives for unification. A universal fellowship arises, in which men are open to all things and everything concerns them. Reason quickens dormant springs, frees what is hidden, makes possible authentic struggles. It presses toward the One that is all, it does away with the delusions that fixate the One prematurely, incompletely, in partisanship.

Reason demands boundless *communication*, it is itself the total will to communicate. Because, in time, we cannot have objective possession of a truth that is the eternal truth, and because being-here is possible only with other being-there, and existence can come into its own only with other existence, communication is the form in which truth is revealed in time.

The great seductions are: through belief in God to withdraw from men; through supposed knowledge of the absolute truth to justify one's isolation; through supposed possession of being itself to fall into a state of complacency that is in truth lovelessness. And to these may be added the assertion that every man is a self-contained monad, that no one can emerge from himself, that communication is a delusion.

In opposition to these stands philosophical faith, which may also be called faith in communication. For it upholds these two propositions: Truth is what joins us together; and, truth has its origin in communication. The only reality with which man can reliably and in self-understanding ally himself in the world, is his fellow man. At all the levels of communication among men, companions in fate lovingly find the road to the truth. This road is lost to the man who shuts himself off from others in stubborn self-will, who lives in a shell of solitude.

[190]

JEANS, JAMES HOPWOOD

JEANS, JAMES HOPWOOD (1877-1946). Jeans, one of the most eminent savants and an international authority in mathematics, theoretical physics and astronomy, has also been called "the Edgar Wallace of cosmology." Very few scientists of his rank have ever had his talents for combining profundity with a colorful, popular style. While his earlier books *The Dynamical Theory of Gases* (1904), *Theoretical Mechanics* (1906), *Mathematical Theory of Electricity and Magnetism* (1908) and numerous learned papers were written for experts, his later works *The Stars in Their Courses* (1931), *The New Background of Science* (1933) and *Through Space and Time* (1934) have been admired by tens of thousands of readers who were not prepared to read other scientific books. Jeans himself was fond of fiction and detective stories, and he knew how to charm the public, although he never made a confession to his readers which he could not justify before his scientific conscience.

Towards the end of his life, Jeans became more and more convinced that the scientific viewpoint was synonymous with that of the astronomer. Human life was to be seen as a chain of causes and effects. The problems of the day were to be set against a background of time into which the whole of human history shrinks to the twinkling of an eye. Abstract problems of philosophy did not trouble him. Nor did he feel a need for seeking a rational basis for morals. According to Jeans, neither science nor philosophy has a voice in the region of moral acting. This is left to the Christian religion only.

APPEARANCE AND REALITY

WE may picture the world of reality as a deep-flowing stream, the world of appearance is its surface, below which we cannot see. Events deep down in the stream throw up bubbles and eddies on the surface of the stream. These are the transfers of energy and radiation of our common life which affect our senses and so activate our minds; below these lie deep waters which we can only know by inference. These bubbles and eddies show atomicity. . . .

Many philosophers have regarded the world of appearance as a kind of illusion, some sort of creation or selection of our minds which has in some way less existence in its own right than the underlying world of reality. Modern physics does not confirm this view; the phenomena are seen to be just a part of the real world which affects our senses, while the space and time in which they occur have the same sort of reality as the substratum which orders their motions. . . .

Because we have only complete photons at our disposal, and these form blunt probes, the world of phenomena can never be seen clearly and distinctly, either by us or by our instruments. Instead of seeing clearly defined particles clearly located in space and execution, clear-cut motions, we see only a collection of blurs, like a badly focused lantern side. . . . This is enough of itself to prevent our ever observing strict causality in the world of phenomena.

Each blur represents the unknown entity which the particle-picture depicts as a particle, or perhaps a group of such entities. The blurs may be pictured as wave-disturbances, the intensity of the waves at any point representing the probability that, with infinitely refined probes at our disposal, we should find a particle at that point. Or again, we may interpret the waves as representations of knowledge —they do not give us pictures of a particle, but of what we know as to the position and speed of motion of the particle. Now these waves of knowledge exhibit complete determinism; as they roll on, they show us knowledge growing out of knowledge and uncertainty following uncertainty according to a strict causal law. But this tells us nothing we do not already know. If we had found new knowledge appearing, not out of previous knowledge but spontaneously and of its own accord, we should have come upon something very startling and of profound philosophical significance; actually what we find is merely what was to be expected, and the problem of causality is left much where it was.

[191]

JEFFERSON, THOMAS

JEFFERSON, THOMAS (1743-1826). In accordance with Jefferson's own will, his tombstone reads:

Here was buried Thomas Jefferson
Author of the Declaration of American Independence
Of the Statute of Virginia for religious freedom
And Father of the University of Virginia.

Jefferson did not want to have mentioned that he had been Governor of Virginia, member of Congress, Minister to France, Secretary of State, Vice-President and third President of the United States. Jefferson often protested that he disliked politics and preferred the peaceful life on his farm and among his books. Undoubtedly these declarations were sincere. His was a meditative mind. He was not a man of action. But for decades he was involved in political struggles because they concerned not so much his material interests as his philosophy, and it was his philosophy, at least its broad outline, which caused a great political upheaval, resulting in Jefferson's victory over men of action, and his election to the Presidency.

Jefferson's political philosophy was founded upon his ideas on human nature. His motto was, "I cannot act as if all men were unfaithful because some are so. . . . I had rather be the victim of occasional infidelities than relinquish my general confidence in the honesty of man." His confidence disregarded differences of education, wealth, social position. The aim of his political activity was a life of freedom in which every individual would be able to develop his moral and intellectual nature and pursue his happiness. He was also confident that the common man would give authority to good and wise leaders. He firmly believed that Providence created man for society and endowed him with a sense of right and wrong so that an orderly society could subsist.

Jefferson, who in his youth had been engaged in "dancing, junketing and high jinks," was a man of solid studies in various fields. He was a profound jurist, versed in mathematics, botany and meteorology, interested in zoology, astronomy and ethnology, mechanics and architecture, well-read in classical and modern literature, a talented musician and a model farmer. He was opposed to Calvinist orthodoxy, advocated religious tolerance, emancipation of slaves and public education. Among modern political economists there are some who think it fashionable to deride Jefferson as "a petty bourgeois liberal." It is true, Jefferson, the leader of small farmers, shopkeepers and artisans, disliked big business and large-scale industrialization. But his philosophy was anything but the expression of his material interests or of his prejudices.

CHARACTER OF WASHINGTON

HIS mind was great and powerful, without being of the very first order; his penetration strong, though not so acute as that of a Newton, Bacon, or Locke; and, as far as he saw, no judgment was ever sounder. It was slow in operation, being little aided by invention or imagination, but sure in conclusion. Hence the common remark of his officers of the advantage he derived from councils of war, where, hearing all suggestions, he selected whatever was best; and certainly no general ever planned his battles more judiciously. But if deranged in the course of the action—if any member of his plan was dislocated by sudden circumstances, he was slow in a readjustment. The consequence was that he often failed in the field, and rarely against an enemy in station, as at Boston and York. He was incapable of fear, meeting personal dangers with the calmest unconcern. Perhaps the strongest feature in his character was prudence; never acting until every circumstance, every consideration, was maturely weighed; refraining if he saw doubt; but when once decided going through with his purpose, whatever obstacle interposed.

His integrity was most pure, his justice the most inflexible I have ever known; no motives of interest or consanguinity, of friendship or hatred, being able to bias his decision. He was, indeed, in every sense of the word a wise, a good, and a great man. His temper was naturally irritable and high-toned; but reflection and resolution had obtained a firm and habitual ascendancy over it. If, however, it broke its bonds, he was most tremendous in his wrath. In his expenses he was honorable, but exact; liberal in contributions to whatever promised utility, but frowning and unyielding on all visionary projects and all unworthy calls on his charity. His heart was not warm in its affections; but he exactly calculated every man's value, and gave him a solid esteem proportioned to it.

Although, in the circle of his friends, where he might be unreserved with safety, he took a free share in conversation, his colloquial talents were not above mediocrity, possessing neither copiousness of ideas nor fluency of words. In public, when called upon for a sudden effort, he was unready, short and embarrassed. Yet he wrote readily, rather diffusely, in an easy and correct style. This he had acquired by conversation with the world; for his education was merely reading, writing, and common arithmetic, to which he added surveying at a later day. His time was employed in action chiefly, reading little, and that only in agriculture and English history. His correspondence became necessarily extensive, and, with journalizing his agricultural proceedings, occupied most of his leisure time within doors.

On the whole, his character was, in its mass, perfect; in nothing bad; in few points indifferent; and it may be truly said that never did nature and fortune combine more perfectly to make a man great, and to place him in the same constellation with whatever worthies have merited from man an everlasting remembrance. For his was the singular destiny and merit of leading the armies of his country successfully through an arduous war for the establishment of its independence; of conducting its councils through the birth of a government, new in its forms and its principles, until it had settled down into an orderly train; and of scrupulously obeying the laws through the whole of his career, civil and military, of which the history of the world furnishes no other example.

Letter to Dr. Walter Jones, Thomas Jefferson.

THE PASSAGE OF THE POTOMAC
THROUGH THE BLUE RIDGE

THE passage of the Potomac through the Blue Ridge is perhaps one of the most stupendous scenes in Nature. You stand on a very high point of land. On your right comes up the Shenandoah, having ranged along the foot of the mountain a hundred miles to seek a vent. On your left approaches the Potomac, seeking a passage also. In the moment of their junction they rush together against the mountain, rend it asunder, and pass off to the sea. The first glance at this scene hurries our senses into the opinion that this earth has been created in time; that the mountains were formed first; that the rivers began to flow afterward; that in this place particularly, they have been dammed up by the Blue Ridge of mountains, and have formed an ocean which filled the whole valley; that, continuing to rise, they have at length broken over at this spot, and have torn the mountain down from its summit to its base. The piles of rock on each hand, but particularly on the banks of the Shenandoah; the evident marks of their disrupture and avulsion from their beds by the most powerful agents of Nature corroborate the impression.

But the distant finishing which Nature has given to the picture is of a very different character. It is a true contrast to the foreground. It is as placid and delightful as that is wild and tremendous. For, the mountains being cloven asunder, she presents to your eye, through the cleft, a small patch of smooth blue horizon, at an infinite distance in the plain country, inviting you, as it were, from the riot and tumult roaring around, to pass through the breach and participate of the calm below. Here the eye ultimately composes itself; and that way, too, the road happens actually to lead.

You cross the Potomac above its junction, pass along its side through the base of the mountain for three miles—its terrible precipices hanging in fragments over you—and within about twenty miles reach Fredericktown and the fine country round that. This scene is worth a voyage across the Atlantic. Yet here—as in the neighborhood of the Natural Bridge—are people who have passed their lives within half a dozen miles, and have never been to survey these monuments of a war between rivers and mountains which must have shaken the earth itself to its centre.

THE INFLUENCE AND DOOM OF SLAVERY

THE whole commerce between master and slave is a perpetual exercise of the most boisterous passions; the most unremitting despotism on the one part and degrading submission on the other. Our children see this, and learn to imitate it—for man is an imitative animal. This quality is the germ of all education in him. From his cradle to his grave he is learning to do what he sees others do. If a parent could find no motives, either in his philanthropy or his self-love, for restraining the intemperance of passion toward his slave, it should always be a sufficient one that his child is present. But generally it is not sufficient. The parent storms, the child looks on, catches the lineaments of wrath, puts on the same airs in the circle of smaller slaves, gives loose to his worst passions, and thus, nursed, educated, and daily exercised in tyranny, cannot but be stamped by it with odious peculiarities. The man must be a prodigy who can retain his manners and his morals undepraved by such circumstances.

And with what execration should the statesman be loaded who, permitting one-half of the citizens thus to trample on the other, transforms those into despots and these into enemies; destroys the morals of the one part and the *amor patriae* of the other! For if the slave can have a country in this world, it must be any other in preference to that in which he is born to live and labor for another; in which he must lock up the faculties of his nature, contribute as far as depends on his individual endeavors to the banishment of the human race, or entail his own miserable condition on the endless generations proceeding from him. With the morals of a people their industry also is destroyed. For in a warm climate no man will labor for himself who can make another labor for him. This is so true, that of the proprietors of slaves a very small proportion indeed are ever seen to labor.

What an incomprehensible machine is man, who can endure toil, famine, stripes, imprisonment, and death itself, in vindication of his own liberty and the next moment be deaf to all those motives whose power supported him through his trial, and inflict upon his fellow-men a bondage, one hour of which is fraught with more misery than ages of that which he rose in rebellion to oppose! But we must wait with patience the workings of an over-ruling Providence, and hope that this is preparing the deliverance of these our suffering brethren. When the measure of their tears shall be full, doubtless a God of justice will awaken to their distress, and, by diffusing a light and liberality among their oppressors —or at length by His exterminating thunder—manifest His attention to things of this world, and that they are not left to the guidance of blind fatality.

[192]

JOAD, CYRIL E. M.

JOAD, CYRIL E. M. (1891-1953). As an Oxford student, Joad loathed the idealism in which he had been brought up. He felt himself to be a naive realist. Then, influenced by Bertrand Russell, he became an extreme realist and was satisfied that his views agreed completely with modern physics, although he found out that his realism was also quite compatible with metaphysics. Soon thereafter, Joad, the former grim adversary of idealism, came close to Plato's doctrine of Ideas, which must not necessarily be interpreted in accordance with the idealistic schools. Joad then became conspicuous as an ardent defender of religion against its materialistic and relativistic critics. He especially emphasized the fallacy of assuming that to lay bare the origins of a thing is tantamount to describing its present nature, and he continued, that to show how a belief arises does not constitute a description of it much less its refutation.

Joad's principal works are: *Matter, Life and Value* (1929), *The Present and Future of Religion* (1930) and *Return to Philosophy* (1935).

THE POWER OF THOUGHT

I BELIEVE in the practical efficacy of the intellect; I believe, that is to say, that what you think affects and may determine what you do. It follows that facts are not "hard," since they can be affected by thinking about them. If you change men's moral and political ideas, you can, I hold, thereby change society; if you can change their ideas about what is worth while, you can change their mode of living. It seems to me to be nonsense to suggest that the ideas which lay behind the French Revolution played no part in determining its outbreak or guiding its course, or that the ideas of Christ or Mahomet about how men should live have played no part in changing their modes of living. In no sphere, perhaps, does the student find more impressive verification of the power of the idea not only to persist but in the end to prevail than in victory which the claim to think freely gained over dogmatic religion. To trace the slow history of French free thought from the new springs of Renaissance discovery through Rabelais and Montaigne, thence to the Libertins and Bayle and from them to its full flowering in Holbach and Diderot and Voltaire, is to realize the power over men's minds of ideas that are rooted in objective fact. (Yet the phrase "rooted in objective fact" is, I think, merely a periphrasis for the word "true.") On the one side was all that authority could muster to suppress and destroy with the weapons of exile, imprisonment, torture and death; on the other, there was only the power of the idea. Yet in the last resort the idea prevailed, though only for a time, for the victories of the mind and spirit have to be won afresh in every age.

Nor are the changes which thought brings about negligible; on occasion they have profoundly affected man's way of living, and affected it for the better; indeed, it is the hope of bettering man's life and his societies that has inspired almost every system of philosophy which has concerned itself with human conduct and institutions. Most of us are at some time or other impelled, even if the impulse is brief, to take a hand in solving the problems of our society, and most of us know in our hearts that it is our business to try to leave the world a little better than we found it.

"There are no phenomena," says Herbert Spencer, "which a society presents but what have their origins in the phenomena of individual human life." This, I think, is true. To change men's lives is to change society, and to change their minds is to change their lives. Now, it is by ideas that men's minds are changed.

[193]

JOHN OF SALISBURY

JOHN OF SALISBURY (About 1115-1180). The first to personify the type of a cultivated Englishman who combines statesmanship with humanist learning and philosophical mind was John of Salisbury, who played a very important role in the English foreign and ecclesiastical policy of his days, and proved to be an independent thinker and a gifted writer. Numerous pages of his books strike one as most modern. His judgments on people and the state of culture were rather liberal. His descriptions were colorful, and his manner of expression shows a rare combination of humor and dignity, of restraint and acuteness. In 1148, John became secretary to Archbishop Theobald of Canterbury, and, in 1162, he began to serve in the same capacity to Thomas à Becket. He shared Becket's exile and witnessed his murder. He was a friend of Pope Hadrian IV, the only Englishman who ever was crowned with the tiara, and he directed the diplomatic negotiations between King Henry II of England and the Holy See on the occasion of the conquest of Ireland.

621

While secretary to Archbishop Theobald, John wrote the books *Polycraticus* and *Metalogicus*. The first is a theory of the state, defining the rights of the king who, according to him, is limited by religious laws only, but may be killed when he breaks these laws. The second is a defense and criticism of dialectics and a refutation of exaggerated realism. John also wrote biographies of St. Anselm and of Thomas à Becket, and, in *Metalogicus,* he inserted his charming autobiography. From 1176 until his death, he was Bishop of Chartres, France, and was associated with the famous school of the cathedral.

ON DREAM INTERPRETATION

In describing the methods of the interpreters of dreams I fear it may seem that I am not describing the art but am myself nodding, for it is no art or at best a meaningless one. For whoever involves himself in the deception of dreams is not sufficiently awake to the law of God, suffers a loss of faith, and drowses to his own ruin. Truth is indeed far removed from him, nor can he grasp it any more effectually than he who with blinded eyes gropes his way in broad daylight can lance a boil or treat a cancer.

Although this drowsiness of infidelity in the form of dream interpretation is to be aroused by the goad of faith, and this mockery of craftiness (shall we call it, rather than of a craft) is to be battled with, we do not propose to block the path of the disposition of divine grace nor prevent the Holy Spirit from breathing where it will and according to its will suffusing obedient souls with its truth. But all who are credulous enough to put faith in dreams have patently wandered not only from the orbit of pure belief but also from that of reason.

Surely if ambiguous language is used which lends itself to many interpretations would not one be justly regarded as quite ignorant who, as a result of it, stubbornly makes some particular decision without taking into consideration these meanings? All things involve varied and manifold meanings, as has been stated above. Careful discrimination is to be made amid this multiplicity of meanings, lest by following one line too enthusiastically there be a tendency to fall into error. Hence the dream interpreter which is inscribed with the name of Daniel is apparently lacking in the weight which truth carries, when it allows but one meaning to one thing. This matter really needs no further consideration since the whole tradition of this activity is foolish and the circulating manual of dream interpretation passes brazenly from hand to hand of the curious.

Daniel himself certainly had received from the Lord the gift of interpreting dreams and visions. God forbid that this prophet, who was aware that it had been prohibited by the law of Moses for any of the faithful to pay attention to dreams, should be the one to reduce this insane practice to an art, for he well knew that the accomplice of Satan is transformed into an angel of light for the ruin of man and that the Lord sent upon him wicked angels.

Joseph also, thanks to his gift of interpreting dreams, held the chief place in Egypt. His brothers, as if envying his dreams, sold him into slavery to the Ishmaelites, but the hand of the Lord, by a miracle as pleasant as it was favorable to him, revealed the face of the future which was presented to the king as he slept and, as it were by the medium of dreams, raised Joseph not only from servitude to freedom but to the chief place among the nobles and grandees; so that only in respect to the royal throne was the king above him. Now were this possible with regard to a profession based upon human wisdom, I would be inclined to believe that one of his predecessors had won distinction before him, or I would readily think that a holy man filled with the spirit of piety had bequeathed the knowledge of acquiring distinction, if not to man in general, which would have been but right, at least to his own sons and brothers.

Furthermore Moses, trained in all the wisdom of Egypt, either was not acquainted with this art or scorned it, since in his abhorrence of impiety he banished it from God's people. However Daniel, a holy man, acquired the learning and wisdom of the Chaldeans, which assuredly a pious man would not have done if he had believed that the educational system of the Gentiles were sinful. He had too as fellow students those whom he rejoiced to have as sharers in the law and justice of God. For Ananias, Azariah, and Michael received with him all that the Chaldeans had to teach. They too were inspired by God and refrained from partaking of the royal table. Their diet too was vegetarian; they were content with it and they attended the King on his military expeditions.

But behold! A unique gift which man was unable to confer had been conferred upon Daniel alone; he could solve the riddle of dreams and at the dictation of the Lord clarify the obscurity of allegory. To make his intimacy with divine favor more conspicuous, he knew what the king, when lying in bed, premeditated. Pondering upon his visions Daniel had the wisdom to expound the miracle of salvation, which then lay in shadow and took place or rather was to take place at the end of the ages.

Are interpreters of dreams thus wont to enter even into the thoughts of others, to banish darkness, to disclose the hidden, and to clarify the obscurity of allegory? If there be any who enjoys such special favor let him join Daniel and Joseph and like them attribute it to the Lord. But for him whom the spirit of truth has not illumined it is vain to place trust in the art, since every art has its source in nature and its development in experience and reason. But reason is so undependable in the case of interpreters of dreams that for the most part it knows not where to turn or what decision to make. That this is frequently the case may be gathered from a few instances.

A certain individual (his name escapes me though I remember that the great Augustine narrates the incident), much troubled by a matter which caused him to hesitate, demanded with great insistence the opinion of one to whom he was aware the matter at issue was well known. This person put off the request with promises, thwarting by his cunning the insistence of the other. It chanced that on the same night each had a dream, the one that he was giving the explanation as requested, the other that he was being instructed by his informant. The result was that when he awoke he marveled that he had obtained the knowledge without the help of the other and without effort on his own part. Afterward, when as usual pleading that the promised information be given him, "What you asked," replied the other, "was done the night I came to instruct you." Who can explain such an incident unless on the supposition that good or bad spirits, influenced by the good or bad deeds of men, instruct or lead them astray?

Our Holy Mother the Catholic Church knows on the authority of Jerome himself how he was hurried before the tribunal of God the Judge for the reason that he had been too devoted to pagan books, where he was forced to assert that he would not merely not read them further but would not even keep them. Before this declaration he had been questioned and had said that he was a Christian. His judge rebuked him sharply for being not His disciple but Cicero's.

I do not dare affirm that this should be classed as a dream since this same truthful and learned teacher most solemnly states that it was not a shadowy dream but an actual experience and that the Lord did indeed visit him. To prove his assertion beyond the shadow of a doubt, on arising he displayed the livid welts and scars of wounds upon his body.

When spirits act thus in the case of human beings the devout soul should reject every image except that which leaves its innocence unimpaired. For should the dream add fuel to vice, perchance by inducing lust and avarice or by inspiring greed for dominion or anything of the sort to destroy the soul, undoubtedly it is the flesh or the evil spirit that sends it. This spirit, with the permission of the Lord because of their sins, wreaks its unbridled wickedness upon some men so violently that what they suffer in the spirit they wretchedly but falsely believe comes to pass in the flesh.

For example it is said that some Moon or Herodias or

625

Mistress of the Night calls together councils and assemblies, that banquets are held, that different kinds of rites are performed, and that some are dragged to punishment for their deeds and others raised to glory. Moreover babes are exposed to witches and at one time their mangled limbs are eargly devoured, at another are flung back and restored to their cradles if the pity of her who presides is aroused.

Cannot even the blind see that this is but the wickedness of mocking demons? This is quite apparent from the fact that it is for the weaker sex and for men of little strength or sense that they disport themselves in such a cult. If in fact anyone who suffers from such illusion is firmly censured by someone or by some sign the malign influence is either overcome or yields, and, as the saying is, as soon as one is censured in the light the works of darkness cease. The most effective cure however for this bane is for one to embrace the true faith, refuse to listen to such lies, and never to give thought to follies and inanities of the sort.

[194]

JOHNSON, SAMUEL

JOHNSON, SAMUEL (1709-1784). Johnson was most popular among his British contemporaries, especially the citizens of London, as "the philosopher," but he disliked philosophers just as he disliked country life, music, learned women, Whigs, history for its own sake and a lot of other things. To him, Berkeley was a madman, Hume nothing but an infidel and Voltaire, whose literary skill he admired, a rascal. He was a critic of literature but he held that the fundamental aspects of life were not proper subjects for poetry.

Although Johnson was not a profound thinker, he was a man of deep convictions, acquired by hard experiences. His poem *The Vanity of Human Wishes* (1749) outlines his philosophy of life, which he formulated again and again in satirical and earnest, resigned and irate sayings. To him life is mostly bitter, and rarely sweet. It is endurable only because there are short intervals of satisfaction. The end of writing is to enable mankind "better to enjoy life or better to endure it." Poetry must stand the test of reason and common sense. Fabulous images, Johnson maintained, have worn thin.

In politics, Johnson was a staunch Tory, in religious questions uncompromisingly orthodox. He demanded that literature, in which he was mainly interested, does not have to explain the riddles of existence, but that it should support moral and religious doctrines and defend the king and the Church. Much of this philosophy was expressed by Johnson in casual remarks in his *Lives of the Poets* (1779-81). However, he is best known not by his own writings but rather by the book of his biographer James Boswell, who wrote down Johnson's remarks about daily life, literature, politics, and contemporary history. The biography presents a genial man, who— though difficult to deal with, a sarcastic conversationalist, sometimes sound, sometimes queer—was always sincere and original.

THE CRITIC

CRITICISM is a study by which men grow important and formidable at very small expense. The power of invention has been conferred by nature upon few, and the labor of learning those sciences which may, by mere labor, be obtained is too great to be willingly endured; but every man can exert such judgment as he has upon the works of others; and he whom nature has made weak, and idleness keeps ignorant, may yet support his vanity by the name of a critic.

I hope it will give comfort to great numbers who are passing through the world in obscurity, when I inform them how easily distinction may be obtained. All the other powers of literature are coy and haughty, they must be long courted, and at last are not always gained; but criticism is a goddess easy of access, and forward of advance, who will meet the slow, and encourage the timorous; the want of meaning she supplies with words, and the want of spirit she recompenses with malignity.

This profession has one recommendation peculiar to itself, that it gives vent to malignity without real mischief. No genius was ever blasted by the breath of critics. The poison which, if confined, would have burst the heart, fumes away in empty hisses, and malice is set at ease with very little danger to merit. The critic is the only man whose

627

triumph is without another's pain, and whose greatness does not rise upon another's ruin.

THE UNIVERSAL FALLACY

WE always make a secret comparison between a part and the whole; the termination of any period of life reminds us that life itself has likewise its termination; when we have done anything for the last time, we involuntarily reflect that a part of the days allotted us is past, and that as more is past there is less remaining.

It is very happily and kindly provided, that in every life there are certain pauses and interruptions, which force considerations upon the careless, and seriousness upon the light; points of time where one course of action ends and another begins; and by vicissitude of fortune, or alteration of employment, by change of place, or loss of friendship, we are forced to say of something, *this is the last*.

An even and unvaried tenor of life always hides from our apprehension the approach of its end. Succession is not perceived but by variation; he that lives today as he lived yesterday, and expects that, as the present day is, such will be the morrow, easily conceives time as running in a circle and returning to itself. This uncertainty of our duration is impressed commonly by dissimilitude of condition; it is only by finding life changeable that we are reminded of its shortness.

This conviction, however forcible at every new impression, is every moment fading from the mind; and partly by the inevitable incursion of new images, and partly by voluntary exclusion of unwelcome thoughts, we are again exposed to the universal fallacy; and we must do another thing for the last time, before we consider that the time is nigh when we shall do no more.

[195]